KUMĀRASAMBHAVA OF KĀLIDĀSA

कालिदास-विरचित

कुमारसंभव

Kumārasambhava

of

Kālidāsa

CANTOS I-VIII

Edited with Commentary of Mallinātha,
a Literal English Translation,
Notes and Introduction
by

M. R. KALE

MOTILAL BANARSIDASS PUBLISHERS
PRIVATE LIMITED • DELHI

Reprint : Delhi, 1986, 1991, 1995, 1999, 2004, 2011
Seventh Edition: Delhi, 1981

ISBN: 978-81-208-0160-8 (Cloth)
ISBN: 978-81-208-0161-5 (Paper)

MOTILAL BANARSIDASS
41 U.A. Bungalow Road, Jawahar Nagar, Delhi 110 007
8 Mahalaxmi Chamber, 22 Bhulabhai Desai Road, Mumbai 400 026
203 Royapettah High Road, Mylapore, Chennai 600 004
236, 9th Main III Block, Jayanagar, Bangalore 560 011
Sanas Plaza, 1302 Baji Rao Road, Pune 411 002
8 Camac Street, Kolkata 700 017
Ashok Rajpath, Patna 800 004
Chowk, Varanasi 221 001

Printed in India
By Jainendra Prakash Jain at Shri Jainendra Press,
A-45, Naraina Phase-I, New Delhi 110 028
and Published by Narendra Prakash Jain for
Motilal Banarsidass Publishers Private Limited,
Bungalow Road, Delhi 110 007

PREFACE

At the suggestion of some professors and readers from several parts of India where this poem is studied as a text-book, I have added the 8th canto in this edition, thus giving the complete poem in one volume. As regards the additional cantos (9-17) found in some copies of the Kumârasambhava, scholars are now generally agreed that they are spurious, being the work of some other poet. I have also taken this opportunity to submit the whole work to a thorough revision, with special attention to the needs of the class of students for whom this edition is intended.

As in other books edited by me, the prose order of each śloka has been given in the commentary by using bold type, the words not actually repeated by Mallinâtha being enclosed within rectangular brackets. The notes explain all allusions, and grammatical peculiarities not noticed by Mallinâtha, copious extracts from other commentaries being given for this purpose. The introduction also gives a summary of all the eight cantos in English. The main outline of the story, as found in the Śiva-Purāṇa, has also been given in original Sanskrit. Important additions have been made in the Notes, and in this respect I thankfully acknowledge the help derived from the *Trivandrum Sanskrit Series* edition with the commentaries of Aruṇagirinâtha and Nârâyaṇa. As before, I am indebted also to the editions of Deshpande and Chakravarti. Any suggestions etc. to further increase the usefulness of this edition will be most thankfully received.

Bombay,
January 1923 — M. R. Kale

PUBLISHER'S NOTE

Inconsistencies in the use of diacritics are regretted as the recomposition of the text would amount to increase in the price which may make the book unaffordable to the students.

— Publisher

PREFACE TO THE SIXTH EDITION

The edition of Kumârasambhava was not available for past several years. Some editions of other authors contain only five or less cantos and therefore need to have a complete poem was much felt. This edition which is a reprint of Fifth edition containing all the eight cantos of the poem, is hoped to be of special use to students. I am much thankful to Shri Sundarlal Jain of M/s Motilal Banarsidass of Delhi-7, who undertook to publish the sixth edition in a short time.

25, Goodwill Building,
Mahim, Bombay-16,
Jan. 1967.

V. M. Kale

CONTENTS

INTRODUCTION.

I. THE SANSKRIT KÂVYA.

Before the student enters upon a critical and detailed study of the Kumârasambhava it is necessary that he should be acquainted with the salient features of what is called Kâvya in Sanskrit.[1] Sanskrit rhetoricians have divided all kinds of literary compositions into two main divisions, दृश्य (what is capable of being seen) and श्रव्य (what can only be heard or chanted). All the varieties of dramatic pieces come under the दृश्य class, while everything else can be broadly described as श्रव्य. The श्रव्य Kávya[2], again, has been further sub-divided, on consideration of its form, according as it is written in verse, or in prose, or in mixed verse and prose.[3] (1) Compositions in verse or metrical form are the commonest specimens of श्रव्य Kâvya. They generally fall into two classes, the distinction being based chiefly on their length[4]:—(a) महाकाव्यs or 'Great Poems', such as the Raghuvaṃśa, the Śiśupâlavadha &c., (b) and खण्डकाव्यs or 'Small Poetical Pieces', a class which includes all minor lyrical poetry and such works as the Meghadûta, the Bhâminîvilâsa, the Amaruśataka, &c. (2) Prose works are comparatively rare in Sanskrit; their main kinds are two[5]—Kathâ (*e. g.* the Kâdambarí of Báṇabhaṭṭa) and Âkhyâyiká (*e.g.* the Harshacharita of the same author). (3) Works in which prose and verse are mixed are

---

1 The information given here has been briefly summarized from the Kāv.-D. and the Sāh.-D. For a *historical* outline of Kāvya literature the student is recommended to consult any standard History (*e. g.* Macdonell's) of Sanskrit Literature.

2 The student should remember that Kāvya, according to Sanskrit writers does not mean '*Metrical* composition,' only. Kāvya signifies any literary piece which is highly sentimental, whether in prose or in verse; in popular usage it has been chiefly applied to verse.

3 पद्यं गद्यं च मिश्रं च तत्त्रिधैव व्यवस्थितम् । Daṇḍin.

4 This is clear from the words of Vis'vanâtha who says खण्डकाव्यं भवेत्काव्यस्यैकदेशानुसारि च; 'a Khaṇḍa kāvya treats of some *portion* of (the subjects that fill a whole) Mahákāvya.'

5 अपादः पदसंतानो गद्यमाख्यायिकाकथे। इति तस्य प्रभेदौ द्वौ ॥ Daṇḍin. The Agnipurāṇa mentions five kinds, *viz.* आख्यायिका कथा खण्डकथा परिकथा तथा । कथानिकेति मन्यन्ते गद्यकाव्यं च पञ्चधा ॥

classed as Champûs (*e. g.* the Bhâratachampû, the Viśvaguṇâdarśa-champú)[6]

The student will thus notice that, along with dramas, the महाकाव्यs and खण्डकाव्यs have been the most popular forms of literary composition, and have attracted the best geniuses to try their hand at them. It is true that the Khaṇḍa Kâvya attracted more attention, chiefly because it is short and requires less expenditure of time and energy; and that the number of extant Mahâkâvyas, therefore, is not very large. But what is here lacking in quantity has been amply made up in quality. For in dignity of style, depth of thought and majesty of movement, the Mahâkâvya is by far the best expression which the Sanskrit literary artist has found for his genius. The Kumârasambhava is a Mahákâvya, which the Sâh.-D.[7] defines as follows:—

सर्गबन्धो महाकाव्यं तत्रैको नायकः सुरः ।
सद्वंशः क्षत्रियो वापि धीरोदात्तगुणान्वितः ॥
एकवंशभवा भूपाः कुलजा बहवोऽपि वा ।
शृङ्गारवीरशान्तानामेकोऽङ्गी रस इष्यते ॥
अङ्गानि सर्वेऽपि रसाः सर्वे नाटकसंधयः ।
इतिहासोद्भवं वृत्तमन्यद्वा सज्जनाश्रयम् ॥
चत्वारस्तस्य वर्गाः स्युस्तेष्वेकं च फलं भवेत् ।
आदौ नमस्क्रियाऽऽशीर्वा वस्तुनिर्देश एव वा ॥
क्वचिन्निन्दा खलादीनां सतां च गुणकीर्तनम् ।
एकवृत्तमयैः पद्यैरवसानेऽन्यवृत्तकैः ॥

---

6 गद्यपद्यमयं काव्यं चम्पूरित्यभिधीयते । Sah.—D. If we set aside the distinction between श्रव्य and दृश्य, and consider *form* alone, it is also possible to class dramas as 'mixed Kāvya,' as indeed has been done by Daṇḍin, who says मिश्राणि नाटकादीनि (K.-D. I. 31).

7 We give above the definition of the Sáh.—D., which is more detailed, since its author, who lived in the fifteenth century, had all the famous Mahákávyas before him, including even the later specimens. The definition of Daṇḍin (of the sixth century) is earlier and concise, and we give it below for comparison with that of Viśvanátha :—

सर्गबन्धो महाकाव्यमुच्यते तस्य लक्षणम् ।आशीर्नमस्क्रियावस्तुनिर्देशो वापि तन्मुखम्॥
इतिहासकथोद्भूतमितरद्वा सदाश्रयम् । चतुर्वर्गफलायत्तं चतुरोदात्तनायकम् ॥
नगरार्णवशैलर्तुचन्द्रार्कोदयवर्णनैः । उद्यानसलिलक्रीडामधुपानरतोत्सवैः ॥
विप्रलम्भैर्विवाहैश्च कुमारोदयवर्णनैः । मन्त्रदूतप्रयाणाजिनायकाभ्युदयैरपि ॥
अलंकृतमसंक्षिप्तं रसभावनिरन्तरम् । सर्गैरनतिविस्तीर्णैः श्रव्यवृत्तैः सुसंधिभिः ॥
सर्वत्र भिन्नवृत्तान्तैरुपेतं लोकरञ्जनम् । काव्यं कल्पान्तरस्थायि जायते सदलंकृति ॥

Other definitions, more or less similar, will be found in Agnipurâṇa (337), Kâvyâlamkāra (I.), Sarasvatî-Kaṇṭhâbharaṇa (V.), &c.

नातिस्वल्पा नातिदीर्घा सर्गा अष्टाधिका इह ।
नानावृत्तमयः क्वापि सर्गः कश्चन दृश्यते ॥
सर्गान्ते भाविसर्गस्य कथायाः सूचनं भवेत् ।
संध्यासूर्येन्दुरजनीप्रदोषध्वान्तवासराः ॥
प्रातर्मध्याह्नमृगयाशैलर्तुवनसागराः ।
संभोगविप्रलम्भौ च मुनिस्वर्गपुराध्वराः ॥
रणप्रयाणोपयममन्त्रपुत्रोदयादयः ।
वर्णनीया यथायोगं साङ्गोपाङ्गा अमी इह ॥
कवेर्वृत्तस्य वा नाम्ना नायकस्येतरस्य वा ।
नामास्य सर्गोपादेयकथया सर्गनाम तु ॥ 315–325.

(*Parichchheda VI.*)

Thus, a Mahákávya should be divided into chapters, called सर्गs or cantos. The hero should be either a divine personage, or a Kshatriya of noble descent and possessed of the qualities of a Dhîrodâtta[8] Hero. This is when the poem is concerned with the description of the life of a single hero (as in the Śiśupálavadha or the Vikramâṅkadevacharita); if like the Raghuvaṃśa it has for its theme a number of Heroes, then they should all be Kshatriya princes sprung from the same race, and of pure descent. The prominent sentiment (रस) should be either शृङ्गार, वीर or शान्त, others being introduced as accessories. The subject-matter should be arranged as in a náṭaka with the necessary changes. The plot may be historical, or may have for its subject-matter the glorious deeds of the good and the virtuous. The object of such compositions should be the attainment of the four aims of human pursuit—*i. e.*, they should be written in such a way that their study would point out the means of attaining them. It should open with a verse or verses expressive of a salutation to a deity, or a blessing conferred on the readers, or a hinting of the subject-matter; these may sometimes be followed by censure of villains and praise of the good (as in the Vikramâṅkadevacharita). A Mahákávya should be divided into सर्गs not less than eight,[9] which should be neither too long nor

---

8 A 'Dhîrodâtta' ('self-controlled and exalted') Hero is one who is magnanimous, exceedingly grave, forbearing, not boastful, resolute, one whose high spirit is concealed, and who is faithful to his promise (महासत्त्वोऽतिगम्भीरः क्षमावानविकत्थनः । स्थिरो निगूढाहंकारो धीरोदात्तो दृढव्रतः ॥ D.—R. III.).

9 Some restrict the number to thirty; *cf.* अष्टसर्गान्न तु न्यूनं त्रिंशत्सर्गाच्च नाधिकम् । I'śânasaṃhitâ; but the *Haravijaya* possesses as many as fifty cantos. So the rule is not absolute.

too short.[10] They should be composed in the same metre, which should change only at the end; sometimes (as a variety) a सर्ग may be written in a number of metres. The contents of the next canto should be indicated at the end of the preceding one. It should describe, at more or less length, such incidents and topics as twilight, the rise of the sun and the moon, the night, the evening, darkness, the day, morning, noon, hunting, mountains, seasons, forests, oceans, the union and separation of lovers, ages, heaven, cities, sacrifices, battles, invasions, marriage-ceremonies, advice, the birth of a son, &c. &c. It should be named after the poet, or the plot, or the Hero, or some other person; while each Sarga should be named in accordance with its own contents (*e. g.* the 3rd canto of the Kum. is named मदनदहन).

It should be borne in mind that these elaborate rules were evolved after a minute examination of all available specimens. The works of early poets like **Kálidása** will not therefore be found to conform strictly to the definition given above, nor is it necessary that they should do so, provided they follow the broad lines laid down. For Dandin himself says, न्यूनमप्यत्र यैः कैश्चिदङ्गैः काव्यं न दुष्यति । यद्युपात्तेषु संपत्तिराराधयति तद्विदः ॥ (I. 20). Thus the Kumârasambhava, though it does not describe each one of all thos incidents and topics, still conforms mostly to the definition given, as the student can verify for himself. Thus, it has for its theme the doings of god Śiva who is a deity. The predominent sentiment is शृङ्गार, though करुण is introduced as an accessory (*e. g.* in Canto IV.). It is named after the chief incident of the theme, *viz.* the birth of Kumâra, the War-god. The subject of the next Canto is indicated towards the close of the previous one; *e. g.* it is evident from what is said at the end of canto VI. that the wedding of Śiva and Párvatî would be described in canto VII. The metre changes at the end of each canto. शैल is described in canto I., ऋतु in canto III., संभोग in VIII., उपयम in VII. Each canto is named after the most important event described in it. Other particulars the student can find out for himself. Technically, the Kumârasambhava is a representative specimen of its class; as regards its other merits and distinguishing features, we shall have a few remarks to make, but these more properly belong to a subsequent Section.

---

10 The Íśána-Saṃhitá explains that the number of stanzas in a single canto should not exceed 200, and should not be less than 30.

II. KA'LIDA'SA.

(A) HIS LIFE, WORKS AND POETRY.

His Life

To turn now to the poet it must be admitted that we have absolutely no trustworthy information regarding the personal history of Kálidâsa, by universal consent the greatest of Indian poets. The curiosity of the querist who would ask–'Where and when was he born?' 'Who were his parents?' 'When did he die?' &c.—must ever remain unsatisfied. The poet has studiously observed complete silence about himself in his works. Read them howsoever we may, we find no allusion, no incident mentioned, that may directly shed any light either on his personal history or on any remarkable event of his life. Under these circumstances we have to content ourselves with gathering what little information we can about a poet of world-wide repute from external sources, and a few incidents found here and there in his works, which may be supposed to have a distant bearing upon the history of his life. Reserving for another Section the question of the date of the poet, we proceed here to state the few facts that can thus be known about him. A time-honoured tradition, supported by internal and external evidence, associates the name of Kâlidâsa with that of the epoch-making king Vikramâditya of Ujjayinî. The keen interest and admiration with which the poet describes the Mahâkâla, the Śiprâ, and other beauties of Ujjayinî, unmistakably point to the conclusion that he must have been a native of that city. And the various covert references[11] to the name of Vikrama in fully eulogistic terms, which are doubtless meant to immortalize king Vikramâditya, are inexplicable if that monarch be not regarded as the poet's patron. Kâlidâsa also betrays considerable acquaintance with court-life in his works. This circumstance, coupled with the fact that there is no allusion in his writings to the goddess of wealth having ever frowned upon him, shows that he was in affluent circumstances, and had not the misfortune ever to drink the bitter cup of poverty. He was a Brâhmaṇa by caste and was a devout worshipper of Śiva, though by no means a sectarian. He seems to have travelled a good deal, at least in Northern India. For, as Dr. Bhau Dâjî remarks, he is the only poet who describes a living saffron flower,

---

11 *E. g.*, अनुत्सेकः खलु विक्रमालंकारः (Vikr.), विक्रममाहिम्ना वर्धते भवान् (*Ibid.*) &c.

the plant of which grows in Kashmir. His graphic description of the Himâlayan scenes looks very much like that of one who was an eye-witness. Unlike Bhavabhûti and many other brother poets, he appears to have enjoyed great popularity during his lifetime. He was 'an admirer of field-sports,' and 'describes their beneficial effects with the exactness of a true sportsman.' Though fond of pleasures he was not the unscrupulous voluptuary he is supposed to be by some critics, as is clear from the many noble sentiments expressed in the Śákuntala[12]. It also appears from the same play that he was against love-marriages, though always actuated with the most generous sentiments towards the fair sex. His works bear further testimony to his considerable acquaintance with the Vedas, the philosophy taught by the Upanishads, the Epics and the Puráṇas, the Bhagavadgîtá, the systems of Sáṃkhya, Yoga, and Vedánta as propounded by Bâdarâyaṇa, Medicine, and the rudiments of Astronomy. Beyond these few facts nothing is known for certain about our poet at present. It is inevitable that, during the course of time, a number of fanciful stories and legends should have clustered round the popular hero of literary India. Thus there is a story which relates how the poet was born a blockhead and a dunce, but had wisdom bestowed upon him in consequence of his subsequent propitiation of the goddess Kâlî, whence his name *Kálidása.* Another story makes him a friend of King Kumáradása of Ceylon, in whose city Kálidása was murdered by a courtesan. No reliance need be placed on such accounts. Many such stories will be found in the Sanskrit *Bhojaprabandha*, and in a collection which, under the title of *Tales of King Bhoja and Poet Kálidása*, is a popular book in many Indian vernaculars. A few conjectures have been advanced as to some other particulars, but to test their veracity falls strictly within the province of the antiquary.

His Works

The poet's silence about himself in his works gave an opportunity to many unscrupulous inferior poets to father their own works upon him. The following is a list of the works generally attributed to him:— (1) शाकुन्तल (2) विक्रमोर्वशी (3) मालविकाग्निमित्र (4) रघुवंश (5) कुमारसंभव (6) मेघदूत (7) कुन्तेश्वरदौत्य (8) ऋतुसंहार (9) अम्बास्तव (10) कल्याणस्तव (11) कालीस्तोत्र (12) काव्यनाटकालंकाराः (?) (13) and (14) two गङ्गाष्टकs (15) घटकर्पर (16) चण्डिकादण्डकस्तोत्र (17) चर्चास्तव (18) ज्योतिर्विदाभरण (19) दुर्घटकाव्य (20) नलोदय (21) नवरत्नमाला (22) पुष्पबाणविलास

12 *Cf.* अनिर्वर्णनीयं परकलत्रं &c. S'âk. V. and our note *ad loc.*

(23) मकरन्दस्तव (24) and (25) two मङ्गलाष्टकs (?) (26) महापद्यषट्क (27) रत्नकोश (28) राक्षसकाव्य (29) लक्ष्मीस्तव (30) लघुस्तव (31) विद्वद्विनोदकाव्य (32) वृन्दावनकाव्य (33) वैद्यमनोरमा (34) शुद्धिचन्द्रिका (35) शृङ्गारतिलक (36) शृङ्गाररसाष्टक (37) शृङ्गारसारकाव्य (38) श्यामलादण्डक (39) श्रुतबोध (40) सप्तश्लोकीरामायण and (41) सेतुबन्ध. Of these the first six are acknowledged by all critics to be undoubtedly his. (7) is not yet discovered, but is known only in a quotation by the Kâshmirian scholar Kshemendra, in his Auchityavichâracharchá. The authorship of (8) is somewhat doubtful; while the remaining ones are certainly to be dismissed as the productions of other poets. There is another fact also which should be borne in mind in this connexion. In Sanskrit literary history there have been *many poets who bore the name Kâlidâsa*, and at least three were known to Râjas'ekhara who wrote एकोऽपि जीयते हन्त कालिदासो न केनचित् । शृङ्गारे ललितोद्गारे कालिदासत्रयी किमु ॥ It is possible, therefore, that other Kálidásas than the author of the Raghuvaṃśa are responsible for the trifling pieces mentioned above. Here, then, we are concerned with the first six only. The most convenient and reliable method of studying the development of a poet's mind and relation to his productions would be to read his works in their chronological order. But we have no external evidence, whatsoever, to ascertain the chronology of Kâlidâsa's works. It must, therefore, be based wholly on internal evidence. Judged as such the works would stand in this order—Poems—कुमार॰, मेघदूत and रघुवंश; Plays—मालविका॰, विक्रमो॰ and शाकुन्तल; or, both indiscriminately, as—कुमार॰, मालविका॰, विक्रमो॰, मेघदूत, शाकुन्तल and रघुवंश. Space will not permit us even to refer to these briefly. We will only remarl in passing that the last three are the outcome of the poet's matured poetic faculties and riper years.

His Poetry

Kálidása is indisputably the greatest master-mind in Sanskrit poetry. His genius has been recognized in India from very early times. He has been and will ever be enshrined in the hearts of his countrymen as the Prince of Indian poets. Most Indian successors of Kálidása have expressed in suitable words their admiration of the poet who stood far ahead of them in the perfection of his art. Thus Báṇabhaṭṭa, the famous author of the Kádambarî, speaks of him in the following words:—

निर्गतासु न वा कस्य कालिदासस्य सूक्तिषु ।
प्रीतिर्मधुरसार्द्रासु मञ्जरीष्विव जायते ॥

"When Kâlidâsa's sweet sayings, charming with sweet sentiment, went forth, who did not feel delight in them as in honey-laden flowers?" Kumârila, who flourished about the first half of the eighth century, has quoted with approval the passage from the Śâkuntala, "सतां हि संदेहपदेषु वस्तुषु प्रमाणमन्तःकरणप्रवृत्तयः." There is a Subháshita which says :—

पुरा कवीनां गणनाप्रसङ्गे कनिष्ठिकाऽधिष्ठितकालिदासा ।
अद्यापि तत्तुल्यकवेरभावादनामिका साऽर्थवती बभूव ॥

"While once the poets were being counted, Kâlidása (as being the first) occupied the last finger. But the ring-finger remained true to its name (अनामिका=nameless), since his second has not yet been found (by whom it can be occupied)". Pandit Govardhanâchârya thus speaks of our poet:—

साकूतमधुरकोमलविलासिनीकण्ठकूजितप्राये ।
शिक्षासमयेऽपि मुदे रतलीलाकालिदासोक्ती ॥

"Two things only, *viz.* love-sport and Kálidása's poetry, delight the heart even at the time of instruction, as they mostly consist of the sweet, tender and touching words of a sportful girl." Almost every Pandit has in his mouth the following memorable verse—

काव्येषु नाटकं रम्यं तत्र रम्या शकुन्तला ।
तत्रापि च चतुर्थोऽङ्कस्तत्र श्लोकचतुष्टयम् ॥

"Among Kávyas the drama is the most charming. Among dramas Śákuntala is specially charming. Even there the fourth Act is the best; and lastly, four ślokas[13] therein are especially most beautiful". The highest place is assigned to Kálidása among poets for the construction of happy similes, when it is said—

उपमा कालिदासस्य भारवेरर्थगौरवम् ।
दण्डिनः पदलालित्यं माघे सन्ति त्रयो गुणाः ॥

Among later writers, Jayadeva has called our poet कविकुलगुरु 'the lord of poets' and the विलास or 'Graceful Play' of the Muse of Poetry.[14]

That his countrymen should place him at the head of all Sanskrit poets, unparalleled and unsurpassed by those who have preceded or followed him, is natural enough; but he has evoked spontaneous outpourings of praise and manifestations of admiration even from foreign scholars and poets who had access to his works either directly or through translations. Goethe has voluntarily

13 They are—यास्यत्यद्य शकुन्तलेति &c.; शुश्रूषस्व गुरून् &c.; अभिजनवतो भर्तुः श्लाघ्ये &c.; and भूत्वा चिराय चतुरन्तमहीसपत्नी &c.

14 भासो हासः कविकुलगुरुः कालिदासो विलासः ।

oestowed the highest meed of praise on him—so much was he enraptured by the charms of Kâlidâsa's Muse and struck with his poetic genius. This is what he says about the Śákuntala—

"Wouldst thou the young year's blossoms and the fruits of its decline,

And all by which the soul is charmed, enraptured, feasted, fed?

Wouldst thou the earth and heaven itself in one sole name combine?

I name thee, O Śakuntalâ, and all at once is said." [15]

When we remember that Goethe himself was the greatest poet of Germany and one of the greatest of the world, we realize the importance of his estimate of our poet. The well-known philosopher and traveller, Humboldt, pronounces the following judgment—"Kâlidása is a masterly describer of the influence which Nature exercises upon the minds of lovers. Tenderness in the expression of feelings and richness of creative fancy have assigned to him his lofty place among the poets of all nations." The celebrated critic, Schlegel, has assigned him a very high position amongst the glorious company of the 'Sons of Song'. Several eminent modern orientalists have also offered their tribute of praise to our Indian Shakespeare, as Sir William Jones was the first to call him—the very comparison of Kâlidâsa to Shakespeare is the highest form of eulogy that could be bestowed upon him by foreign critics. Sir Monier-Williams, while writing about the Śâkuntala, thus expresses himself:—"No composition of Kâlidása displays more the richness of his poetical genius, the exuberance of his imagination, the warmth and play of his fancy, his profound knowledge of the human heart, his delicate appreciation of its most refined and tender emotions, his familiarity with the workings and counter-workings of its conflicting feelings—in short more entitles him to rank as the Shakespeare of India." Prof. Lassen calls him "the brightest star in the firmament of Indian poetry."

We thus find that Kâlidâsa has established his sovereignty in the hearts of all alike. Now it may be asked, 'What is that in Kâlidâsa which establishes his undisputed claim to the highest honour which is thus bestowed upon him?' Unless this question is satisfactorily answered Kâlidâsa's merits as a poet cannot be

15 As translated from the German by Mr. E. B. Eastwick.

said to be determined.[16] His poetic genius has brought Sanskrit poetry to the highest elegance and refinement. His style is peculiarly pure and chaste. It has neither the laxity of the Puránas nor the extravagant colouring of later poems. It is unartificial and characterized by brevity consistent with perspicuity. An unaffected simplicity of expression and an easy-flowing language mark his writings which are embellished with similes unparalleled for their beauty and appropriateness, and with pithy general sayings. His diction is marked by the absence of long compounds, involved constructions, over-wrought rhetoric, and artificial puns. Kâlidâsa excels other poets in his description of the sublime and the beautiful. It is a principle recognized by all modern critics that 'Nature must be the life and essence of poetry'; and in respect of this, Kâlidâsa may be said to be essentially a poet of Nature (of course in the limited sense of the term which it is possible to attach to it in those times of gay luxury and general prosperity). He describes with most effective touches the gorgeous scenery of the mountain Himálaya—its snow-clad and mineral-covered summits, the peaks where sunshine ever reigns, the fragrant and cool breezes blowing there, the wilds with the hunters, the musk-deer, the potent herbs shedding lustre at night, the *chamara* deer, the Mânasa lake &c.; and his description of the Ganges and the peaceful hermitage-life is very striking and life-like. His descriptive powers are great, and some of the scenes in the Śák., the Megh., and the Ragh. are so enchanting as to hold his readers spell-bound. And as regards ध्वनिकाव्य, the kind of poetry which suggests even more than what it expresses, he is a master of acknowledged skill.

(B) HIS DATE.

The problem of the date of Kâlidâsa is a vexed one and it has yet to be finally settled. The earliest mention of Kâlidâsa by name is in the Aihole Inscription dated 634 A. D., and it furnishes the 7th Century A. D. as the downward limit of the poet's date. Tradition mentions Kálidâsa as a contemporary and a court-poet of king Vikramāditya. One king of that name founded the era known after him, which is accepted as commencing with 57 B. C. Some antiquarians once did not accept this date as the correct one, but brought Vikramāditya down to A. D. 544,

16 For this the student is referred to pp. 27-29 of our Introduction to the S'ákuntala, 5th ed.

propounding what was known as the *Korur Theory*. The battle of Korur marked a turning-point in Indian history, Vikramâditya having defeated the Mlechchhas in it. Curiously enough, Mr. Fergusson held that to commemorate the battle an era was invented, and that its beginning was placed back 600 years. So he put the true date of Vikramâditya at 544 A. D., and this theory for a time held sway, since no Inscription was discovered bearing a date prior to 600 of the Vikrama era. But the discovery of the Mandasor Inscription, which is dated Samvat 529, made this theory untenable, and the traditionary date remained unshaken. Then there is the theory of the *Nine Gems*. Nine eminent men called the 'Nine Gems' adorned the court of king Vikramáditya—

धन्वन्तरिक्षपणकामरसिंहशङ्कुवेतालभट्टघटकर्परकालिदासाः ।
ख्यातो वराहमिहिरो नृपतेः सभायां रत्नानि वै वररुचिर्नव विक्रमस्य ॥

Of these अमरसिंह is said to have lived between 414 A. D. and 642 A. D. Varâhamihira is believed to have died in 587 A. D. On the strength of these dates of Kâlidâsa's supposed contemporaries, Dr. Kern placed him in the latter half of the sixth century. But in this there are many *a priori* conclusions and speculations as to probabilities. If the tradition proves anything definitely, it proves the connexion of Kâlidâsa with king Vikramâditya; but as regards the contemporaneity of the nine authors, the tradition cannot be true. Next there is the theory of *Renaissance* propounded by Prof. Max Müller. He divided the whole Sanskrit literary period into two parts. The first began with the Vedas and ended with the first century A. D. Then came an *interregnum*, a period during which foreigners invaded India and so literary activity was dormant. The Professor placed the 'Renaissance of Sanskrit learning' in the sixth century A. D. with the reign of Vikramâditya. But, as has been shown by Drs. Peterson and Bühler, the period called *interregnum* was really not destitute of literary productivity, and, therefore, if Kâlidâsa is to be considered as the first poet of the new school, he must be placed considerably earlier than Prof. Max Müller has done

There are some minor things which have been pushed into the controversy. They are—(1) the alleged covert references to Diñnâga and Nichula in the Meghadûta, the former a foe and the latter a friend of Kâlidâsa; (2) the identity of Mâtṛigupta, a king of Kashmir, and Kâlidâsa (for, names in Sanskrit are often titles, and Mátṛigupta, *lit.* 'protected by the mother,' may also be taken as Kâligupta or Kâlidâsa); (3) and the supposed astronomical references in the works of Kâlidâsa to the astronomical theories of A'ryabhata, who lived in 476 A. D. Prof. R. N. Apte has examined all these at some length, and on the first point he comes to the conclusion that Diṅnâga and Nichula were not contemporaries of the great Kâlidâsa, but must have been contemporaries of *some other* Kâlidása. On the second point he observes that Mátṛigupta and Kálida'sa were two different persons, since they are differently quoted by Kshemendra and other writers and commentators. The supposed astronomical references have really no astronomical significance at all, and it cannot be said that Kálidása was acquainted with the astronomical works of A'ryabhata. Mr. K. B. Pathak, the latest exponent of the 6th century theory, repeats the arguments given above, but principally bases his conclusion on his theory about the Húṇa kings, allusion to whom is made by the poet in the Raghuvaṃśa. He argues that since there is no mention made of the Húṇas in the Rámâyaṇa, the conclusion follows that Kálidása unconsciously refers to the Hu'ṇa kings of his own time, who held sway over the Punjab and Kashmir in the second quarter of the sixth century. But this rests merely on assumption; for there are references to the Húṇas even in the Mahábhárata. Prof. Apte has also shown that just beyond Bactria or the threshold of ancient India, the Hûṇas had constituted a powerful empire from the middle of the 3rd century B. C. to the end of the 1st or the 2nd century A. D.

Modern European scholars are generally inclined to hold that Kâlidâsa must have flourished under one or more of the Gupta kings. The Gupta period (about 300–650 A. D.) was noted in ancient Indian history for a revival of Sanskrit learning and arts. The late Mr. Vincent A. Smith (see his *Early History of India* p. 304, 3rd ed. 1914) believed that Kâlidâsa must have lived in the reigns of the first two, or even in that of the third, of these Gupta Kings:—

Chandragupta II. (*c.* 357–413)
Kumâragupta I. (413–455)
Skandagupta (455–480)

Both Chandragupta II. and Skandagupta had adopted the title of *Vikramâditya*. To quote the words of Mr. Smith, "It is not unlikely that the earliest works of Kâlidâsa............may have been composed before A. D. 413, that is to say, while Chandragupta II. was on the throne; but I am inclined to regard the reign of Kumâragupta I. (413–455) as the time during which the poet's later works were composed, and it seems possible, that the whole of his literary career fell within the limits of that reign. It is also possible that he may have continued writing after the accession of Skandagupta". Mr. Smith thus makes Kâlidâsa's literary career extend over a period of not less than thirty years. Note that, even according to Mr. Smith, there is nothing wrong in the tradition about a Vikramáditya having been our poet's patron; only we must arrive at an understanding as to *which* Vikramâditya is meant, because various kings in the history of ancient India called themselves by that title. We ourselves hold, for reasons given below, that we must accept as our poet's patron that king Vikramáditya whose traditional era commences at 56 B. C. The attempt to place Kālidāsa in the court of the Gupta kings rests merely on the fact that Chandragupta II. was named Vikramáditya. But the existence of prior kings of that title is now a certainty.[17]

Vatsabhúti, the author of the Mandasor inscription, copies several ideas from Kālidâsa; the latter must, therefore, have lived prior to 472 A. D. Again, Aśvaghosha, the author of the *Buddhacharita*, which is a life of the great Buddha in Sanskrit, has numerous passages similar to those occurring in the works of Kâlidâsa. Now, Kâlidâsa was an original poet borrowing his subjects from Válmîki and other ancient authors. Aśvaghoshe was more a philosopher than a poet, and may, with greater probability, be supposed to have borrowed his ideas from Kālidāsa. The date of Aśvaghosha is given as 78 A. D.; and, if we suppose him to have borrowed from Kâlidâsa, the latter will have to be placed earlier than 78 A. D. And in this view Dr. Peterson also concurs when he says '*Kâlidâsa stands near the beginning of the Christian era, if, indeed, he does not overtop it.*'

There is also internal evidence pointing to the same conclusion. We have first the evidence obtained from the state of the law of inheritance and the penalty for theft as they are indicated in passages in the Śâkuntala. The passage in the sixth Act of the drama, announcing the death of the merchant Dhanamitra who died heirless, seems to Prof. Apte to refer to a period when the widow of a deceased person could not inherit his estate. Such a

17 The Râjataraṃgiṇī mentions an earlier Vikramâditya, a contemporary of King Pratâpâditya of Kashmir.

period is to be found only before the Christian era, when Manu, Âpastamba and Vasishṭha held sway, and Bṛihaspati, Śaṅkha, Likhita and Yájñavalkya had not yet written their Codes. The penalty for theft, as indicated in the prologue to the sixth Act, seems to have been the extreme one, and there is also a passage of similar import in the Vikramorvaśîya (आत्मनो वधमाहर्ता &c. V. 1). The penalty for theft has been from time to time mitigated with the progress of civilization. Manu and Âpastamba lay down the extreme penalty, the option of fine being introduced later on, as we find it in the Smṛiti of Bṛihaspati. These two circumstances tend to show that Kálidâsa flourished at a period which is anterior to Bṛihaspati, the latter being generally placed in the first century A. D.

Prof. Apte further calls attention to the fact that there is no reference to the Nyâya philosophy in the works of Kâlidâsa [except perhaps in Ragh. XIII. 1, in which the word शब्दगुणं (आकाशं) occurs, but which the poet might have borrowed from the Sámkhyas], and concludes that he must have lived *before* the development of that philosophy. Then again we have the evidence of style. The artificiality of diction and the fondness for long compounds and double-meaning words which mark the writings of Daṇḍin (who in his Kâvyádarśa says that an abundance of compounds constitutes the quality of *ojas* in poetry), Bâṇa, Bhavabhúti (7th century A. D.) and other mediæval writers, are entirely absent in Kâlidâsa's writings—a fact which shows that he must be placed some six or seven centuries before them, a period necessary to cause such a revolution in the art of literary composition, considering the scanty means of the propagation of learning in those times. It thus becomes clear that Kâlidâsa lived in the first century B. C. at the latest.[18]

---

18 Prof. S. Ray refers to the discovery in 1909–10 of the Bhita medallion, which pictures a scene which looks exactly like the opening scene of the S'âkuntala. The medallion is assigned to the Sunga period (184 B. C.–72 B. C.), and Prof. Ray assumes that Kâlidâsa is anterior to the date of the medallion, though the Archæological Survey authorities, holding to the Vincent Smith date, are inclined to dispute the identification of the scene with the one in the Play.

III.—THE POEM.

(1) Summary of the Story.

Before the student begins the study of his actual text, it is advisable that he should make himself familiar with the contents of the poem as a connected whole. We, therefore, give below briefly the story of the poem as presented in its eight Cantos :—

Canto I.—The poet begins with a description of the mountain Himâlaya, deservedly called the King of all mountain-ranges. From his wife Menâ he had a son named Mainâka and a daughter called Párvatî, who was in her former birth Satî, the daughter of Daksha and wife of S'iva. Párvatî's childhood and budding youth are then described. When she has attained the marriageable age, the sage Nárada, who is on a visit to Himálaya, foretells that she would win S'iva for her husband. Relying on this prophecy, Himálaya does not particularly bestir himself in the matter of his daughter's marriage. In the meanwhile, the god S'iva, after he had lost his wife Satî, had betaken himself to a peak of the Himálaya and was practising penance there. When Himálaya comes to know of this, he arranges that his daughter, accompanied by her two companions, should wait upon S'iva and do worshipful homage to him.

Canto II.—At about this time the gods in Heaven were very much harassed by the demon Târaka and they therefore go to Brahmá in a body. Having first propitiated him by a suitable hymn of praise, they narrate to him their grievances. Táraka, who had become master of the three worlds by virtue of a boon he had obtained from Brahmâ, had pressed all the gods into his service, and even the mighty Indra was powerless against him. The only person capable of ridding the world of this demon would be the son of S'iva. As, however, that puissant deity had no son, the obvious course was to bring about the birth of a son to him. Brahmá points out that Párvatî, daughter of the mountain Himálaya, was the only suitable mate to S'iva; if their marriage would be brought about, the gods could accomplish what they sought.

Canto III.—Now, in order to induce the sentiment of passion in the anchorite S'iva and thereby make him marry Párvatî,

Indra deputes Káma (the god of Love). The latter, accompanied by his friend and helper Vasanta (the Vernal Season), repairs to the place where S'iva was practising penance and Párvatî was in attendance on him. When Káma appears there, all of a sudden the trees and plants put forth fresh sprouts, the earth becomes clad with untimely vernal glory, the beasts of the forest and the birds of the air show the influence of love, and even the ascetics find it hard to control their senses. The sudden descent of Spring and the near presence of the lovely maiden combine for a moment to slightly disturb the concentration of S'iva, but for a moment only. He immediately controls himself; and finding that Káma was responsible for that momentary deflection of his fixity, he becomes wrathful; all of a sudden fire bursts forth from his third eye (on the forehead), which consumes Káma, reducing him to a heap of white ashes. Frightened at this unexpected catastrophe, Himálaya carries away his daughter to a safer place; S'iva immediately vanishes from the scene; and the *coup* planned by Indra comes to naught for the time being.

Canto IV.—Rati, the wife of Káma, had accompanied her lord on his fateful mission and was an eye-witness of his sad end. She now laments long and piteously. She calls upon Vasanta to arrange a funeral pyre, on which she intends to immolate herself. The preparations are being made, when suddenly a voice from the celestial void assures her that her separation from Káma is only temporary; for, when S'iva would wed Párvatî, he would bestow upon him his corporeal form, and thus would Rati be re-united with her husband.

Canto V.—Now Párvatî, who had fallen in love with Śiva and secretly cherished a desire to become his wife, found herself sorely disappointed; and to achieve her object she could think of no other means than to practise austere penance. With difficulty she obtains the permission of her parents and repairs to a peak of the Himálaya which later came to be called *Gaurî-s'ikhara* after her. Here she continues mortifying the flesh by all kinds of processes, and is not daunted by even the severest forms of penance known to ascetics. These austerities win for her the love of Śiva who comes to her hermitage in the disguise of a young ascetic, in order to test the strength of her attachment. On learning the object of her penance he argues with her skilfully for a long while, pointing out the various faults of Śiva, such as his love for odious and horrid objects, his deformed bouy, his poverty, &c., and generally proving his entire unsuitability for the hand of such a pure, noble-born, delicate and cultured maiden as Párvatî. The latter, however, attaches no importance to the so-called faults of Śiva; on the contrary, in her eyes those very faults constitute his charms; and, in short, speaking through her attendant maid, she makes it clear to the visitor that his arguments were unavailing and his presence unwelcome. At this the ascetic discovers himself in his real form and declares himself as her slave. When Párvatî sees Śiva before her, she is filled with supreme joy.

CANTO VI.—Párvatî then asks S'iva to obtain her father's formal sanction for the marriage. S'iva deputes the Seven heavenly Sages for this purpose. Accompanied by Vasishṭha's wife Arundhatî, they go to the capital city (Oshadhiprastha) of Himàlaya, which they much admire. Himálaya receives them with proper respect and veneration; and, after mutual greetings are exchanged, he asks them in courteous terms the purpose of their visit. Thereupon they make known their business. Himálaya is only too pleased at their request and gives his consent. Fixing the date of the marriage as being the fourth day from that day, the sages return to S'iva, inform him accordingly, and, permitted by him, go back to their celestial abode.

CANTO VII.—The city of Himâlaya is now gaily decorated in honour of the coming marriage-celebrations. On the appointed day the ladies in Himâlaya's palace bathed Pa'rvatî, put on her the customary marriage-dress, and decked her with various auspicious things for the holy ceremony; and on Kaila'sa, S'iva too was suitably dressed and decked by the Holy Mothers. Afterwards he starts for Oshadhiprastha on his famous bull, accompanied by the Mothers, by his attendant Gaṇas, and by Indra and other gods. He is received at the gates of the city by Hima'laya and the bride's party. His beauty is much admired by the spectators, and in particular by the ladies of the city. Then inside the palace the holy rites connected with wedding are all duly performed, including the final blessing pronounced by Sarasvatî. After the conclusion of the ceremony the guests disperse and S'iva stays at his father-in-law's house.

CANTO VIII.—The amorous sports of the newly-wedded pair are now described at some length. In all, S'iva spends one month at Oshadhiprastha and then leaves it in the company of his wife. He next wanders over many regions, including among them the mountains Meru, Kailâsa, Mandara, and Malaya, the celestial Ganges, and the Nandana Garden. Finally he comes to the mountain Gandhamadana at evening time. He proceeds to describe the beauty of sunset to his consort, the evening gradually giving place to a moonlit night. They then both drink the wine brought to them by the guardian-deity of the mountain Gandhamádana, and spend the night in connubial pleasures. He then makes that place his abode thenceforth, and lives there for twenty-five years, enjoying the company of his beloved without break or hindrance in his happiness. With this statement the poem concludes.

(2) The Sources of the Poem.

The plots of all the works of Kálidâsa, excepting the Meghadúta and the Mâlavikâgnimitra, are borrowed from legendary or historical sources; on the bare outlines of these stories he built splendid structures out of his poetic imagination, changing and altering as suited his purpose. The story of the marriage of Śiva and Pârvatî is an ancient one in ancient Hindu Mythology. It is found in the Brahma-Purâṇa, in the Kâliká-Purâṇa and in the Śiva-Puráṇa; the two former versions are comparatively meagre, while the one in the Śiva-Puráṇa is more detailed. For the benefit of the student we subjoin from that work the following extracts[1] corresponding to the various Cantos:—

Canto I. राजते स्म हरिस्तत्र (=सृष्टौ) वैराजः पुरुषः प्रभुः । सत्यं पदमुपश्रित्य स्थितोऽसौ पुरुषोत्तमः ॥ तपोलोकं समास्थाय ब्रह्मातिष्ठत्तपोधनः । तपश्च मानसाः पुत्रा ब्रह्मणा निर्मिताः पुरा ॥ ते चोर्ध्वरेतसः सर्वे पश्चादन्यानृषीन्प्रभुः । ते विरक्ताश्च संजाताः पश्चात्क्रोधमवाप सः ॥ तेनैव रोदनं चक्रे ततश्चैवाभवद्धरः । रोदनाद्रुद्रनाम्नेति प्रसिद्धो भगवान्भवः ॥ ततो ब्रह्मा ऋषीन्सप्त भृग्वादीन्निर्ममे तदा । उत्सङ्गान्नारदं श्रेष्ठं छायायां कर्दमं पुनः ॥ अङ्गुष्ठाच्च तदा दक्षं ...... ॥ षष्टिः कन्यास्तथा जाता दक्षाच्चैव महात्मनः । दत्ता दक्षेण ताः कन्या विधिवदृषिसत्तमाः ॥ देवाश्च दनुजाश्चैव... ॥ प्रसूतौ दक्षकन्याभिर्व्याप्तमेतच्चराचरम् । सती नाम तथा कन्या रुद्राय च महात्मने ॥ दत्ता दक्षेण सा देवी भवानीति प्रकीर्तिता । गुणरूपा महाकाली या वै रुद्रमुपाश्रिता ॥ पुनश्च पार्वती जाता सा शिवं समुनागता ॥ पूर्वं दक्षस्य रुद्रस्य स्पर्धा जाता महात्मनः । ततो दक्षः स्वयं यज्ञं कृतवान्देवसंनिधौ ॥ अनाहूय तथा रुद्रं पूर्वमृषिसमन्वितः ।

1 In these extracts lines giving unnecessary and lengthy details have been omitted, but care has been taken to preseve the thread of the narrative intact.

ततो देवी सती नाम्नी पित्रा नाकारिता यदा ॥ तदा गता पुनस्तत्र नाहूतापि पितुर्गृहे । प्राप्यावज्ञां तु सा तत्र देहत्यागमथाकरोत् ॥ सतीदेहसमुत्पन्ना ज्वाला लोकभयावहा । पतिता पर्वते यत्र पूजिता सुखदायिनी ॥ ज्वालामुखीति सा प्रोक्ता सर्वकामफलप्रदा । इदानीं पूज्यते लोकैः सर्वकामफलाप्तये ॥ सा देवी शैलराजस्य पत्नी मेनेति विश्रुता । पितॄणां मानसी कन्या तस्यां जन्म समादधे ॥ ततश्च पार्वती नाम प्रसिद्धमभवत्तदा । सा पुनः शिवमाराध्य भर्तारं समुपाश्रिता ॥ (अ० ५, ६)

Canto II. ब्रह्मा सर्वं सुनिश्चित्य देवाज्ञापरिसाधकः । वरं दातुं तदा तत्राजगाम हंसवाहनः ॥ यत्रैष तारको नाम तपस्तप्यति दारुणम् । उवाच वचनं तस्मै वरं ब्रूहि यथेप्सितम् ॥ दैत्य उवाच—यदि प्रसन्नो देवेशो यदि देयो वरो मम । वरद्वयं तदा देयं श्रूयतां च पितामह ॥ त्वया च निर्मिते लोके मत्तुल्यो बलवान्न हि । शिववीर्यसमुत्पन्नः पुत्रः सेनापतिर्यदा । भूत्वा शस्त्रं क्षिपेन्मह्यं तदा मे मरणं भवेत् ॥ दैत्योऽपि (=तारकः) तपसस्तस्माद्विरराम महामुने । वरं लब्ध्वा शुभं तत्र शोणिताख्यं पुरं गतः ॥ सर्वे वै पीडितास्तेन तारकेण दुरात्मना । देवा वा दानवाश्चान्ये यक्षाः किंपुरुषास्तदा ॥ पीडिताः सर्व एवैते तेभ्यो रत्नान्युपाददे । इन्द्रादिभिश्च दिक्पालैः स्वीयं रत्नं समर्पितम् ॥ इन्द्रेणोच्चैःश्रवास्तस्मै धर्मेण दण्डरत्नकम् । कुबेरेण गदा तस्मै निधयो नव एव च ॥ वरुणेन हयाः शुद्धा ऋषिभिः कामधुक्तथा । यत्र यत्र शुभं दृष्टं तत्तदानीतवांस्तदा ॥ समुद्रश्च तथा रत्नान्यदात्तस्मै पुरा मुने । सूर्यश्च तप्यते तावद्यावद्दुःखं न जायते ॥ चन्द्रस्तत्र सदा दृश्यो वायुः सर्वानुकूलवान् । देवानां चैव यद्द्रव्यं पितॄणां कव्यमेव च ॥ त्रैलोक्यं चैव तत्सर्वं तारकाज्ञापरायणम् । ते देवाश्च सदा तत्र सेवामार्गपरायणाः ॥ देवोद्यानानि सर्वाणि तीर्थान्यपि महामुने । आनीतानि गृहे तेन न किंचिदवशेषितम् ॥ एवं वर्षाण्यनेकानि गतानि पीडितास्तदा । सर्वे देवा मिलित्वा च ब्रह्माणं शरणं गताः ॥ ते सर्वे च तदा गत्वा ब्रह्माणं जगतः प्रभुम् । नमस्कृत्य स्थितास्तत्र नम्रीभूता ऋषीश्वराः ॥ तान्विषण्णांस्तदा तत्र दृष्ट्वोवाच पितामहः । यूयमत्र कथं प्राप्ताः किं दुःखं भवतां पुनः ॥ तदहं स्फोटयाम्यद्य साध्यं यदि भवेदिह । इत्येतद्वचनं श्रुत्वा तदीयं परमर्षयः ॥ देवाः सानुचराः सर्वे वचनं चेदमब्रुवन् । भवतः किमविज्ञातं दुःखं च यदुपस्थितम् ॥ तारकाच्चैव यद्दुःखं संभूतं परमेश्वर । इत्येवं वचनं श्रुत्वा ब्रह्मा वचनमाददे ॥ मत्तो नैव वधो योग्यो मत्तो वृद्धिमुपागतः । उपायं वो दिशाम्यद्य श्रूयतां ऋषिसत्तमाः ॥ शिववीर्यसमुत्पन्नः पुत्रश्चैनं हनिष्यति ! हिमवच्छिखरे रम्ये शंभुस्तप्यति नित्यशः ॥ सखीभ्यां सहिता तत्र परिचर्यां शिवस्य ह । वचनान्नारदस्यैव उमा पित्रानुशासिता ॥ करोतीह ऋषिश्रेष्ठास्तस्याः संयोगतां व्रजेत् । शिववीर्यं समाधातुं क्षमा नान्या शिवां विना ॥ यथा वीर्यं मदीयं वै जलरूपधरः शिवः । समाधातुं समर्थोऽस्ति तस्मादन्यो न वै पुनः ॥ तथोपायं करिष्यध्वं तदा सिद्धिर्भविष्यति । इत्येवं वचनं तस्य श्रुत्वा ते सर्व एव हि ॥ नमस्कृत्य सुरास्तत्र विचार्य तु परस्परम् । जग्मुस्ते मुनयो देवाः स्वं स्वं स्थानं मुदान्विताः ॥ गतेषु तेषु देवेन्द्रः सस्मार मकरध्वजम् । आगतस्तत्क्षणादेव रत्या युक्तः स वै प्रभुः ॥ (अ. ९, १०)

Canto III. (स्मरः) प्रणामं च ततः कृत्वा स्थित्वा प्राञ्जलिरब्रवीत् । किं कार्यं ते समुत्पन्नं स्मृतोऽहं केन हेतुना ॥ तत्त्वं कथय देवेश तत्कर्तुं समुपागतः । इत्युक्त्वा तु महेन्द्राय स्थितस्तूष्णीं प्रियया सह ॥ इन्द्रोऽपि वचनं श्रुत्वा कंदर्पस्य महात्मनः । उवाच वचनं तं वै युक्तं युक्तमिति स्तुवन् ॥ त्वया साधु समारब्धं यत्ते कार्यमुपस्थितम् । तत्कर्तुमुद्यतोऽसि त्वं धन्यस्त्वं मकरध्वज ॥ जयार्थं मम देवेन निर्मितं वज्रमुत्तमम् । अन्यदस्त्रं भवानेव देवेन निर्मितः पुरा ॥ वज्रं हिंसात्मकं विद्धि भवान्सुखकरं मम । द्वयोरपि भवानत्र श्रेष्ठः सर्वेषु चोत्तमम् ॥ वज्रं च निष्फलं स्याद्वै त्वं तु नैव कदापि हि । यतः कार्यं प्रजायेत ततः किं नु प्रियः सदा ॥ तस्मान्मित्रवरस्त्वं च कार्यं कर्तुं ममार्हसि ॥ ...न केवलं मदीयं च कार्यं देवसुखावहम् ॥ वयं च याचितारः स्मः कार्यं कार्यं त्वया शुभम् । इत्येवं मघवद्वाक्यं श्रुत्वा तु मकरध्वजः ॥ उवाच प्रेमगम्भीरं गद्गदं स्मितपूर्वकम् । किमर्थं भाषसे देव नान्तरं ह्यावयोरिह ॥ तथापि च महाराज कथयामि शृणुष्व तत् । मुक्तिमार्गं समापन्नं ते शत्रुं पातयाम्यहम्॥ ते पदं कर्षितुं यो वै तपस्तप्यति दारुणम्। क्षणेन पातयाम्यद्य कटाक्षेण स्त्रियास्तथा ॥ देवं वा दानवं वापि ऋषिं वा देवसत्तमान् ॥ मानुषाणां न वै मेऽद्य गणना पातने मता ॥ वज्रं तिष्ठतु दूरे वै शस्त्राण्यन्यान्यनेकशः ॥ किं ते कार्यं करिष्यन्ति मयि मित्रे स्थिते प्रभो । अन्येषां गणना नास्ति पातयामि हरं यदि ॥ एवं तु वचनं तस्य श्रुत्वा हर्षमुपागतः । उवाच प्रणियन्वाचा कामं कामिसुखावहम् ॥ यत्कार्यं मनसोद्दिष्टं तत्कार्यं कथितं त्वया । शृणु काम प्रवक्ष्यामि यदर्थं स्मरणं तव ॥ तारकाख्यो महादैत्यो ब्रह्मणो वरमुत्तमम् । संप्राप्य पीड्यते लोकान्नष्टा धर्मा ह्यनेकशः ॥ दुःखिता देवताः सर्वा ऋषयश्च तथामलाः । देवानां चायुधान्यत्र विफलान्यभवन्प्रभो ॥ मरणं नैव तस्येत्थं भविष्यति कदाचन । एतस्य मरणं प्रोक्तं शंभुवीर्योद्भवात्मनः ॥ एतत्कार्यं त्वया साध्यं देवानां परमं सुखम् । ममापि हि हितं लोके कर्तुमर्हसि सांप्रतम् ॥ शंभुश्च गिरिराजे वै तपः परममास्थितः । तत्समीपे च सेवार्थं पार्वती सखिसंयुता ॥ संतिष्ठति महाराज पित्राज्ञया मया श्रुतम् । यथा तस्यां रुचिस्तस्य शिवस्य परमात्मनः ॥ जायते नितरां काम तथा कार्यं त्वया ध्रुवम् । इत्युक्तो वचनं तस्मै तथेत्योमिति तद्वचः ॥ गृहीत्वा शिरसा कामः सदारः सवसन्तकः । यत्र चैव हरः साक्षात्तपते परमं तपः ॥ तत्र गत्वा मधुश्चादौ धर्मान्विस्तारयन्स्थितः । वसन्तस्य च ये धर्मास्ते धर्मास्तद्वने गताः ॥ वनानि च प्रफुल्लानि पलाशानां च तद्वने ॥ पुष्पाणि सहकारेषु अशोकवनिकासु च । बकुलेषु च पुष्पाणि भ्रमराकुलितानि च ॥ तिलकेषु तथैतेषु कोकिलाकलकूजितम् । भ्रमराणां तथा शब्दो ह्यनेकोऽभून्महामुने ॥ चन्द्रस्य विशदा ह्यासन्किरणा दूतिका इव । मानिनः प्रेरयामासुर्ह्यकाले कामदर्पितान् ॥ मारुतश्च सुखश्चात्र ववौ विरहिणां प्रियः । कामो वनौकसां तत्र मुनीनां दुःसहो ह्यभूत् ॥ अचेतनानां तत्रैव कामशक्तिः सचेतसाम् । अकालिनीं प्रवृत्तिं च मधोर्वीक्ष्य हरस्तदा ॥ आश्चर्यं परमं गत्वा तपः परमदुष्करम् । तपयामास तत्रैव हरो दुःखहरः परः ॥ वसन्ते प्रसृते तत्र कामो रतिसमन्वितः । चूतबाणं समाकृष्य स्थितः पार्श्वे तु वामतः ॥ रत्या युक्तस्तदा कामं दृष्ट्वा को वा न मोहितः । एतस्मिन्नन्तरे देवी पुष्पाभरणभूषिता ॥ सखीभ्यां संयुता तत्र यत्रातिष्ठद्धरः स्वयम् । जगाम शिवपूजार्थं नीत्वा पुष्पा-

ण्यनेकशः ॥ पृथिव्यां यादृशं लोके सौन्दर्यं विविधं महत् । तत्सर्वं चैकतस्तस्यां पार्वत्यां समुपस्थितम् ॥ आर्तवाणि च पुष्पाणि धृतानि च तया यदा । तत्सौन्दर्यं कथं वर्ण्यमपि वर्षशतैरपि ॥ यदा शिवसमीपे तु गता सा पर्वतात्मजा । तदेवाकर्षयच्चापं रुच्यर्थं शूलपाणिनः ॥ तच्चापं पतितं हस्तात्पार्श्वे तस्य महात्मनः । तयागत्योत्पलाक्ष्या वै दृष्टः शंभुः स्वयं यदा ॥ नमस्कृत्य तदा पूजां कृत्वासीत्पुरतः स्थिता । सा दृष्टा प्रभुणा तत्र सुन्दराङ्गं विवृण्वती ॥ शिवोऽपि वर्णयामास तदङ्गं सुन्दरं तदा । इत्येवं वर्णयित्वा तु तपसो विरराम ह ॥ स्त्रीस्वभावात्तदा सा च लज्जिता सुन्दरी स्वयम् । विवृण्वती तथाङ्गानि पश्यन्ती च मुहुर्मुहुः ॥ एवं चेष्टां तदा दृष्ट्वा शंभुर्मोहमुपागमत् । यद्यालिङ्गनमेतस्याः करोमि किं पुनः सुखम् ॥ क्षणमात्रं विचिन्त्यैवं किमहं मोहमागतः । एवं विवेकमासाद्य पर्यङ्कबन्धनं दृढम् ॥ रचयामास सर्वात्मा ईश्वरः किं पतेदिह । धैर्यस्य च्यवनं दृष्ट्वा विचारे तत्परः शिवः ॥ कारणं किंचिदुत्पन्नं नान्यथेदं भवेदिति । दिशो विलोकयामास परितः शंकरस्तदा ॥ वामभागे स्थितं कामं ददर्श बाणकर्षिणम् । तं दृष्ट्वा क्रोधसंयुक्तः संजातस्तत्क्षणादपि ॥ तृतीयात्तस्य नेत्राद्वै निःससाराग्निरुच्छलः । भस्मसात्कृतवांस्तेन मदनं तावदेव हि ॥ यावच्च मरुतां वाचः क्षम्यतां वै प्रभो त्वया । भवेन च ततः पूर्वं हतोऽसौ मकरध्वजः । शिवोऽपि तत्क्षणादेव विहायाश्रममुत्थितः ॥ वेगदीर्घीकृतात्मा च गिरिराजः सुतां तदा । समादाय सखीयुक्तां जगाम मन्दिरं स्वकम् ॥ क्षणमात्रं रतिस्तत्र विसंज्ञा ह्यभवत्तदा । भर्तृजन्यं च यद् दुःखं न ज्ञातमृषिसत्तमाः ॥ (अ. १०,११)

Canto IV. जातायां चैव संज्ञायां रतिर्दुःखसमन्विता । विललाप तदा तत्र वनमासीत्सुदुःखितम् ॥ मयूराश्चैव नृत्यं हि वृक्षाश्च चलनं जहुः । मृगाश्च भ्रमणं भ्रमन्भृङ्गा गुञ्जारवं पुनः ॥ पक्षिणश्च तदा विप्रा मूकाश्च मुनयो यथा । वायवश्चलनं हित्वा वान्ति नैव दिशो दश ॥ रतिरुवाच—किं करोमि क्व गच्छामि किं कृतं दैवतैरिह । स्वामिनं तु समाहूय हाहा प्रिय प्रियेति च ॥ हस्तौ पादौ तथास्फाल्य केशानत्रोटयत्तदा । ब्रह्मणा सदृशो योगो न सोढो मम कर्मणा ॥ तद्विलापं तदा श्रुत्वा देवाः शिवमुपाययुः । प्रसन्नं कृतवन्तस्ते शिवं लोकसुखावहम् ॥ प्रसन्नो भगवांस्तत्र वचनं चेदमब्रवीत् । अनङ्गस्तावदेव स्याद्यावच्च रुक्मिणीपतिः ॥ द्वारकायां स्वयं स्थित्वा पुत्रानुत्पादयिष्यति । इत्युक्त्वान्तर्दधे रुद्रो देवानां स्तुवतां तदा ॥ देवास्तां च समासाद्य रुद्रस्य वचनाद्रतिम् । उक्त्वा वचस्तदीयं च स्वं स्वं भुवनमाययुः ॥ (अ. ११)

Canto V. पितुर्गृहं तदा गत्वा मिलित्वा मातरं मुदा । पुनर्जातं तदात्मानं मेने सा पर्वतात्मजा ॥ निनिन्द च स्वकं रूपं हा हतास्मि तदाऽब्रवीत् । तिष्ठन्ती च सखीमध्ये धिग्रूपं च मदीयकम् ॥ इति सा दुःखिता तत्र स्मरन्ती हरचेष्टितम् । एतस्मिन्समये तत्र नारदो ह्यगमत्तदा ॥ पूजितः सुखमासीनः पृष्टः प्राप्तौ शिवस्य च । उक्तवान्वचनं ह्येतत्तपःसाध्यो हरः स्वयम् ॥ नान्यथा लभ्यते देवि देवैर्ब्रह्मादिकैरपि । पार्वती च तदा श्रुत्वा वचनं नारदस्य च ॥ तपःसाध्यं हरं मेने तपोर्थं मन आददे । मातरं पितरं

चैव सखीभ्यां पर्यपृच्छत ॥ सख्यावूचतुः—हिमवञ्छ्रूयतां पुत्र्या वचनं बुध्यतेऽधुना । साफल्यं नैव देहस्य रूपस्य च तथा पुनः ॥ भवतश्च कुलस्यास्य साफल्यं कर्तुमिच्छति । इत्येवं च तदा पृष्टे गिरिराजोऽब्रवीदिदम् ॥ मह्यं च रोचते सख्यौ मेनायै रुच्यतां पुनः । जग्मतुर्मातरं सख्यौ तदाज्ञप्ते मुनीश्वराः ॥ गत्वा तु मातरं तस्या वचनं प्रोचतुस्तदा । तप्तुकामास्ति ते पुत्री शिवार्थे परमं तपः ॥ प्राप्तानुज्ञा पितुश्चैव तुभ्यं च परिपृच्छति । समाकर्ण्य वचस्त्वेतन्मेना दुःखमुपागता ॥ समाहूय तदा पुत्रीमुवाच विह्वला सती । कुत्र यासि तपः कर्तुं देवाः सन्ति गृहे मम ॥ तीर्थानि च विचित्राणि सन्ति किं न पितुर्गृहे । शरीरं कोमलं वत्से तपस्तु कठिनं महत् ॥ इत्येवं बहुधा पुत्री मात्रापि वारिता सती । सुखं नैवात्र संवेदे ह्यनाराध्य शिवं तदा ॥ दुःखं ज्ञात्वा तदीयं सा मात्राज्ञप्ता जगाम ह । सखीभ्यां सहिता तत्र तपस्तप्तुमुपाययौ ॥ हित्वाभरणान्यनेकानि वस्त्राणि विविधानि च । वल्कलं च तदा धृत्वा मौञ्जीं बद्ध्वा सुशोभनाम् ॥ हित्वा हारं तदा चर्म मृगस्य परमं शुभम् । जगाम तपसे तत्र शृङ्गे स्यात्तीर्थमुत्तमम् ॥ गौरीशिखरनामासीत्तपसः करणादिह । सुन्दराश्च द्रुमास्तत्र पवित्राः फलभाजिनः ॥ भूमिशुद्धिं ततः कृत्वा विधाय वेदिकां शुभाम् । उपविश्यासने तत्र चकार परमं तपः ॥ तया तपः समारब्धं मुनीनामपि दुष्करम् । चाञ्चल्यं च तदा त्यक्त्वा शरीरस्य विशेषतः ॥ दीप्तानां च तथाग्नीनां मध्ये स्थित्वा तु घर्मके । वर्षासु स्थण्डिले स्थित्वा शीते जलसमीपगाः । एवं तपः प्रकुर्वाणा वृक्षानारोपयत्तदा । सिञ्चती प्रत्यहं तत्र ह्यातिथ्यं चाप्यकल्पयत् ॥ वातश्चैव तथा शीतो वृष्टिश्च विविधा तदा । दुःखं च विविधं तत्र गणितं न तया तदा ॥ तथा तपस्तया तप्तं मुनिभिश्च सुदुष्करम् । श्रुत्वा च ऋषयस्तत्र विस्मयं परमं गताः ॥ दर्शनार्थं समाजग्मुः कीदृक् तप्तं तपोऽनया । महतां धर्मवृद्धेषु गमनं श्रेष्ठमुच्यते ॥ प्रमाणं तपसो नास्ति मान्यो धर्मः सदा बुधैः । श्रुत्वा दृष्ट्वा तपस्तस्याः किमन्यैः क्रियते तपः ॥ जल्पन्तस्ते तदा तत्र कठिनाङ्गाश्च ये पुनः । तदाश्रमगता ये च विरोधरहितास्तदा ॥ सिंहा गावस्तथान्ये च रागादिदोषसंयुताः । तन्महिम्ना च ते तत्र न बाध्यन्ते परस्परम् ॥ वृक्षाश्च सफलास्तत्र तृणानि विविधानि च । पुष्पाणि च विचित्राणि तत्रासन् ऋषिसत्तमाः ॥ तद्वनं च तदा सर्वं कैलासेन समन्वितम् । जातं च तपसस्तस्याः सिद्धिरूपमभूत्तदा ॥ एतस्मिन्समये देवा ऋषयो नारदादयः । पार्वत्यास्तत्तपो दृष्ट्वा तेजसा व्यापितास्तथा । जग्मुस्ते च तदा तत्र यत्रास्ते वृषभध्वजः ॥ (त ऊचुः)—पार्वत्या तु तपस्तप्तं दारुणं लोकशोषणम् । अपूर्वदृष्टं नो भाविं देवदानवदुर्लभम् ॥ कुरु कार्यं तथा शीघ्रं शिव त्वं परिपालकः । इत्युक्ते नारदप्रख्यैः शंभुर्वचनमब्रवीत् ॥ तया पर्वतराजस्य सुतया तपसा ह्यहम् । क्रीतोऽस्मि वचनं तस्याः करिष्यामि भवत्प्रियम् ॥ इत्युक्त्वा च तदा देवान् विसृज्य शंकरस्तदा । जटिलं रूपमास्थाय जगाम पार्वतीवनम् ॥ तमागतं तदा दृष्ट्वा शिवाप्यपूजयत्तदा । पार्वती कुशलं तं वै पप्रच्छ त्वं कुतो गतः ॥ इति पृष्टे तया तत्र प्रुक्त्वा स्वीयं च तां पुनः । पृष्टवान् कपटेनैव गोपयन् रूपमुत्तमम् ॥ अयि देवि जलं ह्येतत् फलादि च निरन्तरम् । अविच्छिन्नं भवेदत्र यथाशक्ति तपस्यसि ॥ नवेऽपि देवि वयसि कृतं वै तप उत्तमम् । अतः किंचिदिह पृच्छेयं कथनीयं त्वयाधुना ॥ पूजा

विधिस्त्वया देवि कृतो वै सर्वथात्मना । तस्मान्मैत्री च संजाता रहस्यं नैव गोप्यताम् ॥ किं वाञ्छसि वरं देवि प्रष्टुमिच्छाम्यतः परम् । वरार्थे च तपश्चेद्धि तिष्ठतु तप एव तत् ॥ रत्नं तु ग्रहीतारं वै न पृच्छति ग्रहीष्यति । ईदृशं चैव सौन्दर्यं तत्तु व्यर्थं कृतं त्वया ॥ हित्वाभरणान्यनेकानि चर्मादि च धृतं त्वया । तत्सर्वं कारणं ब्रूहि दृष्ट्वा हर्षमुपागमे ॥ इति पृष्टा तदा तेन सखीं प्रेरयती तदा । तन्मुखेनैव तत्सर्वं कथयामीति सुव्रता ॥ तया च प्रेरिता तत्र सखी जटिलमाह तत् । शृणु साधो प्रवक्ष्यामि यदि त्वं श्रोतुमिच्छसि ॥ यदर्थमेतया सख्या ह्यारब्धं तप उत्तमम् । हित्वेन्द्रप्रमुखान् देवानैश्वर्यसयुतानपि ॥ पतिं पिनाकपाणिं वै प्राप्तुमिच्छति सांप्रतम् । इयं सखी मदीया वै वृक्षानारोपयत् पुरा ॥ तेषु वृक्षेषु संजातं फलं पश्य पुरः प्रभो । मनोरथाङ्कुरं त्वस्याः पश्यामि न कथंचन ॥ रूपहार्यं शिवं देवं मदनस्यानुहारिणम् । तस्माच्च नारदादेशात्तपस्तप्यति दारुणम् ॥ यत्ते पृष्टं मयाख्यातं सख्याश्च समभीप्सितम् । इत्येवं वचनं श्रुत्वा जटिलो वाक्यमब्रवीत् ॥ सख्येदं कथितं सत्यं परिहास उतापि वा । यथार्थं न कथं देवि मुखेन परिभाषसे ॥ इत्युक्ते च तदा तेन जटिलेन महात्मना । उवाच पार्वती देवी तत्तथैव न चान्यथा ॥ मनसा वचसा साक्षाद्वृतो वै शंकरो मया । जानामि दुर्लभं वस्तु कथं प्राप्यं मया भवेत् ॥ तथापि मन-सौत्सुक्यात्तप्यते च मयाधुना । इत्युक्ते च तया तत्र स्थितस्तोवाच स दण्डधृक् ॥...हित्वा सुवर्णमुद्रां च काचं ग्रहीतुमिच्छसि । हित्वा च चन्दनं शुभ्रं कर्दमं लेप्तुमीहसे ॥ इन्द्रा-दिलोकपालांश्च हित्वा शिवमनुव्रता । नैतद्युक्तं हि लोकेषु विरुद्धं दृश्यतेऽधुना ॥ त्वं कमलपत्राक्षि क्व चासौ च त्रिलोचनः । शशाङ्कवदना त्वं च पञ्चवक्त्रः शिवः स्मृतः ॥ कबर्यांश्चैव ते रूपं वर्णितुं नैव शक्यते । जटाजूटं शिवस्यैव प्रसिद्धं परिचक्षते ॥ चन्दनं च त्वदीयाङ्गे चिताभस्म शिवस्य च । क्व दुकूलं त्वदीयं वै गजाजिनमथाशुभम् ॥ काङ्क्ष-दादीनि दिव्यानि क्व सर्पाः शंकरस्य च । क्व वरा देवताः सर्वाः क्व च भूतावलिः प्रिये ॥ भवत्याश्च शिवस्यैव न युक्तं रूपमुत्तमम् । वपुश्चैव विरूपाक्षं जन्म न ज्ञायते कदा ॥ यदि धनं भवेत्तस्य कथं दिगम्बरो भवेत् । वरेषु ये गुणाः प्रोक्ता नैकोऽपि च शिवे स्मृतः ॥ वाहनं च बलीवर्दो वसनं चर्म एव च । यदि गृही भवेत्सो वै कथं च मदनं दहेत् ॥ जातिर्न लभ्यते तस्य विद्या ज्ञानं न दृश्यते । क्व च हारस्त्वदीयो वै क्व च वै मुण्डमा-लिका ॥ सर्वं विरोधि रूपं च तव चैव शिवस्य च । मह्यं न रोचते देवि यदिच्छसि तथा कुरु ॥ स मया विदितो देवः श्मशाने वासमीहते । असद्वस्तु च यत्किंचित्तत्सर्वं सेवते स्वयम् ॥ निवर्तय मनस्तस्मान्मो चेद्गच्छेः समीपतः । इत्येतद्वचनं श्रुत्वा पार्वती क्रोधसंयुता ॥ उवाच क्रुध्यमानासौ शिवनिन्दापरं च तम् । त्वयोक्तं विदितो देवस्तदलीकं वचस्तव ॥ यदि च विदितः स्याद्वै विरुद्धं नोच्यते त्वया । कुतो जातिर्भवेत्तस्य निर्गु-णस्य गुणात्मनः ॥ सर्वासामपि विद्यानामधिष्ठानं सदाशिवः । किं तस्य विद्यया कार्यं पूर्णस्य परमात्मनः ॥ सर्वेषां चादिभूतस्य वयोमानं कुतः स्मृतम् । कल्याणरूपिणस्तस्य सेवया किं भवेदिह ॥ सप्तजन्म दरिद्रः स्यात्सेवते यदि शंकरम् । तस्यैव दुर्लभा लोके लक्ष्मीः स्यादनपायिनी ॥ यदग्रे सिद्धयोऽष्टौ च नृत्यन्ति प्रतिवासरम् । अवाङ्मुखाः सदा तत्र कुतो वित्तं सुदुर्लभम् ॥ यद्यप्यमङ्गलानीह सेवते शंकरः सदा । तथापि मङ्गलं

तस्य स्मरणादेव जायते ॥ यद्यपूतं भवेद्भस्म चिताया‌श्च त्वयोदितम् । नृत्यस्यापगमे देवैः शिरोभिर्धार्यते कथम् ॥ कथं तत्त्वं विजानन्ति त्वादृशा हि बहिर्मुखाः । शिवनिन्दां करोतीह तत्त्वमज्ञाय यः पुमान् ॥ आजन्म संचितं पुण्यं तस्य भस्मीभविष्यति । त्वत्पूजा च कृता यस्मात्तस्मात्पापं भजाम्यहम् ॥...यथा तथा भवेत्सो वै ममाभीष्टतमो मतः । पुनर्वचनमादातुं प्रक्रमे तावदेव हि ॥ उवाच गिरिजा देवी सखीं दुष्टमना ह्यसौ । वारणीयः प्रयत्नेन शिवनिन्दां करिष्यति ॥ न केवलं भजेत्पापं निन्दाकर्ता शिवस्य च । यो वै शृणोति तां निन्दां पापभाक् स भवेदिह ॥ स्थलमेतत्तथा हित्वा यास्यामोऽन्यत्र मा चिरम् । इत्युक्त्वा चलनायासौ पदमुत्क्षिपते यदा ॥ तदासौ च शिवः साक्षादाललम्बे प्रियां सतीम् । कृत्वा स्वीयं स्वरूपं च यथाध्यातं तया तथा ॥ दर्शयित्वा पुनस्तां च सुवाचावाङ्मुखीं शिवाम् । कुत्र यास्यसि मां हित्वा न त्वं त्याज्या मया पुनः ॥ अद्यप्रभृति ते दासस्तपोभिः प्रेमनिर्भरः । क्रीतोऽस्मि तव सौन्दर्यात्क्षणमेकं युगायते ॥ इत्युक्ते देवदेवेन जहौ दुःखं पुरातनम् । तपसश्चैव यज्जातं महद् दुःखं गतं तदा । फले जाते श्रमः पूर्वं जातो नाशमवाप्नुयात् ॥ (अ. १२,१४)

Canto VI. उवाच व्रीडिता देवी वचः स्मृत्वा पुरातनम् । सखीमुखेन सा तत्र शिवं सम्यग्व्यवस्थितम् ॥ एहि यामो गृहं देवि कथं चैवं विलम्बसे । एवं ब्रुवन्तं तं देवं पार्वतीवचनात्सखी ॥ यदि प्रसन्नो देवेश करोषि च कृपां यदि । तदैवं च त्वया कार्यं कृपां कृत्वा ममोपरि ॥ पितुर्गृहे मया सम्यग् गम्यते त्वदनुज्ञया । पितुर्मे सफलं जन्म कुरुष्वेव गृहाश्रमम् ॥ इत्येवं वचनं श्रुत्वा शिवोऽपि च शिवां तदा । उवाच वचनं त्वं च यदिच्छसि तथेति तत् ॥ इत्युक्त्वान्तर्दधे शंभुर्गत्वा काशीं विचारयन् । सस्मार च ऋषीन् सप्त विरहाविष्टमानसः ॥ पार्वत्यपि सखीयुक्ता रूपं कृत्वा तु सार्थकम् । जगाम च स्वकं धाम पितुर्विरहकातरा ॥ आश्रमं सफलं मेने कुपुत्रात्पुत्रिका वरा । हिमवान्नारदं तत्र प्रस्तुवन्साधु साध्विति ॥ ऋषयश्चैव ते सर्वे शंभुना च स्मृता यदा । तदाजग्मुश्च ऋषयः कल्पवृक्षा इवापरे ॥ परं ब्रह्म गृणन्तश्च हेमवल्कलधारिणः । मुक्ताफलैर्विचित्रैश्च भूषिता भूषणैः परैः ॥ अरुन्धत्या तथा युक्ताः साक्षात्सिद्धिरिवापरा । तान् दृष्ट्वा सूर्यसंकाशान् जहौ लज्जां हरः स्वयम् ॥ स्थित्वाग्रे ऋषयः श्रेष्ठा नमस्कृत्य शिवं मुदा । मेनिरे च तदात्मानं कृतार्थं ते तपस्विनः ॥ इति विस्मयमापन्ना नमस्कृत्य स्थिताः पुरः । प्रोचुः प्राञ्जलयस्ते वै शिवं लोकमलापहम् ॥ व्यापकाय नमस्तुभ्यं व्याप्यरूपाय ते नमः । पराय पररूपाय सर्वोत्कृष्टाय ते नमः ॥ इत्येवं च स्तुवन्तस्ते पुनरूचुः परात्मने । भाग्यं किं वर्ण्यतेऽस्माभिः स्वीय किं तु पुनः पुनः ॥ तपस्तप्तं त्रिधा पूर्वं वेदाध्ययनमुत्तमम् । अग्नयश्च हुताः पूर्वं यज्ञाश्च विविधाः कृताः ॥ तपांसि च विचित्राणि सर्वाण्यपि विशेषतः । दानानि च तथा पूर्वं तीर्थानि त्रिविधानि च ॥ वाङ्मनःकायजं किंचित्पुण्यं वा कर्मसंभवम् । यो वै भजति नित्यं त्वां कृतकृत्यो भवेन्नरः ॥ किं भाग्यं वर्ण्यतेऽस्माकं कृतं नः स्मरणं त्वया । सर्वोत्कृष्टास्तथा जाताः स्मरणान्ते सदाशिव ॥ दर्शनं भवतोऽद्यैव जातं तद्वस्तुदुर्लभम् । अद्यप्रभृति लोकेषु मान्याः पात्रतमा वयम् ॥ जातास्तेऽनुमहादेव उच्चैःपदमुपाश्रिताः । अत्र किं बहुनोक्तेन जन्म साफल्यतां गतम् ॥ पूर्णानां किं च कर्तव्यमस्ति चेत्परमा कृपा ।

सदृशं सेवकानां तु देयं कार्यं शुभं तथा ॥ इत्येवं वचनं श्रुत्वा तेषां वचनमाददे । ऋषयश्च सदा पूज्याः कारणात्स्मरणं कृतम् ॥ ममावस्था भवद्भिश्च ज्ञायन्ते ह्युपकारकाः । देवानां दुःखमुत्पन्नं तारकास्युदुरात्मनः॥ ब्रह्मणा च वरो दत्तः किं करोमि दुरासदः। मूर्तयोऽष्टौ च याः प्रोक्ता मदीयाः परमर्षयः ॥ ताः सर्वा उपकारार्थं न तु स्वार्थमिति स्फुटम्। तथात्र कर्तुकामोऽहं विवाहं शिवया सह ॥ तयापि च तपस्तप्तं दुष्करं परमर्षिभिः । तस्याः फलं वरं देयमभीष्टं तद्धितावहम् ॥ तस्माद्भवन्तो गच्छन्तु हिमाचलगृहं ध्रुवम् । तत्र गत्वा हितं चैतत्तत्पत्नीं तु पुनस्तथा ॥ कथनीयं प्रयत्नेन यथा स्यात्कार्यमुत्तमम् । हिमाचलगृहे पुत्री पार्वती च गुणान्विता ॥ अस्मदर्थे च तां तत्र प्रार्थनीयो हिमाचलः । तत्तथा च प्रवक्तव्यं देवानां च हितं भवेत् ॥ भवद्भिः कल्पितो यो वै विधिः स्यादविकल्पकः । भवतां नैव कथ्येत भवन्तः कार्यभाजिनः ॥ इत्येवं वचनं श्रुत्वा मुनयस्तेऽमलाशयाः । आनन्दं लेभिरे सर्वे प्रभुणानुग्रहीकृताः ॥ गताश्चाकाशमार्गेण यत्र स्याद्धिमवत्पुरम् । ततो दृष्ट्वा पुरं दिव्यमृषयस्तेऽतिविस्मिताः ॥ ऊचुः परस्परं सर्वे किमेतदिति संस्फुटम् । अलकायाश्च स्वर्गाया भोगवत्यास्तथा पुनः ॥ विशेषोऽत्रामरावत्या दृश्यते ऋषिसत्तमाः । किं गृहाणि सुरम्याणि स्फाटिकैर्विविधैरिह ॥ मणिभिश्चो विचित्राणि रचितान्यङ्गणानि च । गृहे गृहे विचित्राश्च वृक्षाः स्वर्गसमुद्भवाः ॥ तोरणानां तथा लक्ष्मीर्दृश्यते च गृहे गृहे । वितानानि विचित्राणि चैलपल्लवतोरणैः ॥ उद्यानानि विचित्राणि पुष्पैश्च भरितानि वै । नराश्च देवताः सर्वे स्त्रियश्चाप्सरसस्तथा ॥ कर्ममार्गपरा नित्यं सदा यौवनशालिनः । यावन्न दृष्टमेतच्च तावत्स्वर्गपरा नराः ॥ इत्येवमृषिवर्यास्ते वर्णयन्तस्तथा पुरम् । गता हिमालयस्याथ गृहं सर्वसमृद्धिमत् ॥ तान् दृष्ट्वा सूर्यसंकाशान् हिमवान्विस्मितस्तु॥ । सूर्याः सप्त कथं चात्र आयान्तीमे गृहं प्रति ॥ एतस्मिन्नन्तरे ते वै ह्याकाशादपतंस्तदा । सन्मुखो हिमवान् दृष्ट्वा ययौ मानपुरःसरम् ॥ पूजां विधाय तेषां च दण्डवत्प्रपपात ह । ...इत्युक्त्वासनमानीय ददौ भक्तिपुरःसरम् ॥ आसनेषूपविष्टेषु तदाज्ञप्तः स्वयं स्थितः । उवाच हिमवांस्तत्र ऋषीन् ज्योतिर्मयांस्तदा ॥ लोकेषु दर्शनीयोऽहं बहुतीर्थसमो मतः । यस्माद्भवन्तो मद्गेहं ह्यागता विष्णुरूपिणः ॥ पूर्णानां चैव किं कार्यं कृपणानां गृहेषु च । तेषां च दुःखनाशार्थं गृहेषु गमनं सताम् ॥ मद्गेहपावनार्थं च भवन्तः सुसमागताः । तथापि किंचित्कार्यं हि सदृशं सेवकस्य च ॥ कथनीयं भवद्भिश्च सफलोऽस्तु ममाश्रमः । महताज्ञया लोको मान्यतां गच्छति ध्रुवम् ॥ तस्माच्च कुत्रचित्कार्ये योज्योऽहमृषिसत्तमाः । एवं वचनमाकर्ण्य ऋषयस्ते प्रहर्षिताः ॥ ऊचुस्ते गिरिराजं वै स्मृत्वा स्मृत्वा शिवस्य च । शिवः परोपकारार्थं कर्तुकामः प्रजासुखम् ॥ अस्मन्मुखेन ते पुत्रीं याचते शंकरः स्वयम् । जगद्गुरोर्गुरुस्त्वं च भविष्यसि न संशयः ॥ जगन्माता तु ते पुत्री तस्यैवानुग्रहाद्भवेत् । जगत्पिता शिवः प्रोक्तो जगन्माता शिवा स्मृता ॥ तस्मै देया त्वया कन्या सार्थक्यं ते भविष्यति । एवं वचनमाकर्ण्य गिरिराजोऽब्रवीदिदम् ॥ मदीयं च शरीरं वै पत्नी मेना च या मता । ऋद्धिः सिद्धिर्निधिश्चान्यो श्रीर्मदीया न चान्यथा ॥ एवमुक्त्वा तदा पुत्रीं ज्ञात्वा लोकस्य मातरम् । भूषयित्वा तदङ्कं च ऋष्युत्सङ्गे न्यवेशयत् । इदं भैक्ष्यमुमा नाम दत्तं वै ऋषिसत्तमाः ॥ ऋषय ऊचुः—अस्माद्विधा भिक्षुकाश्च दाता चैव भवान् स्वयम् । भैक्ष्यं

च पार्वती प्रोक्तं किमतः परमुत्तमम् ॥ हिमवच्छिखराणां ते मनसः सदृशी गतिः । एवमुक्त्वा तु तां कन्यामृषयो विमलाशयाः ॥ आशिषं दत्तवन्तस्ते शिवाय सुखदो भव । मिलित्वा च गृहं तेऽद्य वर्धयिष्यन्ति नित्यशः ॥ इत्युक्त्वा ऋषयः सर्वे गिरिराजं परस्परम् । पुष्पाणि फलयुक्तानि व्यत्ययं चक्रिरे तदा ॥ अरुन्धती तत्र दृष्ट्वा मेनां साश्रुमुखीं तदा । गुणैश्च लोभयामास शिवस्य परमा सती ॥ ततश्च ते चतुर्थेऽह्नि निर्धार्य लग्नमुत्तमम् । परस्परं च संहृष्य जग्मुस्ते शिवसंनिधिम् ॥ महाकोशीं प्रयातास्ते यत्रास्ते शंकरः स्वयम् । विवाहस्य विधिं सम्यगूचुस्ते ऋषिसत्तमाः ॥ तदाज्ञप्ताश्च ते तत्र गताश्चागमनाय वै । शिवोऽपि सगणस्तत्र प्रसन्नमुखपङ्कजः । कैलासमगमद्देवो विवाहरचनाय वै ॥ (अ. १५)

Canto VII. हिमवानपि तत्रैव स्वानाहूय सुहृद्वृतः । विधिवत्कारयामास मण्डपादिविधिं क्रमात् ॥ विविधानि विचित्राणि तोरणानि तथा पुनः । ध्वजांश्चैव विचित्रांश्च चकार परया मुदा ॥ वस्त्रालंकारसंयुक्ताः सर्वे हर्षसमाकुलाः । कार्ये चक्रुश्च तत्रत्यं हिमवद्गृहसंभवम् ॥ कन्यां चैव तु दानार्थं सुस्नाप्यालंचकार सः । विवाहविधियोग्यं च वेषं संपाद्य संस्थितः ॥ देवतापूजनं कृत्वा नानोपकरणानि च । प्रतीक्षां वरवर्गस्य कृत्वा च हिमवान् स्थितः ॥ मातरः सप्त तास्तत्र शिवभूषाविधिं परम् । चक्रिरे च मुदा युक्ता यथायोग्यं तथा पुनः ॥ चन्द्रस्तु मुकुटस्थाने सांनिध्यमकरोत्तदा । तिलकं सुन्दरं ह्यासीन्नयनं तु तृतीयकम् ॥ भूतिश्च चन्दनं ह्यासीद् दुकूलं चर्म उच्यते । सर्पा ह्याभरणान्यासन्मणयो विविधाश्च ये ॥ एतस्मिन्समये देवा आजग्मुः प्रभुसेवया । ब्रह्मा तु हंसमारुह्य ऋषिभिः सहितस्तदा ॥ नमस्कृत्य स्थितस्तत्र तावद्विष्णुः समागतः । इन्द्रश्चैव यमश्चैव कुबेरो वरुणस्तथा ॥ अन्ये ते लोकपालाश्च स्वीयचिह्नसमन्विताः । नद्यो गङ्गादयः सर्वा नागाः सर्वे तथाविधाः ॥ सेवावसरमाज्ञाय समाजग्मुर्मुदान्विताः । निःससार ततस्तस्मात्कैलासात्पर्वतोत्तमात् ॥ शिवः परमसंतुष्टो देवान्कृत्वा पुरस्तदा । आजगाम महावीर्यः सर्वसिद्धिसमन्वितः ॥ तमागतं तदा श्रुत्वा हिमवान् बलसंयुतः । जगाम संमुखस्तत्र धन्योऽहमिति चिन्तयन् ॥ देवसेनां तथा दृष्ट्वा हिमवान् विस्मयं गतः । देवा हि तद्बलं दृष्ट्वा विस्मयं परमं गताः ॥ पर्वतानां तथा सेना देवानां च तथा पुनः । मिलित्वा तु तथा रेजे मन्यते सागरावुभौ ॥ रचित्वा शिबिरं सम्यक् संस्थाप्य देवताबलम् । जगाम पर्वतस्तत्र यत्र स्याद्विधिवेदिका ॥ कारयित्वा विशेषेण चतुष्कं तोरणैर्युतम् । एतस्मिन्नन्तरे तावद्गुरेण रूपमुत्तमम् ॥ धृतं तु भक्तवात्सल्यात्कृपालुत्वं प्रदर्शितम् । सूर्यकोटिप्रतीकाशं सुनेत्रैर्भूषणैर्युतम् ॥ मुकुटेन विराजन्तं विचित्रवसनं शुभम् । सूर्येण छत्रितो योऽसौ चन्द्रेण वीजितस्तथा ॥ सिद्धयोऽष्टौ प्रनृत्यं च कुर्वन्ति स्म तदग्रतः । गङ्गा च यमुना चैव चामरे दधतुः शुभे ॥ शिवोऽपि च तथा द्वारि गतो देवगणैः सह । मेना तं पूजयामास ब्रह्मविष्णुसमन्वितम् ॥ तावत् स्त्रियः समाजग्मुर्हित्वा कामाननेकशः । मज्जनं कुर्वती काचिच्चूर्णेन संयुता ययौ ॥ काचित्तु बालकं हित्वा अतृप्तं द्रष्टुमाययौ । रशनां बध्नती काचित्तयैव संयुता ययौ ॥ वस्त्रं च विपरीतं च धृत्वा काचिदुपाययौ । काचिद्धस्ते शलाकां च धृत्वाञ्जनसमन्विताम् ॥ आदर्शं च तथान्यस्मिन् नीत्वा नेत्रमुपाययौ । काचित्तु [illegible]नी पादं रञ्जयन्ती यदा तदा ॥

श्रुत्वोद्वोषं च तांद्दृष्ट्वा दर्शनार्थमुपागता । इत्यादि विविधं कार्यं हित्वान्याः समुपागताः ॥ दृष्ट्वा च शांकरं रूपं मोहं प्राप्ताश्च पुत्रिकाः । सम्यक् कृतं तु पार्वत्या नान्यथा यद्भवेदिह ॥ अहो पश्यत किं रूपं वर्णनीयं कथं भवेत् । नेत्राणि सफलान्यासन हिमवत्पुरवासिनाम् ॥......पार्वत्या साधितं सर्वं शिवार्थे तु तपः कृतम् । यदीदं युगलं ब्रह्मा संगमायाक्षमो भवेत ॥ तदा च सफलोऽप्यस्य श्रमो निष्फलतामियात् । सम्यक् कृतं तथा तेन मेलितं युगममुत्तमम् ॥ कथास्तथाविधाः शृण्वन् शिवो द्वारि समागतः । सर्वे देववरास्तत्र ह्यच्युताद्याः शिवं प्रति ॥ स्थितास्तत्र शिवस्यार्थे...॥ तावच्च हिमवान् स्नात्वा सपत्नीकः स्वयं गतः । ब्रह्मा सर्वं च तत्रत्यं कारयामास वै तदा ॥ आवाहनं तथा पाद्यं सर्वं च विधिपूर्वकम् । दुकूलं सुन्दरं तेन दत्तं तस्मै महात्मने ॥ तिलकं पुष्पहारं च काञ्चनस्य यथाविधि । संस्थाप्याग्निं पुनस्तत्र वैवाहमकरोद्विधिम् ॥ अक्षतारोपणं तत्र स्त्रियश्चक्रुस्तदाज्ञया । प्रदक्षिणं तथा चाग्नेश्चतुर्धा च कृतं तदा ॥ अनुज्ञां चैव दत्त्वा तु कन्यायै स पितामहः । ध्रुवस्य दर्शनं तत्र कारयामास वै तदा ॥........गिरिराजोऽपि तत्रैवं संपाद्य विधिमुत्तमम् । मेने कृतार्थमात्मानं सफलं च गृहाश्रमम् ॥ तौ दंपती तदा तत्र संपूज्य कुलदेवताम् । वर्धाप्य मण्डपं तत्र ब्रूहुच्य कौतुकौषधिम् ॥ ऋषीन्प्रणम्य सर्वांस्ताश्चकारानुग्रहं शिवः । हिमवानपि तत्रैव यथायोग्यमपूजयत् ॥ गिरिराजं तथैवात्र संप्रार्थ्य देवतागणाः । दत्त्वा च ह्याशिषस्तस्मै वन्दितास्ते ययुर्मुदा ॥ हिमवत्पुत्रिकाः सर्वे वाद्यगानपरायणाः । अन्वगच्छन्त ते तत्र गिरिराजादयश्च ये ॥ अच्युताद्याश्च ये देवा ऋषयो निर्मलाश्रयाः । समागत्य तु कैलासं संस्थाप्य मन्दिरे शिवम् । पत्न्या युक्तं च संप्रार्थ्य दत्तानुज्ञा ययुश्च ते ॥

[It is by no means certain, however, that Kâlidâsa followed this version of the legend when he composed the Kum. Most of the extant recensions of the Purâṇas are evidently modern compilations, probably based upon earlier ones. The language of the extracts given above seems to show that their author had our poem before him when writing his story. We should therefore hesitate to assert that Kâlidâsa copied the very expressions of the S. P.; it is more likely that the compiler, or some reviser, of the Purâṇa copied Kâlidâsa. For the plot of the Kum. our author was most probably indebted to an earlier recension of the S. P.]

---

(3) CRITICAL AND GENERAL REMARKS.

The Kumârasambhava or "the poem descriptive of the birth of Kumâra," has all the requirements of a Mahâkâvya and is classed as such by Sanskritists. The hero of this poem is a divine being, and one of the Dhîrodâtta class. The prevailing sentiment is Sriṅgâra, Karuṇa and Śânta, though not very prominent, being accessories to it. The 3rd and the 5th Cantos are a good illustration of Vipralambha, the 4th that of Karuṇa, the 7th of Vivâha, and the 8th of Saṃbhoga. The subject of each following canto is hinted at the end of each preceeding one. The description of cities, seasons &c. can be easily marked by the student. It must, however, be remarked here that the poet, in his zeal to describe a lover just married, has spoiled the character of Śiva, which he had well maintained in the first six Cantos.

The available recension of the Kâvya consists of 17 cantos or Sargas, though some believe that it has twenty-two in all. It has a commentary by Mallinâtha upto eight cantos only. It is now generally believed that only these eight are the work of the poet, and that the rest were written either by some later writer or by some disciple of Kálidása. The commentator Râmagovinda states that the Kumârasaṃbhava extends to eight cantos only. Again, it may be remarked that the title "the Birth of Kumâra" cannot very well apply to the whole of the poem. The eighth canto properly leads up to the संभव (not actual but potential) of the War-God, and the poem naturally ends there. If the poet goes on describing the war against the demon Târaka in Heaven, as is done in the succeeding cantos, it would be inconsistent with the scope and plan of the poem as suggested by its title. If the defeat and the death of Târaka were to be its subject-matter, it should have been called by some other name, such as तारकवध. The evidence of style also conclusively proves that cantos 9–17 are certainly not written by the author of the first eight.

Such is not the opinion of Dr. Ryder, however. He accepts the later cantos as genuine on what seem to us to be trifling and inconclusive arguments. The learned Doctor argues, for instance, that the last nine cantos are worse poetry than the first eight, because love, and not fighting, was Kâlidâsa's *forte*. Does Dr. Ryder forget the spirited fighting scenes in the Raghuvaṃśa?

As a matter of fact, scholars are now generally coming round to agree to treat the later cantos as interpolated.

In the Kumârasaṃbhava Kâlidâsa chooses a higher plane for the play of his genius. In the Raghuvaṃs'a his heroes are men ; in the Meghadûta the story refers to the Yakshas who occupy in their semi-divine nature a position midway between men and gods. In the '*Birth of Kumâra*' the poet deals solely with gods and beings of another world, thoug in so doing he does not fail to invest them with human sentiments, without which, indeed. the poem would have lost most of its charm. The scene is laid among the valleys and on the slopes of the Himâlaya, a mountain which is, as we are told in the very first verse, देवतात्मा ; and all subsequent actions that take place there are divine and superhuman. Then follows a description of Pârvatî, and this is done so skilfully that the master-hand for a while makes us forget that we are reading about a goddess and not about a woman on earth. The scene of the second canto is laid in *Brahmaloka,* and here, as in the tenth canto of the Raghuvaṃśa, Kâlidâsa shows his intimate knowledge of the leading ideas of Hindu philosophy. The third Canto gives him an opportunity for a description of spring and he has wonderfully succeeded in drawing a picture true to Nature and at the same time of an unsurpassed poetic beauty. Very few descriptions by other poets would compare with this in the Kumâra, beginning with कुबेरगुप्तां दिशमुष्णरश्मौ गन्तुं प्रवृत्ते समयं विलङ्घ्य । दिग्दक्षिणा गन्धवहं मुखेन व्यलीकनिःश्वासमिवोत्ससर्ज ॥ (III. 25). The fourth Canto shows Kâlidása to be a master of *Karuṇa rasa,* and the lament of Rati is so splendid that some timorous rhetoricians have considered that the excess and recurrence of emotion has here become a fault (रसगतो दोषः । पुनः पुनर्दीप्तिः । यथा कुमारसंभवे रतिविलापे ।). The student will find that this lament has its counterpart in the अजविलाप of the 8th canto of the *Raghuvaṃśa.* In the fifth canto Párvatî is described in the *rôle* of a *tapasvinî* where Śiva comes to visit her, disguised as a *Brahmachârin.* Their dialogue is one of the best-known passages in Kálidâsa's works, where his powers of repartee, humour and piquancy of style are seen at their best. The sixth Canto is rather a tame one, only enlivened by the fine description of Oshadhiprastha, the capital city of Himâlaya. The seventh Canto is devoted to a very detailed description of the marriage-ceremony and the processions, and he has given it a human touch again by the prevailing tone of domesticity throughout. The eight and the last canto is considered by many to be a crowning achievement of Kálidása's poetic skill, and the quotations from this canto occurring in standard critical works like the Kávyálaṃkárasûtras and the Sarasvatîkaṇṭhábharaṇa and others are more numerous than from any other canto. Indeed, it may be said without exaggeration that in the descriptions of the sunset, twilight and nightfall on the mountain, Kálidâsa has excelled himself; they abound with the finest similes and the grandest imagery.

One chief reason of Kálidása's superiority over other poets is his brilliantly-polished style; there is no other Sanskrit poet who possesses an equal command over language so simple and withal so graceful. In fact, all the works of Kâlidâsa are written in what the later rhetoricians have called the *Vaidarbhî* style, the ten chief excellences belonging to which are thus given by Daṇḍin :— श्लेषः प्रसादः समता माधुर्यं सुकुमारता । अर्थव्यक्तिरुदारत्वमोजःकान्तिसमाधयः॥ (K. D. I. 41). Kâlidâsa abhors the looseness and laxity of the epics, the superfluous piling of epithets found in lesser poets, and the artificiality of diction which is observable even in writers like Báṇa and Mâgha. He studiously avoids all meretricious ornament and the cheap tinsel of verbal tricks. His strength lies in the music of his words and in the swift conveying of precise and beautiful ideas. He employs no figures of speech except the commonest ones, and in particular he delights in *Upamá*, of which he is a recognized master. He is a great lover of nature, and all his similes and illustrations are drawn from his close observation of natural phenomena (*e. g.* Kum. III. 21, IV. 44, V. 5, VII. 26 &c.)

It is difficult to judge, owing to its shortness, whether the *Kumárasambhava* is as great a poetic triumph as the *Raghuvaṃs'a*; in this difficulty itself lies, we think, the evidence of the greatness of Kálidâsa's genius. Dr. Ryder rightly prefers the *Raghuvaṃs'a*, but is constrained to remark that "there are passages in *The Birth of the War-God* of a piercing beauty which the world can never let die."

---

(4) MALLINA'THA.

There exist a large number of commentaries on this poem, but none of them is so well-known or so often studied as that of Mallinâtha, who enjoys a supreme position as the standard authority in the interpretation of Kàlidâsa's poems. While writing about Kálidása we had to remark above that he says absolutely nothing about himself in his writings, and the same is true of his great scholiast Mallinâtha. Pandit Vámanácharya Jhalkikar, the the editor of the Kávya-Prakás'a, wrote that Mallinátha was a Bráhmaṇa of the Kásyapa *gotra*, and that his descendants were still living at Gajendragad in the Satara District. But the learned Pandit was hasty in his identification; for Mr. M. S. Sâstrî (in his "Second Report on the Search of Sanskrit MSS.") has shown that Mallinâtha was a native of Tailangana (Ândhra), which fact is now accepted as established. He had a son named Kumârasvâmin, who was also an erudite scholar, and wrote a commentary on the Pratâparudrîya. In addition to his three commentaries on the three poems of Kâlidâsa, Mallinâtha is credited to have written (*a*) commentaries on अमरकोश, एकावली, काव्यादर्श, किरातार्जुनीय, तन्त्रवार्तिक, तार्किकरक्षा, नलोदय, नैषधीयचरित, प्रशस्तपादभाष्य, भट्टिकाव्य, लघुशब्देन्दुशेखर, शिशुपालवध, and सारमञ्जरी, and (*b*) independently, these works :—उदारकाव्य, रघुवीरचरितकाव्य, वैश्यकल्पतरु and वैद्यरत्नमाला. It is possible that some of these productions belong to some other Mallinâtha than our commentator; for there have been many Mallinâthas, just as there have been many Kâlidâsas.

The date of Mallinâtha can be fixed with tolerable certainty. He has written a com. on the Ekâvalî, a work on rhetorics which frequently refers to king Vîra-Narasimha, whose reign extended up to 1314 A.D. Mallinâtha also often quotes the Pratâparudrîya, another work on rhetorics, which mentions king Pratâparudra who reigned from 1295 to 1323 A.D Sir Dr. Bhandarkar has shown (p. xxi of his Preface to his second Ed. of the Mâlatî-Mâdhava) that Mallinâtha must be placed before the lexicographer Medinikara, the latest limit for whose date is 1431 A.D. Hence it is clear that the date of Mallinâtha approximately falls somewhere between 1325 and 1425 A.D. Most probably he belongs to the latter half the 14th century.

Mallinâtha is a commentator of great merit and literary acumen. He was a profound grammarian, well-versed in the Nyâya and Vaiśeshika philosophies, and thoroughly acquainted with Pâuranic as well as secular literature, as he himself tells us in his introductory ślokas to the commentary on the Ragh., and the extreme popularity of his commentaries shows that this is not an idle boast. His commentaries are pre-eminently adapted to the needs of the advanced general reader. They are sufficiently expressive without being prolix. He never makes an unnecessary display of his knowledge, but strictly follows the principle he himself lays down, *viz.* नामूलं लिख्यते किंचिन्नानपेक्षितमुच्यते. He has modestly expressed his inability to grasp the real pith of Kâlidâsa's poetry, but he says that he would follow in the footsteps of Dakshiṇâvarta-nâtha and others, the older commentators who preceded him.[1] Still, Mallinâtha is perhaps the only commentator on the poems of Kâlidâsa who shows a critical appreciation of poetry, and endeavours to preserve, as far as possible, the genuine readings of the poet, studiously rejecting the spurious substitutions of single words and phrases, and the occasional interpolations of whole ślokas. To his commentaries on the three poems of Kâlidâsa he has given the title संजीवनी, meaning thereby that his commentaries *re-inspire with life* the words of Kâlidâsa "that lay *in a swoon* under the effect of the poison of bad commentaries." Every student of Kâlidâsa now recognizes that this was no vain presumption; Mallinâtha's commentaries have eclipsed all others, and now he stands unrivalled as *the* commentator of Kâlidâsa's poetical works.

---

1 The commentaries of Dakshiṇâvartanâtha have been recently discovered in South India and begun to be published in the Triv. S. Series. From what we have seen of them they are not undeserving of the praise bestowed upon them by Mallinâtha

Important Abbreviations.

—:o:—

A. G.—Apte's Guide to Sanskrit Composition.
Ak., Amar.—Amarakośa.
Ar., Aruna.—Arunagirinâtha (com.)
Av.—Avachûri (com.)
Bg.—Bhagavadgîtâ.
Bhar.—Bhartṛihari's Śatakas (N. and V.).*
Bhatti.—Bhaṭṭi-Kāvya.*
Bh.-P.—Bhâgavata-Purâṇa.
Bṛih.-Sam.—Bṛihatsaṃhitâ.
Bṛih.-Up.—Bṛihadâraṇyakopanishad.
Cha'r.-Châritravardhana (com.)
Chh.-Up.—Chhândogyopanishad.
D.—Deshpande's Ed. of the Kum.
D.-K.—Daśakumâracharita.*
D.-R.—Daśarûpaka.
Gi't.—Gîtagovinda.
Hitop.—Hitopadeśa.*
H. S. Gr.—Higher Sanskrit Grammar (by M. R. Kâle).
Hv.—Harivaṃśa.
Jin.—Jinasamudra (Com.)
Ka'd.—Kâdambarî.*
Ka's'.—Kâśikâ of Vâmana.
Katha's.—Kathásaritságara.
Ka'v., K.-D.—Kâvyâdarśa.
Kir.—Kirâtârjunîya.*
K.-P.—Kâvya-Prakâśa.
Kum.—Kumârasambhava.*
Kuv.—Kuvalayânanda.
Mah.-Bh.—Mahá-Bhárata.
Ma'lav.—Mâlavikâgnimitra.*
Malli.—Mallinâtha.
Ma'l.-Ma'dh.—Mâlatî-Mâdhava
Ma'rk.-P.—Mârkaṇḍeya-Purâṇa
Megh.—Meghadûta.*
Mṛich.—Mṛichchhakaṭika.
Mud.—Mudrârâkshasa.*
Mv.—Mahâvîracharita.
M. W—Monier Williams.
Na'g.—Nâgânanda.*
Naish.—Naishadhîyacharita.
Na'r.—Nârâyaṇa (Com).
Pa'n.—Pâṇini's Ashṭâdhyâyî.
Pa'r.-P.—Parvatî-Pariṇaya.
Ragh.—Raghuvaṃśa.*
Ra'm.—Râmâyaṇa of Vâlmîki.
Ratn.—Ratnâvalî.*
Ṛitu.—Ṛitusaṃhâra.*
Ṛ.-V.—Ṛig-Veda.
Śa'k.—Śâkuntala.*
S.-D.—Sâhitya-Darpaṇa.
Sid.-K.—Siddhāntakaumudî.
Śis'.—Śiśupâlavadha.
Ś.-P.—Śiva-Puráṇa.
Up.—Upanishad.
Utt.—Uttararâmacharita.*
Va'rt.—Vârttika.
Veni'.—Veṇîsaṃhâra.*
Vg —Vijayagaṇi (Com.)
Vik.—Vikramorvas'îya.*
V.-P.—Vishṇu-Purâṇa.
Yog.-S.—Yogasûtras.

* Annotated by the Editor.

॥ श्रीः ॥

कुमारसंभवम् ।

॥ संजीवन्या समेतम् ॥

प्रथमः सर्गः ।

मातापितृभ्यां जगतो नमो वामार्धजानये ।
सद्यो दक्षिणदक्पातसंकुचद्वामदृष्टये ॥

अन्तरायतिमिरोपशान्तये शान्तपावनमचिन्त्यवैभवम् ।
तन्नरं वपुषि कुञ्जरं मुखे मन्महे किमपि तुन्दिलं महः ॥

शरणं करवाणि शर्मदं ते चरणं वाणि चराचरोपजीव्यम् ।
करुणामसृणैः कटाक्षपातैः कुरु मामम्ब कृतार्थसार्थवाहम् ॥

इहान्वयमुखेनैव सर्वं व्याख्यायते मया ।
नामूलं लिख्यते किंचिन्नानपेक्षितमुच्यते ॥

भारती कालिदासस्य दुर्व्याख्याविषमूर्छिता ।
एषा संजीवनी व्याख्या तामद्योज्जीवयिष्यति ॥

तत्रभवान्कालिदासः कुमारसंभवं काव्यं चिकीर्षुः 'आशीर्नमस्क्रियावस्तुनिर्देशो वापि तन्मुखम्' इति शास्त्रात्काव्यादौ वक्ष्यमाणार्थानुगुणं वस्तु निर्दिशति—

अस्त्युत्तरस्यां दिशि देवतात्मा हिमालयो नाम नगाधिराजः ।
पूर्वापरौ तोयनिधी[2] वगाह्य[3] स्थितः पृथिव्या इव मानदण्डः ॥ १ ॥

अस्तीति ॥ **उत्तरस्यां दिशि** । अनेनास्य देवभूमित्वं सूच्यते । [**देवतात्मा**] देवता आत्मा अधिष्ठाता यस्य सः । एतेनास्य वक्ष्यमाणमेनकापारिणयपार्वतीजननादिचेतनव्यवहारयोग्यत्वसिद्धिः । हिमस्यालयः स्थानमिति **हिमालयः नाम** हिमालय इति प्रसिद्धः । अधिको राजा अधिराजः 'राजाहः सखिभ्यष्टच्' । न गच्छन्तीति नगा अचलास्तेषामधिराजो **नगाधिराजः अस्ति** । कथंभूतः । **पूर्वापरौ** प्राच्यपाश्चिमौ तोय-

१ कुमारोत्पत्तिपर्यन्तं काव्यं न कृतं तस्मादनुपपन्नमिदं नामेत्यत्र उच्यते–तादिच्छामो विभो स्रष्टुं–(२. ५१) इति देवैः कुमारसृष्टिमात्रस्यैव ब्रह्माणं प्रति प्रार्थितत्वात्कुमारसंभव इत्येव संज्ञा युक्ता । न चैवं सतितत्पर्यन्तं काव्यं प्रवर्तितव्यमिति वाच्यम् । उमारूपेण ते यूयं संयमास्तिमितं मनः । शंभोर्यतध्वमाक्रष्टुमिति ब्रह्मणः प्रतिवचनेन शंभोश्चित्ताकर्षणमात्रस्यैव परमसाध्यत्वेन प्रतिपादनात् तच्चाष्टमसर्गे विस्तरतः प्रतिपादितम् ।...संभोगवर्णनेन कुमारोत्पत्तेर्बिन्दूत्क्षेपोपि कृत इति सर्वमनवद्यम् । इति वि०. २ वारिनिधी. ३ विगाह्य. ४ उत्तरस्यां दिशि देवभूमयः दक्षिणस्यां दिश्यसुरभूमयो मध्ये मनुष्यभूमय इति पुराणप्रसिद्धिः । इति वि०.

निधी समुद्रौ **वगाह्य** प्रविश्य अत एव **पृथिव्याः** भूमेर्मानं हस्तादिना परिच्छेदः ; भावे ल्युट् । तस्य दण्डः । यद्वा मीयतेऽनेनेति मानम् । करणे ल्युट् । स चासौ दण्डश्च **[मानदण्डः] स इव स्थितः** । आयामपरिच्छेदक दण्ड इव स्थित इत्यर्थः । पूर्वापरसागरावगाहित्वं चास्य हिमालयस्यास्त्येव । उक्तं च ब्रह्माण्डपुराणे—'कैलासो हिमवांश्चैव दक्षिणे वर्षपर्वतौ । पूर्वपश्चिमगावेतावर्णवान्तरुपस्थितौ ॥' इति । अत्र हिमाचलस्योभयाब्धिव्याप्तिसाम्यान्मानदण्डत्वेनोत्प्रेक्षालंकारः । प्रकृतेऽप्रकृतगुणक्रियादिसंबन्धादप्रकृतत्वेन प्रकृतस्य संभावनमुत्प्रेक्षा इत्यलंकारसर्वस्वकारः । अस्मिन्सर्गे प्रायेण वृत्तमुपजातिः । क्वचिदिन्द्रवज्रोपेन्द्रवज्रे च । तल्लक्षणं तु—'स्यादिन्द्रवज्रा यदि तौ जगौ ग उपेन्द्रवज्रा जतजास्ततो गौ । अनन्तरोदीरितलक्ष्मभाजौ पादौ यदीयावुपजातयस्ताः ॥' इति ॥

इतः परं षोडशभिः श्लोकैर्हिमाद्रिं वर्णयति । तत्र नगाधिराजत्वं निर्वोढुमाह—

यं सर्वशैलाः परिकल्प्य वत्सं मेरौ स्थिते दोग्धरि दोहदक्षे ।
भास्वन्ति रत्नानि महौषधीश्च पृथूपदिष्टां दुदुहुर्धरित्रीम् ॥ २ ॥

यमिति ॥ सर्वे च ते शैलाश्च **सर्वशैलाः** ॥ 'पूर्वकालैकसर्वजरत्पुराणनवकेवलाः समानाधिकरणेन ।' इति समासः ॥ **यं** हिमालयं **वत्सं परिकल्प्य** विधाय **दोहदक्षे** दोहनसमर्थे **मेरौ दोग्धरि स्थिते** सति ॥ 'यस्य च भावेन भावलक्षणम्' इति सप्तमी । **पृथूपदिष्टां** पृथुना वैन्येनोपदिष्टामित्युक्त्या प्रदर्शितां **धरित्रीम्** । गोरूपधरामिति शेषः । 'गौर्भूत्वा तु वसुंधरा' इति विष्णुपुराणात् । 'अकथितं च' इति कर्मत्वम् ॥ भास्वन्ति च भास्वत्यश्च **भास्वान्ति** द्युतिमन्ति । ओषधिविशेषणं चैतत् ॥ 'नपुंसकमनपुंसकेन'–इत्यादिना नपुंसकैकशेषः । **रत्नानि** मणीञ्जातिश्रेष्ठवस्तूनि च । 'रत्नं श्रेष्ठे मणावपि' इति विश्वः ॥ 'जातौ जातौ यदुत्कृष्टं तद्रत्नमिति कथ्यते ।' इति यादवः ॥ **महौषधीश्च** संजीवनीप्रभृतीश्च । क्षीरत्वेन परिणता इति शेषः । 'ताः क्षीरपरिणामिनीः' इति विष्णुपुराणात् ॥ **दुदुहुः** ॥ 'दुहियाचि–' इत्यादिना द्विकर्मकत्वम् ॥ अत्र प्रयोजकत्वेऽपि शैलानां 'पञ्चभिर्हलैः कर्षति ग्रामं ग्रामणीः' इतिवत्तत्समर्थाचरणात्कर्तृत्वेन व्यपदेशः । दुहेः स्वरितेत्त्वेऽप्यकर्त्रभिप्रायविवक्षायां परस्मैपदम् । अत्रार्थे प्रमाणम्—'गौर्भूमिरचलाः सर्वे कर्तारोऽत्र पयांसि च । ओषध्यश्चैव भास्वन्ति रत्नानि विविधानि च ॥ वत्सश्च हिमवानासीद्दोग्धा मेरुर्महागिरिः ।' इति ॥ एतेन वत्सस्य मातुः प्रेमास्पदत्वादस्य सारग्राहित्वं गम्यते । तथा चास्य नगस्य रत्नविशेषभोक्तृत्वान्नगाधिराजत्वं युक्तमिति भावः ॥ अत्र हिमवद्वर्णनस्य प्रकृतत्वात्तद्गतौषधिरत्नानां द्वयानामपि प्रकृतत्वात्तेषां दोहनक्रियारूपसमानधर्मसंबन्धादौपम्यस्य गम्यत्वात्केवलप्राकरणिकविषयस्तुल्ययोगिता नामालंकारः । तदुक्तम्—'प्रस्तुतानां तथान्येषां केवलं तुल्यधर्मतः । औपम्यं गम्यते यत्र सा मता तुल्ययोगिता ॥' इति । न चात्र रूपकपरिणामाद्यलंकारशङ्का कार्या तेषामारोपहेतुत्वात् । हिमहेमाचलादिषु वत्सत्वदोग्धृत्वादीनामागमसिद्धत्वेनानारोप्यमाणत्वादिति ॥

नतु हिमदोषदूषितस्य तस्यात्यन्तमनभिगम्यत्वाच्छिद्रात्रेण इव सर्वमपि सौभाग्यं विफलमित्याशङ्क्याह—

अनन्तरत्नप्रभवस्य यस्य हिमं न सौभाग्यविलोपि जातम् ।
एको हि दोषो गुणसंनिपाते निमज्जतीन्दोः किरणेष्विवाङ्कः ॥ ३ ॥

अनन्तेति ॥ प्रभवत्यस्मादिति प्रभवः कारणम् । [**अनन्तरत्नप्रभवस्य**] अनन्तानामपरिमितानां रत्नानां श्रेष्ठवस्तूनां प्रभवस्य **यस्य** हिमाद्रेः **हिमम्** ॥ कर्तृ ॥ सुभगस्य भावः सौभाग्यम् ॥ ' हृद्भगसिन्ध्वन्ते पूर्वपदस्य च ' इत्युभयपदवृद्धिः ॥ तद्विलुम्पतीति **सौभाग्यविलोपि** सौन्दर्यविघातकं **न जातं** नाभूत् । तथा **हि** । **एकः दोषः गुणसंनिपाते इन्दोः किरणेष्वङ्क इव निमज्जति** । अन्तर्लीयत इत्यर्थः । न हि स्वल्पो दोषोऽमितगुणाभिभावक एव किं तु कश्चिदिन्दुकलङ्कादिवद्गुणैरभिभूयते । अन्यथा सर्वरम्यवस्तुहानिप्रसङ्गादिति भावः । अत्रोपमानुप्राणितोऽर्थान्तरन्यासालंकारः । तल्लक्षणं तु—' ज्ञेयः सोऽर्थान्तरन्यासो वस्तु प्रस्तुत्य किंचन । तत्साधनसमर्थस्य न्यासो योऽन्यस्य वस्तुनः ॥ ' इति दण्डी ॥

यश्चाप्सरोविभ्रममण्डनानां संपादयित्रीं शिखरैर्बिभर्ति ।
बलाहकच्छेदविभक्तरागामकालसंध्यामिव धातुमत्ताम् ॥ ४ ॥

यश्चेति ॥ [**च**] किंचेति चकारार्थः । **यः** हिमाद्रिः [**अप्सरोविभ्रममण्डनानां**] अप्सरसां विभ्रममण्डनानि विलासालंकरणानि । अथ वा विभ्रमो विपरीतन्यासः । ' विभ्रमस्त्वरयाकाले भूषास्थानविपर्ययः । ' इति दशरूपकात् ॥ तेन मण्डनानि तेषां **संपादयित्रीम्** । एतद्धातुरागदर्शिन्योऽप्सरसः संध्याभ्रमेण प्रसाधनाय त्वरन्त इति भावः ॥ तथात्वे भ्रान्तिमदलंकारो व्यज्यते ॥ ' कर्तृकर्मणोः कृति ' इति कर्मणि षष्ठी ॥ [**बलाहकच्छेदविभक्तरागां**] वारीणां वाहका बलाहकाः ॥ पृषोदरादित्वात्साधुः ॥ तेषां छेदेषु खण्डेषु विभक्तः संक्रमितो रागो यया ताम् । एतेनाद्रेरभ्रंकषत्वं गम्यते ॥ इदं विशेषणद्वयं संध्यायामपि योज्यम् ॥ धातवः सिन्दूरगैरिकादयोऽस्य सन्तीति धातुमान् । नित्ययोगे मतुप् ॥ तस्य भावो धातुमत्ता तां [**धातुमत्ताम्**] । धातुयोगित्वमिति संबन्धोऽपि वाच्यार्थः ॥ ' समासकृत्तद्धितेषु संबन्धाभिधानं भावप्रत्ययेन ' इति वचनात् । लक्षणया नित्यानुषङ्गिकधातुमित्यर्थः ॥ **अकालसंध्यामिव** अनियतकालप्राप्तसंध्यामिव **शिखरैः बिभर्ति** धत्ते ॥ अत्र संध्याशब्दस्य जातिवाचित्वाज्जात्युत्प्रेक्षा ॥

आमेखलं संचरतां घनानां छायामधः[3]सानुगतां निषेव्य ।
उद्वेजिता वृष्टिभिराश्रयन्ते शृङ्गाणि यस्यातपवन्ति सिद्धाः ॥ ५ ॥

आमेखलमिति ॥ **सिद्धाः** अणिमादिसिद्धा देवयोनिविशेषाश्च ॥ ' पिशाचो गुह्यकः सिद्धो भूतोऽमी देवयोनयः । ' इत्यमरः । आ मेखलाभ्यः **आमेखलं** नितम्बपर्यन्तम् ॥ ' मेखला खण्डबन्धे स्यात्काञ्चीशैलनितम्बयोः । ' इति विश्वः ॥ ' आङ् मर्यादाभिविध्योः ' इत्यव्ययीभावः । **संचरतां घनानां** मेघानाम् [**अधःसानुगतां**] अधःसानूनि मेघमण्डलादधस्तटानि गतां प्राप्ताम् ॥ ' द्वितीया श्रितातीतपतितगतात्यस्तप्राप्तापन्नैः ' इति समासः ॥ **छायाम्** अनातपम् ॥ ' छाया सूर्यप्रिया कान्तिः प्रतिबिम्बमनातपः । '

---

१ विविक्त. २ छायामिषे इ. पा. इषे आश्विने । स्यादाश्विन इषोऽप्याश्वयुजोऽपि स्यादित्यमरः । ३ सानुगताः

इत्यमरः ॥ **निषेव्य वृष्टिभिः उद्वेजिताः** क्लेशिताः सन्तः ॥ 'उद्वेगः स्तिमिते क्लेशे भये मन्थरगामिनि ।' इति शब्दार्णवः ॥ **यस्य** हिमाद्रेः **आतपवन्ति** सातपानि **शृङ्गाणि आश्रयन्ते** । आश्रित्य स्थिता इत्यर्थः । अतिमेघमण्डलमस्यौन्नत्यमिति भावः॥

पदं तुषारस्रुतिधौतरक्तं यस्मिन्नदृष्ट्वापि हतद्विपानाम् ।
विदन्ति मार्गं नखरन्ध्रमुक्तैर्मुक्ताफलैः केसरिणां किराताः ॥ ६ ॥

पदमिति ॥ **यस्मिन्** अद्रौ **किराताः [तुषारस्रुतिधौतरक्तं]** तुषारस्रुतिभिर्हिमनिस्यन्दैर्धौतं क्षालितं रक्तं शोणितं यस्य तत्तथोक्तम् । अतो दुर्ग्रहमिति भावः । हता द्विपा गजा यैस्तेषां **हतद्विपानां केसरिणां** सिंहानां **पदं** पादप्रक्षेपस्थानम् **अदृष्ट्वापि [नखरन्ध्रमुक्तैः]** नखरन्ध्रैर्नखद्रोणिभिर्मुक्तैः **मुक्ताफलैः मार्गं विदन्ति** जानन्ति । अत्र व्याधाः सिंहघातिनो गजेन्द्राश्च मुक्ताकरा इति भावः ॥ 'करीन्द्रजीमूतवराहशङ्खमत्स्याहिशुक्त्युद्भववेणुजानि । मुक्ताफलानि प्रथितानि लोके तेषां तु शुक्त्युद्भवमेव भूरि ॥'

न्यस्ताक्षरा धातुरसेन यत्र भूर्जत्वचः कुञ्जरबिन्दुशोणाः ।
व्रजन्ति विद्याधरसुन्दरीणामनङ्गलेखक्रिययोपयोगम् ॥ ७ ॥

न्यस्ताक्षरा इति ॥ **यत्र** हिमाद्रौ **धातुरसेन** सिन्दूरद्रवेण ॥ 'शृङ्गारादौ विषे वीर्ये गुणे रागे द्रवे रसः ।' इत्यमरः । **न्यस्ताक्षराः** लिखितवर्णा अत एव **[कुञ्जरबिन्दुशोणाः]** कुञ्जरस्य ये बिन्दवः काये वयोविशेषभाविनः पद्मकाख्याः । 'पद्मकं बिन्दुजालकम् ।' इत्यमरः ॥ ते इव शोणा रक्तवर्णाः । लिखितभागेष्विति शेषः । **भूर्जत्वचः** भूर्जपत्रवल्कलानि ॥ 'भूर्जे पत्रो भुजा भूर्जो मृदुत्वक्चर्मिका अपि ।' इति यादवः ॥ **विद्याधरसुन्दरीणाम्** । **[अनङ्गलेखक्रियया]** लिख्यते येषु ते लेखाः पत्रिकाः । अनङ्गस्य लेखास्तेषां क्रियया । कामव्यञ्जकलेखकरणेनेत्यर्थः । **उपयोगम्** उपकारं **व्रजन्ति** । दिव्याङ्गनाविहारयोग्योऽयं शैल इति भावः ॥

यः पूरयन्कीचकरन्ध्रभागान्दरीमुखोत्थेन समीरणेन ।
उद्गास्यतामिच्छति किंनराणां तानप्रदायित्वमिवोपगन्तुम् ॥ ८ ॥

य इति ॥ **यः** हिमाद्रिः । **[दरीमुखोत्थेन]** दरी गुहा सैव मुखं तस्मादुत्थेनोत्पन्नेन । 'आतश्चोपसर्गे' इति कप्रत्ययः । **समीरणेन** वायुना । **[कीचकरन्ध्रभागान्]** कीचका वेणुविशेषाः । 'वेणवः कीचकास्ते स्युर्ये स्वनन्त्यनिलोद्धताः ।' इत्यमरः ॥ तेषां रन्ध्रभागाञ्छिद्रप्रदेशान् **पूरयन्** धमयन् । वांशिकोऽपि वंशरन्ध्राणि मुखमारुतेन पूरयतीति प्रसिद्धिः । **उद्गास्यतां** देवयोनित्वादुच्चैर्गान्धारग्रामेण गानं करिष्यताम् ॥ उक्तं च नारदेन—'षड्जमध्यमनामानौ ग्रामौ गायन्ति मानवाः । न तु गान्धारग्रामाख्यं स लभ्यो देवयोनिभिः ॥' इति ॥ **किंनराणां** देवगायकानां **तानप्र-**

---

१ विन्दन्ति. २ स्थान

दायित्वम् । तानो नाम स्वरान्तरप्रवर्तको रागस्थितिप्रवृत्त्यादिहेतुरंशापरनामा वंशवाद्यसाध्यः प्रधानभूतः स्वरविशेषः ॥ 'तानस्त्वंशस्वरो मतः' इत्यभिनवगुप्तः ॥ 'गाता यं यं स्वरं गच्छेत्तं तं वशेन तानयेत् ।' इति भरतः ॥ तत्प्रदानशीलत्वं तानप्रदायित्वं वांशिकत्वम् **उपगन्तुमिच्छति इव** इत्युत्प्रेक्षा । सा च दरीमुखोत्थेनेत्येकदेशविवर्तिरूपकोज्जीविता । मुखसाध्यत्वात्तानप्रदायित्वस्य । यत्रावयवरूपणादवयविरूपणं गम्यते तदेकदेशविवर्ति रूपकम् । गम्यते चात्रावयविनः पुंसो रूपणं यच्छब्दनिर्दिष्टे हिमाद्रावित्यलं बहुना ॥

कपोलकण्डूः[1] करिभिर्विनेतुं विघट्टितानां सरलद्रुमाणाम् ।
यत्र स्नुतक्षीरतया प्रसूतः[2] सानूनि गन्धः[3] सुरभीकरोति ॥ ९ ॥

कपोलेति ॥ **यत्र** हिमाद्रौ **करिभिः** गजैः **कपोलकण्डूः** गण्डस्थलकण्डूः **विनेतुम्** अपनेतुं **विघट्टितानां** घर्षितानां **सरलद्रुमाणां** संबन्धीनि स्नुतानि करिकपोलघर्षणात्क्षरितानि क्षीराणि येषां तेषां भावस्तत्ता तया [**स्नुतक्षीरतया**] हेतुना **प्रसूतः** उत्पन्नः **गन्धः सानूनि सुरभीकरोति** ॥ एतेनास्य गजाकरत्वं गम्यते । तथा च गजायुर्वेदे—' हिमवद्विन्ध्यमलया गजानां प्रभवा नगाः । ' इति ॥

वनेचराणां वनितासखानां दरीगृहोत्सङ्गनिषक्तभासः ।
भवन्ति यत्रौषधयो रजन्यामतैलपूराः सुरतप्रदीपाः ॥ १० ॥

वनेचराणामिति ॥ **यत्र** हिमाद्रौ **रजन्यां** [**दरीगृहोत्सङ्गनिषक्तभासः**] दर्यः कन्दरा एव गृहास्तेषामुत्सङ्गेष्वभ्यन्तरेषु निषक्ताः संक्रान्ता भासो यासां ताः **ओषधयः** तृणज्योतींषि । 'अमावोषधीषु च तेजो निधाय रविरस्तं याति' इत्यागमः । वनितानां सखायो वनितासखाः । 'राजाहःसखिभ्यष्टच् । ' [**वनितासखानां**] रममाणानामित्यर्थः । वने चरन्तीति वनेचराः किराताः । ' चरेष्टः ' इति टप्रत्ययः । 'तत्पुरुषे कृति बहुलम् ' इत्यलुक् । तेषां **वनेचराणाम्** । **अतैलपूराः** अनपेक्षिततैलसेका इत्यर्थः । [**सुरतप्रदीपाः**] सुरते सुरतकर्मणि प्रदीपाः **भवन्ति** । अत्रौषधीष्वारोप्यमाणस्य प्रदीपत्वस्य प्रकृतसुरतोपयोगित्वात्परिणामालंकारः । तदुक्तम्—' आरोप्यमाणस्य प्रकृतोपयोगित्वे परिणामः । ' इति । तथा प्रदीपकारणतैलपूरणनिषेधादकारणकार्योत्पत्तिलक्षणा विभावना चेत्युभयोः संसृष्टिः ॥

उद्वेजयत्यङ्गुलिपार्ष्णिभागान्मार्गे शिलीभूतहिमेऽपि यत्र ।
न दुर्वहश्रोणिपयोधरार्ता भिन्दन्ति मन्दां गतिमश्वमुख्यः ॥ ११ ॥

उद्वेजयतीति ॥ **यत्र** हिमाद्रौ । शिलीभूतं घनीभूतं हिमं यत्र तस्मिन् [**शिलीभूतहिमे**] अत एव [**अङ्गुलिपार्ष्णिभागान्**] अङ्गुलीनां पार्ष्णीनां च भागान्प्रदेशान् **उद्वेजयति** अतिशैत्यात्क्लेशयति **अपि मार्गे** श्रोणयश्च पयोधराश्च श्रोणिपयोधरम् । दुर्वहेण दुर्धरेण श्रोणिपयोधरेणार्ताः पीडिताः [**दुर्वहश्रोणिपयोधरार्ताः**] । आङ्पूर्वादृच्छतेः क्तः । ' उपसर्गादृति धातौ ' इति वृद्धिः । अश्वानां मुखानीव मुखानि

---

1 कण्डूम्. 2 समीरः. 3 गन्धैः.

यासां ताः **अश्वमुख्यः** किंनरस्त्रियः ॥ उष्ट्रमुखवत्समासः ॥ 'स्यात्किंनरः किंपुरुष-स्तुरङ्गवदनो मयुः ।' इत्यमरः । **मन्दां** मन्थरां **गतिं न भिन्दन्ति** न त्यजन्ती-त्यर्थः । पादपीडाकरेऽप्यतिभारभङ्गुरशरीरतया न शीघ्रं गन्तुं शक्यत इति भावः ॥

दिवाकराद्रक्षति यो गुहासु लीनं दिवाभीतमिवान्धकारम् ।
क्षुद्रेऽपि नूनं शरणं प्रपन्ने ममत्वमुच्चैःशिरसां सतीव ॥ १२ ॥

दिवाकरादिति ॥ **यः** हिमाद्रिः **दिवा** दिवसे **भीतं** भयाविष्टम् **इव** । उलूकमिवेति च ध्वनिः । **गुहासु लीनम् अन्धकारं** ध्वान्तम् । दिवा दिनं करोतीति दिवाकरस्तस्माद् **दिवाकरात्** । 'दिवाविभानिशाप्रभाभास्कर'- इत्यादिना टप्रत्ययः । 'भीत्रार्थानां भयहेतुः' इत्यपादानत्वात्पञ्चमी ॥ **रक्षति** त्रायते ॥ ननु क्षुद्रसंरक्षणमनर्हमित्याशङ्क्याह–क्षुद्रे इति । **उच्चैःशिरसां** उन्नतानां **शरणं प्रपन्ने** शरणागते **क्षुद्रे** नीचे **अपि सति** सज्जने **इव नूनं ममत्वं** ममायमित्यभिमानः । अस्तीति शेषः । ममशब्दात्त्वप्रत्ययः । अर्थान्तरन्यासोऽलंकारः ॥

लाङ्गूलविक्षेपविसर्पिशोभैरितस्ततश्चन्द्रमरीचिगौरैः ।
यस्यार्थयुक्तं गिरिराजशब्दं कुर्वन्ति बालव्यजनैश्चमर्यः ॥ १३ ॥

लाङ्गलेति ॥ **चमर्यः** मृगीविशेषाः । **इतस्ततः** [**लाङ्गूलविक्षेपविसर्पिशोभैः**] लाङ्गलानि बालधयः । 'पुच्छोऽस्त्री लोमलाङ्गूले बालहस्तश्च बालधिः ।' इत्यमरः ॥ तेषां विक्षेपैर्विधूननैर्विसर्पिण्यो विसृमराः शोभाः कान्तयो येषां तैः । [**चन्द्रमरीचिगौरैः**] चन्द्रमरीचिभिरिव गौरैः शुभ्रैः । 'गौरः करीरे सिद्धार्थे शुक्ले पीतेऽरुणेऽपि च ।' इति यादवः ॥ 'उपमानानि सामान्यवचनैः' इति समासः । **बालव्यजनैः** चामरैः **यस्य** हिमाद्रेः **गिरिराजशब्दं** गिरिराज इति संज्ञाम् । **अर्थयुक्तम्** अभिधेयवन्तं **कुर्वन्ति** । राजानो हि छत्रचामरादिचिह्निता इति भावः ॥

यत्रांशुकाक्षेपविलज्जितानां यदृच्छया किंपुरुषाङ्गनानाम् ।
दरीगृहद्वारविलम्बिबिम्बास्तिरस्करिण्यो जलदा भवन्ति ॥ १४ ॥

यत्रेति ॥ **यत्र** हिमाद्रौ । [**अंशुकाक्षेपविलज्जितानाम्**] अंशुकाक्षेपेण वस्त्रापहरणेन विलज्जितानां **किंपुरुषाङ्गनानां** किंनरस्त्रीणां **यदृच्छया** दैवगत्या [**दरीगृहद्वारविलम्बिबिम्बाः**] दरीगृहद्वारेषु विलम्बिबिम्बाः लम्बमानमण्डलाः **जलदाः तिरस्करिण्यः** जवनिकाः **भवन्ति** ॥ 'प्रतिसीरा जवनिका स्यात्तिरस्करिणी च सा ।' इत्यमरः । 'तिरसोऽन्यतरस्याम्' इति सत्वम् । अत्र जलदेष्वारोप्यमाणस्य तिरस्करिणीत्वस्य प्रकृतोपयोगित्वात्परिणामालंकारः ॥

भागीरथीनिर्झरशीकराणां वोढा मुहुः कम्पितदेवदारुः ।
यद्वायुरन्विष्टमृगैः किरातैरासेव्यते भिन्नशिखण्डिबर्हः ॥ १५ ॥

---

१ अतीव. २ चान्द्र. ३ द्वारि. ४ बर्हैः.

भागीरथीति ॥ **भागीरथीनिर्झरशीकराणां** गङ्गाप्रवाहपाथःकणानाम् । कर्मणि षष्ठी । **वोढा** प्रापकः ॥ वहेस्तृच् ॥ **मुहुः** पुनः पुनः सद्यो वा । 'पौनःपुन्ये भृशार्थे च सद्यो वा स्यान्मुहुःपदम् ।' इति वैजयन्ती ॥ [**कम्पितदेवदारुः**] कम्पिता देवदारवो येन स तथोक्तः । [**भिन्नशिखण्डिबर्हः**] भिन्नानि विश्लेषितानि शिखण्डिनां बर्हाणि गतिलाघवार्थं किरातकटिबद्धानि येन स तथोक्तः । क्रमाद्विशेषणत्रयेण शैत्यसौरभ्यमान्द्यान्युक्तानि । यस्य हिमाद्रेर्वायुः [**यद्वायुः**] **अन्विष्टमृगैः** मार्गितमृगैः । श्रान्तैरिति भावः ॥ 'अन्विष्टं मार्गितं मृगितम्' इत्यमरः ॥ **किरातैः आसेव्यते** ॥

सप्तर्षिहस्तावचितावशेषाण्यधो विवस्वान्परिवर्तमानः ।
पद्मानि यस्याग्रसरोरुहाणि प्रबोधयत्यूर्ध्वमुखैर्मयूखैः ॥ १६ ॥

सप्तर्षीति ॥ [**सप्तर्षिहस्तावचितावशेषाणि**] सप्त च ते ऋषयश्च सप्तर्षयः । 'दिक्संख्ये संज्ञायाम्' इति समासः । तेषां हस्तैरवचितेभ्यो लूनेभ्योऽवशेषाण्यवशिष्टानि । 'शेषोऽप्रधाने संतापे त्रिष्वन्यत्रोपयुज्यते ।' इति केशवः । कर्मण्यण्प्रत्ययः । अनेन पद्मानां साफल्यं सूचितम् । **यस्य** हिमाद्रेः । [**अग्रसरोरुहाणि**] रोहन्तीति रुहाणि ॥ 'इगुपधज्ञाप्रीकिरः कः' इति कप्रत्ययः ॥ अग्रे उपरि यानि सरांसि तेषु रुहाणि **पद्मानि अधः परिवर्तमानः** भ्रमन् **विवस्वान्** सूर्यः **ऊर्ध्वमुखैः मयूखैः प्रबोधयति** विकासयति । न कदाचिदधोमुखैः । अतिमार्तण्डमण्डलत्वादप्रभूमेरिति भावः । सप्तर्षिमण्डलं ध्रुवादप्यूर्ध्वमिति ज्यौतिषिकाः । अतस्तेषामग्रसरोरुहभागित्वं युक्तम् ॥

यज्ञाङ्गयोनित्वमवेक्ष्य यस्य सारं धरित्रीधरणक्षमं च ।
प्रजापतिः कल्पितयज्ञभागं शैलाधिपत्यं स्वयमन्वतिष्ठत् ॥१७॥

यज्ञाङ्गेति ॥ **यस्य** हिमाद्रेः [**यज्ञाङ्गयोनित्वम्**] यज्ञाङ्गानां यज्ञसाधनानां सोमलतादीनां योनिः प्रभवस्तस्य भावस्तत्त्वम् । 'यज्ञाङ्गार्थं मया सृष्टो हिमवानचलेश्वरः ।' इति विष्णुपुराणात् ॥ **धरित्रीधरणक्षमं** भूभारधरणयोग्यं **सारं** बलं **च** ॥ 'सारो बले स्थिरांशे च' इत्यमरः ॥ **अवेक्ष्य** ज्ञात्वा **प्रजापतिः स्वयम्** एव [**कल्पितयज्ञभागं**] कल्पितो यज्ञभागो यस्मिंस्तत्तथोक्तम् ॥ 'सोमस्य राज्ञः कुरङ्ग इन्दोः शृङ्गी समुद्रस्य शिशुमारो हिमवतो हस्ती ।' इति श्रुतेरिति भावः । [**शैलाधिपत्यम्**] शैलानामाधिपत्यमधिपतित्वम् । 'पत्यन्तपुरोहितादिभ्यो यक्' इति यक्प्रत्ययः ॥ **अन्वतिष्ठत्** । ददाति स्मेत्यर्थः । उक्तं च ब्रह्माण्डपुराणे—'शैलानां हिमवन्तं च नदीनां चैव सागरम् । गन्धर्वाणामधिपतिं चक्रे चित्ररथं विधिः ॥' इति ॥

संप्रति कथां प्रस्तौति—

स मानसीं मेरुसखः पितॄणां कन्यां कुलस्य स्थितये स्थितिज्ञः ।
मेनां मुनीनामपि माननीयामात्मानुरूपां विधिनोपयेमे ॥ १८ ॥

---

१ आचरित. २ भागः. ३ हस्तिरूपांशः.

स इति ॥ मेरोः सखा **मेरुसखः** । बन्धुसंपन्न इति भावः । **स्थितिज्ञः** मर्यादाभिज्ञः । अनेन श्रुतसंपत्तिः सूच्यते । **सः** हिमवान् **पितॄणां मानसीं** मनःसंकल्पजन्यां **मुनीनामपि माननीयाम्** । योगब्रह्मवादाभ्यां पूज्यामित्यर्थः । उक्तं च विष्णुपुराणे 'तेभ्यः शुभास्पदं जज्ञे मेनका हरिणी तथा । ते उभे ब्रह्मवादिन्यौ योगिन्यौ चाप्युभे द्विज ॥' इति ॥ **आत्मानुरूपां** कुलशीलसौन्दर्यादिभिः सदृशीं **मेनां** मेनकादेवीति नामवतीं **कन्याम्** । **कुलस्य स्थितये** प्रतिष्ठायै । **विधिना** यथाशास्त्रेण **उपयेमे** परिणीतवान् ॥ 'उपाद्यमः स्वकरणे' इत्यात्मनेपदम् ॥ 'तेषां तु मानसी कन्या मेना नाम महागिरेः । पत्नी हिमवतो यस्याः पुत्रो मैनाक उच्यते ॥' इति ब्रह्माण्डपुराणात् ॥

कालक्रमेणाथ तयोः प्रवृत्ते स्वरूपयोग्ये सुरतप्रसङ्गे ।
मनोरमं यौवनमुद्वहन्त्या गर्भोऽभवद्भूधरराजपत्न्याः ॥ १९ ॥

कालक्रमेणेति ॥ **अथ कालक्रमेण** । गच्छता कालेनेत्यर्थः । **तयोः** मेनकाहिमवतोः **स्वरूपयोग्ये** सौन्दर्यानुगुणे । रूप्यते निश्चीयतेऽनेनेति रूपं ज्ञानं तद्योग्ये । शास्त्रानुसारिणीत्यर्थः । **सुरतप्रसङ्गे** सुरतकर्मणि **प्रवृत्ते** सति **मनोरमं यौवनमुद्वहन्त्याः भूधरराजपत्न्याः** मेनकायाः **गर्भः अभवत्** ॥

असूत सा नागवधूपभोग्यं मैनाकमम्भोनिधिबद्धसख्यम् ।
क्रुद्धेऽपि पक्षच्छिदि वृत्रशत्राववेदनाज्ञं कुलिशक्षतानाम् ॥२०॥

असूतेति ॥ **सा** मेना **नागवधूपभोग्यम्** । नागकन्यापरिणेतारमित्यर्थः । [**अम्भोनिधिबद्धसख्यं**] अम्भोनिधिना बद्धसख्यं समुद्रकृतमैत्रीकम् । सख्यमूलं सूचयति—**पक्षच्छिदि** पक्षच्छेत्तरि ॥ '-सत्सूद्विष' इत्यादिना क्विप्प्रत्ययः ॥ **वृत्रशत्रौ क्रुद्धे** कुपिते सति **अपि कुलिशक्षतानां** वज्रप्रहाराणाम् । संबन्धसामान्ये षष्ठी । [**अवेदनाज्ञं**] जानातीति ज्ञः ॥ 'इगुपधज्ञा—' इति कप्रत्ययः ॥ वेदनानां ज्ञः । अथ वा वेदनां जानातीति वेदनाज्ञः ॥ 'आतोऽनुपसर्गे कः' इति कप्रत्ययः ॥ 'उपपदमतिङ्' इति समासः ॥ स न भवतीत्यवेदनाज्ञस्तम् । कुलिशक्षतवेदनानभिज्ञमित्यर्थः ॥ सापेक्षत्वेऽपि गमकत्वात्समासः ॥ पक्षच्छेदोद्यतशक्रात् त्राणाय शरणागमनमनयोः सख्यमूलमिति भावः । **मैनाकं** पुत्रम् **असूत** । सर्वपर्वतपक्षच्छेदेऽप्ययमच्छिन्नपक्ष एवेति मैनाकस्योत्कर्षः । तादृक्पुत्रवत्त्वं हिमाद्रेरिति सार्थकं मैनाकस्य वर्णनम् ॥ 'पिता न ज्ञायते यस्या भ्राता यदि न विद्यते । नोपयच्छेत्तु तां कन्यां धर्मलोपभयात्सुधीः ॥' इत्यभ्रातृककन्यापरिणयनिषेधात्प्रकृते पार्वती भ्रातृमत्येवेति सूचनार्थं मैनाकवर्णनमिति तात्पर्यार्थः ॥

अथावमानेन पितुः प्रयुक्ता दक्षस्य कन्या भवपूर्वपत्नी ।
सती सती योगविसृष्टदेहा तां जन्मने शैलवधूं प्रपेदे ॥ २१ ॥

अथेति ॥ **अथ** मैनाकजननानन्तरं **दक्षस्य** प्रजापतेः **कन्या** [**भवपूर्वपत्नी**] भवस्य महादेवस्य पूर्वपत्नी पूर्वभार्या **सती** पतिव्रता ॥ 'सती साध्वी पतिव्रता' इत्यमरः ।

---

१ पितरो ब्रह्मणा सृष्टा व्याख्याता ये मया पुरा । अग्निष्वात्ता बर्हिषदोऽनाग्नयः साग्नयश्च ये । तेभ्यः स्वधासुता जज्ञे मेना वैतरणी–वैधारणी-तथा । इ. २ ०सौख्यं इ. ३ अपमानेन.

सती नाम देवी पितुः दक्षस्य ॥ कर्तरि षष्ठी ॥ **अवमानेन** स्वभर्त्रवज्ञया **प्रयुक्ता** प्रेरिता [**योगविसृष्टदेहा**] योगेन योगमार्गेण विसृष्टदेहा त्यक्तदेहा सती । **जन्मने** पुनरुद्भवाय **तां शैलवधूं** मेनकां **प्रपेदे** । अत्र ' पुरा किल सती देवी दक्षाध्वरे तत्कृतां स्वभर्त्रवज्ञामसहमाना पितरं प्रसूं चोपेक्ष्य मत्कर्तव्यकार्यं त्वज्जामातैव करिष्यतीति निर्धार्य देवकार्याणि साधयितुं च योगाग्निना स्वशरीरं ददाह ' इति पुरावृत्तकथानुसंधेया ॥

सा भूधराणामधिपेन तस्यां समाधिमत्यामुदपादि भव्या ।
सम्यक्प्रयोगादपरिक्षतायां नीताविवोत्साहगुणेन संपत् ॥ २२ ॥

सेति ॥ **भव्या** कल्याणी **सा** सती **भूधराणामधिपेन** हिमवता **समाधिमत्यां** नियमवत्यां **तस्यां** मेनकायां **सम्यक्प्रयोगात्** साध्वाचरणाद्धेतोः **अपरिक्षतायाम्** अभ्रष्टायां **नीतौ उत्साहगुणेन** उत्साहशक्त्या । कर्त्रा । **संपद् इव उदपादि** । उत्पादिता । उत्पद्यतेर्ण्यन्तात्कर्मणि लुङ् । ' चिण्भावकर्मणोः ' इति चिण्प्रत्ययः । ' चिणो लुक् ' इति तस्य लुक् ॥

प्रसन्नदिक्पांशुविविक्तवातं शङ्खस्वनानन्तरपुष्पवृष्टि ।
शरीरिणां स्थावरजङ्गमानां सुखाय तज्जन्मदिनं बभूव ॥ २३ ॥

प्रसन्नेति ॥ प्रसन्ना निर्मला दिशो यस्मिंस्तत् **प्रसन्नदिक्** । [**पांशुविविक्तवातं**] पांशुविविक्ता रजोरहिता वाता यस्मिंस्तत्तथोक्तम् । [**शङ्खस्वनानन्तरपुष्पवृष्टि**] शङ्खस्य स्वनात्स्वनस्य वा अनन्तरं पुष्पवृष्टिर्यस्मिंस्तत्तथोक्तम् । [**तज्जन्मदिनं**] तस्याः पार्वत्या जन्मदिनम् । [**स्थावरजङ्गमानां**] स्थितिशीलाः स्थावराः शैलवृक्षादयः । ' स्थेशभासपिशकसो वरच् ' इति वरच्प्रत्ययः ॥ जङ्गम्यन्ते भृशं गच्छन्तीति जङ्गमा देवतिर्यङ्मनुष्यादयः । स्थावराश्च तेषां द्वयानामपि **शरीरिणां सुखाय** आनन्दाय **बभूव** ॥

तया दुहित्रा सुतरां सवित्री स्फुरत्प्रभामण्डलया चकासे ।
विदूर[3]भूमिर्नवमेघशब्दा[4]दुद्भिन्नया रत्नशलाकयेव ॥ २४ ॥

तयेति ॥ **स्फुरत्प्रभामण्डलया तया दुहित्रा सवित्री** जनयित्री । ' स्वरतिसूतिसूयतिधूञूदितो वा ' इतीडागमः । विदूरस्याद्रेः प्रान्तभूमिः **विदूरभूमिः** । ' अविदूरे विदूरस्य गिरेरुत्तुङ्गरोधसः । काकतालीयसंमान्ते मणीनामाकरो भवेत् ॥ ' इति बुद्धः ॥ **नवमेघशब्दादुद्भिन्नया रत्नशलाकया** रत्नाङ्कुरेण **इव सुतरां चकासे** रराज ॥

दिने दिने सा परिवर्धमाना लब्धोदया चान्द्रमसीव लेखा ।
पुपोष लावण्यमयान्विशेषाञ्ज्योत्स्नान्तराणीव कलान्तराणि ॥ २५ ॥

दिन इति ॥ लब्ध उदयो यया सा **लब्धोदया** । उत्पन्नेत्यर्थः । अभ्युदितेत्यन्यत्र । **दिने दिने** प्रतिदिनम् ॥ ' नित्यवीप्सयोः ' इति वीप्सायां द्विरुक्तिः । **परिवर्धमाना** ।

१ तूर्य. २ धरित्री. ३ वैदूर्यभूमिः. ४ नादात्.

उभयत्र समानमेतत् । सा बाला । चन्द्रमस इयं **चान्द्रमसी लेखेव लावण्यमयान्** कान्तिविशेषप्रचुरान् ॥ 'मुक्ताफलेषु च्छायायास्तरलत्वमिवान्तरा । प्रतिभाति यदङ्गेषु तल्लावण्यमिहोच्यते ॥ ' इति भूपालः ॥ **विशेषान्** अवयवान् ॥ 'विशेषोऽवयवे व्यक्तौ ' इत्युत्पलमालायाम् ॥ ज्योत्स्नायामन्तरमन्तर्धानं येषां तानि **ज्योत्स्नान्तराणि** ज्योत्स्नयान्तर्हितानि । तन्मयानीति यावत् । अन्याः कलाः **कलान्तराणि इव** ॥ सुप्सुपेति समासः । 'स्थानात्मीयान्यतादर्थ्यरन्ध्रान्तर्धिषु चान्तरम् ।' इति शाश्वतः । **पुपोष** उपचितवती ॥ इयं वाक्योपमेत्याह दण्डी । तल्लक्षणं तु—"वाक्यार्थेनैव वाक्यार्थः कोऽपि यद्युपमीयते । एकानेकेवशब्दत्वात्सा तु वाक्योपमा द्विधा ॥ " इति ॥

तां पार्वतीत्याभिजनेन नाम्ना बन्धुप्रियां बन्धुजनो जुहाव ।
उ मेति मात्रा तपसो निषिद्धा पश्चादुमाख्यां सुमुखी जगाम ॥२६॥

तामिति ॥ **बन्धुप्रियां तां** बालां **बन्धुजनः** पित्रादिः । अभिजनादागतेन **आभिजनेन** । पित्रादिपूर्वसंबन्धोपाधिकेनेत्यर्थः । 'अभिजनाः पूर्वबान्धवाः ' इति काशिका ॥ **नाम्ना** । पर्वतस्यापत्यं स्त्री **पार्वती** । 'तस्यापत्यम् ' इत्यण्प्रत्ययः ॥ **इति जुहाव** आहूतवान् ॥ ह्वयतेर्लिटि रूपम् । पर्वतजन्यत्वोपाधिना पार्वतीति नाम्ना प्रसिद्धिरिति भावः । **पश्चाद्** अभिजननामप्रवृत्त्यनन्तरं **मात्रा** जनन्या ॥ उ इति संबोधने ॥ 'उ इति वितर्कसंबोधनपादपूरणेषु ' इति गणव्याख्याने ॥ माशब्दो निषेधे ॥ उ हे वत्से **मा** मा कुरु **इति** एवंरूपेण । **तपसः** तपश्चर्यायाः ॥ 'वारणार्थानामीप्सितः ' इत्यपादानत्वात्पञ्चमी ॥ **निषिद्धा** निवारिता सती **सुमुखी** सा बाला उमेत्याख्यां नामधेयं **उमाख्यां जगाम** ॥

महीभृतः पुत्रवतोऽपि दृष्टिस्तस्मिन्नपत्ये न जगाम तृप्तिम् ।
अनन्तपुष्पस्य मधोर्हि चूते द्विरेफमाला सविशेषसङ्गा ॥ २७ ॥

महीभृत इति ॥ पुत्राश्च दुहितरश्च पुत्राः ॥' भ्रातृपुत्रौ स्वसृदुहितृभ्याम् ' इत्येकशेषः । तेऽस्य सन्तीति पुत्रवान् ॥ भूमार्थे मतुप् ॥ तस्य **पुत्रवतोऽपि** बह्वपत्यस्यापीत्यर्थः । **महीभृतः** हिमाद्रेः **दृष्टिः** चक्षुः **तस्मिन् अपत्ये** तोके । 'अपत्यं तोकं तयोः समे ' इत्यमरः ॥ तस्यां पार्वत्यामित्यर्थः । **तृप्तिं न जगाम** । तथा हि । **अनन्तपुष्पस्य** नानाविधकुसुमस्यापि **मधोः** वसन्तस्य संबन्धिनी **द्विरेफमाला** भृङ्गपङ्क्तिश्चूतस्य विकारे **चूते** चूतकुसुमे ॥ 'अवयवे च प्राण्योषधिवृक्षेभ्यः ' इति विकारार्थोत्पन्नस्याण्प्रत्ययस्य लुक्प्रकरणे 'पुष्पमूलेषु बहुलम् ' इति पठनाल्लुक् ॥ [**सविशेषसङ्गा**] सविशेषः सातिशयः सङ्गो यस्याः सा तथोक्ता । अत्यन्तासक्तेत्यर्थः ॥

प्रभामहत्या शिखयेव दीपस्त्रिमार्गयेव त्रिदिवस्य मार्गः ।
संस्कारवत्येव गिरा मनीषी तया स पूतश्च विभूषितश्च ॥२८॥

प्रभेति ॥ **प्रभामहत्या** प्रकाशाधिकया **शिखया** ज्वालया **दीपः इव** । शिखादीपयोरवयवावयविभावाद्भेदेन व्यपदेशः ॥ त्रयो मार्गा यस्यास्तया **त्रिमार्गया** मन्दा-

१ सङ्ग संज्ञा

कन्या । [**त्रिदिवस्य**] तृतीया द्यौर्लोकः इति त्रिदिवः स्वर्गः ॥ वृत्तिविषये त्रिशब्दस्य त्रिभागवत्पूरणार्थत्वम् । पृषोदरादित्वाद्दिवृशब्दादकारागमः । पुंस्त्वं लोकात् । दीव्यतेर्घञर्थे कविधानम् । दीव्यन्त्यत्र जना इति क्षीरस्वामी । तस्य **मार्गः इव** । [**संस्कारवत्या**] संस्कारो व्याकरणजन्या शुद्धिस्तद्वत्या **गिरा** वाचा । 'भद्रैषां लक्ष्मीर्निहिताधि वाचि' इति श्रुतेरिति भावः । मनस ईषा मनीषा सास्यास्तीति **मनीषी** विद्वान् **इव** ॥ शकन्ध्वादित्वात्साधुः ॥ **तया** पार्वत्या **स** हिमवान् **पूतः** शोधितः **च विभूषितश्च** ॥ अत्र शिखागिरोरविशिष्टयोरुपमानानर्हत्वान्न विशेषणाधिक्यदोषः । इयं मालोपमा ॥

मन्दाकिनीसैकतवेदिकाभिः सा कन्दुकैः कृत्रिमपुत्रकैश्च ।
रेमे मुहुर्मध्यगता सखीनां क्रीडारसं निर्विशतीव बाल्ये ॥ २९ ॥

मन्दाकिनीति ॥ **सा** पार्वती **बाल्ये** वयसि क्रीडानां रसः स्वादः । रुचिरिति यावत् । तं **क्रीडारसम्** ॥ 'रसो गन्धे रसः स्वादे' इति विश्वः । **निर्विशतीव** भुञ्जानेव । 'निर्वेशो भृतिभोगयोः' इत्यमरः 'आच्छीनद्योर्नुम्' इति विकल्पान्नुमभावः । **सखीनां मध्यगता** सती [**मन्दाकिनीसैकतवेदिकाभिः**] मन्दाकिन्याः सैकतेषु पुलिनेषु वेदिकाभिः । **कन्दुकैः** । [**कृत्रिमपुत्रकैः**] क्रियया निर्वृत्तैः कृत्रिमैः । 'ड्वितः क्त्रिः' इति क्त्रिप्रत्ययः । 'क्त्रेर्मम्नित्यम्' इति मबागमश्च । पुत्रकैः पाञ्चालिकाभिः । 'पाञ्चालिका पुत्रिका स्याद्वस्त्रदन्तादिभिः कृता ।' इत्यमरः । 'संज्ञायां कन्' इति कन्प्रत्ययः । **च मुहुः** पुनः पुनः **रेमे** ॥

तां हंसमालाः शरदीव गङ्गां महौषधिं नक्तमिवात्मभासः ।
स्थिरोपदेशामुपदेशकाले प्रपेदिरे प्राक्तनजन्मविद्याः ॥ ३० ॥

तामिति ॥ [**स्थिरोपदेशां**] स्थिरः स्थेयानुपदेशः प्राग्भवीयो यस्यास्तादृशीम् । मेधाविनीमित्यर्थः । **तां** पार्वतीम् । **उपदेशकाले प्राक्तनजन्मविद्याः** । पूर्वजन्माभ्यस्तविद्या इत्यर्थः । **शरदि गङ्गां हंसमालाः इव नक्तं** रात्रौ **महौषधिं** तृणविशेषम् **आत्मभासः** स्वदीप्तयः **इव प्रपेदिरे** ॥ उपमानसामर्थ्यादुपदेशमन्तरेणैवेति गम्यते ॥

असंभृतं मण्डनमङ्गयष्टेरनासवाख्यं करणं मदस्य ।
कामस्य पुष्पव्यतिरिक्तमस्त्रं बाल्यात्परं साथ वयः प्रपेदे ॥ ३१ ॥

असंभृतमिति ॥ **अथ सा** पार्वती । **अङ्गयष्टेः असंभृतम्** अयत्नसिद्धं **मण्डनं** प्रसाधनम् **अनासवाख्यम्** आसवाख्यारहितं **मदस्य करणं** साधनं **कामस्य पुष्पव्यतिरिक्तम् अस्त्रम्** अस्त्रभूतं **बाल्यात्** शैशवात् **परम्** अनन्तरभावि **वयः** यौवनं **प्रपेदे** प्राप ॥ यौवनेनैव हि युवतयः प्रसाध्यन्ते माद्यन्ते काम्यन्ते चेति भावः । अत्र द्वितीयपाद आसवरूपकारणाभावेऽपि तत्कार्यमदोक्तेर्विभावनालंकारः । तदुक्तम्—'कारणा-

---

१ बाल्यम्. २ महौषधीः. ३ साधु.

भावे कारणात्पत्तिर्विभावना ' इति ॥ प्रथमतृतीययोस्त्वारोप्यमाणयोर्मण्डनमदनास्त्रत्वयोः प्रकृतोपयोगात्परिणामालंकारः । तल्लक्षणं तु [१० श्लोकव्याख्याने] उक्तम् ॥

उन्मीलितं तूलिकयेव चित्रं सूर्यांशुभिर्भिन्नमिवारविन्दम् ।
बभूव तस्याश्चतुरस्रशोभि वपुर्विभक्तं नवयौवनेन ॥ ३२ ॥

उन्मीलितमिति ॥ **नवयौवनेन** प्रथमयौवनेन **विभक्तम्** अभिव्यञ्जितम् । पीनजघनादिसंस्थानमित्यर्थः ॥ **तस्याः** पार्वत्याः **वपुः** । **तूलिकया** कूर्चिकया । शलाकयेत्यर्थः । 'तूलिका कथितालेख्यकूर्चिकातूलशय्ययोः ।' इति विश्वः ॥ **उन्मीलितं** रञ्जनद्रव्येणोद्भासितं समुत्कीर्णरूपमिति यावत् **चित्रम्** आलेख्यम् **इव** । **सूर्यांशुभिः भिन्नं** विकसितम् **अरविन्दं** पद्मम् **इव** । चतस्रः अस्रयो यस्य तच्चतुरस्रमन्यूनातिरिक्तं यथा तथा शोभत इति **चतुरस्रशोभि** ॥ ताच्छील्ये णिनिः । **बभूव** । चित्रारविन्दयोस्तूलिकातरणिकिरणसंबन्ध इव स्वतःसिद्धस्यैवाङ्गसौष्ठवस्य यौवनप्रादुर्भावोऽभिव्यञ्जको बभूवेत्यर्थः ॥

देवतानां रूपं पादाङ्गुष्ठप्रभृति वर्ण्यते मानुषाणां केशादारभ्येति धार्मिकाः । संप्रति सप्तदशभिः श्लोकैः पार्वत्याः पादादिकेशान्तवर्णनमारभते—

अभ्युन्नताङ्गुष्ठनखप्रभाभिर्निक्षेपणाद्रागमिवोद्गिरन्तौ ।
आजहतुस्तच्चरणौ पृथिव्यां स्थलारविन्दश्रियमव्यवस्थाम् ॥ ३३ ॥

अभ्युन्नतेति ॥ [**अभ्युन्नताङ्गुष्ठनखप्रभाभिः**] अभ्युन्नतयोरङ्गुष्ठनखयोः प्रभाभिर्निमित्तेन **निक्षेपणात्** निर्भरन्यासाद्धेतोः । **रागम्** अन्तर्गतं लौहित्यम् । 'रागः क्लेशादिके रक्ते मात्सर्ये लोहितादिषु ।' इति शाश्वतः ॥ **उद्गिरन्तौ** वमन्तौ । बहिर्निःसारयन्तौ **इव** स्थितावित्यर्थः ॥ अत्रोद्गिरतेर्गौणार्थत्वान्न ग्राम्यतादोषः । प्रत्युत गुण एव । यथाह दण्डी—'निष्ठ्यूतोद्गीर्णवान्तादि गौणवृत्तिव्यपाश्रयम् । अतिसुन्दरमन्यत्र ग्राम्यकक्षां विगाहते ॥' इति । तस्याश्चरणौ **तच्चरणौ** । **पृथिव्याम् अव्यवस्थां** व्यवस्थारहिताम् । संचारिणीमित्यर्थः । **स्थलारविन्दश्रियम् आजहतुः** । स्थलविशेषणान्नियतलौहित्यलाभः । अत्र सामुद्रिकाः—'यस्या रक्ततलौ पादावुन्नताग्रौ तलस्पृशौ । निगूढगुल्फौ निहतौ सा स्यान्नृपतिसंमता ॥' इति । अत्रोपमानधर्मस्यारविन्दश्रियश्चरणयोरुपमेययोरसंभवादरविन्दश्रियमिव श्रियमिति प्रतिबिम्बीकरणाक्षेपान्निदर्शनालंकारः । सा च संबन्धेऽप्यसंबन्धलक्षणातिशयोक्त्यनुप्राणिता । अव्यवस्थामित्यनेन स्थलारविन्दस्य स्थैर्यसंबन्धेऽप्यसंबन्धाभिधानात् । निदर्शनालक्षणं तु—'असंभवद्धर्मयोगादुपमानोपमेययोः । प्रतिबिम्बक्रिया गम्या यत्र सा स्यान्निदर्शना ॥' इति ॥

सा राजहंसैरिव संनताङ्गी गतेषु लीलाञ्चितविक्रमेषु ।
व्यनीयत प्रत्युपदेशलुब्धैरादित्सुभिर्नूपुरसिञ्जितानि ॥ ३४ ॥

सेति ॥ **प्रत्युपदेशलुब्धैः** ॥ 'गुरुशुश्रूषया विद्या पुष्कलेन धनेन वा । अथ वा विद्यया विद्या चतुर्थी नोपपद्यते ॥' इति न्यायादिति भावः । तदेव व्यनक्ति—**नूपुरसिञ्जितानि आदित्सुभिः** आदातुमिच्छुभिः । मञ्जीरसिञ्जितमञ्जुकूजितोपदेशमिच्छद्भिरित्यर्थः । **राजहंसैः संनताङ्गी** । कुचभारादिति भावः । **सा** पार्वती [**लीला-**

१ अत्युन्नता. २ संनतांसा. ३ विभ्रमेषु. ४ लब्धैः.

ञ्चितविक्रमेषु] लीलाभिर्विलासैरञ्चिताः पूजिता विक्रमाः पादन्यासा येषु तेषु । 'अञ्चेः पूजायाम्' इतीडागमः । 'लीला विलासक्रिययोः' इत्यमरः ॥ गतेषु विषयेषु व्यनीयत इव विनीता किमु । अन्यथा कथमस्या हंसगमनमित्युत्प्रेक्षा ॥

वृत्तानुपूर्वे च न चातिदीर्घे जङ्घे शुभे सृष्टवतस्तदीये ।
शेषाङ्गनिर्माणविधौ विधातुर्लावण्य उत्पाद्य इवास यत्नः ॥ ३५ ॥

वृत्तेति ॥ वृत्ते वर्तुले पूर्वमनुगते अनुपूर्वे । गोपुच्छाकारे इत्यर्थः । वृत्ते च ते अनुपूर्वे च वृत्तानुपूर्वे न अतिदीर्घे च । महाविभाषया न समासः । नञो विशेषणत्वं चशब्दप्रयोगादेव ज्ञेयम् । शुभे मङ्गले । तस्याः इमे तदीये जङ्घे प्रसृते ॥ 'जङ्घा तु प्रसृता' इत्यमरः ॥ सृष्टवतः निर्मितवतः विधातुः स्रष्टुः शेषाङ्गनिर्माणविधौ । जङ्घाव्यतिरिक्तावयवनिर्माणार्थमित्यर्थः । उत्पाद्ये पुनः संपाद्ये लावण्ये कान्तिविशेषविषये । लावण्यलक्षणं तु (२५ श्लोकटीकायां) उक्तम् । यत्नः आस इव बभूवेवेत्युत्प्रेक्षा । उपादानमन्तरेण कार्यस्य दुष्करत्वात्तदङ्गानां च लावण्योपादानकत्वात्पूर्वसंपादितस्य च जङ्घार्थमेव कार्त्स्न्येन विनियोगात्पुनर्लावण्यसंपादने यत्नः स्यादेवेत्येतादृक्सौन्दर्ये तज्जङ्घे इति भावः । आसेति बभूवार्थे तिङन्तप्रतिरूपकमव्ययमित्याह शाटाकयनः ॥ वल्लभस्तु—"न तिङन्तप्रतिरूपकमव्ययम् अस्तेर्भूः इति भ्वादेशनियमात्तादृक्तिङन्तस्यैवाभावात् । किंतु कवीनामयं प्रामादिकः प्रयोगः" इत्याह । वामनस्तु—"अस गतिदीप्त्यादानेष्विति धातोर्लिटि रूपमिदम् ।" इत्याह । अस इत्यनुदात्तेद्दीप्त्यर्थे । आस दिदीपे । प्रवृत्त इत्यर्थः ॥

नागेन्द्रहस्तास्त्वचि कर्कशत्वादेकान्तशैत्यात्कदलीविशेषाः ।
लब्ध्वापि लोके परिणाहि रूपं जातास्तदूर्वोरुपमानबाह्याः ॥ ३६ ॥

नागेन्द्रेति [नागेन्द्रहस्ताः] नागेन्द्राणामैरावतादीनां हस्ताः कराः त्वचि चर्मणि कर्कशत्वात् कदलीविशेषाः राजरम्भादयः एकान्तशैत्यात् हेतोः लोके परिणाहि वैपुल्ययुक्तम् ॥ 'परिणाहो विशालता' इत्यमरः । रूपं लब्ध्वापि । अपिशब्दात्करिकदलीमात्रस्य तादृक्परिणाहो नास्तीति भावः । तस्या ऊर्वोः तदूर्वोः उपमानबाह्याः जाताः उपमानक्रियानर्हा बभूवुः । तदूर्वोर्न कार्कश्यं नाप्येकान्तशैत्यमिति भावः ॥

एतावता नन्वनुमेयशोभि काञ्चीगुणस्थानमनिन्दितायाः ।
आरोपितं यद्गिरिशेन पश्चादनन्यनारीकमनीयमङ्कम् ॥ ३७ ॥

एतावतेति ॥ अनिन्दितायाः अनवद्यायाः पार्वत्याः काञ्चीगुणस्थानं नितम्बबिम्बम् एतावता ननु एतावतैव । 'प्रश्नावधारणानुज्ञानुनयामन्त्रणे ननु ।' इत्यमरः । (अवश्यं) शोभत इति शोभि ॥ आवश्यके णिनिः । ततस्त्यप्रत्ययः ॥ अनुमेयं

---

१ ण्यमुत्पन्नं. २ शोभं; कान्ति.

शोभित्वं शोभा यस्य तद् **अनुमेयशोभि**। त्वप्रत्ययस्तु गतार्थत्वान्न प्रयुक्तः इत्याह वामनः ॥ **पश्चात्**। आदौ नैःस्पृह्येऽपि तयोरानन्तरमित्यर्थः। गिरौ शेते इति गिरिशः शिवः ॥ 'गिरौ डश्छन्दसि' इति डप्रत्ययः ॥ भाषायामपि क्वचिदिष्यते। अथ वा गिरिः कैलासोऽस्यास्ति गिरिशः ॥ लोमादित्वाच्छप्रत्ययः। तेन **गिरिशेन [अनन्यनारीकमनीयम्]** अन्यासां नारीणां कमनीयः कामयितुं शक्यो न भवतीत्यनन्यनारीकमनीयस्तम् **अङ्कं** निजोत्सङ्गम् **आरोपितम्** इति **यत्**। **एतावता** लिङ्गेनेति पूर्वेणान्वयः ॥ रोहतेर्ण्यन्तात्कर्मणि क्तः। 'रुहः पोऽन्यतरस्याम्' इति हकारस्य पकारः। गत्यर्थविवक्षायां द्विकर्मकत्वम्। प्रधाने कर्मणि क्तः। गिरिजानितम्बबिम्बं विश्वातिशायिसौन्दर्यं गिरिशाङ्कारूढत्वाद्व्यतिरेकेण नार्यन्तरनितम्बबिम्बवत्। विपक्षे हेत्वनुक्तिरेव बाधिका। दाक्षायणीनितम्बबिम्बस्य तु पक्षसपक्षयोरन्यतरभावानतिवृत्तेर्निष्कलङ्कमनुमानमित्यलमस्थानसंरम्भेण ॥

तस्याः प्रविष्टा नतनाभिरन्ध्रं रराज तन्वी नवलोमराजिः।
नीवीमतिक्रम्य सितेतरस्य तन्मेखलामध्यमणेरिवार्चिः ॥ ३८ ॥

तस्या इति ॥ **नीवीं** वस्त्रग्रन्थिम् ॥ 'स्त्रीकटीवस्त्रबन्धेऽपि नीवी परिपणेऽपि च।' इत्यमरः ॥ **अतिक्रम्य** अतीत्य **[नतनाभिरन्ध्रं]** नतं निम्नं नाभिरन्ध्रं **प्रविष्टा** प्रविशन्ती **तन्वी** सूक्ष्मा **तस्याः** पार्वत्याः **नवलोमराजिः सितेतरस्य** असितस्य इन्द्रनीलस्येत्यर्थः। **[तन्मेखलामध्यमणेः]** तस्याः पार्वत्या मेखला तन्मेखला। तस्या इत्यनुवृत्तौ पुनस्तच्छब्दोपादानं वाक्यान्तरत्वात्सोढव्यम्। यद्वा तस्या नीव्या मेखला तन्मेखला तत्र तदवस्थानात्। तस्या मध्यमणेः **अर्चिः** प्रभा **इव रराज** ॥ 'ज्वालाभासोर्नपुंस्यर्चिः' इत्यमरः ॥

मध्येन सा वेदिविलग्नमध्या वलित्रयं चारु बभार बाला।
आरोहणार्थं नवयौवनेन[3] कामस्य सोपानमिव प्रयुक्तम् ॥ ३९ ॥

मध्येनेति ॥ 'वेदिः परिष्कृता भूमिः' इत्यमरः ॥ **वेदिविलग्नमध्या** वेदिवत्कृशमध्या। तनुमध्येति यावत्। **सा बाला** पार्वती। **मध्येन** मध्यभागेन **चारु** सुन्दरं **वलित्रयं कामस्य आरोहणार्थं नवयौवनेन प्रयुक्तं** रचितं **सोपानमिव बभार** इत्युत्प्रेक्षा ॥

अन्योन्यमुत्पीडयदुत्पलाक्ष्याः स्तनद्वयं पाण्डु तथा प्रवृद्धम्।
मध्ये यथा श्याममुखस्य तस्य मृणालसूत्रान्तरमप्यलभ्यम् ॥ ४० ॥

अन्योन्यमिति ॥ **अन्योन्यं** परस्परम् ॥ 'कर्मव्यतिहारे सर्वनाम्नो द्वे वाच्ये' इति द्विरुक्तिः ॥ 'समासवच्च बहुलम्' इति बहुलवचनादसमासपक्षेऽपि पूर्वपदस्थस्य सुपः

१ नीला. २ राजी. ३ नवयौवनस्य कामेन. ४ चारु. ५ विवृद्धम्. ६ सूत्रेण पदं न लभ्यम्; प्यलभ्यम्. ३८ श्लोकस्य स्थानेऽयं श्लोको दृश्यते—गम्भीरनाभी (भि) ह्रदसंनिधाने (वेशे) रराज नीला (तन्वी) नवलोमराजिः। मुखेन्दुभीरु(त)स्तनचक्रवाकचञ्चुच्युतेव (शव-)रीव ॥

सुवेक्ष्यः ॥ उत्पीडयद् उपरुन्धत पाण्डु गौरम् उत्पलाक्ष्याः स्तनद्वयम् तथा तेन प्रकारेण प्रवृद्धम् । कर्तरि क्तः । श्याममुखस्य कृष्णचूचुकस्येति स्वरूपवर्णनं तस्य स्तनद्वयस्य मध्ये यथा येन प्रकारेण मृणालसूत्रान्तरं बिसतन्तुमात्रावकाशः अपि अलभ्यं लब्धुमशक्यम् ॥ 'अन्तरमवकाशावधिपरिधानान्तर्धिभेदतादर्थ्ये ।' इत्यमरः ॥ अत्र संबन्धेऽसंबन्धरूपातिशयोक्त्यलंकारः । कुचयोः पीवरत्वातिशयार्थमवकाशसंबन्धेप्यसंबन्धाभिधानादिति ॥

लोके सुकुमारत्वमेव कुसुमास्त्रस्य साधकत्वमिति स्थिते सत्याह—

शिरीषपुष्पाधिकसौकुमार्यौ बाहू तदीयाविति मे वितर्कः ।
पराजितेनापि कृतौ हरस्य यौ कण्ठपाशौ मकरध्वजेन ॥ ४१ ॥

शिरीषेति ॥ तस्या इमौ तदीयौ बाहू [शिरीषपुष्पाधिकसौकुमार्यौ] शिरीषपुष्पादधिकं सौकुमार्यं मार्दवं ययोस्तथोक्तौ इति मे वितर्कः ऊहः । कुतः । यौ बाहू पराजितेनापि पूर्वं निर्जितेनापि मकरध्वजेन कामेन हरस्य कण्ठपाशौ कण्ठबन्धनरज्ज्वौ कृतौ । कण्ठालिङ्गनं प्रापिताविन्यर्थः । तदसाध्यसाधनात्तत आधिक्यमिति भावः ॥ अत्र बाह्वोरारोपितकण्ठपाशत्वस्य प्रकृतवैरनिर्यातनोपयोगात्परिणामालंकारः ॥

कण्ठस्य तस्याः स्तनबन्धुरस्य मुक्ताकलापस्य च निस्तलस्य ।
अन्योन्यशोभाजननाद्बभूव साधारणो भूषणभूष्यभावः ॥ ४२ ॥

कण्ठस्येति ॥ स्तनबन्धुरस्य स्तनाभ्यां बन्धुरस्योन्नतस्य तस्याः पार्वत्याः कण्ठस्य गलस्य निस्तलस्य वर्तुलस्य मुक्ताकलापस्य मुक्ताभूषणस्य च । 'वर्तुलं निस्तलं वृत्तं बन्धुरं तून्नतानतम् ।' 'कलापो भूषणे बर्हे तूणीरे संहतावपि ।' इति चामरः ॥ अन्योन्यशोभाजननाद् भूषणभूष्यभावः अलंकारालंकार्यभावः साधारणः समानो बभूव । उभावप्यन्योन्यस्य भूष्य भूषणे च बभूवतुरित्यर्थः ॥ अत्र कण्ठमुक्ताकलापयोः शोभाक्रियाद्वारेणान्योन्यभूषाजनकत्वादन्योन्यालंकारः । तदुक्तम् 'परस्परक्रियाजननमन्योन्यम् ।' इति ॥

चन्द्रं गता पद्मगुणान्न भुङ्क्ते पद्माश्रिता चान्द्रमसीमभिख्याम् ।
उमामुखं तु प्रतिपद्य लोला द्विसंश्रयां प्रीतिमवाप लक्ष्मीः ॥ ४३ ॥

चन्द्रमिति ॥ लोला चपला । परिभ्रमणशीलेत्यर्थः । लक्ष्मीः कान्त्यभिमानिनी देवता चन्द्रं गता प्राप्ता सती पद्मगुणान् सौगन्ध्यादीन् न भुङ्क्ते नानुभवति । पद्माश्रिता सती चन्द्रमस इमां चान्द्रमसीम् अभिख्यां शोभाम् ॥ आभिख्या नामशोभयोः' इत्यमरः । अमृतवदानन्दिनीं न भुङ्क्ते । उमामुखं प्रतिपद्य तु द्वे

१ माला. २ प्रतर्कः. ३ तस्यास्तनु. ४१—४२ श्लोकयोर्मध्यऽयं श्लोको दृश्यते—

निर्भर्त्सिताशोकदलप्रसूति पाणिद्वयं चारुनखं तदीयम् ।
नवोदितेन्दुप्रतिमस्य शोभां व्योम्नः प्रदोषे विफलीचकार ॥

चन्द्रपद्मे संश्रयः कारणं यस्यास्तां द्विसंश्रयां प्रीतिम् आनन्दम् अवाप । तत्रोभयगुणसंभवादिति भावः। अत्रोपमानभूतचन्द्रपद्मापेक्षयापेमपेयस्योमामुखस्याधिकगुणवस्त्वोक्त्या व्यतिरेकालंकारः ॥ तदुक्तम्—'भेदप्राधान्येनोपमानादुपमेयस्याधिक्ये विपर्यये वा व्यतिरेकः' इति ॥

पुष्पं प्रवालोपहितं यदि स्यान्मुक्ताफलं वा स्फुटविद्रुमस्थम् ।
ततोऽनुकुर्याद्विशदस्य तस्यास्ताम्रौष्ठपर्यस्तरुचः स्मितस्य ॥४४॥

पुष्पमिति ॥ पुष्पं पुण्डरीकादिकं [प्रवालोपहितं] प्रवाले बालपल्लव उपहितं निहितं स्याद्यदि । 'प्रवालो वल्लकीदण्डे विद्रुमे बालपल्लवे ।' इति विश्वः ॥ मुक्ताफलं वा स्फुटे निर्मले विद्रुमे तिष्ठतीति स्फुटविद्रुमस्थं स्याद्यदि । ततः तर्हि विशदस्य शुभ्रस्य [ताम्रौष्ठपर्यस्तरुचः] ताम्रे अरुणे ओष्ठे पर्यस्ता प्रसृता रुक्कान्तिर्यस्य तथोक्तस्य तस्याः पार्वत्याः स्मितस्य अनुकुर्यात् । स्मितमनुकुर्यादित्यर्थः । अत्र 'माषाणामश्नीयात्' इतिवत्संबन्धमात्रविवक्षया षष्ठी । अत्र पुष्पप्रवालयोर्मुक्ताविद्रुमयोश्चासंबन्धेऽपि संबन्धोक्त्या अतिशयोक्तिः सा च संभावना इत्यलंकारसर्वस्वकारः । विशेषतस्तु पुष्पमुक्ताफलयोरुपमानयोः प्रकृतोत्कर्षार्थमुपमेयताकल्पनात्प्रतीपालंकारः । तदुक्तम्—'उपमानस्याक्षेप उपमेयताकल्पनं वा प्रतीपः ।' इति । स च पूर्वोक्तातिशयोक्त्यनुप्राणित इति ॥

स्वरेण तस्याममृतस्रुतेव प्रजल्पितायामभिजातवाचि ।
अप्यन्यपुष्टा प्रतिकूलशब्दा श्रोतुर्वितन्त्रीरिव ताड्यमाना ॥ ४५ ॥

स्वरेणेति ॥ अभिजातवाचि मधुरभाषिण्यां तस्यां पार्वत्याम् अमृतस्रुता अमृतस्राविणा इव ॥ क्विप् ॥ स्वरेण नादेन प्रजल्पितायाम् आलपन्त्याम् । कर्तरि क्तः ॥ अन्यैः काकादिभिः पुष्टा अन्यपुष्टा कोकिला अपि ॥ मुख्यया वृत्त्या जातिवचनस्वाभावाद् क्लीबभावः ॥ ताड्यमाना वाद्यमाना विषमबद्धा तन्त्रीः वितन्त्रीः इव । 'अवितृस्तृतन्त्रिभ्य ईः' इति तन्त्रीधातोरौणादिक ईप्रत्ययः । क्लीबभावात्र 'हल्ङ्याब्भ्यः—'इति सुलोपः । तदुक्तम्—'अवीलक्ष्मीतरीतन्त्रीह्रीधीश्रीणामुणादितः । स्त्रीलिङ्गानाममीषां तु न सुलोपः कदाचन ॥' इति । एते क्लीबन्ता न भवन्तीत्यर्थः ॥ श्रोतुः जनस्य प्रतिकूलशब्दा कर्णकठोरनादा भवतीति शेषः ॥

प्रवातनीलोत्पलनिर्विशेषमधीरविप्रेक्षितमायताक्ष्या ।
तया गृहीतं नु मृगाङ्गनाभ्यस्ततो गृहीतं नु मृगाङ्गनाभिः ॥४६॥

---

१ ताम्रोष्ठ. २ अन्यपुष्टा...शब्दाः. ४५–४६ श्लोकयोर्मध्ये इमौ श्लोकौ अन्योन्यस्य पाठान्तरीभूतौ दृश्येते—कर्णद्वयस्थं नगराजपुत्र्यास्ताटङ्कयुग्मं सु(नि)तरां रराज (बभासे, चकासे)। म(ज्ञा)त्वा भवित्रीं त्रिपुरारिपत्नीं तां सेवमाना(सेवासमेता)विव पुष्पवन्तौ ॥ ताटङ्कपत्रं (–युग्मं) विरराज तस्याः शैलात्मजायाः श्रवणद्वयस्थम् । मत्वा भवित्रीं मदनारिपत्नीं सेवासमेताविव पुष्पवन्तौ ॥

प्रवातेति ॥ [**प्रवातनीलोत्पलनिर्विशेषम्**] प्रवाते प्रभूतवातस्थले यन्नीलोत्पलं ततो निर्विशेषं निर्भेदम् । तत्सदृशमित्यर्थः । **अधीरविप्रेक्षितं** चकितविलोकितम् **आयताक्ष्या** विशालनेत्रया **तया** पार्वत्या **मृगाङ्गनाभ्यः** हरिणीभ्यः **गृहीतम्** अभ्यस्तं **नु** ॥ अथ वा **मृगाङ्गनाभिः** ततः तस्याः पार्वत्याः ॥ 'पञ्चम्यास्तसिल्' ॥ **गृहीतं नु** ॥ अत्र विवक्षितस्य परस्परग्रहणस्योत्प्रेक्षणादुत्प्रेक्षेति केचित् । तदुपजीविसंदेहालंकार इत्यन्ये । उभयोः संकर इत्यपरे ॥

तस्याः शलाकाञ्जननिर्मितेव कान्तिर्भ्रुवोरायतलेखयोर्या ।
तां वीक्ष्य लीलाचतुरामनङ्गः स्वचापसौन्दर्यमदं मुमोच ॥४७॥

तस्या इति ॥ **आयतलेखयोः** दीर्घरेखयोः **तस्याः** पार्वत्या **भ्रुवोः** संबन्धिनी [**शलाकाञ्जननिर्मिता**] शलाकयाञ्जनेन निर्मिता **इव** स्थिता **या कान्तिः लीलाचतुरां** विलाससुभगां **तां** कान्तिं **वीक्ष्य अनङ्गः** [**स्वचापसौन्दर्यमदं**] स्वचापसौन्दर्येण यो मदः तं **मुमोच** ॥ इह सौन्दर्यातिशयोक्तिः ॥

लज्जा तिरश्चां यदि चेतसि स्यादसंशयं पर्वतराजपुत्र्याः ।
तं केशपाशं प्रसमीक्ष्य कुर्युर्बालप्रियत्वं शिथिलं चमर्यः ॥४८॥

लज्जेति ॥ **तिरश्चां** तिर्यग्जातीनां **चेतसि लज्जा स्याद्यदि** । संशयाभावः **असंशयम्** । संदेहो नास्तीत्यर्थः । **पर्वतराजपुत्र्याः** । 'शार्ङ्गरवाद्यञो ङीन्' इति ङीन् ॥ **तं** प्रसिद्धं **केशपाशं** केशकलापम् ॥ 'पाशः पक्षश्च हस्तश्च कलापार्थाः कचात्परे ।' इत्यमरः ॥ **प्रसमीक्ष्य** दृष्ट्वा **चमर्यः** मृगीविशेषाः । बालाः प्रिया यासामिति विग्रहे बालप्रियास्तासां भावः **बालप्रियत्वम्** । प्रियबालत्वमित्यर्थः । आहिताग्न्यादिपाठाद्वा परनिपातः । 'त्वतलोर्गुणवचनस्य' इति पुंवद्भावः । **शिथिलं कुर्युः** । निर्लज्जत्वान्न शिथिलयन्तीत्यर्थः ॥ अत एवात्र निर्लज्जत्वकरणहेतोराद्यपादे वाक्यार्थत्वेनोक्त्या काव्यलिङ्गाख्यालंकारः । तदुक्तम्—'हेतोर्वाक्यपदार्थत्वे काव्यलिङ्गमुदाहृतम् ।' इति ॥

सर्वोपमाद्रव्यसमुच्चयेन यथाप्रदेशं विनिवेशितेन ।
सा निर्मिता विश्वसृजा प्रयत्नादेकस्थसौन्दर्यदिदृक्षयेव ॥ ४९॥

सर्वोपमेति ॥ किंबहुना । **सा** पार्वती **विश्वसृजा** विधात्रा [**एकस्थसौन्दर्यदिदृक्षया**] एकत्र तिष्ठतीत्येकस्थं तस्य सौन्दर्यस्य । सर्ववस्तुगतस्येत्यर्थः । दिदृक्षया **इव प्रयत्नात् यथाप्रदेशं** क्रमाद् **विनिवेशितेन** स्थापितेन [**सर्वोपमाद्रव्यसमुच्चयेन**] सर्वेषामुपमाद्रव्याणां चन्द्रारविन्दाद्युपमानवस्तूनां समुच्चयेन समाहारेण **निर्मिता** ॥ दिदृक्षयेवेति फलोत्प्रेक्षा दर्शनार्थित्वाद्विश्वसृज इति ॥

तां नारदः कामचरः कदाचित्कन्यां किल प्रेक्ष्य पितुः समीपे ।
समादिदेशैकवधूं भवित्रीं प्रेम्णा शरीरार्धहरां हरस्य ॥ ५० ॥

१ योः सा यां. २ लोलाम्. ३ तत्. ४ एकवधूः भवित्री ...हरा. ५ प्रीत्या.

तामिति ॥ कामेनेच्छया चरतीति **कामचरः नारदः कदाचित्** पितुः हिमवतः **समीपे कन्यां तां** पार्वतीं **प्रेक्ष्य किल प्रेम्णा** न त्वन्यथा **हरस्य** शिवस्यार्धं हरतीत्यर्धहरा ॥ 'हरतेरनुद्यमनेऽच्' इत्यच्प्रत्ययः ॥ शरीरस्यार्धहरां **शरीरार्धहराम्** । कुलधुरन्धरादिवदवयवद्वारा समुदायविशेषकत्वात्समासः । अन्यथा त्वर्धस्य समप्रविभागवचनत्वादर्धशरीरेति स्यात् ॥ **एकवधूम्** असपत्नीकां भार्याम् । 'पूर्वकाल-इत्यादिना समासः ॥ **भविनीं** भाविनीं **समादिदेश** । हरस्यार्धाङ्गहारिण्येकपत्नी भविष्यतीत्यादिष्टवानित्यर्थः ॥

गुरुः प्रगल्भेऽपि वयस्यतोऽस्यास्तस्थौ निवृत्तान्यवराभिलाषः ।
ऋते कृशानोर्न हि मन्त्रपूतमर्हन्ति तेजांस्यपराणि हव्यम् ॥५१॥

गुरुरिति ॥ **गुरुः** पिता । 'गुरू गीष्पतिपित्राद्यौ' इत्यमरः । **अतः** नारदवचनाद्धेतोः **अस्याः** पार्वत्याः **प्रगल्भे वयसि अपि** यौवने सत्यपि [**निवृत्तान्यवराभिलाषः**] निवृत्तोऽन्यस्मिन्वरे जामातर्यभिलाषो यस्य स तथोक्तः सन् । 'वरो ना रूपजामात्रोः' इति वैजयन्ती । **तस्थौ** । वरान्तरं नान्विष्टवानित्यर्थः ॥ ननु कुतोऽसौ निर्बन्ध इत्यत आह ऋते इति ॥ तथाहि [**मन्त्रपूतं**] मन्त्रैः पूतं संस्कृतं हूयत इति **हव्यम्** आज्यादिकं **कृशानोः** पावकाद् **ऋते** कृशानुं विना ॥ 'अन्यारादितर'–इत्यादिना पञ्चमी ॥ **अपराणि तेजांसि** सुवर्णादीनि **न अर्हन्ति** । न भजन्तीत्यर्थः । ईश्वरादन्यस्य तद्योग्यस्याभावादुपेक्षेति भावः ॥

तर्हि तमेवाहूय दीयतामित्याशङ्क्याह—

अयाचितारं न हि देवदेवमद्रिः सुतां ग्राहयितुं शशाक ।
अभ्यर्थनाभङ्गभयेन साधुर्माध्यस्थ्यमिष्टेऽप्यवलम्बतेऽर्थे ॥ ५२ ॥

अयाचितारमिति ॥ **अद्रिः** हिमवान् **अयाचितारम्** अयाचमानं **देवदेवं** महादेवं **सुतां** पार्वतीं **ग्राहयितुं** स्वयमाहूय परिग्राहयितुं **न शशाक** नोत्सेहे । ग्रहेर्द्विकर्मकत्वम् । **तथा हि** । **साधुः** सज्जनः ॥ 'साधुर्वार्धुषिके चारौ सज्जने चाभिधेयवत् ।' इति विश्वः । **अभ्यर्थनाभङ्गभयेन** याच्ञावैफल्यभीत्या **इष्टे अपि अर्थे** विषये **माध्यस्थ्यम्** औदासीन्यम् **अवलम्बते** ॥

न च तथैव स्थितः किं तूपायान्तरं चिन्तितवानिति वक्तुं प्रस्तौति—

यदैव पूर्वे जनने शरीरं सा दक्षरोषात्सुदती ससर्ज ।
तदाप्रभृत्येव विमुक्तसङ्गः पतिः पशूनामपरिग्रहोऽभूत् ॥५३॥

यदेति ॥ शोभना दन्ता यस्याः सा **सुदती** ॥ 'वयसि दन्तस्य दतृ' इति दत्रादेशः ॥ 'उगितश्च' इति ङीप् । **सा** पार्वती **पूर्वे जनने** पूर्वस्मिञ्जन्मनि ॥ 'पूर्वादिभ्यो नवभ्यो वा' इति स्मिन्नादेशविकल्पः ॥ पूर्वे ज्वलने इति पाठे पूर्वं दाक्षायणीत्वे ज्वलने योगाग्नौ । **यदा** यस्मिन्काले **दक्षरोषात् शरीरं** देहं **ससर्ज** तत्याज । **तदाप्रभृत्येव** तदाद्येव यथा तथा **पशूनां पतिः** शिवः **विमुक्तसङ्गः** त्यक्तवि-

१ अन्यतर. २ स्वयमुत्ससर्ज. ४ ततः प्रभृति.

प्रयासङ्गः सन् । **अपरिग्रहः** अपत्नीकः **अभूत्** । कन्यन्तरं न परिजग्राहेत्यर्थः । 'पत्नीपरिजनादानमूलशापाः परिग्रहाः' । इत्यमरः ॥

स कृत्तिवासास्तपसे यतात्मा गङ्गाप्रवाहोक्षितदेवदारु ।
प्रस्थं हिमाद्रेर्मृगनाभिगन्धि किंचित्क्वणत्किंनरमध्युवास ॥ ५४ ॥

स इति ॥ **कृत्तिवासाः** चर्माम्बरः । 'अजिनं चर्म कृत्तिः स्त्री' इत्यमरः । **यतात्मा** नियतचित्तः **स** पशुपतिः **तपसे** तपोऽर्थं [**गङ्गाप्रवाहोक्षितदेवदारु**] गङ्गाप्रवाहेणोक्षिताः सिक्ता देवदारवो यस्मिंस्तत्तथोक्तम् । **मृगनाभिगन्धि** कस्तूरीगन्धवत् । कस्तूरीमृगसंचारादिति भावः । 'मृगनाभिर्मृगमदः कस्तूरी चाथ कोलकम् । इत्यमरः । [**क्वणत्किंनरं**] क्वणन्तो गायन्तः किंनरा यस्मिंस्तत्तथोक्तम् । **किंचित्** किमपि **हिमाद्रेः प्रस्थं** सानुम् **अध्युवास** । कुत्रचित्प्रस्थ उवासेत्यर्थः । 'उपान्वध्याङ्वसः' इत्याधारस्य कर्मत्वम् ॥ 'प्रस्थोऽस्त्री सानुमानयोः' इत्यमरः ॥

गणा नमेरुप्रसवावतंसा भूर्जत्वचः स्पर्शवतीर्दधानाः ।
मनःशिलाविच्छुरिता निषेदुः शैलेयनद्धेषु शिलातलेषु ॥ ५५ ॥

गणा इति ॥ **गणाः** प्रमथगणाः ॥ 'गणाः प्रमथसंख्यौघाः' इति वैजयन्ती । **नमेरुप्रसवावतंसाः** सुरपुन्नागकुसुमशेखराः ॥ 'नमेरुः सुरपुन्नागः' इति विश्वः । **स्पर्शवतीः** सुखस्पर्शाः । मृद्वीरित्यर्थः । प्रशंसायां मतुप् ॥ **भूर्जत्वचः** भूर्जवल्कलानि । **दधानाः** । वसाना इत्यर्थः । [**मनःशिलाविच्छुरिताः**] मनःशिलाभिर्धातुविशेषैर्विच्छुरिता अनुलिप्ताश्च सन्तः । [**शैलेयनद्धेषु**] शिलायां भवं शैलेयं गन्धौषधिविशेषः । 'शिलायाः स्त्रीभ्यो ढक्' इति भावार्थे ढक् ॥ 'शिलाजतु च शैलेयम्' इति यादवः । तेन नद्धेषु व्याप्तेषु **शिलातलेषु निषेदुः** । उपविविशुरित्यर्थः ॥

तुषारसंघातशिलाः खुराग्रैः समुल्लिखन्दर्पकलः ककुद्मान् ।
दृष्टः कथंचिद्गवयैर्विविग्नैरसोढसिंहध्वनिरुन्ननाद ॥ ५६ ॥

तुषारेति ॥ [**तुषारसंघातशिलाः**] तुषारसंघाता हिमघनास्त एव शिलास्ताः **खुराग्रैः समुल्लिखन्** विदारयन्दर्पेण कलो मधुरध्वनिर्यस्य स **दर्पकलः विविग्नैः** भीतैः **गवयैः** गौसदृशमृगविशेषैः **कथंचित्** कृच्छ्रेण **दृष्टः** ककुदमस्यास्तीति **ककुद्मान्** वृषभः असोढः सिंहानां ध्वनिर्येन सः [**असोढसिंहध्वनिः**] सिंहध्वनिमसहमानः सन् । **उन्ननाद** उच्चैर्ननाद जगर्जेत्यर्थः । स्वभावोक्तिरलंकारः । तदुक्तम्—'स्वभावोक्तिरसौ चारु यथावद्वस्तुवर्णनम् ।' इति ॥

तत्राग्निमाधाय समित्समिद्धं स्वमेव मूर्त्यन्तरमष्टमूर्तिः ।
स्वयं विधाता तपसः फलानां केनापि कामेन तपश्चचार ॥ ५७ ॥

तत्रेति ॥ **तपसः फलानाम्** इन्द्रत्वादीनां **स्वयं विधाता** जनयिता । दाते-

१ जितात्मा. २ प्रपातोत्थित. ३ वसानाः. ४ गन्धेषु. ५ अयम्. ६ समृद्धं. ७ चकार.

त्यर्थः । अष्टौ मूर्तयो यस्य सः अष्टमूर्तिः ईश्वरः । 'भूतार्कचन्द्रयज्वानो मूर्तयोऽष्टौ प्रकीर्तिताः' । इति ॥ तत्र प्रस्थे स्वं स्वकीयम् एव मूर्त्यन्तरं मूर्तिभेदं समित्समिद्धं समिद्भिः समिद्धं दीपितम् अग्निम् आधाय प्रतिष्ठाप्य केनापि कामेन कयापि फलकामनया तपः चचार चक्रे ॥ 'प्रयोजनमनुद्दिश्य न मन्दोऽपि प्रवर्तते ।' इति न्यायात्कामेनेत्युक्तम् । तस्यावाप्तसमस्तकामत्वात्केनापीत्युक्तम् ॥

अनर्घ्यमर्घ्येण तमद्रिनाथः स्वर्गौकसामर्चितमर्चयित्वा ।
आराधनायास्य सखीसमेतां समादिदेश प्रयतां तनूजाम् ॥ ५८ ॥

अनर्घ्यमिति ॥ अद्रीणां नाथः अद्रिनाथः हिमवान् । अर्घं मूल्यमर्हतीत्यर्घ्यः । 'मूल्ये पूजाविधावर्घः' इत्यमरः ॥ 'दण्डादिभ्यो यत्' इति यत्प्रत्ययः ॥ अर्घ्यो न भवतीत्यनर्घ्यस्तम् अनर्घ्यम् । अमूल्यमित्यर्थः । स्वर्ग ओकः स्थानं येषां तेषां स्वर्गौकसां देवानाम् अर्चितम् । दैवैः पूज्यमानमित्यर्थः । 'मतिबुद्धिपूजार्थेभ्यश्च' इति वर्तमाने क्तः ॥ 'क्तस्य च वर्तमाने' इति षष्ठी ॥ तम् ईश्वरम् अर्घ्येण पूजार्थोदकेन । 'पादार्घाभ्यां च' इति यत्प्रत्ययः । 'षट् तु त्रिष्वर्घ्यमर्घार्थे पाद्यं पादाय वारिणि' । इत्यमरः । अर्चयित्वा पूजयित्वा अस्य ईश्वरस्य आराधनाय सखीभ्य] जयाविजयाभ्यां समेतां [सखीसमेतां] प्रयतां नियतां तनूजां सुतां समादिदेश आज्ञापयामास ॥

प्रत्यर्थिभूतामपि तां समाधेः शुश्रूषमाणां गिरिशोऽनुमेने ।
विकारहेतौ सति विक्रियन्ते येषां न चेतांसि त एव धीराः ॥ ५९ ॥

प्रत्यर्थीति ॥ गिरिशः शिवः समाधेः प्रत्यर्थिभूतां प्रतिपक्षभूताम् । सुप्सुपेति समासः । अपि श्रोतुमिच्छन्तीं शुश्रूषमाणां सेवमानाम् । सेवका हि सेव्ये दत्तकर्णा भवन्ति । इच्छार्थे सन्प्रत्ययः । 'ज्ञाश्रुस्मृदृशां सनः' इत्यात्मनेपदम् । तां पार्वतीम् अनुमेने अङ्गीचकार । न प्रतिषिद्धवानित्यभिप्रायः । न चैतावता धीरस्य कश्चिद्विकार इत्याशयः ॥ धीरत्वमेवार्थान्तरन्यासेनाह–विकारेति ॥ [विकारहेतौ । विकारस्य प्रकृतेरन्यथात्वस्य हेतौ स्त्रीसन्निधानादिकारणे सति विद्यमाने अपि येषां चेतांसि न विक्रियन्ते न विकृतिं नीयन्ते ते एव धीराः । विक्रियन्ते इति कर्मणि लट् ॥

शुश्रूषाप्रकारमेवाह—

अवचितबलिपुष्पा वेदिसंमार्गदक्षा
　　नियमविधिजलानां बर्हिषां चोपनेत्री ।
गिरिशमुपचचार प्रत्यहं सा सुकेशी
　　नियमितपरिखेदा तच्छिरश्चन्द्रपादैः ॥ ६० ॥

---

१ अनर्घं. २ समग्राम्. ३ अत्र कालिकापुराणम्–एवमुक्त्वा तु तां देवीं सेवायै जगृहे हरः । इदमेव महद्धैर्यं यद्विभो न हि विभ्रयेत् ॥ इति ।

अवचितेति ॥ **सुकेशी** शोभनमूर्धजा ॥ 'स्वाङ्गाच्चोपसर्जनादसंयोगोपधात्' इति ङीप् ॥ **सा** पार्वती अवचितानि लूनानि बलिपुष्पाणि पूजाकुसुमानि यया सा [**अवचितबलिपुष्पा**] [**वेदिसंमार्गदक्षा**] वेदेर्नियमवेदिकायाः संमार्गे संमार्जने दक्षा । [**नियमविधिजलानां**] नियमविधेर्नित्यकर्मानुष्ठानस्य यानि जलानि तेषां **बर्हिषां** कुशानां **च उपनेत्री** आनेत्री सती [**तच्छिरश्चन्द्रपादैः**] तस्य गिरिशस्य शिरसि चन्द्रस्य पादै रश्मिभिः । 'पादा रश्म्यङ्घ्रितुर्यांशाः' इत्यमरः । **नियमितपरिखेदा** निवर्तितपरिश्रमा सती अहन्यहनि **प्रत्यहम्** । 'अव्ययं विभक्तिसमीपसमृद्धि'— इत्यादिना यथार्थेऽव्ययीभावः । 'नपुंसकादन्यतरस्याम्' इत्यच्प्रत्ययः । **गिरिशम् उपचचार** शुश्रूषांचक्रे ॥

इति श्रीमन्महामहोपाध्यायकोलाचलमल्लिनाथसूरिविरचितया
संजीवनीसमाख्यया व्याख्यया समेतः श्रीकालिदासकृतौ
कुमारसंभवे महाकाव्ये
उमोत्पत्तिर्नाम प्रथमः सर्गः ॥

द्वितीयः सर्गः ।

तस्मिन्विप्रकृताः काले तारकेण दिवौकसः ।
तुरासाहं पुरोधाय धाम स्वायंभुवं ययुः ॥ १ ॥

तस्मिन्निति ॥ **तस्मिन्काले** पार्वतीशुश्रूषाकाले **तारकेण** तारकनाम्ना वज्रणखपुत्रेण केनाचिदसुरेण **विप्रकृताः** उपप्लुता दिवमोकः स्थानं येषां ते **दिवौकसः** देवाः । 'दिवं स्वर्गेऽन्तरिक्षे च' इति विश्वः । द्यौरोक इति पक्षे पृषोदरादित्वात्साधुः । तुरं त्वरितं साहयत्यभिभवतीति तुराषाट् । साहयतेश्चौरादिकात्क्विप् । 'नहिवृतिवृषि—'इत्यादिना पूर्वपदस्य दीर्घः । प्रकृतिग्रहणे प्रातिपदिकस्यापि ग्रहणात् । मुग्धबोधकारस्तु तुराशब्दष्टाबन्त इत्याचष्टे ॥ तं **तुरासाहं** देवेन्द्रम् । अजादिषु साड्रूपत्वाभावात् 'सहेः साडः सः' इति षत्वं न भवति ॥ **पुरोधाय** पुरस्कृत्य । स्वयंभुवो ब्रह्मण इदं **स्वायंभुवम्** । संज्ञापूर्वकविधेरनित्यत्वात् 'ओर्गुणः' इति गुणो न । **धाम** स्थानं **ययुः** । ब्रह्मलोकं जग्मुरित्यर्थः ॥

तेषामाविरभूद्ब्रह्मा परिम्लानमुखश्रियाम् ।
सरसां सुप्तपद्मानां प्रातर्दीधितिमानिव ॥ २ ॥

तेषामिति ॥ [**परिम्लानमुखश्रियाम्**] परिम्लाना पारिक्षीणा मुखश्रीः मुखकान्तिः येषां तथोक्तानां **तेषां** देवानां **ब्रह्मा सुप्तपद्मानां** मुकुलितारविन्दानां **सरसां प्रातः दीधितिमान्** सूर्यः **इव आविरभूत्** । प्रकाशोऽभूदित्यर्थः । 'प्रकाशे प्रादु-

राविः स्यात्' इत्यमरः ॥ सूर्योपमानेन तेषां म्लानिहरणत्वं सूचितम् । अत्रोपमालंकारः । तल्लक्षणं तु—' स्वतःसिद्धेन भिन्नेन संमतेन च धर्मतः । साम्यमन्येन वर्ण्यस्य वाच्यं चैकपदोपमा ॥ ' इति ॥

अथ सर्वस्य धातारं ते सर्वे सर्वतोमुखम् ।
वागीशं वाग्भिरर्थ्याभिः प्रणिपत्योपतस्थिरे ॥ ३ ॥

अथेति ॥ **अथ** आविर्भावानन्तरं **सर्वे ते** देवाः सर्वतः समन्ततो मुखानि यस्य तं **सर्वतोमुखम्** । चतुर्मुखमित्यर्थः । [**वागीशं**] वाचां विद्यानामीशं **सर्वस्य** जगतः **धातारं** स्रष्टारं ब्रह्माणं **प्रणिपत्य** नमस्कृत्य । अर्थादनपेताभिः **अर्थ्याभिः** । अर्थयुक्ताभिरित्यर्थः । ' धर्मपथ्यर्थन्यायादनपेते ' इति यत्प्रत्ययः । **वाग्भिः उपतस्थिरे** । तुष्टुवुरित्यर्थः । ' उपाद्देवपूजासंगतिकरणमित्रकरणपथिष्विति वक्तव्यम् ' इत्यात्मनेपदम् । ॥

स्तुतिप्रकारमाह ' नमः ' इत्यादिभिर्द्वादशभिः श्लोकैः—

नमस्त्रिमूर्तये तुभ्यं प्राक्सृष्टेः केवलात्मने ।
गुणत्रयविभागाय पश्चाद्भेदमुपेयुषे ॥ ४ ॥

नम इति ॥ हे भगवन्नित्यध्याहार्यं व्याख्येयम् । **सृष्टेः प्राक्** ॥ ' अन्यारात्–' इत्यादिनाऽञ्चूत्तरपदयोगे पञ्चमी ॥ **केवलात्मने** एकरूपाय ॥ ' आत्मा वा इदमेक एवाग्र आसीत्' इति श्रुतेः ॥ ' निर्णीते केवलमिति त्रिलिङ्गं त्वेककृत्स्नयोः । ' इत्यमरः । **पश्चात्** सृष्टिप्रवृत्तिकाले । [**गुणत्रयविभागाय**] विभज्यतेऽनेनेति विभागः । गुणानां सत्त्वादीनां त्रयमेव विभागो यस्य तस्मै । ' गुणाः सत्त्वं रजस्तमः ' इत्यमरः ॥ **भेदम्** उपाधिम् । स्रष्टृत्वादिकमित्यर्थः । **उपेयुषे** प्राप्तवते । ' उपेयिवाननाश्वाननूचानश्च ' इति निपातः । अत एव **त्रिमूर्तये** ब्रह्मविष्णुरुद्ररूपिणे **तुभ्यं नमः** । ' नमःस्वस्ति–'इत्यादिना चतुर्थी । उक्तं च—'नमो रजोजुषे सृष्टौ स्थितौ सत्त्वमयाय च । तमोरूपाय संहारे त्रिरूपाय स्वयंभुवे ॥ ' इति ॥

यदमोघमपामन्तरुप्तं बीजमज त्वया ।
अतश्चराचरं विश्वं प्रभवस्तस्य गीयसे ॥ ५ ॥

यदिति ॥ न जायत इत्यजः । हे **अज** । अपां जलानाम् **अन्तः त्वया यद् अमोघम्** अवन्ध्यं **बीजं** वीर्यम् **उप्तं** निक्षिप्तम् । मुक्तम् इति पाठे विसृष्टमित्यर्थः । ' शुक्रं तेजोरेतसी च बीजवीर्येन्द्रियाणि च ' । इत्यमरः ॥ **अतः** ते बीजात् **चराचरं** स्थावरजङ्गमात्मकम् । समाहारे द्वन्द्वैकवद्भावः ॥ **विश्वं** जगत् । उत्पन्नमिति शेषः । **तस्य** विश्वस्य । प्रभवत्यस्मादिति **प्रभवः** कारणं **गीयसे** ॥ अदश्चराचरं विश्वं प्रसवस्तस्य गीयते ' इति पाठे अद इदं चराचरं विश्वं तस्य बीजस्य प्रसवो गीयते । लोके इति शेषः ॥ अत्र मनुः—'अप एव ससर्जादौ तासु बीजमवासृजत् । तदण्डमभवद्धैमं सहस्रांशुसमप्रभम् ॥ ' इति ॥

तिसृभिस्त्वमवस्थाभिर्महिमानमुदीरयन् ।
प्रलयस्थितिसर्गाणामेकः कारणतां गतः ॥ ६ ॥

तिसृभिरिति ॥ **एकः** सृष्टेः प्राक्केवलस्त्वं **तिसृभिः अवस्थाभिः** त्रैगुण्यमयीभिर्हरिहरब्रह्मस्वरूपाभिः **महिमानं** निजशक्तिम् **उदीरयन्** विजृम्भयन् **प्रलयस्थितिसर्गाणाम्** अन्तस्थित्युत्पत्तीनां **कारणतां गतः** । इदं पश्चाद्भेदमुपेयुषे (२।४) इत्यस्य विवरणमतो न गतार्थत्वदोषः ॥

भूतसृष्टिकर्तृत्वमुक्त्वा मिथुनसृष्ट्यर्थं मूर्तिमतो ब्रह्मणो भेदमाह—

स्त्रीपुंसावात्मभागौ ते भिन्नमूर्तेः सिसृक्षया ।
प्रसूतिभाजः सर्गस्य तावेव पितरौ स्मृतौ ॥ ७ ॥

स्त्रीपुंसाविति ॥ स्त्री च पुमांश्च **स्त्रीपुंसौ** ॥ ' अचतुर ' इत्यादिनाच्प्रत्ययान्तो निपातः । **सिसृक्षया** स्रष्टुमिच्छया **भिन्नमूर्तेः** द्विधाकृतविग्रहस्य **ते** तवात्मनो देहस्य भागौ **आत्मभागौ** । ' आत्मा जीवे धृतौ देहे स्वभावे परमात्मनि । ' इति विश्वः । **तावेव** भागौ **प्रसूतिभाजः** उत्पत्तिभाजः । [**सर्गस्य**] सृज्यत इति सर्गस्तस्य । निजसृष्टेरित्यर्थः । माता च पिता च **पितरौ** ॥ पिता मात्रा इत्येकशेषः । **स्मृतौ** । वृद्धैरिति शेषः ॥ अत्र मनुः—' द्विधा कृत्वात्मनो देहमर्धेन पुरुषोऽभवत् । अर्धेन नारी तस्यां स विराजमसृजत्प्रभुः ॥ ' इति ॥

स्वकालपरिमाणेन व्यस्तरात्रिंदिवस्य ते ।
यौ तु स्वप्नावबोधौ तौ भूतानां प्रलयोदयौ ॥ ८ ॥

स्वकालेति ॥ [**स्वकालपरिमाणेन**] स्वकालस्य परिमाणेन ' चतुर्युगसहस्राणि ब्रह्मणो दिनमुच्यते । ' इत्युक्तरूपेण । [**व्यस्तरात्रिंदिवस्य**] व्यस्तं विभक्तं रात्रिंदिवं रात्र्यहनी यस्य तस्य । यद्यपि ' अचतुर ' इत्यादिसूत्रेण रात्रौ च दिवा च रात्रिंदिवमिति सप्तम्यर्थे वृत्तौ द्वन्द्व इत्युक्तं तथापि ' दोषामन्यमहः ' ' दिवामन्या रात्रिः ' इत्यादौ कर्मवदत्रापि प्रातिपदिकार्थवृत्तित्वं कथंचित्प्रयोगबलादाश्रयणीयम् ॥ **ते** तव **यौ तु स्वप्नावबोधौ तौ** एव **भूतानां प्रलयोदयौ** संहारसृष्टी । यदाहुः—' यदा स देवो जागर्ति तदेदं चेष्टते जगत् । यदा स्वपिति शान्तात्मा तदा सर्वं प्रलीयते ॥ ' इति ॥ एतच्च दैनंदिनसृष्टिप्रलयाभिप्रायकं महाप्रलयस्य ब्रह्मणो वर्षशतान्ते भावित्वात् ॥

जगद्योनिरयोनिस्त्वं जगदन्तो निरन्तकः ॥
जगदादिरनादिस्त्वं जगदीशो निरीश्वरः ॥ ९ ॥

जगदिति ॥ हे भगवन् ! त्वं **जगद्योनिः** जगत्कारणं स्वयम् **अयोनिः** अनादि-

---

१ भावौ. २ परिणामेन. ३ यावेव स्वप्नबोधौ तौ; यौ स्वप्नबोधौ तावेव; स्वप्नावबोधौ भूतानां तावेव. ४ भवन्तो जगदन्तकः; जगदन्तोऽप्यनन्तकः. ५ जगदीशोऽप्यनीश्वरः.

त्वादकारणकस्त्वम् । [जगदन्तः] अन्तयतीत्यन्तः । पचाद्यच् । जगतोऽन्तो जगत्संहर्ता स्वयं **निरन्तकः** नित्यत्वादन्तरहितः । त्वं जगतामादिः **जगदादिः** । सृष्टेः प्रागपि सन्नित्यर्थः । अत एव त्वम् **अनादिः** आदिरहितः । त्वं [**जगदीशः**] जगतामीशो नियन्ता स्वयं **निरीश्वरः** । अनियम्य इत्यर्थः । ' यतो वा इमानि भूतानि जायन्ते ' इत्यादिश्रुतिरेवात्र प्रमाणम् ॥ अत्रायोनिरित्यादौ नञ्तत्पुरुषाश्रयणे विरोधः । बहुव्रीहिणा तु तत्परिहार इति विरोधाभासालंकारः । यथाहुः—'विरोधाभासत्वे विरोधः' इति ॥

तव तु न प्रपञ्चस्येव जन्मतिरोधानज्ञानेषु परापेक्षेत्याह—

आत्मानमात्मना वेत्सि सृजस्यात्मानमात्मना ।
आत्मना कृतिना च त्वमात्मन्येव प्रलीयसे ॥ १० ॥

आत्मानमिति ॥ हे भगवन् । **त्वमात्मानं** लोकानुग्रहार्थं ब्रह्मरूपेणोत्पिपादयिषितं स्वस्वरूपम् **आत्मना एव वेत्सि** जानासि । सर्वोपि क्रिया कर्तव्यार्थज्ञानपूर्विकेति भावः । तथा **आत्मानम् आत्मना एव** । आत्मन्येवेत्यत्रापि संबध्यते । स्वस्मिन्नेव **सृजसि** । अधिष्ठानमपि स्वयमेवेत्यर्थः । ' स्वे महिम्नि प्रतिष्ठितम्' इति श्रुतेः ॥ **कृतिना** समर्थेन । इदं सर्वत्र संबध्यते । **आत्मना** स्वेनैव **आत्मन्येव प्रलीयसे** स्वस्मिन्नेव प्रलीनो भवसि । लीयतेर्दैवादिकात्कर्तरि लट् । 'प्रकृत्यादिभ्य उपसंख्यानम्' इति वार्तिकात्सर्वत्रात्मनेति तृतीया । न हि ते प्रपञ्चस्येव ज्ञानोत्पत्तिलयेषु परापेक्षेति फलितार्थः॥

द्रवः संघातकठिनः स्थूलः सूक्ष्मो लघुर्गुरुः ।
व्यक्तो व्यक्तेतरश्चासि प्राकाम्यं ते विभूतिषु ॥ ११ ॥

द्रव इति ॥ त्वमित्यनुषज्यते । हे भगवन् । त्वं **द्रवः** सरित्समुद्रादिवद्रसात्मकोऽसि । [**संघातकठिनः**] संघातेन निबिडसंयोगेन कठिनो महीधरादिवत् । **स्थूलः** इन्द्रियग्रहणयोग्यो घटादिवत् । **सूक्ष्मः** अतीन्द्रियः परमाण्वादिवत् । **लघुः** उत्पतनयोग्यस्तूलादिवत् । **गुरुः** हेमाद्रिवदचलनीयः । **व्यक्तः** कार्यरूपोसि । **व्यक्तेतरः** कारणरूपः **च असि** । एवं **विभूतिषु** अणिमादिषु **ते** तव । प्रकामस्य भावः **प्राकाम्यं** यथाकामत्वम् ॥

उद्घातः प्रणवो यासां न्यायैस्त्रिभिरुदीरणम् ।
कर्म यज्ञः फलं स्वर्गस्तासां त्वं प्रभवो गिराम् ॥ १२ ॥

उद्घात इति ॥ हे भगवन् । **यासां** गिरां वाचाम् **उद्घातः** उपक्रमः **प्रणवः** ओंकारात्मकः । 'ओङ्कारप्रणवौ समौ' इति । 'स्यादभ्यादानमुद्घात आरम्भः' इति चामरः । इदमुपसंहारस्याप्युपलक्षणम् ॥ ' ब्रह्मणः प्रणवं कुर्यादादावन्ते च सर्वतः । दहत्येनः कृतं पूर्वं परस्ताच्च विशेषतः ॥' इति निरुक्तपरिशिष्टयोर्यास्कः ॥ नीयन्त एभिरर्थविशेषा इति न्यायाः स्वराः । उक्तं च—'स्वरविशेषादर्थप्रतिपत्तिः' । 'यथेन्द्रशत्रुः स्वरतोऽपराधात्' इति ॥ यासां

---

१ गुरुर्लघुः. २ उद्गीथः.

गिरां त्रिभिः न्यायैः उदात्तानुदात्तस्वरितैः स्वरैः उदीरणम् उच्चारणम् । यासां कर्म । प्रतिपाद्यमित्यर्थः । यज्ञः ज्योतिष्टोमादिः । न तु चैत्यवन्दनादिरिति भावः । फलं स्वर्गः । कर्मद्वारेति शेषः । कर्मस्वर्गौ ब्रह्मापवर्गयोरप्युपलक्षणे । त्वं तासां गिराम् । वेदानामित्यर्थः । प्रभवत्यस्मादिति प्रभवः कारणम् । प्रणेता स्मर्ता वा मतभेदेन ॥

सांख्यमतेन स्तुवन्ति—

त्वामामनन्ति प्रकृतिं पुरुषार्थप्रवर्तिनीम् ।
तद्दर्शिनमुदासीनं त्वामेव पुरुषं विदुः ॥ १३ ॥

त्वामिति ॥ हे भगवन् । त्वां पुरुषस्यार्थौ भोगापवर्गरूपस्तदर्थं प्रवर्तत इति तां पुरुषार्थप्रवर्तिनीं प्रकृतिं त्रैगुण्यात्मकं मूलकारणम् । 'प्रकृतिः पञ्चभूतेषु प्रधाने मूलकारणे'। इति यादवः । आमनन्ति कथयन्ति ॥ 'म्ना अभ्यासे' इति धातोर्लट् । 'पाघ्राध्मास्थाम्ना'—इत्यादिना मनादेशः ॥ प्रकृतिपुरुषभेदाग्रहणात्प्रकृतिपुरुषभेदव्यपदेशः । त्वामेव तां प्रकृतिं साक्षित्वेन पश्यतीति तद्दर्शिनम् उदासीनं कूटस्थं पुरुषं विदुः विदन्ति ॥ 'विदो लटो वा' इति झेर्जुसादेशः । 'अजामेकां लोहितशुक्लकृष्णाम्' इति श्रुतिरत्र प्रमाणम् ॥

त्वं पितॄणामपि पिता देवानामपि देवता ।
परतोऽपि परश्चासि विधाता वेधसामपि ॥ १४ ॥

त्वमिति ॥ हे भगवन् । त्वं पितॄणाम् अग्निष्वात्तादीनाम् अपि पिता । तेषामपि तर्पणीय इत्यर्थः । देवानाम् इन्द्रादीनाम् अपि देवता । तेषामपि यजनीयः इत्यर्थः । परतोऽपि परश्चासि । सर्वोत्तरोऽसीत्यर्थः ॥ 'इन्द्रियेभ्यः परा ह्यर्था अर्थेभ्यश्च परं मनः । मनसश्च परा बुद्धिर्बुद्धेरात्मा महान्परः ॥ महतः परमव्यक्तमव्यक्तात्पुरुषः परः । पुरुषान्न परं किंचित्सा काष्ठा सा परा गतिः ॥' इति सर्वोत्तरत्वाभिधानात् । वेधसां दक्षादीनाम् अपि विधाता स्रष्टा असि ॥

त्वमेव हव्यं होता च भोज्यं[2] भोक्ता च शाश्वतः ।
वेद्यं[3] च वेदिता चासि ध्याता ध्येयं च यत्परम्[4] ॥ १५ ॥

त्वमेवेति ॥ शश्वत्सिद्धः शाश्वतः । शैषिकोऽण्प्रत्ययः । यद्यपि 'कालाट्ठञ्' इति ठञपवादः अत एव सूत्रकारस्यापि प्रयोगः—'येषां च विरोधः शाश्वतिकः' इति । तथापि प्रयोगवशात्साधुरिति वामनः इति शाश्वतः प्रयुक्तः । शश्वतः त्वमेव । हूयत इति हव्यं हविराज्यादिकम् । जुहोतीति होता । यजमानः च असि । भोज्यम् अभ्यवहार्यमन्नम् । 'भोज्यं भक्ष्ये' इति निपातनात्कुत्वाभावः । भोक्ता अन्नादः च असि । वेद्यं साक्षात्कार्यं वस्तु च वेदिता साक्षात्कर्ता च असि । ध्याता स्मर्ता च यत्परं वस्तु ध्येयं तत् च असि । साक्षात्कारसाधनभूतप्रत्ययविशेषप्रवाहो ध्यानम् ॥

इति तेभ्यः स्तुतीः श्रुत्वा यथार्थाः[5] हृदयंगमाः ।
प्रसादाभिमुखो वेधाः प्रत्युवाच दिवौकसः ॥ १६ ॥

---

१ देवतम्. २ भोग्यं. ३ वेद्यं वेदयिता, वेद्यश्च वेदिता. ४ तत्प. ५ यथार्थ-याथार्थ्य-६ अमा.

इतीति ॥ **वेधाः** ब्रह्मा इति **तेभ्यः** देवेभ्यः । 'आख्यातोपयोगे' इत्यपादानत्वात्पञ्चमी ॥ **यथार्थाः** सत्या अत एव हृदयं गच्छन्तीति **हृदयंगमाः** मनोहराः । 'खच्प्रकरणे गमेः सुप्युपसंख्यानम्' इति खच्प्रत्ययः । 'अरुर्द्विषदजन्तस्य मुम्' इति मुमागमः । **स्तुतीः** स्तोत्राणि **श्रुत्वा प्रसादाभिमुखः** अनुग्रहप्रवणः सन् । **दिवौकसः** देवान् **प्रत्युवाच** ॥

अथ कविराह—

पुराणस्य कवेस्तस्य चतुर्मुखसमीरिता ।
प्रवृत्तिरासीच्छब्दानां चरितार्था चतुष्टयी ॥ १७ ॥

पुराणस्येति ॥ द्रव्यगुणक्रियाजातिभेदेन चत्वारोऽवयवा यस्या इति **चतुष्टयी** चतुर्विधा ॥ 'संख्याया अवयवे तयप्' इति तयप् । 'टिड्ढाणञ्द्वयसच्'—इत्यादिना ङीप् ॥ **शब्दानां प्रवृत्तिः** वैखरीप्रमुखा वाग्वृत्तिः । उक्तं च–'वैखरी शब्दनिष्पत्तिर्मध्यमा श्रुतिगोचरा । द्योतितार्था च पश्यन्ती सूक्ष्मा वागनपायिनी ॥' इति । **पुराणस्य** पुरातनस्य । पृषोदरादित्वात्साधुः । **कवेः** कवयितुः **तस्य** ब्रह्मणः [**चतुर्मुखसमीरिता**] चतुर्भिर्मुखैः समीरिता सती । 'तद्धितार्थ—' इत्यादिनोत्तरपदसमासः । समाहारे चतुर्मुखीति स्यात् ॥ **चरितार्था** अन्वर्था **आसीत्** । चतुर्मुखोच्चारणाच्चातुर्विध्यं सफलमासीदित्यर्थः ॥

भगवानाह—

स्वागतं स्वानधीकारान्प्रभावैरवलम्ब्य वः ।
युगपद्युगबाहुभ्यः प्राप्तेभ्यः प्राज्यविक्रमाः ॥ १८ ॥

स्वागतमिति ॥ हे **प्राज्यविक्रमाः** प्रभूतपराक्रमा देवाः । 'प्राज्यं भूरि प्रभूतं च' इति यादवः । **स्वान्** स्वकीयान् **अधीकारान्** नियोगान् ॥ 'उपसर्गस्य घञि'–इति वा दीर्घः ॥ **प्रभावैः** सामर्थ्यैः **अवलम्ब्य** आस्थाय । यथाधिकारं स्थित्वापीत्यर्थः । **युगपत्** समकालं **प्राप्तेभ्यः** । युगपत्प्राप्त्या महत्कार्यमनुमीयते इति भावः । **युगबाहुभ्यः** । दीर्घबाहुभ्य इत्यर्थः । आजानुबाहुत्वं भाग्यलक्षणम् । **वः** युष्मभ्यम् । 'बहुवचनस्य वस्नसौ' इति वसादेशः । 'कर्मणा यमभिप्रैति'–इत्यत्र कर्मपदेन क्रियाग्रहणात्संप्रदानत्वम् ॥ **स्वागतं** शोभनमागमनम् । काकुरत्रानुसंधेया ॥

किमिदं द्युतिमात्मीयां न बिभ्रति यथा पुरा ।
हिमक्लिष्टप्रकाशानि ज्योतींषीव मुखानि वः ॥ १९ ॥

किमिति ॥ वत्साः इत्युत्तरश्लोकीयं (श्लो० २८) संबोधनमत्राप्यनुषञ्जनीयम् । हे वत्साः पुत्रकाः । [**हिमक्लिष्टप्रकाशानि**] हिमेन नीहारेण क्लिष्टप्रकाशानि मन्दप्रभाणि **ज्योतींषि** नक्षत्राणि **इव** ॥ 'दीप्तिताराहुताशेषु ज्योतिः' इति शाश्वतः । **वः** युष्माकं **मुखानि पुरा यथा** पूर्वमिव **आत्मीयां द्युतिं न बिभ्रति** । **इदं किम्** । किंनिबन्धनमित्यर्थः । किमिदमित्यनेन वाक्यार्थः परामृश्यते ॥

---

१ किमिमां, किमिति. २ यथापुरं. ३ प्रभावाणि, प्रसादानि.

उक्तमेव प्रपञ्चयति सप्तभिः श्लोकैः—

प्रशमादर्चिषामेतदनुद्गीर्णसुरायुधम् ।
वृत्रस्य हन्तुः कुलिशं कुण्ठिताश्रीव लक्ष्यते ॥ २० ॥

प्रशमादिति ॥ अर्चिषां तेजसां प्रशमात् निर्वाणात् अनुद्गीर्णसुरायुधम् अनुदितचित्रप्रभमित्यर्थः । एतद् वृत्रस्य हन्तुः इन्द्रस्य कुलिशं वज्रम् । कुण्ठिताः अश्रयो यस्य तत् कुण्ठिताश्रि कुण्ठितकोटि इव लक्ष्यते दृश्यते ॥

किं चायमरिदुर्वारः पाणौ पाशः प्रचेतसः ।
मन्त्रेण हतवीर्यस्य फणिनो दैन्यमाश्रितः ॥ २१ ॥

किं चेति ॥ किं च अयम् अरिदुर्वारः रिपुदुष्प्रधर्षः प्रचेतसः वरुणस्य । 'प्रचेता वरुणः पाशी' इत्यमरः ॥ पाणौ पाशः रज्जुरायुधविशेषः । मन्त्रेण गारुडेन हतवीर्यस्य प्रतिबद्धशक्तेः फणिनः सर्पस्य दैन्यं शोच्यत्वम् आश्रितः ॥ अत्र फणिनिष्ठदैन्यस्य पाशेऽसंभवाद्दैन्यमिव दैन्यमिति कल्पनादसंभवद्वस्तुसंबन्धो निदर्शनालंकारः ॥

कुबेरस्य मनःशल्यं शंसतीव पराभवम् ।
अपविद्धगदो बाहुर्भग्नशाख इव द्रुमः ॥ २२ ॥

कुबेरस्येति ॥ अपविद्धा त्यक्ता गदा येन सः अपविद्धगदः । अत एव भग्नशाखः द्रुमः इव स्थितः कुबेरस्य बाहुः मनःशल्यम् । दुःखहेतुत्वान्मनसः शल्यप्रायमित्यर्थः । पराभवम् । शत्रुकृतमिति शेषः । शंसति इव कथयतीव । लक्षणयानुमापयतीत्यर्थः ॥ बाहौ मुख्यकथनस्यासंभवादिवशब्दोऽप्यत एव ॥

यमोऽपि विलिखन्भूमिं दण्डेनास्तमितत्विषा ।
कुरुतेऽस्मिन्नमोघेऽपि निर्वाणालातलाघवम् ॥ २३ ॥

यम इति ॥ [अस्तमितत्विषा] अस्तं नाशमितः प्राप्तः ॥ अस्तमिति मकारान्तमव्ययम् । तस्य 'द्वितीया श्रितातीतपतितगतात्यस्तप्राप्तापन्नैः' इति समासः । अस्तमितास्त्विषो यस्य तेन निस्तेजस्केन दण्डेन यमोऽपि भूमिं विलिखन् अमोघेऽपि । प्रागिति भावः । अस्मिन् दण्डे [निर्वाणालातलाघवम्] निर्वाणालातस्य शान्तोल्मुकस्य । अलातं नाम भूलेखनशलाका तस्य यल्लाघवं क्लैब्यं तत् कुरुते ॥ 'अलातमुल्मुकं ज्ञेयम्' इति हलायुधः । 'निर्वाणोऽवाते' इति निपातनान्निष्ठानत्वम् ॥ अत्रापि लाघवमिव लाघवमिति कल्पनान्निदर्शनालंकारः ॥

अमी च कथमादित्याः प्रतापक्षतिशीतलाः ।
चित्रन्यस्ता इव गताः प्रकामालोकनीयताम् ॥ २४ ॥

१ अनुदगूर्ण, अनुगूर्ण. २ कुण्ठितश्रि. ३ अपि. ४ शूलं. ५ क्षय. ६ आयाता. ७ दर्शिनः, दर्शनम.

अमी इति ॥ [**प्रतापक्षतिशीतलाः**] प्रतापक्षत्या तेजसां क्षयेण शीतलाः **अमी आदित्याश्च** । द्वादशेति शेषः । **कथम्** । केन हेतुनेत्यर्थः । **चित्रन्यस्ताः** चित्रलिखिताः **इव** । [**प्रकामालोकनीयताम्**] प्रकाममत्यन्तमालोकनीयतां दृश्यतां **गताः** प्राप्ताः ॥

पर्याकुलत्वान्मरुतां वेगभङ्गोऽनुमीयते ।
अम्भसामोघसंरोधः प्रतीपगमनादिव ॥ २५ ॥

पर्याकुलेति ॥ **मरुतां** वायूनाम् । सप्तसप्तानामिति शेषः । **पर्याकुलत्वात** स्खलितगतित्वाद्धेतोः [**वेगभङ्गः**] वेगस्य भङ्गः **अम्भसां** जलानां **प्रतीपगमनात्** उत्तानावरोहादित्यर्थः । [**ओघसंरोधः**] ओघस्य संरोधः प्रवाहप्रतिबन्धः **इव अनुमीयते** ॥

आवर्जितजटामौलिविलम्बिशशिकोटयः ।
रुद्राणामपि मूर्धानः क्षतहुंकारशंसिनः ॥ २६ ॥

आवर्जितेति ॥ [**आवर्जितजटामौलिविलम्बिशशिकोटयः**] आवर्जितेषु पारिभवदुःखावनम्रेषु जटानां मौलिषु जटाजूटेषु विलम्बिन्यः स्रंसिन्यः शशिकोटयश्चन्द्ररेखा येषां ते तथोक्ताः । **रुद्राणामपि** । एकादशानामिति शेषः । **मूर्धानः** [**क्षतहुंकारशंसिनः**] क्षतं हुंकारं शंसन्तीति तथोक्ताः । हुंकारक्षत्यनुमापका इत्यर्थः । हुंकारशस्त्रा हि रुद्रा इति भावः ॥

लब्धप्रतिष्ठाः प्रथमं यूयं किं बलवत्तरैः ।
अपवादैरिवोत्सर्गाः कृतव्यावृत्तयः परैः ॥ २७ ॥

लब्धेति ॥ **प्रथमं** पूर्वं **लब्धप्रतिष्ठाः** लब्धास्थितयः । लब्धावकाशा इत्यन्यत्र । **यूयं बलवत्तरैः** पौरुषातिरेकात्प्रबलतरैः । निरवकाशैरित्यपरत्र । **परैः** शत्रुभिः । **उत्सर्गाः** सामान्यशास्त्राणि 'मा हिंस्यात्' इत्येवमादीनि । अपोह्यन्त एभिरिति **अपवादैः** 'गामालभेत' इत्यादिभिर्विशेषशास्त्रैः **इव किं कृतव्यावृत्तयः** कृतप्रतिष्ठाभङ्गाः । कृतविषयसंकोचरूपबाधा इत्यन्यत्र । 'विषयसंकोच एव बाधः' इत्याचार्याः । निषेधशास्त्रस्य वैदिकहिंसापरिहारेण लौकिकमात्रे व्यवस्थापनाद्विषयसंकोच इत्यलमतिगहनावगाहनेन ॥

तद्ब्रूत वत्साः किमितः प्रार्थयध्वं समागताः ।
मयि सृष्टिर्हि लोकानां रक्षा युष्मास्ववस्थिता ॥ २८ ॥

तदिति ॥ **तत्** तस्मात्कारणात् । हे **वत्साः** पुत्रकाः । 'वत्सस्त्वर्भकपुत्राद्योर्वर्षे वत्सं तु वक्षसि' इति विश्वः । स्वयं पितामहत्वाद्वत्सा इत्यामन्त्रयते ॥ संभूयागताः **समा-**

---

१ ताहंकार. २ न खलु स्थ बलोत्तरैः. ३ प्रार्थयध्वे. ४ भूतानाम्. २६–२७ मध्ये क्षेपकोऽयं दृश्यते–निशाकरोऽपि मलिनः सुप्तोत्थितमिवाननम् । कलाशेषेऽपि या लक्ष्मीर्न सा पूर्तेऽपि विद्यते ॥

गताः इतः मत्तः किं प्रार्थयध्वम् । किमिच्छतेत्यर्थः । ब्रूत । लोकरक्षणे यूयमेव कर्तार इत्याह—मयि लोकानां सृष्टिः रक्षा युष्मासु अवस्थिता हि । अतस्तदर्थमपि नास्ति मदपेक्षेत्यर्थः ॥

ततो मन्दानिलोद्धूतकमलाकरशोभिना ।
गुरुं नेत्रसहस्रेण नोदयामास वासवः ॥२९॥

तत इति ॥ ततः भगवत्प्रश्नानन्तरं वासवः इन्द्रः गुरुं बृहस्पतिम् ॥ ' गुरुर्गीष्पतिपित्राद्यौ ' इत्यमरः । [मन्दानिलोद्धूतकमलाकरशोभिना] मन्दानिलोद्धूतो यः कमलाकरः स इव शोभत इति तेन तथोक्तेन [नेत्रसहस्रेण] नेत्राणां सहस्रेण नोदयामास प्रेरयामास । सहस्रग्रहणमास्थातिशयार्थम् । अनिमेषाणामपि प्रयत्नवशादक्षिस्पन्दो न विरुध्यते ॥

स द्विनेत्रं हरेश्चक्षुः सहस्रनयनाधिकम् ।
वाचस्पतिरुवाचेदं प्राञ्जलिर्जलजासनम् ॥ ३० ॥

स इति ॥ हरेः इन्द्रस्य । ' इन्द्रो दुश्च्यवनो हरिः ' इति हलायुधः । सहस्रान्नयनेभ्योऽधिकं सहस्रनयनाधिकम् । तदगोचरदर्शित्वादिति भावः । द्वे नेत्रे यस्य तद् द्विनेत्रम् । प्रसिद्धाच्चक्षुषोऽयं विशेष इत्यर्थः । चक्षुः चक्षुर्भूतः । चक्षुष्ट्वारोपस्य प्रकृतोपयोगात्परिणामालंकारः । स वाचस्पतिः ॥ कस्कादित्वादलुक्सत्वे ॥ षष्ठ्याः 'पतिपुत्र'—इत्यादिना सत्वमिति स्वामी तन्न छन्दोविषयत्वात् ॥ प्राञ्जलिः सन् । जलजासनं ब्रह्माणम् इदम् उवाच ॥

एवं यदात्थ भगवन्नामृष्टं नः परैः पदम् ।
प्रत्येकं विनियुक्तात्मा कथं न ज्ञास्यसि प्रभो ॥ ३१ ॥

एवमिति । हे भगवन् षड्गुणैश्वर्यसंपन्न । यदात्थ 'कृतव्यावृत्तयः परैः' (२।२७) इति यद्ब्रवीषि ॥ 'ब्रुवः पञ्चानाम्'—इत्यादिनाहादेशः । 'वर्तमानसामीप्ये वर्तमानवद्वा इति वर्तमानप्रयोगः । वामनस्तु भ्रान्तोऽयं प्रयोग इत्याह । 'आहेति भूते णलन्तभ्रमवर्तं' इति । आहेत्युपलक्षणम् ॥ तद् एवं सत्यम् । नः अस्माकं पदम् अधिकारः परैः शत्रुभिः आमृष्टम् आक्षिप्तम् । हे प्रभो प्रत्येकं प्रतिपुरुषं विनियुक्तात्मा प्रवेशितस्वरूपः । सर्वान्तर्यामीत्यर्थः । कथं न ज्ञास्यसि न वेत्सि । वर्तमानेऽपि वचनभङ्ग्या भविष्यन्निर्देशः प्रसिद्धः ॥ ' अपह्नवे ज्ञः ' । अकर्मकाच्च ' इत्यात्मनेपदविकल्पः ॥

उक्तमेव प्रपञ्चयति—

भवल्लब्धवरोदीर्णस्तारकाख्यो महासुरः ।
उपप्लवाय लोकानां धूमकेतुरिवोत्थितः ॥ ३२ ॥

---

१ चोदयामास; प्रेरयामास. २ वृत्रहा. ३ द्विनेत्रः, विनेतृ. ४ दशचक्षुःशताधिकम्. ५ यथा. ६ ज्ञास्यति प्रभुः । ७ त्वया दत्त, भवदत्त.

भवदिति ॥ [**भवल्लब्धवरोदीर्णः**] भवतस्त्वत्तो लब्धेन वरेणोदीर्ण उद्धतः। तारकः इत्याख्या नामधेयं यस्य स **तारकाख्यः**। महानसुरो **महासुरः**। 'सन्महत्परमोत्तमोत्कृष्टाः पूज्यमानैः' इति तत्पुरुषः। **धूमकेतुः** उत्पातविशेषः **इव लोकानाम् उपप्लवाय** उपद्रवाय **उत्थितः** उत्पन्नः ॥

पुरे तावन्तमेवास्य तनोति रविरातपम्।
दीर्घिकाकमलोन्मेषो यावन्मात्रेण साध्यते ॥ ३३ ॥

पुर इति ॥ **अस्य** तारकस्य **पुरे रविः** सूर्यः **तावन्तं** तावन्मात्रम् **एव आतपं तनोति यावन्मात्रेण** यावतैव। यावती मात्रा मितिर्यस्य यावन्मात्रं तेन वा। अल्पपरिमाणेनेत्यर्थः। 'मात्रा परिच्छदे। अल्पे च परिमाणे स्यान्मात्रं कार्त्स्न्येऽवधारणे॥' इत्यमरः। [**दीर्घिकाकमलोन्मेषः**] दीर्घिकासु क्रीडावापीषु कमलानामुन्मेषो विकाशः **साध्यते** निष्पाद्यते। कठोरकिरणोऽपि मन्दोष्णः सन्नेव तद्भीत्या पुरे प्रकाशते इत्यभिप्रायः॥

सर्वाभिः सर्वदा चन्द्रस्तं कलाभिर्निषेवते।
नादत्ते केवलां लेखां हरचूडामणीकृताम् ॥ ३४ ॥

सर्वाभिरिति ॥ **चन्द्रः तं** तारकं **सर्वदा**। कृष्णपक्षेऽपीत्यर्थः। **सर्वाभिः कलाभिः निषेवते**। 'कला तु षोडशो भागः' इत्यमरः॥ **केवलां हरचूडामणीकृतां** शिवशिरोमणीकृतां **लेखां न आदत्ते** न गृह्णाति॥

व्यावृत्तगतिरुद्याने कुसुमस्तेयसाध्वसात्।
न वाति वायुस्तत्पार्श्वे तालवृन्तानिलाधिकम् ॥ ३५ ॥

व्यावृत्तेति ॥ **वायुः** [**कुसुमस्तेयसाध्वसात्**] स्तेनस्य भावः कर्म वा स्तेयं चौर्यम्॥ 'स्तेनाद्यन्नलोपश्च' इति यत्प्रत्ययो नलोपश्च॥ कुसुमानां स्तेयं तस्मात्स्तेयाभियोगाद्दण्डाद्वा साध्वसं भयं तस्माद्धेतोः **उद्याने व्यावृत्तगतिः**। निवृत्तोद्यानसंचारः सन्नित्यर्थः॥ सापेक्षत्वेऽपि गमकत्वात्समासः॥ **तत्पार्श्वे** तत्समीपे [**तालवृन्तानिलाधिकम्**] तालस्य वृन्तैरुद्बध्यते तालस्येव वृन्तमस्येति वा तालवृन्तं तस्यानिलाद्व्यजनसंचारपवनादधिकं यथा तथा **न वाति**॥ 'व्यजनं तालवृन्तकम्' इत्यमरः॥

पर्यायसेवामुत्सृज्य पुष्पसंभारतत्पराः।
उद्यानपालसामान्यमृतवस्तमुपासते ॥ ३६ ॥

पर्यायेति ॥ **ऋतवः** षड् वसन्तादयः **पर्यायसेवां** क्रमसेवाम् **उत्सृज्य** [**पुष्पसंभारतत्पराः**] पुष्पाणां संभारे संग्रहे तत्पराः। आसक्ताः सन्तः इत्यर्थः। 'तत्परे प्रसितासक्तौ' इत्यमरः। [**उद्यानपालसामान्यं**] उद्यानपालैरुद्यानाधिकृतैः सामान्यं साधारणं यथा भवति तथा **तं** तारकम् **उपासते** सेवन्ते। शीतोष्णादिदोषप्रकाशनं तु दूरापास्तमित्यर्थः॥

---

१ करोति, आत०. २ सिध्यति. ३ साह.

तस्योपायनयोग्यानि रत्नानि सरितां पतिः ।
कथमप्यम्भसामन्तरा निष्पत्तेः प्रतीक्षते ॥ ३७ ॥

तस्येति ॥ **सरितां पतिः** समुद्रः **तस्य** तारकस्य [**उपायनयोग्यानि**] उपायनानां प्राभृतानां योग्यानि । 'प्राभृतं तु प्रदेशनम् । उपायनम् ।' इत्यमरः । **रत्नानि अम्भसाम् अन्तः आनिष्पत्तेः** परिपाकपर्यन्तम् ॥ विकल्पादसमासः । **कथमपि** महता यत्नेन **प्रतीक्षते** । कदा वा परिपच्येरन्निर्त्येकाग्रेण पालयतीत्यर्थः ॥

ज्वलन्मणिशिखाश्चैनं वासुकिप्रमुखा निशि ।
स्थिरप्रदीपतामेत्य भुजङ्गाः पर्युपासते ॥ ३८ ॥

ज्वलदिति ॥ किं च इति चार्थः । [**ज्वलन्मणिशिखाः**] ज्वलन्त्यो मणीनां शिरोरत्नानां शिखा ज्वाला येषां ते **वासुकिप्रमुखाः भुजङ्गाः** सर्पाः । सिद्धाश्च ध्वन्यन्ते ॥ 'भुजङ्गः सिद्धसर्पयोः' इत्यमरः ॥ **निशि स्थिरप्रदीपताम्** अनिर्वाणदीपत्वम् **एत्य एनं** तारकं **पर्युपासते** परिवृत्य सेवन्ते ॥

तत्कृतानुग्रहापेक्षी तं मुहुर्दूतहारितैः ।
अनुकूलयतीन्द्रोऽपि कल्पद्रुमविभूषणैः ॥ ३९ ॥

तत्कृतेति ॥ **इन्द्रः अपि** [**तत्कृतानुग्रहापेक्षी**] तेन तारकेण कृतं तत्कृतमनुग्रहं प्रसादमपेक्षते इति तथोक्तः सन् । **मुहुः दूतहारितै** दूतप्रापितैः [**कल्पद्रुमविभूषणैः**] कल्पद्रुमाणां विभूषणैः । तत्प्रसूनैरित्यर्थः । **तं** तारकम् **अनुकूलयति** अनुकूलं करोति ॥

इत्थमाराध्यमानोऽपि क्लिश्नाति भुवनत्रयम् ।
शाम्येत्प्रत्यपकारेण नोपकारेण दुर्जनः ॥ ४० ॥

इत्थमिति ॥ **इत्थम्** उक्तप्रकारेण रविशशिपवनोदधिभुजङ्गसुरेन्द्रैः **आराध्यमानः अपि भुवनत्रयं क्लिश्नाति** पीडयति । तथा हि । **दुर्जनः प्रत्यपकारेण** प्रतीकारेणैव **शाम्येत्** शान्तो भवेत् । **उपकारेण तु न** शाम्येत् । प्रत्युत प्रकुप्यतीति भावः ॥

तेनामरवधूहस्तैः सदयालूनपल्लवाः ।
अभिज्ञाश्छेदपातानां क्रियन्ते नन्दनद्रुमाः ॥ ४१ ॥

तेनेति ॥ **तेन** तारकेण **अमरवधूहस्तैः** । सुकुमारैरिति भावः । तैरपि [**सदयालूनपल्लवाः**] सदयमालूना अवतंसार्थं छिन्ना पल्लवा येषां ते **नन्दनद्रुमाः** [**छेदपातानाम्**] छेदाश्च पाताश्च छेदपातास्तेषाम् । अभिजानन्तीति **अभिज्ञाः** । कृद्योगात्कर्मणि षष्ठी । **क्रियन्ते** ॥

वीज्यते स हि संसुप्तः श्वाससाधारणानिलैः ।
चामरैः सुरबन्दीनां बाष्पशीकरवर्षिभिः ॥ ४२ ॥

---

१ मथिताः. २ प्रत्यहं. ३ स्वर्गद्रु०. ४ प्रत्युपकारेण. ५ हस्तस०. ६ छिन्नपा. ७ संतप्तः

वीज्यत इति ॥ **हि** यस्मात्कारणात्त **स** तारकः **संस्तुतः** सन् । [**श्वाससाधारणानिलैः**] श्वाससाधारणो निःश्वाससमानोऽनिलो येषां तैः । ततोऽप्याधिक्ये निद्राभङ्गभयादिति भावः । **बाष्पशीकरवर्षिभिः** । तासां स्त्रीणां रोदनस्याथमवसर इति भावः । **सुरबन्दीनां** सुरप्रग्रहस्त्रीणां संबन्धिभिः । 'प्रग्रहोपग्रहौ बन्द्याम्' इत्यमरः । **चामरैः वीज्यते** ॥

उत्पाट्य मेरुशृङ्गाणि क्षुण्णानि हरितां खुरैः ।
आक्रीडपर्वतास्तेन कल्पिताः स्वेषु वेश्मसु ॥ ४३ ॥

उत्पाट्येति ॥ **तेन** तारकेण **हरितां** सूर्याश्वानाम् ॥ 'हरित्सूर्ये च सूर्याश्वे वर्णे च हरिते दिशि ।' इति विश्वः । **खुरैः** शफैः **क्षुण्णानि** चूर्णितानि । एतेन तेषामत्यौन्नत्यं सूचितम् । **मेरुशृङ्गाणि उत्पाट्य स्वेषु वेश्मसु** । वेश्मास्विति बहुवचनेनास्य भुवनत्रयनिवासः सूचितः । [**आक्रीडपर्वताः**] आक्रीडन्ते एष्विस्याक्रीडाः । ते च ते पर्वताः **कल्पिताः** कृताः ॥

मन्दाकिन्याः पयः शेषं दिग्वारणमदाविलम् ।
हेमाम्भोरुहसस्यानां तद्वाप्यो धाम सांप्रतम् ॥ ४४ ॥

मन्दाकिन्या इति ॥ **सांप्रतं** संप्रति **मन्दाकिन्याः** भागीरथ्याः [**दिग्वारणमदाविलं**] दिग्वारणानां दिग्गजानां मदैराविलं कलुषं **पयः** जलमेव शिष्यत इति **शेषं** शिष्टम् । कर्मणि घञ् प्रत्ययः । 'त्रिष्वन्यत्रोपयुज्यते' इति नपुंसकत्वम् । तर्हि कनककमलानि क्व गतानीत्याह—हेमेति । [**हेमाम्भोरुहसस्यानां**] हेमाम्भोरुहाण्येव सस्यानि तेषां तु तस्य वाप्यः **तद्वाप्यः** एव **धाम** स्थानम् । सर्वाण्यप्युत्पाट्य स्वदीर्घिकास्वेव प्रतिरोपितवानित्यर्थः ॥

भुवनालोकनप्रीतिः स्वर्गिभिर्नानुभूयते ।
खिलीभूते विमानानां तदापातभयात्पथि ॥ ४५ ॥

भुवनेति ॥ [**तदापातभयात्**] तस्य तारकस्यापातात्समापत्तेर्भयात् **विमानानां पथि खिलीभूते** अप्रहतीभूते सति ॥ 'द्वे खिलाप्रहते समे' इत्यमर ॥ **स्वर्गिभिः** देवैः [**भुवनालोकनप्रीतिः**] भुवनानामालोकने प्रीति **नानुभूयते** ॥

यज्वभिः संभृतं हव्यं विततेष्वध्वरेषु सः ।
जातवेदोमुखान्मायी मिषतामाच्छिनत्ति नः ॥ ४६ ॥

यज्वभिरिति ॥ **यज्वभिः** विधिवदिष्टवद्भिः । 'यज्वा तु विधिनेष्टवान्' इत्यमरः । 'सुयजोर्ङ्वनिप्' इति ङ्वनिप्प्रत्ययः । **विततेषु अध्वरेषु** यज्ञेषु **संभृतं** दत्तं **हव्यं** हविः **मायी** मायावी । व्रीह्यादित्वादिनिप्रत्ययः । **स** तारकः **नः** अस्माकं **मिषतां** पश्यताम् । पश्यत्सु सत्स्वित्यर्थः । 'षष्ठी चानादरे' इति षष्ठी । जातवेदाः वह्निरेव मुखं तस्मात् **जातवेदोमुखात् आच्छिनत्ति** । आक्षिप्य गृह्णातीत्यर्थः ॥

---

१ पाम्बु. २ कृते. ३ दाघात, तदपाय. ४ पिबताम्.

उच्चैरुच्चैःश्रवास्तेन हयरत्नमहारि च ।
देहबद्धमिवेन्द्रस्य चिरकालार्जितं यशः ॥ ४७ ॥

उच्चैरिति ॥ किं च इति चार्थः । तेन तारकेण उच्चैः उन्नतः उच्चैःश्रवाः नाम । हयो रत्नमिव हयरत्नम् अश्वश्रेष्ठः । 'रत्नं श्रेष्ठे मणावपि' इति विश्वः । अस्य शुभ्रत्वादुत्प्रेक्षते—देहबद्धं बद्धदेहम् । मूर्तिमदित्यर्थः ॥ आहिताग्न्यादित्वान्निष्ठायाः परनिपातः। चिरकालार्जितम् इन्द्रस्य यशः इव अहारि अपहृतम् ॥

तर्हि सामाद्युपायास्तत्र कथं न प्रयुक्ता इत्यत्राह—

तस्मिन्नुपायाः सर्वे नः क्रूरे प्रतिहतक्रियाः ।
वीर्यवन्त्यौषधानीव विकारे सांनिपातिके ॥ ४८ ॥

तस्मिन्निति ॥ क्रूरे घातुके । 'नृशंसो घातुकः क्रूरः' इत्यमरः । तस्मिन् असुरे नः अस्माकं सर्वे उपायाः संनिपातदोषत्रयस्य प्रकोपजे सांनिपातिके विकारे ज्वरादौ ॥ 'संनिपाताच्च' इति वक्तव्याट्ठक् ॥ वीर्यवन्ति सारवन्ति औषधानि इव प्रतिहतक्रियाः विफलप्रयोगा भवन्ति ॥

तदेव प्रतिहतक्रियत्वमाह—

जयाशा यत्र चास्माकं प्रतिघातोत्थितार्चिषा ।
हरिचक्रेण तेनास्य कण्ठे निष्कमिवार्पितम् ॥ ४९ ॥

जयाशेति ॥ [च] किं च इति चार्थः । नूनमनेन हरिचक्रेण वयं जेष्याम इति यत्र हरिचक्रे अस्माकं जयाशा विजयाशंसा । आसीदिति शेषः । [प्रतिघातोत्थितार्चिषा] प्रतिघातेन प्रतिहत्योत्थितार्चिषोद्गततेजसा तेन हरिचक्रेण विष्णोः सुदर्शनेन अस्य तारकस्य कण्ठे निष्कम् उरोभूषणम् अर्पितमिव इत्युत्प्रेक्षा । स्वयमेव निष्कमिव स्थितमित्यर्थः । तारकशिरश्छेदाय हरिणा चक्रं त्यक्तं तदपि नष्टशक्ति जातमिति भावः ॥ 'साष्टे शते सुवर्णानां हेम्न्युरोभूषणे पले । दीनारेऽपि च निष्कोऽस्त्री' इत्यमरः ॥

तदीयास्तोयदेष्वद्य पुष्करावर्तकादिषु ।
अभ्यस्यन्ति तटाघातं निर्जितैरावता गजाः ॥ ५० ॥

तदीया इति ॥ अद्य संप्रति [निर्जितैरावताः] निर्जित ऐरावतो यैस्ते तथोक्ताः । तस्य तारकस्येमे तदीयाः गजाः पुष्कराश्चावर्तकाश्च नाम आदयो येषां तेषु [पुष्करावर्तकादिषु] तोयदेषु मेघेषु तटाघातं वप्रक्रीडाम् अभ्यस्यन्ति ॥

तदिच्छामो विभो स्रष्टुं सेनान्यं तस्य शान्तये ।
कर्मबन्धच्छिदं धर्मं भवस्येव मुमुक्षवः ॥ ५१ ॥

---

१ बन्ध. २ द्रुता. ३ निष्क इवार्पितः. ४ तटाघातान्, तडाघाते [तडिति निपातः तडिति शब्दपूर्वमाघातम्]. ५ स्रष्टं.

तदिति ॥ तत् तस्मात्कारणात् । हे विभो स्वामिन । मोक्तुं भवं त्यक्तुमिच्छवः मुमुक्षवः विरक्ताः भवस्य संसारस्य शान्तये निवृत्तये [कर्मबन्धच्छिदं] कर्मैव बन्धस्तं छिनत्तीति कर्मबन्धच्छित्तं धर्मम् इव । आत्मज्ञानहेतुभूतमिति शेषः । 'तमेव विदित्वातिमृत्युमेति ' इति ज्ञानादेव मुक्तिः । तस्य तारकस्य शान्तये नाशाय । सेनां नयतीति सेनानीश्चमूपतिः । ' सत्सूद्विष '—इत्यादिना क्विप् ॥ तं सेनान्यं कंचित् स्रष्टुम् इच्छामः ॥ वयमिति शेषः ॥

सेनानीसृष्टेः फलमाह—

गोप्तारं सुरसैन्यानां यं पुरस्कृत्य गोत्रभित् ।
प्रत्यानेष्यति शत्रुभ्यो बन्दीमिव जयश्रियम् ॥ ५२ ॥

गोप्तारमिति ॥ सुरसैन्यानां देवतासेनानां गोप्तारं रक्षितारं यं सेनान्यं पुरस्कृत्य पुरोधाय ॥ ' पुरोऽव्ययम् ' इति गतित्वात् ' नमस्पुरसोर्गत्योः ' इति सकारः । गां पृथ्वीं त्रायन्ते इति गोत्रास्तान्भिनत्तीति गोत्रभित् इन्द्रः जयश्रियं बन्दीमिव बन्दीकृतां स्त्रियमिव शत्रुभ्यः सकाशात् प्रत्यानेष्यति प्रत्याहरिष्यति । तं स्रष्टुमिति पूर्वेण संबन्धः ॥

वचस्यवसिते तस्मिन्ससर्ज गिरमात्मभूः ।
गर्जितानन्तरां वृष्टिं सौभाग्येन जिगाय सा ॥ ५३ ॥

वचसीति ॥ तस्मिन् बार्हस्पत्ये वचसि अवसिते परिसमाप्ते सति आत्मभूः ब्रह्मा गिरं वाचं ससर्ज जगादेत्यर्थः । सा गीः सौभाग्येन मनोहरत्वेन । हृद्भगसिन्ध्वन्ते पूर्वपदस्य च ' इत्युभयपदवृद्धिः । [गर्जितानन्तरां] गर्जिताद्गर्जितस्य वानन्तरं प्रवृत्तां वृष्टिं जिगाय जितवती । गर्जितपरत्वाद्वृष्टेरिव तद्विज्ञापनफलत्वाद्गिरः सुभगत्वमिति भावः ॥

संपत्स्यते वः कामोऽयं कालः कश्चित्प्रतीक्ष्यताम् ।
न त्वस्य सिद्धौ यास्यामि सर्गव्यापारमात्मना ॥ ५४ ॥

संपत्स्यत इति ॥ अयं वः युष्माकं कामः मनोरथः सेनानीरूपः संपत्स्यते सेत्स्यति । कश्चित् कियानपि कालः प्रतीक्ष्यताम् । तु किं तु अस्य सेनान्यः सिद्धौ विषये आत्मना स्वयं [सर्गव्यापारं] सर्गः सृष्टिरेव व्यापारस्तं न यास्यामि । नाहं स्रक्ष्यामीत्यर्थः ॥

कुत इत्याशङ्क्याह—

इतः स दैत्यः प्राप्तश्रीर्नेत एवार्हति क्षयम् ।
विषवृक्षोऽपि संवर्ध्य स्वयं छेत्तुमसांप्रतम् ॥ ५५ ॥

इत इति ॥ इतः मत्त एव प्राप्तश्रीः लब्धोदयः स दैत्यः तारकासुरः इतः

१ सुर०. २ व्यपरतें. ३ तस्य. ४ या. ५ न कामो वः कालोयं तु (यत्नु) प्र०. ६ सिद्धये.

मत्त एव **क्षयं** नाशं **न अर्हति** । तथा हि—अन्यो वृक्षस्तावदास्ताम् । विषस्य वृक्षः **विषवृक्षः अपि संवर्ध्य** कुतश्चित्कारणात्सम्यग्वर्धयित्वा **स्वयं छेत्तुम् असांप्रतम्** अनर्हः । असांप्रतमित्यनेन निपातेनाभिहितत्वाद् वृक्ष इति द्वितीयान्तो न भवति अनभिहिते कर्मणि द्वितीयाभिधानात् । यथाह वामनः—'निपातेनाप्यभिहिते कर्मणि न कर्मविभक्तिः । परिगणनस्य प्रायिकत्वात्' इति ॥

वृतं तेनेदमेव प्राक्मया चास्मै प्रतिश्रुतम् ।
वरेण शमितं लोकानलं दग्धुं हि तत्तपः ॥ ५६ ॥

वृतमिति ॥ **प्राक्** पूर्वं **तेन** असुरेण **इदमेव** देवैरवध्यत्वमेव **वृतं** प्रार्थितम् । **मया च अस्मै** तारकाय **प्रतिश्रुतं** प्रतिज्ञातम् ॥ 'प्रत्याङ्भ्यां श्रुवः पूर्वस्य कर्ता' इति संप्रदानत्वाच्चतुर्थी ॥ कर्तव्यं चैतदित्याह—**लोकान्दग्धुम् अलं** शक्तम् , 'पर्याप्तिवचनेष्वलमर्थेषु' इति तुमुन्प्रत्ययः । तस्य तपः **तत्तपः वरेण** वरदानेन **शमितं हि** । मयेति शेषः ॥

संयुगे सांयुगीनं तमुद्यन्तं प्रसहेत कः ।
अंशादृते निषिक्तस्य नीललोहितरेतसः ॥ ५७ ॥

संयुग इति ॥ **संयुगे** युद्धे **उद्यन्तं** व्याप्रियमाणम् । संयुगे साधुं **सांयुगीनम्** । 'प्रतिजनादिभ्यः खञ्' इति खञ्प्रत्ययः ॥ **तं** तारकं **निषिक्तस्य** क्वचित्क्षेत्रे क्षारितस्य । [**नीललोहितरेतसः**] 'नीलः कण्ठे लोहितश्च केशेष्विति नीललोहित इति पुराणम् ।' इति स्वामी । तस्य नीललोहितस्य धूर्जटे रेतसः शुक्रस्य **अंशाद् ऋते** अंशं विना अन्यः **कः प्रसहेत** अभिभवेत् ॥ 'प्रसहनमभिभवः' इति वृत्तिकारः ॥

कथमसावीदृक्शक्तिरित्याह—

स हि देवः परं ज्योतिस्तमःपारे व्यवस्थितम् ।
परिच्छिन्नप्रभावर्द्धिर्न मया न च विष्णुना ॥ ५८ ॥

स इति ॥ **स देवः** नीललोहितः [**तमःपारे**] तमसः पारे परतः **व्यवस्थितं** तमोगुणातीतं **परं ज्योतिः** परमात्मा **हि** । अत एव **मया परिच्छिन्नप्रभावर्द्धिः** अवगाढमहिमातिशयः **न** भवति तथा **विष्णुना च न** । अतस्तस्यासाध्यं नास्तीत्यर्थः ॥

संप्रति तदंशोत्पत्तावुपायं दर्शयति—

उमारूपेण ते यूयं संयमस्तिमितं मनः ।
शंभोर्यतध्वमाक्रष्टुमयस्कान्तेन लोहवत् ॥ ५९ ॥

उमेति ॥ **ते** कार्यार्थिनः **यूयं संयमस्तिमितं** समाधिनिश्चलं **शंभोः मनः उमारूपेण** उमासौन्दर्येण । 'रूपं स्वभावे सौन्दर्ये नाणके पशुशब्दयोः । ग्रन्थावृत्तौ

---

१ वृतस्ते...वाह. २ अशमितः शमितुम्. ३ सम्मुखीनं. ४ दधतं, डम्रद. ५ निषिक्तात् तु. ६ प्रतिष्ठितम्.

ना ।काादावाकारश्लोकयोरपि ॥' इति विश्वः ॥ **अयस्कान्तेन** मणिविशेषेण । 'कस्कादिषु च' इति सकारः । **लोहवत्** अयोधातुमिव । 'तेन तुल्यं क्रिया चेद्वतिः' इति वतिप्रत्ययो मृग्यः । **आक्रष्टुम्** आहर्तुं **यतध्वम्** उद्युक्ता भवत ॥

उभे एव क्षमे वोढुमुभयोर्बीजमाहितम् ।
सा वा शंभोस्तदीया वा मूर्तिर्जलमयी मम ॥ ६० ॥

उभे इति ॥ **उभयोः** शंभोर्मम च **आहितं** निषिक्तं **बीजं** तेजः **वोढुं सा वा** उमा **शंभोः** अष्टमूर्तेः तस्य इयं **तदीया जलमयी मूर्तिः वा मम** । **उभे एव क्षमे** । न तृतीयेत्यर्थः ॥ वाशब्दो द्वन्द्वार्थे, न त्वन्यार्थे । एतदेवोदाहृत्येत्थमेव व्याख्यातं गणव्याख्याने ॥ अत्र दीपकालंकारः प्राकरणिकयोरुमामहेश्वरयोरप्राकरणिकयोर्ब्रह्मजलमूर्त्योश्चौपम्यस्य गम्यत्वात । यथाह भोजराजः—'प्रस्तुतानामप्रस्तुतानां चौपम्यस्य गम्यत्वे दीपकम्' इति ॥ न चेयं तुल्ययोगिता तस्याः केवलप्रस्तुतविषयत्वेन केवलाप्रस्तुतविषयत्वेन चोत्थानादिति ॥

तस्यात्मा शितिकण्ठस्य सैनापत्यमुपेत्य वः ।
मोक्ष्यते सुरबन्दीनां वेणीर्वीर्यविभूतिभिः ॥ ६१ ॥

तस्येति ॥ **तस्य शितिकण्ठस्य** अष्टमूर्तेः **आत्मा** । पुत्र इत्यर्थः ॥ 'आत्मा वै पुत्रनामासि' इति श्रुतेः । **वः** युष्माकं सेनापतेर्भावः **सैनापत्यम्** ॥ 'पत्यन्त-पुरोहितादिभ्यो यक्' इति यक्प्रत्ययः । **उपेत्य** प्राप्य **वीर्यविभूतिभिः** शौर्यसंपत्तिभिः **सुरबन्दीनां वेणीः मोक्ष्यते** विस्रंसयिष्यति ॥ तारकासुरं हनिष्यतीति भावः ॥

इति व्याहृत्य विबुधान्विश्वयोनिस्तिरोदधे ।
मनस्याहितकर्तव्यास्तेऽपि देवा दिवं ययुः ॥ ६२ ॥

इतीति ॥ [**विश्वयोनिः**] विश्वस्य योनिः कारणम् ॥ 'योनिः स्त्रीणां भगस्थाने कारणे ताम्रिके पणे ।' इति वैजयन्ती । **विबुधान्** सुरान् **इति व्याहृत्य** अभिधाय **तिरोदधे** अन्तर्हितवान् । **ते देवाः अपि मनसि** [**आहितकर्तव्याः**] आहितं कर्तव्यं यैस्ते तथोक्ताः सन्तः **दिवं** स्वर्गं **ययुः** प्रापुः ॥

तत्र निश्चित्य कन्दर्पमगमत्पाकशासनः ।
मनसा कार्यसंसिद्धौ त्वराद्विगुणरंहसा ॥ ६३ ॥

तत्रेति ॥ [**पाकशासनः**] पाको नाम कश्चिदसुरस्तस्य शासन इन्द्रः **तत्र** हरचित्ताकर्षणकृत्ये **कन्दर्पं निश्चित्य** । साधकत्वेनेति शेषः ॥ **कार्यसंसिद्धौ** [**त्वराद्विगुणरंहसा**] त्वरयौत्सुक्येन द्वौ गुणौ यस्य तद्विगुणं द्विरावृत्तं रंहो वेगो यस्य तेन तथोक्तेन । 'गुणस्तु वृत्तिशब्दादिज्येन्द्रियामुख्यतन्तुषु' इति वैजयन्ती ॥ **मनसा अगमत** । सस्मारेत्यर्थः। गमेर्लुङ् । लृदित्वाच्च्लेरङादेशः ॥

---

१ सोढुम्. २ वीर्यं, ३ सेनापत्यम्. ४ वेणिबन्धानदूषितान्. ५ प्रतिययुर्दिवम्. ६ कर्म-कार्य-संसिद्धि-, कार्यसंसिद्धये.

अथ स ललितयोषिद्भ्रूलताचारुशृङ्गं
रतिवलयपदाङ्के चापमासज्य कण्ठे।
सहचरमधुहस्तन्यस्तचूताङ्करास्त्रः
शतमखमुपतस्थे प्राञ्जलिः पुष्पधन्वा ॥ ६४ ॥

अथेति ॥ **अथ** स्मरणानन्तरम्। **सः** स्मृत इत्यर्थः। पुष्पं धनुर्यस्य स **पुष्पधन्वा** कामः। 'वा संज्ञायाम्' इत्यनङ्। [**ललितयोषिद्भ्रूलताचारुशृङ्गं**] 'ललितं त्रिषु सुन्दरम्' इत्यमरः। ललितायाः सुन्दर्या योषितो भ्रुवौ लते इव चारुणी शृङ्गे कोटी यस्य तत्तथोक्तं **चापम्**। [**रतिवलयपदाङ्के**] रतिः स्मरप्रिया। 'रतिः स्मरप्रिया' इत्यमरः। तस्या वलयपदानि कङ्कणस्थानान्यङ्काश्चिह्नं यस्य तथोक्ते **कण्ठे आसज्य** लगयित्वा ॥ चापकण्ठविशेषणाभ्यां शृङ्गारैकनिधेस्त्रिभुवनैकवीरस्य शृङ्गारवीरोपकरणेषु तुल्यरसत्वं व्यज्यते। [**सहचरमधुहस्तन्यस्तचूताङ्कुरास्त्रः**] सहचरस्य सख्युर्मधोर्वसन्तस्य हस्ते न्यस्तं चूताङ्कुरमेवास्त्रं यस्य स तथोक्तः। **प्राञ्जलिः** सन्। **शतमखम् इन्द्रं उपतस्थे** संगतवान् ॥ संगतिकरणार्थादात्मनेपदम् ॥ अत्र स्वभावोक्तिः—'स्वभावोक्तिरसौ चारु यथावद्वस्तुवर्णनम्।' इति ॥ मालिनीवृत्तमेतत्—'ननमयययुतेयं मालिनी भोगिलोकैः।' इति तल्लक्षणात् ॥

इति श्रीमन्महामहोपाध्यायकोलाचलमल्लिनाथसूरिविरचितया संजीवनीसमाख्यया व्याख्यया समेतः श्रीकालिदासकृतौ कुमारसंभवे महाकाव्ये ब्रह्मसाक्षात्कारो नाम द्वितीयः सर्गः ॥

तृतीयः सर्गः।

तस्मिन्मघोनस्त्रिदशान्विहाय सहस्रमक्ष्णां युगपत्पपात।
प्रयोजनापेक्षितया प्रभूणां प्रायश्चलं गौरवमाश्रितेषु ॥ १ ॥

तस्मिन्निति ॥ **मघोनः** इन्द्रस्य **अक्ष्णां सहस्रं** त्रिरावृत्ता दश परिमाणमेषामिति **त्रिदशान्** देवान्। 'संख्ययाव्ययासन्नादूराधिकसंख्याः संख्येये' इति बहुव्रीहिः। 'बहुव्रीहौ संख्येये'—इति डच्प्रत्ययः। उक्तार्थत्वात्सुचो निवृत्तिः। **विहाय** त्यक्त्वा **तस्मिन्** कामे **युगपत् पपात**। सहस्रेणाक्षिभिरद्राक्षीदित्यादरातिशयोक्तिः। ननु सुचिरपरिचितानेकसुरपरित्यागेन भगवतो महेन्द्रस्य कथमकाण्डे तस्मिन्नेकस्मिन्पक्षपात इत्याशङ्कयार्थान्तरं न्यस्यति—**प्रायः** भूम्ना **प्रभूणाम् आश्रितेषु** सेवकेषु विषये **गौरवं** आदरः **प्रयोजनापेक्षितया** कार्यार्थित्वेन हेतुना **चलं** चञ्चलम्। फलतन्त्राः प्रभवो न तु गुणतन्त्रा इति भावः ॥

---

१ सुललित. २ शार्ङ्गम्. ३ आसाद्य. ४ पुष्पकेतुः. ५ ब्रह्माभिगमनः. ६ तंऽपि.

स वासवेनासनसंनिकृष्टमितो निषीदेति विसृष्टभूमिः ।
भर्तुः प्रसादं प्रतिनन्द्य मूर्ध्ना वक्तुं मिथः प्राक्रमतैवमेनम् ॥२॥

स इति ॥ **स** कामः **वासवेन** इन्द्रेण आसनस्य सिंहासनस्य संनिकृष्टं संनिहितम् **आसनसंनिकृष्टं** यथा तथा ॥ शेषषष्ठ्यायं समासः कृद्योगलक्षणया तु न । 'न लोकाव्ययनिष्ठाखलर्थतृनाम्' इति षष्ठीनिषेधात् ॥ **इतः निषीद** इहोपविश **इति विसृष्टभूमिः** दत्तावकाशः सन् । **भर्तुः** स्वामिनः **प्रसादम्** अनुग्रहं **मूर्ध्ना प्रतिनन्द्य** संभाव्य **मिथः** रहसि ॥ 'मिथोऽन्योन्यं रहस्यपि ।' इत्यमरः ॥ **एनम्** इन्द्रम् **एवं** वक्ष्यमाणप्रकारेण **वक्तुं प्राक्रमत** उपक्रान्तवान् ॥ 'प्रोपाभ्यां समर्थाभ्याम्' इत्यात्मनेपदम् ॥

आज्ञापय ज्ञातविशेष पुंसां लोकेषु यत्ते करणीयमस्ति ।
अनुग्रहं संस्मरणप्रवृत्तमिच्छामि संवर्धितमाज्ञया ते ॥ ३ ॥

आज्ञापयेति ॥ हे **पुंसां ज्ञातविशेष** ज्ञातसार । ज्ञातपुंविशेषेत्यर्थः । सापेक्षत्वेऽपि गमकत्वात्समासः ॥ **आज्ञापय** । तदिति शेषः । उत्तरवाक्ये यच्छब्दप्रयोगान्न पूर्ववाक्ये तच्छब्दप्रयोगनिर्बन्धः ॥ किं तदित्याह—**लोकेषु ते** तव **यत् करणीयं** कर्तव्यम् **अस्ति** । [**संस्मरणप्रवृत्तं**] संस्मरणेन प्रवृत्तं उत्पन्नं **ते** तव **अनुग्रहं** प्रसादम् **आज्ञया** नियोगेन **संवर्धितं** वृद्धिं गमितम् **इच्छामि** । संस्मरणकृतमनुग्रहं केनचिन्नियोगेन वर्धय । क्वचित्कर्मणि नियुङ्क्ष्वेत्यर्थः । अन्यथा मे नास्ति परितोष इति भावः ॥ तुमुन्नन्तपाठे णिजर्थे यत्नः कार्यः ॥

न च मे किंचिदसाध्यमस्तीत्याह—

केनाभ्यसूया पदकाङ्क्षिणा ते नितान्तदीर्घैर्जनिता तपोभिः ।
यावद्भवत्याहितसायकस्य मत्कार्मुकस्यास्य निदेशवर्ती ॥४॥

केनेति ॥ **पदकाङ्क्षिणा** राज्यकामेन **केन** पुंसा **नितान्तदीर्घैः** अतिप्रभूतैः **तपोभिः ते** तव **अभ्यसूया** ईर्ष्या **जनिता** । ब्रूहीति शेषः । किमर्थम् । **यावत्** यतः स भवद्वैरी **आहितसायकस्य** संहितबाणस्य **अस्य मत्कार्मुकस्य** निदेशे वर्तत इति **निदेशवर्ती** आज्ञावशः **भवति** । अविलम्बेनैव भविष्यतीत्यर्थः । 'वर्तमानसामीप्ये वर्तमानवद्वा' इति लट् ॥

संप्रति चतुर्वर्गे मोक्षमधिकृत्याह—

असंमतः कस्तव मुक्तिमार्गं पुनर्भवक्लेशभयात्प्रपन्नः ।
बद्धश्चिरं तिष्ठतु सुन्दरीणामारेचितभ्रूचतुरैः कटाक्षैः ॥ ५ ॥

असंमत इति ॥ **तव असंमतः कः** [**पुनर्भवक्लेशभयात्**] पुनर्भवः पुनरुत्पत्तिः । संसार इति यावत् । तत्र ये क्लेशा जन्मजरामरणादयस्तेभ्यो भयात् **मुक्तिमार्गं प्रपन्नः**

---

१ विसृष्ट. २ प्रतिवन्द्य–पद्य. ३ तैरुप. ४ संवर्धितुम्. ५ फल. ६ तावत्. ७ कामिनीनां ८ आरोपित. ९ ललितैः. १० विलासैः

तं वद। यतः सोऽपि [**आरेचितभ्रूचतुरैः**] आरेचिताभिरेकैकशो विवर्तिताभिर्भ्रूभिश्चतुरैः **सुन्दरीणां कटाक्षैः बद्धः चिरं तिष्ठतु**। आरेचितलक्षणं तु—'स्याद्भ्रुवोर्ललिताक्षेपादेकस्या एव रेचितम्। तयोर्मूलसमुत्क्षेपं कौटिल्याद् भ्रूकुटिं विदुः॥' इति॥

धर्मार्थावधिकृत्याह—

अध्यापितस्योशनसापि नीतिं प्रयुक्तरागप्रणिधिर्द्विषस्ते।
कस्यार्थधर्मौ वद पीडयामि सिन्धोस्तटावोघ इव प्रवृद्धः॥६॥

अध्यापितस्येति॥ **उशनसा** शुक्रेण **नीतिं** नीतिशास्त्रम् **अध्यापितस्य अपि**। अपिशब्दाच्छुक्रशिष्याणामप्रधृष्यत्वं गम्यते। 'गतिबुद्धि—' इत्यादिना द्विकर्मकादिङ्धातोर्ण्यन्तात्प्रधाने कर्मणि क्तः। 'अप्रधाने दुहादीनां ण्यन्ते कर्तुश्च कर्मणः' इति वचनात्। **ते द्विषः** तव शत्रोः **कस्य अर्थधर्मौ** [**प्रयुक्तरागप्रणिधिः**] प्रयुक्तः प्रहितो रागो विषयाभिलाष एव प्रणिधिर्दूतो येन सोऽहम्। 'प्रणिधिः प्रार्थने चरे' इति यादवः। **प्रवृद्धः ओघः** प्रवाहः **सिन्धोः** नद्याः **तटौ इव पीडयामि वद**॥

काममधिकृत्याह—

कामैकपत्नीव्रतदुःखशीलां लोलं मनश्चारुतया प्रविष्टाम्।
नितम्बिनीमिच्छसि मुक्तलज्जां कण्ठे स्वयंग्राहनिषक्तबाहुम्॥७॥

कामिति॥ [**एकपत्नीव्रतदुःखशीलां**] एकः पतिर्यस्याः सैकपत्नी पतिव्रता। 'नित्यं सपत्न्यादिषु' इति ङीप्। तस्या व्रतं पातिव्रत्यं तेन दुःखशीलां दुःखस्वभावाम्। दृढव्रतामित्यर्थः। 'शीलं स्वभावे सद्वृत्ते' इत्यमरः। **चारुतया** सुन्दरत्वेन हेतुना **लोलं मनः** त्वच्चित्तं **प्रविष्टां कां नितम्बिनीं** नारीं **मुक्तलज्जां** सतीं **कण्ठे स्वयंग्राहनिषक्तबाहुम्**। स्वयं गृह्णातीति स्वयंग्राहा। 'विभाषा ग्रहः' इति णप्रत्ययः। न च जलचर एव ग्राह इति नियमो जलचरे ग्राह एवेति नियमादिति। स्वयंग्राहा च सा निषक्तबाहुश्च तां तथाभूताम् **इच्छसि**। त्वदर्थे पतिव्रतामपि व्रताद् भ्रंशयिष्यामीत्यर्थः। एतच्चेन्द्रस्य पारदारिकत्वादुक्तम्। तथा च श्रुतिः—'अहल्यायै जारः' इति॥

त्रिविधा नायिका। स्वकीया परकीया साधारणी चेति। तत्र परकीयां प्रत्युक्तम्। इतरे प्रत्याह—

कयासि कामिन्सुरतापराधात्पादानतः कोपनयाऽवधूतः।
तस्याः करिष्यामि दृढानुतापं प्रवालशय्याशरणं शरीरम्॥८॥

कयेति॥ हे **कामिन्** कामुक **सुरतापराधात्**। अन्यासङ्गादित्यर्थः। **पादानतः** प्रणतः सन्। **कोपनया** कोपनशीलया **कया** स्त्रिया **अवधूतः** तिरस्कृतः **असि**। **तस्याः शरीरं दृढानुतापं** गाढपश्चात्तापमत एव **प्रवालशय्याशरणं करिष्यामि** इति॥

---

१ प्रणिधेः. २ यानि. ३ पत्नीम्. ४ विलम्बिनीम्. ५ विषक्त. ६ सहसापराध:-धात्. ७ यस्याः.

प्रसीद विश्राम्यतु वीर वज्रं शरैर्मदीयैः कतमः सुरारिः ।
बिभेतु मोघीकृतबाहुवीर्यः स्त्रीभ्योऽपि कोपस्फुरिताधराभ्यः ॥ ९ ॥

प्रसीदेति ॥ हे **वीर प्रसीद** प्रसन्नो भव । **वज्रं** कुलिशं **विश्राम्यतु** । उदास्तामित्यर्थः । **मदीयैः शरैः मोघीकृतबाहुवीर्यः** विफलीकृतभुजशक्तिः **कतमः** दैत्यदानवादिषु यः कश्चन **सुरारिः** ॥ 'वा बहूनां जातिपरिप्रश्ने डतमच्' इति डतमच्प्रत्ययः ॥ [**कोपस्फुरिताधराभ्यः**] कोपेन स्फुरिताधराभ्यः **स्त्रीभ्योऽपि बिभेतु** । किमु वक्तव्यं पुंभ्य इत्यर्थः । सकृद्भीतः सर्वतो बिभेतीति भावः । भीत्रार्थानां 'भयहेतुः' इत्यपादानत्वात्पञ्चमी ॥

तव प्रसादात्कुसुमायुधोऽपि सहायमेकं मधुमेव लब्ध्वा ।
कुर्यां हरस्यापि पिनाकपाणेर्धैर्यच्युतिं के मम धन्विनोऽन्ये १०

तवेति ॥ किं बहुना । **तव प्रसादात्** अनुग्रहात् **कुसुमायुधोऽपि** अतिदुर्बलास्त्रोऽप्यहम् **एकं** मधुं वसन्तम् **एव सहायं लब्ध्वा** [**पिनाकपाणेः**] पिनाकः पाणौ यस्य स पिनाकपाणिः । 'प्रहरणार्थेभ्यः परे निष्ठासप्तम्यौ ।' तस्य **हरस्यापि** । हरः पिनाकी चेत्यतिदारुण इति भावः । **धैर्यच्युतिं** धैर्यहानिं **कुर्याम्** । कर्तुं शक्नुयामित्यर्थः । 'शकि लिङ् च' इति शक्यार्थे लिङ् । **अन्ये धन्विनः** धनुर्भृतः **मम के** । न केऽपि इत्यर्थः । किंशब्दः कुत्सायाम् । 'कुत्साप्रश्नवितर्केषु क्षेपे किंशब्द इष्यते' इति शाश्वतः ॥

अथोरुदेशादवतार्य पादमाक्रान्ति[1]संभावित[2]पादपीठम् ।
संकल्पितार्थे[3] विवृतात्मशक्तिराखण्डलः काममिदं बभाषे ॥ ११ ॥

अथेति ॥ अथ स्मरवाक्यश्रवणानन्तरम् । **आखण्डलः** सहस्राक्षः **ऊरुदेशात् पादम्** [**आक्रान्तिसंभावितपादपीठम्**] आक्रान्त्या आक्रमणेन संभावितं पादपीठं यस्मिंस्तद्यथा तथा **अवतार्य संकल्पितार्थे** हराचित्ताकर्षणरूपे विषये **विवृतात्मशक्तिम्** 'कुर्यां हरस्यापि'—इत्यादिना प्रकटीकृतस्वसामर्थ्यं **कामं** स्मरम् **इदं** वक्ष्यमाणं **बभाष** ॥

सर्वं सखे त्वय्युपपन्नमेतदुभे ममास्त्रे कुलिशं भवांश्च ।
वज्रं[4] तपोवीर्यमहत्सु कुण्ठं त्वं सर्वतोगामि च साधकं च ॥ १२ ॥

सर्वमिति ॥ हे **सखे** । सखे इति संबोधनं गौरवार्थम् । **सर्वमेतत् त्वयि उपपन्नं** सिद्धम् । **मम कुलिशं** वज्रं **भवान् च उभे अस्त्रे** । तत्र **वज्रं** [**तपोवीर्यमहत्सु**] तपोवीर्येण तपोबलेन महत्सु प्रबलेषु **कुण्ठं** प्रतिबद्धप्रसरम् । **त्वम्** अस्त्रं **सर्वतोगामि च साधकं च** । तापसेष्वप्यकुण्ठमित्यर्थः ॥

अवैमि ते सारमतः खलु त्वां कार्ये गुरुण्यात्मसमं नियोक्ष्ये ।
व्यादिश्यते भूधरतामवेक्ष्य कृष्णेन देहोद्वहनाय शेषः ॥ १३ ॥

---

१ आक्रान्त. २ संभावितपादपीठं. ३ संकल्पिते. ४ पूर्वं.

अवैमीति ॥ हे सखे **ते सारं** बलम् **अवैमि** वेद्मि । **अतः खलु** अत एव **आत्मसमं** मत्तुल्यं **त्वां गुरुणि** महति **कार्ये** 'तस्मै हिमाद्रेः—(३।१६) इति वक्ष्यमाणे **नियोक्ष्ये** । 'स्वराद्यन्तोपसर्गादिति वक्तव्यम्' इति वार्तिकादात्मनेपदनियमः । तथा हि । सारपरीक्षापूर्वक एव सर्वत्र नियोग इत्याह—**कृष्णेन** विष्णुना ध तीति धरः पचाद्यच् । भुवो धरो भूधरस्तस्य भावस्तत्तां **भूधरताम्** । भूधरणशक्तिमित्यर्थः । अवेक्ष्य ज्ञात्वा शेषः सर्पराजो **देहोद्वहनाय** स्वदेहमुद्वोढुम् । 'क्रियार्थोपपदस्य—' इत्यादिना चतुर्थी । **व्यादिश्यते** नियुज्यते । शेषशायी हि भगवान् ॥

नियोगाङ्गीकारं सिद्धवत्कर्तुमाह—

आशंसता बाणगतिं वृषाङ्के कार्यं त्वया नः प्रतिपन्नकल्पम् ।
निबोध यज्ञांशभुजामिदानीमुच्चैर्द्विषामीप्सितमेतदेव ॥ १४ ॥

आशंसतेति ॥ **वृषाङ्के** हरे **बाणगति** बाणप्रसरम् **आशंसता** कथयता । 'कुर्यां हरस्यापि पिनाकपाणेः' (३।१०) इत्यादिनेति शेषः । **त्वया नः** अस्माकं **कार्यं प्रतिपन्नकल्पम्** अङ्गीकृतप्रायम् । 'ईषदसमाप्तौ'—इत्यादिना कल्पप्प्रत्ययः । कथमेतदत आह—**इदानीं** उच्चैः उन्नता द्विषो येषां तेषाम् **उच्चैर्द्विषां यज्ञांशभुजां** देवानाम् । एतेन द्विषल्लुप्तयज्ञभागत्वं सूच्यते । **ईप्सितम्** आप्तुमिष्टम् **एतदेव** हरेः बाणप्रयोगरूपमेव **निबोध** हरायत्तं बुध्यस्वेत्यर्थः । 'बुध बोधने' इति धातोर्लोट् । अत्र आशंसता प्रार्थयमानेन इति नाथव्याख्यानमनाथव्याख्यानम् । आङ्पूर्वयोः शास्तिशंसत्योरिच्छार्थत्वे आत्मनेपदनियमात् । याच्ञार्थत्वस्याप्रामाणिकत्वात् 'कुर्यां हरस्यापि'—(३।१०) इत्यत्रानयोरभावादयोगाच्चेति ॥

किं तत्कार्यं कथं वा तस्य हरायत्तत्वं कुतो वा मदपेक्षेत्यत्राह—

अमी हि वीर्यप्रभवं भवस्य जयाय सेनान्यमुशन्ति देवाः ।
स च त्वदेकेषुनिपातसाध्यो ब्रह्माङ्गभूर्ब्रह्मणि योजितात्मा ॥ १५ ॥

अमी हीति ॥ **हि** यस्मात् **अमी देवाः जयाय** शत्रुजयार्थं **भवस्य** हरस्य **वीर्यप्रभवं** तेजःसंभूतं **सेनान्यं** सेनापतिम् **उशन्ति** कामयन्ते । 'वश कान्तौ' इति धातोर्लट् । ब्रह्मणां सद्योजातादिमन्त्राणामङ्गानां हृदयादिमन्त्राणां भूः स्थानं **ब्रह्माङ्गभूः** । कृतमन्त्रन्यास इत्यर्थः । **ब्रह्मणि** निजतत्त्वे । 'वेदस्तत्त्वं तपो ब्रह्म ।' इत्युभयत्राप्यमरः । **योजितात्मा** नियमितचित्तः । मन्त्रन्यासपूर्वं ब्रह्म ध्यायन्नित्यर्थः । **स** भवः **च** [**त्वदेकेषुनिपातसाध्यः**] त्वदेकेषोस्तवैकबाणस्य निपातेन साध्यः । अनन्यसाध्योऽयमस्मिन्नवसर इति भावः ॥

तस्मै हिमाद्रेः प्रयतां तनूजां यतात्मने रोचयितुं यतस्व ।
योषित्सु तद्वीर्यनिषेकभूमिः सैव क्षमेत्यात्मभुवोपदिष्टम् ॥ १६ ॥

---

१ यज्ञाङ्ग. २ मुच्चैस्तरामीप्सितमर्थमत्र. ३ अर्थमत्र. ४ हरस्य ५ हार्यः. ६ ब्रह्मनियोजितात्मा. ७ जितात्मने.

तस्मा इति ॥ **यतात्मने** नियतचित्ताय **तस्मै** भवाय । ' रुच्यर्थानां प्रीयमाणः ' इति संप्रदानत्वाच्चतुर्थी । **प्रयतां हिमाद्रेस्तनूजां** पार्वतीं **रोचयितुं यतस्व** । भवितव्यं चात्र पार्वत्यैवेत्याह-**योषित्सु** स्त्रीषु मध्ये । ' यतश्च निर्धारणम् ' इति सप्तमी । **क्षमा** शक्ता [**तद्वीर्यनिषेकभूमिः**] तस्य हरस्य वीर्यं रेतः तस्य निषेकः क्षरणं तस्य भूमिः क्षेत्रं **सा** पार्वती **एव इति आत्मभुवा** ब्रह्मणा **उपदिष्टम्** । ' उभे एव क्षमे वोढुम् ' (२।६०) इत्यादिनोक्तमित्यर्थः ॥

सापीदानीं संनिकृष्टैव तस्येत्याह—

गुरोर्नियोगाच्च नगेन्द्रकन्या स्थाणुं तपस्यन्तमधित्यकायाम् ।
अन्वास्त इत्यप्सरसां मुखेभ्यः श्रुतं मया मत्प्रणिधिः स वर्गः ॥ १७

गुरोरिति ॥ **नगेन्द्रकन्या** पार्वती **च गुरोः** पितुः **नियोगात्** शासनात् **अधित्यकायां** हिमाद्रेरूर्ध्वभूमौ । ' भूमिरूर्ध्वमधित्यका ' इत्यमरः । ' उपाधिभ्यां त्यकन्नास-न्नारूढयोः ' इति त्यकन्प्रत्ययः । **तपस्यन्तं** तपश्चरन्तम् । ' कर्मणो रोमन्थतपोभ्यां वर्तिचरोः ' इति क्यङ्प्रत्ययः । ततः शतृप्रत्ययः । **स्थाणुं** रुद्रम् **अन्वास्ते** उपास्त इत्यर्थः । **इति इदं मया अप्सरसां मुखेभ्यः श्रुतम्** । न चैतदैतिह्यमात्र-मित्याह—**स वर्गः** सोऽप्सरसां गणः **मत्प्रणिधिः** मम गूढचरः । ' प्रणिधिः प्रार्थने चरे ' इति यादवः ॥

तद्गच्छ सिद्ध्यै कुरु देवकार्यमर्थोऽयमर्थान्तरभाव्य[2] एव ।
अपेक्षते प्रत्ययमुत्तमं[3] त्वां बीजाङ्कुरः प्रागुदयादिवाम्भः ॥ १८ ॥

तदिति ॥ **तत्** तस्मात् **सिद्ध्यै** कार्यसिद्ध्यर्थं **गच्छ** । **देवकार्यं कुरु** । आशिषि लोट् ॥ **अयमर्थः** प्रयोजनम् **अर्थान्तरभाव्यः** कारणान्तरसाध्यः **एव** । तच्च कारणान्तरं पार्वतीसंनिधानमिति भावः । 'अर्थः प्रकारे विषये वित्तकारणवस्तुषु । अभि-धेये च शब्दानां वृत्तौ चापि प्रयोजने ॥ ' इति विश्वः ॥ तथापि बीजसाध्यः अङ्कुरः **बीजाङ्कुरः उदयात्** उत्पत्तेः **प्राक् अम्भः इव त्वाम् उत्तमं प्रत्ययं** चरमं कार-णम् **अपेक्षते** ॥ ' प्रत्ययोऽधीनशपथज्ञानविश्वासहेतुषु । ' इत्यमरः । तस्मादस्मिन्नर्थे तत्र चरमसहकारित्वादनन्यसाध्योऽयमर्थ इति भावः ॥

तस्मिन्[4]सुराणां विजयाभ्युपाये तवैव नामास्त्रगतिः[5] कृती त्वम् ।
अप्यप्रसिद्धं यशसे हि पुंसामनन्यसाधारणमेव कर्म ॥ १९ ॥

तस्मिन्निति ॥ **सुराणां विजयाभ्युपाये** जयस्योपायभूते **तस्मिन्** हरे **अस्त्र-गतिः** अस्त्रप्रसरः **तव एव नाम** ॥ नामेति संभावनायाम् । अन्येषां तु संभावनापि नास्तीति भावः । अतः **त्वं कृती** कृतमस्यास्तीति कृती कृतार्थः । तथा हि । **अप्रसिद्धम् अपि अनन्यसाधारणम् एव कर्म पुंसां यशसे हि** । इदं तु प्रसिद्धमसाधारणं चेत्यतियशस्करमिति भावः ॥

---

१ अध्यास्त. २ लभ्य. ३ प्रत्ययसङ्गलब्धां. ४ अस्मिन्. ५ काम.

प्रोत्साहनार्थं स्तौति—

सुराः समभ्यर्थयितार एते कार्यं त्रयाणामपि विष्टपानाम् ।
चापेन ते कर्म न चातिहिंस्रमहो बतासि स्पृहणीयवीर्यः ॥२०॥

सुरा इति ॥ **एते सुराः समभ्यर्थयितारः** याचितारः । **कार्यं** प्रयोजनं **त्रयाणां विष्टपानामपि** संबन्धि । सर्वलोकार्थमित्यर्थः । **कर्म ते** तव **चापेन** । न त्वन्येनेति भावः । **अतिहिंस्रम्** अतिघातुकं **च न** । **अहो बत** इति संबोधने । 'अहो बतानुकम्पायां खेदे संबोधनेऽपि च ।' इति विश्वः ॥ अथ वा अहो आश्चर्ये । बतेत्यामन्त्रणे संतोषे चेति । 'बतामन्त्रणसंतोषखेदानुक्रोशविस्मये ।' इति विश्वः । **स्पृहणीयवीर्यः असि** आश्चर्यविक्रमोऽसि ॥ 'आश्चर्यं स्पृहणीयं च' इति नानार्थकोशः ॥

मधुश्च ते मन्मथ साहचर्यादसावनुक्तोऽपि सहाय एव ।
समीरणो नोदयिता भवेति व्यादिश्यते केन हुताशनस्य ॥२१॥

मधुरिति ॥ हे **मन्मथ** । **असौ मधुः च** वसन्तोऽपि **ते साहचार्यात्** सहचरत्वात् **एव अनुक्तः अपि** अप्रेरितोऽपि **सहायः** सहकारी **एव** । तथा हि । **समीरणः** वायुः **हुताशनस्य** अग्नेः **नोदयिता** प्रेरकः **भव इति केन व्यादिश्यते** ॥ अत्र मधुसमीरणयोरुक्तिमन्तरेण सहायताकरणं सामान्यधर्मः । स च वाक्यद्वये वस्तुप्रतिवस्तुभावेन पृथग्निर्दिष्ट इति प्रतिवस्तूपमालंकारोऽयम् । तदुक्तम्—'यत्र सामान्यनिर्देशः पृथग्वाक्यद्वये यदि । गम्यौपम्याश्रिता सा स्यात्प्रतिवस्तूपमा मता ॥' इति ॥

तथेति शेषामिव[3] भर्तुराज्ञामादाय मूर्ध्ना मदनः प्रतस्थे ।
ऐरावतास्फालनकर्कशेन हस्तेन पस्पर्श तदङ्गमिन्द्रः ॥ २२ ॥

तथेति ॥ **तथा** अस्तु **इति भर्तुः** स्वामिनः **शेषाम् इव** प्रसाददत्तां मालामिव । 'प्रसादान्निजनिर्माल्यदाने शेषेति कीर्तिता ।' इति विश्वः ॥ 'माल्याक्षतादिदाने त्री शेषा' इति वैजयन्तीकेशवौ । **आज्ञां मूर्ध्ना आदाय** शिरसा गृहीत्वा **मदनः प्रतस्थे** । 'समवप्रविभ्यः स्थः' इत्यात्मनेपदम् । **इन्द्रः [ऐरावतास्फालनकर्कशेन]** ऐरावतास्फालनेन प्रोत्साहनार्थेन ताडनेन कर्कशेन परुषेण **हस्तेन तदङ्गं** मदनदेहं **पस्पर्श** । हस्तस्पर्शेन संभावयामासेत्यर्थः । शेषामिवाज्ञाम् इत्यत्र साधकबाधकप्रमाणाभावादुपमोत्प्रेक्षयोः संदेहसंकर इति । यदि भर्त्रा शेषापि दत्ता तदा तामाज्ञामिवेत्युपमा । अथ न दत्ता तर्हि शेषात्वेनोत्प्रेक्षिता । शेषादानं तु संदिग्धमिति ॥

स माधवेनाभिमतेन सख्या रत्या च साशङ्कमनुप्रयातः ।
अङ्गव्ययप्रार्थितकार्यसिद्धिः स्थाण्वाश्रमं हैमवतं जगाम ॥२३॥

---

१ यथा. २ समीरणश्चादयिता; प्रेरयिता. २१–२२ मध्ये क्षेपकोऽयं लभ्यते—
ततः स्फुरत्केसरलग्नभृङ्गां सौरभ्यसंक्रान्तदिगन्तरालाम् ।
ददौ हरिः सादरमीक्षमाणो मन्दारमालां मकरध्वजाय ॥
३ माला०. ४ दिग्वारणा. ५ कर्म.

स इति ॥ **स** मदनः **अभिमतेन** प्रियेण **सख्या** सुहृदा **माधवेन** वसन्तेन **रत्या** स्वदेव्या **च साशङ्कं** संकटमापतितमिति सभयम् **अनुप्रयातः** सन् । तथा [**अङ्गव्ययप्रार्थितकार्यसिद्धिः**] अङ्गस्य व्ययेनापि प्रार्थिता कार्यसिद्धिर्येन स तथोक्तः । शरीरं मृत्वापि सर्वथा देवकार्यं साधयिष्यामीति कृतनिश्चयः सन्नित्यर्थः । **हैमवत** हिमवति भवं [**स्थाण्वाश्रमं**] स्थाणो रुद्रस्याश्रमं **जगाम** ॥

तस्मिन्वने संयमिनां मुनीनां तपःसमाधेः प्रतिकूलवर्ती ।
संकल्पयोनेरभिमानभूतमात्मानमाधाय मधुर्जजृम्भे ॥ २४ ॥

तस्मिन्निति ॥ **तस्मिन्वने** स्थाण्वाश्रमे **संयमिनां** समाधिमतां **मुनीनां** [**तपःसमाधेः**] तपसः समाधेरेकाग्रतायाः प्रतिकूलं वर्तत इति **प्रतिकूलवर्ती** विरोधी **मधुः** वसंतः **संकल्पयोनेः** मनोभवस्य **अभिमानभूतम्** । गर्वहेतुभूतमित्यर्थः । कार्यकारणयोरभेदोपचारः । **आत्मानं** निजस्वरूपम् **आधाय** संनिधाय **जजृम्भे** प्रादुर्बभूव । वसन्तधर्मान् प्रवर्तयामसेत्यर्थः ॥

वसन्तधर्मानाह—

कुबेरगुप्तां दिशमुष्णरश्मौ गन्तुं प्रवृत्ते समयं विलङ्घ्य ।
दिग्दक्षिणा गन्धवहं मुखेन व्यलीकनिःश्वासमिवोत्ससर्ज ॥ २५ ॥

कुबेरेति ॥ **उष्णरश्मौ** सूर्ये साहसिके च नायके **समयं** दक्षिणायनकालं संगमकालं च **विलङ्घ्य** अकाण्डे व्यतिक्रम्य **कुबेरगुप्तां** धनपतिपालितां कुत्सितशरीरेण केनचिद्रक्षितां च **दिशम्** उदीचीं स्त्रीलिङ्गाक्षिप्तां कांचिन्नायिकां च **गन्तुं** चलितुं संगन्तुं च **प्रवृत्ते** सति **दक्षिणा दिक्** दाक्षिण्यवती नायिका च **मुखेन** अग्रभागेन वक्त्रेण च । वहतीति वहः । पचाद्यच् । गन्धस्य वहं **गन्धवहम्** अनिलं व्यलीकेन दुःखेन निःश्वासस्तं **व्यलीकनिःश्वासम् इव** । 'दुःखे वैलक्ष्ये व्यलीकमप्रियाकार्यवस्तुनोः ।' इति वैजयन्ती । **उत्ससर्ज** प्रवर्तयामास । स्वभर्तरि समयोल्लङ्घनेन पराङ्गनासंगतिं प्रवृत्ते सति स्त्रियो दाक्षिण्यादकिंचिद्वदा दुःखान्निश्वसन्तीति भावः । उत्तरायणे सति मलयानिलाः प्रवृत्ता इति वाक्यार्थः । अत्रोत्प्रेक्षालंकारः । न च समासोक्तिरेवेयमुत्प्रेक्षानुप्रविष्टेति शङ्कितव्यम् । केवलविशेषणसामर्थ्यादेवाप्रस्तुतप्रतीतौ सोक्तिष्ठते । अत्र तु दक्षिणेति विशेष्यसामर्थ्यादपि नायिका प्रतीयते । न च श्लेष एव प्रकृताप्रकृतविषयः उभयश्लेषे श्लिष्टविशेष्यानङ्गीकारात् । तस्माच्छब्दशक्तिमूलोऽयं ध्वनिः । स च व्यलीकनिःश्वासरूपचेतनधर्मसंभावनार्थं दक्षिणस्या दिशो नायिकया सहाभेदमासादयन्नभेदलक्षणातिशयोक्त्युपजीविनीं निश्वासमिवेति वाच्योत्प्रेक्षां निर्वहतीति वाच्यलिङ्गभूत इत्युत्पश्यामः ॥

असूत सद्यः कुसुमान्यशोकः स्कन्धात्प्रभृत्येव सपल्लवानि ।
पादेन नापैक्षत सुन्दरीणां संपर्कमासिञ्जितनूपुरेण ॥ २६ ॥

असूतेति ॥ **अशोकः** वृक्षविशेषः **सद्यः स्कन्धात्** प्रकाण्डात् **प्रभृति एव** ।

---

१ धिया०. २ मादाय. ३ नाथां, जुष्टाम्. ४ आशि०.

स्कन्धादारभ्येत्यर्थः । भाष्यकारवचनात्प्रभृतियोगे पञ्चमीति कैयटः । भाष्यं च ' मूलात्प्रभृत्यग्राद्वृक्षास्तक्ष्णुवन्ति ' इति । 'कार्तिक्याः प्रभृत्याग्रहायणी मासे ।' इत्यादि । **सपल्लवानि कुसुमानि असूत** । उभयमप्यजीजनदित्यर्थः । [**आसिञ्जितनूपुरेण**] आसिञ्जितो नूपुरो यस्य तेन । सिञ्जधातोरकर्मकात् ' गत्यर्थाकर्मक'–इत्यादिना कर्तरि क्तः । **सुन्दरीणां पादेन संपर्कं** ताडनं **न अपैक्षत** । 'सनूपुररवेण स्त्रीचरणेनाभिताडनम् । दोहदं यदशोकस्य ततः पुष्पोद्गमो भवेत् ॥' इति । तथा हि–'पदाहतः प्रमदया विकसत्यशोकः शोकं जहाति बकुलो मुखसीधुसिक्तः । आलोकितः कुरबकः कुरुते विकाशमालोडितस्तिलक उत्कलिको विभाति ॥' इति ॥

सद्यः प्रवालोद्गमचारुपत्रे नीते समाप्तिं नवचूतबाणे ।
निवेशयामास मधुर्द्विरेफान्नामाक्षराणीव मनोभवस्य ॥ २७ ॥

सद्य इति ॥ **मधुः** वसन्त एवेषुकारः [**प्रवालोद्गमचारुपत्रे**] प्रवालोद्गमाः पल्लवाङ्कुरा एव चारूणि पत्राणि पक्षा यस्य तस्मिन् । ' पत्रं वाहनपक्षयोः ' इत्यमरः । नवं चूतं चूतकुसुमं तदेव बाणस्तस्मिन् **नवचूतबाणे समाप्तिं नीते** सति **सद्यः मनोभवस्य** धन्विनः **नामाक्षराणीव द्विरेफान्** भ्रमरान् **निवेशयामास** निदधौ ॥ अत्र प्रवालपत्रे इत्याद्येकदेशविवर्तिरूपकं मधोरिषुकारत्वनिरूपणं सूचयन्नामाक्षराणीवेत्युत्प्रेक्षायां निमित्तमित्येकदेशविवर्तिरूपकोत्थापितेयमुत्प्रेक्षा ॥

वर्णप्रकर्षे सति कर्णिकारं दुनोति निर्गन्धतया स्म चेतः ।
प्रायेण सामग्र्यविधौ गुणानां पराङ्मुखी विश्वसृजः प्रवृत्तिः ॥२८॥

वर्णेति ॥ **कर्णिकारं** कर्णिकारकुसुमम् । ' अवयवे च प्राण्योषधिवृक्षेभ्यः ' इत्युत्पन्नस्य तद्धितस्य 'पुष्पफलमूलेषु बहुलं' इति लुक् । एवमन्यत्रापि द्रष्टव्यम् । **वर्णप्रकर्षे** वर्णोत्कर्षे **सति** अपि **निर्गन्धतया** हेतुना **चेतः दुनोति स्म** पर्यतापयत् । ' लट् स्मे ' इति भूतार्थे लट् । तथा हि । **प्रायेण विश्वसृजः** विधातुः **प्रवृत्तिः गुणानां सामग्र्यविधौ** साकल्यसंपादनविषये **पराङ्मुखी** । सर्वत्रापि वस्तुनि किंचिद्वैकल्यं संपादयति । यथा चन्द्रे कलङ्कः । अतः कर्णिकारेऽपि नैर्गन्ध्यं युज्यत इति भावः । सामान्येन विशेषसमर्थनरूपोऽर्थान्तरन्यासोऽलंकारः ॥

बालेन्दुवक्राण्यविकाशभावाद्बभुः पलाशान्यतिलोहितानि ।
सद्यो वसन्तेन समागतानां नखक्षतानीव वनस्थलीनाम् ॥२९॥

बालेन्द्विति ॥ **अविकाशभावात्** निर्विकाशत्वात् मुकुलभावाद्धेतोः [**बालेन्दुवक्राणि**] बालेन्दुरिव वक्राणि **अतिलोहितानि** अतिरक्तानि **पलाशानि** किंशुकपुष्पाणि । ' पलाशे किंशुकः पर्णः ' इत्यमरः । **वसन्तेन** पुंसा **समागतानां** संगतानां **वनस्थलीनां** स्त्रीणां **सद्यः** सद्यो दत्तानि । पुराणेष्वातिलौहित्याभावा-

---

१ सख्युः. २ निर्गन्धामिति.

दिति भावः । **नखक्षतानीव बभुः** । अत्र वसन्तस्य वनस्थलीनां च विशेषणसाधारण्यान्नायकव्यवहारप्रतीतेः समासोक्तिस्तावदस्ति । नखक्षतानीव इति जातिस्वरूपोत्प्रेक्षा वक्रत्वलौहित्यगुणनिर्मित्ता जागर्ति । सा च नायकव्यवहाराश्रितसमासोक्तिगर्भिण्येवोत्तिष्ठत इत्युभयोरेककालत्वैव । ' विशेषणसामर्थ्यादप्रस्तुतस्य गम्यत्वे समासोक्तिरिष्यते ' इति हि लक्षणम् ॥

लग्नद्विरेफाञ्जनभक्तिचित्रं[1] मुखे मधुश्रीस्तिलकं प्रकाश्य[2] ।
रागेण बालारुणकोमलेन चूतप्रवालोष्ठमलंचकार ॥ ३० ॥

लग्नेति ॥ **मधुश्रीः** वसन्तलक्ष्मीः [**लग्नद्विरेफाञ्जनभक्तिचित्रं**] लग्नद्विरेफा एवाञ्जनभक्तयः कज्जलरचनास्ताभिश्चित्रं चित्रवर्णं **तिलकं** पुष्पविशेषमेव तिलकं विशेषकम् । मुखं प्रारम्भस्तस्मिन्नेव **मुखे** वक्त्रे **प्रकाश्य** प्रकटय्य **बालारुणकोमलेन** बालार्कसुन्दरेण **रागेण** अरुणिम्ना तेनैव लाक्षारागेण चूतप्रवाल एवौष्ठस्तं **चूतप्रवालोष्ठम् अलंचकार** प्रसाधयामास ॥ अत्र रूपकालंकारः ॥

मृगाः प्रियाल[3]द्रुममञ्जरीणां रजःकणैर्विघ्नितदृष्टिपाताः ।
मदोद्धताः प्रत्यनिलं विचेरुर्वनस्थलीर्मर्मरपत्रमोक्षाः ॥ ३१ ॥

मृगा इति ॥ [**प्रियालद्रुममञ्जरीणां**] प्रियालद्रुमा राजादनवृक्षाः । ' राजादनः प्रियालः स्यात् ' इत्यमरः । तेषां मञ्जर्यस्तासां **रजःकणैः** [**विघ्नितदृष्टिपाताः**] विघ्निताः संजातविघ्ना दृष्टीनां पाताः प्रसादा येषां ते तथोक्ताः । **मदोद्धताः मृगाः प्रत्यनिलम्** अनिलाभिमुखं [**मर्मरपत्रमोक्षाः**] मर्मरा मर्मरशब्दवन्तः पत्रमोक्षा जीर्णपर्णपाता यासु ताः **वनस्थलीः विचेरुः** वनप्रदेशेषु चरन्ति स्म । ' देशकालाध्वगन्तव्याः कर्मसंज्ञा ह्यकर्मणाम् । ' इति चरतेः सकर्मकत्वम् ॥

चूताङ्कुरास्वादकषायकण्ठः पुंस्कोकिलो यन्मधुरं चुकूज ।
मनस्विनीमानविघातदक्षं तदेव जातं वचनं स्मरस्य ॥ ३२ ॥

चूताङ्कुरेति ॥ [**चूताङ्कुरास्वादकषायकण्ठः**] चूताङ्कुराणामास्वादेन कषायकण्ठो रक्तकण्ठः । ' सुरभावपथे रक्ते कषायः ' इति केशवः । पुमान्कोकिलः **पुंस्कोकिलः** । पुंग्रहणं प्रागल्भ्यद्योतनार्थम् । **मधुरं चुकूज** इति **यत् तत्** कूजनम् **एव** [**मनस्विनीमानविघातदक्षं**] मनस्विनीनां मानविघाते रोषनिरासे दक्षं **स्मरस्य वचनं** मानं त्यजतेत्याज्ञानवचनं **जातम्** । कोकिलकूजितश्रवणानन्तरं स्मराज्ञया इव मानं जहुरित्यर्थः ॥

हिमव्यपायाद्विशदाधराणामापाण्डरीभूत[4]मुखच्छवीनाम् ।
स्वेदोद्गमः किंपुरुषाङ्गनानां चक्रे पदं पत्रविशेषकेषु ॥ ३३ ॥

हिमेति ॥ [**हिमव्यपायात्**] हिमस्य व्यपायादपगमात् [**विशदाधराणां**] विशदा नीरुजा अधरा ओष्ठा यासां तासाम् । **आपाण्डरीभूतमुखच्छवीनाम्**

---

१ चित्रे. २ निवेश्य. ३ पियाल; प्रियालु. ४ आपाण्डुरीभूत.

कुङ्कमपरिहारादिति भावः । **किंपुरुषाङ्गनानां पत्त्रविशेषकेषु** पत्त्ररचनासु **स्वेदोद्गमः पदं चक्रे** । घर्मोदयात्स्वेदोदयोऽभूदित्यर्थः । विशदाधरत्वं मधुच्छिष्टराहित्यादिति भावः । हेमन्तेषु नार्यो बिम्बोष्ठेषु मधूच्छिष्टं शीतभयाद्दधतीति प्रसिद्धम् ॥

तपस्विनः स्थाणुवनौकसस्तामाकालिकीं वीक्ष्य मधुप्रवृत्तिम् ।

प्रयत्नसंस्तम्भितविक्रियाणां कथंचिदीशा मनसां बभूवुः ॥ ३४ ॥

तपस्विन इति ॥ [**स्थाणुवनौकसः**] स्थाणोर्वनमोको येषां ते **तपस्विनः** तत्रत्या मुनयः समानकाल आद्यन्तावस्या आकालिकीम् । अकालभवत्वादुत्पत्त्यनन्तरविनाशिनीमित्यर्थः । 'आकालिकडाद्यन्तवचने' इति समानकालादिकट्प्रत्ययः । प्रकृतेराकाल आदेशश्च निपातितः । 'टिड्ढाणञ्'—इत्यादिना ङीप् । केचिदकालोद्द्वाध्यात्मादित्वाद्भवार्थे ठगित्याहुः । **ताम् आकालिकीं मधुप्रवृत्तिं वीक्ष्य** [**प्रयत्नसंस्तम्भितविक्रियाणां**] प्रयत्नेन संस्तम्भितविक्रियाणां निरुद्धविकाराणां **मनसां कथंचिद् ईशाः** नियन्तारो **बभूवुः** ॥

तं देशमारोपितपुष्पचापे रतिद्वितीये मदने प्रपन्ने ।

काष्ठागतस्नेहरसानुविद्धं द्वंद्वानि भावं क्रियया विवव्रुः ॥ ३५ ॥

तमिति ॥ [**आरोपितपुष्पचापे**] आरोपितमाधिज्यं कृतं पुष्पचापं येन तस्मिन् । [**रतिद्वितीये**] रतिर्द्वितीया यस्य तस्मिन् रतिसहाये **मदने तं देशं** स्थाण्वाश्रमं **प्रपन्ने** प्राप्ते सति **द्वन्द्वानि** स्थावराणि जङ्गमानि च मिथुनानि [**काष्ठागतस्नेहरसानुविद्धं**] काष्ठा उत्कर्षः । 'काष्ठोत्कर्षे स्थितौ दिशि' इत्यमरः । तां गतो यः स्नेहः इष्टसाधननिबन्धनः प्रेमापरनामा ममताभिमानः । 'प्रेमा ना प्रियता हार्दं प्रेम स्नेहः' इत्यमरः । स एव रसस्तेनानुविद्धं संपृक्तं **भावं** रत्याख्यं शृङ्गारभावं **क्रियया** कार्यभूतया चेष्टया **विवव्रुः** प्रकटीचक्रुः । शृङ्गारचेष्टाः प्रावर्तन्तेत्यर्थः ॥

ताश्चेष्टा आह 'मधु' इत्यादिभिश्चतुर्भिः—

मधु द्विरेफः कुसुमैकपात्रे पपौ प्रियां स्वामनुवर्तमानः ।

शृङ्गेण च स्पर्शनिमीलिताक्षीं मृगीमकण्डूयत कृष्णसारः ॥ ३६ ॥

मध्विति ॥ द्वौ रेफौ वर्णविशेषौ यस्य स **द्विरेफः** भ्रमरः । उपचारात्तदर्थोऽपि द्विरेफ उच्यते । यथाह कैयटः—'शब्दधर्मेणाप्यर्थस्य व्यपदेशो दृश्यते । यथा भ्रमरशब्दस्य द्विरेफो भ्रमरः' । [**कुसुमैकपात्रे**] कुसुममेवैकं साधारणं पात्रं तस्मिन् **मधु** मकरन्दम् । 'मधु मद्ये पुष्परसे' इति विश्वः । **स्वां प्रियां** भृङ्गीम् **अनुवर्तमानः** अनुसरन् **पपौ** । तत्पीतशेषं पपावित्यर्थः । कृष्णश्चासौ सारः शबलश्च **कृष्णसारः** कृष्णमृगः । 'वर्णो वर्णेन' इति समासः । [**च**] [**स्पर्शनिमीलिताक्षीं**] स्पर्शेन स्पर्शसुखेन निमीलिताक्षीं **मृगीं शृङ्गेण अकण्डूयत** कषितवान् ॥ 'कण्ड्वादिभ्यो यक्' इति यक् । ततः कर्तरि लङ् ॥

---

१ संस्पर्श.

दौ रसात्पङ्कजरेणुगन्धि गजाय गण्डूषजलं करेणुः।
अर्धोपभुक्तेन बिसेन जायां संभावयामास रथाङ्गनामा॥ ३७॥

ददाविति॥ रसात् अतिरागात् करेणुः करिणी। 'करेणुरिभ्यां स्त्री नेभे' इत्यमरः। पङ्काज्जायत इति पङ्कजं तस्य रेणुः पङ्कजरेणुस्तस्य गन्धोऽस्यास्तीति पङ्कजरेणुगन्धि गण्डूषजलं मुखान्तर्धृतजलं गजाय ददौ। रथाङ्गनामा चक्रवाकः अर्धं यथा तथोपभुक्तेन [अर्धोपभुक्तेन] अर्धजग्धेन बिसेन जायां संभावयामास। स्वजग्धशेषं ददावित्यर्थः॥

गीतान्तरेषु श्रमवारिलेशैः किंचित्समुच्छ्वासितपत्रलेखम्।
पुष्पासवाघूर्णितनेत्रशोभि प्रियामुखं किंपुरुषश्चुचुम्ब॥ ३८॥

गीतान्तरेष्विति॥ किंपुरुषः किंनरः श्रमवारिलेशैः स्वेदोदबिन्दुभिः [किंचित्समुच्छ्वासितपत्रलेखम्] किंचिदीषत्समुच्छ्वासिता विश्लेषिताः पत्रलेखा यस्य तत्। [पुष्पासवाघूर्णितनेत्रशोभि] पुष्पाणामासवो मद्यं पुष्पासवः पुष्पोद्भवमद्यमित्यर्थः। वसन्ते मधूकस्य संभवात्। पुष्पवासितमिति केचित्। तेनाघूर्णिताभ्यामुद्भ्रान्ताभ्यां नेत्राभ्यां शोभत इति तथोक्तं प्रियामुखं गीतान्तरेषु गीतमध्येषु चुचुम्ब॥

पर्याप्तपुष्पस्तबकस्तनाभ्यः स्फुरत्प्रवालोष्ठमनोहराभ्यः।
लतावधूभ्यस्तरवोऽप्यवापुर्विनम्रशाखाभुजबन्धनानि॥३९॥

पर्याप्तेति॥ [पर्याप्तपुष्पस्तबकस्तनाभ्यः] पर्याप्ताः समग्राः पुष्पस्तबका एव स्तना यासां ताभ्यः॥ 'स्वाङ्गाच्चोपसर्जनादसंयोगोपधात्' इति विकल्पान्न ङीष्। [स्फुरत्प्रवालोष्ठमनोहराभ्यः] स्फुरन्तः प्रवालाः पल्लवाः एवौष्ठास्तैर्मनोहराभ्यः [लतावधूभ्यः] लता एव वध्वस्ताभ्यः सकाशात् तरवोऽपि लिङ्गादेव पुंस्त्वं गम्यते। [विनम्रशाखाभुजबन्धनानि] विनम्राः शाखा एव भुजास्तैर्बन्धनानि अवापुः। ताभिरालिङ्गिता इत्यर्थः। स्थावराणामपि मदनविकारोऽभूत्किमुतान्येषामिति भावः। एतच्च तरुलतानामपि चेतनत्वादुक्तम्। यथाह मनुः—'अन्तःसंज्ञा भवन्त्येते सुखदुःखसमन्विताः।' इति। अत्र रूपकालंकारः॥

श्रुताप्सरोगीतिरपि क्षणेऽस्मिन्हरः प्रसंख्यानपरो बभूव।
आत्मेश्वराणां न हि जातु विघ्नाः समाधिभेदप्रभवो भवन्ति॥४०॥

श्रुतेति॥ अस्मिन्क्षणे वसन्providविर्भावकाले भगवान् हरः श्रुताप्सरोगीतिरपि। दिव्याङ्गनागानमाकर्णयन्नपीत्यर्थः। प्रसंख्यानपरः आत्मानुसंधानपरः बभूव। तथा हि। [आत्मेश्वराणाम्] आत्मनश्चित्तस्येश्वराणां नियन्तॄणाम्। वशिनामित्यर्थः। विहन्यन्त एभिरिति विघ्नाः प्रत्यूहाः। घञर्थे कप्रत्ययः। जातु कदाचिदपि। [समाधिभेदप्रभवः] समाधिभेदे समाधिभञ्जने प्रभवः समर्थाः न भवन्ति॥

१ सरःपङ्कज. २ युक्तेन. ३ ईषत्स०. ४ शोभं. ५ चुचुम्बे. ६ संजात. ७ आनम्र.

लतागृहद्वारगतोऽथ नन्दी वामप्रकोष्ठार्पितहेमवेत्रः ।
मुखार्पितैकाङ्गुलिसंज्ञयैव मा चापलायेति गणान्व्यनैषीत् ॥ ४१ ॥

लतेति ॥ **अथ** [**लतागृहद्वारगतः**] लतागृहद्वारं गतः [**वामप्रकोष्ठार्पितहेमवेत्रः**] वामे प्रकोष्ठेऽर्पितहेमवेत्रो धारितहेमदण्डः **नन्दी** नन्दिकेश्वरः । 'नन्दी भृङ्गिरिटस्तण्डुनन्दिनौ नन्दिकेश्वरे ।' इति कोशः । [**मुखार्पितैकाङ्गुलिसंज्ञया**] मुखेऽर्पितायाः सरोषविस्मयस्तिमितावलोकं निहिताया एकस्या अङ्गुलेस्तर्जन्याः संज्ञया सूचनया **एव** । 'संज्ञा स्याच्चेतना नाम हस्ताद्यैरर्थसूचना'। इत्यमरः। **गणान्** प्रमथान् **चापलाय** चापलं कर्तुं **मा** भवत **इति** । 'क्रियार्थोपपदस्य'—इत्यादिना चतुर्थी । **व्यनैषीत्** शिक्षितवान् ॥

न केवलं गणा एव विनीताः किं तु जरायुजादिचतुर्विधं प्राणिजातमपीत्याह—

निष्कम्पवृक्षं निभृतद्विरेफं मूकाण्डजं शान्तमृगप्रचारम् ।
तच्छासनात्काननमेव सर्वं चित्रार्पितारम्भमिवावतस्थे ॥ ४२ ॥

निष्कम्पेति ॥ **निष्कम्पवृक्षम्** । इदमुद्भिज्जोपलक्षणम् । **निभृतद्विरेफं** निश्चलभृङ्गम् । स्वेदजोपलक्षणमेतत् । **मूकाण्डजं** निःशब्दपक्षिसरीसृपादिकम् । एतेनाण्डजजातिरुक्ता । **शान्तमृगप्रचारम्** । जरायुजोपलक्षणमेतत् । **सर्वम् एव काननं तच्छासनात्** नन्दीश्वराज्ञया **चित्रार्पितारम्भं** चित्रलिखितारम्भम् **इव अवतस्थे** ॥ 'नृगवाद्या जरायुजाः । स्वेदजाः कृमिदंशाद्याः पक्षिसर्पादयोऽण्डजाः । उद्भिदस्तरुगुल्माद्याः' इत्यमरः ॥

दृष्टिप्रपातं परिहृत्य तस्य कामः पुरःशुक्रमिव प्रयाणे ।
प्रान्तेषु संसक्तनमेरुशाखं ध्यानास्पदं भूतपतेर्विवेश ॥ ४३ ॥

दृष्टिप्रपातमिति ॥ **कामः प्रयाणे** यात्रायां पुरोगतः शुक्रो यस्मिन्देशे तं **पुरःशुक्रं** देशम् **इव** । 'प्रतिशुक्रं प्रतिबुधं प्रत्यङ्गारकमेव च । अपि शक्रसमो राजा हतसैन्यो निवर्तते ॥' इति प्रतिषेधात् । **तस्य दृष्टिप्रपातं** दृग्विषयं **परिहृत्य प्रान्तेषु** पार्श्वदेशेषु [**संसक्तनमेरुशाखं**] संसक्ता अन्योन्यसंसृष्टा नमेरूणां सुरपुंनागानां शाखा यस्य तत् । तिरोधानयोग्यमिति भावः । **भूतपतेः** शिवस्य **ध्यानास्पदं** समाधिस्थानम् । 'आस्पदं प्रतिष्ठायाम्' इति निपातः । **विवेश** ॥

स देवदारुद्रुमवेदिकायां शार्दूलचर्मव्यवधानवत्याम् ।
आसीनमासन्नशरीरपातस्त्रियम्बकं संयमिनं ददर्श ॥ ४४ ॥

स इति ॥ **आसन्नशरीरपातः** आसन्नमृत्युः **स** कामः [**शार्दूलचर्मव्यवधानवत्याम्**] शार्दूलचर्मणा व्यवधानवत्याम् । व्याघ्रचर्मास्तृतायामित्यर्थः । 'मोक्षश्रीर्व्याघ्रचर्मणि' इति प्राशस्त्यादिति भावः ॥ **देवदारुद्रुमवेदिकायाम् आसीनम्** उपविष्टं **संयमिनं** समाधिनिष्ठं **त्रियम्बकं** त्रिनेत्रं **ददर्श** । केचित्साहसिकाः 'त्रिलो-

१ द्वारि. २ नासा०. ३ न्यषेधीत्. ४ रण्य०. ५ प्रतीपं, प्रदीपं. ६ तं त्र्यम्बकं, त्रिलोचनम्.

चनम्' इति पेठुः । त्र्यम्बकमित्युक्ते पादपूरणव्यत्यासात्त्रियम्बकमिति पादपूरणार्थोऽयङादेशश्छान्दसो महाकविप्रयोगादभियुक्तैरङ्गीकृतः ॥

तमेव देवं षड्भिः श्लोकैर्वर्णयति—

पर्यङ्कबन्धस्थिरपूर्वकायमृज्वायतं संनमितोभयांसम् ।
उत्तानपाणिद्वयसंनिवेशात्प्रफुल्लराजीवमिवाङ्कमध्ये ॥ ४५ ॥

पर्यङ्केति ॥ [**पर्यङ्कबन्धस्थिरपूर्वकायं**] पर्यङ्कबन्धेन वीरासनेन स्थिरपूर्वकायं निश्चलोत्तरार्धम् [**ऋज्वायतं**] ऋजुरायतश्चर्ज्वायतस्तं [**संनमितोभयांसं**] संनमितावुभावंसौ यस्य तं तथोक्तम् । वृत्तिविषये उभशब्दस्थाने उभयशब्दप्रयोग इत्युक्तं कैयटेन । [**उत्तानपाणिद्वयसंनिवेशात्**] उत्तान ऊर्ध्वतलो यः पाणिद्वयस्य संनिवेशः संस्थानं तस्मात् **अङ्कमध्ये** [**प्रफुल्लराजीवं**] प्रफुल्लं राजीवं पङ्कजं यस्य तम् इव स्थितम् । वीरासने वसिष्ठः—'एकं पादमथैकस्मिन्विन्यस्योरौ तु संस्थितम् । इतरस्मिंस्तथैवोरुं वीरासनमुदाहृतम् ॥' इति । तथा योगसारे—'उत्तानिते करतले करमुत्तानितं परम् । आदायाङ्कगतं कृत्वा ध्यायेद्यस्तस्य सोऽन्तरम् ॥' इति ॥

भुजङ्गमोन्नद्धजटाकलापं कर्णावसक्तद्विगुणाक्षसूत्रम् ।
कण्ठप्रभासङ्गविशेषनीलां कृष्णत्वचं ग्रन्थिमतीं दधानम् ॥ ४६ ॥

भुजङ्गमेति ॥ [**भुजङ्गमोन्नद्धजटाकलापं**] भुजङ्गमेनोन्नद्ध उन्नमय्य बद्धो जटाकलापो येन तं तथोक्तम् । [**कर्णावसक्तद्विगुणाक्षसूत्रं**] कर्णावसक्तम् । कर्णावलम्बीत्यर्थः । अत एव द्विगुणं द्विरावृत्तमक्षसूत्रमक्षमाला यस्य तम् । [**कण्ठप्रभासङ्गविशेषनीलां**] कण्ठप्रभाणां सङ्गेन मिश्रणेन विशेषनीलामतिनीलां **ग्रन्थिमतीं** बन्धनयुक्तां **कृष्णत्वचं** कृष्णमृगाजिनं **दधानम्** ॥

किंचित्प्रकाशस्तिमितोग्रतारैर्भ्रूविक्रियायां विरतप्रसङ्गैः ।
नेत्रैरविस्पन्दितपक्ष्ममालैर्लक्ष्यीकृतघ्राणमधोमयूखैः ॥ ४७ ॥

किंचिदिति ॥ [**किंचित्प्रकाशस्तिमितोग्रतारैः**] किंचित्प्रकाशा ईषत्प्रकाशा स्तिमिता निश्चला उग्राश्च ताराः कनीनिका येषां तैः । 'तारकाक्ष्णः कनीनिका' इत्यमरः । **भ्रूविक्रियायां** भ्रूविक्षेपे **विरतप्रसङ्गैः** प्रसक्तिरहितैः । **अविस्पन्दितपक्ष्ममालैः** अचलितपक्ष्मपङ्क्तिभिरधः प्रसृता मयूखा येषां तैः **अधोमयूखैः नेत्रैः** । त्रिनेत्रत्वाद्बहुवचनम् । **लक्ष्यीकृतघ्राणं** नासाग्रनिविष्टदृष्टिमित्यर्थः । करणान्यबहिष्कृत्य स्थाणुवन्निश्चलात्मकः । आत्मानं हृदये ध्यायेन्नासाग्रन्यस्तलोचनः '॥ इति योगसारे ॥

अवृष्टिसंरम्भमिवाम्बुवाहमपामिवाधारमनुत्तरङ्गम् ।
अन्तश्चराणां मरुतां निरोधान्निवातनिष्कम्पमिव प्रदीपम् ॥ ४८ ॥

१ उद्बद्ध, आबद्ध, आविद्ध. २ करा, कर्णावतंस०. ३ मृगत्वचम्. ४ भ्रुवोः क्रि०. ५ विगत. ६ लक्षीकृत. ७ निर्वाण, निवात.

अवृष्टीति ॥ [अन्तश्चराणां] अन्तश्चरन्तीत्यन्तश्चराः तेषां मरुतां प्राणादीनां निरोधात् हेतोः अवृष्टिसंरम्भम् अविद्यमानवर्षसंभ्रमम् अम्बुवाहम् इव स्थितम् । एतेन प्राणनिरोधः सूचितः । अनुत्तरङ्गम् अनुद्भूततरङ्गम् अपामाधारं ह्रदं इव स्थितम् । एतेनापाननिरोधः सूचितः । तथा [निवातनिष्कम्पम्] निवाते निर्वातदेशे निष्कम्पं निश्चलं प्रदीपम् इव स्थितम् । एतेन शेषवायुनिरोधः सूचितः । 'निवातावाश्रयावातौ' इत्यमरः ॥

कपालनेत्रान्तरलब्धमार्गैर्ज्योतिःप्ररोहैरुदितैः शिरस्तः ।
मृणालसूत्राधिकसौकुमार्यां बालस्य लक्ष्मीं ग्लपयन्तमिन्दोः ॥४९॥

कपालेति ॥ [कपालनेत्रान्तरलब्धमार्गैः] कपालनेत्रान्तरेण ब्रह्मकरोटिनेत्रविवरेण लब्धमार्गैः शिरस्तः ब्रह्मरन्ध्रात् । 'पञ्चम्यास्तसिल्' । उदितैः उद्भूतैः ज्योतिःप्ररोहैः तेजोङ्कुरैः [मृणालसूत्राधिकसौकुमार्यां] मृणालसूत्राधिकं सौकुमार्यं मार्दवं यस्यास्तां बालस्य इन्दोः शिशुश्चन्द्रस्य लक्ष्मीं ग्लपयन्तम् ॥

मनो नवद्वार[2]निषिद्धवृत्ति हृदि व्यवस्थाप्य समाधिवश्यम् ।
यमक्षरं क्षेत्र[3]विदो विदुस्तमात्मानमात्मन्यवलोकयन्तम् ॥ ५० ॥

मन इति ॥ [नवद्वारनिषिद्धवृत्ति] नवभ्यो द्वारेभ्यो निषिद्धा निवर्तिता वृत्तिः संचारो यस्य तत्तथोक्तम् । [समाधिवश्यं] समाधिना प्रणिधानेन वश्यं वशंगतम् । यत्प्रत्ययः । 'प्रणिधानं समाधानं समाधिश्च समाश्रयः ।' इति हलायुधः । मनः हृदि हृदयाख्येऽधिष्ठाने व्यवस्थाप्य । तथा च वसिष्ठः—'यतो निर्याति विषयान्यस्मिंश्चैव प्रलीयते । हृदयं तद्विजानीयान्मनसः स्थितिकारणम् ॥' इति । क्षेत्रविदः क्षेत्रज्ञाः पुरुषाः यं न क्षरति इति अक्षरम् अविनाशिनं विदुः विदन्ति । 'विदो लटो वा' इति झेर्जुस् । तम् आत्मानम् आत्मनि स्वस्मिन् अवलोकयन्तं साक्षात्कुर्वन्तम् । स्वातिरेकेण परमात्मनोऽभावादिति भावः ॥

स्मरस्तथाभूतमयुग्मनेत्रं पश्यन्नदूरान्मनसाप्यधृष्यम् ।
नालक्षयत्साध्वससन्न[4]हस्तः स्रस्तं शरं चापमपि स्वहस्तात् ॥५१॥

स्मर इति ॥ स्मरः कामः तथाभूतं पूर्वोक्तरूपं मनसा अपि अधृष्यम् अयुग्मनेत्रं विषमाक्षम् अदूरात् पश्यन् । [साध्वससन्नहस्तः] साध्वसेन सन्नहस्तो विश्लथपाणिः सन् । स्वहस्तात् स्रस्तं शरं चापम् अपि चापं च न अलक्षयत् न विवेद । भीतो मुह्यतीति भावः ॥

निर्वाणभूयिष्ठमथास्य वीर्यं संधुक्षयन्तीव वपुर्गुणेन ।
अनुप्रयाता वनदेवताभ्यामदृश्यत स्थावरराजकन्या ॥ ५२ ॥

निर्वाणेति ॥ अथ निर्वाणेन नाशेन भूयिष्ठं निर्वाणभूयिष्ठम् । नष्टप्रायमित्यर्थः । अस्य स्मरस्य वीर्यं बलं वपुर्गुणेन सौन्दर्येण संधुक्षयन्ती इव पुनरुज्जीवयन्तीव

१ भार्यान् बालस्य रश्मीन्. २ द्वारि. ३ वेद-ब्रह्म-विदः. ४ स्विन्न.

स्थिता **वनदेताभ्यां** सखीभूताभ्याम् **अनुप्रयाता** अनुगता **स्थावरराजकन्या** पार्वती **अदृश्यत** दृष्टा ॥

तामेवाह चतुर्भिः—

अशोकनिर्भर्त्सितपद्मरागमाकृष्टहेमद्युतिकर्णिकारम् ।
मुक्ताकलापीकृतसिन्धुवारं वसन्तपुष्पाभरणं वहन्ती ॥ ५३ ॥

अशोकेति ॥ [**अशोकनिर्भर्त्सितपद्मरागम्**] अशोकपुष्पेण निर्भर्त्सितास्तिरस्कृताः पद्मरागा येन तत्तथोक्तम् । [**आकृष्टहेमद्युतिकर्णिकारम्**] आकृष्टहेमद्युतीनि आहृतस्वर्णाभरणवर्णानि कर्णिकाराणि यस्मिंस्तत्तथोक्तम् । [**मुक्ताकलापीकृतसिन्धुवारं**] मुक्ताकलापीकृतानि सिन्धुवाराणि निर्गुण्डीकुसुमानि यस्मिंस्तत् । 'सिन्धुवारेन्द्रसुरसौ निर्गुण्डीन्द्राणिकेत्यपि ।' इत्यमरः । वसन्तपुष्पाण्येवाभरणं [**वसन्तपुष्पाभरणं**] **वहन्ती** ॥

आवर्जिता किंचिदिव स्तनाभ्यां वासो वसाना तरुणार्करागम् ।
पर्याप्तपुष्पस्तबकावनम्रा संचारिणी पल्लविनी लतेव ॥ ५४ ॥

आवर्जितेति ॥ **स्तनाभ्यां किंचद् आवर्जिता** ईषदानमिता **इव** । तरुणार्कस्य राग इव रागो यस्य तत् [**तरुणार्करागं**] बालार्कारुणमित्यर्थः । उपमानपूर्वपदो बहुव्रीहिरुत्तरपदलोपश्च । **वासो वसाना** आच्छादयन्ती । अत एव **पर्याप्तपुष्पस्तबकावनम्रा पल्लविनी** किसलयवती **संचारिणी लतेव** । स्थितेति शेषः ॥

स्रस्तां नितम्बादवलम्बमाना पुनः पुनः केसरदामकाञ्चीम् ।
न्यासीकृतां स्थामविदा स्मरेण मौर्वीं द्वितीयामिव कार्मुकस्य ॥५५

स्रस्तामिति ॥ **स्थानविदा** निक्षेपयोग्यस्थानवेदिना **स्मरेण न्यासीकृतां** निक्षेपीकृताम् । [**कार्मुकस्य**] कर्मणि प्रभवतीति कार्मुकं धनुः । 'कर्मण उकञ्' इत्युकञ्प्रत्ययः । तस्य । **द्वितीयां मौर्वीम् इव** स्थिताम् । अत्र हि न्यस्ता मौर्व्युत्तरत्र हरवैरनिर्यातनायोपयुज्यत इति भावः । **नितम्बात्स्रस्तां** चलितां [**केसरदामकाञ्चीम्**] केसरदाम बकुलमाला सैव काञ्ची तां **पुनः पुनः अवलम्बमाना** हस्तेन धारयन्ती ॥

सुगन्धिनिःश्वासविवृद्धतृष्णं बिम्बाधरासन्नचरं द्विरेफम् ।
प्रतिक्षणं संभ्रमलोलदृष्टिर्लीलारविन्देन निवारयन्ती ॥ ५६ ॥

सुगन्धीति ॥ [**सुगन्धिनिःश्वासविवृद्धतृष्णं**] सुगन्धिभिर्निःश्वासैर्विवृद्धतृष्णम् [**बिम्बाधरासन्नचरं**] बिम्बतुल्योऽधरो बिम्बाधरः । 'वृत्तौ मध्यपदलोपः स्यात्' इति वामनः । तस्यासन्नचरं संनिकृष्टचरं **द्विरेफं** भृङ्गं **प्रतिक्षणं** [**संभ्रमलोलदृष्टिः**] संभ्रमेण लोलदृष्टिश्चलाक्षी सती **लीलारविन्देन निवारयन्ती** ॥

---

१ आकृष्ट. २ सिन्दुवारम्. ३ सुजात-संजात-पुष्प. ४ पल्लविता. ५ अवरोपयन्ती. ६ पुष्प. ७ द्वितीयमौर्वीमिव. ८ स्तम्भितलो०.

तां वीक्ष्य सर्वावयवानवद्यां रतेरपि ह्रीपदमादधानाम् ।
जितेन्द्रिये शूलिनि पुष्पचापः स्वकार्यसिद्धिं पुनराशशंसे ॥ ५७ ॥

तामिति ॥ [**सर्वावयवानवद्याम्**] सर्वावयवेष्वनवद्यामगर्ह्याम् । 'अवद्यपण्य-' इति निपातः । **रतेः** कामकलत्रस्य **अपि ह्रीपदं** लज्जानिमित्तम् । **आदधानाम्** । न्यूनतामावहन्तीमित्यर्थः । **तां** पार्वतीं **वीक्ष्य पुष्पचापः** कामः **जितेन्द्रिये** । दुर्जयेऽपीत्यर्थः । **शूलिनि** शिवे विषये **स्वकार्यसिद्धिं पुनः आशशंसे** चकमे । पूर्वं साध्वससन्नहस्तः (३।५१) इत्यादिना कार्यसिद्धेरुन्मूलितत्वाभिधानादिह पुनरित्युक्तम् ॥

भविष्यतः पत्युरुमा च शंभोः समाससाद प्रतिहारभूमिम् ।
योगात्स चान्तः परमात्मसंज्ञं दृष्ट्वा परं ज्योतिरुपारराम ॥ ५८ ॥

भविष्यत इति ॥ **उमा च भविष्यतः पत्युः शंभोः प्रतिहारभूमिं** द्वारदेशं **समाससाद** । 'स्त्री द्वार्द्वारं प्रतीहारः' इत्यमरः । **स** शंभुः **च अन्तः** [**परमात्मसंज्ञम्**] परमात्मेति संज्ञा यस्य तत् **परं** मुख्यम् । 'परं दूरान्यमुख्येषु' इति यादवः । **ज्योतिः दृष्ट्वा** साक्षात्कृत्य **योगात्** ध्यानात् । 'योगः संनहनोपायध्यानसंगतियुक्तिषु ।' इत्यमरः । **उपारराम** उपारतः । 'व्याङ्परिभ्यो रमः' इति परस्मैपदम् ॥

ततो भुजङ्गाधिपतेः फणाग्रैरधः कथंचिद्धृतभूमिभागः ।
शनैः कृतप्राणविमुक्तिरीशः पर्यङ्कबन्धं निबिडं बिभेद ॥ ५९ ॥

तत इति ॥ **ततः भुजङ्गाधिपतेः** शेषस्य **फणाग्रैः अधः** भूमेरधः **कथंचित्** अतियत्नेन **धृतभूमिभागः** धृतो भूमिभागः स्वोपवेशनभूभागो यस्य स तथोक्तः । वायुधारणाहितलाघवनिवृत्त्या भगवतो गुरुत्वादिति भावः । **शनैः** कृता प्राणानां प्राङ्निरुद्धानां विमुक्तिः पुनः संचारो येन स **कृतप्राणविमुक्तिः ईशः निबिडं** दृढं **पर्यङ्कबन्धं** वीरासनं **बिभेद** शिथिलीचकार ॥

तस्मै शशंस प्रणिपत्य नन्दी शुश्रूषया शैलसुतामुपेताम् ।
प्रवेशयामास च भर्तुरेनां भ्रूक्षेपमात्रानुमतप्रवेशाम् ॥ ६० ॥

तस्मा इति ॥ अथ **नन्दी तस्मै** भगवते । क्रियाग्रहणाच्चतुर्थी । **प्रणिपत्य** नमस्कृत्य **शुश्रूषया** सेवया निमित्तेन **उपेताम्** सेवार्थमागतामित्यर्थः । **शैलसुतां शशंस** निवेदयामास । **भर्तुः** स्वामिनः [**भ्रूक्षेपमात्रानुमतप्रवेशां**] भ्रूक्षेपमात्रेण भ्रूसंज्ञयैवानुमतप्रवेशामङ्गीकृतप्रवेशाम् **एनां** शैलसुतां **प्रवेशयामास च** ॥

तस्याः सखीभ्यां प्रणिपातपूर्वं स्वहस्तलूनः शिशिरात्ययस्य ।
व्यकीर्यत त्र्यम्बकपादमूले पुष्पोच्चयः पल्लवभङ्गभिन्नः ॥ ६१ ॥

---

१ ह्रीमतिमा०, ह्रीतिमिवा. २ पुष्प–केतुः–धन्वा. ३ स्वकर्म. ४ आशशंस. ५ उपासितुं सा च पिनाकपाणिम्. ६ अन्तर्गतमा०. ७ फणाभिः. ८ अनुमित. ९ पत्य०, त्य मूर्ध्ना.

तस्या इति ॥ **तस्याः** पार्वत्याः **सखीभ्यां** पूर्वोक्ताभ्यां [**स्वहस्तलूनः**] स्वहस्तेन लूनः उपचितः **पल्लवभङ्गभिन्नः** किसलयशकलमिश्रः **शिशिरात्ययस्य** वसन्तस्य संबन्धी **पुष्पोच्चयः** पुष्पप्रकरः । 'हस्तादाने चेरस्तेये' इति घञ्विधानात्कवीनामयं प्रामादिकः प्रयोगः इति वल्लभः । **त्र्यम्बकपादमूले प्रणिपातपूर्वं** नमस्कारपूर्वकं **व्यकीर्यत** विक्षिप्तः ॥

उमापि नीलालकमध्यशोभि विस्रंसयन्ती नवकर्णिकारम् ।
चकार कर्णच्युतपल्लवेन मूर्ध्ना प्रणामं वृषभध्वजाय ॥ ६२ ॥

उमेति ॥ **उमा अपि** [**नीलालकमध्यशोभि**] नीलालकानां मध्ये शोभत इति तथोक्तम् । अलकन्यस्तमित्यर्थः । **नवकर्णिकारं विस्रंसयन्ती** [**कर्णच्युतपल्लवेन**] कर्णात् च्युतः पल्लवो यस्य तेन कर्णच्युतपल्लवेन **मूर्ध्ना वृषभध्वजाय प्रणामं चकार** । क्रियाग्रहणात्संप्रदानत्वम् ॥

अनन्यभाजं पतिमाप्नुहीति सा तथ्यमेवाभिहिता भवेन ।
न हीश्वरव्याहृतयः कदाचित्पुष्णन्ति लोके विपरीतमर्थम् ॥ ६३ ॥

अनन्येति ॥ **सा** कृतप्रणामा देवी **भवेन** हरेण । अन्यां न भजतीति तम् **अनन्यभाजम्** । 'भजो ण्विः' इति ण्विप्रत्ययः । सर्वनाम्नो वृत्तिमात्रे पूर्वपदस्य पुंवद्भावः । **पतिमाप्नुहीति तथ्यं** सत्यम् **एव अभिहिता** उक्ता । उत्तरत्र तथैव संभवादिति भावः । अभिदधातेर्ब्रुवर्थस्य दुहादित्वादप्रधाने कर्मणि क्तः । तथा **हि** । **ईश्वरव्याहृतयः** महापुरुषवाक्यः **कदाचित्** अपि **लोके** भुवने । 'लोकस्तु भुवने जने' इत्यमरः ॥ **विपरीतं** विसंवादिनम् **अर्थम्** अभिधेयं **न पुष्णन्ति** न बोधयन्तीत्यर्थः ॥

कामस्तु बाणावसरं प्रतीक्ष्य पतङ्गवद्वह्निमुखं विविक्षुः ।
उमासमक्षं हरबद्धलक्ष्यः[3] शरासनज्यां मुहुराममर्श ॥ ६४ ॥

काम इति ॥ **कामस्तु बाणावसरं प्रतीक्ष्य** उमासंनिधानादयमेव बाणप्रयोगसमय इति ज्ञात्वा पतङ्गेन तुल्यं **पतङ्गवत्** शलभवत् । 'समौ पतङ्गशलभौ' इत्यमरः । 'तेन तुल्यं क्रिया चेद्वतिः' इति वतिप्रत्ययः । **वह्निमुखं विविक्षुः** प्रवेष्टुमिच्छुः । विशतेः सन्नन्तादुप्रत्ययः । उमायाः समक्षमक्ष्णः समीपम् **उमासमक्षम्** । 'अव्ययीभावे शरत्प्रभृतिभ्यः' इति समासान्तोऽच्प्रत्ययः । [**हरबद्धलक्ष्यः**] हरे बद्धलक्ष्यः सन् । [**शरासनज्यां**] शरासस्य ज्यां मौर्वी **मुहुः आममर्श** परामृष्टवान् ॥

अथोपनिन्ये गिरिशाय गौरी तपस्विने ताम्ररुचा करेण ।
विशोषितां भानुमतो मयूखैर्मन्दाकिनीपुष्करबीजमालाम् ॥ ६५ ॥

अथेति ॥ **अथ गौरी** । तपोऽस्यास्तीति तपस्वी । 'अस्मायामेधास्रजो विनिः' इति विनिप्रत्ययः । तस्मै **तपस्विने गिरिशाय ताम्ररुचा** रक्तवर्णेन **करेण भानुमतः** अंशुमतः **मयूखैः विशोषितां** [**मन्दाकिनीपुष्करबीजमालाम्**]

---

१ भव्यम्. २ नार्क. ३ लक्ष्य.

मन्दाकिन्याः पुष्कराणि पद्मानि तेषां बीजानि तेषां मालां जपमालिकाम् उपनिन्ये समर्पितवती ॥

प्रतिग्रहीतुं प्रणयिप्रियत्वात्त्रिलोचनस्तामुपचक्रमे च ।
संमोहनं नाम च पुष्पधन्वा धनुष्यमोघं समधत्त बाणम् ॥६६॥

प्रतिग्रहीतुमिति ॥ त्रिलोचनः च प्रणयिप्रियत्वाद् अर्थिप्रियत्वात् ताम् अक्षमालां प्रतिग्रहीतुं स्वीकर्तुम् उपचक्रमे । पुष्पं धनुर्यस्य स पुष्पधन्वा कामः च । 'वा संज्ञायाम्' इत्यनङादेशः । संमोह्यतेऽनेनेति संमोहनं नाम । नामेति प्रसिद्धौ । अमोघं बाणं सायकं धनुषि समधत्त संहितवान् ॥

हरस्तु किंचित्परिलुप्तधैर्यश्चन्द्रोदयारम्भ इवाम्बुराशिः ।
उमामुखे बिम्बफलाधरोष्ठे व्यापारयामास विलोचनानि ॥६७॥

हर इति ॥ हरस्तु हरोऽपि चन्द्रोदयारम्भे अम्बुराशिः इव किंचित् ईषत् परिलुप्तधैर्यः । न तु प्राकृतजनवदत्यन्तलुप्तधैर्य इति भावः । [बिम्बफलाधरोष्ठे] बिम्बफलतुल्योऽधरोष्ठो यस्य तस्मिन् उमामुखे विलोचनानि व्यापारयामास । त्रिभिरपि लोचनैः साभिलाषमद्राक्षीदित्यर्थः । एतेन भगवतो रतिभावोदय उक्तः ॥

विवृण्वती शैलसुतापि भावमङ्गैः स्फुरद्बालकदम्बकल्पैः ।
साचीकृता चारुतरेण तस्थौ मुखेन पर्यस्तविलोचनेन ॥६८॥

विवृण्वतीति ॥ शैलसुतापि स्फुरद्बालकदम्बकल्पैः विकसत्कोमलनीपसदृशैः पुलकितैरित्यर्थः । 'ईषदसमाप्तौ—' इत्यादिना कल्पप्प्रत्ययः । अङ्गैः भावं रत्याख्यं विवृण्वती प्रकाशयन्ती चारुतरेण पर्यस्तविलोचनेन व्रीडाविभ्रान्तनेत्रेण मुखेन असाचि साचि संपद्यमाना साचीकृता तिर्यक्कृता । 'तिर्यगर्थे साचि तिरः' इत्यमरः । तस्थौ । ह्रिया मुखं साचीकृत्य स्थितेत्यर्थः । न केवलं हरस्यैव देव्या अप्युदितो रतिभाव इति भावः ॥

अथेन्द्रियक्षोभमयुग्मनेत्रः पुनर्वशित्वाद्बलवन्निगृह्य ।
हेतुं स्वचेतोविकृतेर्दिदृक्षुर्दिशामुपान्तेषु ससर्ज दृष्टिम् ॥६९॥

अथेति ॥ अथ अयुग्मानि नेत्राणि यस्य सः अयुग्मनेत्रः त्रिनेत्रः वशित्वात् जितेन्द्रियत्वात् इन्द्रियक्षोभं पूर्वोक्तमिन्द्रियविकारं पुनर्बलवत् दृढं निगृह्य निवार्य स्वचेतोविकृतेः स्वचित्तविकारस्य हेतुं कारणं दिदृक्षुः द्रष्टुमिच्छुः दिशाम् उपान्तेषु दृष्टिं ससर्ज प्रसारयामास ॥

स दक्षिणापाङ्गनिविष्टमुष्टिं नतांसमाकुञ्चितसव्यपादम् ।
ददर्श चक्रीकृतचारुचापं प्रहर्तुमभ्युद्यतमात्मयोनिम् ॥७०॥

---

१ परिवृत्त. २ क्वचित्, कुचद्वा. ३ साचिक्रियाचा०. ४ निषक्त. ५ ईषत्स०. ६ वक्री.

स इति ॥ स भगवान् [**दक्षिणापाङ्गनिविष्टमुष्टिं**] दक्षिणापाङ्गे निविष्टा स्थिता मुष्टिर्यस्य तं **नतांसम्** [**आकुञ्चितसव्यपादम्**] आकुञ्चितः सव्यपादो यस्य तम् । आलीढाख्यस्थानके स्थितमित्यर्थः । **चक्रीकृतचारुचापं** मण्डलीकृतसौम्यकोदण्डं **प्रहर्तुम् अभ्युद्यतम् आत्मयोनिं** मनोभवं **ददर्श** । आलीढलक्षणमाह यादवः— 'स्थानानि धन्विनां पञ्च तत्र वैशाखमस्त्रियाम् । वितस्त्यन्तरगौ (त्रिवितस्त्यन्तरौ) पादौ मण्डलं तोरणाकृती ॥ समानौ (अन्वर्थे) स्यात्समपदमालीढं तु ततोऽग्रतः । दक्षिणे वाममाकुञ्च्य प्रत्यालीढं विपर्यये ॥' इति ॥

तपःपरामर्शविवृद्धमन्योर्भ्रूभङ्गदुष्प्रेक्ष्यमुखस्य तस्य ।
स्फुरन्नुदर्चिः सहसा तृतीयादक्ष्णः कृशानुः किल निष्पपात ॥७१॥

तप इति ॥ [**तपःपरामर्शविवृद्धमन्योः**] तपःपरामर्शेन तपस आस्कन्दनेन विवृद्धमन्योः प्रवृद्धकोपस्य [**भ्रूभङ्गदुष्प्रेक्ष्यमुखस्य**] भ्रूभङ्गेण दुष्प्रेक्ष्यं दुर्दर्शं मुखं यस्य । **तस्य** हरस्य **तृतीयाद् अक्ष्णः स्फुरन्** उद्दीप्यमानः **उदर्चिः** उद्भूतज्वालः **कृशानुः** अग्निः **सहसा** अतर्कितमेव । 'अतर्किते तु सहसा' इत्यमरः । **निष्पपात किल** निश्चकाम खलु ॥

क्रोधं प्रभो संहर संहरेति यावद्गिरः खे मरुतां चरन्ति ।
तावत्स वह्निर्भवनेत्रजन्मा भस्मावशेषं मदनं चकार ॥७२॥

क्रोधमिति ॥ हे **प्रभो** स्वामिन् **क्रोधं संहर संहर** निवर्तय निवर्तय । 'चापले द्वे भवत इति वक्तव्यम्' इति वार्तिकेन द्वित्वम् । 'संभ्रमेण प्रवृत्तिश्चापल्यम्' इति काशिका । **इति** एवं **मरुतां** देवानां **गिरः** वाचः **खे** व्योम्नि **यावत् चरन्ति** प्रवर्तन्ते **तावत्** तत्कालमेव भवस्य नेत्राज्जन्म यस्य स **भवनेत्रजन्मा** । 'अवर्ज्यो बहुव्रीहिर्व्यधिकरणो जन्माद्युत्तरपदः' इति वामनः । **स वह्निः मदनं** भस्मैवावशेषो यस्य तं **भस्मावशेषं चकार** । ददाहेत्यर्थः ॥

तीव्राभिषङ्गप्रभवेण वृत्तिं मोहेन संस्तम्भयतेन्द्रियाणाम् ।
अज्ञातभर्तृव्यसना मुहूर्तं कृतोपकारेव रतिर्बभूव ॥ ७३ ॥

तीव्रेति ॥ **तीव्राभिषङ्गप्रभवेण** अतिदुःसहाभिभवसंभवेन । 'अभिषङ्गस्त्वभिभवे सङ्ग आक्रोशनेऽपि च ।' इति वैजयन्ती । **इन्द्रियाणां** चक्षुरादीनां **वृत्तिं** व्यापारं **संस्तम्भयता** प्रतिबध्नता **मोहेन** मूर्छया कर्त्रा । **रतिः** मदनभार्या । **मुहूर्तम्** [**अज्ञातभर्तृव्यसना**] अज्ञातं भर्तृव्यसनं भर्तृनाशो यया सा तथोक्ता सती **कृतोपकारा इव बभूव** । सहसा दुःखोपनिपातान्मुमूर्छेत्यर्थः । मोहेन दुःखसंवेदनाभावात्तस्योपकारकत्वोक्तिः ॥

तमाशु विघ्नं तपसस्तपस्वी वनस्पतिं वज्र इवावभज्य ।
स्त्रीसंनिकर्षं परिहर्तुमिच्छन्नन्तर्दधे भूतपतिः सभूतः ॥ ७४ ॥

---

१ दुष्प्रेक्ष्य. २ कोपं. ३ अथाशु. ४ रुज्य, वदह्य. ५ परिहर्तुकामः सोन्तर्दधे.

तमिति ॥ **तपस्वी** तपोनिष्ठः **भूतपतिः** शिवः **तपसः विघ्नम्** अन्तरायभूतं **तं** **कामम् आशु वज्रः** अशनिः **वनस्पतिं** वृक्षम् **इव अवभज्य** भङ्क्त्वा **स्त्रीसंनिकर्षं** स्त्रीसंनिधानं **परिहर्तुमिच्छन्**। तस्यानर्थहेतुत्वादिति भावः। **सभूतः** सगणः सन् **अन्तर्दधे** ॥

शैलात्मजापि पितुरुच्छिरसोऽभिलाषं
व्यर्थं समर्थ्य ललितं वपुरात्मनश्च ।
सख्योः समक्षमिति चाधिकजातलज्जा
शून्या जगाम भवनाभिमुखी कथंचित् ॥ ७५ ॥

शैलात्मजेति ॥ **शैलात्मजा** पार्वती **अपि उच्छिरसः** उन्नतशिरसो महतः **पितुः** **अभिलाषं** हरो वरोऽस्त्विति मनोरथं **ललितं** सुन्दरम् **आत्मनः वपुः च व्यर्थं** निष्फलं **समर्थ्य** विचार्य **सख्योः समक्षं** पुरः **इति च** हेतुना अधिकं जातलज्जा [**अधिकजातलज्जा**]। समानजनसमक्षमवमानस्यातिदुःसहत्वादिति भावः। **शून्या** निरुत्साहा सती **कथंचित्** कृच्छ्रेण भवनस्याभिमुखी [**भवनाभिमुखी**] **जगाम** ॥

सपदि मुकुलिताक्षीं रुद्रसंरम्भभीत्या
दुहितरमनुकम्प्यामद्रिरादाय दोर्भ्याम् ।
सुरगज इव बिभ्रत्पद्मिनीं दन्तलग्नां
प्रतिपथगतिरासीद्वेगदीर्घीकृताङ्गः ॥ ७६ ॥

सपदीति ॥ **सपदि अद्रिः** हिमवान् [**रुद्रसंरम्भभीत्या**] रुद्रस्य संरम्भात्कोपाद्भीत्या। 'संरम्भः संभ्रमे कोपे' इति विश्वः। **मुकुलिताक्षीं** निमीलितनेत्राम्। 'बहुव्रीहौ सक्थ्यक्ष्णोः स्वाङ्गात्षच्' इति षच्प्रत्ययः। 'षिद्गौरादिभ्यश्च' इति ङीष्। अनुकम्पितुमर्हाम् **अनुकम्प्याम्**। 'ऋहलोर्ण्यत्' इति ण्यत्प्रत्ययः। **दुहितरं** **दोर्भ्यामादाय** [**दन्तलग्नां**] दन्तयोर्लग्नां **पद्मिनीं** नलिनीं **बिभ्रत् सुरगज इव** [**वेगदीर्घीकृताङ्गः**] वेगेन रयेण दीर्घीकृताङ्ग आयतीकृतशरीरः सन्। पन्थानं प्रतिगता मार्गानुसारिणी गतिर्यस्य स **प्रतिपथगतिः आसीत्** ॥

इति श्रीमन्महामहोपाध्यायकोलाचलमल्लिनाथसूरिविरचितया संजीवनीसमाख्यया व्याख्यया समेतः श्रीकालिदासकृतौ कुमारसंभवे महाकाव्ये मदनदहनः नाम तृतीयः सर्गः ॥

---

१ समीक्ष्य. २ अभिमुखं. ३ अथ स. ४ दीर्घीकृतात्मा–ताश्रः. ५ मदननिग्रहः.

चतुर्थः सर्गः ।

मूर्च्छिता रतिरित्युक्तम् । संप्रति तद्वृत्तान्तमेवाह—

अथ मोहपरायणा सती विवशा कामवधूर्विबोधिता ।
विधिना प्रतिपादयिष्यता नववैधव्यमसह्यवेदनम् ॥ १ ॥

अथेति ॥ **अथ** अनन्तरं मोहो मूर्च्छा परमयनमाश्रयो यस्याः सा **मोहपरायणा** मोहैकशरणा **सती** । 'परायणमभिप्रेते तत्परे परमाश्रये ।' इति यादवः- **विवशा** मूढत्वान्निश्चेष्टा **कामवधूः** रतिः । [**असह्यवेदनम्**] असह्या दुःसहा वेदना यस्मिंस्तत्तथोक्तम् । विधवाया गतभर्तृकाया भावो वैधव्यम् । नवं च तद्वैधव्यं चेति **नववैधव्यम्** । नवग्रहणं दुःसहत्वद्योतनार्थम् । **प्रतिपादयिष्यता** अनुभावयिष्यता । क्रियार्थक्रियायां लृट् । **विधिना** दैवेन । 'विधिर्विधाने दैवे च' इत्यमरः । **विबोधिता** । वैधव्यानुफलोऽयं विधिरिति भावः । अस्मिन्सर्गे वियोगिनीवृत्तानि— 'विषमे ससजा गुरुः समे सभरा लोऽथ गुरुर्वियोगिनी ।' इति लक्षणात् ॥

अवधानपरे चकार सा प्रलयान्तोन्मिषिते विलोचने ।
न विवेद तयोरतृप्तयोः प्रियमत्यन्तविलुप्तदर्शनम् ॥ २ ॥

अवेति ॥ **सा** रतिः [**प्रलयान्तोन्मिषिते**] प्रलयान्ते मूर्च्छावसाने । 'प्रलयो नष्टचेष्टता' इत्यमरः । उन्मिषिते उन्मीलिते **विलोचने** । अवधानं परं प्रधानं ययोस्ते **अवधानपरे** दिदृक्षयावहिते **चकार** । द्रष्टव्याभावात्तु न विवेदेत्याह—नेति ॥ **प्रियं** कामम् **अतृप्तयोः** तृप्तिं न गतयोः । नित्यदिदृक्षमाणयोरित्यर्थः । **तयोः** लोचनयोः । दर्शनक्रियापेक्षया संबन्धे षष्ठी । अत्यन्तविलुप्तं दर्शनं स्वलोचनयोः करणयोर्यस्य कर्मभूतस्य तम् **अत्यन्तविलुप्तदर्शनं** सन्तं **न विवेद** न ज्ञातवती । प्रियनाशापरिज्ञानाद्दिदृक्षां चक्रे इति तात्पर्यार्थः ॥

अयि जीवितनाथ जीवसीत्यभिधायोत्थितया तया पुरः ।
ददृशे पुरुषाकृति[2] क्षितौ हरकोपानलभस्म केवलम् ॥ ३ ॥

अयीति ॥ अयीति प्रश्ने । ' अयि प्रश्नानुनययोः ' इति विश्वः । **अयि जीवितनाथ जीवसि** प्राणिषि कच्चिद् **इति अभिधाय उत्थितया तया** रत्या **पुरः** अग्रे **क्षितौ** पुरुषस्य आकृतिरिवाकृतिर्यस्य तत् **पुरुषाकृति केवलं** एकं **हरकोपानलभस्म ददृशे** दृष्टम् । न तु पुरुष इति भावः ॥

अथ सा पुनरेव विह्वला वसुधालिङ्गनधूसरस्तनी[3] ।
विललाप विकीर्णमूर्धजा समदुःखामिव कुर्वती स्थलीम् ॥ ४ ॥

अथेति ॥ **अथ** भस्मदर्शनानन्तरम् **पुनरेव विह्वला** विक्लवा **वसुधालिङ्गनधूसरस्तनी** वसुधालिङ्गनेन क्षितिलुण्ठनेन धूसरौ धूसरवर्णौ स्तनौ कुचौ यस्याः

१ . निमग्न । २ कृतिः. ३ धूसराकृतिः.

सा तथोक्ता । 'स्वाङ्गाच्चोपसर्जनादसंयोगोपधात्' इति ङीष् । **विकीर्णमूर्धजा** विकीर्णा विक्षिप्ता मूर्धजाः केशाः यस्याः सा तथोक्ता **सा** रतिः **स्थलीं** वनभूमिम् । तत्रत्यान्प्राणिन इत्यर्थः । 'जानपदकुण्डगोणस्थल'—इत्यादिना ङीष् । **समदुःखां** स्वतुल्यशोकां **कुर्वती इव विललाप** परिदेवितवती । 'विलापः परिदेवनम्' इत्यमरः ॥

उपमानमभूद्विलासिनां करणं यत्तव कान्तिमत्तया ।
तदिदं गतमीदृशीं दशां न विदीर्ये कठिनाः खलु स्त्रियः ॥ ५ ॥

उपेति ॥ **तव यत्करणं** गात्रम् । 'करणं साधकतमं क्षेत्रगात्रेन्द्रियेष्वपि ।' इत्यमरः । **कान्तिमत्तया** सौन्दर्येण हेतुना **विलासिनां** विलसनशीलानां कामिनाम् । 'वौ कषलस'—इत्यादिना घिनुण्प्रत्ययः । उपमीयते येन तद् **उपमानम् अभूत्** । **तत् करणम् इदम् ईदृशीं दशाम्** अवस्थां **गतं** प्राप्तम् । भस्मीभूतमित्यर्थः । तथापि **न विदीर्ये** न विदीर्णा भवामि । कर्तरि लट् । तथा हि—**स्त्रियः कठिनाः खलु** । कठिनत्वादविदीर्यमाणत्वमित्यर्थः । कारणात्कार्यसमर्थनरूपोऽर्थान्तरन्यासः । 'धीरसंचारिणी दृष्टिर्गतिर्गोवृषभाञ्चिता । स्मितपूर्वं तथालापो विलास इति कीर्तितः ॥' इति ॥

क नु मां त्वदधीनजीवितां विनिकीर्य क्षणभिन्नसौहृदः ।
नलिनीं क्षतसेतुबन्धनो जलसंघात इवासि विद्रुतः ॥ ६ ॥

क्वेति ॥ हे प्रिय । **क्षतसेतुबन्धनः** भग्नसेतुबन्धनः **जलसंघातः** जलौघः **नलिनीमिव** । जलैकायत्तजीवितामिति शेषः । **त्वदधीनजीवितां** त्वदायत्तप्राणां **मां क्व नु विनिकीर्य** कुत्र वा निक्षिप्य **क्षणभिन्नसौहृदः** क्षणत्यक्तसौहार्दः सन् । **विद्रुतः** पलायितः **असि** । नु विषादे । यथा पद्मिनीं परित्यज्य वारिपूरो गच्छति तथा मां विहाय गतोऽसीति । सौहृदस्य सेतुरुपमानम् । सेतुसौहृदयोः स्थितिहेतुत्वेन साम्यम् । सुहृदो भावः सौहृदम् । युवादित्वादण्प्रत्ययः । 'हृदयस्य हृल्लेखयदण्लासेषु' इति हृदादेशः । अणि हृद्भावान्न 'हृद्भगसिन्ध्वन्ते पूर्वपदस्य च' इत्युभयपदवृद्धिः । हृद्भूतस्याण्विधाने तूभयपदवृद्धिः स्यात् । यथा सुहृदो भावः सौहार्दमिति । तदेवाह वामनः—'सौहृददौर्हृदशब्दावणि हृद्भावात्' इति ॥

कृतवानसि विप्रियं न मे प्रतिकूलं न च ते मया कृतम् ।
किमकारणमेव दर्शनं विलपन्त्यै रतये न दीयते ॥ ७ ॥

कृतेति ॥ हे प्रिय त्वं **मे** मम **विप्रियम्** अप्रियं **कृतवान् न असि** । **मया च ते** तव **प्रतिकूलम्** अप्रियं **न कृतम्** । परस्परजीवितस्य परस्पराधीनत्वात्कुतः परिभवशङ्केति भावः । **अकारणं** निष्कारणम् **एव** । परस्परापकाररूपकारणाभावेऽपीत्यर्थः । क्रियाविशेषणमेतत् । **विलपन्त्यै** । त्वद्दर्शनार्थिन्या अपीति भावः । **रतये किं** कथं **दर्शनं न दीयते** । क्रियाग्रहणाच्चतुर्थी ॥

---

१ च दीर्ये.

विप्रियमाशङ्कते—

स्मरसि स्मर मेखलागुणैरुत गोत्रस्खलितेषु बन्धनम् ।
च्युतकेशरदूषितेक्षणान्यवतंसोत्पलताडनानि वा ॥ ८ ॥

स्मरसीति ॥ हे **स्मर** । **गोत्रस्खलितेषु** नामव्यत्यासेषु । अन्यस्त्रीनाम्ना ममाह्वानेषु । 'गोत्रं नाम्न्यचले कुले' इति विश्वः । **मेखलागुणैः बन्धनं स्मरसि उत** स्मरसि वा । 'विकल्पे किं किमूत च' इत्यमरः । च्युतकेशरैर्भ्रष्टकिञ्जल्कैर्दूषिते ईक्षणे येषु तानि [**च्युतकेशरदूषितेक्षणानि**] **अवतंसोत्पलताडनानि** । सधूलिक्षेपताडनानीत्यर्थः । स्मरसि **वा** । अपकारस्मरणादिदमदर्शनमिति भावः ॥

हृदये वससीति मत्प्रियं यदवोचस्तदवैमि कैतवम् ।
उपचारपदं न चेदिदं त्वमनङ्गः कथमक्षता रतिः ॥ ९ ॥

हृदय इति ॥ **हृदये वससि इति** स्मरवाक्यानुवादः । इत्येवंरूपं **मत्प्रियं यदवोचः** उक्तवानसि । ब्रूञो लुङि 'वच उम्' इत्युमागमः । **तत्कैतवम् अवैमि** मिथ्येति मन्ये । **इदं** वचनम् **उपचारपदं** परस्य रञ्जनार्थं यदसत्यभाषणं स उपचारस्तस्य पदं स्थानम् । कैतवस्थानमिति यावत् । **न चेत् त्वमनङ्गः** अशरीरः **कथं रतिः अक्षता** अविनष्टा । आश्रयनाशेऽप्याश्रितमविनष्टमिति विरोधादिति भावः ॥

न च मे कश्चिद्विचारः किं तु लोकः शोच्यत इत्याह—

परलोकनवप्रवासिनः प्रतिपत्स्ये पदवीमहं तव ।
विधिना जन एप वञ्चितस्त्वदधीनं खलु देहिनां सुखम् ॥ १० ॥

परलोकेति ॥ [**परलोकनवप्रवासिनः**] परलोकं प्रति नवप्रवासिनः अचिरप्रोषितस्य । अनेनानुगमनकालानतिपातः सूच्यते । **तव पदवीं** मार्गं **अहं प्रतिपत्स्ये** । त्वामनुगमिष्यामीत्यर्थः । अतो मे नास्ति विचार इति भावः । किं **तु विधिना** दैवेन **एष जनः** लोकः **वञ्चितः** प्रतारितः । **देहिनां सुखं त्वदधीनं** त्वय्यधीनं **खलु** । अधिशब्दस्य शौण्डादिकत्वात् 'सप्तमी शौण्डैः' इति समासः । 'अध्युत्तरपदात्' इति खप्रत्ययः । एवमन्यत्रापि । सुखप्रदाभावे कुतः सुखमिति भावः ॥

तदेवाह—

रजनीतिमिरावगुण्ठिते पुरमार्गे घनशब्दविक्लवाः ।
वसतिं प्रिय कामिनां प्रियास्त्वदृते प्रापयितुं क ईश्वरः ॥ ११ ॥

रजनीति ॥ हे **प्रिय** । [**रजनीतिमिरावगुण्ठिते**] रजनीतिमिरेण अवगुण्ठिते आवृते **पुरमार्गे घनशब्दविक्लवाः** गर्जितभीताः **प्रियाः** अभिसारिकाः **कामिनां वसतिं प्रापयितु त्वदृते** त्वां विना । 'अन्यारादितरर्ते'—इत्यादिना पञ्चमी । **कः ईश्वरः** शक्तः । न कश्चिदित्यर्थः । न हि कामान्धानां भीतिरस्तीति भावः ॥

---

१ ष.

नयनान्यरुणानि घूर्णयन्वचनानि स्खलयन्पदे पदे ।
असति त्वयि वारुणीमदः प्रमदानामधुना विडम्बना ॥ १२ ॥

नयनानीति ॥ अरुणानि नयनानि घूर्णयन् भ्रमयन् । तथा पदे पदे प्रतिपदम् । वीप्सायां द्विरुक्तिः । वचनानि स्खलयन् विपर्यासयन् । प्रमदानां वारुणीमदः मद्यमदः अधुना त्वयि असति विडम्बना अनुकृतिमात्रम् । मदनाभावे मदस्य निष्फलत्वादिति भावः । तथा च शिशुपालवधे—'तां मदो दयितसङ्गमभूषः' (१० । ३३) इति ॥

अवगम्य कथीकृतं वपुः प्रियबन्धोस्तव निष्फलोदयः ।
बहुलेऽपि गते निशाकरस्तनुतां दुःखमनङ्ग मोक्ष्यति ॥ १३ ॥

अवगम्येति ॥ हे अनङ्ग अशरीर । प्रियबन्धोः प्रियसखस्य तव वपुः शरीरं कथीकृतम् अन्यथा कथा संपद्यमानं कृतं शब्दमात्रावशिष्टम् अवगम्य ज्ञात्वा निष्फलोदयः । उद्दीप्याभावादुद्दीपनवैफल्यमिति भावः । निशाकरः चन्द्रः बहुले कृष्णपक्षे गते अपि तनुतां कार्श्यं दुःखं यथा तथा कृच्छ्रात् मोक्ष्यति । वृथा वृद्धिरिति दुःखायिष्यत इत्यर्थः ॥

हरितारुणचारुबन्धनः कलपुंस्कोकिलशब्दसूचितः ।
वद संप्रति कस्य बाणतां नवचूतप्रसवो गमिष्यति ॥ १४ ॥

हरितेति ॥ [हरितारुणचारुबन्धनः] हरितं च अरुणं च । 'वर्णो वर्णेन' इति तत्पुरुषः । हरितारुणं चारु बन्धनं वृन्तं पुष्पस्य यस्य तथोक्तः । [कलपुंस्कोकिलशब्दसूचितः] । कलेन मधुरेण पुंस्कोकिलशब्देन पुरुषकोकिलनादेन सूचितोऽनुमापितश्च, चूतचर्वणकार्यत्वात्कलशब्दस्येति भावः । नवचूतप्रसवः नवचूतकुसुमं संप्रति कस्य बाणतां शरत्वं गमिष्यति वद । अन्यस्य पुष्पबाणस्याभावादिति भावः ॥

अलिपङ्क्तिरनेकशस्त्वया गुणकृत्ये धनुषो नियोजिता ।
विरुतैः करुणस्वनैरियं गुरुशोकामनुरोदितीव माम् ॥ १५ ॥

अलीति ॥ त्वया अनेकशः बहुशः धनुषः कार्मुकस्य गुणकृत्ये मौर्वीकार्ये गुणवत्कर्मणि च नियोजिता अधिकृता इयम् अलिपङ्क्तिः करुणस्वनैः दीनस्वनैः विरुतैः कूजितैः गुरुशोकां दुर्भरदुःखाम् । 'गुरुस्तु गीष्पतौ श्रेष्ठे गुरौ पितरि दुर्भरे ।' इति शब्दार्णवः । माम् अनुरोदिति इव । उपसर्गात्सकर्मकत्वम् । 'रुदादिभ्यः सार्वधातुके' इतीडागमः ।

प्रतिपद्य मनोहरं वपुः पुनरप्यादिश तावदुत्थितः ।
रतिदूतिपदेषु कोकिलां मधुरालापनिसर्गपण्डिताम् ॥ १६ ॥

१ कृत्ये. २ विततैः. ३ स्वरैः. ४ दूत. ५ कोकिलान्...पण्डिताम्.

प्रतिपद्येति ॥ **तावत्पुनरपि मनोहरं वपुः** शरीरं **प्रतिपद्य** प्राप्य **उत्थितः** सन् [**मधुरालापनिसर्गपण्डिताम्**] । मधुरालापेषु प्रियोक्तिषु निसर्गपण्डितां स्वभावप्रगल्भां **कोकिलां रतिदूतिपदेषु** सुरतदूतीस्थानेषु **आदिश** आज्ञापय । प्रगल्भानामेव दौत्याधिकार इति भावः । ङीबन्तस्यापि दूतीशब्दस्य छन्दोभङ्गभयाद् ह्रस्वः । 'अपि माषं मषं कुर्याच्छन्दोभङ्गं त्यजेद्गिरम् ।' इति केचित् । 'उणादयो बहुलम्' इति बहुलग्रहणाद् ह्रस्व इति वल्लभः ॥

शिरसा प्रणिपत्य याचितान्युपगूढानि सवेपथूनि च ।
सुरतानि च तानि ते रहः स्मर संस्मृत्य न शान्तिरस्ति मे ॥ १७ ॥

शिरसेति ॥ **स्मर** । **शिरसा प्रणिपत्य याचितानि सवेपथूनि** सकम्पानि । 'द्वितोऽथुच्' इत्यथुच्प्रत्ययः । सात्त्विकान्तरोपलक्षणमेतत् । 'स्तम्भप्रलयरोमाञ्चाः स्वेदो वैवर्ण्यवेपथू । अश्रुवैस्वर्यमित्यष्टौ सात्त्विकाः परिकीर्तिताः ॥ इति । **उपगूढानि** आलिङ्गनानि **च** । 'नपुंसके भावे क्तः' । **तानि** अनुभूतप्रकाराणि **ते रहः** एकान्ते **सुरतानि च संस्मृत्य मे शान्तिः न अस्ति** । अत्र समानकर्तृकत्वं दुर्घटम् समानक्रियापेक्षास्तीति केचित् ॥

रचितं रतिपण्डित त्वया स्वयमङ्गेषु ममेदमार्तवम् ।
ध्रियते कुसुमप्रसाधनं तव तच्चारु वपुर्न दृश्यते ॥ १८ ॥

रचितमिति ॥ हे **रतिपण्डित** रतिकुशल **त्वया मम अङ्गेषु** अवयवेषु **स्वयं रचितम्** । ऋतुरस्य प्राप्तः **आर्तवं** वासन्तम् । 'ऋतोरण्' इत्यण्प्रत्ययः । **कुसुमप्रसाधनं** पुष्पाभरणम् **इदम् ध्रियते** अवतिष्ठते । 'धृञ् अवस्थाने' इति धातोस्तौदादिकात्कर्तरि लट् । **तव तत्** प्रसाधकं **चारु** सुन्दरं **वपुः** तु **न दृश्यते** ॥

विबुधैरसि यस्य दारुणैरसमाप्ते परिकर्मणि स्मृतः ।
तमिमं कुरु दक्षिणेतरं चरणं निर्मितरागमेहि मे ॥ १९ ॥

विबुधैरिति ॥ **दारुणैः** क्रूरैः । प्राणान्तिके कर्मणि नियोगादिति भावः । **विबुधैः** देवैः । अनभिज्ञत्वं च ध्वन्यते । **यस्य** मच्चरणस्य **परिकर्मणि** प्रसाधने । 'परिकर्म प्रसाधनम्' इत्यमरः । **असमाप्ते** सति **स्मृतः असि** । **तमिमं दक्षिणेतरं** वामं **मे चरणं निर्मितरागं** रचितलाक्षारागं **कुरु** । **एहि** आगच्छ ॥

अहमेत्य पतङ्गवर्त्मना पुनरङ्काश्रयणी भवामि ते ।
चतुरैः सुरकामिनीजनैः प्रिय यावन्न विलोभ्यसे दिवि ॥ २० ॥

अहमिति ॥ **अहं पतङ्गवर्त्मना** शलभमार्गेण । अग्निप्रवेशेनेत्यर्थः । 'पतङ्गः शलभे चाग्नौ मार्जारेऽर्के शरे खगे ।' इति वैजयन्ती । **एत्य** आगत्य **पुनः ते अङ्काश्रयणी** उत्सङ्गवर्तिनी **भवामि** संप्रत्येव भाविष्यामि । 'वर्तमानसामीप्ये वर्तमानवद्वा' इति लट् ।

---

१ नवं. २ स्वमनङ्ग०,रापि यत्सुदा०-तादिमं. ३ प्रति०. ४ अयिणी. ५ विलुप्यसे; विकल्प्यसे.

हे प्रिय । दिवि स्वर्गे चतुरैः सुरकामिनीजनैः अप्सरोगणैः यावन्न विलोभ्यसे विलोभयिष्यसे । 'यावत्पुरानिपातयोर्लट्' इति लट् ॥

मदनेन विनाकृता रतिः क्षणमात्रं किल जीवितेति मे ।
वचनीयमिदं व्यवस्थितं रमण त्वामनुयामि यद्यपि ॥ २१ ॥

मदनेनेति ॥ हे रमण । त्वामनुयामि यद्यपि अनुगमिष्याम्येव । 'वर्तमानसामीप्ये वर्तमानवद्वा' इति लट् । 'यद्यपीत्यवधारणे' इति केशवः । किं तु रतिः मदनेन बिनाकृता । वियोजिता सतीत्यर्थः । सुप्सुपेति समासः । क्षणमात्रं जीविता किल इति इदं वचनीयं निन्दा मे मम व्यवस्थितं स्थिरमभूत् ॥

क्रियतां कथमन्त्यमण्डनं परलोकान्तरितस्य ते मया ।
सममेव गतोऽस्यतर्कितां गतिमङ्गेन च जीवितेन च ॥ २२ ॥

क्रियतामिति ॥ [परलोकान्तरितस्य] परलोकेऽन्तरितस्य व्यवहितस्य । मृतस्येत्यर्थः । ते तव मया अन्त्यमण्डनं कथं केन प्रकारेण क्रियताम् । क्रियतामित्यत्र कामचारे लोट् बोध्यः । द्रुतदग्धस्य ते यथेच्छमण्डनमपि न संभवतीत्यर्थः । कुतः । अङ्गेन च जीवितेन च समं सह एव अतर्किताम् अविचारितां गतिं गतोऽसि । इह मृतशरीरमपि नास्ति कस्य मण्डनमिति भावः ॥

ऋजुतां नयतः स्मरामि ते शरमुत्सङ्गनिषण्णधन्वनः ।
मधुना सह सस्मितां कथां नयनोपान्तविलोकितं च यत् ॥ २३ ॥

ऋजुतामिति ॥ शरम् ऋजुताम् आर्जवं नयतः [उत्सङ्गनिषण्णधन्वनः] उत्सङ्गे निषण्णमङ्कगतं धनुर्यस्य तस्य । 'धनुषश्च' इत्यनङ्गादेशः । ते तव मधुना वसन्तेन सह । 'मधुर्दैत्ये वसन्ते च चैत्रे च' इति विश्वः । सस्मितां कथाम् आलापं तथा यत् नयनोपान्तविलोकितम् अपाङ्गवीक्षणम् । ते इत्यनुषङ्गः । तत च स्मरामि ॥

क नु ते हृदयंगमः सखा कुसुमायोजितकार्मुको मधुः ।
न खलूग्ररुषा पिनाकिना गमितः सोऽपि सुहृद्गतां गतिम् ॥ २४ ॥

क्वेति ॥ हृदयं गच्छतीति हृदयंगमः हृद्यः । 'खच्प्रकरणे गमेः सुप्युपसंख्यानम्' इति खच्प्रत्ययः । 'अरुर्द्विषदजन्तस्य मुम्' इति मुमागमः । ते तव सखा [कुसुमायोजितकार्मुकः] कुसुमैरायोजितमारचितं कार्मुकं येन । कार्मुकनिर्माता मधुः वसन्तः क नु क वा । गत इति शेषः । अथ वा सः अपि उग्ररुषा तीव्रकोपेण पिनाकिना ईश्वरेण [सुहृद्गतां] सुहृदा मदनेन गतां प्राप्तां गतिम् । भस्मतामित्यर्थः । न गमितः खलु न प्रापितः किम् । 'जिज्ञासानुनये खलु' इत्यमरः ॥

---

१ जीवतीति. २ भ्रियते. ३ कत्वरितस्य. ४ निषङ्ग, निषक्त; ५ विलोकितानि च. ६ तत्.

अथ तैः परिदेविताक्षरैर्हृदये दिग्धशरैरिवाहतः ।
रतिमभ्युपपत्तुमातुरां मधुरात्मानमदर्शयत्पुरः ॥ २५ ॥

अथेति ॥ **अथ तैः परिदेविताक्षरैः** विलापवचनैः **हृदये दिग्धशरैः** विषलिप्तमुखैः शरैः **इव आहतः** सन् । 'विषाक्ते दिग्धलिप्तकौ' इत्यमरः । **मधुः** वसन्तः **आतुराम्** आपन्नां **रतिम् अभ्युपपत्तुम्** अनुग्रहीतुम् । आश्वासयितुमित्यर्थः । 'अभ्युपपत्तिरनुग्रहः' इत्यमरः । **आत्मानं पुरः अदर्शयत्** । आविरभूदित्यर्थः ॥

तमवेक्ष्य रुरोद सा भृशं स्तनसंबाधमुरो जघान च ।
स्वजनस्य हि दुःखमग्रतो विवृतद्वारमिवोपजायते ॥ २६ ॥

तमिति ॥ **सा** रतिः **तं** मधुम् **अवेक्ष्य** दृष्ट्वा **भृशं रुरोद** । स्तनौ संबाध्य **स्तनसंबाधम्** । 'परिक्लिश्यमाने च' इति णमुल् । **उरः जघान** ताडितवती **च** । तथा हि । **स्वजनस्य अग्रतः दुःखं** [**विवृतद्वारं**] विवृतमपसारितं द्वारं कपाटं यस्य तत् **इव उपजायते** आविर्भवति । उच्छृङ्खलं प्रवर्तत इत्युत्प्रेक्षाभिप्रायः ॥

इति चैनमुवाच दुःखिता सुहृदः पश्य वसन्त किं स्थितम् ।
तदिदं कणशो विकीर्यते पवनैर्भस्म कपोतकर्बुरम् ॥ २७ ॥

इतीति ॥ दुःखमस्याः संजातं **दुःखिता** । संजातदुःखेत्यर्थः । तारकादित्वादितच् । सा रतिः **एनं** वसन्तम् **इत्युवाच च** । चकारः पूर्वोक्तसमुच्चयार्थः । हे **वसन्त पश्य** । **सुहृदः** त्वत्सखस्य **किं स्थितम्** किमुपस्थितम् । **तद् इदं कपोतकर्बुरं** पारावतशबलं **कणशः** चूर्णीभूतम् । अल्पार्थाच्छस्प्रत्ययः । **भस्म पवनैः विकीर्यते** विक्षिप्यते । पश्य भस्मीभूतस्ते सुहृदित्यर्थः ॥

अयि संप्रति देहि दर्शनं स्मर पर्युत्सुक एष माधवः ।
दयितास्वनवस्थितं नृणां न खलु प्रेम चलं सुहृज्जने ॥ २८ ॥

अयीति ॥ **अयि स्मर संप्रति दर्शनं देहि** । **एष माधवः** वसन्तः **पर्युत्सुकः** त्वद्दर्शनोत्कण्ठितः । त्वामप्यनादृतवतोऽस्य को माधव इत्याशङ्क्याह—**नृणां** पुरुषाणां **दयितासु प्रेम अनवस्थितम्** अस्थिरम् । चलमित्यर्थः । **सुहृज्जने** प्रेम **तु न चलं खलु** ॥

ईदृशाः सुहृदः कति न सन्तीत्याशङ्क्य न कोऽपीत्याह —

अमुना ननु पार्श्ववर्तिना जगदाज्ञां ससुरासुरं तव ।
बिसतन्तुगुणस्य कारितं धनुषः पेलवपुष्पपत्रिणः ॥ २९ ॥

अमुनेति ॥ **ननु** मदन । **पार्श्ववर्तिना** सहचरेण **अमुना** वसन्तेन **ससुरासुरं** सुरासुरसहितं **जगत् बिसतन्तुगुणस्य** मृणालसूत्रमौर्वीकस्य [**पेलवपुष्पप-**

१ दिग्धफलैः. २ इवार्दितः; वार्पितः. ३ अभ्यवप०. ४ गुरु. ५ सुहृदं. ६ यद्. ७ प्रकीर्यते. ८ कापित्थक०; पाण्डुरम्. ९ सुहृत्सु चंचलम्. १० कोमल, पेशल.

त्रिणः] पेलवानि कोमलानि पुष्पाण्येव पत्रिणो बाणा यस्य तस्य तव **धनुषः आज्ञां कारितम्** । जगदाज्ञाकारितेत्यर्थः । 'हृक्रोरन्यतरस्याम्' इति जगतः कर्मत्वम् ॥

गत एव न ते निवर्तते स सखा दीप इवानिलाहतः ।
अहमस्य दशेव पश्य मामविषह्य[1]व्यसनेन धूमिताम् ॥ ३० ॥

गत इति ॥ **स ते सखा अनिलाहतः** वायुताडितः **दीपः इव गत एव न निवर्तते** । **अहमस्य** दीप्यमानस्य **दशा** वर्तिः **इव** । तिष्ठामीति शेषः । "दशा वर्ताववस्थायां वस्त्रान्ते स्युर्दशा अपि ।" इति विश्वः । कुतः । **अविषह्यव्यसनेन** सोढुमशक्यदुःखप्रकर्षेण **धूमितां** संजातधूमां **मां पश्य** । धूमवत्त्वान्नष्टदीपदशासाम्यं धूमश्च व्यसनमेवेत्यर्थः । वर्तिरपि दीपे नष्टे धूमिता भवति ॥

विधिना कृतम[2]र्धवैशसं ननु मां काम[3]वधे विमुञ्चता ।
अ[4]नपायिनि संश्रय[5]द्रुमे गजभग्ने पतनाय वल्लरी ॥ ३१ ॥

विधिनेति ॥ **ननु** वसन्त **कामवधे** मदनवधे **मां विमुञ्चता** वर्जयता । अमारयतेत्यर्थः । **विधिना** दैवेन । विशसति हिनस्तीति विशसो घातुकः । पचाद्यच् । विशसस्य कर्म वैशसम् । युवादित्वादण्प्रत्ययः । **अर्धवैशसम्** अर्धवधः **कृतम्** । 'अर्धो वा एष आत्मनो यत्पत्नी' इति श्रुतेः । पत्युः स्वस्य चाश्रयाश्रयीभूतयोरेकपदार्थत्वाभिप्रायेणार्धोक्तिः । तथा चैकदेशवधे देशान्तरस्यापि वधनियमनान्मामपि विधिरघ्नन्नेव हतवानिति तात्पर्यम् । एतदेवोपपादयति—**अनपायिनि** अनपायित्वेन विश्वस्ते **संश्रयद्रुमे** आश्रयवृक्षे **गजभग्ने** सति **वल्लरी** लता **पतनाय** भवतीति शेषः । पतितुमेव सालमित्यर्थः । 'तुमर्थाच्च भाववचनात्' इति चतुर्थी ॥

तदिदं क्रियतामनन्तरं भवता बन्धुजनप्रयोजनम् ।
विधुरां ज्वलनातिसर्जना[6]न्ननु मां प्रापय प[7]त्युरन्तिकम् ॥ ३२ ॥

तदिति ॥ **तत्** तस्मात्कारणादुक्तप्रकारेण । अन्यथापि मरणस्यावश्यंभावादित्यर्थः । **अनन्तरं भवता इदं** वक्ष्यमाणं **बन्धुजनप्रयोजनं** बन्धुकृत्यं **क्रियताम्** । प्रार्थनायां लोट् । तदेवोपदिशति—**ननु** वसन्त । **विधुरां** विवशां **मां ज्वलनातिसर्जनात्** अग्निदानात् **पत्युः अन्तिकं प्रापय** । अग्निप्रवेशनं कारयेत्यर्थः ॥

कर्तव्यश्चायमर्थः स्त्रीणामित्याह—

शशिना सह याति कौमुदी सह मेघेन तडित्[8]प्रलीयते ।
प्रमदाः पतिवर्त्मगा इति प्रतिपन्नं हि विचेतनैरपि ॥ ३३ ॥

शशिनेति ॥ **कौमुदी** चन्द्रिका **शशिना सह याति** । शशिन्यस्तमिते स्वयं नश्यतीत्यर्थः । **तडित्** सौदामनी **मेघेन सह प्रलीयते** प्रणश्यति । कर्तरि लट् । **प्रमदा**

---

१ व्यसनप्रधूमिताम्. २ मध. ३ वधेऽपि मु०. ४ अनघापि हि; अहतापि हि. ५ संश्रिता द्रुमे. ६ दनु. ७ भर्तुः. ८ विलीयते.

स्त्रियः पतिवर्त्म गच्छन्तीति **पतिवर्त्मगाः** पतिमार्गानुगामिन्यः **इति एतत् विचेतनैः** अल्पचेतनैः **अपि** । अविवेकिभिरपीत्यर्थः । नाथस्तु पृथग्जनैरिति पपाठ । **प्रतिपन्नं** ज्ञातं **हि** । 'अलवणा यवागूः' 'अनुदरा कन्या' इतिवदल्पत्वाभिप्रायेण विचेतनैरपीति निर्देशः । पतिवर्त्मगा इत्यत्र स्मृतिः—'आर्तार्ते मुदिते हृष्टा प्रोषिते मलिना कृशा । मृते म्रियेत या पत्यौ सा स्त्री ज्ञेया पतिव्रता ॥' इति ॥

अमुनैव कषायितस्तनी सुभगेन प्रियगात्रभस्मना ।
नवपल्लवसंस्तरे यथा रचयिष्यामि तनुं विभावसौ ॥ ३४ ॥

अमुनेति ॥ **अमुना** पुरोवर्तिना **सुभगेन** शोभनेन **प्रियगात्रभस्मना एव** । एवकारो मण्डनान्तरनिवृत्त्यर्थः । **कषायितस्तनी** रञ्जितस्तनी । 'रागे क्वाथे कषायोऽस्त्री निर्यासे सौरभे रसे ।' इति वैजयन्ती । **नवपल्लवसंस्तरे यथा** नवपल्लवतल्पे इव **विभावसौ** वह्नौ **तनुं** शरीरं **रचयिष्यामि** । निधास्यामीत्यर्थः ॥

कुसुमास्तरणे सहायतां बहुशः सौम्य गतस्त्वमावयोः ।
कुरु संप्रति तावदाशु मे प्रणिपाताञ्जलियाचितश्चिताम् ॥ ३५ ॥

कुसुमेति ॥ हे **सौम्य** साधो । **त्वम् आवयोः** रतिपञ्चबाणयोः **बहुशः** बहुवारं **कुसुमास्तरणे** पुष्पशयने **सहायतां गतः** । **संप्रति** [**प्रणिपाताञ्जलियाचितः**] प्रणिपाताञ्जलिना याचितः अञ्जलिपूर्वकं प्रार्थितः सन्नित्यर्थः । **आशु तावत् मे चितां** काष्ठचयं **कुरु** कुरुष्व । यथेह तथामुत्रोपकर्तव्यं मित्रेणेत्यर्थः ॥

तदनु ज्वलनं मदर्पितं त्वरयेर्दक्षिणवातवीजनैः ।
विदितं खलु ते यथा स्मरः क्षणमप्युत्सहते न मां विना ॥ ३६ ॥

तदन्विति ॥ **तत्** चिताकरणम् **अनु** अनन्तरं मय्यर्पितं **मदर्पितं ज्वलनम्** अग्निं **दक्षिणवातवीजनैः** मलयमारुतसंचारणैः **त्वरयेः** । त्वरितं ज्वलयेत्यर्थः । त्वराहेतुमाह—**ते** तव **विदितं खलु** । 'मतिबुद्धिपूजार्थेभ्यश्च' इति वर्तमाने क्तः । तद्योगात्कर्तरि षष्ठी । **यथा** येन प्रकारेण **स्मरः मां विना क्षणम् अपि न उत्सहते** न हृष्यति । तथा त्वया ज्ञातमेवेत्यर्थः ॥

इति चापि विधाय दीयतां सलिलस्याञ्जलिरेक एव नौ ।
अविभज्य परत्र तं[3] मया सहितः पास्यति ते स बान्धवः ॥ ३७ ॥

इतीति ॥ **अपि च इति** एवं **विधाय** कृत्वा **नौ** आवाभ्याम् **एक एव सलिलस्याञ्जलिः दीयताम्** । **तम् अञ्जलिं स ते बान्धवः** सखा स्मरः **परत्र** परलोके **मया सहितः अविभज्य पास्यति** ॥

परलोकविधौ च माधव स्मरमुद्दिश्य विलोलपल्लवाः ।
निवपेः सहकारमञ्जरीः प्रियचूतप्रसवो हि ते सखा ॥ ३८ ॥

---

१ विनि० याचितां. २ मद्विना. ३ तत्.

परलोकेति ॥ किं च । माधव वसन्त । परलोकविधौ पिण्डोदकादिकर्मणि स्मरम् उद्दिश्य [विलोलपल्लवाः] विलोलाः पल्लवाः यासु ताः सहकारमञ्जरीः चूतवल्लरीः निवपेः देहि । हि यस्मात्कारणात् ते सखा स्मरः [प्रियचूतप्रसवः] प्रियाः चूतप्रसवा यस्य स तथोक्तः ॥

इति देहविमुक्तये स्थितां रतिमाकाशभवा सरस्वती ।
शफरीं ह्रदशोषविक्लवां प्रथमा वृष्टिरिवान्वकम्पयत् ॥ ३९ ॥

इतीति ॥ इति [देहविमुक्तये] देहस्य विमुक्तये शरीरस्य विसर्गाय स्थिताम् । कृतानिश्चयामिति यावत् । रतिम् आकाशभवा सरस्वती अशरीरा वाक् ह्रदशोषविक्लवां ह्रदस्य जलाधारस्य शोषेण विक्लवां शफरीं प्रोष्ठीम् । 'प्रोष्ठी तु शफरी द्वयोः' इत्यमरः । प्रथमा वृष्टिः वर्षम् इव अन्वकम्पयत् अनुकम्पितवती । सदयमुवाचेत्यर्थः । 'कृपा दयानुकम्पा स्यात्' इत्यमरः ॥

कुसुमायुधपत्नि दुर्लभस्तव भर्ता न चिराद्भविष्यति ।
शृणु येन स कर्मणा गतः शलभत्वं हरलोचनार्चिषि ॥ ४० ॥

कुसुमेति ॥ हे कुसुमायुधपत्नि रते । तव भर्ता चिरात् चिरं दुर्लभः न भविष्यति । किं त्वचिरमेव सुलभो भविष्यतीत्यर्थः । शृणु । तत्कर्मेति शेषः । येन कर्मणा स ते भर्ता [हरलोचनार्चिषि] हरलोचनस्यार्चिर्ज्वाला । 'ज्वालाभासो न पुंस्यर्चिः' इत्यमरः । तस्मिन् शलभत्वं गतः । 'समौ पतङ्गशलभौ' इत्यमरः ॥

तदेव कर्मोपाचष्टे—

अभिलाषमुदीरितेन्द्रियः स्वसुतायामकरोत्प्रजापतिः ।
अथ तेन निगृह्य विक्रियामभिशप्तः फलमेतदन्वभूत् ॥ ४१ ॥

अभिलाषमिति ॥ उदीरितेन्द्रियः प्रेरितेन्द्रियः । स्मरेणेति शेषः । प्रजापतिः ब्रह्मा स्वसुतायां सरस्वत्याम् अभिलाषम् अनुरागम् अकरोत् । अथ तेन प्रजापतिना विक्रियाम् इन्द्रियविकारं निगृह्य निरुध्य अभिशप्तः सन् । एतत्फलम् दाहात्मकं स्वकर्मफलम् अन्वभूत ॥

शापावधिरपि तेनैवोक्त इत्याह श्लोकद्वयेन—

परिणेष्यति पार्वतीं यदा तपसा तत्प्रवणीकृतो हरः ।
उपलब्धसुखस्तदा स्मरं वपुषा स्वेन नियोजयिष्यति ॥ ४२ ॥
इति चाह स धर्मयाचितः स्मरशापावधिदां सरस्वतीम् ।
अशनेरमृतस्य चोभयोर्वशिनश्चाम्बुधराश्च योनयः ॥ ४३ ॥

परिणेष्यतीति ॥ इतीति च ॥ [धर्मयाचितः] धर्मेण धर्माख्यप्रजापतिना याचितः प्रार्थितः स ब्रह्मा भगवान् तपसा करणेन [तत्प्रवणीकृतः] तस्यां पार्वत्यां प्रवणीकृ-

---

१ स्थिराम्. २ विह्वलाम्. ३ अन्वकम्पत. ४ हरलोचनार्चिषाम्. ५ स योजयिष्यति, समग्रयिष्यति. ६ ०चारिणि. ७ स्मरशापान्तभवां, सधर्मचारिणीं स्मरशापान्तभवा सरस्वती.

तोऽभिमुखीकृतः **हरः** शिवः **यदा** पार्वतीं **परिणेष्यति** उद्वक्ष्यति । **तदा उपलब्धसुखः** प्राप्तानन्दः सन् । **स्मरं** कामं **स्वेन वपुषा नियोजयिष्यति ।** संगमयिष्यति । **इति** एवं [**स्मरशापावधिदां**] स्मरशापस्यावधिदामवसानदायिनीं **सरस्वतीं** वाचं **च आह** । एवं शापावधिमप्युक्तवानित्यर्थः । ननु तथा क्रुद्धस्य कथमीदृशी शान्तिरत आह—**वशिनः** जितेन्द्रियाः **च अम्बुधराः च अशनेः अमृतस्य च** इति **उभयोः योनयः** प्रभवाः । वशिपक्षेऽशन्यमृतशब्दौ कोपप्रसादपरौ । अन्यत्र वैद्युताग्न्युदकपरौ ॥ युग्मकम् ॥

तदिदं परिरक्ष शोभने भवितव्यप्रियसंगमं वपुः ।
रविपीतजला तपात्यये पुनरोघेन हि युज्यते नदी ॥ ४४ ॥

तदिति ॥ हे **शोभने तत्** तस्मात्कारणात् [**भवितव्यप्रियसंगमं**] भवितव्यो भविष्यन्प्रियसंगमो यस्य तत्तथोक्तम् **इदं वपुः परिरक्ष** । तथा हि । **रविपीतजला नदी तपात्यये** प्रावृषि । 'प्रावृट् तपात्यये' इति हलायुधः । **पुनः ओघेन** प्रवाहेण **युज्यते** संगच्छते **हि** ॥

इत्थं रतेः किमपि भूतमदृश्यरूपं मन्दीचकार मरणव्यवसायबुद्धिम् ।
तत्प्रत्ययाच्च कुसुमायुधबन्धुरेनां[3] आश्वासयत्सुचरितार्थपदैर्वचोभिः[4] ॥ ४५

इत्थमिति ॥ **इत्थम्** अनेन प्रकारेण **अदृश्यरूपं किमपि भूतं** कश्चित्प्राणी । 'युक्ते क्ष्मादावृते भूतं प्राण्यतीते समे त्रिषु ।' इत्यमरः । **रतेः** मदनदाराणां **मरणव्यवसायबुद्धिं** मरणोद्योगबुद्धिं **मन्दीचकार** । निवारयामासेत्यर्थः । 'मूढाल्पापटुनिर्भाग्या मन्दाः' इत्यमरः । अथ **कुसुमायुधबन्धुः** वसन्तः **च तत्प्रत्ययात्** तस्मिन्भूते विश्वासात् । 'प्रत्ययोऽधीनशपथज्ञानविश्वासहेतुषु ।' इत्यमरः । **एनां** रतिं [**सुचरितार्थपदैः**] सुष्ठु चरितार्थानि पदानि येषां तैः **वचोभिः** वाक्यैः **आश्वासयत्** । सर्वथा ते देवताप्रसादात्प्रियसंगमो भविष्यतीत्यादिवचनैरस्या दुःखमपाचकारेत्यर्थः ॥

अथ मदनवधूरुपप्लवान्तं व्यसनकृशा परिपालयांबभूव[5] ।
शशिन इव दिवातनस्य लेखा[6] किरणपरिक्षयधूसरा प्रदोषम्[7] ॥ ४६ ॥

अथेति ॥ **अथ** अनन्तरं [**व्यसनकृशा**] व्यसनेन दुःखेन कृशा **मदनवधूः** रतिः **उपप्लवान्तं** विपदवधिं [**किरणपरिक्षयधूसरा**] किरणपरिक्षयेण धूसरा मलिना **दिवातनस्य** दिनभवस्य । 'सायंचिरम्'—इत्यादिना ट्युप्रत्ययः । **शशिनः** चन्द्रस्य **लेखा प्रदोषं** रात्रिम् **इव परिपालयांबभूव** प्रतीक्षांचक्रे । पुष्पिताग्रावृत्तम् । 'अयुजि नयुगरेफतो यकारो युजि च नजौ जरगाश्च पुष्पिताग्रा ।' इति लक्षणात् ॥

इति श्रीमन्महामहोपाध्यायकोलाचलमल्लिनाथसूरिविरचितया
संजीविनीसमाख्यया व्याख्यया समेतः श्रीकालिदासकृतौ
कुमारसंभवे महाकाव्ये रतिविलापः नाम चतुर्थः सर्गः ॥

---

१ अपि वीत० २ पूर्यते. ३ एताम्. ४ समभिवृद्धरसैः. ५ प्रतिपाल०. ६ रेखा. ७ दिनान्तम्.

पञ्चमः सर्गः ।

तथा समक्षं दहता मनोभवं पिनाकिना भग्नमनोरथा सती ।
निनिन्द रूपं हृदयेन पार्वती प्रियेषु सौभाग्यफला हि चारुता ॥ १ ॥

तथेति ॥ पर्वतस्यापत्यं स्त्री **पार्वती तथा** तेन प्रकारेण अक्ष्णोः समीपे **समक्षं** पुरतः । 'अव्ययं विभक्तिसमीपसमृद्धि'–इत्यादिनाव्ययीभावः । **मनोभवं** मन्मथं **दहता** भस्मीकुर्वता **पिनाकिना** ईश्वरेण [**भग्नमनोरथा**] भग्नः खण्डितो मनोरथः अभिलाषो यस्याः सा तथोक्ता **सती हृदयेन** मनसा **रूपं** सौन्दर्यं **निनिन्द** । धिङ् मे रूपं यद्धरमनोहरणाय नालमिति गर्हितवतीत्यर्थः । युक्तं चैतदित्याह–तथा **हि** । **चारुता** सौन्दर्यं **प्रियेषु** पतिषु विषये [**सौभाग्यफला**] सौभाग्यं प्रियवाल्लभ्यं फलं यस्याः सा तथोक्ता । सौन्दर्यस्य तदेव फलं यद्भर्तृसौभाग्यं लभ्यते । नो चेद्विफलं तदिति भावः । अस्मिन्सर्गे वंशस्थं वृत्तम् –'जतौ तु वंशस्थमुदीरितं जरौ' इति लक्षणात् ॥

इयेष सा कर्तुमवन्ध्यरूपतां समाधिमास्थाय तपोभिरात्मनः ।
अवाप्यते वा कथमन्यथा द्वयं तथाविधं प्रेम पतिश्च तादृशः ॥ २ ॥

इयेषेति ॥ सा पार्वती **समाधिम्** एकाग्रताम् **आस्थाय** अवलम्ब्य **तपोभिः** वक्ष्यमाणनियमैः करणभूतैः **आत्मनः** स्वस्य **अवन्ध्यरूपतां** सफलसौन्दर्यं **कर्तुम् इयेष** इच्छति स्म । तपसा शिवं वशीकर्तुमुद्युक्तेत्यर्थः । **अन्यथा** ततोऽन्यप्रकारेण **कथं वा** तत् **द्वयम् अवाप्यते** । किं तद् द्वयम् । तथाभूता विधा प्रकारो यस्य तत् **तथाविधं प्रेम** स्नेहः । येनार्धाङ्गहरा हरस्य भवेदिति भावः । **तादृशः पतिश्च** । यो मृत्युंजय इति भावः । द्वयमेव खलु स्त्रीणामपेक्षितं यद्भर्तृवाल्लभ्यं जीवद्भर्तृकत्वं चेति । तच्च तपश्चर्यैकसाध्यमिति निश्चिकायेत्यर्थः । अत्र मनुः–' यद्दुष्करं यद्दुरापं यद्दुर्गं यच्च दुस्तरम् । तत्सर्वं तपसा प्राप्यं तपो हि दुरतिक्रमम् ॥ ' इति ॥

निशम्य चैनां तपसे कृतोद्यमां सुतां गिरीशप्रतिसक्तमानसाम् ।
उवाच मेना परिरभ्य वक्षसा निवारयन्ती महतो मुनिव्रतात् ॥ ३ ॥

निशम्येति ॥ **मेना** मेनका च **गिरीशप्रतिसक्तमानसां** हरासक्तचित्तां **तपसे** तपश्चरणाय **कृतोद्यमां** कृतोद्योगां **सुतां निशम्य** श्रुत्वा **एनां** पार्वतीं **वक्षसा परिरभ्य** आलिङ्ग्य **महतः मुनिव्रतात्** तपसः **निवारयन्ती उवाच** । मुनिव्रतादित्यत्र यद्यपि मुनिव्रतस्य मेनकाया अनीप्सितत्वात् ' वारणार्थानामीप्सितः ' इति नापादानत्वं तथापि कृतोद्यमामिति मानसप्रवेशोक्तत्वात् ' ध्रुवमपायेऽपादानं ' इत्यपादानत्वमेव स्यात् । यथाह भाष्यकारः–' यच्च मिथ्या संप्राप्य निवर्तते तच्च ध्रुवमपायेऽपादानम् इति प्रसिद्धम् । ' इति ॥

---

१ प्रिये सुसौ०. २ कामतां. ३ तत्. ४ गिरीशं प्रति सक्त०, त्रिनेत्र प्रतिसक्त.

सामान्यनिषेधमुक्त्वा विशेषनिषेधमाह—

मनीषिताः सन्ति गृहेषु देवतास्तपः क्व वत्से क्व च तावकं वपुः ।
पदं सहेत भ्रमरस्य पेलवं शिरीषपुष्पं न पुनः पतत्रिणः ॥ ४ ॥

मनीषिता इति ॥ हे **वत्से** । मनस ईषिता इष्टाः **मनीषिताः** । शकन्ध्वादित्वात्साधुः । **देवताः** शच्यादयः **गृहेषु सन्ति** । त्वं ता आराधयेति शेषः । **तपः क्व** । तवेदं **तावकम्** । ' युष्मदस्मदोरन्यतरस्यां खञ्च ' इत्यण्प्रत्ययः । ' तवकममकावेकवचने ' इति तवकादेशः । **वपुः च क्व** । तथा हि । **पेलवं** मृदुलं **शिरीषपुष्पं भ्रमरस्य** भृङ्गस्य **पदं** पदस्थितिं **सहेत** । **पतत्रिणः पुनः** पक्षिणस्तु पदं **न** सहेत । अतिसौकुमार्याद्दिव्योपभोगयोग्यं ते वपुर्न दारुणतपःक्षममित्यर्थः । अत्र दृष्टान्तालंकारः ॥

इति ध्रुवेच्छामनुशासती सुतां शशाक मेना न नियन्तुमुद्यमात् ।
क ईप्सितार्थस्थिरनिश्चयं मनः पयश्च निम्नाभिमुखं प्रतीपयेत् ॥ ५ ॥

इतीति ॥ **इति** एवम् **अनुशासती** उपदिशन्ती **मेना ध्रुवेच्छां** स्थिरव्यवसायां **सुतां** पार्वतीम् **उद्यमात्** उद्योगात्तपोलक्षणात् **नियन्तुं** निवारयितुं **न शशाक** समर्था नाभूत् । तथा हि । [**ईप्सितार्थस्थिरनिश्चयं**] इष्टार्थे ईप्सितार्थे स्थिरनिश्चयं **मनः निम्नाभिमुखं पयः च कः प्रतीपयेत्** प्रतिकूलयेत् । प्रतिनिवर्तयेदित्यर्थः । निम्नप्रवणं पय इवेष्टार्थाभिनिविष्टं मनो दुर्वारमिति भावः । अत्र दीपकानुप्राणितः अर्थान्तरन्यासोऽलंकारः ॥

कदाचिदासन्नसखीमुखेन सा मनोरथज्ञं पितरं मनस्विनी ।
अयाचतारण्यनिवासमात्मनः फलोदयान्ताय तपःसमाधये ॥ ६ ॥

कदाचिदिति ॥ अथ **कदाचित् मनस्विनी** स्थिरचित्ता **सा** पार्वती **मनोरथज्ञम्** अभिलाषाभिज्ञं **पितरं** हिमवन्तम् [**आसन्नसखीमुखेन**] आसन्नसख्याप्तसखी सैव मुखमुपायः । ' मुखं निःसरणे वक्त्रे प्रारम्भोपाययोरपि । ' इति विश्वः । तेन । [**फलोदयान्ताय**] फलोदयः फलोत्पत्तिरन्तोऽवधिर्यस्य तस्मै **तपःसमाधये** तपोनियमार्थम् **आत्मनः** स्वस्य **अरण्यनिवासं** वनवासम् **अयाचत** । ' दुह्याच्—' इत्यादिना द्विकर्मकत्वम् ॥

अथानुरूपाभिनिवेशतोषिणा कृताभ्यनुज्ञा गुरुणा गरीयसा ।
प्रजासु पश्चात्प्रथितं तदाख्यया जगाम गौरी शिखरं शिखण्डिमत् ॥ ७ ॥

अथेति ॥ **अथ गौरी** [**अनुरूपाभिनिवेशतोषिणा**] अनुरूपेण योग्येन अभिनिवेशेनाग्रहेण तुष्यतीति तथोक्तेन **गरीयसा** पूज्यतमेन **गुरुणा** पित्रा **कृताभ्यनुज्ञा** तपः कुर्विति कृतानुमतिः सती **पश्चात्** तपःसिद्ध्युत्तरकालं **प्रजासु**

१. ० तायार्चे, षिता अर्च. २ गृहेऽपि. ३ स्थिरे०, व्रते०, श्रुते०.

जनेषु **तदाख्यया** तस्या गौर्याः संज्ञया **प्रथितम्** । गौरीशिखरमिति प्रसिद्धमित्यर्थः । **शिखण्डिमत्** । न तु हिंस्रप्राणिप्रचुरमिति भावः । **शिखरं** शृङ्गं **जगाम** ययौ ॥

विमुच्य सा हारमहार्यनिश्चया विलोलयष्टिप्रविलुप्तचन्दनम्[1] ।
बबन्ध बालारुणबभ्रु वल्कलं पयोधरोत्सेधविशीर्णसंहति ॥ ८ ॥

विमुच्येति ॥ **अहार्यनिश्चया** अनिवार्यनिश्चया **सा** गौरी [**विलोलयष्टिप्रविलुप्तचन्दनम्**] विलोलाभिश्चलाभिर्यष्टिभिः प्रतिसरैः प्रविलुप्तं प्रमृष्टं चन्दनं स्तनान्तरगतं येन तं तथोक्तं **हारं** मुक्तावलीं **विमुच्य** विहाय **बालारुणबभ्रु** बालार्कपिङ्गलं [**पयोधरोत्सेधविशीर्णसंहति**] पयोधरयोः स्तनयोरुत्सेधेनोच्छ्रायेण विशीर्णा विघटिता संहतिरवयवसंश्लेषो यस्य तत्तथोक्तं **वल्कलं** कण्ठलम्बि स्तनोत्तरीयभूतं **बबन्ध** । धारयामासेत्यर्थः ॥

यथा प्रसिद्धैर्मधुरं शिरोरुहैर्जटाभिरप्येवमभूत्तदाननम् ।
न षट्पदश्रेणिभिरेव पङ्कजं सशैवलासङ्गमपि प्रकाशते ॥ ९ ॥

यथेति ॥ तस्या देव्या आननं **तदाननं प्रसिद्धैः** भूषितैः । 'प्रसिद्धौ ख्यातभूषितौ' इत्यमरः । रोहन्तीति रुहाः । 'इगुपधज्ञाप्रीकिरः कः' इति कप्रत्ययः । शिरसि रुहास्तैः **शिरोरुहैः** मूर्धजैः **यथा मधुरं** प्रियम् **अभूत्** । 'स्वादुप्रियौ तु मधुरौ' इत्यमरः । **जटाभिः अपि एवं** मधुरमभूत् । तथा हि । **पङ्कजं** पद्मं **षट्पदश्रेणिभिः** भ्रमरपङ्क्तिभिः **एव न** किं तु सह शैवलासङ्गेन **सशैवलासङ्गम् अपि** । 'तेन सहेति तुल्ययोगे' इति बहुव्रीहिः । **प्रकाशते** । शैवलेनापि शोभत एवेत्यर्थः ॥

प्रतिक्षणं सा कृतरोमविक्रियां[2] व्रताय मौञ्जीं त्रिगुणां[4] बभार याम् ।
अकारि तत्पूर्वनिबद्धया तया सरागमस्या रसनागुणास्पदम् ॥ १० ॥

प्रतीति ॥ **सा** देवी **प्रतिक्षणं** क्षणे क्षणे **कृतरोमविक्रियां** पारुष्यात्कृतरोमाञ्चां **त्रिगुणां** त्रिरावृत्तां **यां मौञ्जीं** मुञ्जमयीं मेखलां **व्रताय** तपसे **बभार** । [**तत्पूर्वनिबद्धया**] तदेव पूर्वं प्रथमं यस्य तत्पूर्वं यथा तथा निबद्धया **तया** मौञ्ज्या **अस्याः** देव्याः [**रसनागुणास्पदम्**] रसनागुणस्यास्पदं स्थानं जघनम् । सह रागेण **सरागं** सलोहितम् **अकारि** कृतम् । सौकुमार्यातिशयादिति भावः ॥

विसृष्टरागादधरान्निवर्तितः[5] स्तनाङ्गरागारुणिताच्च कन्दुकात्[6] ।
कुशाङ्कुरादानपरिक्षताङ्गुलिः कृतोऽक्षसूत्रप्रणयी तया करः ॥ ११ ॥

विसृष्टेति ॥ **तया** देव्या **विसृष्टरागात्** त्यक्तलाक्षारसरञ्जनात् **अधरात्** अधरोष्ठात् **निवर्तितः** । निसृष्टरागात् इति पाठे नितरां त्यक्तलाक्षारागात् । रागत्यागेन निष्प्रयोजनत्वादिति भावः । तथा [**स्तनाङ्गरागारुणितात्**] स्तनाङ्गरागेणारुणितादरुणीकृतात् पतनसमये तस्य स्तनयोरुपरोधादिति भावः । **कन्दुकात् च** निवर्तितः [**कुशाङ्कु-**

---

१ दृष्टिः परिलुप्तचन्दना. २ चन्दना. ३ रूप. ४ द्विगुणाम्. ५ निसृष्ट. ६ कञ्चुकात्.

रादानपरिक्षताङ्गुलिः] कुशाङ्कुराणामादानेन लवनेन परिक्षताः व्रणिताः अङ्गुल्यो यस्य स तथोक्तः करः पाणिः अक्षसूत्रप्रणयी अक्षमालासहचरः कृतः ॥

महार्हशय्यापरिवर्तनच्युतैः स्वकेशपुष्पैरपि या स्म दूयते ।
अशेत सा बाहुलतोपधायिनी निषेदुषी स्थण्डिल एव केवले ॥ १२ ॥

महार्हेति ॥ [महार्हशय्यापरिवर्तनच्युतैः] महानर्हो मूल्यं यस्याः सा महार्हा श्रेष्ठा या शय्या तस्यां परिवर्तनेन लुण्ठनेन च्युतैर्भ्रष्टैः स्वकेशपुष्पैः अपि या देवी दूयते स्म क्लिश्यति स्म । पुष्पाधिकसौकुमार्यादिति भावः । सा देवी बाहुलतामुपधत्ते उपधानीकरोतीति बाहुलतोपधायिनी सती केवले संस्तरणरहिते स्थण्डिले भूमौ एव अशेत शयितवती । तथा निषेदुषी उपविष्टा च । 'क्सुश्च' इति क्सुः । 'उगितश्च' इति ङीप् । भूमावेव शयनादिव्यवहारो न जातूपरीत्यर्थः ॥

पुनर्ग्रहीतुं नियमस्थया तया द्वयेऽपि निक्षेप[1] इवार्पितं द्वयम् ।
लतासु तन्वीषु विलासचेष्टितं विलोलदृष्टं हरिणाङ्गनासु च ॥ १३ ॥

पुनरिति ॥ नियमस्थया व्रतस्थया तया देव्या द्वये अपि द्वयं पुनः ग्रहीतुं पुनरानेतुं निक्षेपः अर्पितमिव निक्षेपत्वेनार्पितं किमु । क्वचित् द्वयीषु इति प्रामादिकः पाठः । कुत्र द्वये किं द्वयमर्पितमित्याह--तन्वीषु लतासु विलास एव चेष्टितं विलासचेष्टितं हरिणाङ्गनासु विलोलदृष्टं चञ्चलावलोकितं च । व्रतस्थायां तस्यां तयोरदर्शनाल्लतादिषु दर्शनाच्च र्पितमिवेत्युत्प्रेक्षा न तु वस्तुतोऽर्पणमस्तीति भावः ॥

अतन्द्रिता सा स्वयमेव वृक्षकान्घटस्तनप्रस्रवणै[4]र्व्यवर्धयत्[3] ।
गुहोऽपि येषां प्रथमाप्तजन्मनां न पुत्रवात्सल्यमपाकरिष्यति ॥ १४ ॥

अतन्द्रितेति ॥ सा देवी स्वयम् एव अतन्द्रिता असंजाततन्द्रा सती । तारकादित्वादितच्प्रत्ययः । वृक्षकान् स्वल्पवृक्षान् ['अल्पे ' इत्यल्पार्थे कप्रत्ययः । [घटस्तनप्रस्रवणैः] घटाविव स्तनौ तयोः प्रस्रवणैः प्रस्नुतपयोभिः व्यवर्धयत् । गुहः कुमारः अपि प्रथमाप्तजन्मनां प्रथमलब्धजन्मनाम् । अग्रजातानामित्यर्थः । येषां वृक्षकाणां संबन्धि पुत्रवात्सल्य सुतप्रेम न अपाकरिष्यति । उत्तरत्र कुमारोदयेऽपि न तेषु पुत्रवात्सल्यं निवर्तिष्यत इत्यर्थः ॥

अरण्यबीजाञ्जलिदानलालितास्तथा च तस्यां हरिणा विशश्वसुः ।
यथा तदीयैर्नयनैः कुतूहलात्पुरः सखीनाममिमीत लोचने ॥ १५ ॥

अरण्येति ॥ [अरण्यबीजाञ्जलिदानलालिताः] अरण्यबीजानां नीवारादीनामञ्जलयस्तेषां दानेन लालिताः हरिणाः च तस्यां देव्यां तथा विशश्वसुः विस्रम्भं जग्मुः । 'समौ विस्रम्भविश्वासौ ' इत्यमरः । यथा कुतूहलात् औत्सुक्यात् तदीयैः हरिणसबन्धिभिः नयनैः नेत्रैः करणैः । स्वकीये लोचने सखीनां पुरः

---

१ द्वयीषु. २ निक्षेपम्. ३ दाद्यः. ४ प्रस्नविनां.

पुरतः । अनेन तेषां संबन्धसहत्वमुक्तम् । **अमिमीत** । अक्षिपरिमाणतारतम्यज्ञानाय मानं चकारेत्यर्थः । केचित्तु सा पार्वती तदीयैर्नेत्रैः कुतूहलात्पुरोऽग्रे वर्तमानानां सखीनां लोचने अमिमीत व्रतस्थत्वान्नात्मन इत्याहुः । 'माङ् माने' इत्यस्माद्धातोर्लङ् । इयमेव खलु विश्वासस्य परा काष्ठा यदक्षिपीडनेऽपि न क्षुभ्यन्तीति भावः ॥

तपःप्रभावमाह—

कृताभिषेकां हुतजातवेदसं त्वगुत्तरासङ्गवतीमधीतिनीम् ।
दिदृक्षवस्तामृषयोऽभ्युपागमन्न धर्मवृद्धेषु वयः समीक्ष्यते ॥ १६ ॥

कृतेति ॥ **कृताभिषेकां** कृतस्नानां **हुतजातवेदसं** हुताग्निकाम् । कृतहोमामित्यर्थः । त्वचा वल्कलेनोत्तरासङ्गवतीमुत्तरीयवतीं **त्वगुत्तरासङ्गवतीम्** । अधीतमस्या अस्तीति **अधीतिनीं** स्तुतिपाठादि कुर्वतीम् । 'इष्टादिभ्यश्च' इतीनिप्रत्ययः । **तां** देवीं **दिदृक्षवः** द्रष्टुमिच्छवः **ऋषयः** मुनयः **अभ्युपागमन्** समुपागताः । न चात्र कनिष्ठसेवादोष इत्याह—**धर्मवृद्धेषु वयः न समीक्ष्यते** न प्रमाणीक्रियते । सति धर्मज्यैष्ठ्ये वयोज्यैष्ठ्यं न प्रयोजकमित्यर्थः । तथा च मनुः—'न तेन वृद्धो भवति येनास्य पलितं शिरः । यो वा युवाप्यधीयानस्तं देवाः स्थविरं विदुः ॥' इति ॥

विरोधिसत्त्वोज्झितपूर्वमत्सरं द्रुमैरभीष्टप्रसवार्चितातिथि ।
नवोटजाभ्यन्तरसंभृतानलं तपोवनं तच्च बभूव पावनम् ॥ १७ ॥

विरोधीति ॥ [**विरोधिसत्त्वोज्झितपूर्वमत्सरं**] विरोधिभिः सत्त्वैर्गोव्याघ्रादिभिरुज्झितपूर्वमत्सरं त्यक्तपूर्ववैरम् । हिंसारहितमित्यर्थः । **द्रुमैः** [**अभीष्टप्रसवार्चितातिथि**] अभीष्टप्रसवेनेष्टफलेनार्चिताः पूजिताः अतिथयो यस्मिंस्तत्तथोक्तम् । [**नवोटजाभ्यन्तरसंभृतानलं**] नवानामुटजानां पर्णशालानामभ्यन्तरेषु संभृताः संचिता अनला अग्नयो यस्मिंस्तत्तथोक्तं **तत् च तपोवनं** पावयतीति **पावनं बभूव** । अहिंसातिथिसत्काराग्निपरिचर्याभिर्जगत्पावनं बभूवेत्यर्थः ॥

यदा फलं पूर्वतपःसमाधिना न तावता लभ्यममंस्त काङ्क्षितम् ।
तदानपेक्ष्य स्वशरीरमार्दवं तपो महत्सा चरितुं प्रचक्रमे ॥ १८ ॥

यदेति ॥ **सा** देवी **यदा** यस्मिन् काले **तावता** तावत्प्रमाणेन **पूर्वतपःसमाधिना**] पूर्वेणानुष्ठीयमानप्रकारेण तपोनियमेन **काङ्क्षितं फलं लभ्यं** लब्धुं शक्यं **न अमंस्त** अशक्यममंस्तेत्यर्थः । **तदा** तत्काले । अविलम्बेनेत्यर्थः । [**स्वशरीरमार्दवं**] स्वशरीरस्य मार्दवं मृदुत्वं सौकुमार्यम् **अनपेक्ष्य** अविगणय्य **महत्** दुश्चरं तपः **चरितुं** साधयितुं **प्रचक्रमे** उपचक्रमे ॥

क्लमं ययौ कन्दुकलीलयापि या तया मुनीनां चरितं व्यगाह्यत ।
ध्रुवं वपुः काञ्चनपद्मनिर्मितं मृदु प्रकृत्या च ससारमेव च ॥ १९ ॥

---

१ निवीतिनीम्. २ संस्कृता०. ३ तत्र. ४ सर्वसमा समा०; सर्वसमाधिसाधनम्. ५ सेवया. ६ संनिभं,-धर्मि यत्. ७ हि.

क्रममिति ॥ **या** देवी **कन्दुकलीलया** कन्दुकक्रीडया **अपि क्लमं ययौ** ग्लानिं प्राप । **तया** देव्या **मुनीनां चरितं** तीव्रं तपः **व्यगाह्यत** प्रविष्टम् । अत्रोत्प्रेक्षते— **ध्रुवम्** अस्याः **वपुः [काञ्चनपद्मनिर्मितं]** काञ्चनपद्मेन सुवर्णकमलेन निर्मितं घटितम् । अत एव **प्रकृत्या** पद्मस्वभावेन **मृदु च** सुकुमारमपि काञ्चनस्वभावेन **ससारं च** कठिनं **एव** । तथा च तदुपादानकत्वाद्देव्या वपुषः सुकुमारस्यापि तीव्रतपःक्षमत्वमित्युत्प्रेक्षार्थः ॥

शुचौ चतुर्णां ज्वलतां हविर्भुजां शुचिस्मिता मध्यगता सुमध्यमा।
विजित्य नेत्रप्रतिघातिनीं प्रभामनन्यदृष्टिः सवितारमैक्षत ॥ २० ॥

शुचाविति ॥ **शुचौ** ग्रीष्मे **शुचिस्मिता** विशदमन्दहासा **सुमध्यमा** पार्वती **ज्वलतां** दीप्तिमतां **चतुर्णां हविर्भुजाम्** अग्नीनां **मध्यगता** सती । नेत्रे प्रतिहन्तीति तां **नेत्रप्रतिघातिनीं प्रभां** सावित्रं तेजः **विजित्य** । न विद्यतेऽन्यत्र दृष्टिर्यस्याः सा **अनन्यदृष्टिः** सती **सवितारं** सूर्यम् **ऐक्षत** ददर्श । 'ग्रीष्मे पञ्चाग्निमध्यस्थो वर्षासु स्थण्डिलेशयः ।' इति स्मरणात् । पञ्चाग्निमध्ये तपश्चचारेत्यर्थः । सवितैव पञ्चमोऽग्निः—'अग्निः सविता सवितैवाग्निः' इति श्रौतलिङ्गात् ॥

तथातितप्तं[1] सवितुर्गभस्तिभिर्मुखं तदीयं कमलश्रियं दधौ ।
अपाङ्गयोः केवलमस्य दीर्घयोः शनैः शनैः श्यामिकया कृतं पदम् २१

तथेति ॥ **सवितुः** सूर्यस्य **गभस्तिभिः** किरणैः **तथा** पूर्वोक्तप्रकारेण **अतितप्तं** संतप्तं तस्या इदं **तदीयं मुखं कमलश्रियं** कमलस्य शोभां **दधौ** प्राप । यथा रवितापात्कमलं न म्लायति प्रत्युत विकसति तथा तदीयं मुखमासीदिति भावः । किं तु **अस्य** मुखस्य **दीर्घयोः अपाङ्गयोः केवलं** नेत्रान्तयोरेव **शनैः शनैः** मन्दं मन्दं **श्यामिकया** कालिम्ना **पदं** स्थानं **कृतम्** । तयोः सौकुमार्यादित्यर्थः ॥

अयाचितोपस्थितमम्बु केवलं रसात्मकस्योडुपतेश्च रश्मयः ।
बभूव तस्याः किल[2] पारणाविधिर्न वृक्षवृत्तिव्यतिरिक्तसाधनः[3][4] ॥२२॥

अयाचितेति ॥ **अयाचितोपस्थितम्** अप्रार्थितोपनतं **केवलम् अम्बु** उदकं **रसात्मकस्य** अमृतमयस्य [**उडुपतेः**] उडूनां नक्षत्राणां पतिश्चन्द्रस्तस्य **रश्मयः च तस्याः** पार्वत्याः **पारणाविधिः** अभ्यवहारकर्म **बभूव** । तावन्मात्रसाधनकोऽभूदित्यर्थः । साध्यसाधनयोरभेदेन व्यपदेशः साधनान्तरव्यावृत्त्यर्थः । **किल** इति प्रसिद्धौ । [**वृक्षवृत्तिव्यतिरिक्तसाधनः**] वृक्षाणां या वृत्तिर्जीवनोपायस्तद्व्यतिरिक्तं साधनमुपायो यस्य स तथोक्तः पारणाविधिः **न** बभूव । वृक्षोऽप्ययाचितोपस्थितेन मेघोदकेनेन्दुकिरणैश्च जीवतीति प्रसिद्धम् । अम्बिकापि तावन्मात्रम[म्बुपि]बतेत्यर्थः ॥

निकामतप्ता विविधेन[5] वह्निना नभश्चरेणेन्धनसंभृतेन सा[6] ।
तपात्यये वारिभिरुक्षिता नवैर्भुवा सहोष्माणममुञ्चदूर्ध्वगम् ॥२३॥

---

1 तथाभितप्तं, तथापि तप्तम्. २ खलु. ३ वृक्षवृत्तिः. ४ साधनम्. ५ द्विविधेन. ६ च.

निकामेति ॥ **विविधेन** । पञ्चविधेनेत्यर्थः । **नभश्चरेण** खेचरेण । आदित्यरूपेणेत्यर्थः । **इन्धनसंभृतेन** काष्ठसमिद्धेन **वह्निना** [**निकामतप्ता** निकामं अत्यन्तं तप्ता **सा** अम्बिका **तपात्यये** ग्रीष्मान्ते । प्रावृषीत्यर्थः । **नवैः वारिभिः उक्षिता** सिक्ता सती **भुवा** पञ्चाग्नितप्तया **सह ऊर्ध्वगम्** ऊर्ध्वप्रसृतम् **ऊष्माणं** बाष्पम् **अमुञ्चत** । 'ग्रीष्मोष्मबाष्पा ऊष्माणः' इति यादवः ॥

स्थिताः क्षणं पक्ष्मसु ताडिताधराः पयोधरोत्सेधनिपातचूर्णिताः ।
वलीषु तस्याः स्खलिताः प्रपेदिरे चिरेण नाभिं प्रथमोदबिन्दवः ॥२४॥

स्थिता इति ॥ [**प्रथमोदबिन्दवः**] उदकस्य बिन्दवः उदबिन्दवः । 'मन्थौदन–' इत्यादिनोदकशब्दस्योदादेशः । प्रथमे उदबिन्दवः । प्रथमविशेषणाद्बिन्दूनां विरलत्वं बहुवचनान्नातिविरलत्वं च गम्यते । तथा च चिरत्वनाभ्यन्तरगमनयोर्निर्वाहः । **तस्याः** पार्वत्याः **पक्ष्मसु** नेत्रलोमसु **क्षणं स्थिताः** स्थितिं गताः । स्थिता इत्यनेन पक्ष्मणां सान्द्रत्वं क्षणमिति स्नैग्ध्यं च गम्यते । अनन्तरं [**ताडिताधराः**] ताडितो व्यथितोऽधर ओष्ठो यैस्ते तथोक्ताः । एतेनाधरस्य मार्दवं गम्यते । ततः [**पयोधरोत्सेधनिपातचूर्णिताः**] पयोधरयोः स्तनयोः उत्सेधे उपरिभागे निपातेन पतनेन चूर्णिता जर्जरिताः । कुचकाठिन्यादिति भावः । तदनु **वलीषु** उदररेखासु **स्खलिताः** । निम्नोन्नतत्वादिति भावः । इत्थं **चिरेण** न तु शीघ्रम् । प्रतिबन्धबाहुल्यादिति भावः । **नाभिं प्रपेदिरे** प्रविष्टाः । न तु निर्जग्मुः । एतेन नाभेर्गाम्भीर्यं गम्यते । अत्र प्रतिपदमर्थवत्त्वात्परिकरालंकारः ॥

शिलाशयां तामनिकेतवासिनीं निरन्तरास्वन्तरवातवृष्टिषु ।
व्यलोकयन्नुन्मिषितैस्तडिन्मयैर्महातपःसाक्ष्य इव स्थिताः क्षपाः ॥२५॥

शिलाशयामिति ॥ **निरन्तरासु** नीरन्ध्रासु अन्तरे मध्ये वातो यासां तादृश्यो या वृष्टयस्तासु **अन्तरवातवृष्टिषु** । न निकेते गृहे वसतीति **अनिकेतवासिनीम्** । अनावृतदेशवासिनीमित्यर्थः । शिलायां शेत इति **शिलाशयां** शिलातलशायिनीम् । 'अधिकरणे शेतेः' इत्यच्प्रत्ययः । **तां** पार्वतीं [**महातपःसाक्ष्ये**] साक्षाद्द्रष्टा साक्षी । 'साक्षाद्द्रष्टरि संज्ञायाम्' इतीनिप्रत्ययः । तस्य कर्म साक्ष्यम् । महातपसः साक्ष्ये **स्थिताः क्षपाः तडिन्मयैः** विद्युद्रूपैः **उन्मिषितैः** अवलोकनैः **व्यलोकयन् इव** । इवेति चक्षुषा विलोकनमेवोत्प्रेक्ष्यते । साक्ष्यं तु 'आदित्यचन्द्रावनिलोऽनलश्च द्यौर्भूमिरापो हृदयं यमश्च । अहश्च रात्रिश्च उभे च संध्ये धर्मश्च जानाति नरस्य वृत्तम् ॥' इति प्रमाणसिद्धत्वान्नोत्प्रेक्ष्यमित्यनुसंधेयम् ॥

एवं वर्षासु विहितं तपःप्रकारमुक्त्वा संप्रति हेमन्ते तपश्चरणप्रकारमाह—

निनाय सात्यन्तहिमोत्किरानिलाः सहस्यरात्रीरुदवासतत्परा ।
परस्पराक्रन्दिनि चक्रवाकयोः पुरो वियुक्ते मिथुने कृपावती ॥२६॥

१ ०रोत्सङ्ग. २ सात्यन्त, अत्यर्थ०; अत्यर्थहिमोत्करानिलाः.

निनायेति ॥ **सा** पार्वती । [**अत्यन्तहिमोत्किरानिलाः**] उत्किरन्ति क्षिपन्तीत्युत्किराः । 'इगुपधज्ञा-' इत्यादिना कः । अत्यन्तं हिमानामुत्किरा अनिला यासु ताः **सहस्यरात्रीः** पौषरात्रीः । 'पौषे तैषसहस्यौ द्वौ' इत्यमरः । [**उदवासतत्परा**] उदके वास उदवासः । 'पेषंवासवाहनाधिषु च' इत्युदादेशः । उदवासे तत्परा आसक्ता तथा [**परस्पराक्रन्दिनि**] परस्परमाक्रन्दिन्यन्योन्यमाक्रोशिनि **पुरः** अग्रे **वियुक्ते** विरहिणि । वियोगं प्राप्ते इति यावत् । चक्रवाकी च चक्रवाकश्च चक्रवाकौ तयोः **चक्रवाकयोः मिथुने** द्वन्द्वे **कृपावती** सती **निनाय** । दुःखिषु कृपालुत्वं महतां स्वभाव इति चक्रवाकमिथुने कृपा न तु कामितयेति वाच्यानवकाशः । 'अप्सु वासस्तु हेमन्ते क्रमशो वर्धयेत्तपः ।' इति मनुः ॥

मुखेन सा पद्मसुगन्धिना निशि प्रवेपमानाधरपत्रशोभिना ।
तुषारवृष्टिक्षतपद्मसंपदां सरोजसंधानमिवाकरोदपाम् ॥ २७ ॥

मुखेनेति ॥ **सा** पार्वती **निशि** रात्रौ [**पद्मसुगन्धिना**] पद्मवत्सुगन्धिना सुरभिणा । 'गन्धस्येत्'—इत्यादिनेकारः । [**प्रवेपमानाधरपत्रशोभिना**] प्रवेपमानः कम्पमानोऽधर ओष्ठ एव पत्रं दलं तेन शोभत इति तथोक्तेन **मुखेन** [**तुषारवृष्टिक्षतपद्मसंपदां**] तुषारवृष्ट्या तुहिनवर्षेण क्षता नाशिताः पद्मसंपदो यासां तासाम् **अपां सरोजसंधानं** पद्मसंघट्टनम् **अकरोद् इव** । इत्युत्प्रेक्षालंकारः । पद्मान्तरं तुहिनेनोपहन्यते तन्मुखपद्मं तु न तथेति व्यतिरेकालंकारो व्यज्यते इत्युभयोः संकरः ॥

स्वयंविशीर्णद्रुमपर्णवृत्तिता[1] परा हि काष्ठा तपसस्तया पुनः ।
तदप्यपाकीर्णमतः प्रियंवदां[3] वदन्त्यपर्णेति[4] च तां पुराविदः ॥२८॥

स्वयमिति ॥ [**स्वयंविशीर्णद्रुमपर्णवृत्तिता**] स्वयं विशीर्णानि स्वतश्च्युतानि द्रुमपर्णान्येव वृत्तिर्जीवनं यस्य तस्य भावस्तत्ता **तपसः परा काष्ठा** परमुत्कर्षो **हि** । 'काष्ठोत्कर्षे स्थितौ दिशि' इत्यमरः । **तया** देव्या **पुनः तत्** पर्णवर्तनम् **अपि अपाकीर्णम्** अपाकृतम् । **अतः** पर्णापाकरणाद्धेतोः । [**प्रियंवदां**] प्रियं वदतीति प्रियंवदा ताम् । 'प्रियवशे वदः खच्' इति खच्प्रत्ययः । 'अरुर्द्विषदजन्तस्य मुम्' इति मुमागमः । **तां** पार्वतीं **पुराविदः** पुराणज्ञास्तपःकरणसमयेऽविद्यमानं पर्णभक्षणं यस्याः सा **अपर्णा इति वदन्ति च** । नामान्तरसमुच्चयार्थश्चकारः । स्वयं प्रियंवदाः परेषामपि प्रियवादभाजनानि भवन्तीति भावः । अत्र अपर्णाम् इत्यपपाठ इतिशब्दाभिहिते द्वितीयानुपपत्तेः । यथाह वामनः–' निपातेनाप्यभिहिते कर्मणि न कर्मविभक्तिः परिगणनस्य प्रायिकत्वात् ' इति ॥

मृणालिकापेलवमेवमादिभिर्व्रतैः स्वमङ्गं ग्लपयन्त्यहर्निशम् ।
तपः शरीरैः कठिनैरुपार्जितं तपस्विनां दूरमधश्चकार सा ॥ २९ ॥

---

१ संतानं. २ पत्र. ३ प्रियंवदाः. ४ न्त्यपर्णां किल. ५ कोमल. ६ तदङ्गम्. ७ क्षपयन्ती.

मृणालिकेति ॥ **मृणालिकापेलवं** पद्मिनीकन्दकोमलं **स्वं** स्वकीयम् **अङ्गं** शरीरम् [**एवमादिभिः**] एवमुक्तप्रकारतोयाग्निमध्यवासव्रतमादिर्येषां तैः **व्रतैः** । अहश्च निशा च **अहर्निशम्** । समाहारे द्वन्द्वैकवद्भावः । अत्यन्तसंयोगे द्वितीया । **ग्लपयन्ती** कर्शयन्ती **सा** पार्वती **कठिनैः** । क्लेशसहैरित्यर्थः । **शरीरैः उपार्जितं** संपादितं **तपस्विनाम्** ऋषीणां **तपः दूरम्** अत्यन्तम् **अधश्चकार** । अतिशिश्ये इत्यर्थः । तपस्विभिरप्येवं तपः कर्तुं न शक्यत इति तात्पर्यार्थः ॥

अथाजिनाषाढधरः प्रगल्भवाग्ज्वलन्निव ब्रह्ममयेन तेजसा ।
विवेश कश्चिज्जटिलस्तपोवनं शरीरबद्धः[2] प्रथमाश्रमो यथा ॥ ३० ॥

अथेति ॥ **अथ** अनन्तरम् [**अजिनाषाढधरः**] अजिनं कृष्णमृगत्वक् । आ ऽढः प्रयोजनमस्येत्याषाढः पालाशदण्डः । 'पालाशो दण्ड आषाढः' इत्यमरः । 'विशाखाषाढादण्मन्थदण्डयोः' इत्यण्प्रत्ययः । तयोर्धरस्तथोक्तः । **प्रगल्भवाक्** प्रौढवचनः **ब्रह्ममयेन** वैदिकेन **तेजसा** । ब्रह्मवर्चसेनेत्यर्थः । **ज्वलन् इव** स्थितः । इवशब्दो निर्धारणार्थः । **कश्चिद्** अनिर्दिष्टः **जटिलः** जटावान् । ब्रह्मचारीति शेषः । पिच्छादित्वादिलच्प्रत्ययः । **शरीरबद्धः** बद्धशरीरः । शरीरवानित्यर्थः । आहिताग्न्यादिषु पाठात्साधुः । **प्रथमाश्रमः यथा** ब्रह्मचर्याश्रम इव । यथाशब्द इवार्थे । **तपोवनम्** । देव्या इति शेषः । **विवेश** प्रविष्टवान् ॥

तमातिथेयी बहुमानपूर्वया सपर्यया प्रत्युदियाय पार्वती ।
भवन्ति साम्येऽपि[3] निविष्टचेतसां वपुर्विशेषेष्वतिगौरवाः क्रियाः ॥ ३१ ॥

तमिति ॥ अतिथिषु साध्वी **आतिथेयी** । 'पथ्यतिथि'—इत्यादिना ढञ्प्रत्ययः । 'टिड्ढाणञ्' इत्यादिना ङीप् । **पार्वती तं** ब्रह्मचारिणं **बहुमानपूर्वया** बहुमानः पूर्वो यस्यास्तया । गौरवपूर्वयेत्यर्थः । **सपर्यया** अर्चया । 'सपर्यार्चार्हणाः समाः' इत्यमरः । **प्रत्युदियाय** प्रत्युज्जगाम । कथं समानेऽपि तस्यास्तादृशी प्रतिपत्तिरत आह—**साम्ये** सति **अपि निविष्टचेतसां** स्थिरचित्तानां **वपुर्विशेषेषु** व्यक्तिविशेषेषु अतिशयितं गौरवं यासु ताः **अतिगौरवाः** अतिगौरवसहिताः **क्रियाः** चेष्टाः **भवन्ति** । प्रवर्तन्ते इत्यर्थः । साधवो न साम्याभिनिवेशिन इति भावः ॥

विधिप्रयुक्तां परिगृह्य सत्क्रियां परिश्रमं नाम विनीय च क्षणम् ।
उमां स पश्यन्नृजुनैव चक्षुषा प्रचक्रमे वक्तुमनुज्झितक्रमः ॥ ३२ ॥

विधीति ॥ **स** ब्रह्मचारी [**विधिप्रयुक्तां**] विधिना प्रयुक्तामनुष्ठितां **सत्क्रियां** पूजां **परिगृह्य** स्वीकृत्य **क्षणं परिश्रमं** विश्रामं **च विनीय नाम** । नामेत्यपरमार्थे । अथ

२९–३० श्लोकयोर्मध्ये क्षेपकोऽयं दृश्यते—

सुराः समु(तदु-)दीक्ष्य नगेन्द्रकन्यया कृतं तपः शंभुवशक्रियाक्षमम् ।
ययाचिरे तं प्रणिपत्य दुःखिताः पतिं चमूनां सुतमाजिहेतुम् (हेतवे) ॥

१ वर्षता. २ बन्धः. ३ म्येऽप्रभिनि०. ४ अधि०. ५ प्रतिगृह्य.

उमाम् ऋजुना एव विलासरहितेनैव **चक्षुषा पश्यन् अनुज्झितक्रमः** अत्यक्तोचितपरिपाटीकः सन्। **वक्तुं प्रचक्रमे** प्रारेभे ॥

अपि क्रियार्थं सुलभं समित्कुशं जलान्यपि स्नानविधिक्षमाणि ते ।
अपि स्वशक्त्या तपसि प्रवर्तसे शरीरमाद्यं खलु धर्मसाधनम् ॥ ३३

अपीति ॥ अत्रापिशब्दः प्रश्ने । **क्रियार्थं** होमादिकर्मानुष्ठानार्थम्। समिधश्च कुशाश्च **समित्कुशम्** । 'जातिरप्राणिनाम्' इति द्वन्द्वैकवद्भावः। **सुलभम् अपि** सुलभं कच्चित् । **जलानि ते** तव **स्नानविधिक्षमाणि** स्नानक्रियायोग्यानि **अपि** कच्चित्। किं च **स्वशक्त्या** निजसामर्थ्यानुसारेण **तपसि प्रवर्तसे अपि** । देहमपीडयित्वा तपश्चरसि कच्चिदित्यर्थः । युक्तं च नामैतत्। **खलु** यस्मात् **शरीरम् आद्यं धर्मसाधनम्** । धर्मस्तु कायेन वाचा बुद्धया धनादिना च बहुभिः साध्यते । तेषु च वपुरेव मुख्यं साधनम् । सति देहे धर्मार्थकाममोक्षलक्षणाश्चतुर्वर्गाः साध्यन्ते । अत एव 'सततमात्मानमेव गोपायीत' इति श्रुतिः । 'अयथाबलमारम्भो निदानं क्षयसंपदाम् ।' इति भावः ॥

अपि त्वदावर्जितवारिसंभृतं प्रवालमासामनुबन्धि वीरुधाम् ।
चिरोज्झितालक्तकपाटलेन ते तुलां यदारोहति दन्तवाससा ॥३४॥

अपीति ॥ [**त्वदावर्जितवारिसंभृतं**] त्वयावर्जितेन सिक्तेन वारिणा संभृतं जनितम् **आसां वीरुधां** लतानां **प्रवालं** पल्लवम् **अनुबन्धि अपि** अनुस्यूतं किम्। **यत्** प्रवालं चिरोज्झितश्चिरकालत्यक्तो लाक्षारागो येन तत्तथापि पाटलम् । स्वभावरक्तमित्यर्थः । तेन **चिरोज्झितालक्तकपाटलेन ते** तव **दन्तवाससा** अधरेण । 'ओष्ठाधरौ तु रदनच्छदौ दशनवाससी ।' इत्यमरः। **तुलां** साम्यम् **आरोहति** । गच्छतीत्यर्थः । अत्र तुलाशब्दस्य सादृश्यवाचित्वात्तद्योगेऽपि 'तुल्यार्थैरतुलोपमाभ्याम्' इति न तृतीयाप्रतिषेधः तत्र सूत्रे सदृशवाचिन एव ग्रहणादिति ॥

अपि प्रसन्नं हरिणेषु ते मनः करस्थदर्भप्रणयापहारिषु ।
य उत्पलाक्षि प्रचलैर्विलोचनैस्तवाक्षिसादृश्यमिव प्रयुञ्जते ॥ ३५ ॥

अपीति ॥ [**करस्थदर्भप्रणयापहारिषु**] करस्थान्दर्भान्प्रणयेन स्नेहेनापहरन्तीति ते तथोक्तेषु । सापराधेष्विति भावः । 'करस्थदर्भप्रणयापराधिषु' इति पाठे दर्भाणां प्रणयेन प्रार्थनयापराधिषु। **हरिणेषु** विषये **ते मनः प्रसन्नम् अपि** । न क्षुभितं किम् । सापराधेष्वपि न कोपितव्यं तपस्विभिरिति भावः । हे **उत्पलाक्षि ये** हरिणाः **प्रचलैः** चञ्चलैः **विलोचनैः** नेत्रैः **तवाक्षिसादृश्यं प्रयुञ्जते इव** अभिनयन्तीव । प्रदर्शयन्त्यान्मृगनेत्राणि त्वन्नयनाभ्यां साम्यमुपयान्तीति भावः । 'उत्पलक्षेपचलैः' इति पाठान्तरे उत्पलकम्पचलैः। भावानयने द्रव्यानयनमिति न्यायेन क्षिप्यमाणोत्पलचलैरित्यर्थः ॥

---

१ अयि. २ क्रियार्थे. ३ विधौ. ४ पराधिषु. ५ ०लाक्षेपचलैः. ६ सापत्न्यम्.

यदुच्यते पार्वति पापवृत्तये न रूपमित्यव्यभिचारि तद्वचः ।
तथा हि ते शीलमुदारदर्शने तपस्विनामप्युपदेशतां गतम् ॥ ३६ ॥

यदिति ॥ हे **पार्वति रूपं** सौम्याकृतिः **पापवृत्तये** पापाचरणाय **न** भवति । **इति यदुच्यते** । लोकैरिति शेषः । **तद्वचः** न व्यभिचरति न स्खलतीति **अव्यभिचारि** सत्यम् । ‘यत्राकृतिस्तत्र गुणाः’ । ‘न सुरूपाः पापसमाचारा भवन्ति ।’ इत्यादयो लोकवादा न विसंवादमासादयन्तीत्यर्थः । किमिति ज्ञायते—**तथा हि** । हे **उदारदर्शने** आयताक्षि । सुरूपे इत्यर्थः । अथ वा उन्नतज्ञाने । विवेकवतीत्यर्थः । **ते** तव **शीलं** सद्वृत्तम् । ‘शीलं स्वभावे सद्वृत्ते’ इत्यमरः । **तपस्विनाम् अपि** उपदिश्यते अनेनेत्युपदेशः प्रवर्तकं प्रमाणं तत्ताम् **उपदेशतां गतं** प्राप्तम् । मुनयोऽपि त्वां वीक्ष्य स्ववृत्ते प्रवर्तन्त इति भावः ॥

विकीर्णसप्तर्षिबलिप्रहासिभि[1]स्तथा न गाङ्गैः सलिलैर्दिवश्च्युतैः ।
यथा त्वदीयैश्चरितैरनाविलैर्महीधरः पावित एष सान्वयः ॥ ३७ ॥

विकीर्णेति ॥ **एष महीधरः** हिमवान् । [**विकीर्णसप्तर्षिबलिप्रहासिभिः**] सप्त च ते ऋषयश्च सप्तर्षयः । ‘दिक्संख्ये संज्ञायाम्’ इति समासः । विकीर्णैः पर्यस्तैः सप्तर्षीणां संबन्धिभिर्बलिभिः । पुष्पोपहारैः प्रहसन्ति तैः तथोक्तैः **दिवः** अन्तरिक्षात् **च्युतैः गाङ्गैः सलिलैः तथा न पावितः** । **अनाविलैः** अकलुषैः **त्वदीयैः चरितैः यथा सान्वयः** सपुत्रपौत्रः पावितः पवित्रीकृतः ॥

अनेन धर्मः सविशेषमद्य मे त्रिवर्गसारः प्रतिभाति भाविनि[2] ।
त्वया मनोनिर्विषयार्थकामया यदेक एव प्रतिगृह्य सेव्यते ॥ ३८ ॥

अनेनेति ॥ हे **भाविनि** प्रशस्ताभिप्राये । **अनेन** कारणेन **धर्मः सविशेषं** सातिशयम् **अद्य मे** । [**त्रिवर्गसारः**] त्रयाणां धर्मकामार्थानां वर्गस्त्रिवर्गः । ‘त्रिवर्गो धर्मकामार्थैश्चतुर्वर्गः समोक्षकैः ।’ इत्यमरः । तत्र सारः श्रेष्ठः **प्रतिभाति** । **यत्** यस्मात्कारणात् [**मनोनिर्विषयार्थकामया**] मनसो निर्विषयावर्थकामौ यस्यास्तया **त्वया एकः** धर्मः **एव प्रतिगृह्य** स्वीकृत्य **सेव्यते** । यत्त्वयार्थकामौ विहाय धर्म एवावलम्बितः । अतः सर्वेषां नः स श्रेयानिति प्रतिपद्यत इत्यर्थः ॥

संप्रति मनोरथं जिज्ञासुः प्रस्तौति—

प्रयुक्तसत्कारविशेषमात्मना न मां परं संप्रतिपत्तुमर्हसि[3] ।
यतः[4] सतां संनतगात्रि संगतं मनीषिभिः साप्तपदीनमुच्यते ॥ ३९ ॥

प्रयुक्तेति ॥ **आत्मना** त्वया प्रयुक्तः कृतः सत्कारविशेषः पूजातिशयो यस्य तं [**प्रयुक्तसत्कारविशेषं**] **मां परम्** अन्यं **संप्रतिपत्तुम्** अवगन्तुं **न अर्हसि** । हे **संनतगात्रि** संनताङ्गि । ‘अङ्गगात्रकण्ठेभ्यः’ इति वक्तव्यात् ङीष् । **यतः** कारणान्मनस

१ प्रवाहिभिः, प्रकाशिभिः. २ भामिनि. ३ सा प्र०. ४ यदा यथा.

ईषिभिः **मनीषिभिः** विद्वद्भिः । शकन्ध्वादित्वात्साधुः । **सतां संगतं** सख्यं सप्तभिः पदैरवाप्यत इति **साप्तपदीनं** सप्तपदोच्चारणसाध्यम् **उच्यते** । तच्चावयोस्त्वत्कृतसत्कारप्रयोगादेव सिद्धमित्यर्थः । 'साप्तपदीनं सख्यम्' इति निपातनात्साधु ॥

अतोऽत्र[1] किंचिद्भवतीं बहुक्षमां द्विजातिभावादुपपन्नचापलः ।
अयं जनः प्रष्टुमनास्तपोधने न चेद्रहस्यं[2] प्रतिवक्तुमर्हसि ॥ ४० ॥

अत इति ॥ हे **तपोधने अतः** सख्याद्धेतोः **अत्र** प्रस्तावे **बहुक्षमां** बहूक्तिसहाम् । यद्वा क्षमावतीम् । **भवतीं** त्वां **द्विजातिभावाद्** ब्राह्मणत्वाद् **उपपन्नचापलः** सुलभधार्ष्ट्यः **अयं जनः** । स्वयमित्यर्थः । **किंचित्** प्रष्टुं मनो यस्य स **प्रष्टुमनाः** प्रष्टुकामः । 'तुंकाममनसोरपि' इति मकारलोपः । रहसि भवं **रहस्यं** गोप्यं **न चेत् प्रतिवक्तुम् अर्हसि** ॥

प्रष्टव्यमाह—

कुले प्रसूतिः प्रथमस्य वेधसस्त्रिलोकसौन्दर्यमिवोदितं[3] वपुः ।
अमृग्यमैश्वर्यसुखं नवं वयस्तपःफलं स्यात्किमतः परं वद[4] ॥ ४१ ॥

कुल इति ॥ **प्रथमस्य वेधसः** हिरण्यगर्भस्य **कुले** अन्ववाये **प्रसूतिः** उत्पत्तिः । 'यज्ञार्थं हि मया सृष्टो हिमवानचलेश्वरः' । इति ब्रह्मपुराणवचनात् । **वपुः** शरीरं [**त्रिलोकसौन्दर्यं**] त्रयाणां लोकानां सौन्दर्यम् **इव उदितम्** एकत्र समाहृतम् । **ऐश्वर्यसुखं** संपत्सुखम् **अमृग्यम्** अन्वेषणीयं न भवति । किं तु सिद्धमेवेत्यर्थः । **वयः नवम्** । यौवनमित्यर्थः । **अतः परम्** अतोऽन्यत् **किं तपःफलं स्याव वद** अस्ति चेदिति शेषः । न किंचिदस्तीत्यर्थः ॥

भवत्यनिष्टादपि नाम दुःसहान्मनस्विनीनां प्रतिपत्तिरीदृशी ।
विचारमार्गप्रहितेन चेतसा न दृश्यते तच्च कृशोदरि[5] त्वयि ॥ ४२ ॥

भवतीति ॥ **दुःसहात्** सोढुमशक्याद् **अनिष्टाद्** भर्त्रादिकृतात् **अपि मनस्विनीनां** धीरस्त्रीणाम् **ईदृशी** तपश्चरणलक्षणा **प्रतिपत्तिः** प्रवृत्तिः । 'प्रतिपत्तिस्तु गौरवे । प्राप्तौ प्रवृत्तौ प्रागल्भ्ये' इति केशवः । **भवति नाम** । नामेति संभावनायाम् । [**विचारमार्गप्रहितेन**] विचारमार्गे प्रहितेन **चेतसा** चित्तेन **तद्** अनिष्टं **च** हे **कृशोदरि त्वयि न दृश्यते** । विचार्यमाणे तदपि नास्त्यसंभावितत्वादित्यर्थः ॥

अनिष्टाभावमेव प्रपञ्चयति—

अलभ्यशोकाभिभवेयमाकृतिर्विमानना[6] सुभ्रु कुतः पितुर्गृहे ।
पराभिमर्शो[7] न तवास्ति कः करं प्रसारयेत्पन्नगरत्नसूचये[8] ॥ ४३ ॥

अलभ्येति ॥ हे **सुभ्रु** । **इयं** त्वदीया **आकृतिः** मूर्तिः [**अलभ्यशोकाभि-**

---

१ अथ. २ प्रतिगोप्तुम०, प्रतिबोध–गोप–यिष्यसि. ३ उच्छ्रितं. ०वोर्जितम्. ४ तव. ५ तलोदरि, तनूदरि. ६ अनन्यशोभा. ७ परावमर्शः. ८ सूचिषु, सूतये.

भवा] अलभ्यो लब्धुमनर्हः शोकेन भर्त्रायवमानजेन दुःखेनाभिभवस्तिरस्कारो यस्याः सा तथोक्ता । दृश्यत इति शेषः । असंभावितश्चायमर्थ इत्याह—**पितुः गृहे विमानना** अवमानः **कुतः** । न संभाव्यत एवेत्यर्थः । न चाप्यन्यस्माद्भावीत्याह—**पराभिमर्शः** परधर्षणं तु **तव न अस्ति** । **पन्नगरत्नसूचये** फणिशिरोमणिशलाकां ग्रहीतुमित्यर्थः । 'क्रियार्थोपपदस्य च कर्मणि स्थानिनः' इति चतुर्थी । **करं** हस्तं **कः प्रसारयेत्** । सुभ्रु इत्यत्र भ्रूशब्दस्योवङ्स्थानीयत्वात् 'नेयङुवङ्स्थानावस्त्री' इति नदीसंज्ञाप्रतिषेधात् 'अम्बार्थनद्योर्ह्रस्वः' इति ह्रस्वत्वं नास्ति । तेन ह्रस्वः प्रामादिक इति केचित् । अन्ये तु 'अप्राणिजातेश्चारज्ज्वादीनाम्' इत्यत्र अलावूः कर्कन्धूः इत्युकारान्तादप्यूङ्प्रत्ययमुदाजहार भाष्यकार एतस्मादेव ज्ञापकात्क्वचिदूकारान्तस्याप्यूङन्तत्वान्नदीत्वे ह्रस्वत्वमित्याहुः । अत एवाह वामनः—'ऊकारान्तादप्यूङ्प्रवृत्तेः' इति । ' 'सुभ्रूः कुतस्तातगृहेऽवमाननम्' इति पाठान्तरकरणं तु साहसमेवोक्तोपपत्तिसंभवात् । अन्यत्रापि 'सुभ्रु त्वं कुपितेत्यपास्तमशनं त्यक्त्वा कथा योषिताम्' इत्यादिप्रयोगदर्शनाद्वंशस्थवृत्ते पादादौ जगणभङ्गप्रसङ्गाच्चेत्यलं गोष्ठीभिः ॥

किमित्यपास्याभरणानि यौवने धृतं त्वया वार्धकशोभि वल्कलम् ।
वद प्रदोषे स्फुटचन्द्रतारका विभावरी यद्यरुणाय कल्पते ॥ ४४ ॥

किमिति ॥ हे गौरि **किमिति** केन हेतुना **यौवने त्वया आभरणानि अपास्य** विहाय । वृद्धस्य भावो वार्धकम् । मनोज्ञादित्वाद् वुञ्प्रत्ययः । 'वार्धकं वृद्धसंघाते वृद्धत्वे वृद्धकर्मणि ।' इति विश्वः । तत्र शोभत इति **वार्धकशोभि वल्कलं धृतम्** । **प्रदोषे** रजनीमुखे स्फुटाः प्रकटाश्चन्द्रस्तारकाश्च यस्याः सा **स्फुटचन्द्रतारका विभावरी** रात्रिः **अरुणाय** सूर्यसुताय **कल्पते यदि** अरुणं गन्तुं कल्पते किम् । **वद** ब्रूहि । 'क्रियार्थोपपदस्य' इत्यादिना चतुर्थी । दीप्यमानशशाङ्कतारके प्रदोषे यद्यरुण उदेति ततो विभूषणापहारेण तव वल्कलधारणं संघटत इति भावः ॥

तपःप्रयोजनं निराकर्तुमाह—

दिवं यदि प्रार्थयसे वृथा श्रमः पितुः प्रदेशास्तव देवभूमयः ।
अथोपयन्तारमलं समाधिना न रत्नमन्विष्यति मृग्यते हि तत् ॥ ४५ ॥

दिवमिति ॥ **दिवं** स्वर्गं **प्रार्थयसे** कामयसे **यदि** तर्हि **श्रमः** तपश्चरणप्रयासः **वृथा** निष्फलः । यदि स्वर्गार्थं तप्यसे ततः श्रमं मा कार्षीः । कुतः । **तव पितुः** हिमवतः **प्रदेशाः देवभूमयः** । स्वर्गपदार्थास्तत्रत्या इत्यर्थः । **अथ उपयन्तारं** वरं प्रार्थयसे तर्हि **समाधिना** तपसा **अलम्** । न कर्तव्यमित्यर्थः । निषेध्यस्य निषेधं प्रति करणत्वात्तृतीया । तथा **हि** । **रत्नम्** । कर्तृ । **न अन्विष्यति** न मृगयते । ग्रहीतारमिति शेषः । किं तु **तत्** रत्नं **मृग्यते** । ग्रहीतृभिरिति शेषः । न हि वरार्थं त्वया तपसि वर्तितव्यं किं तु तेनैव त्वदर्थमिति भावः ॥

---

१ विनिकीर्णता०, विनकीर्य ता०, ०तारके. २ अन्विच्छति.

वरवाचकाक्षरश्रवणानन्तरमेव देव्या उष्णोच्छ्वासमालक्ष्य प्रश्नेषु च प्रत्युत्तरमनुपलभ्य स्वयमेवाशङ्क्याह—

निवेदितं निःश्वसितेन सोष्मणा मनस्तु मे संशयमेव गाहते ।
न दृश्यते प्रार्थयितव्य एव ते भविष्यति प्रार्थितदुर्लभः कथम् ॥४६॥

निवेदितमिति ॥ **सोष्मणा निःश्वसितेन** निःश्वासवायुना **निवेदितम्** । चिन्तानुभावेनोष्णोच्छ्वासेन ते वरार्थित्वं सूचितमित्यर्थः । तर्हि किं प्रश्नव्यसनेनेत्याह । **मे मनः तु** तथापि **संशयम् एव गाहते** प्राप्नोति । कुतः । **ते** तव । 'कृत्यानां कर्तरि वा' इति षष्ठी । **प्रार्थयितव्यः** प्रार्थयितुमर्ह **एव न दृश्यते** । **प्रार्थितदुर्लभः** प्रार्थितो दुर्लभः स **कथं भविष्यति** । नास्त्येवेत्यर्थः ॥

अथ पतिप्रार्थनामेव सिद्धवत्कृत्वाह—

अहो स्थिरः कोऽपि तवेप्सितो युवा चिराय कर्णोत्पलशून्यतां गते ।
उपेक्षते यः श्लथलम्बिनीर्जटाः[1] कपोलदेशे कलमाग्रपिङ्गलाः ॥४७॥

अहो इति ॥ **अहो** चित्रम् । **तव ईप्सितः** आप्तुमिष्टः **युवा कः अपि स्थिरः** कठिनः । वर्तत इति शेषः । कुतः । **यः युवा चिराय** चिरात्प्रभृति **कर्णोत्पलशून्यतां गते** प्राप्ते **कपोलदेशे** गण्डस्थले श्लथाः शिथिलबन्धना अत एव लम्बिन्यस्ताः **श्लथलम्बिनीः [कलमाग्रपिङ्गलाः]** कलमाः शालिविशेषास्तेषामग्राणि तद्वत्पिङ्गलाः **जटाः उपेक्षते** । यस्त्वामीदृशीं दृष्ट्वा न व्यथते स नूनं वज्रहृदय इत्यर्थः ॥

मुनिव्रतैस्त्वमतिमात्रकर्शितां दिवाकराप्लुष्टविभूषणास्पदाम्[2] ।
शशाङ्कलेखामिव[3] पश्यतो दिवा सचेतसः कस्य मनो न दूयते[4] ॥ ४८॥

मुनिव्रतैरिति ॥ **मुनिव्रतैः** चान्द्रायणादिभिः **[अतिमात्रकर्शिताम्]** अतिमात्रमत्यन्तं कर्शितां कृशीकृतां **[दिवाकराप्लुष्टविभूषणास्पदां]** दिवाकरेण सूर्येणाप्लुष्टानि दग्धानि वातातपसंस्पर्शान्मृदुत्वाच्च श्यामीकृतानि विभूषणास्पदानि भूषणस्थानानि यस्यास्तां तथोक्ताम् । अत एव **दिवा** अहनि **शशाङ्कलेखामिव** स्थितां **त्वां पश्यतः सचेतसः** जीवतः **कस्य** पुंसः **मनः न दूयते** न परितप्यते । अपि तु सर्वस्यैवेत्यर्थः ॥

अवैमि सौभाग्यमदेन वञ्चितं तव प्रियं यश्चतुरावलोकिनः ।
करोति लक्ष्यं[5] चिरमस्य चक्षुषो न वक्त्रमात्मीयमरालपक्ष्मणः ॥४९॥

अवैमीति ॥ **तव प्रियं** वल्लभं **सौभाग्यमदेन** सौन्दर्यगर्वेण । कर्त्रा । **वञ्चितं** विप्रलब्धम् **अवैमि** वेद्मि **यः** । प्रियश्चतुरं मधुरमवलोकत इति **चतुरावलोकिनः अरालपक्ष्मणः** कुटिलरोम्णः । 'अरालं वृजिनं जिह्मम्' इत्यमरः । **अस्य**

---

१ बन्धिनीर्जटाः; बन्धलम्बिनीर्जटाः कपोल. २ करस्पृष्ट, रप्लुष्ट. ३ रेखा. ४ दीयते. ५ लक्षं रविम०

त्वदीयस्य **चक्षुषः आत्मीयं वक्त्रं मुखं चिरं लक्ष्यं** विषयं **न करोति** । दृष्टिपथं न गच्छतीत्यर्थः । तदयं गर्वेण हतो निष्फलात्मलाभो जात इति भावः ॥

कियच्चिरं श्राम्यसि गौरि विद्यते ममापि पूर्वाश्रमसंचितं तपः ।
तदर्धभागेन लभस्व काङ्क्षितं वरं तमिच्छामि च साधु वेदितुम् ५०

कियदिति ॥ हे **गौरि** । **कियत्** किंप्रमाणकम् । किमवधिकमित्यर्थः । **चिरं श्राम्यसि** तपस्यसि । अत्यन्तसंयोगे द्वितीया । **ममापि [पूर्वाश्रमसंचितं]** पूर्वाश्रमः प्रथमाश्रमो ब्रह्मचर्याश्रमस्तत्र संचितं संपादितं **तपः विद्यते** । **[तदर्धभागेन]** अर्धश्चासौ भागश्च तेन तस्य तपसोऽर्धभागेनैकदेशेन **काङ्क्षितम् इष्टं वरम्** उपयन्तारं **लभस्व** । **तं** वरं **साधु** सम्यक् **वेदितुं** ज्ञातुम् **इच्छामि च** । यद्यसौ योग्यो भवति तदा ममापि संमतिरिति भावः ॥

इति प्रविश्याभिहिता द्विजन्मना मनोगतं सा न शशाक शंसितुम् ।
अथो वयस्यां परिपार्श्ववर्तिनीं विवर्तितानञ्जननेत्रमैक्षत ॥ ५१ ॥

इतीति ॥ **इति** इत्थं **द्विजन्मना** द्विजेन **प्रविश्य** अन्तर्गत्वा । आप्तवद्रहस्यमुद्भाव्येत्यर्थः । **अभिहिता** उक्ता **सा** पार्वती **मनोगतं** हृदिस्थं वरं **शंसितुं** वक्तुं **न शशाक** समर्था नाभूत् । लज्जयेति शेषः । **अथो** अनन्तरं **परिपार्श्ववर्तिनीं वयस्यां** सखीं **[विवर्तितानञ्जननेत्रं]** विवर्तितं विचालितमनञ्जनं व्रतवशाद्वर्जितकज्जलं नेत्रं यस्मिन्कर्मणि तत्तथा **ऐक्षत** । नेत्रसंज्ञयैव प्रत्युत्तरं वाचयाञ्चकारेत्यर्थः ॥

सखी तदीया तमुवाच वर्णिनं निबोध साधो तव चेत्कुतूहलम् ।
यदर्थमम्भोजमिवोष्णवारणं कृतं तपःसाधनमेतया वपुः ॥ ५२ ॥

सखीति ॥ तस्याः पार्वत्या इयं **तदीया सखी** वयस्या **तम्** । 'वर्णः प्रशस्तिः' इति क्षीरस्वामी । सोऽस्यास्तीति **वर्णिनं** ब्रह्मचारिणम् । 'वर्णाद्ब्रह्मचारिणि' इतीनिप्रत्ययः । **उवाच** ब्रूते स्म । किमिति । हे **साधो** विद्वन् **तव कुतूहलं चेत्** । श्रोतुमस्तीति शेषः । तर्हि **निबोध** अवगच्छ । आकर्णयेत्यर्थः । 'बुध अवगमने' इति धातोर्भौवादिकाल्लोट् । श्रोतव्यं किं तदाह—यस्मै लाभायेदं **यदर्थम्** । 'अर्थेन सह नित्यसमासः सर्वलिङ्गता चेति वक्तव्यम्' इति वार्तिकनियमात्क्रियाविशेषणम् । **एतया** पार्वत्या **अम्भोजं** पद्मम् **उष्णवारणम्** आतपत्रम् **इव वपुः** शरीरं **तपःसाधनं कृतम्** । तपःप्रवृत्तिकारणमुच्यते श्रूयतामित्यर्थः ॥

'दृङ्मनःसङ्गसंकल्पा जागरः कृशताऽरतिः । ह्रीत्यागोन्मादमूर्च्छान्ता इत्यनङ्गदशा दश ॥' इति । तत्रास्याः काश्चिद्दशाः क्रममनादृत्यैव योजयति—इयमित्यादिभिः षड्भिः श्लोकैः—

इयं महेन्द्रप्रभृतीनधिश्रियश्चतुर्दिगीशानवमत्य मानिनी[3] ।
अरूपहार्यं मदनस्य निग्रहात्पिनाकपाणिं पतिमाप्तुमिच्छति ॥ ५३ ॥

---

१ निव० २ वाञ्छितं. ३ भामिनी.

इयमिति ॥ **मानिनी** इन्द्राणीप्रभृतीरतिशय्य वर्तितव्यमित्यभिमानवती **इयं** पार्वती **अधिश्रियः** अधिकैश्वर्यान् **महेन्द्रप्रभृतीन्** इन्द्रादींश्चतसृणां दिशामीशान् [**चतुर्दिगीशान्**] इन्द्रवरुणयमकुबेरान् । 'तद्धितार्थ'–इत्यादिनोत्तरपदसमासः । **अवमत्य** अवधूय **मदनस्य निग्रहात्** निबर्हणाद्धेतोः । अकामुकत्वादित्यर्थः । रूपेण सौन्दर्येण हार्यो वशीकरणीयो न भवतीति **अरूपहार्यं** पिनाकः पाणौ यस्य तं **पिनाकपाणिं** हरम् । 'प्रहरणार्थेभ्यः परे निष्ठासप्तम्यौ भवतः' इति साधु । **पतिं** भर्तारम् **आप्तुम् इच्छति** । एतेन संकल्पावस्था सूचिता ॥

असह्यहुंकारनिवर्तितः पुरा पुरारिमप्राप्तमुखः शिलीमुखः ।
इमां हृदि व्यायतपातमक्षिणोद्विशीर्णमूर्तेरपि पुष्पधन्वनः ॥ ५४ ॥

असह्येति ॥ **पुरा** पूर्वं [**असह्यहुंकारनिवर्तितः**] असह्येन सोढुमशक्येन हुंकारेण रौद्रेण निवर्तितः । अत एव **पुरारिं** हरम् **अप्राप्तमुखः** अप्राप्तफलः **विशीर्णमूर्तेः** नष्टशरीरस्य **अपि पुष्पधन्वनः** कामस्य **शिलीमुखः** बाणः **इमां** पार्वतीं **हृदि** [**व्यायतपातम्**] व्यायतः । सुदूरावगाढ इति यावत् । तादृक्पातः प्रहारो यस्मिन् कर्मणि तत्तथा **अक्षिणोत्** अकर्शत् । दग्धदेहस्यापि मार्गणो लग्नः । 'मृदुः सर्वत्र बाध्यते' इति भावः । अनेन 'विवृण्वती शैलसुतापि भावम्' (३।६८) इत्यत्रोक्तं चक्षुःप्रीतिमनःसङ्गाख्यमवस्थाद्वयमनन्तरावस्थोपयोगितयानूद्य कार्श्यावस्था सूचिता ॥

तदा प्रभृत्युन्मदना पितुर्गृहे ललाटिकाचन्दनधूसरालका ।
न जातु बाला लभते स्म निर्वृतिं तुषारसंघातशिलातलेष्वपि ॥ ५५ ॥

तदेति ॥ तदेति च्छेदः । **तदा प्रभृति** । तत आरभ्येत्यर्थः । सप्तम्यर्थस्यापि दाप्रत्ययस्य पञ्चम्यर्थे लक्षणा प्रभृतियोगे पञ्चमीनियमात् । **पितुः गृहे उन्मदना** उत्कटमन्मथा [**ललाटिकाचन्दनधूसरालका**] ललाटस्यालंकारो ललाटिका तिलकः । 'कर्णललाटात्कनलंकारे' इति कन्प्रत्ययः । तस्याश्चन्दनेन धूसरा धूसरवर्णा अलकाश्चूर्णकुन्तला यस्याः सा तथोक्ता । **बाला** पार्वती **जातु** कदाचिदपि [**तुषारसंघातशिलातलेषु**] तुषारसंघातास्तुषारघनास्त एव शिलास्तासां तलेषूपरिभागेषु **अपि निर्वृतिं** सुखं **न लभते स्म** । एतेनारत्यपरसंज्ञा विषयविद्वेषावस्था द्वादशावस्थापक्षे संज्वरश्च व्यज्यते ॥

उपात्तवर्णे चरिते पिनाकिनः सबाष्पकण्ठस्खलितैः पदैरियम् ।
अनेकशः किंनरराजकन्यका वनान्तसंगीतसखीररोदयत् ॥ ५६ ॥

उपात्तेति ॥ **इयं पिनाकिनः** शंभोः **चरिते** त्रिपुरविजयादिचेष्टिते **उपात्तवर्णे** प्रारब्धगीतक्रमे । 'गीतक्रमे स्तुतौ वेदे वर्णशब्दः प्रयुज्यते ।' इति हलायुधः । [**सबाष्पकण्ठस्खलितैः**] सबाष्पे गद्गदे कण्ठे स्खलितैर्विशीर्णैः **पदैः** सुप्तिङन्तरूपैः । करणैः । [**वनान्तसंगीतसखीः**] वनान्ते संगीतेन निमित्तेन सखीर्वयस्याः

१ स्मरारिम्. २ अक्षणोत्. ३ उदात्त. ४ कण्ठः. ५ कार्श्यरो०.

किंनरराजकन्यकाः अनेकशः बहुशः **अरोदयत्** अश्रुमोक्षमकारयत् । हरच-रितगानजनितमदनवेदनामेनां वीक्ष्य किंनर्योऽपि रुरुदुरिति भावः । अत्र वर्णस्खलनलक्षण-कार्योक्त्या पुनः पुनस्तत्कारणीभूतमूर्च्छावस्थाप्रादुर्भावो व्यज्यतेऽन्यथा सखीरोदनानु-पपत्तेरिति । द्वादशावस्थापक्षे तु प्रलापावस्था च व्यज्यते । 'प्रलापो गुणकीर्तनम्' इत्यालंकारिकाः ॥

त्रिभागशेषासु निशासु च क्षणं निमील्य नेत्रे सहसा व्यबुध्यत[१] ।
क नीलकण्ठ व्रजसीत्यलक्ष्यवागसत्यकण्ठार्पितबाहुबन्धना ॥५७॥

त्रिभागेति ॥ [च] किं च इति चार्थः । [त्रिभागशेषासु] शिष्यत इति शेषः । कर्मणि घञ् । त्रिभ्यो भागेभ्यः शेषास्त्ववशिष्टासु । यद्वा रात्रेस्त्रियामत्वेन प्रसिद्धत्वात् तृतीयो भागस्त्रिभागः । संख्याशब्दस्य वृत्तिविषये पूरणार्थत्वमिष्यते । यथा शतांशः सहस्रांश इति । त्रिभागः शेषो यासां तासु **निशासु क्षणं** क्षणमात्रं **नेत्रे निमील्य** मीलयित्व **सहसा** सद्यः हे **नीलकण्ठ क व्रजसि** कुत्र गच्छसि **इति** [**अलक्ष्यवाक्** । अलक्ष्या निर्विषया वाग्वचनं यस्याः सा तथोक्ता । तथा [**असत्यकण्ठार्पितबाहु-बन्धना**] असत्ये मिथ्याभूते कण्ठे अर्पितं बाहुबन्धनं यस्याः सा तथा सती **व्यबुध्यत** विबुद्धवती । एतेन जागरोन्मादौ सूचितौ ॥

स्वप्नसादृश्यप्रतिकृतिदर्शनतदङ्गस्पृष्टस्पर्शाख्याश्चत्वारो विरहिणां विनोदाः । तत्र स्वप्न-संदर्शनमुक्त्वा प्रतिकृतिदर्शनमाह—

यदा[२] बुधैः सर्वगतस्त्वमुच्यसे न वेत्सि भावस्थमिमं कथं जनम् ।
इति स्वहस्तोल्लिखित[३]श्च मुग्धया रहस्युपालभ्यत चन्द्रशेखरः ॥५८॥

यदेति ॥ **यदा** यत इत्यर्थः । 'यदेति हेतौ' इत्युक्त्वा गणव्याख्यानेऽस्योदा-हृतत्वात् । **त्वं बुधैः** मनीषिभिः **सर्वगतः** सर्वव्यापीति **उच्यसे** । तत इत्यध्याहारः । भावे रत्याख्ये तिष्ठतीति **भावस्थम्** । त्वय्यनुरागिणमित्यर्थः । **इमं जनम्** । इममित्यात्मनिर्देशः । **कथं न वेत्सि** न जानासि । **इति मुग्धया** मूढया । अकिंचि-त्करश्चित्रगतोपालम्भः इत्यजानानयेत्यर्थः । तया [**स्वहस्तोल्लिखितः**] स्वहस्तेनोल्लि-खिताश्चित्रे लिखितः **चन्द्रशेखरः रहसि** एकान्ते । सखीमात्रसमक्षमित्यर्थः । **उपालभ्यत** साधिक्षेपमुक्तः **च** । उक्तसमुच्चयार्थश्चकारः । यद्यपि रहसीत्युक्तं तथापि सखीसमक्षकरणाल्लज्जात्यागो व्यज्यत एव ॥

यदा च[४] तस्याधिगमे जगत्पतेरपश्यदन्यं न विधिं विचिन्वती[५] ।
तदा सहास्माभिरनुज्ञया गुरोरियं प्रपन्ना तपसे तपोवनम् ॥ ५९ ॥

यदेति ॥ **जगत्पतेः तस्य** ईश्वरस्य **अधिगमे** प्राप्तौ **अन्यं विधिं** उपायं **विचिन्वती** मृगयमाणा **यदा न अपश्यत्** तदा **इयं** पार्वती **गुरोः** पितुः **अनुज्ञया अस्माभिः सह तपसे** तपश्चरितुं **तपोवनं प्रपन्ना** प्राप्ता **च** ॥

---

१ विबुध्यते. २ यतः सदा. ३ चित्रे लि०, हस्तालि०. ४ हि. ५ वितन्वती.

द्रुमेषु सख्या कृतजन्मसु स्वयं फलं तपःसाक्षिषु दृष्टमेष्वपि ।
न च प्ररोहाभिमुखोऽपि दृश्यते मनोरथोऽस्याः शशिमौलिसंश्रयः ॥६०॥

द्रुमेष्विति ॥ **सख्या** पार्वत्या **स्वयं** [**कृतजन्मसु**] कृतं जन्म येषां तेषु । स्वयं रोपितेष्वित्यर्थः । [**तपःसाक्षिषु**] तपसः साक्षिषु साक्षाद्द्रष्टृषु **एषु द्रुमेषु अपि फलं दृष्टं** लब्धम् । जनितमित्यर्थः । **अस्याः** पार्वत्याः **च शशिमौलिसंश्रयः** चन्द्रशेखरविषयः **मनोरथः** तु **प्ररोहाभिमुखः** अङ्कुरोन्मुखः **अपि न दृश्यते** । 'प्ररोहस्त्वङ्कुरः' इति वैजयन्ती । स्वयं रोपितवृक्षफलकालेऽप्यस्या मनोरथस्य नाङ्कुरोदयोऽप्यस्ति । फलाशा तु दूरापास्तेत्यर्थः ॥

न वेद्मि स प्रार्थितदुर्लभः कदा सखीभिरस्रोत्तरमीक्षितामिमाम्[2] ।
तपःकृशामभ्युपपत्स्यते[3] सखीं वृषेव सीतां तदवग्रहक्षताम् ॥ ६१ ॥

नेति ॥ प्रार्थितः सन्दुर्लभः **प्रार्थितदुर्लभः स** देवः **तपःकृशां** तपसा कृशां क्षीणामत एव **सखीभिः अस्रोत्तरम्** अश्रु प्रधानं यथा भवति तथा **ईक्षिताम् इमां** नः **सखीं** [**तदवग्रहक्षतां**] तस्येन्द्रस्यावग्रहेणानावृष्ट्या क्षतां पीडिताम् । 'वृष्टिर्वर्षे तद्विघातेऽवग्राहावग्रहौ समौ ।' इत्यमरः । 'अवे ग्रहो वर्षप्रतिबन्धे' इत्यप् प्रत्ययः । **सीतां** कृष्टभूमिम् । 'सीता लाङ्गलपद्धतिः' इत्यमरः । **वृषा** वासवः **इव** । 'वासवो वृत्रहा वृषा' इत्यमरः ॥ **कदा अभ्युपपत्स्यते** कदा अनुग्रहीष्यति **न वेद्मि** । अत्र वाक्यार्थः कर्म । तदवग्रहक्षतामित्यत्रावग्रहक्षतामित्यनेनैव गतार्थत्वे तत्पदस्य वैयर्थ्यापत्तेस्तदिति भिन्नं पदं वेद्मीत्यस्य कर्मेति युक्तमुत्पश्यामः ॥

अगूढसद्भावमितीङ्गितज्ञया निवेदितो नैष्ठिकसुन्दरस्तया ।
अयीदमेवं परिहास इत्युमामपृच्छदव्यञ्जितहर्षलक्षणः ॥ ६२ ॥

अगूढेति ॥ **इङ्गितज्ञया** पार्वतीहृदयाभिज्ञया । 'इङ्गितं हृद्गतो भावः' इति सज्जनः । **तया** गौरीसख्या **इति** एवम् **अगूढसद्भावं** प्रकाशितसदभिप्रायं यथा तथा **निवेदितः** ज्ञापितः । [**नैष्ठिकसुन्दरः**] निष्ठा मरणमवधिर्यस्य स नैष्ठिको यावज्जीवब्रह्मचारी । सुन्दरो विलासी । नैष्ठिकश्चासौ सुन्दरश्चेति तथोक्तः । द्वयोरन्यतरस्य विशेषणत्वविवक्षायां विशेषणसमासः । किं तु नैष्ठिकत्वविशेषणेन कामित्वविरोधः । अथ वा देवस्यालौकिकमहिमत्वादुभयं तात्त्विकमिति न विरोधः । [**अव्यञ्जितहर्षलक्षणः**] अभ्यञ्जितं हर्षलक्षणं मुखरागादि हर्षलिङ्गं यस्य तथाभूतः सन् । **अयि गौरी** । अयीति कोमलामन्त्रणे । **इदं** त्वत्सखीभाषितम् **एवम्** । सत्यं किमित्यर्थः । **परिहासः** केलिर्वा । 'द्रवकेलिपरीहासाः' इत्यमरः । **इति** एवम् **उमाम् अपृच्छत्** पृष्टवान् ॥

अथाग्रहस्ते मुकुलीकृताङ्गुलौ समर्पयन्ती स्फटिकाक्षमालिकाम् ।
कथंचिदद्रेस्तनया मिताक्षरं चिरव्यवस्थापितवागभाषत ॥ ६३ ॥

---

१ बद्धम्. २ अस्राकुल; अस्रान्तरवी०, अभ्रान्त-अस्रान्त-निरी०. ३ अभ्यवप०. ४ अपाद०. ५ मण्डलम्.

अथेति ॥ **अथ** अनन्तरम् **अद्रेः तनया** पार्वती **मुकुलीकृताङ्गुली** संपुटीकृताङ्गुली । अग्रश्चासौ हस्तश्चेति समाधानाधिकरणसमासः । 'हस्ताग्राग्रहस्तयोर्गुणगुणिनोर्भेदाभेदात्' इति वामनः । तस्मिन् **अग्रहस्ते** [**स्फटिकाक्षमालिकाम्**] स्फटिकानामक्षमालिकां जपमालिकाम् **समर्पयन्ती** आमुञ्चती **कथंचित्** महता कष्टेन **चिरव्यवस्थापितवाक्** चिरेण स्वीकृतवाक् । एतेन लज्जोपरोधो व्यज्यते । **मिताक्षरं** परिमितवर्णं यथा तथा **अभाषत** बभाषे ॥

किमुवाचेत्याह—

यथा श्रुतं वेदविदां वर त्वया जनोऽयमुच्चैःपदलङ्घनोत्सुकः ।
तपः किलेदं तदवाप्तिसाधनं मनोरथानामगतिर्न विद्यते ॥ ६४ ॥

यथेति ॥ हे **वेदविदां वर** वैदिकश्रेष्ठ । **त्वया यथा श्रुतं** सम्यक्श्रुतम् । श्रुतार्थमेवाह–**अयं जनः** । स्वयमित्यर्थः । [**उच्चैःपदलङ्घनोत्सुकः**] उच्चैःपदस्य शिवलाभरूपोन्नतस्थानस्य लङ्घने आक्रमणे उत्सुकः । किमत्रायुक्तमित्यत्राह—**इदं तपः** [**तदवाप्तिसाधनं**] तदवाप्तेस्तस्योच्चैःपदस्यावाप्तेः प्राप्तेः साधनं **किल** । किलेत्यलीके । अतितुच्छत्वादसाधकमेवेत्यर्थः । तर्हि त्यज्यतामित्याशङ्क्य दुराशा मां न मुञ्चतीत्याशयेनाह—**मनोरथानां** कामानाम् **अगतिः** अविषयः **न विद्यते** । न हि स्वशक्तिपर्यालोचनया कामाः प्रवर्तन्त इति भावः ॥

अथाह वर्णी विदितो महेश्वरस्तदर्थिनी त्वं पुनरेव वर्तसे ।
अमङ्गलाभ्यासरतिं विचिन्त्य तं तवानुवृत्तिं न च कर्तुमुत्सहे ॥ ६५ ॥

अथेति ॥ **अथ वर्णी** ब्रह्मचारी । 'वर्णिनो ब्रह्मचारिणः' इत्यमरः । **आह** । उवाचेत्यर्थः । 'आहेति भूतार्थे लट्प्रयोगो भ्रान्तिमूलः' इत्याह वामनः । किमित्याह—**महेश्वरः** महादेवः **विदितः** । मया ज्ञायत इत्यर्थः । बुद्ध्यर्थत्वाद्वर्तमाने क्तप्रत्ययः । तद्योगात्षष्ठी च । येन त्वं प्राग्भग्नमनोरथा कृतेति भावः । **पुनरेव त्वं** तमीश्वरमर्थयते **तदर्थिनी** एव तत्कामैव **वर्तसे** । तत्प्रभावमनुभूयापीति भावः । अनुसरणे को दोषस्तत्राह—[**अमङ्गलाभ्यासरतिं**] अमङ्गलाभ्यासे अमङ्गलाचारे रतिर्यस्य तं तथोक्तं **तम्** ईश्वरं **विचिन्त्य** विचार्य **तवानुवृत्तिम्** अनुसरणं **कर्तुं न उत्सहे च** । नानुमन्तुं शक्नोमीत्यर्थः ॥

अवस्तुनिर्बन्धपरे कथं नु ते करोऽयमामुक्तविवाहकौतुकः ।
करेण शंभोर्वलयीकृताहिना सहिष्यते तत्प्रथमावलम्बनम् ॥ ६६ ॥

अवस्त्विति ॥ अवस्तुनि तुच्छवस्तुनि निर्बन्धोऽभिनिवेशः परं प्रधानं यस्यास्तस्याः संबुद्धिः **अवस्तुनिर्बन्धपरे** पार्वति । [**आमुक्तविवाहकौतुकः**] आमुक्तमासञ्जितं विवाहे यत्कौतुकं हस्तसूत्रं तद्यस्य सः **ते अयं करः** । 'कौतुकं मङ्गले हर्षे

१ पुर एव. २ ननु. ३ तु. ४ भुजग.

हस्तसूत्रे कुतूहले ।' इति शाश्वतः । **वलयीकृताहिना** भूषणीकृतसर्पेण **शंभोः** महादेवस्य **करेण** करणभूतेन [**तत्प्रथमावलम्बनं**] तदेव प्रथमं तत्प्रथमम् । अपरिचितत्वादतिभयंकरमिति भावः । तच्च तदवलम्बनं ग्रहणं चेति **कथं नु सहिष्यते** । न कथंचिदपि सहिष्यत इत्यर्थः । अग्रतो यद्भावि तद्दूरेऽवतिष्ठतां प्रथमं करग्रह एव दुःसह इति भावः ॥

त्वमेव तावत्परिचिन्तय स्वयं कदाचिदेते यदि योगमर्हतः ।
वधूदुकूलं कलहंसलक्षणं गजाजिनं शोणितबिन्दुवर्षि च ॥ ६७ ॥

त्वमेवेति ॥ हे गौरि । **त्वम् एव स्वयम्** आत्मना । **तावत्** इति मानार्थे । यावन्मात्रं विचारणीयं तावन्मात्रमित्यर्थः । इदमेवोदाहृतं च गणव्याख्याने । **परिचिन्तय** पर्यालोचय । किमिति । **कलहंसलक्षणं** कलहंसाचिह्नम् । 'चिह्नं लक्ष्म च लक्षणम्' इत्यमरः । वध्वा नवोढाया दुकूलं **वधूदुकूलम्** । 'वधूः स्नुषा नवोढा स्त्री' इति विश्वः । तथा [**शोणितबिन्दुवर्षि**] शोणितबिन्दून्वर्षतीति तथोक्तम् । आर्द्रमित्यर्थः । **गजाजिनं च** कृत्तिवासश्च । तत्पिनाकिनः इत्याशयः । **एते कदाचित्** जात्वपि **योगं** संगतिम् **अर्हतः यदि** अर्हतः किम् । एतत्त्वमेव चिन्तयेति पूर्वेणान्वयः । पाणिग्रहणकाले वधूवरयोर्वस्त्रान्तग्रन्थिः क्रियते । कृत्तिवाससा पाणिपीडने तु दुकूलधारिण्यास्तव स कथं संघटिष्यत इति भावः ॥

चतुष्कपुष्पप्रकरावकीर्णयोः परोऽपि को नाम तवानुमन्यते ।
अलक्तकाङ्कानि पदानि पादयोर्विकीर्णकेशासु परेतभूमिषु ॥ ६८ ॥

चतुष्केति ॥ [**चतुष्कपुष्पप्रकरावकीर्णयोः**] चतुष्के गृहविशेषे यः पुष्पप्रकरस्तत्रावकीर्णयोर्न्यस्तयोः । कुसुमास्तृतदिव्यभवनभूसंचारोचितयोरित्यर्थः । **तव पादयोः अलक्तकाङ्कानि** लाक्षारञ्जितानि **पदानि** पादाकाराणि पादन्यासाचिह्नानि । 'पदं शब्दे च वाक्ये च व्यवसायापदेशयोः । पादतच्चिह्नयोः' इति विश्वः । विकीर्णा विक्षिप्ताः केशाः शवशिरोरुहा यासु तासु **विकीर्णकेशासु** । 'अतस्थं तत्र दृष्टं च' इति वचनात् 'स्वाङ्गाच्चोपसर्जनादसंयोगोपधात्' इति विकल्पान्न ङीप् । **परेतभूमिषु** प्रेतभूमिषु । श्मशानेष्वित्यर्थः । **परः अपि** शत्रुरपि **कः नाम अनुमन्यते** । न कोऽपीत्यर्थः । नामेति कुत्सायाम् । पिनाकपाणिपाणिग्रहणे तस्य परेतभूसंचारित्वेन साहचर्यात्तवापि तत्र संचारोऽवश्यंभावीति भावः ॥

अयुक्तरूपं किमतः परं वद त्रिनेत्रवक्षः सुलभं तवापि यत् ।
स्तनद्वयेऽस्मिन्हरिचन्दनास्पदे पदं चिताभस्मरजः करिष्यति ॥ ६९ ॥

अयुक्तेति ॥ **त्रिनेत्रवक्षः** । त्र्यम्बकालिङ्गनमित्यर्थः । **तव** तत्संबन्धितया **सुलभम् अपि** सुप्रापं च । भवतीति शेषः । तवेति शेषे षष्ठी । 'न लोकाव्यय-' इत्या-

---

१ स्वतः; द्वयं. २ च सहं०; क च हं०... क चाजिनं...तत्. ३ अनुमंस्यते. ४ प्रकीर्ण° ५ भवेत्. ६ अङ्किते.

दिना कृद्योगलक्षणषष्ठ्या निषेधात् । **अतः परम्** अस्मात्त्रिनेत्रवक्षोलाभादन्यद् **अयुक्तरूपम्** अत्यन्तायुक्तं **किं वद** । न किंचिदित्यर्थः । 'प्रशंसायां रूपप्' इति रूपप्रत्ययः । कुतः । **यत्** यस्मात्कारणात् **हरिचन्दनास्पदे** हरिचन्दनस्यास्पदे स्थानभूते **अस्मिन् स्तनद्वये [चिताभस्मरजः]** चिताभस्म श्मशानभस्म तदेव रजश्चूर्णम । कर्तृ । **पदं करिष्यति** पदं निधास्यति । भर्तुर्भवस्य भस्माङ्गरागादिति भावः ॥

इयं च तेऽन्या पुरतो विडम्बना यदूढया वारणराजहार्यया ।
विलोक्य वृद्धोक्षमधिष्ठितं त्वया महाजनः स्मेरमुखो भविष्यति ७०

इयमिति ॥ **इयं च ते** तव **पुरतः** आदावेव **अन्या विडम्बना** । परिहास इत्यर्थः । का सेत्यत्राह—**ऊढया** परिणीतया । वहेः कर्मणि क्तः । **वारणराजहार्यया त्वया अधिष्ठितम्** आरूढं वृद्धमुक्षाणं **वृद्धोक्षम्** । 'अचतुर–' इत्यादिना निपातः । **विलोक्य महाजनः** साधुजनः **स्मेरमुखः** स्मितमुखः **भविष्यति** उपहसिष्यति **यत्** । इयमिति पूर्वेण संबन्धः । स्मेरेति 'नमिकम्पिस्म्यज–' इत्यादिना रप्रत्ययः ॥

द्वयं गतं संप्रति शोचनीयतां समागमप्रार्थनया पिनाकिनः[२] ।
कला च सा कान्तिमती कलावतस्त्वमस्य लोकस्य च नेत्रकौमुदी ॥७१॥

द्वयमिति ॥ **पिनाकिनः** ईश्वरस्य **समागमप्रार्थनया** प्राप्तिकामनया । क्रियमाणयेति शेषः । **संप्रति द्वयं शोचनीयतां** शोच्यत्वं **गतम्** । किं तदाह—**सा** प्रागेव हरशिरोगता । अत्र सेति प्रसिद्धार्थत्वान्न यच्छब्दापेक्षा । तदुक्तं काव्यप्रकाशे— 'प्रक्रान्तप्रसिद्धानुभूतार्थविषयस्तच्छब्दो यदुपादानं नापेक्षते ।' इति । **कान्तिमती** । नित्ययोगे मतुप् । **कलावतः** चन्द्रस्य **कला** षोडशो भागः **च** । **अस्य लोकस्य नेत्रकौमुदी** । नेत्रानन्दिनीत्यर्थः । **त्वं च** । कान्तिमतीत्वनेत्रकौमुदीत्वविशेषणयोरुभयत्राप्यन्वयः । प्रागेकैव शोच्या । संप्रति तु त्वमप्यपरेति द्वयं शोच्यमिति पिण्डितार्थः । शोच्यत्वं च निकृष्टाश्रयणादिति भावः ॥

'कन्या वरयते रूपं माता वित्तं पिता श्रुतम् । बान्धवाः कुलमिच्छन्ति मिष्टान्नमितरे जनाः ॥' इति लोकानामाभाषणम् । तत्र किंचिदपि नास्तीत्याह—

वपुर्विरूपाक्षमलक्ष्यजन्मता दिगम्बरत्वेन निवेदितं वसु ।
वरेषु यद्बालमृगाक्षि मृग्यते तदस्ति किं व्यस्तमपि त्रिलोचने ॥७२॥

वपुरिति ॥ **वपुः** तवादस्य विरूपाणि विकृतरूपाण्यक्षीणि नेत्राणि यस्य तद् **विरूपाक्षम्** । 'बहुव्रीहौ सक्थ्यक्ष्णोः स्वाङ्गात्षच्' इति षच्प्रत्ययः । वैरूप्यं च त्रिनेत्रत्वादिति क्षीरस्वामी । अतो न सौन्दर्यवार्तापीत्यर्थः । **[अलक्ष्यजन्मता]** अलक्ष्यम-

---

१ भार्यया. २ कपालिनः. ३ कलात्मनः.

ज्ञातं जन्म यस्य तस्य भावस्तत्ता । कुलमपि न ज्ञायत इत्यर्थः । 'अलक्षिता जनिः' इति पाठे जनिरुत्पत्तिरलक्षिता न ज्ञाता । 'जनिरुत्पत्तिरुद्भवः' इत्यमरः । **वसु** वित्तं **दिगम्बरत्वेन एव निवेदितम्** । नास्तीति ज्ञापितमित्यर्थः । यदि वित्तं भवति तदा कथं दिगम्बरो भवति । अतो ज्ञेयं निर्धनोऽयमिति । किंबहुना । हे **बालमृगाक्षि** पार्वति **वरेषु** वोढृषु । 'वरौ जामातृवोढारौ' इति विश्वः । **यत्** रूपवित्तादिकं **मृग्यते** कन्यातद्बन्धुभिरन्विष्यते **तत् त्रिलोचने** त्र्यम्बके **व्यस्तम्** एकम् **अपि** । समस्तं मा भूदिति भावः । **अस्ति किम्** । नास्त्येवेत्यर्थः ॥

निवर्तयास्मादसदीप्सितान्मनः क्व तद्विधस्त्वं क्व च पुण्यलक्षणा ।
अपेक्ष्यते[1] साधुजनेन वैदिकी श्मशानशूलस्य न यूपसत्क्रिया॥७३॥

निवर्तयेति ॥ **अस्माद् असदीप्सितात्** अनिष्टमनोरथात् **मनः निवर्तय** निवारय । [**तद्विधः**] सा पूर्वोक्ता विधा प्रकारो यस्य तथोक्तः । अमङ्गलशील इत्यर्थः । **क्व** । महदन्तरमित्यर्थः । **पुण्यलक्षणा** प्रशस्तभाग्यचिह्ना **त्वं च क्व** । अतो न तवायमर्ह इत्यर्थः । तथा हि । **साधुजनेन** । 'साधुर्वार्धुषिके चारौ सज्जने चाभिधेयवत् ।' इति विश्वः । **श्मशानशूलस्य** श्मशानभूमिनिखातस्य मध्यशङ्कोः **वैदिकी** वेदोक्ता । यूपो नाम पशुबन्धनसाधनभूतः संस्कृतदारुविशेषस्तस्य सत्क्रिया प्रोक्षणाभ्युक्षणादिसंस्कारः **यूपसत्क्रिया न अपेक्ष्यते** नेष्यते । यथा श्मशानशूले यूपसत्क्रिया न क्रियते तथा त्वमपि तस्मै न घटस इति तात्पर्यार्थः ॥

इति द्विजातौ प्रतिकूलवादिनि प्रवेपमानाधरलक्ष्यकोपया ।
विकुञ्चित[2]भ्रूलतमाहिते तया विलोचने तिर्यगुपान्तलोहिते ॥ ७४॥

इतीति ॥ **इति** एवं प्रकारेण **द्विजातौ** द्विजे **प्रतिकूलवादिनि** सति । [**प्रवेपमानाधरलक्ष्यकोपया**] प्रवेपमानेन चञ्चलेनाधरोष्ठेन लक्ष्यः अनुमेयः कोपः क्रोधो यस्यास्तथोक्तया **तया** पार्वत्या **उपान्तलोहिते** प्रान्तरक्ते **विलोचने** [**विकुञ्चितभ्रूलतं**] विकुञ्चिते कुटिलिते भ्रूलते यस्मिंस्तत्तथा । सभ्रूभङ्गमित्यर्थः । **तिर्यक्** साचि **आहिते** निहिते । अनादरात्तिर्यगैक्ष्यतेत्यर्थः ॥

उवाच चैनं परमार्थतो हरं न वेत्सि नूनं यत एवमात्थ माम् ।
अलोकसामान्यमचिन्त्यहेतुकं द्विषन्ति मन्दाश्चरितं महात्मनाम्॥७५॥

उवाचेति ॥ अथ **एनं** ब्रह्मचारिणं **उवाच च** । किमिति । **परमार्थतः** तत्त्वतः **हरं न वेत्सि** न जानासि **नूनम्** । कुतः । **यतः माम् एवम्** उक्तया रीत्या **आत्थ** ब्रवीषि । 'ब्रुवः पञ्चानामादितः–' इति रूपसिद्धिः । अज्ञानादेवायं शिवद्वेषस्तवेत्याशयेनाह–**मन्दाः** मूढाः । 'मूढाल्पापटुनिर्भाग्या मन्दाः' इत्यमरः । लोकसामान्यमितरजनसाधारणं न भवति इति **अलोकसामान्यम् अचिन्त्यहेतुकं** दुर्बोधका-

१ अपेक्षते साधुजनो न वैदिकीं...हि यूपसत्क्रियाम्. २ निकु.,–भ्रूलतया.

रणक महात्मनां चरितं द्विषन्ति हेत्वपरिज्ञानाद्दूषयन्ति। विद्वांसस्तु कोऽप्यत्र हेतुरस्तीति बहु मन्यन्त इत्यर्थः ॥

संप्रति 'अमङ्गलाभ्यासरतिम्' (५।६५) इत्याद्युक्तदूषणजातं विपदित्यादिभिः षड्भिः श्लोकैः परिहर्तुमारभते—

विपत्प्रतीकारपरेण मङ्गलं निषेव्यते भूतिसमुत्सुकेन वा।
जगच्छरण्यस्य निराशिषः सतः किमेभिराशोपहतात्मवृत्तिभिः ॥७६॥

विपदिति ॥ **विपत्प्रतीकारपरेण** । अनर्थपरिहारार्थिनेत्यर्थः । 'उपसर्गस्य घञ्यमनुष्ये बहुलम्' इति दीर्घः । **भूतिसमुत्सुकेन** ऐश्वर्यकामेन **वा मङ्गलं** गन्धमाल्यादिकं **निषेव्यते** । शरणे रक्षणे साधुः शरण्यः । 'तत्र साधुः' इति यत्प्रत्ययः । 'शरणं गृहरक्षित्रोः' इत्यमरः । जगतः शरण्यस्तस्य **जगच्छरण्यस्य निराशिषः** निरभिलाषस्य **सतः** शिवस्य । 'आशीरुरगदंष्ट्रायां विप्रवाक्याभिलाषयोः ।' इति शाश्वतः । [**आशोपहतात्मवृत्तिभिः**] आशया तृष्णयोपहता दूषितात्मवृत्तिरन्तःकरणवृत्तिर्येषां तैः **एभिः** मङ्गलैः **किम्** । वृथेत्यर्थः । पूर्वं मङ्गलमित्येकवचनस्य जात्यभिप्रायत्वादेभिरिति बहुवचनेन परामर्शो न विरुध्यते । इष्टावाप्त्यनिष्टपरिहारार्थिनो हि मङ्गलाचारनिर्बन्धः । तदुभयासंसृष्टस्य तु यथाकथंचिदास्ताम् । को दोष इत्यर्थः । एतेन 'अमङ्गलाभ्यासरतिम्' (५।६५) इत्युक्तं प्रत्युक्तम् ॥

अकिंचनः सन्प्रभवः स संपदां त्रिलोकनाथः पितृसद्मगोचरः ।
स भीमरूपः शिव इत्युदीर्यते न सन्ति याथार्थ्यविदः पिनाकिनः ॥७७॥

अकिंचन इति ॥ **स** हरः । न विद्यते किंचन द्रव्यं यस्य सः **अकिंचनः** दरिद्रः **सन् संपदां** प्रभवत्यस्मादिति **प्रभवः** कारणम् । **पितृसद्मगोचरः** श्मशानाश्रयः सन् [**त्रिलोकनाथः**] त्रयाणां लोकानां नाथः । 'तद्धितार्थ—' इत्यादिनोत्तरपदसमासः । **स** देवो **भीमरूपः** भयंकराकारः सन् **शिवः** सौम्यरूप **इति उदीर्यते** उच्यते । अतः **पिनाकिनः** हरस्य [**याथार्थ्यविदः**] यथाभूतोऽर्थो यथार्थस्तस्य भावो याथार्थ्यं तत्त्वं तस्य विदः **न सन्ति** । लोकोत्तरमहिम्ना निर्लेपस्य यथाकथंचिदवस्थानं न दोषायेति भावः । एतेन 'अवस्तुनिर्बन्धपरे' (५।६६) इति परिहृतं वेदितव्यम् ॥

देवस्य लौकिकमलौकिकं च प्रसाधनं नास्तीत्याशयेनाह—

विभूषणोद्भासि पिनद्धभोगि वा गजाजिनालम्बि दुकूलधारि वा ।
कपालि वा स्यादथ वेन्दुशेखरं न विश्वमूर्तेरवधार्यते वपुः ॥ ७८ ॥

---

१ किमाभिः. २ स लोकनाथः. ३ याथात्म्य. ४ अथ चन्द्रशेखरम्.

विभूषणेति ॥ विश्वं मूर्तिर्यस्येति विश्वमूर्तेः अष्टमूर्तेः शिवस्य वपुः शरीरं भूषणैरुद्भासत इति विभूषणोद्भासि स्यात् । पिनद्धभोगि आमुक्तभुजङ्गमं वा स्यात् । पिनद्धेति नह्यतेरपिपूर्वात्कर्मणि क्तः । 'वष्टि भागुरिरल्लोपमवाप्योरुपसर्गयोः ।' इत्यकारलोपः । गजाजिनालम्बि स्यात् । अथ वा दुकूलधारि स्यात् । कपालमस्यास्तीति कपालि ब्रह्मशिरःकपालशेखरं वा स्यात् । अथ इन्दुशेखरं वा स्यात् । न अवधार्यते न निर्धार्यते । सर्वं संभवतीत्यर्थः । एतेन 'त्वमेव तावत्' (५।६७) श्लोकोक्तं प्रत्युक्तमिति ज्ञेयम् ॥

'अयुक्तरूपं किमतःपरं वद' इति (५।६९) श्लोकोक्तं प्रत्याह—

तदङ्गसंसर्गमवाप्य कल्पते ध्रुवं चिताभस्मरजो विशुद्धये ।
तथा हि नृत्याभिनयक्रियाच्युतं विलिप्यते मौलिभिरम्बरौकसाम् ॥७९॥

तदङ्गेति ॥ [तदङ्गसंसर्गम्] तस्य शिवस्याङ्गं तस्य संसर्गम् अवाप्य आसाद्य [चिताभस्मरजः] चिताभस्मैव रजो विशुद्धये कल्पते । अलं पर्याप्नोतीत्यर्थः । अलमर्थयोगात् 'नमःस्वस्तिस्वाहा'—इत्यादिना चतुर्थी । ध्रुवं शोधकत्वं प्रमाणसिद्धमित्यर्थः । प्रमाणमेवाह—तथा हि । प्रसिद्धमेवेत्यर्थः [नृत्याभिनयक्रियाच्युतं] नृत्ये ताण्डवे योऽभिनयोऽर्थव्यञ्जकचेष्टाविशेषः स एव क्रिया तया निमित्तेन च्युतं पतितम् । चिताभस्मरजः इति शेषः । अम्बरौकसां देवानां मौलिभिः विलिप्यते ध्रियते । अशुद्धं चेत्कथमिन्द्रादिभिर्ध्रियतेत्यर्थापत्तिरनुमानं वा प्रमाणमित्यर्थः ॥

यदुक्तम् 'दिगम्बरत्वेन निवेदितं वसु' (५।७२) 'इयं च तेऽन्या पुरतो विडम्बना' (५।७०) इत्यादि च तत्रोत्तरमाह—

असंपदस्तस्य वृषेण गच्छतः प्रभिन्नदिग्वारणवाहनो वृषा ।
करोति पादावुपगम्य मौलिना विनिद्रमन्दाररजोरुणाङ्गुली ॥८०॥

असंपद इति ॥ [प्रभिन्नदिग्वारणवाहनः] प्रभिन्नो मदस्रावी दिग्वारणो दिग्गजो वाहनं यस्य सः । ऐरावतेनोढ इत्यर्थः । वृषा देवेन्द्रः असंपदः दरिद्रस्य वृषेण गच्छतः वृषभारूढस्य तस्य ईश्वरस्य पादौ मौलिना मुकुटेन उपगम्य प्रणम्येत्यर्थः । [विनिद्रमन्दाररजोरुणाङ्गुली] विनिद्राणां विकसितानां मन्दाराणां कल्पतरुकुसुमानां रजोभिः परागैररुणा अङ्गुलयो ययोस्तौ तथोक्तौ करोति । दिग्गजारोहिणामिन्द्रादीनामपि वन्द्यस्येन्दुमौलेः किं संपदा वृषारोहणे वा को दोष इत्यर्थः ॥

यदुक्तम् 'अलक्ष्यजन्मता' (५।७२) इति तत्रोत्तरमाह—

विवक्षता दोषमपि च्युतात्मना त्वयैकमीशं प्रति साधु भाषितम् ।
यमामनन्त्यात्मभुवोऽपि कारणं कथं स लक्ष्यप्रभवो भविष्यति ॥८१॥

---

१ संस्पर्शम्. २ जोऽपि शु०. ३ नृत्ता. ४ विलुप्यते. ५ उपगम्य. ६ विवृण्वता.

विवक्षतेति ॥ च्युतात्मना ॰॰स्वभावेनात एव दोषं दूषणं विवक्षता वक्तुमिच्छता अपि त्वया ईशं प्रति एकम् अलक्ष्यजन्मता इत्येतदेकम् । वच इत्यर्थः । साधु भाषितं सम्यगुक्तम् । कुतः । यम् ईश्वरम् आत्मभुवः अपि ब्रह्मणोऽपि । ' ब्रह्मात्मभूः सुरज्येष्ठः ' इत्यमरः । कारणम् आमनन्ति उदाहरन्ति । विद्वांस इति शेषः । 'पाघ्राध्मास्थाम्नादाण् '—इत्यादिना मनादेशः । स ईश्वरः कथं लक्ष्यप्रभवः लक्ष्यजन्मा भविष्यति । अनादिनिधनस्य भगवतः कारणशङ्का कलङ्कश्च नान्विष्यत इत्यर्थः ॥

अलं विवादेन यथा श्रुतस्त्वया तथाविधस्तावदशेषमस्तु सः ।
ममात्र भावैकरसं मनः स्थितं न कामवृत्तिर्वचनीयमीक्षते ॥ ८२ ॥

अलमिति ॥ अथ वा विवादेन कलहेन अलम् । त्वया तावत् यथा येन प्रकारेण स ईश्वरः श्रुतः अशेषं कार्त्स्न्येन तथाविधः तावत्प्रकारः एव अस्तु । मम मनः तु अत्र ईश्वरे [भावैकरसं] भावः शृङ्गार एकोऽद्वितीयो रस आस्वाद्यो यस्य तत्तथा स्थितम् । तथा हि । कामवृत्तिः स्वेच्छाव्यवहारी वचनीयम् अस्थानसङ्गापवादं नईक्षते न विचारयति । न हि स्वेच्छासंचारिणो लोकापवादाद्बिभ्यतीति भावः ॥

निवार्यतामालि किमप्ययं बटुः पुनर्विवक्षुः स्फुरितोत्तराधरः ।
न केवलं यो महतोऽपभाषते शृणोति तस्मादपि यः स पापभाक् ॥ ८३ ॥

निवार्यतामिति ॥ हे आलि सखि । ' आलिः सखी वयस्या च ' इत्यमरः । स्फुरितोत्तराधरः स्फुरणभूयिष्ठोष्ठः अयं बटुः माणवकः पुनः किम् अपि विवक्षुः वक्तुमिच्छुः । ब्रुवः सन्नन्तादुप्रत्ययः । निवार्यताम् । तर्हि वक्तुमेव कथं न ददासीत्याह—तथा हि । यः महतः पूज्यान् अपभाषते अपवदति न केवलं स पापभाक् भवति । किं तु तस्मात् अपभाषमाणात्पुरुषात् यः शृणोति सोऽपि पापभाक् । भवतीति शेषः । अत्र स्मृतिः—' गुरोः यत्र परीवादो न श्रोतव्यः कथंचन । कर्णौ तत्र पिधातव्यौ गन्तव्यं वा ततोऽन्यतः ॥ ' इति ॥

संप्रति गन्तव्यपक्षमाश्रयते—

इतो गमिष्याम्यथ वेति वादिनी चचाल बाला स्तनभिन्नवल्कला ।
स्वरूपमास्थाय च तां कृतस्मितः समाललम्बे वृषराजकेतनः ॥ ८४ ॥

इत इति ॥ अथ वा इतः अन्यत्र गमिष्यामि इति वादिनी वदन्ती [स्तनभिन्नवल्कला] स्तनाभ्यां भिन्नवल्कला रयवशात्कुचस्रस्तचीरा बाला पार्वती चचाल । वृषराजकेतनः वृषभध्वजः च स्वरूपम् आस्थाय निजरूपमाश्रित्य कृतस्मितः सन् । तां पार्वतीं समाललम्बे जग्राह ॥

---

१ श्रुतम्. २ तादृक्. ३ वशं. ४ स्थिरम्. ५ प्यसौ. ६ तोन्नताधरः. ७ महतां—तोविभाषते. ८ सा च. ९ रय. १० आधाय.

तं वीक्ष्य वेपथुमती सरसाङ्गयष्टि-
निंक्षेपणाय पदमुद्धृतमुद्वहन्ती ।
मार्गाचलव्यतिकराकुलितेव सिन्धुः
शैलाधिराजतनया न ययौ न तस्थौ ॥ ८५ ॥

तमिति ॥ तं देवं वीक्ष्य वेपथुमती सरसाङ्गयष्टिः स्विन्नगात्री । महादेवदर्शनेन देव्याः सात्त्विकभावोदय उक्तः । निक्षेपणाय अन्यत्र विन्यासाय उद्धृतम् उत्क्षिप्तं पदम् अङ्घ्रिम् उद्वहन्ती । शैलाधिराजतनया पार्वती [मार्गाचलव्यतिकराकुलिता] मार्गेऽचलस्तस्य व्यतिकरेण समाहृत्या । अवरोधनेनेति यावत् । आकुलिता संभ्रमिता सिन्धुः नदी इव ।'देशे नदविशेषेऽब्धौ सिन्धुर्ना सरिति स्त्रियाम् ।' इत्यमरः । न ययौ न तस्थौ । लज्जयेति भावः । वसन्ततिलकावृत्तमेतत् ॥

अद्य प्रभृत्यवनताङ्गि तवास्मि दासः
क्रीतस्तपोभिरिति वादिनि चन्द्रमौलौ ।
अह्नाय सा नियमजं क्लममुत्ससर्ज
क्लेशः फलेन हि पुनर्नवतां विधत्ते ॥ ८६ ॥

अद्येति ॥ चन्द्रमौलौ शिवे । हे अवनताङ्गि पार्वति अद्य प्रभृति अस्माद्दिनादारभ्येत्यर्थः । प्रभृतियोगादद्येति सप्तम्यर्थवाचिना पञ्चम्यर्थो लक्ष्यते । तव तपोभिः क्रीतः । 'दासृ दाने' । दासते आत्मानं ददातीति दासः । अस्मि इति वादिनि वदति सति सा देवी अह्नाय सपदि । 'स्राग्झटित्यञ्जसाह्नाय द्राङ्मङ्क्षु सपदि द्रुतम् ।' इत्यमरः । नियमजं तपोजन्यं क्लमं क्लेशं उत्ससर्ज । फलप्राप्त्या क्लेशं विसस्मारेत्यर्थः । तथा हि क्लेशः फलेन फलसिद्ध्या पुनर्नवतां विधत्ते । पूर्ववदेवाक्लिष्टतामापादयतीत्यर्थः । सफलः क्लेशो न क्लेश इति भावः ॥

इति श्रीमन्महामहोपाध्यायकोलाचलमल्लिनाथसूरिविरचितया संजीवनीसमाख्यया व्याख्यया समेतः श्रीकालिदासकृतौ कुमारसंभवे महाकाव्ये तपःफलोदयो नाम पञ्चमः सर्गः ॥

---

१ निक्षेप एव. २ मर्पयन्ती. ३ त्यनवमाङ्गि. ४ पिधत्ते.

षष्ठः सर्गः ।

अथ विश्वात्मने गौरी संदिदेश मिथः सखीम् ।
दाता मे भूभृतां नाथः प्रमाणीक्रियतामिति ॥ १ ॥

अथेति ॥ **अथ** देवदेवानुग्रहानन्तरं **गौरी** पार्वती विश्वमात्मा स्वरूपं यस्येति विश्वस्यात्मेति वा **विश्वात्मने** शिवाय **मिथः** रहसि । 'मिथोऽन्योन्य रहस्यपि' इत्यमरः । **सखीं संदिदेश** अतिससर्ज । क्रियामात्रप्रयोगेऽपि संप्रदानत्वाच्चतुर्थी । किमिति । **भूभृतां नाथः** हिमवान् **मे** मम **दाता** सन् । **प्रमाणीक्रियताम् इति** । दातृत्वेन प्रमाणीक्रियतामित्यर्थः । प्रार्थनायां लोट् । पित्रा दीयमानायाः परिग्रहो मम महाननुग्रह इति भावः ॥

तया व्याहृतसंदेशा सा बभौ निभृता प्रिये ।
चूतयष्टिरिवाभ्यासे मधौ परभृतोन्मुखी ॥ २ ॥

तयेति ॥ **तया** सख्या । सखीमुखेनेत्यर्थः । **व्याहृतसंदेशा** उक्तवाचिका । **प्रिये** हरविषये **निभृता** निश्चला । परमासक्तेत्यर्थः । **सा** गौरी **मधौ** वसन्ते निभृता स्थिरा परभृतया कोकिलयोन्मुखी मुखरा **परभृतोन्मुखी** । मुखशब्देनाभिभाषणव्यापारो लक्ष्यते । तथा च परभृतामुखेन व्याहरन्तीत्यर्थः । परभृतेति क्रियाशब्दाविवक्षायाम् 'जातेरस्त्री'—इति ङीष्प्रत्ययो न भवति । तयेत्युपमेयस्य व्यस्तत्वादुपमानवाचि परभृताशब्दस्य समासः सोढव्यः । अथ वा भृद्भरणम् । संपदादित्वात्क्विप् । परैर्भृद्यस्यास्तया परभृतेति व्यासेन व्याख्येयम् । पदमञ्जरीकारस्तु परैर्भ्रियत इति कर्मणि क्विपमाह । **चूतयष्टिः** चूतशाखा इव **अभ्यासे** अन्तिके **बभौ** । 'सदेशाभ्याससविधसमर्यादसवेशवत् । उपकण्ठान्तिकाभ्यर्णाभ्यग्रा अप्यभितोऽव्ययम् ॥' इत्यमरः ॥

स तथेति प्रतिज्ञाय विसृज्य कथमप्युमाम् ।
ऋषीञ्ज्योतिर्मयान्सप्त सस्मार स्मरशासनः ॥ ३ ॥

स इति ॥ **स** प्रकृतः । [**स्मरशासनः**] शास्तीति शासनः । बहुलग्रहणात्कर्तरि ल्युट् । स्मरस्य शासनः ईश्वरः **तथा इति प्रतिज्ञाय** । तथा करिष्यामीत्युक्त्वेत्यर्थः । **उमां कथम् अपि** कृच्छ्रेण **विसृज्य** । तत्र गाढानुरागत्वादिति भावः । **ज्योतिर्मयान्** तेजोरूपान् **सप्त ऋषीन्** अङ्गिरःप्रभृतीन् **सस्मार** स्मृतवान् ॥

ते प्रभामण्डलैर्व्योम द्योतयन्तस्तपोधनाः ।
सारुन्धतीकाः[1] सपादि प्रादुरासन्पुरः प्रभोः ॥ ४ ॥ ते

१ अत्र वसिष्ठपत्नीमात्रस्यागमनवर्णनं तत्पातिव्रत्यस्यान्यपत्नीपातिव्रत्येभ्यो व्यतिरेकं द्योतयितुम् । एवं हि पुराणप्रसिद्धिः—सप्तर्षीणां पुरा पत्नीरकामयत पावकः । विज्ञातवृत्ता स्वाहाथ तासां रूपेण पावकम् ॥ रमयामास सुचिरं न शशाक मनागपि । यत्नैररुन्धतीरूपं ग्रहीतुं मुनयस्ततः ॥ अन्ये तु तत्यजुः पत्नीः– इति ना० प०.

त इति ॥ ते तप एव धनं येषां ते **तपोधनाः** सप्तर्षयः **प्रभामण्डलैः** तेजः-पुञ्जैः **व्योम** आकाशं **द्योतयन्तः** प्रकाशयन्तः । अरुन्धत्या सह वर्तन्त इति **सारुन्धतीकाः** सन्तः । ' नद्यृतश्च ' इति कप् । **सपदि प्रभोः** ईश्वरस्य **पुरः** पुरोभागे **प्रादुरासन्** प्रत्यक्षा बभूवुः ॥

इतः परं बहुभिः श्लोकैस्तानेव मुनीन् वर्णयति—

आप्लुतास्तीरमन्दारकुसुमोत्किरवीचिषु ।
व्योमगङ्गाप्रवाहेषु दिङ्नागमदगन्धिषु ॥ ५ ॥

आप्लुता इति ॥ [**तीरमन्दारकुसुमोत्किरवीचिषु**] उत्किरन्ति विक्षिपन्तीत्युत्किराः । 'इगुपध'—इत्यादिना कप्रत्ययः । तीरे ये मन्दाराः कल्पवृक्षास्तेषां कुसुमानामुत्किरा वीचयस्तरङ्गा येषां तेषु । [**दिङ्नागमदगन्धिषु**] दिङ्नागानां दिग्गजानां मदगन्धो येष्विति तथोक्तेषु **व्योमगङ्गाप्रवाहेषु** आकाशगङ्गास्रोतःसु **आप्लुताः** स्नाताः ॥

मुक्तायज्ञोपवीतानि बिभ्रतो हैमवल्कलाः ।
रत्नाक्षसूत्राः प्रव्रज्यां कल्पवृक्षा इवाश्रिताः ॥ ६ ॥

मुक्तेति ॥ [**मुक्तायज्ञोपवीतानि**] मुक्तानां मौक्तिकानां यज्ञोपवीतानि । मुक्तामयानीत्यर्थः । **बिभ्रतः** दधानाः । हेममयानि वल्कलानि येषां ते **हैमवल्कलाः** । रत्नमयान्यक्षसूत्राणि येषां ते **रत्नाक्षसूत्राः** । **प्रव्रज्यां** प्रव्रजनम् । ' व्रजयजोर्भावे क्यप् ' इति क्यप् । **आश्रिताः कल्पवृक्षा इव** स्थिताः । अत्र चतुर्थाश्रमवाचिना प्रव्रज्याशब्देन वानप्रस्थाश्रमो लक्ष्यते । 'जहुः परिग्रहव्रीडां प्राजापत्यास्तपस्विनः' (६ । ३४) इति सपत्नीकत्वाभिधानात् ' सुतविन्यस्तपत्नीकस्तया वानुगतोऽपि सन् । ' इति वानप्रस्थस्योभयथा स्मरणात् ॥

अधःप्रस्थापिताश्वेन समावर्जितकेतुना ।
सहस्ररश्मिना साक्षात्सप्रणाममुदीक्षिताः ॥ ७ ॥

अध इति ॥ **अधःप्रस्थापिताश्वेन** सूर्यमण्डलोपरिवर्तित्वात्सप्तर्षिमण्डलस्येति भावः । **समावर्जितकेतुना** तन्मण्डलाघातशङ्कया नामितध्वजेन **सहस्ररश्मिना** सूर्येण **साक्षात्** स्वयमेव **सप्रणामम् उदीक्षिताः** । गमनाभ्यनुज्ञादानपर्यन्तमित्यर्थः । भगवतः सूर्यस्याप्युपास्या इति भावः ॥

आसक्तबाहुलतया सार्धमुद्धृतया भुवा ।
महावराहदंष्ट्रायां विश्रान्ताः प्रलयापदि ॥ ८ ॥

आसक्तेति ॥ पुनः किंविधाः । **प्रलयापदि** कल्पान्तसंकटे **आसक्तबाहुलतया** दंष्ट्रायामिति शेषः । **उद्धृतया** । दंष्ट्रयेति शेषः । **भुवा सार्धं** धरण्या सह **महावराहदंष्ट्रायां विश्रान्ताः** । महाप्रलयेऽप्यविनाशिन इत्यर्थः ॥

---

१ कुसुमोत्कर. २ आकाशगङ्गास्रोतःसु. ३ हेम. ४ प्रव्रज्याः...आस्थिताः ५ शश्वत्. ६ उद्धतया.

सर्गशेषप्रणयनीद्विश्वयोनेरनन्तरम्।
पुरातनाः पुराविद्भिर्धातार इति कीर्तिताः ॥ ९ ॥

सर्गेति ॥ **विश्वयोनेः** ब्रह्मणः **अनन्तरं** [**सर्गशेषप्रणयनात्**] सर्गशेषस्य प्रणयनात्। ब्रह्मसृष्टावशिष्टसृष्टेः करणाद्धेतोरित्यर्थः। **पुराविद्भिः** पुराणवेदिभिर्व्यासादिभिः **पुरातनाः धातारः इति कीर्तिताः**। विश्वयोनेरिति संबन्धमात्रे षष्ठी तस्यानन्तरमिति भाष्ये दर्शनात्। अपादानत्वविवक्षायां तु पञ्चमी। अयमदःशब्दो यथाशब्दादृत्तादनन्तरस्येति शाबरभाष्ये दर्शनात्। तथा 'अथातो धर्मजिज्ञासा वेदाध्यायादनन्तरम्' इत्याचार्याः। कविश्च 'पुराणपत्रापगमादनन्तरम्' इति। एवमन्यत्रापि द्रष्टव्यम् ॥

प्राक्तनानां विशुद्धानां परिपाकमुपेयुषाम्।
तपसामुपभुञ्जानाः फलान्यपि तपस्विनः ॥ १० ॥

प्राक्तनानामिति ॥ **प्राक्तनानां** जन्मान्तरभवानां **विशुद्धानां** निर्मलानां **परिपाकं** फलदानोन्मुखत्वं **उपेयुषां** गतानां **तपसां फलानि उपभुञ्जानाः अपि तपस्विनः** तपोनिष्ठाः। प्रारब्धभोगिनो निस्पृहाश्चेति भावः ॥ कुलकम् ॥

तेषां मध्यगता साध्वी पत्युः पादार्पितेक्षणा।
साक्षादिव तपःसिद्धिर्बभासे बह्वरुन्धती ॥ ११ ॥

तेषामिति ॥ **तेषाम्** ऋषीणां **मध्यगता साध्वी** पतिव्रता। अत एव **पत्युः** वसिष्ठस्य [**पादार्पितेक्षणा**] पादयोरर्पितेक्षणा निविष्टदृष्टिः **अरुन्धती साक्षात्** प्रत्यक्षा **तपःसिद्धिः इव**। तेषामेवेति शेषः। तेषां मध्यगतेति लिङ्गवचनादिसाम्यादियमुपमा ॥ **बहु** भूयिष्ठं **बभासे** भाति स्म ॥

तामगौरवभेदेन मुनींश्चापश्यदीश्वरः।
स्त्रीपुमानित्यनास्थैषा वृत्तं हि महितं सताम् ॥ १२ ॥

तामिति ॥ **ईश्वरः** भगवान् **ताम्** अरुन्धतीं **मुनीन् च अगौरवभेदेन** समानप्रतिपत्त्या **अपश्यत्** दृष्टवान्। न चायमविवेक इत्याह—**हि** यस्मात् **स्त्री पुमान् च इति एषा अनास्था** स्त्रीपुंसभेदो न विवक्षितः। किं तु **सतां** साधूनां **वृत्तं** चरित्रमेव **महितं** पूज्यम्। 'गुणाः पूजास्थानं गुणिषु न च लिङ्गं न च वयः।' इति भावः ॥

तद्दर्शनादभूच्छंभोर्भूयान्दारार्थमादरः।
क्रियाणां खलु धर्म्याणां सत्पत्न्यो मूलकारणम् ॥ १३ ॥

तदिति ॥ **तद्दर्शनात्** अरुन्धतीदर्शनात् **शंभोः दारार्थं** दारपरिग्रहार्थम् **आदरः भूयान्** बहुतर **अभूत्**। ननु दाराः कुत्रोपयुज्यन्त इत्यत्राह—**धर्म्याणां** धर्मादनपेतानाम्। 'धर्मपथ्यर्थन्यायादनपेते' इति यत्प्रत्ययः। **क्रियाणाम्** इज्यादीनां सत्यः पतिव्रताः पत्न्यः **सत्पत्न्यः**। 'पत्युर्नो यज्ञसंयोगे' इति ङीप्। नकारश्च। **मूलकारणं खलु** ॥

१ भूयः, दाराक्रिया०. २ साधनम्; दाम्पत्यं मूलसाधनम्.

धर्मेणापि पदं शर्वे कारिते पार्वतीं प्रति ।
पूर्वापराधभीतस्य कामस्योच्छ्वसितं मनः ॥ १४ ॥

धर्मेणेति ॥ **धर्मेण** दारसंजिघृक्षालक्षणेन **अपि** । कर्त्रा । **शर्वे** ईश्वरे **पार्वतीं प्रति पदं कारिते** सति । 'हृक्रोरन्यतरस्याम्' इति शर्वस्याणिकर्तुः कर्मत्वम् । **पूर्वापराधभीतस्य कामस्य मनः उच्छ्वसितम्** । पुनरुज्जीवनावकाशो भवतीति सप्रत्याशमभूदित्यर्थः ॥

अथ ते मुनयः सर्वे मानयित्वा जगद्गुरुम् ।
इदमूचुरनूचानाः प्रीतिकण्टकितत्वचः ॥ १५ ॥

अथेति ॥ **अथ अनूचानाः** साङ्गवेदप्रवक्तारः । 'अनूचानः प्रवचने साङ्गेऽधीती गुरोस्तु यः ।' इत्यमरः । 'उपेयिवाननाश्वाननूचानश्च' इति निपातः । [**प्रीतिकण्टकितत्वचः**] प्रीत्या कण्टकिताः पुलकितास्त्वचो येषां ते तथोक्ताः । **ते सर्वे मुनयः जगद्गुरुं** हरं **मानयित्वा** पूजयित्वा **इदं** वक्ष्यमाणम् **ऊचुः** ॥

यद्ब्रह्म सम्यगाम्नातं यदग्नौ विधिना हुतम् ।
यच्च तप्तं तपस्तस्य विपक्वं फलमद्य नः ॥ १६ ॥

यदिति ॥ **ब्रह्म** वेदः । 'वेदस्तत्त्वं तपो ब्रह्म' इत्यमरः । **सम्यक्** नियमपूर्वकम् **आम्नातम्** अधीतमिति **यत्** । **अग्नौ विधिना हुतम्** इति **यत्** । **तपः** चान्द्रायणादिकं **तप्तम्** इति **च यत्** । **तस्य** अध्ययनेज्यातपोरूपस्य आश्रमत्रयसाध्यस्य कृत्स्नस्यापि कर्मण इत्यर्थः । समुदायाभिप्रायकमेकवचनमन्यथा आवृत्त्यान्वयप्रसङ्गात् । न च नपुंसकैकवद्भावः अनपुंसकेनेति नियमात् । **फलं** कार्यम् **अद्य नः** अस्माकं **विपक्वम्** । सुनिष्पन्नमित्यर्थः । कर्मणि क्तः । 'पचो वः' इति निष्ठातस्य वत्वम् ॥

तदेव फलमाह—

यदध्यक्षेण जगतां वयमारोपितास्त्वया ।
मनोरथस्याविषयं मनोविषयमात्मनः ॥ १७ ॥

यदिति ॥ **यत्** यस्मात्कारणात् **जगताम् अध्यक्षेण** अधिपेन **त्वया वयं मनोरथस्य** अभिलाषस्य **अविषयम्** अगोचरम् **आत्मनः** स्वस्य **मनोविषयं** मनोदेशम् **आरोपिताः** प्रापिताः । तस्माद्विपक्वं फलमिति पूर्वेण संबन्धः । सकलजगदन्वेष्टव्यस्य भगवतोऽपि वयमन्वेष्या भवाम इति परमोत्कृष्टा वयमिति भावः ॥

तदेवोपपादयति—

यस्य चेतसि वर्तेथाः स तावत्कृतिनां वरः ।
किं पुनर्ब्रह्मयोनेर्यस्तव चेतसि वर्तते ॥ १८ ॥

---

१ प्रथमे. २ पूजयित्वा; प्रणिपत्य. ३ कित स्वचः. ४ अध्यपथम्. ५ विश्वयोनेः.

यस्येति ॥ यस्य जनस्य चेतसि वर्तेथाः । येन स्मर्यस इत्यर्थः । स तावत एव कृतिनां कृत्यकृत्यानां वरः श्रेष्ठः । [ब्रह्मयोनेः] ब्रह्मणो वेदस्य वेधसो वा योनेः कारणस्य । यद्वा वेदप्रमाणकस्य । तव चेतसि यः वर्तते । त्वया स्मर्यत इत्यर्थः । किं पुनः । स कृतिनां वर इति किमु वक्तव्यमित्यर्थः ॥

सत्यमर्काच्च सोमाच्च परमध्यास्महे पदम् ।
अद्य तूच्चैस्तरं ताभ्यां स्मरणानुग्रहात्तव ॥ १९ ॥

सत्यमिति ॥ अर्कात् सूर्यात् च सोमात् चन्द्रात् च परम् उच्चैः पदं स्थानम् अध्यास्महे तिष्ठामः । वयमिति शेषः । सत्यम् । 'अधिशीङ्स्थासां कर्म' इति कर्मत्वम् । अद्य तु तव । कर्तुः । [स्मरणानुग्रहात्] स्मरणमेवानुग्रहः प्रसादस्तस्माद्धेतोः । ताभ्याम् अर्केन्दुभ्याम् उच्चैस्तरम् अत्युच्चं पदम् । अध्यास्महे इति संबन्धः । उच्चैस्तरमिति द्रव्यप्रकर्षत्वाभावामुप्रत्ययः ॥

त्वत्संभावितमात्मानं बहु मन्यामहे वयम् ।
प्रायः प्रत्ययमाधत्ते स्वगुणेषूत्तमादरः ॥ २० ॥

त्वदिति ॥ वयं त्वया संभावितं सत्कृतं त्वत्संभावितम् आत्मानम् आत्मस्वरूपं बहु अधिकं यथा तथा मन्यामहे । तथा हि । उत्तमादरः सत्पुरुषकर्तृकः सत्कारः स्वगुणेषु विषये प्रायः प्रायेण भूम्ना प्रत्ययं विश्वासम् आधत्ते जनयति । सर्वस्यापि महाजनपरिग्रह एव पूज्यताहेतुरित्यर्थः ॥

या नः प्रीतिर्विरूपाक्ष त्वदनुध्यानसंभवा ।
सा किमावेद्यते तुभ्यमन्तरात्मासि देहिनाम् ॥ २१ ॥

येति ॥ हे विरूपाक्ष । त्वदनुध्यानसंभवा त्वत्कर्तृकस्मरणजन्या नः अस्माकं या प्रीतिः सा प्रीतिः तुभ्यं किमावेद्यते किमर्थं निवेद्यते । तथा हि । देहिनां प्राणिनाम् अन्तरात्मा अन्तर्यामी असि । सर्वसाक्षिणा त्वयास्मत्प्रीतिरनावेदितापि ज्ञायत एव यतस्ततो न बुद्धबोधनं संभवतीति भावः ॥

साक्षाद् दृष्टोऽसि न पुनर्विद्मस्त्वां वयमञ्जसा ।
प्रसीद कथयात्मानं न धियां पथि वर्तसे ॥ २२ ॥

साक्षादिति ॥ हे देव साक्षात् प्रत्यक्षेण दृष्टः असि । अञ्जसा पुनः तत्त्वतस्तु त्वां वयं न विद्मः । दृश्यमानस्य रूपस्याताात्त्विकत्वादिति भावः । अतः प्रसीद अनुगृहाण । आत्मानं निजस्वरूपं कथय । न चाकथितं तत्सुबोधमित्याह—धियां बुद्धीनां पथि न वर्तसे । अतस्त्वयैव त्वद्रूपं कथनीयमित्यर्थः ॥

---

१ नित्यं. २ तरां. ३ तस्मात्. ४ विशालाक्ष. ५ तव निध्यान. ६ आख्यायते. ७ नां विद्मः पुनः.

तात्त्विकं रूपं तावदास्तां न दृश्यमानमपि रूपं तत्त्वतो रूपयितुं शक्यमित्याह—

किं येन सृजसि व्यक्तमुत येन बिभर्षि तत् ।
अथ विश्वस्य संहर्ता भागः कतम एष ते ॥ २३ ॥

किमिति ॥ हे देव । **एष** दृश्यमानः **ते भागः** मूर्तिः **किम्** । **येन** भागेन **व्यक्तं** प्रपञ्चं **सृजसि** सः । यत्तदोर्नित्यसंबन्धात्सर्वत्र तच्छब्दोऽध्याहार्यः । **उत येन** भागेन **तत्** व्यक्तं **बिभर्षि** पालयसि स वा । **अथ यः** भागः । तस्य **विश्वस्य संहर्ता** स वा । किमादयः संदेहे । **कतमः** ब्रह्मविष्णुमहेश्वरेष्वयं कतमः भागः तदुच्यतामित्यर्थः ॥

ननु हर इत्येवं निश्चयात्कथमयं संशयस्तत्राह—

अथ वा सुमहत्येषा प्रार्थना देव तिष्ठतु ।
चिन्तितोपस्थितांस्तावच्छाधि नः करवाम किम् ॥ २४ ॥

अथ वेति ॥ **अथ वा** । हे **देव सुमहती** । गुह्यतमत्वादतिदुर्लभेत्यर्थः । **एषा प्रार्थना** निजरूपनिरूपणप्रार्थना **तिष्ठतु** । किंतु [**चिन्तितोपस्थितान्**] चिन्तितेन चिन्तिताः वोपस्थिताः चिन्तितोपस्थितास्तान् **नः** अस्मान् **तावत् शाधि** आज्ञापय **किं करवाम** । प्रार्थनायां लोट् । अलमप्रस्तुतेन प्रस्तुते तावन्नियुङ्क्ष्वेत्यर्थः ॥

अथ मौलिगतस्येन्दोर्विशदैर्दशनांशुभिः ।
उपचिन्वन्प्रभां तन्वीं प्रत्याह परमेश्वरः ॥ २५ ॥

अथेति ॥ **अथ परमेश्वरः मौलिगतस्य इन्दोः तन्वीम्** अल्पाम् । कलामात्रत्वादिति भावः । **प्रभां** कान्तिं **विशदैः** शुभ्रैः **दशनांशुभिः उपचिन्वन्** वर्धयन् **प्रत्याह** । प्रत्युवाचेत्यर्थः ॥

विदितं वो यथा स्वार्था न मे काश्चित्प्रवृत्तयः ।
ननु मूर्तिभिरष्टाभिरित्थंभूतोऽस्मि सूचितः ॥ २६ ॥

विदितमिति ॥ हे मुनयः **काश्चित्** अपि **मे प्रवृत्तयः** व्यापाराः **स्वार्थाः न** भवन्ति **यथा** तथा **वः** युष्माकं **विदितम्** । वाक्यार्थः **कर्म** । बुद्ध्यर्थत्वाद्वर्तमाने क्तः । तद्योगात्षष्ठी । प्रवृत्तिपारार्थ्ये प्रमाणमाह—**ननु अष्टाभिः मूर्तिभिः इत्थंभूतः** इमं प्रकारं परार्थप्रवृत्तिरूपं प्राप्तः । 'भू प्राप्तौ' इति धातोः कर्तरि क्तः । **सूचितः** ज्ञापितः **अस्मि** । मत्स्वमूर्तिचेष्टया स्वपारार्थ्यमनुमेयमित्यर्थः ॥

सोऽहं तृष्णातुरैर्वृष्टिं विद्युत्वानिव चातकैः ।
अरिविप्रकृतैर्देवैः प्रसूतिं प्रति याचितः ॥ २७ ॥

सोऽहमिति ॥ **सः** परार्थवृत्तिः **अहं तृष्णातुरैः चातकैः वृष्टिं विद्युत्वान्** मेघः **इव अरिविप्रकृतैः** शत्रुपीडितैः **देवैः प्रसूतिं** पुत्रोत्पादनं **प्रति याचितः** । याचतेर्दुहादित्वादप्रधाने कर्मणि क्तः ॥

---

१ अथो यस्तस्य.

अत आहर्तुमिच्छामि पार्वतीमात्मजन्मने ।
उत्पत्तये हविर्भोक्तुर्यजमान इवारणिम् ॥ २८ ॥

अत इति ॥ **अतः** सुरप्रार्थितत्वाद्धेतोः **आत्मजन्मने** पुत्राय । पुत्रमुत्पादयितुमित्यर्थः । 'क्रियार्थोपपदस्य-' इत्यादिना चतुर्थी । **पार्वतीं यजमानः** यष्टा । 'पूङ्यजोः शानन्' इति शानन्प्रत्ययः । **हविर्भोक्तुः** अग्नेः **उत्पत्तये अरणिम्** अग्निमन्थनदारुविशेषम् **इव** । 'निर्मन्थ्यदारुणि त्वरणिर्द्वयोः' इत्यमरः । **आहर्तुं** संग्रहीतुं मिच्छमि ॥

तामस्मदर्थे युष्माभिर्याचितव्यो हिमालयः ।
विक्रियायै न कल्पन्ते संबन्धाः सदनुष्ठिताः ॥ २९ ॥

तामिति ॥ **अस्मदर्थे** अस्मत्प्रयोजने निमित्ते सति **युष्माभिः तां** पार्वतीं **हिमालयः** हिमवान् **याचितव्यः** । याचेर्दुहादित्वादप्रधाने कर्मणि तव्यप्रत्ययः । आवश्यकं चैतदित्याह— [**सदनुष्ठिताः**] सद्भिः सत्पुरुषैरनुष्ठिताः संघटिताः **संबन्धाः** यौनादयो **विक्रियायै** वैकल्योत्पादनाय **न कल्पन्ते** न पर्याप्नुवन्ति । न समर्था इत्यर्थः । अलमर्थयोगाच्चतुर्थी ॥

न चाहं लौल्यात्स्त्रियमिच्छामि किं तु देवोपकाराय । यद्येवं निखिलदेवेषु विद्यमानेषु हिमगिरेः शिलाभूतस्य कन्यापरिणयेच्छा कथमित्युक्ते स एव मे श्लाघ्यसंबन्धोऽत्रभवान्हिमवानित्याह—

उन्नतेन स्थितिमता धुरमुद्वहता भुवः ।
तेन योजितसंबन्धं वित्त मामप्यवञ्चितम् ॥ ३० ॥

उन्नतेनेति ॥ **उन्नतेन** प्रांशुना प्रसिद्धेन च **स्थितिमता** प्रतिष्ठावता **भुवः धुरं** भारम् **उद्वहता** । निर्वाहकेणेत्यर्थः । **तेन** हिमवता [**योजितसंबन्धं**] योजितः संघटितः संबन्धो यौनसंबन्धो यस्य तं **माम् अपि अवञ्चितम्** अव्यामोहितं **वित्त** जानीत । 'विद ज्ञाने' इति धातोर्लोट् ॥

तर्हि स किं वाच्य इत्याशङ्क्याह—

एवं वाच्यः स कन्यार्थमिति वो नोपदिश्यते ।
भवत्प्रणीतमाचारमामनन्ति हि साधवः ॥ ३१ ॥

एवमिति ॥ **कन्यार्थं** कन्याप्रदानाय **स** हिमवान् **एवं वाच्यः इति वः** युष्मभ्यं **न उपदिश्यते** । कुतः **हि** यस्मात् **साधवः** विद्वांसः [**भवत्प्रणीतं**] भवद्भिः प्रणीतं स्मृतिरूपेण निबद्धम् **आचारम् आमनन्ति** उपदिशन्ति । न हि स्वयमुपदेष्टारः परोपदेशमपेक्षन्त इत्यर्थः ॥

आर्याप्यरुन्धती तत्र व्यापारं कर्तुमर्हति ।
प्रायेणैवंविधे कार्ये पुरन्ध्रीणां प्रगल्भता ॥ ३२ ॥

---

१ उत्पादाय. २ हिमाचलः. ३ साहाय्यम्.

आर्येति ॥ **आर्या** पूज्या **अरुन्धती अपि तत्र** विवाहकृत्ये **व्यापारं** साहाय्यं **कर्तुम् अर्हति** । तथा हि । **प्रायेण** प्राचुर्येण **एवंविधे कार्ये** विवाहादिकार्ये । दुर्घट इत्यर्थः । **पुरन्ध्रीणां** कुटुम्बिनीनाम् । ' स्यात्तु कुटुम्बिनी । पुरन्ध्री ' इत्यमरः । **प्रगल्भता** चातुर्यम् । स्त्रीप्रधानेषु कृत्येषु स्त्रीणामेव घटनापाटवमिति भावः ॥

तत्प्रयातौषधिप्रस्थं सिद्धये हिमवत्पुरम् ।
महाकोशीप्रपातेऽस्मिन्संगमः पुनरेव नः ॥ ३३ ॥

तदिति ॥ **तत्** तस्मात्कारणात् **ओषधिप्रस्थं** नाम **हिमवत्पुरं** हिमवन्नगरं **सिद्धये** कार्यसिद्ध्यर्थं **प्रयात** गच्छत । **अस्मिन्** पुरोवर्तिनि [**महाकोशीप्रपाते**] महाकोशी नाम तत्रत्या काचित् नदी तस्याः प्रपाते भृगौ **एव** । सा नदी यत्र पतति तस्मिन्नित्यर्थः । ' प्रपातस्त्वतटो भृगुः ' इत्यमरः । **नः** अस्माकं **पुनः संगमः** । अस्त्विति शेषः । भवत्समागमं प्रतिपालयन्नहमिहैव निवत्स्यामीत्यर्थः ॥

तस्मिन्संयमिनामाद्ये जाते परिणयोन्मुखे ।
जहुः परिग्रहव्रीडां प्राजापत्यास्तपस्विनः ॥ ३४ ॥

तस्मिन्निति ॥ **संयमिनां** योगिनाम् **आद्ये तस्मिन्** ईश्वरे **परिणयोन्मुखे** विवाहोत्सुके **जाते** सति प्रजापतेरिमे **प्राजापत्याः** । ब्रह्मपुत्रा इत्यर्थः । **तपस्विनः** मुनयः [**परिग्रहव्रीडां**] परिग्रहैः पत्नीभिर्व्रीडाम् । गार्हस्थ्यनिमित्तामित्यर्थः । ' पत्नीपरिजनादानमूलशापाः परिग्रहाः ' इत्यमरः । **जहुः** तत्यजुः । जहातेर्लिटि रूपम् । न हि समानगुणदोषेषु व्रीडावकाशोऽस्तीति भावः ॥

ततः परममित्युक्त्वा प्रतस्थे मुनिमण्डलम् ।
भगवानपि संप्राप्तः प्रथमोद्दिष्टमास्पदम् ॥ ३५ ॥

तत इति ॥ **ततः** अनन्तरं **मुनिमण्डलं** मुनिसमूहः **परमम् इति उक्त्वा** ओम् इत्युक्त्वा । अनुमन्येत्यर्थः । अव्ययमेतत् । ' ओमेवं परमं मतम् ' इत्यमरः । **प्रतस्थे** । **भगवान्** ईश्वरः **अपि प्रथमोद्दिष्टं** पूर्वसंकेतितम् **आस्पदं** स्थानं महाकोशीप्रपातं **संप्राप्तः** ॥

ते चाकाशमसिश्यामसुत्पत्य परमर्षयः ।
आसेदुरोषधिप्रस्थं मनसा समरंहसः ॥ ३६ ॥

त इति ॥ **मनसा समरंहसः** मनस्तुल्यवेगा **ते परमर्षयः च** । पूर्वश्लोकोक्तपरसमुच्चयार्थश्चकारः । [**असिश्यामं**] असिवच्छ्यामं नीलं **आकाशं** खं प्रति **उत्पत्य ओषधिप्रस्थं** हिमवत्पुरम् **आसेदुः** । सद्यः प्रापुरित्यर्थः ॥

---

१ कोशी. २ पुनरस्तु. ३ उत्सुके. ४ तपोधनाः. ५ प्रमाणम्. ६ संक्रान्तः. ७ आश्रमम्. ८ व आ०, अथा. ९ मुनिपुंगवाः.

इतः परं दशभिः श्लोकैरोषधिप्रस्थमेव वर्णयति—

अलकामतिवाह्यैव वसतिं वसुसंपदाम् ।
स्वर्गाभिष्यन्दवमनं कृत्वेवोपनिवेशितम् ॥ ३७ ॥

अलकामिति ॥ वसुसंपदां धनसमृद्धीनां वसतिं स्थानम् अलकां कुबेरनगरीम् अतिवाह्य । परिच्छिद्येति यावत् । उपनिवेशितम् इव स्थितम् । तथा [स्वर्गाभिष्यन्दवमनम्] स्वर्गस्याभिष्यन्दोऽतिरेकः । अतिरिक्तजन इति यावत् । तस्य वमनं निःसारणं कृत्वा उपनिवेशितमिव स्थितम् । उभयत्रापि कौटिल्यः—'भूतपूर्वमभूतपूर्वं वा जनपदं परदेशापवाहेन स्वदेशाभिष्यन्दवमनेन वा निवेशयेत् ।' इति । अलकाऽमरावत्यतिशयितसमृद्धिकमित्यर्थः ॥

गङ्गास्रोतःपरिक्षिप्तं वप्रान्तर्ज्वलितौषधि ।
बृहन्मणिशिलासालं गुप्तावपि मनोहरम् ॥ ३८ ॥

गङ्गेति ॥ [गङ्गास्रोतःपरिक्षिप्तं] गङ्गायाः स्रोतोभिः प्रवाहैः परिक्षिप्तं परिवेष्टितम् । तैरेव सपरिखमित्यर्थः । [वप्रान्तर्ज्वलितौषधि] वप्रश्चयः । प्राकारचैत्यमिति यावत् । 'स्याच्चयो वप्रमस्त्रियाम्' इत्यमरः । तस्यान्तर्मध्ये ज्वलिताः प्रकाशमानाः ओषधयो यस्य तत्तथोक्तम् । ज्वलितौषधित्वाद्रात्रिषु संचारिणां दीपनिरपेक्षमित्यर्थः । [बृहन्मणिशिलासालं] बृहद्विपुलो मणिशिलानां माणिक्यानां सालः प्राकारो यस्य तत्तथोक्तम् । 'प्राकारो वरणः सालः' इत्यमरः । अत एव गुप्तावपि संवरणेऽपि मनोहरम् । अकृत्रिमदुर्गसंवरणमिति भावः ॥

जितसिंहभया नागा यत्राश्वा बिलयोनयः ।
यक्षाः किंपुरुषाः पौरा योषितो वनदेवताः ॥ ३९ ॥

जितेति ॥ यत्र पुरे नागाः गजाः [जितसिंहभयाः] जितं सिंहेभ्यो भयं यैस्ते तथोक्ताः । सिंहाधिकबला इत्यर्थः । नाथस्तु 'पदं तुषारस्रुतिधौतरक्तम्' (१।६) इत्येतद्विरोधभयात् 'वीतवीतभयाः' इति पपाठ । तथा न भेतव्यं तत्र वनगजानां सिंहहतत्वाभिधानात् । अत्र त्वोषधिप्रस्थगजानां हिमवन्महिम्ना सिंहातिरेकसंभवेनाविरोधादिति । 'वीतवीतभयाः' इति पाठे वीतं विगतं वीताराद्यङ्कुशकर्मभ्यो भयं येषां ते तथोक्ताः । स्वभावविनीता इत्यर्थः । 'पादकर्म युतं प्रोक्तं यातमङ्कुशवारणम् । उभयं वीतमाख्यातम्' इति यादवः । अश्वाः बिलयोनयः बिलसंभवाः । अन्यत्र तु न तथेति वैचित्र्यम् । उक्तं च—'अमृताद्वाष्पतो वह्नेर्वेदेभ्योऽण्डाच्च गर्भतः । साम्नो हयानामुत्पत्तिः सप्तधा परिकीर्तिता ॥' इति । यक्षाः प्रसिद्धाः किंपुरुषाः किंनराश्च पौराः । वनदेवताः एव योषितः । नतु मानुष्य इत्यर्थः ॥

शिखरासक्तमेघानां व्यज्यन्ते यत्र वेश्मनाम् ।
अनुगर्जितसंदिग्धाः करणैर्मुरजस्वनाः ॥ ४० ॥

१ इव. २ बहुसं०. ३ स्यान्दिव०, स्यन्दिरमणम्. ४ त्वेव विनिवेशितम्. ५ न्तज्व०
६ ज्वलन्म०. ७ स्वर्गादपि. ८ वीत. ९ यक्षाकिं०. १० वेश्मसु. ११ मन्द्रगर्जित०. १२ मुरव.

शिखरेति ॥ यत्र [शिखरासक्तमेघानां] शिखरेष्वासक्ता मेघा येषां तेषां वेश्मनां संबन्धिनः [अनुगर्जितसंदिग्धाः] अनुगर्जितानि प्रतिगर्जितानि तैः संदिग्धाः मुरजस्वनाः करणैः तालव्यवस्थापकैस्ताडनविशेषैः । तदुक्तं राजकन्दर्पेण— ' नृत्यवादित्रगीतानां प्रयोगवशभेदिनाम् । संस्थानं ताडनं रोधः करणानि प्रचक्षते ॥' इति । व्यज्यन्ते स्फुटीक्रियन्ते ॥

यत्र कल्पद्रुमैरेव विलोलविटपांशुकैः ।
गृहयन्त्रपताकाश्रीरपौरादरनिर्मिता ॥ ४१ ॥

यत्रेति ॥ यत्र नगरे [विलोलविटपांशुकैः] । विलोलानि चञ्चलानि विटपेष्वंशुकानि येषां तैः कल्पद्रुमैः एव [अपौरादरनिर्मिता] अपौरादरेण पौरादरं विनैव निर्मिता । अयत्नसिद्धेत्यर्थः । [गृहयन्त्रपताकाश्रीः] गृहेषु यानि यन्त्राण्याधारदारूणि तेषु पताकास्तासां श्रीः । संभवतीति शेषः । तत्र लम्बाम्बराः कल्पतरव एव वैजयन्तीति संभाव्यन्त इत्यर्थः ।

यत्र स्फटिकहर्म्येषु नक्तमापानभूमिषु ।
ज्योतिषां प्रतिबिम्बानि प्राप्नुवन्त्युपहारताम् ॥ ४२ ॥

यत्रेति ॥ यत्र पुरे नक्तं रात्रौ स्फटिकहर्म्येषु आपानभूमिषु पानगोष्ठीप्रदेशेषु ज्योतिषां नक्षत्राणां प्रतिबिम्बानि उपहारतां पुष्पोपहारत्वं मौक्तिकोपहारत्वं वा प्राप्नुवन्ति ॥

यत्रौषधिप्रकाशेन नक्तं दर्शितसंचराः ।
अनभिज्ञास्तमिस्राणां दुर्दिनेष्वभिसारिकाः ॥ ४३ ॥

यत्रेति ॥ यत्र पुरे दुर्दिनेषु मेघाच्छन्नदिवसेषु नक्तम् [ओषधिप्रकाशेन] ओषधीनां तृणज्योतिषां प्रकाशेन संचरन्त एभिरिति संचराः पन्थानः । 'गोचरसंचर '—इत्यादिना घप्रत्ययान्तो निपातः । दर्शितसंचराः प्रकाशितमार्गाः अभिसारिकाः कान्तार्थिन्यः । ' कान्तार्थिनी तु या याति संकेतं साभिसारिका । ' इत्यमरः । तमिस्राणां तमसाम् । कृद्योगात्कर्मणि षष्ठी । अनभिज्ञाः । तमांसि नाभिजानन्तीत्यर्थः ॥

यौवनान्तं वयो यस्मिन्नान्तकः कुसुमायुधात् ।
रतिखेदसमुत्पन्ना निद्रा संज्ञाविपर्ययः॥ ४४ ॥

यौवनान्तमिति ॥ यस्मिन् पुरे वयः यौवनान्तं यौवनावधिकम् । सर्वेऽप्यजरा इत्यर्थः । तथा कुसुमायुधात् कामात् । अन्य इति शेषः । अन्तकः मृत्युः न । अस्तीति शेषः । विरहिणां तादृग्दुःखोत्पादकत्वादन्तकत्वोपचारः । कामं विना मृत्युर्नास्तीत्यर्थः । अत एव तत्कार्यभूतमरणाभाव इत्याशयेनाह—-रतीति । रतिखेदसमु-

१ द्वार. २ सोपान०, ०पङ्क्तिषु; हर्म्याणां शुभ्रसोपानपंक्तिषु. ३ नेऽप्य०. ४ भातंकः—भाग०ः कुसुमायुधः. ५ समुत्थाना.

त्पन्ना निद्रा सुप्तिरेव संज्ञाविपर्ययः चेतनापगमः। न तु दीर्घनिद्रारूप इत्यर्थः। अत्रत्याः सर्वेऽजरामरा इति श्लोकतात्पर्यार्थः। अन्तयत्यन्तं करोतीत्यन्तकः। अन्तयतेस्तत्करोतीति ण्यन्ता प्रत्ययः॥

भ्रूभेदिभिः सकम्पोष्ठैर्ललिताङ्गुलितर्जनैः।
यत्र कोपैः कृताः स्त्रीणामाप्रसादार्थिनः[1] प्रियाः॥ ४५॥

भ्रूभेदिभिरिति॥ यत्र पुरे प्रियाः युवानः भ्रूभेदिभिः भ्रूभङ्गवद्भिः [सकम्पोष्ठैः] सकम्पा ओष्ठा येषु तैः [ललिताङ्गुलितर्जनैः] ललितान्यङ्गुलितर्जनानि येषु तैः स्त्रीणां कोपैः मानाख्यैः आप्रसादार्थिनः आप्रसादं प्रसादपर्यन्तमर्थिनो याचकाः कृताः। न तु शत्रुकोपैरिति भावः॥

संतानकतरुच्छायासुप्तविद्याधराध्वगम्।
यस्य चोपवनं बाह्यं गन्धवद्गन्धमादनम्[2]॥ ४६॥

संतानकेति॥ [च] किं चेति चार्थः। [संतानकतरुच्छायासुप्तविद्याधराध्वगम्] संतानकतरोश्छायासु सुप्ता विद्याधरा देवताविशेषास्त एवाध्वगा यस्मिंस्तत्तथोक्तं गन्धवत् गन्धाढ्यं गन्धमादनं नाम गिरिः यस्य पुरस्य बहिर्भवं बाह्यम् उपवनम् आरामः। संतानकतरुच्छायेत्यत्र पूर्वपदार्थबाहुल्यसंभवेऽपि 'शलभच्छायम्' 'इक्षुच्छायम्' इतिवत्समर्थच्छायानिष्पत्तेस्तदपेक्षाभावात् 'छाया बाहुल्ये' इति नपुंसकत्वं नास्तीत्यनुसंधेयम्। अत्र 'गन्धवद्गन्धमादनम्' इत्यागन्तुकः पाठः। प्राचीनपाठस्तु 'सुगन्धिर्गन्धमादनः' इति पुंल्लिङ्गान्तः। अत एव क्षीरस्वामिना 'गन्धमादनमन्ये च' इत्यत्र गन्धेन मादयतीति गन्धमादनः इति व्याख्याय प्रयोगे च पुंल्लिङ्गता दृश्यत इत्याशयेनोक्तं सुगन्धिर्गन्धमादनः इति कालिदास इति॥

अथ[3] ते मुनयो दिव्याः प्रेक्ष्य हैमवतं पुरम्।
स्वर्गाभिसंधिसुकृतं[4] वञ्चनामिव मेनिरे॥ ४७॥

अथेति॥ अथ ते दिवि भवाः दिव्याः मुनयः हिमवतः इदं हैमवतं पुरं प्रेक्ष्य स्वर्गाभिसंधिना स्वर्गोद्देशेन यत्सुकृतं ज्योतिष्टोमाद्यनुष्ठानं तत् स्वर्गाभिसंधिसुकृतं वञ्चनां प्रतारणाम् इव मेनिरे। हिमवन्नगरमवेक्ष्य स्वर्गस्य पुण्यफलत्वं वदता वेदेन वयं विप्रलब्धा इत्यर्थः। स्वर्गादतिरमणीयमिति भावः॥

ते सद्मनि गिरेर्वेगादुन्मुखद्वाःस्थवीक्षिताः।
अवतेरुर्[5]जटाभारैर्लिखितानलनिश्चलैः[6]॥ ४८॥

त इति॥ लिखितानलनिश्चलैः। चित्रगतज्वलननिष्पन्दैरिति वेगप्रकर्षोक्तिः। जटाभारैः उपलक्षिताः ते मुनयः। [उन्मुखद्वाःस्थवीक्षिताः] द्वारि तिष्ठन्तीति

---

१ मप्रसा०. २ सुगन्धिर्गन्धमादनः. ३ तत्कान्तं; ततस्ते. ४ स्पन्दि सु०, भिसंधि सुकृतां. ५ अवपेतुः. ६ निश्चलाः.

द्वाःस्थाः द्वारपालकाः । 'प्रतीहारे द्वारपालद्वाःस्थद्वाःस्थितदर्शकाः ।' इत्यमरः । उन्मुखैरूर्ध्वमुखैर्द्वाःस्थैर्वीक्षिताः सन्तः । न तु निनिवारिता इत्यर्थः । गिरेः हिमवतः सद्मानि वेगात् अवतेरुः अवतीर्णवन्तः ॥

गगनादवतीर्णा सा यथावृद्धपुरःसरा ।
तोयान्तर्भास्करालीव रेजे मुनिपरंपरा ॥ ४९ ॥

गगनादिति ॥ गगनात् अवतीर्णा अवरूढा [यथावृद्धपुरःसरा] यथावृद्धं वृद्धानुक्रमेण स्थिताः पुरःसरा अग्रेसरा यस्यां सा तथोक्ता । अनुपसर्जनाधिकाराच्च कप् । सा मुनिपरंपरा मुनिपङ्क्तिः तोयान्तः तोयाभ्यन्तरे भास्कराली प्रतिबिम्बितार्कपङ्क्तिः इव रेजे । एतेन मुनीनां तेजस्वित्वेऽपि सुखसंदर्शनं सूचयति । भास्कराणां भूयिष्ठत्वसंभावनार्थं तोयान्तरित्युक्तम् । अत एव बहुत्वसिद्धिश्च ॥

तानर्घ्यानर्घ्यमादाय दूरात्प्रत्युद्ययौ गिरिः ।
नमयन्सारगुरुभिः पादन्यासैर्वसुंधराम् ॥ ५० ॥

तानिति ॥ गिरिः हिमवान् अर्घ्यम् अर्घार्थं जलम् आदाय । सारगुरुभिः अन्तःसारदुर्भरैः पादन्यासैः वसुंधरां नमयन् अधःप्रापयन् । अर्घमर्हन्ति इति अर्घ्यान् पूज्यान् । दण्डादित्वाद्यत्प्रत्ययः । तान् मुनीन् दूरात् प्रत्युद्ययौ ॥

संप्रति हिमवन्तमेव जङ्गमस्थावररूपद्वयसाधारणैर्विशेषणैर्दिशिनष्टि—

धातुताम्राधरः प्रांशुर्देवदारुबृहद्भुजः ।
प्रकृत्यैव शिलोरस्कः सुव्यक्तो हिमवानिति ॥ ५१ ॥

धात्विति ॥ [धातुताम्राधरः] धातुवत्ताम्रोऽधरो यस्य स तथोक्तः । अन्यत्र धातुरेव ताम्रोऽधरो यस्य । प्रांशुः उन्नतः । उभयत्रापि समानम् । [देवदारुबृहद्भुजः] देवदारुवद्बृहन्तौ भुजौ यस्य स तथोक्तः । देवदारव एव बृहन्तौ भुजौ यस्येत्यन्यत्र । प्रकृत्या स्वभावेन एव शिलावदुरो यस्य स शिलोरस्कः । शिलैवोरोऽन्यत्र । 'उरःप्रभृतिभ्यः कप्' इति कप् । अतः हिमवानिति सुव्यक्तः । वर्तमाने क्तः । सत्यं स एवायं हिमवानिति तद्धर्मप्रत्यभिज्ञानादवधारित इत्यर्थः ॥

विधिप्रयुक्तसत्कारैः[1] स्वयं मार्गस्य दर्शकः[2] ।
स तैराक्रमयामास[3] शुद्धान्तं शुद्धकर्मभिः ॥ ५२ ॥

विधीति ॥ स हिमवान् [विधिप्रयुक्तसत्कारैः] विधिना शास्त्रेण प्रयुक्तसत्कारैः कृतार्चनैः शुद्धकर्मभिः अदुष्टचरितैः । शुद्धान्तप्रवेशार्हैरित्यर्थः । तैः मनिभिः स्वयं मार्गस्य दर्शयतीति दर्शकः दर्शयिता सन् । पश्यतेर्ण्यन्तात्कर्तरि ण्वुल्प्रत्ययः । शुद्धान्तम् अन्तःपुरम् आक्रमयामास । प्रवेशयामासेत्यर्थः । अत्र क्रमेरगत्यर्थत्वात् 'गतिबुद्धि-' इत्यादिना तैरित्यस्य न कर्मत्वम् ॥

---

1 सत्कारान्. 2 देशकः. 3 तान्...कर्मणः.

तत्र वेत्रासनासीनान्कृतासनपरिग्रहः ।
ईत्युवाचेश्वरान्[2] वाचं प्राञ्जलिर्भूधरेश्वरः[3] ॥ ५३ ॥

तत्रेति ॥ वेत्रं लताविशेषः । तत्र शुद्धान्ते वेत्रासनासीनान् वेत्रमयविष्टरोपविष्टान् ईश्वरान् प्रभून्मुनीन् भूधरेश्वरः हिमवान् कृतासनपरिग्रहः । उपविष्टः सन्नित्यर्थः । प्राञ्जलिः कृताञ्जलिः सन् । इति एवं वाचम् उवाच ॥

अपमेघोदयं वर्षमदृष्टकुसुमं फलम् ।
अतर्कितोपपन्नं वो दर्शनं प्रतिभाति मे ॥ ५४ ॥

अपेति ॥ अतर्कितोपपन्नम् अविचारितमेवोपगतम् । अत्यन्तासंभावितमित्यर्थः । वः युष्माकं दर्शनम् अपमेघोदयं वर्षम् अनभ्रा वृष्टिस्तथा [अदृष्टकुसुमं] अदृष्टं कुसुमं यस्य तत्तथोक्तं फलं च तत् मे प्रतिभाति । अतिदुर्लभलाभः संवृत्त इत्यर्थः । अत्र मेघोदयकुसुमरूपकारणयोरभावेऽपि वर्षफलरूपकार्ययोरुदयाभिधानाद्विभावना । मुनिदर्शनस्य विशिष्टवृत्तित्वेन च रूपकाद्रूपकालंकारश्चेत्युभयोः संसृष्टिः ॥

मूढं बुद्धमिवात्मानं हैमीभूतमिवायसम्[5] ।
भूमेर्दिवमिवारूढं मन्ये भवदनुग्रहात् ॥ ५५ ॥

मूढमिति ॥ भवदनुग्रहात् आत्मानं मां मूढं (बुद्ध्या विनाकृतं) बुद्धम् इव मूढो भूत्वा यो बुद्धवांस्तमिव । कर्तरि क्तः । आयसम् अयोविकारं हैमीभूतम् इव । आयसत्वं विहाय सौवर्णत्वं प्राप्तमिवेत्यर्थः । भूमेः भूलोकात् दिवं स्वर्गम् आरूढमिव मन्ये । ज्ञानरूपस्थानान्यद्य मे परमुत्कृष्यन्त इति भावः ॥

अद्यप्रभृति भूतानामधिगम्योऽस्मि शुद्धये ।
यदध्यासितमर्हद्भिस्तद्धि तीर्थं प्रचक्षते[6] ॥ ५६ ॥

अद्येति ॥ अद्यप्रभृति इत आरभ्य भूतानां प्राणिनां शुद्धये अधिगम्यः अस्मि शुद्ध्यर्थिनां तीर्थभूतोऽस्मीत्यर्थः । भवदागमनादिति शेषः । हि यस्मात् यत् अर्हद्भिः सद्भिः अध्यासितम् अधिष्ठितम् । जुष्टमिति यावत् । तत्तीर्थं प्रचक्षते । 'निपानागमयोस्तीर्थमृषिजुष्टजले गुरौ ।' इत्यमरः ॥

अवैमि पूतमात्मानं द्वयेनैव द्विजोत्तमाः ।
मूर्ध्नि गङ्गाप्रपातेन धौतपादाम्भसा च वः ॥ ५७ ॥

अवैमीति ॥ हे द्विजोत्तमाः । आत्मानं मां द्वयेन एव पूतं शुद्धम् अवैमि अवगच्छामि । केन द्वयेन । मूर्ध्नि गङ्गाप्रपातेन मन्दाकिनीपातेन वः युष्माकं [धौतपादाम्भसा] धौतयोः क्षालितयोः पादयोरम्भसा च । गङ्गाजलवत्पादाम्भसः पावनत्वमित्यौपम्यं गम्यते । तच्च प्रस्तुताप्रस्तुतयोः इति दीपकालंकारः । 'प्रियः प्रियतराख्यानम्' इति लक्षणात्प्रेयोऽलंकार इति केचित् ॥

---

१ अनासन०; नीचासन०, २ मुनीन्सर्वान्, ३ शशिबांधरः. ४ कृत०, ५ मत्यांनाम्, ६ प्रचक्षते.

जङ्गमं प्रैष्यभावे वः स्थावरं चरणाङ्कितम् ।
विभक्तानुग्रहं मन्ये द्विरूपमपि मे वपुः ॥ ५८ ॥

जङ्गममिति ॥ हे मुनयः । **द्विरूपं** जङ्गमस्थावरात्मकत्वाद्द्विप्रकारकम् **अपि मे वपुः विभक्तानुग्रहं** विभज्य कृतप्रसादं **मन्ये** । कुतः । **जङ्गमं** वपुः **वः** युष्माकं **प्रैष्यभावे** कैंकर्ये । स्थितमिति शेषः । 'प्रादूहोढोढ्येषैष्येषु वृद्धिर्वक्तव्या' इति वृद्धिः । 'नियोज्यकिंकरप्रैष्यभुजिष्यपरिचारकाः ।' इत्यमरः । **स्थावरं** वपुः **चरणाङ्कितम्** । अयमेव हि महाननुग्रहो दासजनस्य यत्कर्मसु नियोजनं मूर्धनि पादन्यासश्चेति तात्पर्यार्थः ॥

भवत्संभावनोत्थाय परितोषाय मूर्च्छते ।
अपि व्याप्तदिगन्तानि नाङ्गानि प्रभवन्ति मे ॥ ५९ ॥

भवदिति ॥ व्याप्ता दिगन्ता यैस्तानि **व्याप्तदिगन्तानि अपि** । महान्त्यपीत्यर्थः । **मे** मम **अङ्गानि भवत्संभावनोत्थाय** युष्मदनुग्रहजन्याय **मूर्च्छते** व्याप्नुवते **परितोषाय न प्रभवन्ति** न पर्याप्नुवन्ति । अलमर्थयोगाच्चतुर्थी । यथा महत्स्वपि मत्पात्रेषु न माति तथा मे हर्षो वर्धत इत्यर्थः ॥

न केवलं दरीसंस्थं भास्वतां दर्शनेन वः ।
अन्तर्गतमपास्तं मे रजसोऽपि परं तमः ॥ ६० ॥

नेति ॥ **भास्वतां** तेजस्विनां विवस्वतां च **वः** युष्माकं **दर्शनेन केवलं दरीसंस्थं** गुहागतं **तमः** ध्वान्तरूपमेव **न अपास्तम्** । किं तु **मे अन्तर्गतम्** अन्तरात्मगतं **रजसः** रजोगुणात् **परम्** अनन्तरं तमः अज्ञानरूपं **अपि** अपास्तम् । रजस्तु पादन्यासैरेवापास्तमिति भावः । प्रसिद्धैर्भास्वद्भिर्बाह्यं तमोऽपास्यत एभिस्त्वान्तरमपीति व्यतिरेको व्यज्यते ॥

कर्तव्यं वो न पश्यामि स्याच्चेत्किं नोपपद्यते ।
मन्ये मत्पावनायैव प्रस्थानं भवतामिह ॥ ६१ ॥

कर्तव्यमिति ॥ **कर्तव्यं** कार्यं **वः** युष्माकं **न पश्यामि** । निस्पृहत्वादिति भावः । अथ **स्यात् चेत्** विद्येत यदि **किं न उपपद्यते** किं नाम न संभवति । सर्वं सुलभमेवेत्यर्थः । अथ वा किमत्र प्रयोजनचिन्तयेत्याह—**मत्पावनाय** मच्छोधनाय **एव भवताम् इह** विषये **प्रस्थानम्** । इमं देशमुद्दिश्येदं प्रयाणमित्यर्थः । **मन्ये** तर्कयामि ॥

तथापि तावत्कस्मिंश्चिदाज्ञां मे दातुमर्हथ ।
विनियोगप्रसादा हि किंकराः प्रभविष्णुषु ॥ ६२ ॥

तथापीति ॥ **तथापि** भवतां निःस्पृहत्वेऽपि **कस्मिंश्चित्** । कर्मणीति शेषः । **आज्ञाम्** इदं कुर्वित्यादेशं **तावत्** इदानीं **मे** मह्यं **दातुम् अर्हथ** । मदनुग्रहबुद्ध्येति भावः । **हि** यस्मात् **किंकराः** भृत्याः । प्रभवन्तीति **प्रभाविष्णुषु** प्रभुषु विषये । 'भुवश्च' इती-

---

१ प्रेष्यभावेन; प्रेष्यपक्षे. २ विरूपं; द्वैरूप्यमपि; द्वैरूप्यं तेन मे कृतम्. ३ अभिगम्य०. उपदिश्यते. ५ शङ्के. ६ इदम्.

ष्णुच्प्रत्ययः । [**विनियोगप्रसादाः**] विशेषेण नियोगो विनियोगः प्रेषणमेव प्रसादः अनुग्रहो येषां ते तथोक्ताः । अन्यथा स्वस्वामिभावो निष्फल इति भावः ॥

एते वयममी दाराः कन्येयं कुलजीवितम् ।
ब्रूत येनात्र वः कार्यमनास्था बाह्यवस्तुषु ॥ ६३ ॥

एत इति ॥ किं बहुना । **एते वयम् अमी दाराः इयं** [**कुलजीवितं**] कुलस्य जीवितं प्राणभूता । परमप्रेमास्पदमित्यर्थः । **कन्या** । **अत्र** एषां मध्ये **येन** जनेन **वः कार्यं** प्रयोजनं **ब्रूत** । तमिति शेषः । येन सोऽपि दीयत इति भावः । रत्नहिरण्यादिकं तु न मे गण्यमित्याह—**बाह्यवस्तुषु** कनकरत्नादिषु **अनास्था** अनादरः । प्रसज्यप्रतिषेधेऽपि नञ्समास इष्यते । अदेयं न किंचिदस्तीति भावः ॥

इत्यूचिवांस्तमेवार्थं गुहामुखविसर्पिणा ।
द्विरिव प्रतिशब्देन व्याजहार हिमालयः ॥ ६४ ॥

इत्येति ॥ **इति ऊचिवान्** उक्तवान् । वचेः क्वसुप्रत्ययः । **हिमालयः** हिमवान् [**गुहामुखविसर्पिणा**] गुहानां मुखेषु विवरेषु विसर्पतीति तथोक्तेन **प्रतिशब्देन तम् एव** पूर्वोक्तमेव **अर्थं द्विः** द्विवारम् । 'द्वित्रिचतुर्भ्यः सुच्' इति सुच्प्रत्ययः । **इव व्याजहार** बभाषे ॥

अथाङ्गिरसमग्रण्यमुदाहरणवस्तुषु ।
ऋषयो नोदयामासुः प्रत्युवाच स भूधरम् ॥ ६५ ॥

अथेति ॥ **अथ** अनन्तरम् **ऋषयः** [**उदाहरणवस्तुषु**] उदाहरणानि कथाप्रसङ्गास्त एव वस्तून्यर्थास्तेषु । अग्रं नयतीत्यग्रणीस्तम् **अग्रण्यं** प्रगल्भम् । 'सत्सूद्विष–' इत्यादिना क्विप् । 'अग्रग्रामाभ्यां नयतेरिति वक्तव्यम्' इति णत्वम् । **अङ्गिरसं** नामर्षिं **नोदयामासुः** प्रतिवक्तुं प्रेरयामासुः । **सः** अङ्गिराः **भूधरं** हिमवन्तं **प्रत्युवाच** ॥

उपपन्नमिदं सर्वमतः परमपि त्वयि ।
मनसः शिखराणां च सदृशी ते समुन्नतिः ॥ ६६ ॥

उपपन्नमिति ॥ **इदम्** 'एते वयममी दाराः' (६ । ६३) इत्याद्युक्तं **सर्वम् अतः परम्** अतोऽधिकम् **अपि त्वयि उपपन्नं** युज्यते । तथा हि । **ते मनसः शिखराणां च समुन्नतिः सदृशी** । शिखराणीव मनो महोन्नतमित्यर्थः । किं नाम दुष्करमुन्नतचित्तानामिति भावः । प्रस्तुताप्रस्तुतयोर्मनःशिखरयोरौपम्यस्य गम्यत्वाद्दीपकालंकारः ॥

स्थाने त्वां स्थावरात्मानं विष्णुमाहुस्तथा हि ते ।
चराचराणां भूतानां कुक्षिराधारतां गतः ॥ ६७ ॥

---

१ कनार्थिनो वयम्. २ उक्तवान्. [illegible] ३ दाराः. ४ हिमालयः. ५ चाद-यामासुः, [illegible]यामासुः. ६ मनसिन

स्थान इति ॥ **त्वां स्थावरात्मानं** स्थावररूपिणं **विष्णुम् आहुः** । ' स्थावराणां हिमालयः ' इति गीतावचनात् । **स्थाने** युक्तम् । युक्तार्थेऽव्ययमेतत् । ' युक्ते द्वे सांप्रतं स्थाने ' इत्यमरः । **तथा हि** । **ते** तव **कुक्षिः चराचराणां** जङ्गमस्थावररूपिणां **भूतानां** पृथिव्यादीनाम् **आधारतां गतः** । तवैव विष्णोः कुक्षिरेवंभूत इति भावः ॥

गामधास्यत्कथं नागो मृणालमृदुभिः फणैः ।
आ रसातलमूलात्त्वमवालम्बिष्यथा न चेत् ॥ ६८ ॥

गामिति ॥ **नागः** शेषाहिः **मृणालमृदुभिः** बिसकोमलैः **फणैः गां** भुवं **कथम् अधास्यत्** धारयेत् । **त्वम् आ रसातलमूलात्** पातालपर्यन्तम् । विकल्पादसमासः **न अवालम्बिष्यथाः चेत्** पादैर्नावलम्बेथा यदि । त्वदवलम्बनादेव भुजगराजोऽपि भुवं बिभर्तीत्यर्थः । अत्र क्रियातिपत्त्यभावाल्लृङ्प्रयोगश्चिन्त्यः ॥

अच्छिन्नामलसंतानाः समुद्रोर्म्यनिवारिताः ।
पुनन्ति लोकान्पुण्यत्वात्कीर्तयः सरितश्च ते ॥ ६९ ॥

अच्छिन्नेति ॥ [**अच्छिन्नामलसंतानाः**] अच्छिन्ना अविच्छिन्ना अमलाश्च संतानाः प्रबन्धाः प्रवाहाश्च यासां तास्तथोक्ताः । [**समुद्रोर्म्यनिवारिताः**] समुद्रोर्मिभिरनिवारिताः । पारगमनादन्तःप्रवेशाच्चेति भावः । **ते** तव **कीर्तयः सरितः च** गङ्गादयः **पुण्यत्वात्** पवित्रत्वात् **लोकान् पुनन्ति** पावयन्ति । लोकपावनाः खलु पुण्यश्लोका इति भावः । केवलप्रकृतविषयस्तुल्ययोगितालंकारः ॥

यथैव श्लाघ्यते गङ्गा पादेन परमेष्ठिनः ।
प्रभवेण द्वितीयेन तथैवोच्छिरसा त्वया ॥ ७० ॥

यथेति ॥ **गङ्गा** भागीरथी । प्रभवत्यस्मादिति प्रभवस्तेन कारणेन । परमे तिष्ठतीति **परमेष्ठिनः** विष्णोः । परमे प्रत्ययः । ' तत्पुरुषे कृति बहुलम् ', इत्यलुक् । परमेवहिर्दिव्यभिभ्यः स्थः ' इति षत्वम् । **पादेन** चरणेन **यथा एव श्लाघ्यते** प्रशस्यते **तथा एव द्वितीयेन प्रभवेण उच्छिरसा त्वया** श्लाघ्यते । हरिचरणवर्तीर्यस्यापि तीर्थभूतस्त्वमिति भावः ॥

तिर्यगूर्ध्वमधस्ताच्च व्यापको महिमा हरेः ।
त्रिविक्रमोद्यतस्यासीत्स तु स्वाभाविकस्तव ॥ ७१ ॥

तिर्यगिति ॥ **तिर्यक् ऊर्ध्वम् अधस्तात् च व्यापकः** । सर्वव्यापीत्यर्थः । **महिमा** महत्त्वं **हरेः** [**त्रिविक्रमोद्यतस्य**] त्रिषु विक्रमेषूद्यतस्य सतः **आसीत्** । त्रिविक्रमोद्यतस्यापि कदाचिदेव । न तु सर्वदेत्यर्थः । **तव तु स** व्यापको महिमा **स्वाभाविकः** नित्यसिद्ध इत्यर्थः ॥

---

१ सदृशैः. २ निवारिताः. ३ लोकम्. ४ श्लाघ्यते. ५ पातेन परमेष्ठिनि प्रथमेन...रसि त्वयि. ६ प्रभावेण. ७ च. ८ तथा.

यज्ञभागभुजां मध्ये पदमातस्थुषा त्वया ।
उच्चैर्हिरण्मयं शृङ्गं सुमेरोर्वितथीकृतम् ॥ ७२ ॥

यज्ञेति ॥ **यज्ञभागभुजाम्** इन्द्रादीनां **मध्ये पदम् आतस्थुषा** निहितवता **त्वया उच्चैः** उन्नतं हिरण्यस्य विकारो **हिरण्मयम्** । 'दाण्डिनायनहास्तिनायन–' इत्यादिनिपातनात्साधु । **सुमेरोः शृङ्गं** शिखरम् । प्राधान्यं च ध्वन्यते । 'शृङ्गं प्राधान्यसान्वोश्च' इत्यमरः । **वितथीकृतं** व्यर्थीकृतम् । तस्य यज्ञभागाभावादिति भावः । अस्य तु तत्सद्भावे प्रमाणम् 'हिमवतो हस्ती' इति श्रुतिः ॥

काठिन्यं स्थावरे काये भवता सर्वमर्पितम् ।
इदं तु ते भक्तिनम्रं सतामाराधनं वपुः ॥ ७३ ॥

काठिन्यमिति ॥ **भवता सर्वं काठिन्यम्** । अनम्रत्वमित्यर्थः । **स्थावरे** स्थिरे **काये** शिलामय इत्यर्थः । **अर्पितं** न्यस्तम् । **सताम्** अर्हताम् **आराधनं** पूजासाधनं **ते इदं वपुः तु** । जङ्गममित्यर्थः । **भक्तिनम्रम्** । काठिन्यलेशोऽप्यत्र नास्त्यन्यथा नम्रत्वासंभवादित्यर्थः । तथा चासाधारण्यं ध्वन्यते ॥

तदागमनकार्यं नः शृणु कार्यं तवैव तत् ।
श्रेयसामुपदेशात्तु वयमत्रांशभागिनः ॥ ७४ ॥

तदिति ॥ **तत्** तस्मात् **नः** अस्माकम् [**आगमनकार्यं**] आगमनस्य कार्यं प्रयोजनं **शृणु** । **तत् कार्यं** च **तव एव** । न त्वस्माकमित्यवधारणार्थ एवकारः । **वयं तु श्रेयसामुपदेशात् अत्र** कार्ये **अंशभागिनः** । त्वमेवात्र फलभाग्वयमुपदेष्टार इति भावः ॥

कार्यमेवाह—

अणिमादिगुणोपेतमस्पृष्टपुरुषान्तरम् ।
शब्दमीश्वर इत्युच्चैः सार्धचन्द्रं बिभर्ति यः ॥ ७५ ॥

अणिमेति ॥ **यः** शंभुः [**अणिमादिगुणोपेतम्**] अणिमादिभिरष्टभिर्गुणैर्वाच्यभूतैरुपेतम् । अष्टैश्वर्यवाचकमित्यर्थः । अत एव [**अस्पृष्टपुरुषान्तरम्**] अस्पृष्टं पुरुषान्तरं येन तं तथोक्तं पुरुषान्तरस्यानभिधायकम् । तस्यैवैवंगुणत्वादित्यर्थः । **उच्चैः** परमम् **ईश्वरः इति शब्दम्** । निरुपपदेश्वरशब्दमित्यर्थः । **सार्धचन्द्रम्** अर्धचन्द्रयुक्तम् । अर्धचन्द्रं चेत्यर्थः । **बिभर्ति** ॥

[10]कलितान्योन्यसामर्थ्यैः पृथिव्यादिभिरात्मभिः ।
[11]येनेदं ध्रियते[12] [13]व्यक्तं धुर्यैर्यानमिवाध्वनि ॥ ७६ ॥

कलितेति ॥ **येन** शंभुना **कलितान्योन्यसामर्थ्यैः** कलितं धृतिसंग्रहादिस्वस्वगुणसंपादितमन्योन्यसामर्थ्यं परस्परसहकाररूपं यैस्तथोक्तैः । स्वस्वरूपसामर्थ्यमन्यो-

---

१ माक्रम्य तस्थुषा. २ भवतः. ३ माराधकं; नम्रमर्हदाराधनम्. ४ यथा; यत्; यदर्थागमनं नो हि. ५ हिं ते तथा. ६ च. ७ अपि. ८ भाजिनः. ९. गुणोत्थानम्. १० कल्पिता. ११ यस्य. १२ धार्यते. १३ विश्वम्.

न्याधेयमेवेति भावः । **पृथिव्यादिभिः आत्मभिः** । अष्टाभिर्मूर्तिभिरित्यर्थः । **इदं व्यक्तं** विश्वं धुरं वहन्तीति **धुर्यैः** अश्वैः । 'धुरो यड्ढकौ' इति यत्प्रत्ययः । **अध्वनि यानं रथः इव ध्रियते** ॥

योगिनो यं विचिन्वन्ति क्षेत्राभ्यन्तरवर्तिनम् ।
अनावृत्तिभयं यस्य पदमाहुर्मनीषिणः ॥ ७७ ॥

योगिन इति ॥ **योगिनः** अध्यात्मवेदिनः **क्षेत्राभ्यन्तरवर्तिनं** शरीरान्तश्चरं सर्वभूतान्तर्यामिनम् । परमात्मस्वरूपिणमित्यर्थः । 'क्षेत्रं पत्नीशरीरयोः' इत्यमरः । **यं** शंभुं **विचिन्वन्ति** मृगयन्ते । **मनीषिणः** विद्वांसः **यस्य** शंभोः **पदं** स्थानम् [**अनावृत्तिभयम्**] अविद्यमानमावृत्तेः पुनः संसारोपत्तेर्भयं यत्र तत्तथाभूतम् **आहुः** ॥

स ते दुहितरं साक्षात्साक्षी विश्वस्य कर्मणाम्[१] ।
वृणुते वरदः शंभुरस्मत्संक्रामितैः[२] पदैः ॥ ७८ ॥

स इति ॥ **विश्वस्य** जगतः **कर्मणां साक्षी** द्रष्टा । 'साक्षाद्द्रष्टरि संज्ञायाम्' इतीनिप्रत्ययः । वरानिष्टान्ददातीति **वरदः** । 'आतोऽनुपसर्गे कः' इति कप्रत्ययः । **स** पूर्वोक्तः **शंभुः अस्मत्संक्रामितैः पदैः** अस्मासु निवेशितैर्वाक्यैः **ते दुहितरं साक्षात् वृणुते** । अस्मन्मुखेन स्वयमेव याचत इत्यर्थः ॥

तमर्थमिव भारत्या सुतया योक्तुमर्हसि ।
अशोच्या हि पितुः कन्या सद्भर्तृ[३]प्रतिपादिता ॥ ७९ ॥

तमिति ॥ **तं** शंभुं **भारत्या** वाचा **अर्थम्** अभिधेयम् **इव सुतया** दुहित्रा **योक्तुं** संघटयितुम् **अर्हसि** । अत्र वागर्थयोरुपमानत्वसामर्थ्याच्छिवयोर्नित्ययोगो विवक्षित इत्युक्तम् । 'वागर्थाविव संपृक्तौ' (रघुवंशे १ । १) इत्यत्रापि । तथा हि । [**सद्भर्तृप्रतिपादिता**] सद्भर्त्रे प्रतिपादिता दत्ता **कन्या पितुः अशोच्या** ॥

गुणान्तरमप्याह—

यावन्त्येतानि[४] भूतानि स्थावराणि चराणि च ।
मातरं कल्पयन्त्वेनामीशो हि जगतः[६] पिता ॥ ८० ॥

यावन्तीति ॥ **स्थावराणि चराणि च यावन्ति एतानि भूतानि** । सन्तीति शेषः । सर्वाणि भूतानीत्यर्थः । **एनां** ते दुहितरं **मातरं कल्पयन्तु** । **हि** यस्मात् **ईशः जगतः पिता** । पितृदारेषु मातृभावो न्याय्य इति भावः ॥

प्रणम्य शितिकण्ठाय विबुधास्तदनन्तरम् ।
चरणौ रञ्जयन्त्वस्या[७]श्चूडामणिमरीचिभिः ॥ ८१ ॥

प्रणम्येति ॥ **विबुधाः** देवाः **शितिकण्ठाय** शिवाय **प्रणम्य तदनन्तरं** नीलकण्ठप्रणामानन्तरम् **अस्याः चरणौ चूडामणिमरीचिभिः रञ्जयन्तु** । ईश्वरपरिग्रहादखिलदेवतावन्द्या भवत्वित्यर्थः ॥

---

१ कर्मणः. २ संक्रामितः. ३ सद्भर्त्रे. ४ यावदङ्ग्यानि. ५ न्त्येना. ६ जगताम्. ७ यन्त्य.

उमा वधूर्भवान्दाता याचितार इमे वयम् ।
वरः शंभुरलं ह्येष त्वत्कुलोद्भूतये विधिः ॥ ८२ ॥

उमेति ॥ **उमा वधूः भवान् दाता । इमे वयं याचितारः** प्रार्थकाः । **शंभुः वरः** वोढा । **एष विधिः** एषा सामग्री [**त्वत्कुलोद्भूतये**] त्वत्कुलस्योद्भूतये उच्छ्रयाय **अलं** पर्याप्तः **हि** । 'नमःस्वस्तिस्वाहास्वधा'—इत्यादिना चतुर्थी ॥

अस्तोतुः स्तूयमानस्य वन्द्यस्यानन्यवन्दिनः ।
सुतासंबन्धविधिना भव विश्वगुरोर्गुरुः ॥ ८३ ॥

अस्तोतुरिति ॥ स्वयमन्यस्तोता न भवतीति **अस्तोतुः** किं तु **स्तूयमानस्य** सर्वस्तुत्यस्य **वन्द्यस्य** जगद्वन्द्यस्य स्वयमन्यं न वन्दत इति **अनन्यवन्दिनः विश्वगुरोः** देवस्य **सुतासंबन्धविधिना** यौनसंबन्धाचरणेन **गुरुः भव** । यो नान्यं स्तौति न वन्दते तस्यापि त्वं स्तुत्यो वन्द्यश्चेत्यहो तव भाग्यवत्तेत्यर्थः ॥

एवंवादिनि देवर्षौ पार्श्वे पितुरधोमुखी ।
लीलाकमलपत्राणि गणयामास पार्वती ॥ ८४ ॥

एवमिति ॥ **देवर्षौ** अङ्गिरसि **एवंवादिनि** सति **पार्वती पितुः पार्श्वे अधोमुखी** सती । लज्जयेति शेषः । **लीलाकमलपत्राणि गणयामास** संचख्यौ । लज्जावशात्कमलदलगणनाव्याजेन हर्षं जुगोपेत्यर्थः । अनेनावहित्थाख्यः संचारी भाव उक्तः । तदुक्तम्—' अवहित्था तु लज्जादेर्हर्षाद्याकारगोपनम् ' इति ॥

शैलः संपूर्णकामोऽपि मेनामुखमुदैक्षत ।
प्रायेण गृहिणीनेत्राः कन्यार्थेषु कुटुम्बिनः ॥ ८५ ॥

शैल इति ॥ **शैलः** हिमवान् **संपूर्णकामोऽपि** । दातुं कृतनिश्चयोऽपीत्यर्थः । **मेनामुखम् उदैक्षत** । उचितोत्तरजिज्ञासयेति भावः । तथा हि । **प्रायेण कुटुम्बिनः** गृहस्थाः । **कन्यार्थेषु** कन्याप्रयोजनेषु [**गृहिणिनेत्राः**] गृहिण्येव नेत्रं कार्यज्ञानकारणं येषां ते तथोक्ताः । कलत्रप्रधानवृत्तय इत्यर्थः ॥

मेने मेनापि तत्सर्वं पत्युः कार्यमभीप्सितम् ।
भवन्त्यव्यभिचारिण्यो भर्तुरिष्टे पतिव्रताः ॥ ८६ ॥

मेन इति ॥ **मेना अपि पत्युः** हिमालयस्य **तत् सर्वम् अभीप्सितं कार्यं मेने** अङ्गीचकार । तथाहि । [**पतिव्रताः**] पतिरेव व्रतं यासां ताः **भर्तुः इष्टे** अभीप्सिते न विद्यते व्यभिचारो यासां ताः **अव्यभिचारिण्यः भवन्ति** । भर्तृचित्ताभिप्रायज्ञा भवन्तीति भावः ॥

इदमत्रोत्तरं न्याय्यमिति बुद्ध्या विमृश्य सः ।
आददे वचसामन्ते मङ्गलालंकृतां सुताम् ॥ ८७ ॥

इदमिति ॥ **स** हिमवान् **वचसाम् अन्ते** मुनिवाक्यावसाने **अत्र** मुनिवाक्ये **इदं** उत्तरश्लोके वक्ष्यमाणं दानमेव **न्याय्यं** न्यायादनपेतम् **उत्तरम् इति बुद्ध्या** चिन्तन

---

१ वरस्य. २ तन्त्राः. ३ कन्यार्थे हि. ४ सयः. ५ समीहितम्.

विमृश्य विचिन्त्य मङ्गलं यथा तथालंकृतां **मङ्गलालंकृतां सुताम् आददे** हस्ताभ्यां जग्राह ॥

एहि विश्वात्मने वत्से भिक्षासि परिकल्पिता ।
अर्थिनो मुनयः प्राप्तं गृहमेधिफलं मया ॥ ८८ ॥

एहीति ॥ हे **वत्से** पुत्रि **एहि** आगच्छ । त्वं **विश्वात्मने** शिवाय **भिक्षा परिकल्पिता असि** निश्चिता असि । 'रत्नादिस्तम्बपर्यन्तं सर्वं भिक्षा तपस्विनः' इति वचनादिति भावः । **अर्थिनः** याचितारः **मुनयः** । **मया** [**गृहमेधिफलं**] गृहमेधिनो गृहस्थस्य फलं **प्राप्तम्** । इह परत्र च तारकत्वात्पात्रे कन्यादानं गार्हस्थ्यस्य फलमित्यर्थः ॥

एतावदुक्त्वा तनयामृषीनाह महीधरः ।
इयं नमति वः सर्वांस्त्रिलोचनवधूरिति ॥ ८९ ॥

एतावदिति ॥ **महीधरः** हिमवान् **तनयाम् एतावत्** पूर्वोक्तम् **उक्त्वा ऋषीन् आह** । किमिति । **इयं त्रिलोचनवधूः** त्र्यम्बकपत्नी **वः सर्वान् नमति इति** । त्रिलोचनवधूरिति सिद्धवदभिधानेनाविप्रतिपन्नं दानमिति सूचयति ॥

ईप्सितार्थक्रियोदारं तेऽभिनन्द्य गिरेर्वचः ।
आशीर्भिरेधयामासुः[3] **पुरःपाकाभिरम्बिकाम् ॥ ९० ॥**

ईप्सितार्थेति ॥ **ते** मुनयः [**ईप्सितार्थक्रियोदारं**] ईप्सितार्थक्रिययेष्टार्थकरणेनोदारं महत् । 'उदारो दातृमहतोः' इत्यमरः । **गिरेः** हिमवतः **वचः** वचनम् **अभिनन्द्य** साध्विति संस्तुत्य **अम्बिकाम्** अम्बाम् । पच्यत इति पाकः फलम् । **पुरःपाकाभिः** पुरस्कृतफलाभिः **आशीर्भिः** आशीर्वादैः **एधयामासुः** संवर्धयामासुः ॥

तां प्रणामादरस्रस्तजाम्बूनदवतंसकाम् ।
अङ्कमारोपयामास लज्जमानामरुन्धती ॥ ९१ ॥

तामिति ॥ [**प्रणामादरस्रस्तजाम्बूनदवतंसकाम्**] प्रणामादरेण नमस्कारासक्त्या स्रस्ते जाम्बूनदे सुवर्णविकारौ वतंसके कनककुण्डले यस्यास्तां **लज्जमानां ताम्** अम्बिकाम् **अरुन्धती अङ्कम् आरोपयामास** । 'रुहः पोऽन्यतरस्याम्' इति पकारः ॥

तन्मातरं चाश्रुमुखीं दुहितृस्नेहविक्लवाम् ।
वरस्यानन्यपूर्वस्य विशोकामकरोद्गुणैः ॥ ९२ ॥

तदिति ॥ [**दुहितृस्नेहविक्लवाम्**] दुहितृस्नेहेन पुत्रिकाप्रेम्णा विक्लवां वियोक्ष्यत इति भीताम् । अत एवाश्रूणि मुखे यस्यास्ताम् **अश्रुमुखीं** तस्या अम्बिकाया मातरं **तन्मातरं** मेनां **च** । अन्या पूर्वं यस्यास्ति सोऽन्यपूर्वः । 'सर्वनाम्नो वृत्तिविषये पुंवद्भावः' इति पूर्वपदस्य पुंवद्भावः । स न भवतीत्यनन्यपूर्वस्तस्य **अनन्यपूर्वस्य** । सापत्न्यदुःखमकुर्वत इत्यर्थः । **वरस्य** वोढुः **गुणैः** मृत्युंजयत्वादिभिः **विशोकां** निर्दुःखाम् **अकरोत्** ॥

---

१ सर्वा०; शैवार्पणे. २ भिक्षा त्वम्. ३ वर्धया. ४ दवस्रस्त…नदाव०. ५ दुहितुः. ६ विह्वलाम्.

वैवाहिकीं तिथिं पृष्टास्तत्क्षणं हरबन्धुना ।
ते[1] त्र्यहादूर्ध्वमाख्याय चेरुश्चीरपरिग्रहाः ॥ ९३ ॥

वैवाहिकीमिति ॥ **चीरपरिग्रहाः** वल्कलमात्रवसनाः **ते** तपस्विनः **तत्क्षणं** तस्मिन्नेव क्षणे **हरबन्धुना** हिमवता **वैवाहिकीं** विवाहयोग्यां **तिथिं पृष्टाः** केत्यनुयुक्ताः सन्तः । त्रयाणामह्नां समाहारस्त्र्यहः । 'तद्धितार्थोत्तरपदसमाहारे च' इति समासः । 'राजाहःसखिभ्यष्टच्' इति टच्प्रत्ययः । द्विगुत्वादेकवचनम् । 'रात्राह्नाहाः पुंसि' इति पुंलिङ्गता । तस्मात् **त्र्यहात् ऊर्ध्वम्** उपरि **आख्याय** चतुर्थेऽहनि विवाहः इत्युक्त्वा **चेरुः** चलिताः ॥

ते हिमालयमामन्त्र्य पुनः प्राप्य[3] च शूलिनम् ।
सिद्धं चास्मै[4] निवेद्यार्थं तद्विसृष्टाः खमुद्ययुः ॥ ९४ ॥

त इति ॥ **ते** मुनयः **हिमालयम् आमन्त्र्य** साधु यामेत्यापृच्छय **पुनः शूलिनं** हरं संकेतस्थानस्थं **प्राप्य च सिद्धं** निष्पन्नम् **अर्थं** प्रयोजनम् **अस्मै निवेद्य च** ज्ञापयित्वा च [**तद्विसृष्टाः**] तेन शूलिना विसृष्टाः **खम्** आकाशं प्रति **उद्ययुः** उत्पेतुः । अत्र संक्षिप्तार्थाभिधानात्संक्षेपो नाम गुण उक्तः । तदुक्तम्—'संक्षिप्तार्थाभिधानं यत्संक्षेपः परिकीर्तितः । ' इति ॥

भगवान्पशुपतिस्त्र्यहमात्रविलम्बमपि सोढुं न शशाक तदौत्सुक्यादित्याह—

पशुपतिरपि तान्यहानि कृच्छ्रादगमयदद्रिसुतासमागमोत्कः ।
कमपरमवशं न विप्रकुर्युर्विभुमपि तं यदमी स्पृशन्ति भावाः ॥ ९५ ॥

पशुपतिरिति ॥ उत्कं मनो यस्य स उत्कः । ' उत्क उन्मनाः ' इति निपातः । **अद्रिसुतासमागमोत्कः** पार्वतीपरिणयोत्सुकः **पशुपतिः अपि तानि** । त्रीणीति शेषः । **अहानि कृच्छ्रात् अगमयत्** अयापयत् । कविराह—**अमी भावाः** औत्सुक्यादयः संचारिणः **अवशम्** इन्द्रियपरतन्त्रम् **अपरं** पृथग्जनं **कं न विप्रकुर्युः** न विकारं नयेयुः । **यत्** यस्मात् **विभुं** समर्थम् । जितेन्द्रियमिति यावत् । **तं** स्मरहरम् **अपि स्पृशन्ति** । विकुर्वन्तीत्यर्थः । अत्र विभुविकारसमर्थनादर्थादितरजनविकारः कैमुतिकन्यायादापततीत्यर्थापत्तिरलंकारः । तथा च सूत्रम्—' दण्डापूपिकयार्थान्तरपतनमर्थापत्तिः । ' इति । अर्थान्तरन्यास इति केचित्तदुपेक्षणीयम् । युक्तिस्तु विस्तरभयान्नोच्यते । पुष्पिताग्रावृत्तम्—' अयुजि नयुगरेफतो यकारो युजि च नजौ जरगाश्च पुष्पिताग्रा । ' इति लक्षणात् ॥

इति श्रीमन्महामहोपाध्यायकोलाचलमल्लिनाथसूरिविरचितया संजीवनीसमाख्यया व्याख्यया समेतः श्रीकालिदासकृतौ
कुमारसंभवे महाकाव्ये उमाप्रदानं नाम
षष्ठः सर्गः ॥

---

१ ताम. २ चेलुः. ३ प्रेक्ष्य. ४ तस्मै.

सप्तमः सर्गः ।

अथौषधीनामधिपस्य वृद्धौ तिथौ च जामित्रगुणान्वितायाम् ।
समेतबन्धुर्हिमवान्सुताया विवाहदीक्षाविधिमन्वतिष्ठत् ॥ १ ॥

अथेति ॥ **अथ** व्यहानन्तरं **हिमवान् ओषधीनाम् अधिपस्य** चन्द्रस्य **वृद्धौ** । शुक्लपक्षे इत्यर्थः । शुभकर्मस्वापूर्यमाणपक्षस्य प्राशस्त्यात् । **तिथौ च** [**जामित्रगुणान्वितायाम्**] जामित्रं लग्नात्सप्तमं स्थानं तस्य गुणः शुद्धिः सा च ग्रहराहित्यं तेनान्वितायां सत्याम् । यद्यपि जामित्रशुद्धिर्लग्नधर्मस्तथापि तद्द्वारा तिथेरपि तथा व्यपदेशे न दोषः । **समेतबन्धुः** युक्तबन्धुः सन् । **सुतायाः** दुहितुः [**विवाहदीक्षाविधिम्**] विवाहदीक्षा विवाहसंस्कारः सैव विधिः कर्म तम् **अन्वतिष्ठत्** कृतवान् ॥

वैवाहिकैः कौतुकसंविधानैर्गृहे गृहे व्यग्रपुरन्ध्रिवर्गम् ।
आसीत्पुरं सानुमतोऽनुरागादन्तःपुरं चैककुलोपमेयम् ॥ २ ॥

वैवाहिकैरिति ॥ **अनुरागात्** प्रीतिवशात् **गृहे गृहे** प्रतिगृहम् । वीप्सायां द्विर्भावः । [**वैवाहिकैः**] विवाहः प्रयोजनमेषामिति वैवाहिकानि तैः । 'प्रयोजनम्' इति ठक् । **कौतुकसंविधानैः** मङ्गलार्थसंपादनैः [**व्यग्रपुरन्ध्रिवर्गम्**] व्यग्रो व्याकुलः पुरन्ध्रिवर्गः कुटुम्बिनीसंघो यस्मिंस्तत्तथोक्तं **सानुमतः** अद्रेः **पुरं** बाह्यमोषधिप्रस्थम् **अन्तःपुरम्** अवरोधनं **च** [**एककुलोपमेयम्**] एककुलेन एकगृहेण वोपमेयम् **आसीत्** । 'सजातीयगणे गोत्रे गृहेऽपि कथितं कुलम्' इति विश्वः । सर्वेषामपि स्वगृह एवेदं शोभनं वर्तत इत्यभिमानोऽभूदित्यर्थः । एतेन हिमाद्रेः प्रजाराग उक्तः । अत्र सर्वं संपन्नमेवेत्यर्थः ॥

संतानकाकीर्णमहापथं[1] तच्चीनांशुकैः कल्पितकेतुमालम् ।
भासोज्ज्वलत्[2]काञ्चनतोरणानां[3] स्थानान्तरं स्वर्ग[4] इवाबभासे ॥ ३ ॥

संतानकेति ॥ [**संतानकाकीर्णमहापथं**] संतानकैर्मन्दारकुसुमैराकीर्णा आस्तृताः महापथाः राजकीयपथाः यस्मिंस्तत्तथोक्तम् । **चीनांशुकैः** पट्टवस्त्रैः [**कल्पितकेतुमालम्**] कल्पिता विरचिताः केतुमाला ध्वजपङ्क्तयो यस्य तत्तथोक्तम् । **काञ्चनतोरणानां भासा** प्रभया **उज्ज्वलत्** दीप्यमानं **तत्** पुरं **स्थानान्तरं** मेरोरन्यत्र स्थितः **स्वर्गः इव आबभासे** । उत्प्रेक्षालंकारः ॥

एकैव सत्यामपि पुत्रपङ्क्तौ चिरस्य[5] दृष्टेव मृतोत्थितेव ।
आसन्नपाणिग्रहणेति[6] पित्रोरुमा विशेषोच्छ्वसितं बभूव ॥ ४ ॥

एकैवेति ॥ [**पुत्रपङ्क्तौ**] पुत्राश्च दुहितरश्च पुत्राः । 'भ्रातृपुत्रौ स्वसृदुहितृभ्याम्'

---

१ चतुःपथम्. २ भासा ज्वलत्. ३ णाङ्कम्. ४ स्थानान्तरस्वर्गः. ५ चिरेण. ६ उपोढपाणि.

इत्येकशेषः । 'पुत्रौ पुत्रश्च दुहिता च' इत्यमरः । तेषां पङ्क्तौ संघे **सत्याम् अपि उमा एका एव चिरस्य दृष्टा इव** चिरान्नष्टलब्धेव **मृतोत्थितेव** मृत्वा पुनरुत्पन्नेव **आसन्नपाणिग्रहणा** आसन्नविवाहा **इति** । भर्तृगृहं गमिष्यतीति हेतोरित्यर्थः । **पित्रोः** मातापित्रोः । 'पिता मात्रा' इत्येकशेषः । [**विशेषोच्छ्वसितं**] विशेषेणोच्छ्वसितं प्राणभूता **बभूव** । पुमपत्यादपि अधिकप्रेमास्पदमभूदित्यर्थः ॥

अङ्काद्ययावङ्कमुदीरिताशीः सा मण्डनान्मण्डनमन्वभुङ्क्त ।
संबन्धिभिन्नोऽपि गिरेः कुलस्य स्नेहस्तदेकायतनं जगाम ॥ ५ ॥

अङ्कादिति ॥ **सा** पार्वती **उदीरिताशीः** प्रयुक्ताशीर्वादा सती **अङ्काद् अङ्कम्** उत्सङ्गं **ययौ** । **मण्डनात्** मण्डनान्तरम् अन्यत् **मण्डनम् अन्वभुङ्क्त** । तदा सर्वे बन्धवः प्रत्येकमेव तामङ्कमारोप्य मण्डनं प्रायच्छन्नित्यर्थः । तच्च स्नेहनिबन्धनमेवेत्याह—**संबन्धिभिन्नः** स्वपुत्रादिभिर्भिन्नो विभक्तः **अपि गिरेः कुलस्य** वंशस्य **स्नेहः तदेकायतनं** सैवैकमायतनं स्थानं तत् **जगाम** । तदिति छेदेऽप्ययमेवार्थः । विधेयप्राधान्यान्नपुंसकत्वमिति । सर्वे बन्धवः स्वापत्येभ्योऽपि तस्यामधिकं स्निह्यन्तीति तात्पर्यार्थः ॥

मैत्रे मुहूर्ते शशलाञ्छनेन योगं गतासूत्तरफल्गुनीषु ।
तस्याः शरीरे प्रतिकर्म चक्रुर्बन्धुस्त्रियो याः पतिपुत्रवत्यः ॥ ६ ॥

मैत्र इति ॥ अथ **मैत्रे** मित्रदैवत्ये **मुहूर्ते** । उदयमुहूर्तात्तृतीयमुहूर्त इत्यर्थः । 'आर्द्रः सार्द्रस्तथा मैत्रः शुभो वासव एव च ।' इति बृहस्पतिस्मरणात् । **उत्तरफल्गुनीषु** फल्गुनीनक्षत्रे । 'फल्गुनीप्रोष्ठपदानां च नक्षत्रे' इत्येकस्मिन्नपि बहुवचनम् । **शशलाञ्छनेन** चन्द्रेण **योगं गतासु** सतीषु **तस्याः** पार्वत्याः **शरीरे बन्धुस्त्रियः प्रतिकर्म** प्रसाधनम् । 'प्रतिकर्म प्रसाधनम्' इत्यमरः । **चक्रुः** । कीदृश्यः । **याः पतिपुत्रवत्यः** । जीवद्भर्तृका जीवदपत्याश्चेत्यर्थः ॥

प्रतिकर्मप्रकारमेव प्रपञ्चयति—

सा गौरसिद्धार्थनिवेशवद्भिर्दूर्वाप्रवालैः प्रतिभिन्नशोभम् ।
निर्नाभिकौशेयमुपात्तबाणमभ्यङ्गनेपथ्यमलंचकार ॥ ७ ॥

सेति ॥ **सा** गौरी **गौरसिद्धार्थनिवेशवद्भिः** श्वेतसर्षपप्रक्षेपवद्भिः **दूर्वाप्रवालैः** दूर्वाङ्कुरैः **प्रतिभिन्नशोभं** विशेषितशोभं [**निर्नाभिकौशेयं**] निर्नाभ्यतिक्रान्तनाभि कौशेयं वस्त्रविशेषो यस्मिंस्तत्तथोक्तम् । 'कौशेयं कृमिकोशोत्थम्' इत्यमरः । **उपात्तबाणं** गृहीतशरम् । 'शरः क्षत्रियया ग्राह्यः' इति मनुस्मरणात् । **अभ्यङ्गनेपथ्यम्** अभ्यङ्गवेशम् **अलंचकार** । अलंकारमप्यलंचकारेत्यर्थः ॥

बभौ च संपर्कमुपेत्य बाला नवेन दीक्षाविधिसायकेन ।
करेण भानोर्बहुलावसाने संधुक्ष्यमाणेव शशाङ्करेखा ॥ ८ ॥

---

१ शरीरप्र०. २ रागम्. ३ उन्नाभि०. ४ विवाहदी०. ५ लेखा.

बभाविति ॥ किं च इति चार्थः । **बाला नवेन** [**दीक्षाविधिसायकेन**] दीक्षाविधौ विवाहकृत्ये यः सायकस्तेन **संपर्कमुपेत्य बहुलावसाने** कृष्णपक्षात्यये । शुक्लपक्षादावित्यर्थः । **भानोः करेण** किरणेन **संधुक्ष्यमाणा** उपचीयमाना । 'सलिलमये शशिनि रवेर्दीधितयो मूर्च्छितास्तमो नैशम् । क्षपयन्ति' इत्यादिवचनात् । **शशाङ्करेखा इव बभौ** ॥

तां लोध्रकल्केन हृताङ्गतैलामाश्यानकालेयकृताङ्गरागाम् ।
वासो वसानामभिषेकयोग्यं नार्यश्चतुष्काभिमुखं व्यनैषुः ॥ ९ ॥

तामिति ॥ **लोध्रकल्केन** लोध्रचूर्णेन [**हृताङ्गतैलां**] हृतमङ्गतैलं यस्यास्ताम् । कृतोद्वर्तनामित्यर्थः । [**आश्यानकालेयकृताङ्गरागाम्**] आश्यानमीषच्छुष्कं तेन कालेयेन गन्धद्रव्येण कृताङ्गरागाम् । कृतस्निग्ध्यामित्यर्थः । 'अथ जायकम् । कालेयकं च कालानुसार्यं च' इत्यमरः । **अभिषेकयोग्यं वासः** वस्त्रं **वसानां** स्नानशाटीमाच्छादयन्तीं **तां** पार्वतीं **नार्यः** [**चतुष्काभिमुखं**] चतुष्कं चतुःस्तम्भगृहं तदभिमुखं **व्यनैषुः** स्नानगृहं निन्युरित्यर्थः ॥

विन्यस्तवैदूर्यशिलातलेऽस्मिन्नाबद्धमुक्ताफलभक्तिचित्रे ।
आवर्जिताष्टापदकुम्भतोयैः सतूर्यमेनां स्नपयांबभूवुः ॥ १० ॥

विन्यस्तेति ॥ [**विन्यस्तवैदूर्यशिलातले**] विन्यस्तं वैदूर्यशिलातलं मरकतशिलाप्रदेशो यस्मिंस्तस्मिन् । [**आबद्धमुक्ताफलभक्तिचित्रे**] आबद्धानां मुक्ताफलानां भक्तिभी रचनाभिश्चित्रे **अस्मिन्** चतुष्के **एनां** पार्वतीम् । [**आवर्जिताष्टापदकुम्भतोयैः**] आवर्जितानामानमितानामष्टापदकुम्भानां कनककलशानां तोयैः **सतूर्यं** मङ्गलवाद्ययुक्तं यथा तथा **स्नपयांबभूवुः** । अष्टसु लोहेषु पदं प्रतिष्ठा यस्येत्यष्टापदम् । 'अष्टनः संज्ञायाम्' इति दीर्घः । 'अष्टापदं स्यात्कनकम्' इति विश्वः ॥

सा मङ्गलस्नानविशुद्धगात्री गृहीतपत्युद्गमनीयवस्त्रा ।
निर्वृत्तपर्जन्यजलाभिषेका प्रफुल्लकाशा वसुधेव रेजे ॥ ११ ॥

सेति ॥ [**मङ्गलस्नानविशुद्धगात्री**] मङ्गलार्थस्नानेन विशुद्धगात्री निर्मलाङ्गी । [**गृहीतपत्युद्गमनीयवस्त्रा**] पत्युर्वरस्योद्गमनीयवस्त्रं धौतवस्त्रम् । 'धौतमुद्गमनीयं स्यात्' इति हलायुधः । 'तत्स्यादुद्गमनीयं यद्धौतयोर्वस्त्रयोर्युगम् ।' इत्यमरः । युगग्रहणं तु प्रायिकाभिप्रायम् । अत एवात्र क्षीरस्वामी 'युगं प्रायशो यल्लक्ष्यं तदेव' इति व्याख्याय 'गृहीतपत्युद्गमनीयवस्त्रा' इत्येतदेवोदाहृतवान् । गृहीतं पतिं प्रत्युद्गमनीयवस्त्रं यया सा । धौतवस्त्रमाच्छादितवतीत्यर्थः । **सा** पार्वती [**निर्वृत्तपर्जन्यजलाभिषेका**] निर्वृत्तो निष्पन्नः पर्जन्यस्य जलेनाभिषेको यस्याः सा तथोक्ता । [**प्रफुल्लकाशा**] प्रफुल्लतीति प्रफुल्लं काशं काशपुष्पं यस्याः सा तथोक्ता **वसुधा इव रेजे** शुशुभे ॥

---

१ श्याम. २ अभिमुखामनैषुः. ३ वैडूर्य. ४ शिले च तस्मिन्. ५ आविद्ध, अविद्धमुक्ताकृतभक्तिलेखे. ६ तोयाः. ७ प्रत्युद्गम०, शुद्धोद्गमनीय; गृहीतवत्युद्गमनीयवस्त्रम्. ८ निवृत्त.

तस्मात्प्रदेशाच्च वितानवन्तं युक्तं मणिस्तम्भचतुष्टयेन ।
पतिव्रताभिः परिगृह्य निन्ये क्लृप्तासनं कौतुकवेदिमध्यम् ॥ १२ ॥

तस्मादिति ॥ किं च इति चार्थः । **तस्मात् प्रदेशात्** स्नानप्रदेशात् **वितानवन्तम्** उल्लोचयुक्तम् । 'अस्त्री वितानमुल्लोचः' इत्यमरः । **मणिस्तम्भचतुष्टयेन युक्तं** [**क्लृप्तासनं**] क्लृप्तं सज्जमानमासनं यस्मिंस्तं **कौतुकवेदिमध्यं पतिव्रताभिः परिगृह्य** दोर्भ्यामालिङ्ग्य **निन्ये** नीता । प्रसाधनार्थमित्यर्थः ॥

तां प्राङ्मुखीं तत्र निवेश्य तन्वीं क्षणं व्यलम्बन्त पुरोनिषण्णाः ।
भूतार्थशोभाह्रियमाणनेत्राः प्रसाधने संनिहितेऽपि नार्यः ॥ १३ ॥

तामिति ॥ **नार्यः** प्रसाधिकाः **तां तन्वीं** पार्वतीं **तत्र** वेदिमध्ये **प्राङ्मुखीं निवेश्य** उपवेश्य **पुरोनिषण्णाः** अग्रे स्थिताः । प्रसाध्यतेऽनेनेति **प्रसाधने** अलंकारसाधनवर्गे **संनिहिते अपि** [**भूतार्थशोभाह्रियमाणनेत्राः**] भूतार्था सत्यरूपा । स्वाभाविकीति यावत् । या शोभा रामणीयकं तया ह्रियमाणान्याकृष्यमाणानि नेत्राणि यासां तास्तथोक्ताः **क्षणं व्यलम्बन्त** । स्वभावसुन्दर्याः किमस्याः प्रसाधनेनेति तूष्णीं तस्थुरित्यर्थः ॥

धूपोष्मणा त्याजितमार्द्रभावं केशान्तमन्तःकुसुमं तदीयम् ।
पर्याक्षिपत्काचिदुदारबन्धं दूर्वावता पाण्डुमधूकदाम्ना ॥ १४ ॥

धूपेति ॥ **काचित्** प्रसाधिका **धूपोष्मणा** करणेन **आर्द्रभावम्** आर्द्रत्वं **त्याजितम्** पचादिषु पाठाद्‌द्विकर्मकत्वम् । त्यजतेर्ण्यन्तादप्रधाने कर्मणि क्तः । **अन्तःकुसुमम्** अन्तर्निक्षिप्तकुसुमं तस्या इमं **तदीयं केशान्तं** केशपाशं **दूर्वावता** मध्ये मध्ये ग्रथितदूर्वेण **पाण्डुमधूकदाम्ना** हरितमधुद्रुमकुसुममाल्येन । 'मधूके तु गुडपुष्पमधुद्रुमौ' इत्यमरः । **उदारबन्धं** रम्यबन्धं यथा तथा **पर्याक्षिपत्** बबन्ध ॥

विन्यस्तशुक्लागुरु चक्रुरङ्गं गोरोचनापत्रविभक्तमस्याः ।
सा चक्रवाकाङ्कितसैकतायास्त्रिस्रोतसः कान्तिमतीत्य तस्थौ ॥ १५ ॥

विन्यस्तेति ॥ **अस्या** गौर्याः **अङ्गं** गात्रं [**विन्यस्तशुक्लागुरु**] विन्यस्तं विरचितं शुक्लागुरु यस्मिंस्तत् [**गोरोचनापत्रविभक्तं**] गोरोचनायाः पत्रैः पत्ररचनाभिर्विभक्तं विशेषितं च **चक्रुः** । **सा** तथाभूता गौरी [**चक्रवाकाङ्कितसैकतायाः**] चक्रवाकैरङ्कितं सैकतं यस्यास्तस्याः **त्रिस्रोतसः** गङ्गायाः **कान्तिं** शोभाम् **अतीत्य** अतिक्रम्य **तस्थौ** । अत्र गोरोचनाचक्रवाकयोः पीतत्वेन साम्यं त्रिस्रोतसो धावल्यं तु प्रसिद्धत्वान्न स्वपदेनोपात्तम् ॥

लग्नद्विरेफं परिभूय पद्मं समेघलेखं शशिनश्च बिम्बम् ।
तदाननश्रीरलकैः प्रसिद्धैश्चिच्छेद सादृश्यकथाप्रसङ्गम् ॥ १६ ॥

---

१ प्रति०. २ भूतात्म०. ३ धूपेन संमार्जितम०; पात्युज्झितसार्द्र०. ४ आसक्त; प्रसन्न. ५ अस्याः. ६ विभक्तपत्त्र. ७ लीन. ८ लक्षं.

लग्नेति ॥ **प्रसिद्धैः** भूषितैः । 'प्रसिद्धौ ख्यातभूषितौ' इत्यमरः । **अलकैः** उपलक्षिता [**तदाननश्रीः**] तस्याः गौर्या आननश्रीः **लग्नद्विरेफं पद्मं समेघलेखं** मेघलेखायुक्तं **शशिनः बिम्बं च परिभूय** तिरस्कृत्य [**सादृश्यकथाप्रसङ्गम्**] सादृश्यमुपमा तस्य कथोक्तिस्तस्याः प्रसङ्गं प्रसक्तिं सादृश्यं वाग्मात्रप्रसक्तमपि **चिच्छेद** अभिनत् । प्रसक्तयोः पद्मचन्द्रयोः परिभूतत्वादन्यत्र चाप्रसङ्गादित्यर्थः । अत्र पूर्वार्धवाक्यार्थस्य सादृश्यकथाच्छेदं प्रति हेतुत्वेनोपन्यासात्काव्यालिङ्गमलंकारः । लक्षणं तूक्तम् ॥

कर्णार्पितो लोध्रकषायरूक्षे गोरोचनाक्षेपनितान्तगौरे ।
तस्याः कपोले परभागलाभाद्बबन्ध चक्षूंषि यवप्ररोहः ॥ १७ ॥

कर्णेति ॥ **तस्याः** गौर्याः [**कर्णार्पितः**] कर्णेऽर्पितो निक्षिप्तो **यवप्ररोहः** यवाङ्कुरः [**लोध्रकषायरूक्षे**] लोध्रस्य वृक्षविशेषस्य कषायेण विलेपनेन रूक्षे विशदे । उद्वर्तिते इत्यर्थः । 'कषायो रसभेदे स्यादङ्गरागे विलेपने ।' इति विश्वः । [**गोरोचनाक्षेपनितान्तगौरे**] गोरोचनायाः क्षेपेण विन्यासेन नितान्तगौरेऽत्यन्तारुणे । 'गौरः श्वेतेऽरुणे पीते' इति विश्वः । **कपोले** गण्डस्थले **परभागलाभात्** वर्णोत्कर्षप्राप्तेः **चक्षूंषि** । द्रष्टृणामिति शेषः । **बबन्ध** जहार । आचकर्षेत्यर्थः । गोरोचनारुणे गण्डस्थले पाण्डुरो यवाङ्कुरो विजातीयवर्णसंनिधानाल्लब्धवर्णोत्कर्षः संश्चक्षुराकर्षकोऽभूदिति भावः ॥

रेखाविभक्तः सुविभक्तगात्र्याः किंचिन्मधूच्छिष्टविमृष्टरागः[३] ।
कामप्यभिख्यां स्फुरितैरपुष्यदासन्नलावण्यफलोऽधरोष्ठः ॥ १८ ॥

रेखेति ॥ **सुविभक्तगात्र्याः** सुसंश्लिष्टावयवायाः पार्वत्याः । [**रेखाविभक्तः**] रेखया मध्यगतया विभक्तः सुश्लिष्टः [**किंचिन्मधूच्छिष्टविमृष्टरागः**] किंचिदीषन्मधूच्छिष्टेन सिक्थकेन विमृष्टो विशेषेण निर्मलीकृतो रागो यस्य स तथोक्तः । 'मधूच्छिष्टं तु सिक्थकम्' इति, 'निर्णिक्तं शोधितं मृष्टम्' इति चामरः । अन्यत्रोक्तम्— अलौहित्यापगमायाधरेषु सिक्थकलेपः क्रियते । [**आसन्नलावण्यफलः**] आसन्नं संनिहितं लावण्यफलं सौन्दर्यप्रयोजनं मुखचुम्बनादिरूपं यस्य स तथोक्तः **अधरोष्ठः स्फुरितैः** भाविशुभशंसिभिः स्पन्दैः **काम् अपि** अनिर्वाच्याम् **अभिख्यां** शोभाम् **अपुष्यत्** पुपोष । 'अभिख्या नामशोभयोः' इत्यमरः ॥

पत्युः शिरश्चन्द्रकलामनेन स्पृशेति सख्या परिहासपूर्वम् ।
सा रञ्जयित्वा चरणौ कृताशीर्माल्येन तां निर्वचनं जघान ॥ १९ ॥

पत्युरिति ॥ **सख्या** । कर्त्र्या । **चरणौ रञ्जयित्वा** लाक्षारसाक्तौ कृत्वा । कृताशीरिति करोतिना समानकर्तृकत्वम् । **अनेन** चरणेन । रञ्जने द्वयोरपि नियमाच्चरणाविद्युक्तत्वाप्यौचित्यात्ताडनविधावेकतरपरामर्श इत्याहुः । **पत्युः** ईश्वरस्य **शिरश्चन्द्रकलाम्** । सुरतविशेष इति शेषः । **स्पृश** ताडय **इति परिहासपूर्वं कृताशीः** प्रयुक्ताशीर्वादा

१ भेद. २ च विभक्त. ३ विमृष्ट.

सा पार्वती तां सखीं माल्येन मालया । 'माल्यं मालास्रजौ' इत्यमरः । निर्वचनं यथा तथा । तूष्णीमित्यर्थः । जघान ताडयामास । निर्वचनमित्यनेन विहृताख्यः शृङ्गारानुभाव उक्तः । तदुक्तम्—'प्राप्तकालं तु यद्ब्रूयात्कुर्याद्वा विहृतं हि तत् ।' इति ॥

तस्याः सुजातोत्पलपत्रकान्ते प्रसाधिकाभिर्नयने निरीक्ष्य ।
न चक्षुषोः कान्तिविशेषबुद्ध्या कालाञ्जनं मङ्गलमित्युपात्तम् २०

तस्या इति ॥ प्रसाधिकाभिः अलंकर्त्रीभिः [सुजातोत्पलपत्रकान्ते] सुजाते सम्यगुत्पन्ने उत्पलपत्रे इव कान्ते रम्ये तस्याः नयने निरीक्ष्य कालाञ्जनम् अञ्जनविशेषः । चक्षुषोः कान्तिविशेषबुद्ध्या । शोभातिशयो भविष्यतीति बुद्ध्येत्यर्थः । न उपात्तं न गृहीतम् । किं तु मङ्गलं शुभम् इति हेतोः उपात्तम् । निसर्गसुभगस्य किमाहार्यकाडम्बरेणेति भावः ॥

सा संभवद्भिः कुसुमैर्लतेव ज्योतिर्भिरुद्यद्भिरिव त्रियामा ।
सरिद्विहङ्गैरिव लीयमानैरामुच्यमानाभरणा चकासे ॥ २१ ॥

सेति ॥ आमुच्यमानाभरणा निबध्यमानाभरणा सा गौरी संभवद्भिः उत्पद्यमानैः कुसुमैः लता इव । अनेन पद्मरागेन्द्रनीलादीन्याभरणानि सूचितानि लताकुसुमानानावर्णत्वात् । उद्यद्भिः उदयं गच्छद्भिः ज्योतिर्भिः उडुभिः त्रियामा रात्रिः इव । अनेन मौक्तिकानि कथितानि । लीयमानैः आश्रयद्भिः । निषीदद्भिरित्यर्थः । विहङ्गैः चक्रवाकैः सरिद् इव । अनेन सुवर्णाभरणानि सूचितानि । विहङ्गाश्च तत्सूचनाय चक्रवाका अभिमताः । चकासे रेजे । अत्र लताकुसुमादीनां सहजसंबन्धिनामुपमानत्वेनोपादानादाहार्यकमपि तस्याः सहजमिवाशोभतेति भावः ॥

आत्मानमालोक्य च शोभमानमादर्शबिम्बे स्तिमितायताक्षी ।
हरोपयाने त्वरिता बभूव स्त्रीणां प्रियालोकफलो हि वेषः ॥ २२ ॥

आत्मानमिति ॥ किं च इति चार्थः । गौरी शोभमानम् आत्मानं निजशरीरम् आदर्शबिम्बे दर्पणमण्डले । 'दर्पणे मुकुरादर्शौ' इत्यमरः । स्तिमितायताक्षी आदरान्निश्चलायतलोचना सती आलोक्य हरोपयाने हरप्राप्तौ त्वरिता व्यग्रा बभूव । स्त्रीणां वेषो नेपथ्यम् [प्रियालोकफलः] प्रियस्य भर्तुरालोको दर्शनं फलं प्रयोजनं यस्य स तथोक्तः हि । अन्यथारण्यचन्द्रिका स्यादिति भावः । अनेन कालाक्षमत्वलक्षणमौत्सुक्यमुक्तमित्यनुसंधेयम् ॥

अथाङ्गुलिभ्यां हरितालमार्द्रं माङ्गल्यमादाय मनःशिलां च ।
कर्णावसक्तामलदन्तपत्रं माता तदीयं मुखमुन्नमय्य ॥ २३ ॥

अथेति ॥ अथ प्रसाधनानन्तरं माता मेनका माङ्गल्यं मङ्गलार्थम् आर्द्रं द्रवं

---

१ समीक्ष्य. २ आरोप्यमाणा०. ३ पानत्व०. ४ अङ्गुलीभ्याम्. ५ मङ्गल्यम्. ६ उन्नि-नाय, उन्नाम.

हरितालं वर्णद्रव्यविशेषं **मनःशिलां** धातुविशेषं **च अङ्गुलिभ्यां** तर्जनीमध्यमाभ्याम् **आदाय** [**कर्णावसक्तामलदन्तपत्रं**] कर्णयोरवसक्ते लग्ने अमले दन्तपत्रे यस्य तत्तथोक्तं तस्याः पार्वत्यां इदं **तदीयं मुखम् उन्नमय्य** । विवाहदीक्षातिलकं चकार इत्युत्तरश्लोकेनान्वयः ॥

उमास्तनोद्भेदमनु प्रवृद्धो मनोरथो यः प्रथमं बभूव ।
तमेव मेना दुहितुः कथंचिद्विवाहदीक्षातिलकं चकार ॥ २४ ॥

उमेति ॥ [**उमास्तनोद्भेदम्**] उमायाः स्तनोद्भेदम् **अनु** । स्तनोदयमारभ्येत्यर्थः । **प्रवृद्धः** वृद्धिं गतः । प्रागेवोत्पन्न इति भावः । **यः मनोरथः** वाञ्छा । 'वाञ्छा लिप्सा मनोरथः' इत्यमरः । **प्रथमं** मनोरथान्तरात्प्राक् । अयमेव प्रथमो मनोरथ इत्यर्थः । **बभूव** । **मेना दुहितुः तमेव** मनोरथभूतमेव । तद्विषये तत्तोपचारः । [**विवाहदीक्षातिलकं**] विवाहदीक्षायां विवाहकृत्ये तिलकं **कथंचित्** कृच्छ्रेण **चकार** । आनन्दबाष्पान्धतयेति शेषः । विवाहानन्तरभावित्वादन्येषामयमेव प्रथमो मनोरथ इति भावः ॥ युग्मकम् ॥

बबन्ध चास्राकुलदृष्टिरस्याः स्थानान्तरे कल्पितसंनिवेशम् ।
धात्र्यङ्गुलीभिः प्रतिसार्यमाणमूर्णामयं कौतुकहस्तसूत्रम् ॥२५॥

बबन्धेति ॥ **अस्याः** पार्वत्याः [**अस्राकुलदृष्टिः**] अस्रैरानन्दबाष्पैराकुलदृष्टिः । अत एव **स्थानान्तरे** [**कल्पितसंनिवेशं**] कल्पितः संनिवेशो निक्षेपो यस्य तत् । स्वस्थानादन्यत्र स्थापितमित्यर्थः । अत एव [**धात्र्यङ्गुलीभिः**] धात्र्या उपमातुरङ्गुलीभिः **प्रतिसार्यमाणं** स्वस्थानं प्राप्यमाणम् **ऊर्णामयं** मेषादिलोमनिर्मितम् । 'ऊर्णा मेषादिलोम्नि स्यात्' इत्यमरः । **कौतुकहस्तसूत्रं** मङ्गलहस्तसूत्रम् । 'कौतुकं मङ्गले हर्षे हस्तसूत्रे कुतूहले' इति शाश्वतः । **बबन्ध च** । मेनेति शेषः । पूर्वोक्ततिलकक्रियासमुच्चयार्थश्चकारः ॥

क्षीरोदवेलेव सफेनपुञ्जा पर्याप्तचन्द्रेव शरत्त्रियामा ।
नवं नवक्षौमनिवासिनी सा भूयो बभौ दर्पणमादधाना ॥ २६ ॥

क्षीरोदेति ॥ नवं नूतनं क्षौमं दुकूलं निवस्त आच्छादयतीति **नवक्षौमनिवासिनी** । वस्तेराच्छादनार्थाण्णिनिः । तथा **नवं दर्पणं आदधाना** बिभ्रती **सा** गौरी **सफेनपुञ्जा** सडिण्डीरपङ्क्तिः । [**क्षीरोदवेला**] क्षीरमुदकं यस्य स क्षीरोदः क्षीरसमुद्रः । 'उदकस्योदः संज्ञायाम्' इत्युदादेशः । तस्य वेला तीरभूमिः **इव** । 'वेला काले च जलधेस्तीरनीरविकारयोः' इति विश्वः । **पर्याप्तचन्द्रा** पूर्णचन्द्रा **शरत्त्रियामा** शरद्रात्रिः **इव भूयः** भूयिष्ठं **बभौ** चकासे ॥

---

१ बाष्पा०. २ धात्र्या०. ३ परिमार्ज्यमानम्. ४ नवं.

तामर्चिताभ्यः कुलदेवताभ्यः कुलप्रतिष्ठां प्रणमय्य माता ।
अकारयत्कारयितव्यदक्षा क्रमेण पादग्रहणं सतीनाम् ॥२७॥

तामिति ॥ [**कारयितव्यदक्षा**] कारयितव्येषु दक्षा कारयित्री । कर्मोपदेशकुशलेत्यर्थः । **माता** मेना । [**कुलप्रतिष्ठां**] प्रतितिष्ठत्यस्यामिति प्रतिष्ठा । 'आतश्चोपसर्गे' इति कः । स्त्रियां टाप् । कुलस्य प्रतिष्ठां कुलालम्बनभूताम् । स्थितिकारिणीमित्यर्थः । **तां** गौरीम् । । **आर्चिताभ्यः** पूजिताभ्यः **कुलदेवताभ्यः** गृहदेवताभ्यः **प्रणमय्य** प्रणामं कारयित्वा । 'ल्यपि लघुपूर्वात्' इति णेरयादेशः । **सतीनां** पतिव्रतानां **पादग्रहणं** पादाभिवन्दनं **क्रमेण अकारयत्** कारयामास । 'हृक्रोरन्यतरस्याम्' इति अणि कर्तुः कर्मत्वम् । अन्यत्र च नमेरकर्मकत्वात् 'गतिबुद्धि'–इत्यादिना ॥

अखण्डितं प्रेम लभस्व पत्युरित्युच्यते ताभिरुमा स्म नम्रा ।
तया तु तस्यार्धशरीरभाजा पश्चात्कृताः स्निग्धजनाशिषोऽपि ॥२८॥

अखण्डितमिति ॥ **नम्रा** प्रणता **उमा ताभिः** सतीभिः **पत्युः** शिवस्य **अखण्डितम्** अक्षतं **प्रेम लभस्व** प्राप्नुहि **इति उच्यते स्म** अभिहिता । 'लट् स्मे' इति भूतार्थे लट् । **तस्य** हरस्य । अर्धं शरीरस्यार्धशरीरम् । 'अर्धं नपुंसकम्' इति समासः । तद्भजतीति **अर्धशरीरभाजा तया** गौर्या **तु स्निग्धजनाशिषः** बन्धुजनाशीर्वादाः **अपि पश्चात्कृताः** अधरीकृताः । ततोऽप्यधिकफललाभादिति भावः ॥

इच्छाविभूत्योरनुरूपमद्रिस्तस्याः कृती कृत्यमशेषयित्वा ।
सभ्यैः सभायां सुहृदास्थितायां तस्थौ वृषाङ्कागमनप्रतीक्षः ॥२९॥

इच्छेति ॥ **कृती** कुशलः । सभायां साधुः **सभ्यः** । 'सभाया यः' इति यप्रत्ययः । **अद्रिः** हिमवान् **इच्छाविभूत्योः** उत्साहैश्वर्ययोः **अनुरूपं** सदृशं यथा तथा **तस्याः** पार्वत्याः **कृत्यं** कर्तव्यम् **अशेषयित्वा** शेषं निःशेषं कृत्वा । समाप्येत्यर्थः । अशेषशब्दात्तत्करोतीति ण्यन्तात् क्त्वाप्रत्ययः । **सुहृदास्थितायां** बन्धुजनाक्रान्तायां **सभायां** संसदि [**वृषाङ्कागमनप्रतीक्षः**] वृषाङ्कस्य हरस्यागमनं प्रतीक्षत इति तथोक्तः सन् । 'कर्मण्यण्' इत्यण् । **तस्थौ** स्थितः ॥

तावद्भवस्यापि कुबेरशैले तत्पूर्वपाणिग्रहणानुरूपम् ।
प्रसाधनं मातृभिरादृताभिर्न्यस्तं पुरस्तात्पुरशासनस्य ॥ ३० ॥

तावदिति ॥ **तावत्** । यावद्गौरीप्रसाधनं क्रियते तत्काल एवेत्यर्थः । **कुबेरशैले** कैलासे । [**तत्पूर्वपाणिग्रहणानुरूपम्**] तदेव पूर्वं तत्पूर्वं तच्च तत्पाणिग्रहणं तस्यानुरूपं **प्रसाधनं** अलंकारसामग्री । **आदृताभिः** सादराभिः । कर्तरि क्तः । **मातृभिः** ब्राह्मीप्रभृतिभिः सप्तमातृकाभिः । पुरं शास्तीति पुरशासनस्तस्य [**पुरशासनस्य** ।] कर्तरि ल्युट् । **भवस्य अपि पुरस्तात्** अग्रे न्यस्तं निहितम् ॥

---

१ अर्गा. २ लाभात्, लाभादधःकृताः. ३ बन्धु. ४ भ्यः. ५ आगमनं प्रतीक्ष्य. ६ तस्य हरस्य. ७ स्मर.

तद्गौरवान्मङ्गलमण्डनश्रीः सा पस्पृशे केवलमीश्वरेण ।
स[1] एव वेषः परिणेतुरिष्टं भावान्तरं तस्य विभोः प्रपेदे ॥ ३१ ॥

तदिति ॥ **ईश्वरेण** शिवेन **सा मङ्गलमण्डनश्रीः** शुभप्रसाधनसंपत् **तद्गौरवात्** तासु मातृष्वादरात् **केवलं पस्पृशे** । स्पृष्टैव न तु दध्रे इत्यवधारणार्थः केवलशब्दः । 'केवलं चावधारणे' इति शाश्वतः । किं तु **तस्य विभोः** देवस्य **स एव वेषः** स्वाभाविको भस्मकपालादिवेष एव **परिणेतुः** लोक उद्वोढुः **इष्टम्** अपेक्षितं **भावान्तरं** रूपान्तरं **प्रपेदे** । अङ्गरागादिरूपतां प्रापेत्यर्थः ॥

भावान्तरापत्तिमेवाह—

बभूव भस्मैव सि[2]ताङ्गरागः कपालमेवामलशेखरश्रीः ।
उपान्तभा[3]गेषु च रोचनाङ्को [4]गजाजिनस्यैव दुकूलभावः ॥ ३२ ॥

बभूवेति ॥ **भस्म एव सिताङ्गरागः** शुभ्रगन्धानुलेपनं **बभूव** । **कपालम् एव** [**अमलशेखरश्रीः**] अमलं शेखरं शिरोभूषणं तस्य श्रीः शोभा बभूव । **गजाजिनस्य एव उपान्तभागेषु** अञ्चलप्रदेशेषु [**रोचनाङ्कः**] रोचनैवाङ्को हंसादिचिह्नं यस्य स तथोक्तः **दुकूलभावः** पट्टांशुकत्वं **च बभूव** । भस्मादिकमेवाङ्गरागादिभावं प्राप्तमित्यर्थः ॥

शं[5]खान्तरद्योति विलोचनं यदन्तर्निविष्टा[6]मलपिङ्गतारम् ।
सांनिध्यपक्षे हरितालमय्यास्तदेव जातं तिलकक्रियायाः ॥ ३३ ॥

शङ्खेति ॥ [**शङ्खान्तरद्योति**] शङ्खान्तरे ललाटास्थिमध्ये द्योतत इति तथोक्तम् । 'शङ्खो निधौ ललाटास्थ्नि' इत्यमरः । [**अन्तर्निविष्टामलपिङ्गतारम्**] अन्तर्निविष्टा मध्यगतामला पिङ्गा तारा कनीनिका यस्य तत्तथोक्तम् । 'तारकाक्ष्णः कनीनिका' इत्यमरः । **यद् विलोचनं तत्** विलोचनम् **एव हरितालमय्याः** वर्णद्रव्यविशेषविकारस्य **तिलकक्रियायाः** तिलकरचनायाः संनिधिरेव सांनिध्यं तदेव । पक्षः साध्यम् । 'पक्षः पार्श्वगरुत्साध्यसहायबलभित्तिषु ।' इति यादवः । तस्मिन् **सांनिध्यपक्षे जातम्** । प्रविष्टमित्यर्थः । अनेन ललाटलोचनमेव तस्य हरितालतिलकमभूदित्युक्तम् ॥

यथाप्रदेशं भुजगेश्वराणां क[7]रिष्यतामाभरणान्तरत्वम् ।
शरीरमात्रं विकृतिं प्रपेदे तथैव तस्थुः फणरत्नशोभाः ॥ ३४ ॥

यथेति ॥ **यथाप्रदेशं** प्रदेशान्प्रकोष्ठादीननतिक्रम्य **आभरणान्तरत्वं** कङ्कणाद्याभरणविशेषत्वं **करिष्यतां** संपादयिष्यतां **भुजगेश्वराणां शरीरमात्रं** शरीरमेव **विकृतिं** रूपान्तरं **प्रपेदे** । **फणरत्नशोभाः तथा एव तस्थुः** । तासां तथैवोपादेयत्वादिति भावः ॥

---

१ स्व एव, स्वभाववे०. २ कृता०. ३ भावेषु. ४ सिंहा०. ५ नेत्रान्तर. ६ अनल. ७ गमिष्यतां.

तस्योपकण्ठे घननीलकण्ठः कुतूहलादुन्मुखपौरदृष्टः ।
स्वबाणचिह्नादवतीर्य मार्गादासन्नभूपृष्ठमियाय देवः ॥ ५१ ॥

तस्येति ॥ तस्य पुरस्य उपकण्ठे अन्तिके घनो मेघ इव नीलः कण्ठो यस्य स घननीलकण्ठः देवः कुतूहलात् दर्शनौत्सुक्यात् [उन्मुखपौरदृष्टः] उन्मुखैः पौरैर्दृष्टः सन् । स्वबाणचिह्नात् त्रिपुरविजयसमये स्वबाणाङ्कात् मार्गात् कुतश्चिदाकाशदेशात् अवतीर्य अवरुह्य आसन्नभूपृष्ठम् निकटभूतलम् इयाय प्राप ॥

तमृद्धिमद्बन्धुजनाधिरूढैर्वृन्दैर्गजानां गिरिचक्रवर्ती ।
प्रत्युज्जगामागमनप्रतीतः प्रफुल्लवृक्षैः कटकैरिव स्वैः ॥ ५२ ॥

तमिति ॥ [आगमनप्रतीतः] आगमनेन शिवागमनेन प्रतीतो हृष्टः गिरिचक्रवर्ती पर्वताधिराजो हिमवान् [ऋद्धिमद्बन्धुजनाधिरूढैः] ऋद्धिमता वस्त्रालंकारादिसमृद्धेन बन्धुजनेनाधिरूढैः । अनेन बन्धूनां समस्वाम्यं सूचितम् । गजानां वृन्दैः [प्रफुल्लवृक्षैः] प्रफुल्ला विकसितकुसुमा वृक्षा येषु तैः स्वैः स्वकीयैः कटकैः नितम्बैः इव तं हरं प्रत्युज्जगाम अभिययौ । 'कटकोऽस्त्री नितम्बोऽद्रेः' इत्यमरः ॥

वर्गावुभौ देवमहीधराणां द्वारे पुरस्योद्घटितापिधाने ।
समीयतुर्दूरविसर्पिघोषौ भिन्नैकसेतू पयसामिवौघौ ॥ ५३ ॥

वर्गाविति ॥ [दूरविसर्पिघोषौ] दूरविसर्पी दूरगामी घोषो ययोस्तौ । देवाश्च महीधराश्च तेषां देवमहीधराणाम् उभौ वर्गौ उद्घटितापिधाने अपनीतकवाटे पुरस्य द्वारे भिन्नो दीर्ण एकसेतुः याभ्यां तौ भिन्नैकसेतू पयसाम् ओघौ प्रवाहौ इव समीयतुः संगतौ ॥

ह्रीमानभूद्भूमिधरो हरेण त्रैलोक्यवन्द्येन कृतप्रणामः ।
पूर्वं महिम्ना स हि तस्य दूरमावर्जितं नात्मशिरो विवेद ॥ ५४ ॥

ह्रीमानिति ॥ भूमिधरः हिमवान् । [त्रैलोक्यवन्द्येन] त्रयो लोकास्त्रैलोक्यम् । चातुर्वर्ण्यादित्वात्ष्यञ्प्रत्ययः । तस्य वन्द्येन नमस्कार्येण हरेण कृतप्रणामः सन् । 'ऋत्विक्पितृव्यश्वशुरमातुलानां यवीयसाम् । प्रवयाः प्रथमं कुर्यात्प्रत्युत्थायाभिवादनम् ॥' इति स्मरणात् । ह्रीमानभूत् । महादेवं प्रति स्वयमल्पत्वात्संकोचं प्रापेत्यर्थः । ननु विदितेश्वरमाहिम्नः स्वयं प्रागेव प्रणतस्य जामातुराचारमात्रस्वीकारे कः संकोच इति शङ्कां निरस्यति—पूर्वमिति ॥ हि यस्मात् स हिमवान् पूर्वं प्रागेव तस्य ईश्वरस्य महिम्ना सामर्थ्येन दूरम् अत्यन्तम् आवर्जितं नमितम् आत्मशिरः न विवेद । सत्यं स्वयं प्रणतत्वानुसंधाने न संकोचः । तदनुसंधानं त्वौत्सुक्यान्नास्तीति भावः ॥

स प्रीतियोगाद्विकसन्मुखश्रीर्जामातुरग्रेसरतामुपेत्य ।
प्रावेशयन्मन्दिरमृद्धमेनमागुल्फकीर्णापणमार्गपुष्पम् ॥ ५५ ॥

---

१ स्ववाह०; स्ववाहवाहात्. २ वाहात्. ३ सम्०. ४ प्रतीक्षः. ५ दूरात्. ६ माङ्गल्य०, आगुल्फपुष्पप्रकरावकीर्णं,० स्फगाढार्पितमा०.

स इति ॥ **प्रीतियोगात्** संतोषसंबन्धात् **विकसन्मुखश्रीः** विकसन्ती मुखश्रीर्यस्य स तथोक्तः **स** हिमवान् । जायां मिमीते जानातीति **जामातुः** वरस्य । पृषोदरादित्वात्साधुः । 'जामाता दुहितुः पतिः ' इत्यमरः । **अग्रेसरतां** पुरोगामित्वम् **उपेत्य एनं** देवम् आगुल्फं पादग्रन्थिपर्यन्तं कीर्णानि पर्यस्तान्यापणमार्गेषु पण्यवीथिकासु पुष्पाणि यस्मिंस्तत **आगुल्फकीर्णापणमार्गपुष्पम्** । ' तद्ग्रन्थी घुटिके गुल्फौ ' इत्यमरः । **ऋद्धं** समृद्धं **मन्दिरं** नगरम् । ' मन्दिरं नगरेऽगारे मन्दिरो मकरालये । ' इति विश्वः । **प्रावेशयत** ॥

तस्मिन्मुहूर्ते पुरसुन्दरीणामीशानसंदर्शनलालसानाम् ।
प्रासादमालासु बभूवुरित्थं त्यक्तान्यकार्याणि विचेष्टितानि ५६

तस्मिन्निति ॥ **तस्मिन्मुहूर्ते** हरपुरप्रवेशसमये [**ईशानसंदर्शनलालसानाम्**] ईशानस्य संदर्शने लालसानां लोलुपानाम् । 'लोलुपो लोलुभो लोलो लालसो लम्पटश्च सः ।' इति यादवः । **पुरसुन्दरीणां प्रासादमालासु इत्थं** वक्ष्यमाणप्रकारेण **त्यक्तान्यकार्याणि** विसृष्टकार्यान्तराणि **विचेष्टितानि** व्यापाराः । ' नपुंसके भावे क्तः ' इति क्तः । **बभूवुः** आसन् ॥

तान्येवाह पञ्चभिः श्लोकैः—

आलोकमार्गं सहसा व्रजन्त्या कयाचिदुद्वेष्टनवान्तमाल्यः[२] ।
बन्द्धुं न संभावित एव तावत्करेण रुद्धोऽपि च[३] केशपाशः ॥५७॥

आलोकमार्गमिति ॥ **आलोकमार्गं** दर्शनपथम् । गवाक्षमित्यर्थः । **सहसा व्रजन्त्या** गच्छन्त्या **कयाचित्** उद्वेष्टनो द्रुतगतिवशादुन्मुक्तबन्धनोऽत एव वान्तमाल्य उद्गीर्णमाल्यश्च यः स **उद्वेष्टनवान्तमाल्यः करेण रुद्धः** गृहीतः **अपि च केशपाशः** केशकलापः । ' पाशः पक्षश्च हस्तश्च कलापार्थाः कचात्परे ' इत्यमरः । **तावत्** आलोकनमार्गप्राप्तिपर्यन्तं **बन्द्धुम्** । बन्धनायेत्यर्थः । **न संभावितः** न स्मृतः **एव** ॥

प्रसाधिकालम्बितमग्रपादमाक्षिप्य काचिद्द्रवरागमेव ।
उत्सृष्टलीलागतिरा[४] गवाक्षादलक्तकाङ्कां पदवीं ततान[५] ॥ ५८ ॥

प्रसाधिकेति ॥ **काचित्** स्त्री [**प्रसाधिकालम्बितं**] प्रसाधिकया अलंकर्त्र्या आलम्बितं रञ्जनार्थं धृतं **द्रवरागम् एव** आर्द्रालक्तकमेव । [**अग्रपादम्**] अग्रश्चासौ पादश्च अग्रपादः इति समानाधिकरणसमासः । ' हस्ताग्राग्रहस्तादयो गुणगुणिनोर्भेदाभेदाभ्याम् ' इति वामनः । तम् **आक्षिप्य** आकृष्य **उत्सृष्टलीलागतिः** त्यक्तमन्दगमना सती **आ गवाक्षात्** गवाक्षपर्यन्तम् । पदद्वयमेतत् । **पदवीम् अलक्तकाङ्कां** लाक्षारसचिह्नां **ततान** चकार ॥

---

१ मुक्ता०. २ दुद्बन्धन. ३ न केशहस्तः; हि केशपाशः, ०केशहस्तः. ४ उन्मृष्ट०. ५ चकार.

विलोचनं दक्षिणमञ्जनेन संभाव्य तद्वञ्चितवामनेत्रा ।
तथैव वातायनसंनिकर्षं ययौ शलाकामपरा वहन्ती ॥ ५९ ॥

विलोचनमिति ॥ **अपरा** स्त्री **दक्षिणं विलोचनम् अञ्जनेन संभाव्य** अलंकृत्य [**तद्वञ्चितवामनेत्रा**] तद्वञ्चितं तेनाञ्जनेन वर्जितं वामनेत्रं यस्याः सा तथोक्ता सती । **तथैव** तेनैव रूपेण **शलाकाम्** अञ्जनकूर्चिकां **वहन्ती** बिभ्रती **वातायनसंनिकर्षं** गवाक्षसमीपं **ययौ** । दक्षिणग्रहणं संभ्रमाद्व्युत्क्रमद्योतनार्थम् । 'सव्यं हि पूर्वं मनुष्या अञ्जते' इति श्रुतेः ॥

जालान्तरप्रेषितदृष्टिरन्या प्रस्थानभिन्नां न बबन्ध नीवीम् ।
नाभिप्रविष्टाभरणप्रभेण हस्तेन तस्थाववलम्ब्य वासः ॥ ६० ॥

जालान्तरेति ॥ **अन्या** स्त्री **जालान्तरप्रेषितदृष्टिः** गवाक्षमध्यप्रसारितदृष्टिः सती [**प्रस्थानभिन्नां**] प्रस्थानेन गमनेन भिन्नां त्रुटितां **नीवीं** वस्त्रग्रन्थिम् । 'नीवी परिपणे ग्रन्थौ स्त्रीणां जघनवाससि ।' इति विश्वः । **न बबन्ध** नाबध्नात् । किं तु [**नाभिप्रविष्टाभरणप्रभेण**] नाभिं प्रविष्टा आभरणानां कङ्कणानां प्रभा यस्य तेन । प्रभैव नाभेरावरणमभूदिति भावः । **हस्तेन वासः अवलम्ब्य** धृत्वा **तस्थौ** ॥

अर्धाचिता सत्वरमुत्थितायाः पदे पदे दुर्निमिते गलन्ती ।
कस्याश्चिदासीद्रसना तदानीमङ्गुष्ठमूलार्पितसूत्रशेषा ॥ ६१ ॥

अर्धाचितेति ॥ **सत्वरं** सवेगम् **उत्थितायाः कस्याश्चित्** अर्धमाचिता मणिभिर्गुम्फिता **अर्धाचिता दुर्निमिते** संभ्रमाद्दुःखेन निक्षिप्ते । 'डुमिञ् प्रक्षेपणे' इति धातोः कर्मणि क्तः । **पदे पदे** प्रतिपदम् । वीप्सायां द्विर्भावः । **गलन्ती** गलद्रत्ना सती **रसना** मेखला **तदानीं** तस्मिन्नवसरे [**अङ्गुष्ठमूलार्पितसूत्रशेषा**] अङ्गुष्ठमूले अर्पितं लगितं सूत्रमेव शेषो यस्याः सा **आसीत्** ॥

तासां मुखैरासवगन्धगर्भैर्व्याप्तान्तराः सान्द्रकुतूहलानाम् ।
विलोलनेत्रभ्रमरैर्गवाक्षाः सहस्रपत्राभरणा इवासन् ॥ ६२ ॥

तासामिति ॥ तदानीं **सान्द्रकुतूहलानां तासां** स्त्रीणाम् [**आसवगन्धगर्भैः**] आसवगन्धो गर्भे येषां तैः । [**विलोलनेत्रभ्रमरैः**] विलोलानि नेत्राण्येव भ्रमरा येषु तैः **मुखैः व्याप्तान्तराः** छन्नावकाशाः **गवाक्षाः सहस्रपत्राभरणा इव आसन्** । कमलालंकृता इव स्थिता इत्यर्थः ॥

तावत्पताकाकुलमिन्दुमौलिरुत्तोरणं राजपथं प्रपेदे ।
प्रासादशृङ्गाणि दिवापि कुर्वञ्ज्योत्स्नाभिषेकद्विगुणद्युतीनि ॥ ६३ ॥

---

१ अर्धाञ्चिता. २ पत्रावरणाः; प्रफुल्लपद्मा. ३ च्छवीनि.

६१—६२ श्लोकयोर्मध्येऽयं श्लोको दृश्यते—

स्तनं धयन्तं तनयं विहाय विलोकनाय त्वरया व्रजन्ती ।
संप्रस्नुताभ्यां पदवीं स्तनाभ्यां सिषेच काचित्पयसा गवाक्षम् ॥

तावदिति ॥ **तावत्** तस्मिन्नवसरे **इन्दुमौलिः** ईश्वरः **दिवा अपि प्रासादशृङ्गाणि** [**ज्योत्स्नाभिषेकद्विगुणद्युतीनि**] ज्योत्स्नाया अभिषेकेण स्नपनेन द्विगुणद्युतीनि द्विरावृत्तकान्तीनि । 'गुणस्त्वावृत्तिशब्दादिज्येन्द्रियामुख्यतन्तुषु ।' इति वैजयन्ती । **कुर्वन्** [**पताकाकुलं**] पताकाभिराकुलं व्याकीर्णम् **उत्तोरणम्** उच्छ्रिततोरणं **राजपथं प्रपेदे** ॥

तमेकदृश्यं नयनैः पिबन्त्यो नार्यो न जग्मुर्विषयान्तराणि ।
तथा हि शेषेन्द्रियवृत्तिरासां सर्वात्मना चक्षुरिव प्रविष्टा ॥ ६४ ॥

तमेति ॥ एक एव दृश्यो दर्शनीयः तम् **एकदृश्यं तम्** ईश्वरं **नयनैः पिबन्त्यः**। अतितृष्णया पश्यन्त्य इत्यर्थः । 'ताः शङ्करं दृष्टिभिरापिबन्त्यः' इति वा पाठः । **नार्यः विषयान्तराणि** ततोऽन्यान् विषयान् । शब्दादीनित्यर्थः । **न जग्मुः** । न विदुरित्यर्थः । **तथा हि** । **आसां** नारीणां **शेषेन्द्रियवृत्तिः** श्रोत्रादिप्रवृत्तिः **सर्वात्मना** स्वरूपकार्त्स्न्येन **चक्षुः प्रविष्टेव** । श्रोत्रादीनीन्द्रियाणि स्वातन्त्र्येण ग्रहणाशक्तेश्चक्षुरेव प्रविश्य कौतुकात्स्वयमप्येनमुपलभन्ते किमु । अन्यथा स्वस्वविषयाधिगमः किं न स्यादिति भावः ॥

अथ पौराङ्गनावचनान्याह—

स्थाने तपो दुश्चरमेतदर्थमपर्णया पेलवयापि तप्तम् ।
या दास्यमप्यस्य लभेत नारी सा स्यात्कृतार्था किमुताङ्कशय्याम् ॥ ६५ ॥

स्थान इति ॥ **पेलवया** कोमलया **अपि अपर्णया** पार्वत्या एतस्मै शिवाय **एतदर्थम्** । 'अर्थेन सह नित्यसमासः सर्वलिङ्गता च' इति विशेष्यनिघ्नत्वम् । **दुश्चरं तपः तप्तं स्थाने** युक्तम् । कुतः । **या नारी अस्य** ईश्वरस्य **दास्यं** दासीत्वम् **अपि लभेत सा कृतार्था स्यात्** । या अङ्क एव शय्या ताम् **अङ्कशय्यां** लभेत **सा किमुत** । कृतार्थेति किमु वक्तव्यमित्यर्थः ॥

परस्परेण स्पृहणीयशोभं न चेदिदं द्वन्द्वमयोजयिष्यत् ।
अस्मिन्द्वये रूपविधानयत्नः पत्युः प्रजानां विफलोऽभविष्यत् ॥ ६६ ॥

परस्परेणेति ॥ **स्पृहणीयशोभं** सर्वैराशास्यमानसौन्दर्यम् **इदं द्वन्द्वं** मिथुनम् । 'द्वन्द्वं रहस्य-' इत्यादिना निपातः । **परस्परेण न अयोजयिष्यत् चेत्** न योजयेद्यदि **प्रजानां पत्युः** विधातुः **अस्मिन्द्वये** द्वन्द्वे [**रूपविधानयत्नः**] रूपविधाने सौन्दर्यनिर्माणे यत्नः प्रयासः **विफलः अभविष्यत्** भवेत् । एतदनुरूपस्त्रीपुंसान्तराभावादिति भावः । 'लिङ्निमित्ते लृङ् क्रियातिपत्तौ' इति लृङ् ॥

न नूनमारूढरुषा शरीरमनेन दग्धं कुसुमायुधस्य ।
व्रीडादमुं देवमुदीक्ष्य मन्ये संन्यस्तदेहः स्वयमेव कामः ॥ ६७ ॥

---

१ धिनापघातेन जडा-खिलो-बभूव. २ कोमलया; याभित०. ३ वितथः. ४ व्रीडावशात्. ५ अवेक्ष्य.

नेति ॥ **आरूढरुषा** प्ररूढकोपेन **अनेन** हरेण **कुसुमायुधस्य** कामस्य **शरीरं न दग्धं नूनम्**। किं तु **कामः अमुं देवम् उदीक्ष्य** दृष्ट्वा **व्रीडात्** सौन्दर्येण जितोऽस्मीति लज्जया **स्वयमेव संन्यस्तदेहः** त्यक्तदेह इति **मन्ये** इत्युत्प्रेक्षा। न स्वयं न्यस्ताकृतेः कोपः संभवतीति भावः ॥

अनेन संबन्धमुपेत्य[1] दिष्ट्या मनोरथप्रार्थितमीश्वरेण।
मूर्धानमालि क्षितिधारणोच्च[2]मुच्चैस्तरं[3] वक्ष्यति शैलराजः ॥ ६८ ॥

अनेनेति ॥ हे **आलि** सखि। 'आलिः सखी वयस्याऽथ' इत्यमरः। **शैलराजः** हिमवान्। **दिष्ट्या** इत्यानन्देऽव्ययम्। [**मनोरथप्रार्थितं**] मनोरथैः प्रार्थितमवरुद्धम्, अभिलाषविषयीकृतमित्यर्थः। 'प्रार्थना याच्ञावरोधयोः' इत्यभिधानात्। **अनेन ईश्वरेण संबन्धम् उपेत्य** अवाप्य [**क्षितिधारणोच्चं**] क्षितिधारणेन उच्चमुन्नतं **मूर्धानम् उच्चैस्तरम्** उन्नततरम्। उच्चैरित्यव्ययात्तरप् प्रत्ययः। मूर्ध्नो द्रव्यत्वान्नामुप्रत्ययान्तो निपातः। 'किमेत्तिङव्ययघादाम्वद्रव्यप्रकर्षे' इत्यनेन द्रव्यप्रकर्षे तस्य विधानादिति। **वक्ष्यति** धारयिष्यति। वहतेर्लृट् ॥

इत्योषधिप्रस्थविलासिनीनां शृण्वन्कथाः श्रोत्रसुखास्त्रिनेत्रः।
केयूरचूर्णीकृतलाजमुष्टिं[4] हिमालयस्यालयमाससाद ॥ ६९ ॥

इतीति ॥ **त्रिनेत्रः** त्र्यम्बकः। त्रिनेत्रत्रिनयनशब्दयोः 'क्षुभ्नादिषु च' इति णत्वाभावः। **इति** इत्थम् **ओषधिप्रस्थविलासिनीनां** संबन्धिनीः **श्रोत्रसुखाः** श्रवणमधुराः **कथाः** आलापान् **शृण्वन्** [**केयूरचूर्णीकृतलाजमुष्टिं**] केयूरैः अङ्गदैश्चूर्णीकृता लाजानां मुष्टयो यस्मिंस्तं तथोक्तम्। तत्रावकीर्णा आचारलाजा अन्तराल एवाङ्गदैश्चूर्णपेषं पिष्यन्त इति पुरंध्रिजनसंबन्धातिशयोक्तिः। **हिमालयस्य** हिमवतः **आलयं** भवनम् **आससाद** ॥

तत्रावतीर्याच्युतदत्तहस्तः शरद्घनाद्दीधितिमानिवोक्ष्णः।
क्रान्तानि[5] पूर्वं कमलासनेन कक्ष्यान्तराण्य[6]द्रिपतेर्विवेश ॥ ७० ॥

तत्रेति ॥ **तत्र** हिमवदालये [**अच्युतदत्तहस्तः**] अच्युतेन विष्णुना दत्तहस्तो वितीर्णहस्तावलम्बः सन् **शरद्घनात्** शरन्मेघात्। शरद्विशेषणान्मेघस्य शुभ्रत्वं गम्यते। **दीधितिमान्** सूर्यः **इव उक्ष्णः** वृषात् **अवतीर्य कमलासनेन पूर्वम्** अग्रे **क्रान्तानि** प्रविष्टानि **अद्रिपतेः कक्ष्यान्तराणि** गेहप्रकोष्ठान्तराणि **विवेश**। 'कक्ष्या कच्छे वरत्रायां काञ्च्यां गेहप्रकोष्ठके' इति यादवः ॥

तमन्वगिन्द्रप्रमुखाश्च देवाः सप्तर्षिपूर्वाः परमर्षयश्च।
गणाश्च गिर्यालयमभ्यगच्छन्[7]प्रशस्तमारम्भमिवोत्तमार्थाः[8] ॥ ७१ ॥

---

१ अवाप्य. २ पालनो. ३ उच्चैस्तराम्; मूर्धानमाक्रम्य महीधराणामुच्चैस्तरां वक्ष्यति शै० इ. पा. ४ मुष्टिः; कर्पूरचूर्णैः; कृतलाजवृष्टिम् इ. पा. ५ नतः. ६ कक्षान्तराणि. ७ अन्वगच्छन्. ८ यशस्यम्.

तमिति ॥ **तम्** ईश्वरम् **अन्वक्** अनुपदम् । अव्ययमेतत् । 'अन्वगन्वक्षमनुगेऽनुपदं क्लीबमव्ययम्' इत्यमरः । **इन्द्रप्रमुखाः देवाः च** । सप्तर्षयः पूर्वे येषां ते **सप्तर्षिपूर्वाः** । 'न बहुव्रीहौ' इति सर्वनामसंज्ञाप्रतिषेधः । **परमर्षयः** सनकादिमहर्षयः च । 'सन्महत्परमोत्तमोत्कृष्टाः पूज्यमानैः' इति तत्पुरुषः । **गणाः** प्रमथाः **च** । **उत्तमार्थाः** महाप्रयोजनाः **प्रशस्तं** प्रकृष्टम् । अमोघमित्यर्थः । आरभ्यत इत्यारम्भ उपायस्तम् **आरम्भम् इव गिर्यालयं** हिमवन्मन्दिरम् **अभ्यगच्छन्** । प्राविशन्नित्यर्थः ॥

तत्रेश्वरो विष्टरभाग्यथावत्सरत्नमर्घ्यं मधुमच्च गव्यम् ।
नवे दुकूले च नगोपनीतं प्रत्यग्रहीत्सर्वममन्त्रवर्जम् ॥ ७२ ॥

तत्रेति ॥ **तत्र** हिमवदालये **ईश्वरः विष्टरभाक्** आसनगतः । उपविष्ट इत्यर्थः । **यथावत्** यथार्हम् । विधिवदित्यर्थः । **सरत्नं** रत्नसहितम् **अर्घ्यम्** अर्घार्थं जलम् । मधु क्षौद्रमस्मिन्नस्तीति **मधुमत्** । गवि भवं **गव्यं** दधि **च** । मधुपर्कमित्यर्थः । 'दधिमधुनी सर्पिर्वा मध्वलाभे' इत्याश्वलायनगृह्यसूत्रात् । **नवे दुकूले च** इति **सर्वं नगोपनीतं** हिमवदानीतमर्घ्यादिकम् । मन्त्रान्वर्जयित्वा मन्त्रवर्जम् । ततो नञ्समासः । **अमन्त्रवर्जम्** । मन्त्रान्न वर्जयित्वेत्यर्थः । 'द्वितीयायां च' इति णमुल्प्रत्यय इत्याह न्यासकारः 'अनुदात्तं पदमेकवर्जम्' इत्यत्र । **प्रत्यग्रहीत्** स्वीकृतवान् ॥

दुकूलवासाः स वधूसमीपं निन्ये विनीतैरवरोधदक्षैः ।
वेलासमीपं स्फुटफेनराजिर्नवैरुदन्वानिव चन्द्रपादैः ॥ ७३ ॥

दुकूलेति ॥ अथ **दुकूलवासाः** दुकूलं वसान इत्यर्थः । **स** हरः **विनीतैः** अनुद्धतैः अवरोधेषु ये दक्षास्तैः **अवरोधदक्षैः वधूसमीपं निन्ये** नीतः । कथमिव । [**स्फुटफेनराजिः**] स्फुटा फेनानां राजिर्यस्य सः । उदकमस्यास्तीति **उदन्वान्** समुद्रः । 'उदन्वानुदधौ च' इति निपातनात्साधुः । **नवैः** अचिरोदितैः **चन्द्रपादैः** चन्द्रकिरणैः **वेलासमीपम् इव** ॥

तया प्रवृद्धाननचन्द्रकान्त्या प्रफुल्लचक्षुःकुमुदः कुमार्या ।
प्रसन्नचेतःसलिलः शिवोऽभूत्संसृज्यमानः शरदेव लोकः ॥ ७४ ॥

तयेति ॥ [**प्रवृद्धाननचन्द्रकान्त्या**] आननं चन्द्र इव इत्युपमितसमासः । प्रवृद्धाऽऽननचन्द्रस्य कान्तिर्यस्यास्तया तथोक्तया **तया कुमार्या शरदा लोक इव संसृज्यमानः** संगच्छमानः **शिवः** [**प्रफुल्लचक्षुःकुमुदः**] चक्षूंषि कुमुदानीव तानि प्रफुल्लानि यस्य स तथोक्तः । **प्रसन्नचेतःसलिलः** चेतः सलिलमिव तत्प्रसन्नं यस्य स तथोक्तः । **अभूत्** । शरल्लोकयोरपि यथोचितं विशेषणानि योज्यानि ॥

---

१ मधुपर्कमहव्यम्. २ ०पनीतं. ३ वन्द्यम्. ४ ०वान्सांऽथ. ५ रक्षैः,-मुख्यैः. ६ सकाशम्. ७ राशिः. ८ विवृद्धा. ९ प्रयुज्यमानः.

तयोः समापत्तिषु कातराणि किंचिद्व्यवस्थापितसंहृतानि ।
ह्रीयन्त्रणां तत्क्षणमन्वभूवन्नन्योन्यलोलानि विलोचनानि ॥ ७५ ॥

तयोरिति ॥ **तयोः** वधूवरयोः **समापत्तिषु** यदृच्छया संगतिषु **कातराणि** चकितानि । ‘ अधीरे कातरः ’ इत्यमरः । द्रष्टुमसमर्थानीति भावः । **किंचित्** ईषत् व्यवस्थापितानि स्थिरीकृतानि पश्चात्संहृतानि निवर्तितानि चेति **व्यवस्थापितसंहृतानि** । ‘ पूर्वकाल० ’ इत्यादिना तत्पुरुषः । [**अन्योन्यलोलानि**] अन्योन्यस्मिन् लोलानि सतृष्णानि । ‘ लोलश्चलसतृष्णयोः ’ इत्यमरः । **विलोचनानि** दृश्यः **तत्क्षणं** तस्मिन्क्षणे **ह्रीयन्त्रणां** ह्रिया निमित्तेन संकोचम् **अन्वभूवन्** ॥

तस्याः करं शैलगुरूपनीतं जग्राह ताम्राङ्गुलिमष्टमूर्तिः ।
उमातनौ गूढतनोः स्मरस्य तच्छङ्किनः पूर्वमिव प्ररोहम् ॥ ७६ ॥

तस्या इति ॥ **अष्टमूर्तिः** शिवः । तस्मादीश्वराच्छङ्कत इति **तच्छङ्किनः** । तद्भीतस्येत्यर्थः । अत एव **उमातनौ** उमाशरीरे **गूढतनोः** गुप्तशरीरस्य **स्मरस्य पूर्वं प्ररोहमिव** प्रथमाङ्कुरमिव स्थितं **शैलगुरूपनीतं** शैलगुरुणा हिमवतोपनीतं प्रापितम् । अथ वा शैलगुरुणा हिमवत्पुरोधसोपनीतं **ताम्राङ्गुलिं** रक्ताङ्गुलिं **तस्याः** पार्वत्याः **करं जग्राह** ॥

रोमोद्गमः प्रादुरभूदुमायाः स्विन्नाङ्गुलिः पुंगवकेतुरासीत् ।
वृत्तिस्तयोः पाणिसमागमेन समं विभक्तेव मनोभवस्य ॥ ७७ ॥

रोमोद्गम इति ॥ **उमायाः रोमोद्गमः** रोमाञ्चः **प्रादुरभूत्** । पुमान्गौः पुंगवो वृषभः । ‘ गोरतद्धितलुकि ’ इति टच् । स केतुश्चिह्नं यस्य स **पुंगवकेतुः** शिवः **स्विन्नाङ्गुलिः आसीत्** । अत्रोत्प्रेक्षते-**पाणिसमागमेन** पाण्योः संस्पर्शेन कर्त्रा । **तयोः** वधूवरयोः **मनोभवस्य वृत्तिः** अवस्थितिः **समं विभक्तेव** समीकृतेवेत्यर्थः । प्राक्सिद्धस्याप्यनुरागसाम्यस्य संप्रति तत्कार्यदर्शनात्पाणिसंस्पर्शकृतत्वमुत्प्रेक्ष्यते । ननु कन्या तु प्रथमसंगमे स्विन्नकरचरणा भवति, पुमांस्तु रोमाञ्चितो भवतीति वात्स्यायनेन विपरीतमुक्तमिति चेन्नैष दोषः । एभिरनयोर्भावं परीक्षेतेति वाक्यशेष एभिरिति बहुवचनेन स्वेदरोमाञ्चग्रहणस्य सकलसात्त्विकोपलक्षणत्वावगमेनानियमावधारणात् । अत एव रघुवंशेऽन्यथाभिधानात्स्वोक्तिविरोध इत्यपास्तम् । तदेतद्रघुवंशसंजीविन्यां (७। २२) सुव्यक्तमवोचम् । सात्त्विकास्तु ‘ स्तम्भप्रलयरोमाञ्चाः स्वेदो वैवर्ण्यवेपथू । अश्रुवैस्वर्यमित्यष्टौ सात्त्विकाः परिकीर्तिताः ॥ ’ इति ॥

प्रयुक्तपाणिग्रहणं यदन्यद्वधूवरं पुष्यति कान्तिमग्र्याम् ।
सांनिध्ययोगादनयोस्तदानीं किं कथ्यते श्रीरुभयस्य तस्य ॥७८॥

---

१ आनाशिरं मुहूर्त-मनोज्ञाम्. २ उमास्तना. ३ शङ्कितः. ४ चिन्ना०. ५ तस्मिन्द्वये तत्क्षणमात्मवृत्तिः समं विभक्तेव मनोभवेन । इ. पा.

प्रयुक्तेति ॥ **यत्** यस्मात्कारणात् [**प्रयुक्तपाणिग्रहणं**] प्रयुक्तं पाणिग्रहणं यस्य तत्तथोक्तम् । **अन्यत्** लौकिकम् । वधूश्च वरश्च **वधूवरम्** । समाहारे द्वन्द्वैकवद्भावः । **तदानीं** पाणिग्रहणकाले **अनयोः** उमाशिवयोः **सांनिध्ययोगात्** संनिधिभावात् **अग्र्याम्** उत्तमां **कान्तिं** शोभां **पुष्यति** पुष्णाति । **तस्य उभयस्य** उमामहेश्वररूपस्य मिथुनस्य **श्रीः किं कथ्यते** यत्प्रसादादन्यस्य शोभालाभस्तस्य शोभा किमु वक्तव्येत्यर्थः । 'विवाहसमये गौरीशिवौ वधूवरावनुप्रविशेताम्' इत्यागमः ॥

प्रदक्षिणप्रक्रमणात्कृशानोरुदर्चिषस्तन्मिथुनं चकासे[१] ।
मेरोरुपान्तेष्विव[२] वर्तमानमन्योन्यसंसक्तमहस्त्रियामम् ॥ ७९ ॥

प्रदक्षिणेति ॥ **तन्मिथुनम् उदर्चिषः** उन्नतज्वालस्य **कृशानोः** कर्मणः **प्रदक्षिणप्रक्रमणात्** प्रदक्षिणीकरणात् **चकासे** । किमिव । **मेरोः उपान्तेषु** परिसरेषु **वर्तमानम्** आवर्तमानम् । मेरुं प्रदक्षिणीकुर्वदित्यर्थः । [**अन्योन्यसंसक्तम्**] अन्योन्येन संसक्तं संगतम् । मिथुनस्याप्येतद्विशेषणम् । अहश्च त्रियामा च **अहस्त्रियामं** रात्रिंदिवम् **इव** । समाहारे द्वन्द्वैकवद्भावः ॥

तौ दंपती त्रिः परिणीय वह्निमन्योन्यसंस्पर्शनिमीलिताक्षौ ।
स कारयामास वधूं पुरोधास्तस्मिन्समिद्धार्चिषि लाजमोक्षम्॥८०॥

ताविति ॥ स पुरस्तादेव हितं विधत्ते इति **पुरोधाः** पुरोहितः । [**अन्योन्यसंस्पर्शनिमीलिताक्षौ**] अन्योन्यस्य संस्पर्शेन स्पर्शसुखेन निमीलिताक्षौ **तौ** जाया च पतिश्च **दंपती** कर्मभूतौ । जायाशब्दस्य दंभावो निपातितः । **वह्निं त्रिः** त्रिवारम् । 'द्वित्रिचतुर्भ्यः सुच्' इति सुच् । **परिणीय** परितो नीत्वा । प्रदक्षिणीकार्येत्यर्थः । नयतेर्द्विकर्मकाल्ल्यप् । **समिद्धार्चिषि** दीप्तज्वाले **तस्मिन्** वह्नौ **वधूं लाजमोक्षम्** लाजविसर्गं **कारयामास** । 'हृक्रोरन्यतरस्याम्' इति विकल्पादणि कर्तुः कर्मत्वम् ॥

सा लाजधूमाञ्जलिमिष्टगन्धं गुरूपदेशाद्वदनं निनाय ।
कपोलसंसर्पिशिखः स तस्या मुहूर्तकर्णोत्पलतां प्रपेदे ॥ ८१ ॥

सेति ॥ **सा** वधूः [**गुरूपदेशात्**] गुरोः पुरोधस उपदेशात् [**इष्टगन्धं**] इष्टः घ्राणतर्पण इत्यर्थः गन्धो यस्य तं **लाजधूमाञ्जलिं वदनं निनाय** । [**कपोलसंसर्पिशिखः**] कपोलसंसर्पिणी शिखा यस्य स तथोक्तः **स** धूमः **तस्याः** गौर्याः **मुहूर्तकर्णोत्पलतां प्रपेदे** । धूमस्य विसृमरत्वान्मुहूर्तग्रहणम् ॥

तदीषदार्द्रारुणगण्डलेखमुच्छ्वासिकालाञ्जनरागमक्ष्णोः ।
वधूमुखं क्लान्तयवावतंसमाचारधूमग्रहणाद्बभूव ॥ ८२ ॥

---

१ बभासे. २ रिवाग्नं.

तदिति ॥ तत् वधूमुखम् आचारधूमग्रहणात् आचारप्राप्तधूमत्वात् [ईषदार्द्रारुणगण्डलेखम्] ईषदार्द्रे स्विन्ने अरुणे च गण्डलेखे गण्डस्थले यस्य तत्तथोक्तम् । अक्ष्णोः [उच्छ्वासिकालाञ्जनरागम्] उच्छ्वास्युद्गच्छन्कालाञ्जनस्य रागः अञ्जनं यस्य तत्तथोक्तम् [क्लान्तयवावतंसं] क्लान्तो यवावतंसो यवाङ्कुरकर्णपूरो यस्य तत्तथाभूतं बभूव । 'लाजाञ्जलिं विसृज्य धूमाग्रं जिघ्रेत्' इति प्रयोगवृत्तिकारः ॥

वधूं द्विजः प्राह तवैष वत्से वह्निर्विवाहं प्रति कर्मसाक्षी ।
शिवेन भर्त्रा सह धर्मचर्या कार्या त्वया मुक्तविचारयेति ॥८३॥

वधूमिति ॥ अथ वधूं द्विजः पुरोधाः प्राह । किमिति । हे वत्से एष वह्निः तव विवाहं प्रति । विवाहकर्मणीत्यर्थः । कर्मसाक्षी कर्मद्रष्टा । भर्त्रा शिवेन सह मुक्तविचारया निर्विचारया त्वया धर्मचर्या धर्माचरणं कार्या कर्तव्या इति । अयं च प्राजापत्यविवाहो द्रष्टव्यः । यथाहाश्वलायनः—'सह धर्मं चरत इति प्राजापत्यः' इति ॥

आलोचनान्तं श्रवणे वितत्य पीतं गुरोस्तद्वचनं भवान्या ।
निदाघकालोल्बणतापयेव माहेन्द्रमम्भः प्रथमं पृथिव्या ॥८४॥

आलोचनान्तमिति ॥ भवस्य पत्न्या भवान्या । 'इन्द्रवरुणभवशर्वरुद्र' इत्यादिना ङीप् । आनुगागमश्च । आलोचनान्तं नेत्रान्तपर्यन्तम् । 'आङ् मर्यादाभिविध्योः' इत्यव्ययीभावः । श्रवणे श्रोत्रे वितत्य विस्तार्य तत् पूर्वोक्तं गुरोः याज्ञिकस्य वचनं 'सह धर्मं चर' इति वाक्यं [निदाघकालोल्बणतापया] निदाघकाले ग्रीष्मकाल उल्बणतापयोत्कटसंतापया पृथिव्या प्रथमम् आद्यं माहेन्द्रं पार्जन्यम् अम्भः इव पीतम् । अत्यादरेण शुश्रावेत्यर्थः ॥

ध्रुवेण भर्त्रा ध्रुवदर्शनाय प्रयुज्यमाना प्रियदर्शनेन ।
सा दृष्ट इत्याननमुन्नमय्य ह्रीसन्नकण्ठी कथमप्युवाच ॥८५॥

ध्रुवेणेति ॥ प्रियं दर्शनं यस्य कर्मभूतस्य । तेन प्रियदर्शनेन ध्रुवेण शाश्वतेन भर्त्रा [ध्रुवदर्शनाय] ध्रुवस्य नक्षत्रविशेषस्य दर्शनाय । 'ध्रुवो भभेदे क्लीबं तु निश्चिते शाश्वते त्रिषु ।' इत्यमरः । प्रयुज्यमाना दृश्यतामिति प्रेर्यमाणा ह्रीसन्नकण्ठी ह्रिया हीनस्वरा सा वधूः कथमपि आननमुन्नमय्य दृष्ट इत्युवाच ॥

इत्थं विधिज्ञेन पुरोहितेन प्रयुक्तपाणिग्रहणोपचारौ ।
प्रणेमतुस्तौ पितरौ प्रजानां पद्मासनस्थाय पितामहाय ॥८६॥

---

१ गिरिः. २ पूर्व. ३ श्रवणौ. ४ विधृत्य, विवृत्य. ५ भेदयेव, तप्तयेव. ६ कण्ठा.

इत्थमिति ॥ **इत्थम्** अनेन प्रकारेण । 'इदमस्थमुः' इति थमुप्रत्ययः । **विधिज्ञेन** विवाहप्रयोगज्ञेन । शास्त्रज्ञेनेत्यर्थः । **पुरोहितेन** हैमवतेन **प्रयुक्तपाणिग्रहणोपचारौ** कृतविवाहकर्माणौ **प्रजानां पितरौ तौ** उमामहेश्वरौ **पद्मासनस्थाय** पद्मासनोपविष्टाय पितॄणां पित्रे **पितामहाय** ब्रह्मणे । 'पितामहो विरिञ्चौ स्यात्तातस्य जनकेऽपि च ।' इति विश्वः । 'पितृव्यमातुलमातामहपितामहाः' इति निपातनात्साधुः । **प्रणेमतुः** नमश्चक्रतुः । पितामहस्य पित्रोरपि पूज्यत्वादिति भावः ॥

वधूर्विधात्रा प्रतिनन्द्यते स्म कल्याणि वीरप्रसवा भवेति ।
वाचस्पतिः सन्नपि सोऽष्टमूर्तौ त्वाशास्यचिन्तास्तिमितो बभूव ॥ ८७ ॥

वधूरिति ॥ **वधूः** कन्या **विधात्रा** ब्रह्मणा । हे **कल्याणि** शोभने । वीरः प्रसवोऽपत्यं यस्याः सा **वीरप्रसवा** वीरसूः **भवेति प्रतिनन्द्यते स्म** । आशिषमुक्तेत्यर्थः । **स** विधाता **वाचस्पतिः** वागीश्वरः **अपि सन्** । कस्कादिषु पाठात् साधुः । **अष्टमूर्तौ** शिवे **तु** [**आशास्यचिन्तास्तिमितः**] आशास्यमाकाङ्क्ष्यं तत्र चिन्ता विचारस्तस्यां स्तिमितो मन्दः **बभूव** । तस्य निरीहस्याशास्याभावादाशिषि स्तिमितत्वमित्यर्थः ॥

कॢप्तोपचारां चतुरस्रवेदीं तावेत्य पश्चात्कनकासनस्थौ ।
जायापती लौकिकमेषणीयमार्द्राक्षतारोपणमन्वभूताम् ॥ ८८ ॥

क्लृप्तेति ॥ **तौ जायापती** वधूवरौ **पश्चात्** नमस्कारानन्तरं [**क्लृप्तोपचारां**] क्लृप्ता रचिता उपचाराः पुष्परचनादयो यस्यां तां **चतुरस्रवेदीमेत्य** प्राप्य **कनकासनस्थौ** सन्तौ **लौकिकं** लोके विदितम् । आचारप्राप्तमित्यर्थः । अत एव **एषणीयम्** आशास्यम् । तथा हि । लौकिकाचारं मनसापि न लङ्घयेत् इति शास्त्रादवश्यकर्तव्यमित्यर्थः । इषेरिच्छार्थादनीयर्प्रत्ययः । **आर्द्राक्षतारोपणं अन्वभूताम्** ॥

पत्रान्तलग्नैर्जलबिन्दुजालैराकृष्टमुक्ताफलजालशोभम् ।
तयोरुपर्यायतनालदण्डमाधत्त लक्ष्मीः कमलातपत्रम् ॥ ८९ ॥

पत्रान्तेति ॥ **लक्ष्मीः** श्रीदेवी [**पत्रान्तलग्नैः**] पत्रान्तेषु दलप्रान्तेषु लग्नैः **जलबिन्दुजालैः** [**आकृष्टमुक्ताफलजालशोभम्**] आकृष्टा आहृता मुक्ताफलजालेन प्रान्तलम्बिना मुक्ताकलापेन या शोभा सा येन तत्तथोक्तम् । [**आयतनालदण्डम्**] आयतं दीर्घं नालमेव दण्डो यस्य तत् [**कमलातपत्रं**] कमलमेवातपत्रं तत् **तयोः उपरि आधत्त** दधौ ॥

द्विधा प्रयुक्तेन च वाङ्मयेन सरस्वती तन्मिथुनं नुनाव ।
संस्कारपूतेन वरं वरेण्यं वधूं सुखग्राह्यनिबन्धनेन ॥ ९० ॥

---

१ मूर्तावाशास्य. २ चतुरन्त. ३ एषितव्यम्. ४ लम्बैः. ५ वृन्दैः, वर्षैः. ६ आकृष्ट. ७ मन्त्रि.

द्विधेति ॥ अथ **सरस्वती** वाग्देवी **च द्विधा** संस्कृतप्राकृतरूपेण द्वैविध्येन **प्रयुक्तेन** उच्चारितेन **वाङ्मयेन** शब्दजालेन **तन्मिथुनं नुनाव** तुष्टाव। 'णु स्तुतौ' इति धातोर्लिट्। केन कमित्याह—संस्कारेति। [**संस्कारपूतेन**] संस्कारेण शास्त्रव्युत्पत्त्या पूतेन प्रकृतिप्रत्ययविभागशुद्धेन। संस्कृतेनेत्यर्थः। **वरेण्यं** वरणीयम्। श्लाघ्यमित्यर्थः। वृणोतेरौणादिक एन्यप्रत्ययः। **वरं** वोढारं शिवम्। [**सुखग्राह्यनिबन्धनेन**] सुखेन ग्राह्यं सुबोधं निबन्धनं रचना यस्य तेन वाङ्मयेन। प्राकृतभाषयेत्यर्थः। **वधूम्** नुनावेत्यनेन संबन्धः॥

तौ संधिषु व्यञ्जितवृत्तिभेदं रसान्तरेषु प्रतिबद्धरागम्।
अपश्यतामप्सरसां मुहूर्तं प्रयोगमाद्यं ललिताङ्गहारम्॥९१॥

ताविति॥ **तौ** दंपती **संधिषु** मुखादिनिर्वहणान्तेषु पञ्चसंधिषु। तदुक्तं दशरूपके—'मुखं प्रतिमुखं गर्भः सावमर्षोपसंहृतिः।' इति। **व्यञ्जितवृत्तिभेदं** स्फुटीकृतकौशिक्यादिवृत्तिविशेषम्। रसानुगुण्येनेति शेषः। तदुक्तं भूपालेन—'कौशिकी स्यात्तु शृङ्गारे रसे वीरे तु सात्वती। रौद्रबीभत्सयोर्वृत्तिर्नियतारभटी पुनः। शृङ्गारादिषु भावेषु रसेष्विष्टा तु भारती॥' तथा 'कौशिक्यारभटी चैव सात्वती भारती तथा। चतस्रो वृत्तयो ज्ञेयास्तासु नाट्यं प्रतिष्ठितम्' इति। **रसान्तरेषु** शृङ्गारादिरसभेदेषु। 'शृङ्गारादौ विषे वीर्ये गुणे रागे द्रवे रसः' इत्यमरः। 'शृङ्गारहास्यकरुणा रौद्रवीरभयानकाः। बीभत्साद्भुतशान्ताख्या रसाः पूर्वैरुदाहृताः' इति। **प्रतिबद्धरागं** प्रति नियमेन प्रवर्तितो वसन्तललितादिरागो यस्मिंस्तत्। यस्मिन्रसे यो रागो विहितस्तदनुसारेण प्रयुक्तरागमित्यर्थः। यथाह कोहलः—'रौद्रेऽद्भुते तथा वीरे पुंरागेण प्रगीयते। शृङ्गारहास्यकरुणाः स्त्रीरागेण प्रकीर्तिताः। भयानके च बीभत्से शान्ते गेयो नपुंसके॥' इति। **ललिताङ्गहारं** मधुराङ्गविक्षेपम्। 'अङ्गहारोऽङ्गविक्षेपः' इत्यमरः। आदौ भवम् **आद्यम्**। रूपकान्तरप्रकृतिभूतमित्यर्थः। तदुक्तम्—'आहुः प्रकरणादीनां नाटकं प्रकृतिं बुधाः' इति। **अप्सरसाम्** उर्वश्यादीनां [**प्रयोगम्**] प्रयुज्यत इति प्रयोगो रूपकम्। नाटकमित्यर्थः। आद्यमिति विशेषणात्। तं **मुहूर्तमपश्यतां** दृष्टवन्तौ। 'पाघ्राध्मास्था०' इत्यादिना दृशेः पश्यादेशः॥

देवास्तदन्ते हरमूढभार्यं किरीटबद्धाञ्जलयो निपत्य।
शापावसाने प्रतिपन्नमूर्तेर्ययाचिरे पञ्चशरस्य सेवाम्॥९२॥*

---

१ दृष्टा. २ सानप्रति०. ३ प्रतिलब्ध.

*९२ श्लोकानन्तरं त्रय एते क्षेपका दृश्यन्ते—

अवाप्य रूपं हरदृष्टिपूतं देव्याः समीपे प्रणिपत्य रुद्रम्।
अनङ्ग ऊर्ध्वं न मुखं निनाय त्रासेन देवैः कृतपाणिसंज्ञः॥
उत्तिष्ठ वत्सेति हरेण चोक्तस्त्वयुक्त्वा भवं तस्य पुरः प्रतस्थे।
भार्यामतः पश्यति माधवं च प्रीत्युन्मुखं चूतशरं वहन्तम्॥
पूर्वं यथा देवपतेर्नियोगं मूर्ध्ना वहन्नाशु तमिन्द्रमेव।
प्राप्तः पुनर्वेन गजेन्द्रगामी प्रोज्झितधामो नवयौवनेन॥

देवा इति ॥ **देवाः** इन्द्रादयः **तदन्ते** तस्य प्रयोगदर्शनस्यान्तेऽवसाने **ऊढभार्यं** परिणीतदारं **हरं** [**किरीटबद्धाञ्जलयः**] किरीटेषु बद्धा अञ्जलयो येषां ते तथोक्ताः सन्तः । **निपत्य** प्रणम्य **शापावसाने प्रतिपन्नमूर्तेः** लब्धशरीरस्य । 'परिणेष्यति पार्वतीं यदा' (४।४२) इत्यादिना शापस्य पार्वतीपरिणयान्तत्वादित्यर्थः । **पञ्चशरस्य** कामस्य कर्तुः **सेवां ययाचिरे** । पुनः समासादितशरीरस्य तस्य सेवा स्वीक्रियतामिति प्रार्थयामासुरित्यर्थः । 'दुह्याच्पच्—' इत्यादिना द्विकर्मकत्वम् ॥

तस्यानुमेने भगवान्विमन्युर्व्यापारमात्मन्यपि सायकानाम् ।
कालेप्रयुक्ता खलु कार्यविद्भिर्विज्ञापना भर्तृषु सिद्धिमेति ॥ ९३ ॥*

तस्येति ॥ **विमन्युः** विगतक्रोधः **भगवान्** ईश्वरः **आत्मन्यपि तस्य** कामस्य **सायकानां व्यापारमनुमेने** । तथा हि । **कार्यविद्भिः** कार्यज्ञैः । अथ वा कालविद्भिः अवसरज्ञैः । [**कालप्रयुक्ता**] काले योग्यावसरे प्रयुक्ता अनुष्ठिता **भर्तृषु** स्वामिषु विषये **विज्ञापना सिद्धिमेति खलु** । सफला भवतीत्यर्थः । अयमेवास्य स्मरसेवास्वीकारो यदात्मन्यपि तत्सायकव्यापारमङ्गीकृतवानिति ॥

अथ विबुधगणांस्तानिन्दुमौलिर्विसृज्य
क्षितिधरपतिकन्यामाददानः करेण ।
कनककलशयुक्तं भक्तिशोभासनाथं
क्षितिविरचितशय्यं कौतुकागारमागात् ॥ ९४ ॥

अथेति ॥ **अथ इन्दुमौलिः** ईश्वरः **तान् विबुधगणान् विसृज्य क्षितिधरपतिकन्यां** पार्वतीं **करेणाददानः कनककलशयुक्तं** मङ्गलार्थमन्तर्निहितहेममयपूर्णकुम्भं [**भक्तिशोभासनाथं**] भक्तयः पुष्पादिरचनास्तासां शोभया सनाथम् । सहितमित्यर्थः । **क्षितिविरचितशय्यं** क्षितौ विरचिता स्थण्डिले कल्पिता शय्या तल्पं यस्मिंस्तत्तथोक्तं **कौतुकागारम् आगात्** शय्यागृहं जगाम । अत्राश्वलायनः— 'अत ऊर्ध्वमक्षारालवणाशिनावधःशायिनौ ब्रह्मचारिणौ स्याताम्' इति । अत ऊर्ध्वं विवाहादूर्ध्वम् । आ त्रिरात्रादिति शेषः । 'त्रिरात्रं द्वादशरात्रं' वा इति वचनात् । तथा कामशास्त्रेऽपि—'अथ परिणयरात्रौ प्रक्रमेणैव किंचित्तिसृषु च रजनीषु स्तब्धभावा दुनोति। त्रिदिनमिह न भिन्द्याद्ब्रह्मचर्यं न चास्या हृदयमननुरुध्य स्वेच्छया नर्म कुर्यात् ॥' इति ॥

---

१ काले. २ कालविद्भिः. ३ रक्षा-रथ्या-भक्ति. रक्षाशक्ति.

*९३-९४ श्लोकयोर्मध्येऽयं क्षेपको लभ्यते—

देवैस्तसंपादितचारुमूर्तिस्तत्संसदि प्रादुरभूत्स कामः ।
लक्ष्यीकृतं शंकरमेव भूयोऽविध्यच्छरैः पुष्पमयैरमोघैः ॥

नवपरिणयलज्जाभूषणां तत्र गौरीं
वदनमपहरन्तीं तत्कृताक्षेपमीशः ।
अपि शयनसखीभ्यो दत्तवाचं कथंचि-
त्प्रमथमुखविकारैर्हासयामास गूढम् ॥ ९५ ॥

नवेति ॥ तत्र कौतुकागारे ईशः ईश्वरः [**नवपरिणयलज्जाभूषणां**] नवपरिणयेन नवोद्वाहेन या लज्जा सा भूषणं यस्यास्तामत एव [**तत्कृताक्षेपं**] तेनेश्वरेण कृताक्षेपं कृताकर्षणम् । उन्नमितमिति यावत् । **वदनमपहरन्तीं** साचीकुर्वतीम् । अयं लज्जानुभावः । अनुभावान्तरमाह–**शयनसखीभ्यः अपि** शयने सहशायिनीभ्यः नर्मसहचरीभ्योऽपीत्यर्थः । **कथंचित्** कृच्छ्रेण **दत्तवाचं** दत्तोत्तरां **गौरीं** [**प्रमथमुखविकारैः**] प्रमथा भृङ्गिरिटिप्रभृतयो हास्यरसाधिदेवताः पशुपतेः पारिषदाः । यथाह भरतः–'शृङ्गारो विष्णुदैवत्यो हास्यः प्रमथदैवतः' इति । 'प्रमथाः स्युः पारिषदाः' इत्यमरः । तेषां मुखविकारैर्मुखविकृतचेष्टितैः **गूढम्** अप्रकाशं **हासयामास** हासाद्युपायैर्लज्जामपाकर्तुं प्रवृत्त इत्यर्थः । यथाह गोनर्दः—'हासेन मधुना नर्मवचसा लज्जितां प्रियाम् । विलुप्तलज्जां कुर्वीत निपुणैश्च सखीजनैः ॥' इति ॥

इति श्रीमन्महामहोपाध्यायकोलाचलमल्लिनाथसूरिविरचितया संजीवनीसमाख्यया व्याख्यया समेतः श्रीकालिदासकृतौ कुमारसंभवे महाकाव्ये उमापरिणयो नाम सप्तमः सर्गः ॥

---

१ कृतोत्क्षेपं. २ प्रथम.

अष्टमः सर्गः ।

अथ शृङ्गारमुभयोर्वर्णयन्नागतः कविः ।
कुमारसंभवफले सर्गेऽस्मिन्नाह संप्रति ॥
सोऽपि संक्षिप्तसंपन्नसंयुक्तश्च समृद्धिमान् ।
इति भेदाच्चतुर्धोक्तश्चतुर्णां च वियोगिनाम् ॥
तत्रावस्थाप्रभेदेन शृङ्गारे नायिका त्रिधा ।
मुग्धा मध्या प्रगल्भा च तत्र ह्रीसाध्वसाविलाम् ॥
मुग्धावस्थां समाश्रित्य देव्याः प्रथमसंगमे ।
आदावेकादशश्लोकाख्याते पूर्वानुरागिणोः ॥
प्रथमं नाम शृङ्गारं तयोः कथितवान्कविः ।
चुम्बनेष्वधरेत्यत्र लक्षणं त्वस्य वक्ष्यते ॥

पाणिपीडनविधेरनन्तरं शैलराजदुहितुर्हरं प्रति ।
भावसाध्वसपरिग्रहादभूत्कामदोहदसुखं मनोहरम्[1] ॥ १ ॥

पाणीति ॥ **पाणिपीडनविधेः अनन्तरं** पाणिग्रहणानन्तरम् । विधेरिति पञ्चमी षष्ठी च । उभयथाप्यनुशासनसंभवादित्युक्तं प्राक् । **शैलराजदुहितुः** पार्वत्याः कर्त्र्याः **हरं प्रति भावसाध्वसपरिग्रहात् मनोहरं** चित्ताकर्षकं कामदोहदम् । कामसंवर्धकमित्यर्थः । 'तरुगुल्मलतादीनामकाले कुशलैः कृतम् । पुष्पाद्युत्पादकं द्रव्यं दोहदं स्यात् ।' इति शब्दार्णवे । तच्च तत्सुखं **कामदोहदसुखं अभूत्** । हरस्येति शेषः । नायिकानायकयोः अन्योन्यानुभावदर्शनात्सुखमाविर्भवति । तच्च मदनोद्दीपकमिति रसविदां स्थितिः । तथा च हरस्य गौर्यां नवोढायां स्वगोचरभावप्रयुक्तसाध्वसदर्शनात्सुखमाविर्भवति । तच्च मदनाकारं प्रादुर्बभूवेत्यर्थः । तत्र रसभावस्थायिनः कार्यमनुभावः । तदुक्तं—'रसा गच्छन्ति संस्थानं यत्कार्यमुपलक्ष्यते । सोऽनुभावः' इति ॥

उक्तं भावसाध्वसम् । तस्य सुखमयत्वं च वर्णयति—

व्याहृता प्रतिवचो न संदधे गन्तुमैच्छदवलम्बितांशुका ।
सेवते स्म शयनं पराङ्मुखी सा तथाऽपि रतये पिनाकिनः ॥ २ ॥

व्याहृतेति ॥ **सा** पार्वती **व्याहृता** यत्किंचिदभिहिता सती **प्रतिवचः** प्रत्युत्तरं **न संदधे** न ददावित्यर्थः । **अवलम्बितांशुका** गृहीतवस्त्रा सती **गन्तुं** उपसर्प्तुं **ऐच्छत्** इच्छति स्म । इषिधातोर्लङ् । 'इषुगमियमां छः' इति छकारः । **पराङ्मुखी** सती **शयनं सेवते स्म** । अनभिमुखमशयिष्टेत्यर्थः । **तथापि** । इत्थं साध्व-

---

[1] मनोहरं वपुः.

सात्प्रतिकूलचेष्टितापीत्यर्थः । **पिनाकिनः** शिवस्य **रतये** सुखाय । बभूवेति शेषः । प्रातिकूल्यमपि तस्यानन्दकरमभूदित्यर्थः । एतेन नवोढाया देव्या मौग्ध्याद्विजितं तन्ममत्वमवसेयम् ॥

कैतवेन शयिते कुतूहलात्पार्वती प्रतिमुखं निपातितम् ।
चक्षुरुन्मिषति सस्मितं प्रिये विद्युदाहतमिव न्यमीलयत् ॥ ३ ॥

कैतवेनेति ॥ **प्रिये** भर्तरि **कुतूहलात्** । एषा किं करिष्यतीति बुभुत्सयेत्यर्थः । **कैतवेन** कपटेन **शयिते** सुप्ते सति **पार्वती** कर्त्री **प्रतिमुखं** यथा तथा **निपातितम्** । प्रियस्वापपरीक्षार्थं तदभिमुखं प्रवर्तितमित्यर्थः । **चक्षुः** स्वदृष्टिं **सस्मितं उन्मिषति** । पुनः प्रिये सहासं पश्यतीत्यर्थः । **विद्युदाहतं** विद्युता प्रतिहतं **इव न्यमीलयत्** । साध्वसादिति भावः । एतेन किंचित्साध्वसस्यापचयो व्यज्यते ॥

नाभिदेशनिहितः सकम्पया शंकरस्य रुरुधे तया करः ।
तद्दुकूलमथ चाभवत्स्वयं दूरमुच्छ्वसितनीविबन्धनम् ॥ ४ ॥

नाभीति ॥ **नाभिदेशनिहितः** । नीवीमोचनायेति शेषः । **शंकरस्य करः सकम्पया** वेपथुमत्या । प्रियकरस्पर्शादुत्पन्नसात्त्विकभावयेत्यर्थः । **तया** पार्वत्या **रुरुधे** निवारितः । **अथ च** । तथापीत्यर्थः । **तद्दुकूलं स्वयं** स्वत एव **दूरं** अत्यन्तं [**उच्छ्वसितनीविबन्धनं**] उच्छ्वसितं स्रस्तं नीविबन्धनं नीविग्रन्थिर्यस्य तत्तथाभूतं **अभवत्** । रतिपारवश्यादिति भावः ॥

एवमालि निगृहीतसाध्वसं शंकरो रहसि सेव्यतामिति ।
सा सखीभिरुपदिष्टमाकुला नास्मरत्प्रमुखवर्तिनि प्रिये ॥ ५ ॥

एवमिति ॥ हे **आलि** सखि पार्वति **रहसि शंकरः एवम्** । स्वोपदिष्टप्रकारेणेत्यर्थः । **निगृहीतसाध्वसं** निरस्तभयं यथा तथा **सेव्यतां इति सखीभिः उपदिष्टं** उक्तं वचनं **सा** पार्वती **प्रिये** शंकरे **प्रमुखवर्तिनि** सति **आकुला** साध्वसविह्वला सती **न अस्मरत्** । न स्मृतवतीत्यर्थः । स हि भयपरिप्लुते चेतसि दृष्टतरोऽप्युपदेशः संसारमाधत्त इति भावः ॥

अप्यवस्तुनि कथाप्रवृत्तये प्रश्नतत्परमनङ्गशासनम् ।
वीक्षितेन परिगृह्य पार्वती मूर्धकम्पमयमुत्तरं ददौ ॥ ६ ॥

अपीति ॥ **कथाप्रवृत्तये** संलापप्रवर्तनाय **अवस्तुनि** अप्रस्तुतार्थे **अपि प्रश्नतत्परम्** । यत्किंचित्पृच्छन्तमित्यर्थः । **अनङ्गशासनं** ईश्वरं **पार्वती वीक्षितेन** न तु वाचेत्यर्थः । **परिगृह्य** अङ्गीकृत्य **मूर्धकम्पमयं** शिरःकम्पस्वरूपम् । स्वार्थे मयट् । **उत्तरं ददौ** । न तु वाङ्मयं, साध्वसादिति भावः । विहृतनामा लज्जानुभाव उक्तः । तदुक्तं—'ईर्ष्यामानातिलज्जाभ्यां न दत्तं योग्यमुत्तरम् । क्रियया व्यज्यते यत्र विहृतं तदुदीरितम् ॥' इति ॥

---

१ शयने. २ विद्युताऽऽहतं; विद्युतेव निहतं. ३ सशङ्कया. ४ तन्नितम्बमभवत्तदा; तन्नितम्बमथ चाभवत्. ५ परिवीक्ष्य.

पुनस्तमेवाह—

शूलिनः करतलद्वयेन सा संनिरुध्य नयने हृतांशुका ।
तस्य पश्यति ललाटलोचने मोघयत्नविधुरा रहस्यभूत् ॥ ७ ॥

शूलिन इति ॥ **सा** पार्वती **रहसि हृतांशुका** प्रियेणाकृष्टवस्त्रा सती **करतलद्वयेन** । स्वकीयेनेत्यर्थः । **शूलिनः** हरस्य **नयने** नेत्रद्वयं **संनिरुध्य** संछाद्य **तस्य** शूलिनः **ललाटलोचने** तृतीयेऽक्षिण **पश्यति** सति [**मोघयत्नविधुरा**] मोघयत्ना खिलप्रयासात एव विधुरा **अभूत्** । तृतीयकराभावादिति भावः । एतेन किंचिद्धार्ष्ट्यादयो व्यज्यन्ते ॥

चुम्बनेष्वधरदानवर्जितं सन्नहस्त[1]मदयोपगूहने ।
क्लिष्टमन्मथमपि प्रियं प्रभोर्दुर्लभ[2]प्रतिकृतं वधूरतम् ॥ ८ ॥

चुम्बनेष्विति ॥ **चुम्बनेषु अधरदानवर्जितं** ओष्ठार्पणरहितं **अदयोपगूहने** निर्दयालिङ्गने [**सन्नहस्तं**] सन्नौ स्तब्धौ हस्तौ करौ यस्मिंस्तत्तथोक्तम् । तथा **दुर्लभप्रतिकृतम्** । प्रगल्भत्वान्नखदन्तताडनाद्यकृतप्रयत्नमित्यर्थः । अत एव **क्लिष्टमन्मथं** लज्जयोपरुद्धमदनं **अपि** वध्वा नवोढाया रतं **वधूरतं प्रभोः** ईश्वरस्य **प्रियम्** । अभूदिति शेषः । 'वधूः स्नुषानवोढास्त्रीभार्यास्पृक्काङ्गनासु च' इति विश्वः । अयं लज्जासाध्वसाभ्यां संकुचितोपचारत्वात्संक्लिष्टसंभोगः । तदुक्तं भूपालेन—'युवानो यत्र संक्षिप्तसाध्वसव्रीडितादिभिः । उपचारान्निषेवन्ते स संक्लिष्ट इतीरितः ॥' इति ॥

यन्मुखग्रहणमक्षताधरं दत्तमव्रणपदं नखं[3] च यत् ।
यद्रतं च सदयं प्रियस्य[4] तत्पार्वती विषहते स्म नेतरत् ॥ ९ ॥

यदिति ॥ **पार्वती प्रियस्य** संबन्धि [**अक्षताधरं**] अक्षतोऽखण्डितोऽधरो यस्मिंस्तत्तथोक्तं **यत् मुखग्रहणं** मुखचुम्बनम् । **अव्रणपदं** लक्ष्मरहितम् । 'पदं व्यवसितत्राणस्थानलक्ष्माङ्घ्रिवस्तुषु' इत्यमरः । **दत्तं यत् च नखं** नखकर्म । **यत् सदयं रतं च तत्** सर्वं **विषहते** सहते **स्म** । **न इतरत्** विपरीतम् । प्रचण्डमिति यावत् । तच्चुम्बनं नखं सुरतं वा न सहते स्म । नवोढात्वादिति हृदयम् । तदुक्तं रतिरहस्ये—'नात्यन्तमानुलोम्येन न चातिप्रातिलोमतः । सिद्धिं गच्छन्ति कन्यासु तस्मान्मध्येन साधयेत्' इति ॥

रात्रिवृत्तमनुयोक्तुमुद्यतं सा विभात[5]समये सखीजनम् ।
नाकरोदपकुतूहलं ह्रिया शंसितुं च[6] हृदयेन तत्वरे ॥ १० ॥

रात्रीति ॥ **सा** पार्वती **विभातसमये** प्रभातकाले **रात्रिवृत्तम्** । सुरतवृत्तान्तमित्यर्थः । **अनुयोक्तुं** प्रष्टुम् । 'प्रश्नोऽनुयोगः पृच्छा च' इत्यमरः । **उद्यतं** प्रवृत्तं

---

१ खिन्नहस्तसदयोपगूहनम्. २ दानम्. ३ नखस्य. ४ हरस्य. ५ प्रभात. ६ तु.

सखीजनं ह्रिया लज्जया **अपकुतूहलं** निराकाङ्क्षं **न अकरोत्** । न किंचिदाचष्ट इत्यर्थः । **हृदयेन** हृदा **च शंसितुं तत्वरे** त्वरिताभूत् । औत्सुक्यादिति भावः । त्वरासंभ्रमादीनामनुभावत्वादिति ॥

दर्पणे च परिभोगदर्शिनी पृष्ठतः प्रणयिनो निषेदुषः ।
प्रेक्ष्य बिम्बमनु बिम्बमात्मनः कानि कानि न चकार लज्जया ११

दर्पण इति ॥ [च] किंचेति चार्थः । **दर्पणे** मुकुरे परिभोगो नखक्षतादिसंभोगचिह्नं पश्यतीति **परिभोगदर्शिनी** सा पार्वती **पृष्ठतः** । पश्चाद्भागे **निषेदुषः** स्थितवतः । सदेः क्वसुः । **प्रणयिनः** प्रियस्य हरस्य **बिम्बं** प्रतिबिम्बम् । दर्पणे संक्रान्तमित्यर्थः । **आत्मनः** स्वस्य **बिम्बं अनु** । प्रतिबिम्बस्य पृष्ठत इत्यर्थः । 'अनुर्लक्षणे' इति कर्मप्रवचनीयत्वात् द्वितीया । **प्रेक्ष्य लज्जया** । स्वचापलप्राकट्यकृतयेत्यर्थः । **कानि कानि** यानि यानि भेदवाच्यानि । अङ्गसंवरणादिचेष्टितानीत्यर्थः । उक्तं च—'लज्जानुभावेन साचीकृता वर्णवैवर्ण्याधोमुखादिकृत' इति । **न चकार** ॥

नीलकण्ठपरिभुक्तयौवनां तां विलोक्य जननी समाश्वसत् ।
भर्तृवल्लभतया हि मानसीं मातुरस्यति शुचं वधूजनः ॥ १२ ॥

नीलकण्ठेति ॥ [**नीलकण्ठपरिभुक्तयौवनां**] नीलकण्ठेन परिभुक्तं यौवनं यस्याः सा तां तथोक्ताम् । प्रियेण भुक्तयौवनामित्यर्थः । **तां** पार्वतीं **विलोक्य जननी** मेना **समाश्वसत्** । संतुतोषेत्यर्थः । श्वसिधातोर्लङ् । 'अङ्गार्ग्यगालवयोः' इति विकल्पादडागमः । तथा हि । **वधूजनः भर्तृवल्लभतया** पतिवात्सल्येन **मातुः मानसीं** मनोभवां **शुचं** शोकं **अस्यति** निरस्यति **हि** । विपर्ययाद्विपर्ययश्चेत्यर्थादवसेयम् । सामान्येन विशेष समर्थनरूपोऽर्थान्तरन्यासः ॥

संप्रति देव्या मुग्धावस्थातो मध्यमावस्थाप्राप्तिमाह—

वासराणि कतिचित्कथंचन स्थाणुना पदमकार्यत प्रिया ।
ज्ञातमन्मथरसा शनैः शनैः सा मुमोच रतिदुःखशीलताम् ॥ १३ ॥

वासराणीति ॥ **स्थाणुना** शंभुना कर्त्रा **प्रिया** पार्वती कर्मभूता **कतिचित् वासराणि** । कैश्चिदहोभिरित्यर्थः । अत्यन्तसंयोगे द्वितीया । **कथंचन** कृच्छ्रेण **पदं** पदप्रक्षेपं **अकार्यत** कारिता । सुरतकर्मणीति शेषः । करोतेर्ण्यन्तात्कर्मणि लुङ् । 'हृक्रोरन्यतरस्याम्' इत्यणि कर्तुः कर्मत्वं 'ण्यन्ते कर्तुश्च कर्मणः' इत्यभिहितत्वं च । **सा** कृतपदा पार्वती **ज्ञातमन्मथरसा** अनुभूतसुरतसुखास्वादा सती । 'आस्वादेऽपि रसं प्राहुः' इति शब्दानुशासने । **शनैः शनैः** क्रमेण [**रतिदुःखशीलतां**] रतौ रते दुःखशीलतां प्रतिकूलस्वभावतां **मुमोच** । 'शीलं स्वभावे सद्वृत्ते' इत्यमरः । मध्यमावस्थां प्रापेत्यर्थः ॥

---

१ मुपबिम्बम्. २ अपि. ३ समाश्वसीत्. ४ रतमकारि चानया. ५ रत.

तुल्यलज्जास्मरत्वमेवाह—

सस्वजे प्रियमुरोनिपीडिता प्रार्थितं मुखमनेन नाहरत् ।
मेखलाप्रणयलोलतां गतं हस्तमस्य शिथिलं रुरोध सा ॥ १४ ॥

सस्वज इति ॥ **सा** पार्वती **उरोनिपीडिता** उरसि गाढमाश्लिष्टा सती **प्रियं सस्वजे** । न तु निष्पन्दमास्तेत्यर्थः । अनेन स्मरातिशयः सूचितः । **अनेन** प्रियेण **प्रार्थितं** चुम्बनार्थं याचितम् । 'याच्ञायामभियाने च प्रार्थना कथ्यते बुधैः' इति केशवः । **मुखं न अहरत्** । [**मेखलाप्रणयलोलतां**] मेखलायां प्रणयः परिचयः । 'प्रणयः स्यात्परिचये याच्ञायां सौहृदेऽपि च' इति यादवः । तत्र लोलतां चञ्चलतां **गतं अस्य** प्रियस्य **हस्तं शिथिलं रुरोध** न्यवारयत् । न तु निर्भरमिति भावः । अत्र सहनप्रतीकाराभ्यां तुल्यलज्जास्मरत्वं व्यज्यते ॥

अथ देव्याः प्रगल्भावस्थां दर्शयितुं तयोः समानरागित्वं तावदाह—

भावसूचितमदृष्टविप्रियं चाटुमत्क्षणवियोगकातरम् ।
कैश्चिदेव दिवसैरभूत्तयोः प्रेम रूढमितरेतराश्रयम् ॥ १५ ॥

भावेति ॥ **तयोः** शिवयोः **कैश्चित्** कतिभिश्चित् **एव दिवसैः** । **भावसूचितं** भावैश्चेष्टाभिः कटाक्षनिक्षेपादिभिः संजातं [**अदृष्टविप्रियं**] अदृष्टं विप्रियमप्रियाचरणं यत्र तत्तथोक्तम् । चाटूनि प्रियोक्तयो यस्मिन्सन्ति तत् **चाटुमत्** । भूमार्थे मतुप् । [**क्षणवियोगकातरं**] क्षणवियोगात्क्षणमात्रविरहादपि कातरं भीरु **इतरेतराश्रयं** अन्योन्यविषयं **प्रेम** । प्रेमपराभिलष्याङ्कुरावस्था भवतीत्यर्थः । **रूढं अभूत्** । क्रमेणानुरागपदाभिलाषं प्राप्तमित्यर्थः । तदेतत्सर्वं स्फुटीकृतं भूपालेन—'अङ्कुरपल्लवकलिकाप्रसूनफलभोगभागियम्' इत्यादिना । एका रतिरेव स्थायीभूता रसीभवति । तस्याश्चाङ्कुरावस्थाभेदोपपत्तौ सा प्रेमादिपदैरभिलष्यत इत्यर्थः । 'स प्रेमा भेदरहितं यूनोर्यद्भावबन्धनम् । राग एव स्वसंवेद्यदशां प्राप्याप्रकाशितः । यावदाश्रयवृत्तिश्चेदनुरागः' इति मानादिलक्षणं विस्तरभयान्न लिख्यत इत्याकर एव द्रष्टव्यम् ॥

तं यथाऽऽत्मसदृशं वरं वधूरन्वरज्यत वरस्तथैव ताम् ।
सागरादनपगा हि जाह्नवी सोऽपि तन्मुखरसैकनिर्वृतिः ॥ १६ ॥

तमिति ॥ **वधूः आत्मसदृशं** स्वानुरूपं **तं वरं** वोढारं प्रति **यथा अन्वरज्यत** अनुरक्ताभूत् । रञ्जेर्दैवादिकात्कर्तरि लकारः । स्वरितत्वादात्मनेपदम् । **तथैव वरः** अपि वोढाप्यात्मनः सदृक्षामात्मसदृशम् । 'त्यदादिषु दृशोऽनालोचने कञ्च' इति चकारात् क्विप्प्रत्ययः । **तां** वधूं प्रत्यन्वरज्यत । वध्वामनुरक्तोऽभूदित्यर्थः । 'गत्यर्थाकर्मक–' इत्यादिना सकर्मकत्वम् । दृष्टान्तमाह—**जाह्नवी** गङ्गा **सागरात्** नापगच्छतीति **अनपगा** अनपेता **हि** । **सोऽपि** सागरः [**तन्मुखरसैकनिर्वृतिः**] तस्या

---

१ निपीडितम्; निपीडनम्. २ दार्ढ्यभाक्क्षण: चाटु तत्क्षण. ३ तदा तयोः; तथा तयोः. ४ गूढम्. ५ वृत्तिभाक्.

जाह्नव्या मुखरसेनाग्रसलिलेन वक्त्रास्वादेनैका मुख्या निर्वृतिरानन्दो यस्य स तथोक्तः। अत्र दृष्टान्तालंकारः। लक्षणं तूक्तम्। इत्थं समानानुरागकथनाद्रसाभासत्वं निरस्तम्। तदुक्तम्—'योषिता बहुसक्तिश्चेद्रसाभासः स उच्यते'। कविनाप्युक्तं मालविकायाम्—अनातुरोत्कण्ठितयोः प्रसिध्यता समागमेनापि रतिर्न मां प्रति। परस्परप्राप्तिनिराशयोर्वरं शरीरनाशोऽपि समानरागयोः॥' इति॥

अथ देव्याः प्रगल्भावस्थामाश्रित्य संभोगमाह—

शिष्यतां निधुवनोपदेशिनः शंकरस्य रहसि प्रपन्नया।
शिक्षितं युवतिनैपुणं तया यत्तदेव गुरुदक्षिणीकृतम्॥ १७॥

शिष्यतामिति॥ **रहसि** एकान्ते निधुवनमुपदिशतीति **निधुवनोपदेशिनः** सुरतविद्यागुरोः। 'व्यवायो ग्राम्यधर्मो मैथुनं निधुवनं रतम्' इत्यमरः। **शंकरस्य शिष्यतां प्रपन्नया** प्राप्तया **तया** पार्वत्या **यत् युवतिनैपुणं** युवतिजनोचितं नैपुणम्। सुरतकौशलमित्यर्थः। **शिक्षितं** अभ्यस्तम्। आचरितमित्यर्थः। **तदेव गुरुदक्षिणीकृतम्**। यथोपदेशकरणाद्दक्षिणासममभूदित्यर्थः। अनेन कृतप्रतिकृतं सूच्यते॥

दष्टमुक्तमधरोष्ठमम्बिका वेदनाविधुतहस्तपल्लवा।
शीतलेन निरवापयत्क्षणं मौलिचन्द्रशकलेन शूलिनः॥ १८॥

दष्टेति॥ **अम्बिका** पार्वती दष्टश्चासौ मुक्तश्च तं **दष्टमुक्तम्**। 'पूर्वकाल—' इत्यादिना समासः। **अधरोष्ठं** [**वेदनाविधुतहस्तपल्लवा**] वेदनया विधुतौ कम्पितौ हस्तपल्लवौ पाणिपल्लवौ यस्याः सा तथोक्ता सती **शीतलेन शूलिनः मौलिचन्द्रशकलेन क्षणं निरवापयत्**। शीतलोपचारेण निर्व्यथमकरोदिति विश्रम्भोक्तिः। निवातेर्धातोर्ण्यन्तात् 'अर्तिह्री—' इत्यादिना पुगागमः। अत्राधरपीडनात्सुखेऽपि दुःखवदुपचारात्कुट्टिमनामानुभाव उक्तः। तदुक्तम्—'केशाधरादिग्रहणे मोदमानापि मानसे। दुःखितेव बहिः कुप्येत्तत्कुट्टिमम्' इति॥

चुम्बनादलकचूर्णदूषितं शंकरोऽपि नयनं ललाटजम्।
उच्छ्वसत्कमलगन्धये ददौ पार्वतीवदनगन्धवाहिने॥ १९॥

चुम्बनादिति॥ अथ **शंकरः अपि चुम्बनात्** चुम्बनार्थितः [**अलकचूर्णदूषितं**] अलकचूर्णेन दूषितमुपहतं **ललाटजं नयनं उच्छ्वसत्कमलगन्धये** विकचारविन्दगन्धधारिणे। 'उपमानाच्च' इतीकारः। [**पार्वतीवदनगन्धवाहिने**] पार्वत्या वदनगन्धवाहिने। फूत्कारमारुतायेत्यर्थः। **ददौ**। रजोनिःसारणार्थं तदाभिमुख्येन स्थापितवानित्यर्थः। एतेन देव्याः प्रियवशंवदत्वमुक्तम्। अत्र हरचक्षुष्यलकचूर्णकथनाद्देव्या उपरिभावः सूचितः॥

---

१ तत्.

एवमिन्द्रियसुखस्य वर्त्मनः[1] सेवनादनुगृहीतमन्मथः ।
शैलराजभवने सहोमया मासमात्रमवसद्वृषध्वजः[2] ॥ २० ॥

एवमिति ॥ **वृषध्वजः** हरः **एवं** उक्तरीत्या [**इन्द्रियसुखस्य**] इन्द्रियाणां सुखस्यानुकूलस्य **वर्त्मनः** मार्गस्य । स्त्रीप्रसङ्गस्येत्यर्थः । **सेवनात्** परिभोगात् **अनुगृहीतमन्मथः** पुनरुज्जीवितमदनः सन् । **उमया सह शैलराजभवने** हिमवद्गेहे **मासमात्रं अवसत्** । अत्यन्तसंयोगे द्वितीया । मासमात्रमिति वधूवशीकरणकालक्लृप्तिः प्रदर्शिता ॥

सोऽनुमान्य[3] हिमवन्तमात्मभूरात्मजाविरहदुःखपीडितम्[4] ।
तत्र तत्र विजहार संचरन्नप्रमेयगतिना ककुद्मता ॥ २१ ॥

स इति ॥ **सः आत्मभूः** शिवः [**आत्मजाविरहदुःखपीडितं**] आत्मजाया दुहितुर्विरहदुःखेन पीडितं **हिमवन्तं अनुमान्य** अनुमतं कृत्वा **अप्रमेयगतिना** अपरिच्छेद्यगतिना **ककुद्मता** वृषेण **संचरन्** संचरमाणः **तत्र तत्र** नानादेशेषु **विजहार** ॥

मेरुमेत्य मरुदाशुवाहनः[6] पार्वतीस्तनपुरस्कृतः[7] कृती ।
हेमपल्लवविभङ्गसंस्तरामन्वभूत्सुरततत्परः क्षपाम्[8] ॥ २२ ॥

मेरुमिति ॥ **मरुदाशुवाहनः** पवनजवनवाहनः । [**पार्वतीस्तनपुरस्कृतः**] पार्वतीस्तनाभ्यां पुरस्कृतः । पार्वत्या पुरोगतयाश्लिष्ट इत्यर्थः । अन्वभूदित्यनेनान्वयः । **कृती** कुशलो हरो **मेरुं एत्य** [**हेमपल्लवविभङ्गसंस्तरां**] हेमपल्लवानां विभङ्गाः खण्डास्त एव संस्तरस्तल्पं यस्यां तां तथोक्तां **क्षपां** रात्रिं **सुरततत्परः** सुरतासक्तः सन् **अन्वभूत्** ॥

पद्मनाभवलयाङ्कितास्मसु[9] प्राप्तवत्स्वमृतविप्रुषो नवाः ।
मन्दरस्य[11] कटकेषु चावसत्पार्वतीवदनपद्मषट्पदः ॥ २३ ॥

पद्मनाभेति ॥ [**पार्वतीवदनपद्मषट्पदः**] पार्वतीवदनपद्मे षट्पदः । प्रियामुखरसास्वादलोल इत्यर्थः । स हरः । [**पद्मनाभवलयाङ्कितास्मसु**] पद्मं नाभिर्यस्य स पद्मनाभो विष्णुः । 'अच्प्रत्यन्ववपूर्वात्सामलोम्नः' इत्यत्राजिति योगविभागात्समासान्तः । तस्य वलयैरङ्किता अश्मानो येषां तेषु । अमृतमथनसमय इति भावः । तथा **नवाः** प्रत्यग्राः **अमृतविप्रुषः** सुधाबिन्दून् **प्राप्तवत्सु मन्दरस्य** मन्थाचलस्य **कटकेषु** नितम्बेषु **च अवसत्** । एतेन मन्दरस्यानेकाद्भुताधारत्वान्मनोविनोदकत्वमुक्तम् ॥

रावणध्वनितभीतया[12] तया कण्ठसक्तमृदुबाहुबन्धनः[13] ।
एकपिङ्गलगिरौ जगद्गुरुर्निर्विवेश विशदाः शशिप्रभाः ॥ २४ ॥

---

१ चात्मनः. २ मासमेकम्. ३ नुमन्त्र्य. ४ खेदितम्. ५ संपतन्. ६ शुगोक्षकः. ७ पुरस्कृतान्. ८ संस्तरान्. ९ मर्दनक्षमान्. १० चरणा. ११ मान्दरेषु. १२ वारणध्वनित. १३ दृढ.

रावणेति ॥ **जगद्गुरुः** । [**रावणध्वनितभीतया**] विश्रवसोऽपत्यं रावणो दशकण्ठः । 'तस्यापत्यम्' इत्यण्प्रत्ययः । वृत्तिविषये विश्रवस्शब्दस्य रवणादेशः । रावणस्य ध्वनितात्कैलासोत्पाटनसमयक्ष्वेडिताद्भीतया **तया पार्वत्या** [**कण्ठसक्तमृदुबाहुबन्धनः**] कण्ठसक्ताभ्यां मृदुबाहुभ्यां बन्धनं यस्य स तथाभूतः । [**एकपिङ्गलगिरौ**] एकनेत्रत्वादेकपिङ्गलः कुबेरस्तस्य गिरौ कैलासे **विशदाः** निर्मलाः **शशिप्रभाः** चन्द्रिकाः **निर्विवेश** बुभुजे । ' निर्वेशो भृतिभोगयोः ' इत्यमरः ॥

तस्य जातु मलयस्थलीरतेर्[1]धूतचन्दनलतः प्रियाक्लमम् ।
आचचाम स[2]लवङ्गकेसरश्चाटुकार इव दक्षिणानिलः ॥ २५ ॥

तस्येति ॥ **जातु** कदाचित् **धूतचन्दनलतः** कम्पितपटीरशाखः । ' समे शाखालते' इत्यमरः । सह लवङ्गस्य केसरैः **सलवङ्गकेसरः** । 'लवङ्गं देवकुसुमम्' इत्यमरः । विशेषणाभ्यां शैत्यसौरभ्ये दर्शिते । **दक्षिणानिलः** मलयमारुतः । **चाटुकारः** चाटुप्रयोगः । प्रियवाद इति यावत् । भावे घञ् । सः **इव** [**मलयस्थलीरतेः**] मलयस्थलीषु मलयाचलप्रदेशेषु रतिः सुरतं यस्य तथोक्तस्य । तत्र रममाणस्येत्यर्थः । **तस्य** शिवस्य **प्रियाक्लमं** प्रियायाः सुरतश्रमं **आचचाम** जहार । यथा लोके महानपि श्रम एकेन प्रियवादेनापैति तद्वद्दक्षिणमारुतेनाप्यस्य सकलोऽपि सुरतक्लमो हृत इत्यर्थः ॥

हेमतामरसताडितप्रिया तत्कराम्बुविनिमीलितेक्षणा ।
खे[3] व्यगाहत तरंगिणीमुमा मीनपङ्क्तिपुनरुक्तमेखला ॥ २६ ॥

हेमेति ॥ **उमा** गौरी [**हेमतामरसताडितप्रिया**] हेमतामरसेन कनककमलेन ताडितः प्रियो यया सा । [**तत्कराम्बुविनिमीलितेक्षणा**] तेनोत्थितस्य प्रियस्य कराम्बुना कराक्षिप्ताम्भसा विनिमीलितेक्षणा मुकुलिताक्षी । [**मीनपङ्क्तिपुनरुक्तमेखला**] मीनपङ्क्त्या पुनरुक्ता द्विगुणिता मेखला यस्याः सा तथाभूता सती **खे तरंगिणीं व्यगाहत** । तत्र तत्र जलक्रीडामकरोदित्यर्थः ॥

तां पुलोमतनयालकोचितैः पारिजातकुसुमैः प्रसाधयन् ।
नन्दने चिरमयुग्मलोचनः सस्पृहं सुरवधूभिरीक्षितः ॥ २७ ॥

तामिति ॥ अयुग्मानि लोचनानि यस्य सः **अयुग्मलोचनः** त्र्यम्बकः । युग्मशब्दो विशेष्यनिघ्नोऽप्यस्ति । ' तास्मिन्युग्मासु संविशेत् ' ' युग्मान्दैवे यथाशक्ति पित्र्येऽयुग्मांस्तथैव च' इत्यादिप्रयोगदर्शनात् । **नन्दने** नन्दनोद्याने [**पुलोमतनयालकोचितैः**] पुलोमतनया शची । 'पुलोम्नस्तु शची सुता' इति हरिवंशे । तस्या अलकानामुचितैः **पारिजातकुसुमैः तां प्रसाधयन्** अलंकुर्वन् **चिरं सुरवधूभिः सस्पृहं ईक्षितः** । केन वा पुण्येनायं लभ्यत इति साभिलाषं दृष्ट इत्यर्थः । अत्र देवस्यानुकूलनायकत्वं देव्याः स्वाधीनपतिकात्वं चावसेयम् ॥

---

१ रते धूत. २ वन:. ३ सतुषारशीतल:. ४ सा. ५ मेखलाम्. ६ वधूभिरैक्ष्यत; वधूनिरीक्षित:.

इत्यभौममनुभूय शंकरः पार्थिवं च वनितासखः सुखम् ।
लोहितायति कदाचिदातपे गन्धमादनगिरिं न्यवर्तत ॥ २८ ॥

इतीति ॥ **इति** इत्थं **शंकरः वनितासखः** सन् । भूमौ भवं भौमम् । न भौमं **अभौमं** दिव्यं पृथिव्यां भवं **पार्थिवं च सुखं अनुभूय कदाचित् आतपे लोहितायति** लोहितवर्णे भवति । अस्तंगते सवितरीत्यर्थः । 'लोहितादिडाज्भ्यः क्यष्' इति क्यष्प्रत्ययः । **गन्धमादनगिरिं न्यवर्तत** । पर्वतमुद्दिश्य निवृत्त इत्यर्थः । उद्देशक्रियां प्रति गिरेः कर्मत्वम् । एतदेवाह भाष्यकारः ॥

तत्र काञ्चनशिलातलाश्रयो नेत्रगम्यमवलोक्य भास्करम् ।
दक्षिणेतरभुजव्यपाश्रयां व्याजहार सहधर्मचारिणीम् ॥ २९ ॥

तत्रेति ॥ **तत्र** ग. श्मादने । [**काञ्चनशिलातलाश्रयः**] काञ्चनविकारः काञ्चनं सौवर्णं तच्च तच्छिलातलं तदाश्रयो यस्य स भगवान् **नेत्रगम्यं** सायंतनम् । अर्धाद्दर्शनयोग्यम् । **भास्करं** सूर्यम् । 'दिवाविभा—' इत्यादिना टप्रत्ययः । **अवलोक्य** [**दक्षिणेतरभुजव्यपाश्रयां**] दक्षिणेतरभुजः सव्यबाहुर्व्यपाश्रयो यस्यास्ताम् । निजवामभुजमवष्टभ्योपविष्टामित्यर्थः । सह धर्मं चरतीति **सहधर्मचारिणीं** पत्नीं **व्याजहार** जगाद ॥

पद्मकान्तिमरुणत्रिभागयोः संक्रमय्य तव नेत्रयोरिव ।
संक्षये जगदिव प्रजेश्वरः संहरत्यहरसावहर्पतिः ॥ ३० ॥

पद्मकान्तिमिति ॥ **असौ** अह्नां पतिः **अहर्पतिः** सूर्यः । 'अहरादीनां पत्यादिषूपसंख्यानम्' इति रेफादेशः । **पद्मकान्तिं** पद्मशोभाम् । [**अरुणत्रिभागयोः**] तृतीयो भागस्त्रिभागः । वृत्तिविषये पूरणार्थत्वं संख्याया इत्युक्तम् । अरुणस्त्रिभागो ययोस्तयोः । अरुणोपान्तयोरिति भाग्यलक्षणोक्तिः । **तव नेत्रयोः संक्रमय्य इव** । तदानीं पद्मानामविकासान्नेत्रयोस्तु विकासाच्चेयमुत्प्रेक्षा । **संक्षये** प्रलयकाले **प्रजेश्वरः** प्रजापतिः **जगत् इव अहः** दिवसं **संहरति** । अस्तं गच्छतीत्यर्थः ॥

सीकरव्यतिकरं मरीचिभिर्दूरयत्यवनते विवस्वति ।
इन्द्रचापपरिवेषशून्यतां निर्झरास्तव पितुर्व्रजन्त्यमी ॥ ३१ ॥

सीकरेति ॥ विवस्तेजोऽस्यास्तीति विवस्वांस्तस्मिन् **विवस्वति** सूर्ये **मरीचिभिः** सहार्थविवक्षायां तृतीयात एव विनापि सहशब्देन तृतीया । **सीकरव्यतिकरं** पयःकणसंपर्कं **दूरयति** दूरीकुर्वति सति । हे **अवनते** पार्वति । **अमी तव पितुः** भवत्पितुर्हिमवतो **निर्झराः** प्रवाहाः । 'प्रवाहो निर्झरो झरः' इत्यमरः । [**इन्द्रचापपरिवेष-**

---

१ दयिता. २ वनम्. ३ व्यगाहत. ४ अरुणात्रिभागयोः. ५ संगमय्य. ६ धूनयति. ७ प्रसवितुः. ८ ते.

शून्यतां] इन्द्रचापं नानावर्णप्रभासमूहस्तस्य परिवेषेण परिवेष्टनेन शून्यतां **व्रजन्ति** । अर्ककिरणसंपर्ककृतत्वादिन्द्रचापस्य तन्निवृत्त्या निवृत्तिरित्यर्थः ॥

दष्टतामरसकेसरस्रजोः[1] क्रन्दतोर्विपरिवृत्तकण्ठयोः[2] ।
निघ्नयोः[3] सरसि चक्रवाकयोरल्पमन्तरमनल्पतां गतम् ॥ ३२ ॥

दष्टेति ॥ [**दष्टतामरसकेसरस्रजोः**] दष्टमर्धजग्धं तामरसकेसरं पद्मकिञ्जल्कम् । मुखद्वयेनैकमिति भावः । तत्स्रजत इति तथोक्तयोः **क्रन्दतोः** कूजतोः **विपरिवृत्तकण्ठयोः** परस्परालोकनार्थं वक्रीकृतग्रीवयोरित्यर्थः । **निघ्नयोः** दैवाधीनयोः । 'अधीनो निघ्न आयत्तः' इत्यमरः । [**चक्रवाकयोः**] चक्रवाकी च चक्रवाकश्च तयोः । 'पुमान्स्त्रिया' इत्येकशेषः । **सरसि अल्पं अन्तरं** व्यवधानं **अनल्पतां** आधिक्यं **गतम्** । सरसि वियुज्यमानयोर्महद्व्यवधानमभूदित्यर्थः ॥

स्थानमाह्निकमपास्य दन्तिनः सल्लकीविटपभङ्गवासितम् ।
आविभातचरणाय[4] गृह्णते वारि वारिरुहबद्धषट्पदम् ॥ ३३ ॥

स्थानमिति ॥ **दन्तिनः** गजाः । अह्नि भवं **आह्निकम्** । 'कालाट्ठञ्' । **स्थानं अपास्य** विहाय [**सल्लकीविटपभङ्गवासितं**] सल्लकी गजप्रिया काचिल्लता । 'सल्लकी स्याद्गजप्रिया' इति हलायुधः । तस्या विटपभङ्गैः पल्लवखण्डैर्वासितं सुरभितं [**वारिरुहबद्धषट्पदं**] वारिरुहेषु बद्धाः संयताः षट्पदा यस्मिंस्तत् **वारि** जलं [**आविभातचरणाय**] आविभातं प्रभातमारभ्य यच्चरणं तस्मै । तत्पर्याप्तमित्यर्थः । **गृह्णते** उपाददते । गजा हि भुक्तिपर्याप्तं जलं सकृदेव सायं पिबन्तीति प्रसिद्धम् ॥

पश्य पश्चिमदिगन्तलम्बिना निर्मितं मितकथे[5] विवस्वता ।
दीर्घया[6] प्रतिमया सरोम्भसां तापनीयमिव सेतुबन्धनम् ॥ ३४ ॥

पश्येति ॥ हे **मितकथे** हे मितभाषिणि । एतेन स्वस्य तत्संलापने लौल्यं सूचयति । **पश्चिमदिगन्तलम्बिना विवस्वता** कर्त्रा **दीर्घया** दिगन्तलम्बित्वादायतया **प्रतिमया** निजप्रतिबिम्बेन । 'प्रतिमानं प्रतिबिम्बं प्रतिमा प्रतियातना प्रतिच्छाया । प्रतिकृतिरर्चा पुंसि प्रतिनिधिरुपमोपमानं स्यात्' इत्यमरः । **सरोम्भसाम्** तपनीयविकारः **तापनीयं** हिरण्मयम् । 'तपनीयं शातकुम्भम्' इत्यमरः । **सेतुबन्धनं निर्मितम् इव** इत्युत्प्रेक्षा । अस्तमयसमये सरःपारावारिणामरुणमायतमर्कप्रतिबिम्बं हिरण्मयसेतुरिव दृश्यत इत्यर्थः । **पश्य** इति वाक्यार्थः कर्म ॥

उत्तरन्ति विनिकीर्य पल्वलं गाढपङ्कमतिवाहितातपाः ।
दंष्ट्रिणो वनवराहयूथपा दष्टभङ्गुरबिसाङ्कुरा इव ॥ ३५ ॥

---

१ स्रजोः. २ विरहदीनकण्ठयोः. ३ भिन्नयोः. ४ आविभाति शरणाय गच्छतः; सांध्यकर्मविधयेऽनुगृह्णते. ५ कथमिदम्. ६ लब्धया.

उत्तरन्तीति ॥ **दंष्ट्रिणः** दंष्ट्रावन्तः । व्रीह्यादित्वादिनिः । अत एव [**दष्टभङ्गुरबिसाङ्कुराः**] दष्टाः भङ्गुराः कुटिला बिसाङ्कुरा मृणालाङ्कुरा यैस्ते ते इव स्थिताः [**वनवराहयूथपाः**] वनवराहाणां यूथपाः । 'यूथनाथस्तु यूथपः' इत्यमरः । **गाढपङ्कं** अतिपङ्किलं **पल्वलं** अल्पसरः । 'वेशन्तः पल्वलं चाल्पसरः' इत्यमरः । **विनिकीर्य** विक्षिप्य **अतिवाहितातपाः उत्तरन्ति** पल्वलान्निर्गच्छन्ति ॥

एष वृक्षशिखरे कृतास्पदो जातरूपरसगौरमण्डलः[1] ।
हीयमानमहरत्ययातपं पीवरोरु पिबतीव बर्हिणः ॥ ३६ ॥

एष इति ॥ हे **पीवरोरु, एषः वृक्षशिखरे** वृक्षाग्रे **कृतास्पदः** कृतस्थितिः **जातरूपरसगौरमण्डलः** आतपरूषणात्काञ्चनद्रववद्रुगबर्हमण्डलः । 'चामीकरं जातरूपं महारजतकाञ्चने' इत्यमरः । बर्हमस्यास्तीति **बर्हिणः** मयूरः । 'फलबर्हाभ्यामिनज्वक्तव्यः' । **हीयमानं** क्षीयमाणं **अहरत्ययातपं** दिनान्तातपं **पिबति इव** । कथमन्यथा क्षीयमाणत्वमिति भावः ॥

पूर्वभागतिमिरप्रवृत्तिभिर्व्यक्त[2]पङ्कमिव जातमेकतः ।
खं हृतातपजलं विवस्वता भाति किंचिदिव शेषवत्सरः ॥३७॥

पूर्वभागेति ॥ [**पूर्वभागतिमिरप्रवृत्तिभिः**] पूर्वभागे प्राचीमूले तिमिरप्रवृत्तिभिर्ध्वान्तप्रसरैः **एकतः व्यक्तपङ्कं** स्फुटपङ्कं **इव जातं** तथा **विवस्वता** [**हृतातपजलं**] हृतमातप एव जलं यस्य तत्तथोक्तं **खं** आकाशं **किंचित्** ईषच्छेषोऽस्यास्तीति **शेषवत्** शुष्कं **सरः इव भाति** ॥

आविशद्भि[3]रुटजाङ्गणं[4] मृगैर्मूलसेकसरसैश्च वृक्षकैः ।
आश्रमाः प्रविशदग्निधेनवो बिभ्रति श्रियमुदीरिताग्नयः ॥ ३८ ॥

आविशद्भिरिति ॥ **उटजाङ्गणं** पर्णशालाङ्गणं **आविशद्भिः** । प्रविशद्भिरित्यर्थः । 'पर्णशालोटजोऽस्त्रियाम्' इत्यमरः । 'उपान्वध्याङ्वसः' इति कर्मत्वम् । **मृगैः** । तथा [**मूलसेकसरसैः**] मूलानां सेकेन सेचनेन सरसैः सद्रवैः **वृक्षकैः च** उपलक्षिताः । अल्पार्थे कप्रत्ययः । प्रविशन्त्यो वनादागच्छन्त्योऽग्निधेनवोऽग्निहोत्रार्था धेनवः येषु ते **प्रविशदग्निधेनवः उदीरिताग्नयः** च **आश्रमाः श्रियं बिभ्रति** ॥

बद्धकोशमपि तिष्ठति क्षणं सावशेषविवरं कुशेशयम् ।
षट्पदाय वसतिं ग्रहीष्यते प्रीतिपूर्वमिव दातुमन्तरम्[6] ॥ ३९ ॥

बद्धकोशमिति ॥ **बद्धकोशं अपि** । मुकुलितमपीत्यर्थः । **कुशेशयं** कर्तृ । 'शतपत्रं कुशेशयम्' इत्यमरः । **वसतिं ग्रहीष्यते** । स्थितिं करिष्यते इत्यर्थः । 'लृटः सद्वा' इति शतृप्रत्ययः । **षट्पदाय प्रीतिपूर्वं अन्तरं** अवकाशं **दातुं इव क्षणं सावशेषविवरं तिष्ठति** ॥

---

१ मण्डलम्. २ लग्न. ३ आवसद्भिः. ४ उटजाङ्कणं. ५ दग्ध. ६ उत्तरम्.

दूरलग्नपरिमेयरश्मिना वारुणी दिगरुणेन भानुना।
भाति केसरवतेव मण्डिता बन्धुजीवतिलकेन कन्यका ॥ ४०॥

दूरलग्नेति ॥ **वारुणी दिक्** प्रतीची [**दूरलग्नपरिमेयरश्मिना**] दूरं लग्ना अत एव परिमेया अल्पावशिष्टा रश्मयो यस्य तेन तथोक्तेन **अरुणेन** लोहितवर्णेन **भानुना केसरवता** किञ्जल्कवता [**बन्धुजीवतिलकेन**] बन्धुजीवं बन्धूककुसुमम्। 'बन्धूको बन्धुजीवकः' इत्यमरः। तदेव तिलकं तेन **मण्डिता** अलंकृता **कन्यका इव भाति** ॥

सामभिः सहचराः सहस्रशः स्यन्दनाश्वहृदयंगमस्वनैः।
भानुमग्निपरिकीर्णतेजसं संस्तुवन्ति किरणोष्मपायिनः ॥४१॥

सामभिरिति ॥ **किरणोष्मपायिनः** किरणोष्माणं पिबन्तीति तथोक्ताः। तथाहारा इत्यर्थः। चरन्तीति चराः। पचाद्यच्। सहभूताश्चराः **सहचराः** वालखिल्यप्रभृतयो महर्षयः [**अग्निपरिकीर्णतेजसं**] अग्नौ परिकीर्णं तेजो यस्य तत्तथोक्तम्। 'अग्निं वावादित्यः सायं प्रविशति' इति श्रुतेः। **भानुम्**। हृदयं गच्छन्तीति हृदयंगमा मनोरमाः। गमेः सुपीति वक्तव्यात्खच्। [**स्यन्दनाश्वहृदयंगमस्वनैः**] स्यन्दनाश्वानां हृदयंगमाः स्वना येषां तैः **सामभिः** सामवेदैः **सहस्रशः संस्तुवन्ति**। 'सामवेदेनास्तमये गीयते' इति श्रुतेः ॥

सोऽयमानतशिरोधरैर्हयैः कर्णचामरविघट्टितेक्षणैः।
अस्तमेति युगभुग्नकेसरैः संनिधाय दिवसं महोदधौ ॥ ४२॥

स इति ॥ **सः अयं** भानुः **दिवसं महोदधौ संनिधाय**। निधायेवेत्यर्थः। दिवसस्यादर्शनादियमुत्प्रेक्षा। **आनतशिरोधरैः** गगनावतरणान्नम्रकन्धरैरत एव **कर्णचामरविघट्टितेक्षणैः युगभुग्नकेसरैः** युगकुटिलितस्कन्धरोमभिः **हयैः अस्तं एति**। 'अस्तस्तु चरमक्ष्माभृत्' इत्यमरः ॥

खं प्रसुप्तमिव संस्थिते रवौ तेजसो महत ईदृशी गतिः।
तत्प्रकाशयति यावदुत्थितं मीलनाय खलु तावतश्च्युतम् ४३

खमिति ॥ **रवौ संस्थिते** अस्तमिते सति **खं** व्योम **प्रसुप्तं इव** निष्प्रकाशत्वान्निद्रितमिव। स्थितमित्यर्थः। युज्यते चैतदित्याह—**महतः तेजसः ईदृशी** वक्ष्यमाणप्रकारा **गतिः**। स्वभाव इत्यर्थः। तां गतिमेवाह—तदिति। **तत्** महत्तेजः **उत्थितं** सत् **यावत्**। स्थानमिति शेषः। **प्रकाशयति**। **तावतः**। स्थानादिति शेषः। अधः **च्युतं** सत्। **मीलनाय** संकोचाय **खलु** भवति। यत्र स्थाने तेजस्तिष्ठति तत्प्रकाशते

१ दूरमग्न; दूरमग्र. २ वारुणा. ३ कुसुमेन. ४स्यन्दनेश्वः स्यन्दनस्य. ५ स्वरैः. ६ शिरोरुहैः. ७ उद्गतम्. ८ तावता.

इति स्थितिः। यतो गच्छति न तत्प्रकाशते। अतः सूर्यापाये खं प्रसुप्तमिति युक्तोत्प्रेक्षेति भावः। अस्यार्थस्य तेजोमात्रसाधारण्येऽपि महति स्फुटमिति महद्ग्रहणं कृतम्॥

संध्ययाऽप्यनुगतं रवेर्वपुर्वन्द्यमस्तशिखरे समर्पितम्।
प्राक्तथेयमुदये पुरस्कृता नानुयास्यति कथं तमापदि॥ ४४॥

संध्ययेति॥ **संध्यया अपि अस्तशिखरे** अस्ताद्रिशृङ्गे **समर्पितं** निहितं **वन्द्यं रवेः वपुः अनुगतं** अन्वगामि। अस्तंगतं रविमन्वगादिति भावः। युक्तं चैतदित्याह—**प्राक्** पूर्वं **उदये तथा** तेन प्रकारेण **पुरस्कृता** अग्रतः कृता। पूजिता चेति गम्यते। प्रातः सूर्योदयात्प्रागेव संध्यागम इति हि प्रसिद्धम्। **इयं** संध्या **तं** रविं **आपदि** अस्तसमये **कथं न अनुयास्यति**। अनुयास्यत्येवेत्यर्थः। संपदसंपदोस्तुल्यरूपत्वमेव साधूनामिति भावः॥

रक्तपीतकपिशाः पयोमुचां कोटयः कुटिलकेशि भान्त्यमूः।
द्रक्ष्यसि त्वमिति सांध्यवेलया वर्तिकाभिरिव साधु वर्तिताः ४५

रक्तेति॥ हे **कुटिलकेशि**। 'स्वाङ्गाच्चोपसर्जनादसंयोगोपधात्' इति ङीप्। **अमूः** पुरोगताः रक्ताः पीताः कपिशाश्च **रक्तपीतकपिशाः**। नानावर्णा इत्यर्थः। 'चार्थे द्वन्द्वः'। न तु 'वर्णो वर्णेन' इति तत्पुरुषः, सामानाधिकरण्याभावात्। **पयोमुचां कोटयः** अभ्रयः। 'स्यात्कोटिरश्रौ चापाग्रे संख्याभेदप्रकर्षयोः' इति विश्वः। **त्वं द्रक्ष्यसि इति** हेतोरनया **सांध्यवेलया**। संध्ययेत्यर्थः। 'संधिवेलया' इति क्वचित्पाठः। **वर्तिकाभिः** चित्रशलाकाभिः **साधु वर्तिताः** उत्पादिताः **इव भान्ति**॥

सिंहकेसरसटासु भूभृता पल्लवप्रसविषु द्रुमेषु च।
पश्य धातुशिखरेषु चात्मना संविभक्तमिव सांध्यमातपम्॥४६॥

सिंहेति॥ [**सिंहकेसरसटासु**] सिंहानां केसराणि स्कन्धरोमाणि तान्येव सटा जटास्तासु। 'सटा जटाकेसरयोः' इति विश्वः। अथ वा सटाशब्देन समूहो लक्ष्यतेऽन्यथा पौनरुक्त्यात्। **पल्लवप्रसविषु** पल्लववत्सु **द्रुमेषु च** तथा **धातुशिखरेषु च भूभृता** अस्ताद्रिणा **आत्मना** स्वयमेव **संविभक्तं इव** स्थितं संध्यायां भवं **सांध्यं आतपं पश्य**। आरुण्यमरुणद्रव्येषु भूयिष्ठमुपलभ्यत इति भावः॥

पार्ष्णिमुक्तवसुधास्तपस्विनः पावनाम्बुरचिताञ्जलिक्रियाः।
ब्रह्म गूढमभिसंध्यमादृताः शुद्धये विधिविदो गृणन्त्यमी ४७

---

१ पदम्. २ घर्मम्. ३ येन पूर्वम्. ४ सांधिवेलया; संध्ययाऽनया. ५ वर्णिकाभिः. ६ मण्डिताः. ७ भूभृताम्. ८ धातुशिखरेषु भानुना; धातुशिखरेषु चात्मनः; चास्तशिखरे विवस्वता ९ अद्रिराजतनये. १० विहिता. ११ सांध्य. १२ सिद्धये.

पार्ष्णीति ॥ [**पार्ष्णिमुक्तवसुधाः**] पार्ष्ण्योर्गुल्फाधोभागास्तैर्मुक्तवसुधास्त्यक्तभूतलाः । पादाग्रस्थिता इत्यर्थः ।'गोशृङ्गमात्रमुद्धृत्य मुक्तपार्ष्णिः क्षिपेज्जलम्'इति स्मरणात् । [**पावनाम्बुरचिताञ्जलिक्रियाः**] पावनैरम्बुभी रचिताञ्जलिक्रियाः । विहितार्घ्यप्रक्षेपा इत्यर्थः । **विधिविदः** । शास्त्रज्ञा इत्यर्थः । **अमी तपस्विनः आदृताः** आदरवन्तः । श्रद्दधाना इत्यर्थः । कर्तरि क्तः । **अभिसंध्यं** संध्यामभि । 'लक्षणेनाभिप्रती आभिमुख्ये' इत्यव्ययीभावः । **शुद्धये** शुद्ध्यर्थं **ब्रह्म** गायत्रीं **गूढं** उपांशु **गृणन्ति** जपन्ति । 'प्रत्यगा तारकोदयात्' इति स्मरणात् ॥

तन्मुहूर्तमनुमन्तुमर्हसि प्रस्तुताय नियमाय मामपि ।
त्वां विनोदनिपुणः सखीजनो वल्गुवादिनि विनोदयिष्यति ४८

तदिति ॥ **तत्** तस्मात्कारणात् **मां अपि प्रस्तुताय नियमाय** प्रकृतसंध्याविधये **मुहूर्तं अनुमन्तुं अर्हसि** । हे वल्गुवादिनि मञ्जुभाषिणि, **विनोदनिपुणः** कालाक्षेपचतुरः **सखीजनः त्वां विनोदयिष्यति** । विनोदशब्दात्तत्करोतीति णिच् ॥

निर्विभुज्य दशनच्छदं ततो वाचि भर्तुरवधीरणापरा ।
शैलराजतनया समीपगामाललाप विजयामहेतुकम् ॥ ४९ ॥

निर्विभुज्येति ॥ **ततः भर्तुः वाचि** वचने **अवधीरणापरा** अवज्ञापरा **शैलराजतनया** पार्वती । छाद्यतेऽनेनेति छदः । 'पुंसि संज्ञायां घः प्रायेण' इति घप्रत्ययः । **दशनच्छदं निर्विभुज्य** कुटिलीकृत्य **समीपगां विजयां** विजयाख्यां सखीं **अहेतुकं** निर्निमित्तं **आललाप** । न तु रोषाद्भर्तुरुत्तरं ददावित्यर्थः ॥

ईश्वरोऽपि दिवसात्ययोचितं मन्त्रपूर्वमनुतस्थिवान्विधिम् ।
पार्वतीमवचनामसूयया प्रत्युपेत्य पुनराह सस्मितम् ॥ ५० ॥

ईश्वर इति ॥ **ईश्वरः अपि दिवसात्ययोचितं** सायंकालोचितं **विधिं** संध्यावन्दनकृत्यं **मन्त्रपूर्वं अनुतस्थिवान्** अनुष्ठितवान् । तिष्ठतेः क्वसुप्रत्ययः । **असूयया** संध्यावन्दनजनितासूयया **अवचनां** अभाषमाणां **पार्वतीं पुनः प्रत्युपेत्य सस्मितं आह** ॥

मुञ्च कोपमनिमित्तकोपने संध्यया प्रणमितोऽस्मि नान्यथा ।
किं न वेत्सि सहधर्मचारिणं चक्रवाकसमवृत्तिमात्मनः ॥ ५१ ॥

मुञ्चेति ॥ हे **अनिमित्तकोपने** अकारणकोपिनि । नन्द्यादित्वात्कर्तरि ल्युः । **कोपं** मानं **मुञ्च** । **संध्यया प्रणमितः अस्मि** प्रणामं कारितोऽस्मि । **अन्यथा** प्रकारान्तरं **न** । धर्माभिसंधायिनं मां कामाभिसंधायिनं मा मन्यस्वेत्यर्थः । **आत्मनः** तव सह धर्मं चरतीति **सहधर्मचारिणं** मां [**चक्रवाकसमवृत्तिं**] चक्रवाकेन समवृत्तिं तुल्यव्यवहारं **न वेत्सि किम्** । अनन्यसङ्गिनं वेत्स्येवेत्यर्थः ॥

---

१ सहेतुकम्. २ अनुतिष्ठवान्. ३ सोऽभ्युपेत्य. ४ प्रयमितः. ५ नान्यथा.

प्रणामकारणमाह—

निर्मितेषु पितृषु स्वयंभुवा या तनुः सुतनु पूर्वमुज्झिता ।
सेयमस्तमुदयं च सेव्यते तेन मानिनि ममात्र गौरवम् ॥ ५२॥

निर्मितेष्विति ॥ हे **सुतनु** सुगात्रि, **पूर्वं** [**स्वयंभुवा**] स्वयं भवतीति स्वयंभूश्चतुराननः । 'भुवः संज्ञान्तरयोः' इति क्विप् । मयूरव्यंसकादित्वात्समासः । तेन **पितृषु** अग्निष्वात्तादिषु **निर्मितेषु** सत्सु **या तनुः उज्झिता सा इयं** तनुः **अस्तं** अस्तमयकाले **उदयं** उदयकाले । अव्ययमेतत् । **सेव्यते** पूज्यते **च** । संध्यारूपेणेति शेषः । हे **मानिनि** । अविमृश्यकारिणीति भावः । **तेन** ब्रह्मतनुत्वेन हेतुना **मम अत्र** संध्यायां **गौरवं** आदरः । तदेतदुक्तं भविष्यपुराणे—'पितामहः पितॄन्सृष्ट्वा मूर्तिं तामुत्ससर्ज ह । प्रातः सायं समागत्य संध्यारूपेण पूज्यते ॥ एतां संध्यां यतात्मानो ये तु दीर्घामुपासते । दीर्घायुषो भविष्यन्ति नीरुजः पाण्डुनन्दन ॥' इति ॥

इत्थं देव्याः कोपमपनीय धातुसंध्यादिवर्णनं करोति—

तामिमां तिमिरवृत्तिपीडितां भूमिलग्नमिव संप्रति स्थिताम् ।
एकतस्तटतमालमालिनीं पश्य धातुरसनिम्नगामिव ॥ ५३ ॥

तामिति ॥ **संप्रति तिमिरवृत्तिपीडितां** तमोवृत्त्युपरुद्धामत एव [**भूमिलग्नं**] भूमौ लग्नं **इव स्थितां तां इमां** संध्यां **एकतः** एकत्र **तटतमालमालिनीं** तीरतमालतरुपङ्क्तिमतीम् । व्रीह्यादित्वादिनिः । **धातुरसनिम्नगां** धातुद्रवनदीं **इव पश्य** ॥

सांध्यमस्तमितशेषमातपं रक्तलेखमपरा बिभर्ति दिक् ।
संपरायवसुधा सशोणितं मण्डलाग्रमिव तिर्यगुत्थितम् ॥ ५४ ॥

सांध्यमिति ॥ **अपरा दिक्** प्रतीची । अस्तमिति मकारान्तमव्ययम् । तस्येतशब्देन समासः । **अस्तमितशेषं** अस्तंगतावशिष्टमत एव [**रक्तलेखं**] रक्तालेखाकृतिर्यस्य तं संध्यायां भवं **सांध्यं आतपं संपरायवसुधा** युद्धभूमिः । 'समरे संपरायः स्यात्' इति विश्वः । **तिर्यगुत्थितं** तिर्यक्फलितं **सशोणितं मण्डलाग्रं** कृपाणं **इव बिभर्ति** । 'कौक्षेयको मण्डलाग्रः करवालः कृपाणवत्' इत्यमरः ॥

यामिनीदिवससंधिसंभवे तेजसि व्यवहिते सुमेरुणा ।
एतदन्धतमसं निरर्गलं दिक्षु दीर्घनयने विजृम्भते ॥ ५५ ॥

यामिनीति ॥ [**यामिनीदिवससंधिसंभवे**] यामिनीदिवसयोः संधिः संध्या तत्र संभवे **तेजसि** संध्यारागे **सुमेरुणा व्यवहिते** सति हे **दीर्घनयने एतत् अन्धतमसम्** । 'अवसमन्धेभ्यस्तमसः' इति समासान्तः । **दिक्षु निरर्गलं विजृम्भते** ॥

---

१ उत्थिता. २ सेवते. ३ वृद्धि. ४ शैलराजतनयेऽधुना स्थिताम्. ५ संप्रतिष्ठिताम्. ६ सांपराय. ७ उज्झितम्. ८ निरङ्कुशम्.

नोर्ध्वमीक्षणगतिर्न चाप्यधो नाभितो न पुरतो न पृष्ठतः ।
लोक एष तिमिरोल्बवेष्टितो गर्भवास इव वर्तते निशि ॥ ५६ ॥

नेति ॥ ऊर्ध्वं उपरि ईक्षणगतिः दृष्टिप्रसारः न अस्ति । अधः अपि च न । अभितः पार्श्वयोश्च न । पुरतः अग्रे च न । पृष्ठतः पश्चादपि न । ईक्षणगतिरिति सर्वत्र संबध्यते । तथापि एषः लोकः निशि [तिमिरोल्बवेष्टितः] तिमिरमेवोल्बं जरायुः । 'गर्भाशयो जरायुः स्यादुल्बं च कललोऽस्त्रियाम्' इत्यमरः । तेन वेष्टितः आवृतः सन् । गर्भ एव वासो वसतिस्तत्र गर्भवासे वर्तते । इव इत्युत्प्रेक्षा ॥

शुद्धमाविलमवस्थितं चलं वक्रमार्जवगुणान्वितं च यत् ।
सर्वमेव तमसा समीकृतं धिङ्महत्त्वमसतां हैतान्तरम् ॥ ५७ ॥

शुद्धमिति ॥ शुद्धं स्वच्छं आविलं मलिनं अवस्थितं स्थावरं चलं जंगमं वक्रं कुटिलं [आर्जवगुणान्वितं] ऋजोर्भाव आर्जवं तदेव गुणस्तेनान्वितं च यत् वस्तुजातम् । तदिति यत्तदोर्नित्यसंबन्धाल्लभ्यते । तत् सर्वं एव तमसा समीकृतं दुर्लक्ष्यविशेषं कृतम् । तथा हि । हतमन्तरं विशेषो येन तत् हतान्तरं असतां असाधूनां महत्त्वं शुद्धि धिक् । धिक्शब्दयोगाद्द्वितीया । समत्वेन परगतिविशेषतिरस्करणमसतां स्वभाव इति सुप्रसिद्धम् । तमसोऽपि तथा महत्त्वं धिगित्यर्थः ॥

नूनमुन्नमति[3] यज्वनां पतिः शार्वरस्य तमसो निषिद्धये ।
पुण्डरीकमुखि पूर्वदिङ्मुखं कैतकैरिव रजोभिरावृतम् ॥ ५८ ॥

नूनमिति ॥ [यज्वनां] यज्वानो विधिनेष्टवन्तः । 'यज्वा तु विधिनेष्टवान्' इत्यमरः । 'सुयजोर्ङ्वनिप्' इति ङ्वनिप्प्रत्ययः । तेषां पतिः प्रियः । दर्शपूर्णमासादियागप्रवृत्तिहेतुत्वादिति भावः । शार्वरस्य शर्वर्या भवस्य तमसः निषिद्धये निरासाय नूनं उन्नमति उदेति । कुतः । हे पुण्डरीकमुखि, पूर्वस्या दिशो मुखं पुरोभागः पूर्वदिङ्मुखं [कैतकैः] केतक्या इमानि कैतकानि तैः रजोभिः परागैः आवृतं इव । दृश्यत इति शेषः । अतो नूनमुदेति चन्द्र इति संबन्धः ॥

मन्दरान्तरितमूर्तिना निशा लक्ष्यते शशभृता सतारका ।
त्वं मया प्रियसखीसमागता श्रोष्यतेव वचनानि पृष्ठतः ॥ ५९ ॥

मन्दरेति ॥ सतारका निशा मन्दरान्तरितमूर्तिना मन्दराद्रिव्यवाहितमण्डलेन शशभृता चन्द्रेण पृष्ठतः पश्चाद्भागे वचनानि श्रोष्यता । श्रोतुं स्थितेनेत्यर्थः । मया प्रियसखीसमागता प्रियसखीभिरावृता त्वं इव लक्ष्यते ॥

---

१ तिमिरौघ. २ हतान्तरम्; अन्तरम्. ३ [illegible] ४ [illegible] दिङ्मुखं [illegible]. ५ आवृतम्.

रुद्धनिर्गमनमा दिनक्षयात्पूर्वदृष्टतनुचन्द्रिकास्मितम् ।
एतदुद्गिरति रात्रिचोदिता दिग्रहस्यमिव चन्द्रमण्डलम् ॥ ६० ॥

रुद्धेति ॥ **दिक्** पूर्वदिक् । नायिका ध्वन्यते । **आ दिनक्षयात्** आ सायं [**रुद्धनिर्गमनं**] रुद्धं निर्गमनं निःसरणं यस्य तत्तथोक्तम् । अन्यत्र बहिरप्रकाशितमित्यर्थः । [**पूर्वदृष्टतनुचन्द्रिकास्मितं**] तनुचान्द्रिका स्मितमिव तनुचन्द्रिकास्मितं पूर्वदृष्टं यस्मात्तत्तथोक्तम् । **एतत् चन्द्रमण्डलं** कर्म **रहस्यं** गोप्यार्थं **इव रात्रिचोदिता** । रात्र्या सख्येव प्रेरिता सतीत्यर्थः । **उद्गिरति** प्रकाशयति । यथा काचिदा सायं मनस्विनी गूहितमभिलाषं प्रदोषे सख्या मह्यं ब्रूहीति निर्बन्धात्पृष्टा सती प्रकटयति तद्वदित्यर्थः ॥

पश्य पक्वफलिनीफलत्विषा बिम्बलाञ्छितवियत्सरोम्भसा ।
विप्रकृष्टविवरं हिमांशुना चक्रवाकमिथुनं विडम्ब्यते ॥ ६१ ॥

पश्येति ॥ **पक्वफलिनीफलत्विषा** उदयरागात [**बिम्बलाञ्छितवियत्सरोम्भसा**] बिम्बाभ्यां प्रतिबिम्बाभ्यां लाञ्छिते चिह्निते वियत्सरोम्भश्च येन तथोक्तेन **हिमांशुना** [**विप्रकृष्टविवरं**] विप्रकृष्टं विवरमन्तरालं यस्य तत्तथोक्तम् । अतिदूरस्थमित्यर्थः । **चक्रवाकमिथुनं विडम्ब्यते** अनुक्रियते **पश्य** । रात्रौ वियति सरोजले चेन्दोर्बिम्बप्रातिबिम्बौ विरहाद्दूरवर्तिनौ चक्रवाकाविव दृश्येते इत्यर्थः ॥

शक्यमोषधिपतेर्नवोदयाः कर्णपूररचनाकृते तव ।
अप्रगल्भयवसूचिकोमलाश्छेत्तुमग्रनखसंपुटैः कराः ॥ ६२ ॥

शक्यमिति ॥ **नवोदयाः** सद्य उत्पादिताः **अप्रगल्भयवसूचिकोमलाः** अकठोरयवाङ्कुरसुकुमाराः **ओषधिपतेः** इन्दोः **कराः तव कर्णपूररचनाकृते** कर्णावतंसनिर्माणक्रियायै । संपदादित्वाद्भावे क्विप् । **अग्रनखसंपुटैः** नखाग्रसंभेदैः **छेत्तुं शक्यम्** । शक्या इत्यर्थः । 'शकिसहोश्च' इति कर्मणि यत्प्रत्ययः । शक्यमिति विपरीतलिङ्गवचनस्यापि सामान्योपक्रमात्कर्माभिधायकत्वम् । पश्चात्कर्मविशेषाकाङ्क्षायां करा इति निर्देशो न विरुध्यते । यथाह वामनः—'शक्यमिति रूपं विलिङ्गवचनस्यापि सामान्योपक्रमात् । अत्र प्रमाणं–शक्यं श्वमांसेनापि क्षुत्प्रतिहन्तुमिति भाष्यकारप्रयोगः' इति ॥

अङ्गुलीभिरिव केशसंचयं संनिगृह्य तिमिरं मरीचिभिः ।
कुड्मलीकृतसरोजलोचनं चुम्बतीव रजनीमुखं शशी ॥ ६३ ॥

अङ्गुलीभिरिति ॥ **शशी** चन्द्रमाः । नायकस्तु प्रतीयते । **अङ्गुलीभिः केशसंचयं इव मरीचिभिः तिमिरं संनिगृह्य** गृहीत्वा । [**कुड्मलीकृतसरोजलो-**

---

१ चन्द्रमण्डलं...मिव रात्रिनोदितम्. २ विप्रकृष्टविधुरम्–विरहम्; विप्रकृष्टविवरम्. ३ शक्यः. ४ नवोदयः. ५ नवः. ६ कोमलः. ७ करः.

चनं] सरोजे लोचने इवेत्युपमितसमासोऽङ्गुलीभिरिवेत्युपमायास्तत्साधकत्वात् । कुङ्कुलीकृते सरोजलोचने यस्य तत्तथोक्तं [रजनीमुखं] रजन्या मुखं प्रारम्भः । वदनं चेति गम्यते । चुम्बति इव । अत्रार्थापत्त्यतिशयोक्तिरलंकार उत्प्रेक्षासंकरश्चेति ॥

पश्य पार्वति नवेन्दुरश्मिभिः सामिभिन्नतिमिरं नभस्तलम् ।
लक्ष्यते द्विरदभोगदूषितं संप्रसीदादिव मानसं सरः ॥ ६४ ॥

पश्येति ॥ हे पार्वति, नवेन्दुरश्मिभिः सामिभिन्नतिमिरं अर्धनिरस्तध्वान्तं नभस्तलं द्विरदभोगदूषितं गजक्रीडाकलुषितं संप्रसीदत् प्रसादं गच्छत् मानसं मानसाख्यं सरः इव लक्ष्यते पश्य ॥

रक्तभावमपहाय चन्द्रमा जात एष परिशुद्धमण्डलः ।
विक्रिया न खलु कालदोषजा निर्मलप्रकृतिषु स्थिरोदया ॥ ६५ ॥

रक्तभावमिति ॥ एषः चन्द्रमाः रक्तभावं रक्तत्वमुदयरागं अपहाय परिशुद्धमण्डलः शुभ्रबिम्बो निष्कण्टको जातः । तथा हि । निर्मलप्रकृतिषु स्वच्छभावेषु शुद्धसचित्तसंपन्नेषु च कालदोषेण जाता कालदोषजा विक्रिया विकारः स्थिरोदया स्थायिनी न भवति खलु । चन्द्रोऽपि स्वभावनिर्मल इति । यथा कश्चिद्राजा कुतश्चिन्निमित्ताद्विरक्तमण्डलः पश्चात्प्रकृतिकृतशुद्धया स्वस्थमण्डलो भवति तद्वदिति भावः । तत्र प्रथमार्थे समासोक्तिरलंकारस्तस्यार्थान्तरन्यासेनाङ्गाङ्गिभावेन संकरः ॥

उन्नतेषु शशिनः प्रभा स्थिता निम्नसंश्रयपरं निशातमः ।
नूनमात्मसदृशी प्रकल्पिता वेधसैव गुणदोषयोर्गतिः ॥ ६६ ॥

उन्नतेष्विति ॥ शशिनः प्रभा चन्द्रिका उन्नतेषु अद्रिशृङ्गादिषु स्थिता । निशातमः तु निम्नसंश्रयपरं गर्तादिनीचस्थानप्रवणम् । तथा हि । वेधसा गुणदोषयोः आत्मसदृशी स्वभावानुरूपा गतिः प्रवृत्तिः प्रकल्पितैव नूनम् । तेजस्विन उन्नमन्ति मलिनास्तु नीचन्तीति भावः ॥

चन्द्रपादजनितप्रवृत्तिभिश्चन्द्रकान्तजलबिन्दुभिर्गिरिः ।
मेखलातरुषु निद्रितानमून्बोधयत्यसमये शिखण्डिनः ॥ ६७ ॥

चन्द्रपादेति ॥ गिरिः हिमाद्रिः [चन्द्रपादजनितप्रवृत्तिभिः] चन्द्रपादैरिन्दुकिरणैर्जनितप्रवृत्तिभिर्जनितप्रसरैः [चन्द्रकान्तजलबिन्दुभिः] चन्द्रकान्तमणीनां जलबिन्दुभिः करणैः मेखलातरुषु निद्रितान् संजातनिद्रान् । तारकादित्वादितच् । अमून् शिखण्डिनः मयूरान् असमये अकाले बोधयति । इन्दुकिरणसंपर्कादुपरि चन्द्रमणिस्पन्देष्वधोवृक्षेशयाः शिखण्डिनो वृष्टिभयाज्जाग्रतीत्यर्थः । शिखण्डिग्रहणमितरशकुन्तानां कुलायनिलयत्वादिति भावः ॥

---

१ भिन्नसान्द्र; भग्नसान्द्र; संविभिन्न. २ संप्रसादम्. ३ एव. ४ इह; हि. ५ इमान्.

कल्पवृक्षशिखरेषु संप्रति प्रस्फुरद्भिरविकल्पसुन्दरि ।
हारयष्टिगणनामिवांशुभिः कर्तुमुद्यतकुतूहलः शशी ॥ ६८ ॥

कल्पवृक्षेति ॥ हे अविकल्पेनाविवादेन सुन्दरि **अविकल्पसुन्दरि, शशी संप्रति [कल्पवृक्षशिखरेषु]** कल्पवृक्षाणां शिखरेष्वग्रेषु **प्रस्फुरद्भिः अंशुभिः** करस्थानीयैरिति भावः । **हारयष्टिगणनां** कल्पतरुलम्बिहारपरिगणनां **कर्तुं उद्यतकुतूहलः इव** उत्पन्नकौतुकः किमु । इत्युत्प्रेक्षा ॥

उन्नतावनतभागवत्तया चन्द्रिका सतिमिरा गिरेरियम् ।
भक्तिभिर्बहुविधाभिरर्पिताऽऽभाति भूतिरिव मत्तदन्तिनः ॥६९॥

उन्नतेति ॥ **गिरेः उन्नतावनतभागवत्तया** निम्नोन्नतप्रदेशवत्त्वेन हेतुना **सतिमिरा** तिमिरमिश्रा । समोन्नतेषु तमसोऽनवकाशादिति भावः । **इयं चन्द्रिका बहुविधाभिः भक्तिभिः** रचनाभिः **अर्पिता** विन्यस्ता **मत्तदन्तिनः भूतिः** भसितं **इव आभाति** । 'भूतिर्मातङ्गशृङ्गारे जातौ भस्मनि संपदि' इति विश्वः । तत्र भक्तिसहितानि गजाङ्गान्येव तिमिरभागोपमानमित्यनुसंधेयम् ॥

एतदुच्छ्वसितपीतमैन्दवं सोढुमक्षममिव प्रभारसम् ।
मुक्तषट्पदविरावमञ्जसा भिद्यते कुमुदमा निबन्धनात् ॥ ७० ॥

एतदिति ॥ **एतत् कुमुदं** कैरवं कर्तृ उच्छ्वसितेन पीतं **उच्छ्वसितपीतम्** । अतितृष्णयोच्छ्वस्योच्छ्वस्य पीतमित्यर्थः । इन्दोरिमं **ऐन्दवं [प्रभारसं]** प्रभा चन्द्रिका सैव रसो द्रवस्तं **सोढुं अक्षमं इव अञ्जसा मुक्तषट्पदविरावं** प्रवर्तितभृङ्गनादं यथा तथा **निबन्धनात् आ** वृन्तात् **भिद्यते** विकसति । कर्मकर्तरि लट् । यथा लोके कस्यचिदतिपानान्निःसहात्मन उच्चैः क्रोशत उदरं भिद्यते तथैतदिति भावः ॥

पश्य कल्पतरुलम्बि शुद्धया ज्योत्स्नया जनितरूपसंशयम् ।
मारुते चलति चण्डि केवलं व्यज्यते विपरिवृत्तमंशुकम् ॥ ७१ ॥

पश्येति ॥ **शुद्धया ज्योत्स्नया [जनितरूपसंशयं]** जनितो रूपसंशयः अंशुकं ज्योत्स्ना वेति स्वरूपसंदेहो यस्य तत्तथोक्तं **कल्पतरुलम्बि अंशुकं** हे **चण्डि** अत्यन्तकोपने । गौरादित्वान्ङीष् । **केवलं मारुते चलति** सति **विपरिवृत्तं** चलं सत् **व्यज्यते पश्य** । ज्योत्स्नासच्छायत्वान्न रूपतो विविच्यते परं तु क्रिययेत्यर्थः ॥

शक्यमङ्गुलिभिरुद्धृतैरधः शाखिनां पतितपुष्पपेशलैः ।
पत्रजर्जरशशिप्रभालवैरेभिरुत्कचयितुं तवालकान् ॥ ७२ ॥

---

१ इव पश्य सुन्दरि; इव शम्भुसुन्दरि. २ रचनाम्. ३ आगत. ४ भागवत्तया. ५ भाति. ६ हस्तिनः. ७ उच्छ्वसितपीतम्. ८ बालुभ्. ९ चण्डिके बलात्; चण्डिके चलम्. १० उत्थितैः. ११ कोमलैः. १२ अलकम्—अलकाः.

शक्यमिति ॥ **अङ्गुलिभिः उद्धृतैः** उच्चितैः **शाखिनां अधः** । [**पतितपुष्पपेशलैः**] पतितपुष्पवत्पेशलैः कोमलैः । तथा भ्रमकरैरित्यर्थः । **एभिः** [**पत्रजर्जरशशिप्रभालवैः**] पत्रैर्जर्जरा शकलिता शशिप्रभा चन्द्रिका तस्या **लवैः** **खण्डैः** । तरुतलेषु पत्रान्तरालक्ष्यज्योत्स्नामण्डलैरित्यर्थः । **तव अलकान् उत्कचयितुं** बन्द्धुम् । 'कच दीप्तिबन्धनयोः' इति धातोस्तुमुन्प्रत्ययः । **शक्यम्** । शक्या इत्यर्थः । शक्यमिति विलिङ्गवचनस्य सामान्योपक्रमादित्याद्युपदमेवोक्तम् ॥

एष चारुमुखि योगतारया युज्यते तरलबिम्बया शशी ।
साध्वसादुपगतप्रकम्पया कन्ययेव नवदीक्षया वरः ॥ ७३ ॥

एष इति ॥ हे **चारुमुखि** हे उज्ज्वलानने । 'स्वाङ्गाच्चोपसर्जनादसंयोगोपधात्' इति ङीष् । **एषः शशी तरलबिम्बया** स्फुरन्मण्डलया **योगतारया** । प्रत्यहं यया युज्यते सा योगतारा । नित्यनक्षत्रेणेत्यर्थः । **साध्वसात्** नवसंगमभयात् **उपगतप्रकम्पया** वेपथुमत्या **नवदीक्षया** नवोद्वाहया **कन्यया वरः** वोढा **इव युज्यते** संगच्छते । युजेर्दैवादिकत्वात्कर्तरि लट् ॥

पाकभिन्नशरकाण्डगौरयोरुल्लसत्प्रतिकृतिप्रदीप्तयोः ।
रोहतीव तव गण्डलेखयोश्चन्द्रबिम्बनिहिताक्षि चन्द्रिका ॥ ७४ ॥

पाकेति ॥ हे **चन्द्रबिम्बनिहिताक्षि** चन्द्रबिम्बनिहितेक्षणे । [**पाकभिन्नशरकाण्डगौरयोः**] पाकभिन्नः पाकविकसितो यः शरकाण्डस्तद्वद्गौरयोः सितयोः । 'अवदातः सितो गौरः' इत्यमरः । [**उल्लसत्प्रतिकृतिप्रदीप्तयोः**] उल्लसन्त्या प्रतिकृत्या चन्द्रिकाप्रतिबिम्बेन प्रदीप्तयोः प्रोज्ज्वलयोः **तव गण्डलेखयोः चन्द्रिका रोहति इव** । गण्डस्थलप्रतिबिम्बसंक्रमणमूर्छिता चन्द्रिका तयोरेव प्ररूढेति प्रतीयत इत्यर्थः ॥

अत्रान्तरे कांचिदवलोक्याह—

लोहितार्कमणिभाजनार्पितं कल्पवृक्षमधु बिभ्रती स्वयम् ।
त्वामियं स्थितिमतीमुपस्थिता गन्धमादनवनाधिदेवता ॥ ७५ ॥

लोहितेति ॥ [**लोहितार्कमणिभाजनार्पितं**] लोहितेऽरुणेऽर्कमणिभाजने सूर्यकान्तपात्रेऽर्पितं **कल्पवृक्षमधु** कल्पतरुप्रसूतं मद्यं **स्वयं बिभ्रती गन्धमादनवनाधिदेवता स्थितिमतीं** अवस्थानवतीम् । इह स्ववने तिष्ठन्तीमित्यर्थः । **त्वां इयं** प्रत्यक्षा **उपस्थिता** प्राप्ता । स्वगृहागतां त्वां संभावयितुमागतेत्यर्थः ॥

आर्द्रकेसरसुगन्धि ते मुखं रक्तमेव नयनं स्वभावतः ।
अत्र लब्धवसतिर्गुणान्तरं कं विलासिनि मदः करिष्यति ॥ ७६ ॥

---

१ चन्द्रमुखि. २ पश्य तारया; योग्यतारया. ३ पाण्डु. ४ प्रकृतिजप्रसादयोः; प्रतिकृतिप्रसन्नयोः. ५ उपागता; समागता. ६ मत्तरक्तनयनम्; प्रान्तरक्तनयनम्; मत्तमेव नयनम्. ७ किमु. ८ मदैः.

आर्द्रेति ॥ हे पार्वति, इदं ते **स्वभावतः आर्द्रकेसरसुगन्धि** सरसकेसरसुगन्धि । 'गन्धस्येत्-' इत्यादिनेकारः । **मुखम्** । **रक्तं एव नयनम्** । हे **विलासिनि** विलसनशीले, **अत्र** त्वन्मुखे **लब्धवसतिः** लब्धानुप्रवेशो **मधुः** मद्यं **कं गुणान्तरं** गुणविशेषं **करिष्यति** । न कंचिदित्यर्थः । केसरसौगन्ध्यादिगुणानां त्वन्मुखे स्वभावसिद्धत्वान्मधुनः फलं न पश्यामीत्यर्थः । 'अर्धर्चाः पुंसि च' इति पुंलिङ्गत्वम् । यदाहुः—'मकरन्दस्य मद्यस्य माक्षिकस्य च वाचकः । अर्धर्चादिगणे पाठात्पुंनपुंसकयोर्मधुः' इति ॥

मान्यभक्तिरथ वा सखीजनः सेव्यतामिदमनङ्गदीपकम्[1] ।
इत्युदारमभिधाय शंकरस्तामपाययत पानमम्बिकाम् ॥ ७७ ॥

मान्यभक्तिरिति ॥ **अथ वा सखीजनः [मान्यभक्तिः]** मान्या भक्तिर्यस्य स तथोक्तः । सखीजनः स्वीकार्य इत्यर्थः । ततः **अनङ्गदीपकं इदं** वक्ष्यमाणं पानं **सेव्यतां इति उदारं** चतुरं **अभिधाय शंकरः तां अम्बिकां** पीयत इति **पानं** मद्यं **अपाययत** पाययामास । पिबतेर्ण्यन्ताल्लुङि तङ् । पिबतेः प्रत्यवसानार्थादणि कर्तुः कर्मत्वम् । पिबतेर्निगरणार्थत्वेऽपि 'न पादम्य-' इति परस्मैपदप्रतिषेधः । ननु मान्यभक्तिरित्यत्र कथं पुंवद्भावः । 'अप्रियादिषु' इति निषेधाद्भक्तिशब्दस्य प्रियादिपाठात् । नैष दोषो नपुंसकपूर्वपदत्वात् । यथाह वृत्तिकारः—'दृढभक्तिरित्येवमादिषु स्त्रीपूर्वपदस्याविवक्षितत्वात्सिद्धम्' इति । भोजराजस्तु—'भज्यत इति कर्मसाधनस्यैव प्रियादिपाठतया दृढभक्तिरिति न तु भजनं भक्तिरिति भावसाधनस्य । अतोऽत्रास्त्रीपूर्वपदत्वेऽपि न दोषः' इत्याह ॥

पार्वती तदुपयोग[2]संभवां विक्रियामपि सतीं[3] मनोहराम् ।
अप्रतर्क्यविधियोगकारितामा[4]म्रतेव[5] सहकारतां ययौ ॥ ७८ ॥

पार्वतीति ॥ **पार्वती [तदुपयोगसंभवाम्]** तस्य मद्यस्य उपयोगेन पानेन संभवः यस्याः तां **विक्रियां अपि सतीं मनोहरां** विकारत्वेऽपि रम्यामित्यर्थः । विक्रियां मदविकारं **ययौ** । अत्र विक्रियाशब्दस्यावृत्तिः । कथमिव । **आम्रता** चूतत्वं **[अप्रतर्क्यविधियोगकारितां]** अप्रतर्क्येण दुरूहेण विधियोगेन दैवबलेन कारितां **सहकारतां इव** सौरभाढ्यं अवस्थाविशेषमिव । 'आम्रश्चूतो रसालोऽसौ सहकारोऽतिसौरभः' इत्यमरः । यथा चूतत्वलक्षणाविकृतिः शोभते तथा तस्या अपि मदविकारोऽशोभतेत्यर्थः ॥

तत्क्षणं[6] विपरिवर्तितह्रियो[7]र्नेष्यतोः[8] शयनमिद्धरागयोः ।
सा बभूव वशवर्तिनी[9] द्वयोः शूलिनः सुवदना मदस्य च ॥ ७९ ॥

---

१ दीपनम्. २ उपभोग. ३ सताम्. ४ निर्मिताम्; निर्मिता. ५ नम्रता. ६ तत्क्षणे. ७ विपरिवृत्तलज्जयोः. ८ वाञ्छतोः. ९ वशवर्तिका.

तदिति ॥ सा सुवदना पार्वती तत्क्षणं तदैव विपरिवर्तितह्रियोः निवर्तितलज्जयोः शयनं तल्पं नेष्यतोः प्रापयिष्यतोरिद्धः प्रवृद्धो रागोऽनुराग आरुण्यं च ययोः इद्धरागयोः शूलिनः प्रियतमस्य भवस्य च इति द्वयोः वशे वर्तत इति वशवर्तिनी अधीना बभूव ॥

मदपारवश्यं तावदाह—

घूर्णमाननयनं स्खलत्कथं स्वेदबिन्दुमदकारणस्मितम् ।
आननेन न तु तावदीश्वरश्चक्षुषा चिरमुमामुखं पपौ ॥ ८० ॥

घूर्णमानेति ॥ ईश्वरः घूर्णमाननयनं भ्राम्यन्नेत्रं स्खलत्कथं स्खलद्वचनं स्वेदबिन्दुमत् स्वेदयुक्तं अकारणस्मितं आकस्मिकहासयुक्तं उमामुखं तावत् । आतृष्णापगमामित्यर्थः । आननेन मुखेन न पपौ । न चुचुम्बेत्यर्थः । किं तु चिरं चक्षुषा पपौ । तृष्णयाद्राक्षीदित्यर्थः । तस्या मदपारवश्यं दृष्ट्वा मुदं तावदन्वभूदित्यर्थः ॥

संप्रति प्रियवशंवदत्वमाह—

तां विलम्बितपनीयमेखलामुद्वहञ्जघनभारदुर्वहाम् ।
ध्यानसंभृतविभूतिसंभृतं प्राविशन्मणिशिलागृहं हरः ॥ ८१ ॥

तामिति ॥ हरः विलम्बितपनीयमेखलां विस्रंसिहेमरसनां [जघनभारदुर्वहां] जघनभारेण दुर्वहां तां पार्वतीं उद्वहन् [ध्यानसंभृताविभूतिसंभृतं] ध्यानसंभृतया संकल्पमात्रसिद्धया विभूत्या भोगसाधनेन संभृतं संपूर्णं मणिशिलागृहं प्राविशत् । रिरंसुरिति भावः ॥

तत्र हंसधवलोत्तरच्छदं जाह्नवीपुलिनचारुदर्शनम् ।
अध्यशेत शयनं प्रियासखः शारदाभ्रमिव रोहिणीपतिः ॥ ८२ ॥

तत्रेति ॥ तत्र मणिभवने [हंसधवलोत्तरच्छदं] हंसवद्धवल उत्तरच्छदः प्रच्छदपटो यस्य तत्तथोक्तं [जाह्नवीपुलिनचारुदर्शनं] जाह्नवीपुलिनमिव चारुदर्शनं शयनं शय्यां रोहिणीपतिः चन्द्रः [शारदाभ्रं] शरदि भवं शारदमभ्रं मेघ इव । शरद्ग्रहणं धावल्यार्थम् । प्रियासखः सन् । प्रियया सहेत्यर्थः । अध्यशेत शायितवान् । 'अधिशीङ्स्थासां कर्म' इति कर्मत्वम् । रोहिणीग्रहणसामर्थ्यादिन्दोरभ्रारोहणे रोहिणीसाहित्यमनुसंधेयम् ॥

क्लिष्टचन्द्रमदयैः कचग्रहैरुत्पथार्पितनखं समत्सरम् ।
तस्य तच्छिदुरमेखलागुणं पार्वतीरतमभूदतृप्तये ॥ ८३ ॥

---

१ स्खलद्वचम्; स्खलत्कथम्. २ संभृतेतिविभूतिरीश्वरः; संभृतिविभूतिसंभृतम्; संभूतिविभूति-शोभितं-गोचरम्. ३ रहः. ४ क्लिष्टकेशमवलुप्तचन्दनम्. ५ व्युत्पथार्पित; व्यत्ययार्पित. ६ न तृप्तये.

क्लिष्टेति ॥ **अदयैः** निर्दयैः **कचग्रहैः** केशकर्षणैः **क्लिष्टचन्द्रं** पीडितहरचन्द्रं [**उत्पथार्पितनखं**] उत्पथमुन्मर्यादमर्पिता नखा यस्मिंस्तत् **समत्सरं** अन्योन्यविजिगीषापूर्वकं [**छिदुरमेखलागुणं**] छिदुराः स्वयमेव छिद्यमाना मेखलागुणा यस्मिंस्तत्तथोक्तम् । 'विदिभिदिच्छिदेः कुरच्' इति कुरच्प्रत्ययः । 'कर्मकर्तरि' इति काशिका । **तत् पार्वतीरतं तस्य** ईश्वरस्य **अतृप्तये अभूत्** । तृप्तये नाभूदिति भावः ॥

केवलं प्रियतमादयालुना ज्योतिषामवनतासु पङ्क्तिषु ।
तेन तत्परिगृहीतवक्षसा नेत्रमीलनकुतूहलं कृतम् ॥ ८४ ॥

केवलमिति ॥ **प्रियतमादयालुना केवलम्** प्रियतमायां दययैव । तस्येश्वरस्यासौकुमार्यादनवरतं सुरतसहिष्णुत्वात् । न तु स्वयं तृप्येत्यर्थः । **तत्परिगृहीतवक्षसा** तया पार्वत्याश्लिष्टवक्षसा **तेन** ईश्वरेण **ज्योतिषां** नक्षत्राणां **पङ्क्तिषु अवनतासु** सतीषु । पश्चिमायामित्यर्थः । **नेत्रमीलनकुतूहलं कृतम्** । निद्रा स्वीकृतेत्यर्थः ॥

स व्यबुध्यत बुधस्तवोचितः शातकुम्भकमलाकरैः समम् ।
मूर्छनापरिगृहीतकैशिकैः किंनरैरुषसि गीतमङ्गलः ॥ ८५ ॥

स इति ॥ **बुधस्तवोचितः** विद्वत्स्तोत्रार्हः **सः** हरः **उषसि** प्रभाते । [**मूर्छनापरिगृहीतकैशिकैः**] स्वराणामारोहक्रमो मूर्छना । 'क्रमयुक्ताः स्वरास्तत्र मूर्छना परिकीर्तिता' इति भरतः । तया मूर्छनया परिगृहीतकैशिकैः स्वीकृतरागविशेषैः **किंनरैः गीतमङ्गलः** सन् । **शातकुम्भकमलाकरैः समं** कनकपद्माकरैः सह । 'तपनीयं शातकुम्भं गाङ्गेयं भर्म कर्बुरम्' इत्यमरः । **व्यबुध्यत** विबुद्धवान् । बुध्यतेर्दैवादिकात्कर्तरि लङ् । अत्र बुध्यतेर्जागरविकासयोर्बोधयोः श्लेषनिमित्तकाभेदाध्यवसायमूला सहोक्तिरलंकारः ॥

तौ क्षणं शिथिलितोपगूहनौ दंपती रचितमानसोर्मयः ।
पद्मभेदनिपुणाः सिषेविरे गन्धमादनवनान्तमारुताः ॥ ८६ ॥

ताविति ॥ **शिथिलितोपगूहनौ** शिथिलितालिङ्गनौ । जाया च पतिश्च **दंपती** । जायाशब्दस्य दंभावो निपातितः । **तौ** शिवौ **रचितमानसोर्मयः** । मानसे सरसि रचिततरङ्गा इत्यर्थः । **पद्मभेदनिपुणाः** । पद्मभेदपिशुना इति यावत् । विकाससूचका इत्यर्थः । **गन्धमादनवनान्तमारुताः क्षणं सिषेविरे** ॥

ऊरुमूलनखमार्गराजिभिस्तत्क्षणं हृतविलोचनो हरः ।
वाससः प्रशिथिलस्य संयमं कुर्वतीं प्रियतमामवारयत् ॥ ८७ ॥

---

१ प्रतिगृहीत. २ तया निशाक्षयं. ३ वंशिकैः. ४ समुपगीत. ५ प्रशिथिलोप. ६ चलित. ७ पिशुनाः. ८ पङ्क्तिभिः. ९ संचयम्.

ऊर्वीति ॥ तत्क्षणं मारुतवीजनसमये [ऊरुमूलनखमार्गराजिभिः] ऊरुमूले नखमार्गराजिभिर्नखपदपङ्क्तिभिः । मरुता प्रसारितवस्त्रतया प्रकाशिताभिरित्यर्थः । हृतविलोचनः आकृष्टदृष्टिः हरः प्रशिथिलस्य वाससः संयमं बन्धनं कुर्वतीं प्रियतमां अवारयत ॥

स प्रजागरकषायलोचनं गाढदन्तपदताडिताधरम् ।
आकुलालकमरंस्त रागवान्प्रेक्ष्य भिन्नतिलकं प्रियामुखम् ॥ ८८ ॥

स इति ॥ रागवान् रागी सः हरः [प्रजागरकषायलोचनं] प्रजागरेण कषायलोचनं रक्तनेत्रं [गाढदन्तपदताडिताधरं] गाढैर्दन्तपदैर्दन्तक्षतैस्ताडिताधरं आकुलालकं भिन्नतिलकं प्रियामुखं प्रेक्ष्य अरंस्त अन्वरज्यत । तादृङ्मुखदर्शनमेव तस्योद्दीपकमित्यर्थः ॥

तेन भङ्गिविषमोत्तरच्छदं मध्यपिण्डितविसूत्रमेखलम् ।
निर्मलेऽपि शयनं निशात्यये नोज्झितं चरणरागलाञ्छितम् ॥ ८९ ॥

तेनेति ॥ तेन हरेण [भङ्गिविषमोत्तरच्छदं] भङ्गिभिर्भङ्गैर्विषमो निम्नोन्नतः उत्तरच्छदः प्रच्छदपटो यस्मिंस्तत् । [मध्यपिण्डितविसूत्रमेखलं] मध्ये पिण्डिता पुञ्जीकृता विसूत्रमेखला छिन्नरसना यस्मिंस्तत्तथोक्तं [चरणरागलाञ्छितं] चरणयोः रागेण लाक्षारागेण लाञ्छितं चिह्नितं शयनं निशात्यये प्रभाते निर्मले अपि । सूर्योदये सत्यपीत्यर्थः । न उज्झितं न त्यक्तम् । अत्र देव्याः सकलसुरतोपचारसंपन्नत्वं पुरुषायितं सूच्यते ॥

स प्रियामुखरसं दिवानिशं हर्षवृद्धिजननं सिषेविषुः ।
दर्शनप्रणयिनामदृश्यतामाजगाम विजयानिवेदितः ॥ ९० ॥

स इति ॥ सः हरः हर्षवृद्धिजननं सुखातिशयकारणं प्रियामुखरसं अधरामृतं दिवा च निशि च दिवानिशम् । द्वन्द्वैकवद्भावः । सिषेविषुः सेवितुमिच्छुः सन् । [विजयानिवेदितः] विजयानाम्नी काचिद्देव्याः सखी तया निवेदितः । एतदर्थमागतमिति ज्ञापितोऽपीत्यर्थः । दर्शनप्रणयिनां अदृश्यतां आजगाम । दर्शनं न ददावित्यर्थः ॥

समदिवसनिशीथं सङ्गिनस्तत्र शंभोः
शतमगमदृतूनां साग्रमेका निशेव ।
न तु सुरतसुखेभ्यश्छिन्नतृष्णो बभूव
ज्वलन इव समुद्रान्तर्गतस्तज्जलौघैः ॥ ९१ ॥

---

१ परिताडिता. २ अपास्तचित्रकम्. ३ भिन्न. ४ सुख. ५ निवेदनात्. ६ साग्रम्. ७ च; तु. ८ सुखेषु. ९ तज्जलेभ्यः; तज्जलेषु.

समेति ॥ निशीथोऽत्र निशामात्रलक्षकः । **समदिवसनिशीथं** तुल्याहर्निशं यथा तथा **तत्र** तस्यां पार्वत्यां **सङ्गिनः** आसक्तस्य । रात्रिंदिवं रममाणस्येत्यर्थः । **शंभोः** शिवस्य **सार्धं** अर्धेन सहितं **ऋतूनां शतं** पञ्चाशदुत्तरं मानुषमानेन पञ्चविंशतिवर्षाणि । **एका निशेव अगमत्** । सः शंभुः **समुद्रान्तर्गतः** समुद्रस्यान्तर्वृत्तिः **ज्वलनः** वडवाग्निरिव **तज्जलौघैः** तस्य समुद्रस्य प्रवाहैः **इव सुरतसुखेभ्यः छिन्नतृष्णः** वृत्ताभिलाषः **न बभूव** । किं तु तत्र तस्य तृष्णा चिरं वर्धतेत्यर्थः ॥

इति श्रीमन्महामहोपाध्यायकोलाचलमल्लिनाथसूरिविरचितया संजीविनिसमाख्यया व्याख्यया समेतः श्रीकालिदासकृतौ कुमारसंभवे महाकाव्ये उमासुरतवर्णनं नामाष्टमः सर्गः ॥

समाप्तं कुमारसंभवम् ।

KUMA'RASAMBHAVA
(TRANSLATION)

CANTO I.

1. There is, in the northern quarter, the deity-souled lord of mountains (*lit.* immovable ones), by name Himâlaya (the mansion of snow), who stands, like the measuring-rod of the earth, spanning (the distance between; *lit.* having entered) the Eastern and the Western oceans.

2. Whom having fixed upon as the calf, while mount Meru, clever in milking, stood as the milker, all the mountains milked from the earth (in the shape of a cow), as directed by Prithu, brilliant jewels and great medicinal herbs.

3. Snow could not be a destroyer of beauty in the case of him who is the source of countless jewels; for, one blemish is lost in a host of virtues, like the spot on the moon (lost) in her rays.

4. Who bears, on his peaks, a richness of metals, appearing like an untimely twilight, with its colours reflected upon patches of clouds, and the cause of the amorous decking of the heavenly nymphs.

5. To whose sunny peaks the Siddhas repair (for comfort) when troubled by showers, after having enjoyed the shadow, fallen on the peaks below, of the clouds floating round the mountain's zone.

6. Where the Kirâtas (mountaineers) track the spoor of the lions that have killed elephants, by the pearls dropping from the cavities of their claws, though they do not see their foot-marks, the blood-stains having been washed away by the streamlets of melted snow.

7. Where the barks of the birch-trees, having characters written on them with mineral fluid, and so resembling the red spots on (the bodies of full-grown) elephants, become useful to the Vidyâdhara damsels for amatory correspondence.

8. Who, by filling the holes of the bamboos with the wind breathed from the mouths of its caves, (appears) as if he wishes to play an accompaniment to (swell the music of) the Kinnaras, singing in a high pitch.

9. Where the odour, born of the milky juice flowing from the cedar (Sarala) trees, rubbed against by elephants to ease the itching sensation of their temples, makes the peaks fragrant.

10. Where the (phosphorescent) herbs with their lustre shed into the interior of caves, serve, at night, as lights requiring no feeding of oil, at the time of the amorous sports of the forest-dwellers accompanied by fair females.

11. Where, on the path on which the snow has formed into blocks, and which therefore bites the sides of the toes and the heels, the As'vamukhî women do not leave off their lazy gait, oppressed (bowed down) as they are by (the weight of) their hips and full breasts difficult to bear.

12. Who in his caves protects from the sun (*lit.* the maker of light) darkness, hiding there for shelter, being as it were afraid of light (like the owl); indeed, with the exalted, a feeling of kinship (that he is their own) extends as much to the lowly suppliant seeking their protection, as to the excellent.

13. Where the *chamarî* deer prove his title, the "Lord of the mountains." to be significant by (waving over him) the *chauries* (in the shape of their tails) which are as white as the rays of the moon, and which have their beauty extended all round by the movements of the tails.

14. Where the clouds, with their forms accidentally hanging over the entrances to the caverns serving as houses, become the screens for the women of the Kiṃpurashas, shy at their garments having been snatched away.

15. From which the wind, which bears along with it the spray of the current of the Ganges, which ever and anon shakes the Devadâru trees, and which agitates the feathers of peacocks (in forests), is enjoyed by the hunters when they have done stalking the deer.

16. Whose lotuses, growing in the lakes on the highest summits, and left after being collected by the hands of the seven sages, the sun, moving on a lower level, blossoms by (means of his) rays shooting upwards.

17. On observing him as the source of sacrificial requisites, and his strength as capable of holding up the earth, the Lord of creation (Brahmá) himself conferred on him the sovereignty of the mountains, with a share in the sacrificial offerings attached to it.

18. To maintain the continuity of his line, he, a kinsman of Meru, knowing rectitude, married, according to (proper) rites, Mená, the mind-born daughter of the Pitṛis, equal to himself and respected even of the sages.

19. In course of time, as they began to enjoy connubial life worthy of their (respective) charms, the consort of the Mountain-lord, possessed of charming youth, conceived a child.

20. She gave birth to Maináka, who wedded a Nága damsel. who contracted friendship with the ocean (to hide himself in it) and who never experienced the pain of the wounds made by the thunderbolt, even when the foe of Vṛitra, the cleaver of pinions, (*i. e.* Indra), was enraged.

21. Then the chaste Satî, the daughter of Daksha and the former wife of Bhava (S'iva), who, driven by the insult offered by her father (to her lord), had abandoned her body by (means of) *Yoga*, resorted to the Mountain's consort (Menâ) for re-birth.

22. That blessed one (Umâ) was begotten on her (Menâ), who was always self-restrained (or, devoted to the performance of holy rites), by the Mountain-lord, as prosperity is produced by the quality of energy from policy not failing (in its operation) on account of its being well-directed.

23. Her birth-day conduced to the happiness of embodied beings, both movable and immovable; a day on which the quarters brightened, on which the winds were free from dust, and wherein there was a shower of flowers following close upon the music of conches (in the sky).

24. The mother (*lit.* the progenitor) shone very brightly by her daughter, having a halo of refulgent lustre ; as shines the land adjoining the Vidúra hills by the rays of gems shooting up at (responsive to) the thunder of the new clouds.

25. She, who had got her birth, growing day by day, developed extra-ordinary graces, as the newly-risen crescent of the moon, waxing day by day, (develops) other digits hidden in her lustre.

26. Her, the darling of her relatives, they called by the patronymic name of Párvatî ; that maiden of a pleasing face came to be called Umà (only) afterwards, when forbidden by her mother to do penance with the words " *U má* (Oh, do not)."

27. The eyes of the Mountain-lord, though having a son, were never satiated with resting on this his child ; the row of bees, indeed, is more fondly attached to the mango tree (blossoms), though the vernal season blooms with countless flowers.

28. By her he received (additional) sanctity and was also glorified, even as the lamp is by its exceedingly brilliant flame, or the heavenly path by the Ganges (*lit.* the river of three courses), or the wise by refined speech.

29. In childhood she, surrounded by her companions, and entering, as it were, into the spirit of sport, often played with balls and dolls (made of cloth &c.) and with altars built on the sands of the Ganges.

30. To her, whose impressions (of the previous life) were permanent, the lores, acquired in the past life, came at the time of instruction, as do the flocks of swans to the Ganges in autumn, or their own lustre to the medicinal herbs at night.

31. Now she reached an age, beyond childhood, which is in itself an embellishment, not artificial, of the slim body, a cause of exhilara-

tion, not known as wine, and a missile of Káma, (but) other than the flowery one.

32. Her body, fully unfolded (developed) by fresh youth, appeared charming in its perfect symmetry, like a painting gradually grown under the brush (of a painter), or like a lotus blooming under the (influence of the) rays of the sun.

33. Her feet, while treading, gave to the earth the ever-shifting beauty of (being decked with) land-lotuses, emitting, as it were, red colour on account of the radiance of her prominent great toe and nails.

34. She, with a body stooping (on account of the weight of her breasts), was instructed as it were, in the matter of her gait, wherein the tread appeared graceful through playful gestures, by the royal swans, themselves desirous of receiving instruction in return as they wanted to learn the music of her anklets.

35. The Creator, after he had fashioned her beautiful thighs, not very long, rounded and symmetrical, had to make an effort, as it were, for the production of excellent beauty, when forming her other limbs.

36. The trunks of lordly elephants through toughness of skin and the plantain-stalks through their extreme coldness, were unfit as (*lit.* out of the question as being) standards of comparison for her thighs, though (both) had a plump, rounded shape in the world.

37. The beauty of the resting-place of the zone (*i. e.* hips) of her, who was faultless, could, indeed, be inferred from this, that it was placed, in after-times (*i. e.* after her austerities were over), by S'iva on his lap, which it was not possible even to be coveted by another female.

38. The delicate line of down which entered her deep navel after passing the knot of her garment (at the waist), appeared like the shooting ray of the blue (*lit.* not-white) central gem (sapphire) of her zone.

39. She, with a slender waist resembling an altar, had three charming folds of skin on her waist, as if they were a flight of stairs raised there by blossoming youth for the God of love to ascend.

40. Of her, the lily-eyed one, the two breasts, yellowish white, having black nipples and pressing against each other, were so rounded that it was impossible to find between them as much space as could be occupied even by a lotus-fibre.

41. I fancy her arms were more delicate than even the S'irisha flower, since they were thrown as chains round the neck of S'iva by the fish-bannered God (Cupid), although vanquished.

42. In the case of her neck gracefully elevated over her breasts and her encircling pearl-necklace, the condition of being the adorned and the

adorner was indifferently exchangeable owing to each bringing beauty to the other.

43. The unsteady Goddess of beauty could not enjoy (possess) the charms of the lotus when with the moon, and of the lunar graces when with the lotus; but when she betook herself to the face of Umá, she enjoyed the pleasure (coming from the charms) peculiar to both.

44. If a white flower were laid upon a tender young leaf or a pearl were to rest on the richest (*lit.* spotless) coral, then only could either vie with the sweet smile which played about (*lit.* whose lustre was shed over) her rosy lip.

45. While she, who had a musical sound, spoke in a voice that distilled nectar as it were, even the female cuckoo (*lit.* bred by others), was to the ears of the listeners full of jarring notes, like a harp, out of tune, when played upon.

46. The timid (unsteady) glances, not at all dissimilar to the blue lotus (tremulous) in a strong wind,—did the female fawns borrow (them) from her, or she, with elongated eyes, from them?

47. On seeing the beauty, charming in its sportiveness, of her long-arching brows, pencilled as it were with black paint, the bodiless God (Cupid) gave up all pride in the beauty of his own (curved) bow.

48. If there can be a sense of shame in the minds of the lower animals, then the female *chamarí* deer will, undoubtedly, grow cold in their fondness for their hair, on seeing the magnificent tresses of the daughter of the Mountain-lord.

49. In short, she was created by the Creator of the universe with great effort, as if with a desire to see all beauty combined in one form, by gathering together all the standards of comparison and placing them, each in its place.

50. Once, it is said, Nárada, who roams at will, on seeing that girl near her father, declared that she would be S'iva's one bride who would share half of his body through love.

51. For this reason her father remained (indifferent), setting aside all thought of another bridegroom for her, although she had reached the age of adolescence: (for) lustrous objects other than fire do not deserve an oblation sanctified by *mantras.*

52. The Mountain could not offer his child to the God of gods unsolicited: a wise man resorts to neutrality even in the matter of his desired object, through fear of his request being refused.

53. When that lady, of pearly teeth, through resentment against Daksha, abandoned her body in her former life, just from that time

the Lord of beings (S'iva), giving up all attachment (to worldly pleasures), lived without a wife.

54. He, with a skin for his garment, and with his mind controlled, dwelt, for the purpose of practising austerities, on some peak of the Snowy Mountain, where the sacred Devadáru trees were laved by the current of the Ganges, which was odoriferous with the fragrance of musk, and where there was the music of heavenly minstrels (Kiṃnaras).

55. And his attendant troops, with the flowers of the Nameru trees for their ear-ornaments, clad in birch-barks soft to the touch, and annointed with mineral (red arsenic) dyes, sat on the rocks coated with fragrant resin.

56. His bull (*lit.* he who had a prominent hump), uttering a pleasing bellow of pride, digging with his hoofs the rocks of collected snow, and looked at with great difficulty by the terrified *gavaya* bulls, bellowed aloud there, intolerant of the roar of the lions.

57. He (S'iva), of eight forms, himself the giver of the fruit of penance, having set up a fire there, which he kindled with sacrificial wood and which was another manifestation of himself, practised austerities with some unknown object.

58. The mountain-lord, having worshipped, with the customary offerings, him who was of inestimable worth and was adored by the gods (*lit.* the denizens of heaven), directed his daughter of restrained soul, together with her (two) female friends, to wait upon (or propitiate) him.

59. S'iva allowed her to serve him according to her desire, although she was an obstruction to contemplation ; for *they* alone are steady whose minds are not affected in the presence of the cause of perturbation.

60. Culling flowers for offerings, assiduous in cleaning the altar and bringing water and the Kus'a grass for the performance of holy rites—thus did she, having lovely tresses, attend upon S'iva every day, her fatigue being allayed by the rays of the lunar digit on his head.

CANTO II.

1. At that time the denizens of heaven, harassed by Ta'raka, went to the abode of the self-existent God (Bramhà), having placed Indra at their head.

2. Brahmà revealed himself to them, the lustre of whose faces had faded away, as does the sun (the possessor of bright rays) to the lakes with sleeping (closed) lotuses in the morning.

3. Then, having bowed to him, who has a face on every side, who is the creator of all, and who is the lord of speech, they propitiated him with appropriate (*lit.* full of sense) speeches.

4. "Salutation to thee of three forms, the one soul existing before creation who afterwards dividedst thyself into the three Guṇas (Sattva, Rajas and Tamas) and manifestedst a variety (of forms).

5. O unborn one, the universe, composed of things that move and that do not move, has sprung from the ever-prolific seed which was cast by thee in the waters; hence art thou glorified as its source.

6. Manifesting thy might by the three forms (*lit.* three states characterized by the three qualities), thou alone hast come to be the cause of the creation, the protection and the retraction (of the universe).

7. Male and female are the separate manifestations of thy own self, (thus) split up through the desire of creating; and these are declared as the parents of the creation that sprang into existence.

8. The waking and slumbering of thee, who hast separated thy day and night by the measure of thy own time, are (*i. e.* represent the period of) the creation and destruction of all things.

9. Thyself without a source, thou art the source of the universe; thyself endless, thou art the end of the universe; without beginning, thou art the beginning of the universe; and thyself lordless, thou art the lord of the universe.

10. Thou knowest thyself in thyself, thou createst thyself by thyself and thou art absorbed in thyself by thy own mighty self.

11. Thou art fluid and hard on account of the close contact of the particles (adhesion); gross and subtile; light and yet heavy; perceptible and yet the opposite of that; thy will is absolute in (the manifestation of) the energies (or miraculous powers).

12. Thou art the source of those speeches (Vedas), the introduction of which is by (the syllable) *Om*, the utterance of which is according to the three accents (acute, grave and circumflex), the rite to be performed by which is sacrifice, and the fruit of which is heaven.

13. They declare thee as the Prakṛiti operating for the benefit of the soul (Purusha); and they know thee alone to be the Purusha, the indifferent (passive) witness of (the operations of) the Prakṛiti.

14. Thou art the father of the manes, god of the gods, higher than the high, and the progenitor of the progenitors of mankind.

15. Thou, the eternal one, art the sacrificial offering and again its offerer (the sacrificer), the enjoyed and the enjoyer, the knowable and also the knower, the meditator and again the supreme object of meditation."

16. Having heard from them these praises, truthful and going (pleasing) to the heart, the Creator, inclined to show favour, answered the gods.

17. Of that primeval bard, the fourfold (*i.e.* having a fourfold excellence) flow of words (speech), being uttered from the four mouths, was successful (or had its object gained).

18. "Welcome to you, O gods of mighty valour, who, having held your (respective) high posts by your might, have come here in a body and who have pole-like (long) arms (*i. e.* reaching upto the knee).

19. Why is it that your faces do not show their wonted glow, as before, like stars with their gleam dimmed by a mist?

20. This thunderbolt of the destroyer of Vṛitra, not displaying its variegated splendour (rain-bow) on account of the loss of its radiance, appears as though it has had its edges blunted.

21. The noose in the hand of Varuṇa, irresistible to the enemy, is reduced to the helplessness of a serpent, whose prowess is repressed by a spell.

22. The arm of Kubera, from which the mace is cast off, and which, therefore, appearing like a tree with its branches broken, hints, as it were at a defeat that has been like a dart (driven) in the heart (*i. e.* rankling in his mind).

23. Even Yama, scratching the ground with his rod having its lustre entirely gone, brings to it the insignificance of a quenched firebrand (for marking the earth), even though it is invincible.

24. How have these A'dityas, cool on account of the loss of their burning lustre, come to the condition of being gazed on at will, as if painted in pictures?

25. The halting of the speed of the Maruts (wind-gods) can be guessed from their faltering motion, as is the stoppage of their current from the refluence of waters.

26. The heads of the Rudras, with their crescents hanging from the knots of matted hair bent low (through shame of defeat), tell of the quelling of their deep guttural sounds (which are their weapons).

27. Have you, who had already gained position (established your pre-eminence), been thrown down from it by your more powerful enemies, as general rules are overthrown (set aside) by special ones (exceptions)?

28. Say then, my children; what crave you, coming here together? For, with me rests the creation of the world, with you its protection."

29. Then Indra urged the preceptor (of the gods to speak), with (a motion of) his thousand eyes, that appeared beautiful like a bed of lotuses shaken by a gentle wind.

30. He, the twofold eye of Indra, greater (more serviceable to him) than his one thousand eyes,—he, Vàchaspati (the lord of speech), spoke to him, the lotus-throned one (Brahmà), with hands folded (in supplication).

31. "O Lord, what you said is so; our high position is snatched away from us by our foes. O mighty One, how should you not know it, when your soul pervades each and every creature!

32. A mighty demon named Ta'raka, grown insolent by a boon obtained from you, has risen to torment the worlds, like a comet.

33. To his city the Sun sends his rays in such numbers only as will suffice to awaken (*i.e.* cause to bloom) the lotuses in his pleasure-lakes.

34. On him the Moon waits with all his digits at all times (in both the halves); he keeps back only the digit that forms the crest-gem of S'iva.

35. The Wind, with his motion in his garden stopped through fear of (punishment for) stealing (bearing away) flowers, does not blow near him any more (with greater force) than is produced by a fan.

36. And the Seasons, ever diligent in providing a stock of flowers, wait upon him, as if they were (nothing more than) his gardeners, giving up for the time a succession of service.

37. The Lord of rivers (the sea) anxiously awaits the developing of precious stones, fit to be offered as presents to him, in the bosom of water.

38. And the serpents, with Vàsukì at their head, wait upon him at night with their blazing jewel-lustres, serving (him) as fixed lamps.

39. Even Indra, desirous of securing favour done by him, tries again and again to win him over with the precious flowers of the desire-granting trees (Kalpadrumas) sent by messengers.

40. Though served in this way, he harasses the three worlds. A wicked person can be put down only by a retaliation of injury, and not by an act of kindness.

41. By him are the trees of the Nandana grove, the leaves of which were tenderly plucked by the wives of the immortals, made to experience cuttings and fallings.

42. When asleep, he is fanned by the captive heavenly damsels with *chauries*, showering the spray of tears, and raising wind light like breathing.

43. He has built pleasure-mountains in his residences, having rooted up peaks of Meru, (formerly) struck by the hoofs of the Sun's coursers.

44. The water of the heavenly Ganges, made turbid by the rut of the elephants of the quarters, is now left alone (*i. e.* without its golden lotuses), while his pleasure-lakes have become the abode of the harvest of golden lotuses.

45. The love of seeing different worlds is no more entertained by the gods, as the path of the aerical cars has become desolate through fear of being attacked by him.

46. He, versed in magic arts, snatches away from the mouth of fire the oblation offered by the sacrificers (in due form) in sacrifices when instituted, while we look on (helplessly).

47. He has borne away the well-known Uchchais'ravas, the jewel of horses, who was, as it were, the long-acquired glory of Indra in a bodily form.

48. All our efforts against the wicked wretch are turned to naught, as herbs of powerful healing virtue against a joint distemper of the three humours malignly disturbed.

49. The discus of Vishṇu, whereon rested our hope of success, offered itself, as it were, like a gold ornament round his neck, with (only) a stream of lustre flashing forth from it as it clashed (against his bosom).

50. Now his elephants, who have vanquished Airâvata, are practising butting against the clouds, such as the Pushkarâvartakas and others.

51. O Almighty God, we, therefore desire to create a leader to destroy him, as those desirous of salvation wish to amass religious virtue, which cuts off the fetters of Karman.

52.—(A leader), having placed whom. in the forefront, as the defender of the heavenly host, the Breaker of-mountains (Indra) will bring back from the enemy the Glory of victory. like one taken captive."

53. When this address was concluded, the Self-existent One (Brahmâ) uttered a speech, which far surpassed, in sweetness (*i. e.* in its refreshing effect), a shower falling after thunder.

54. "This your desire will be gratified; wait some time: but I will not myself undertake the work of creation for its fulfilment (*i. e.* producing a leader).

55. The demon who acquired his glory from here, ought not to have destruction from here; it is improper to cut down even a poisonous tree when (it has been) nurtured by oneself.

56. Formerly this very thing (*viz.* freedom from death at the hands of the gods) he sought (as a boon), and the same I granted him; and (thus) by a boon I made nugatory his penance, capable of burning the worlds.

57. Who but a portion of the energy of the Black-necked one (S'iva) dropped (on favourable ground), can withstand him who is warlike when ready to attack in a battle?

58. That God (S'iva) is the supreme spirit (*lit.* highest lustre) reigning beyond the region of darkness (the quality of Tamas);—he, the extent of whose prowess cannot be accurately gauged either by me or by Vishṇu.

59. So you, who are desirous of achieving your object, should try to draw away (tempt) the mind of S'iva, steadied by self-restraint (or firmly fixed on contemplation) (towards matrimony) by means of the beauty of Umâ, like iron by a magnet.

60. Only these two are capable of bearing the seed of us two when deposited—Umá of S'iva and his watery form of me.

61. The son (*lit.* the self in another form) of that S'iva, having taken up the leadership of your host, will loosen the braids of the captive heavenly damsels by the glory of his might."

62. Having thus addressed the gods the Creator of the universe vanished (from sight); and the gods, too, went back to the celestial world with what-was-to-be-done firmly settled in their minds.

63. Having fixed upon Kaṃdarpa (as the proper agent to be employed) in that business, the chastiser of Pâka (Indra) approached him by the mind, the speed of which was doubled by his eagerness for the accomplishment of his object.

64. Then that flower-bowed god, having his bow, the ends of which were as beautiful as the arching brows of graceful women, slung over his neck bearing the marks of the bracelets of Rati, and having his missile (*viz.* the young sprouts of mango trees) deposited in the hands of his friend Madhu (vernal season), approached with folded hands the Performer-of-hundred-sacrifices (Indra).

CANTO III.

1. The thousand eyes of (Indra) simultaneously alighted on him, leaving the gods ; generally the regard of masters for their dependants changes according to the purpose they desire to be accomplished.

2. He was allowed a place near his own throne by Indra with the words "sit here"; and he, having acknowledged the courtesy of his master by (a reverential inclination of) his head, began to speak to him in private thus—

3. "O you who discern the special qualifications of men, command what you desire to be done for you in the (three) worlds. I should like this favour, shown by your remembrance (of me), to be enhanced by (the bestowing of) a command.

4. By whom, desirous of getting your post, has your vengeance been roused by his mighty (*lit.* exceedingly prolonged) austerities ? For in a trice shall he be brought within the range of this my bow on which an arrow has been fixed.

5. Who, undesired by you, is seeking the path of salvation through fear of re-birth ? Let him long stand fettered down to worldly existence by the side-long glances, bewitching with the play of the eye-brows, of beautiful women.

6. Say, of what foe of yours shall I, employing passion as my messenger, obstruct the temporal and spiritual advancement, although he be instructed in morality by Us'anas himself, as the flooded current of a river obstructs its two banks ?

7. What lady (having full buttocks), austerely sticking to (or, paining you by her keeping) the vow of chastity, who has made a niche in your unsteady (lustful) mind by her beauty, do you wish to twine her arms round your neck, of her own accord, abandoning all (sense of) shame ?

8. O gallant, by what lady, naturally passionate, have you been spurned, although fallen at her feet, for your infidelity in love ? Her body shall I subject to strong repentance and make it (helplessly) resort to a couch of tender sprouts.

9. O mighty one, be pleased; let your bolt rest; what foe of the gods should quail, with the might of his arms rendered unavailing, even before women, with their lower lips curling through anger ?

10. Although flower-armed, taking Madhu (the presiding deity of the vernal season) alone for my associate, I shall break down (through your favour) the self-restraint even of the Trident-holder (S'iva). What are other bowmen before me, then ?"

11. Then A'khaṇḍala (Indra), having taken his leg off his thigh and honoured the footstool by placing it upon it, thus spoke to Káma who had declared his power as equal to the (achievement of the) object he had in view:—

12. "Friend, all this is possible for you to do; I have but two weapons, yourself and my bolt; my bolt (however) is powerless against those who are great on account of their power of austerities, while you go (unchallenged) everywhere and accomplish everything.

13. I know your strength, and hence I employ you, who are like me, in a business of grave import ; (it is) on observing his capability to support the earth that S'esha is asaigned the duty of bearing his body by Kṛishṇa.

14. In talking of the power of your arrow to hit the Bull-emblemed God (S'iva), you have almost undertaken our work : know that at present this is just the desired object of the gods (*lit.* those who have an allotted portion in a sacrifice) who have powerful foes.

15. These gods desire to have a general of their host, sprung from the energy of S'iva, for conquering (their foes). And he, the repository of the principal and accessary *mantras*, who has concentrated his mind on Brahman, can be subdued (managed) by the fall of your arrow only.

16 Strive to make him, who is self-restrained, love the pure daughter of Himálaya; she alone of all women is the proper ground for the depositing of his seed—so has the Self-born (Brahma') declared.

17. And the daughter of the Mountain-lord, at her father's bidding, is (now) waiting upon the Eternal one (S'iva) practising penance on the high region of Himálaya--so have I heard from the lips of the heavenly nymphs; (for) they form my band of spies.

18. So, then, go to accomplish (this business); do the work of the gods. This purpose can only be attained by the achievement of another object : it (therefore) has need of you as its primary cause, as the sprouting up of a seed requires water before it can make its appearance.

19. On him, the means of the attainment of victory by the gods, *your* missile only, we grant, has power; *you* are blessed; (the performance of) a deed, not accomplished by any other person, although (it be) unknown to fame, is the glory of men.

20. These gods are your suppliants; the business (you have to accomplish) is (for the benefit) of the three worlds; and the deed to be done by your bow is not very cruel : O wonder! Your prowess is to be envied!!

21. O Cupid, Spring is your helper, though unasked, through your comradeship. Who asks the wind to be the fanner of fire (*lit.* the devourer of sacrificial offerings) ?"

22. With the words "so be it", the God of love received on his head his master's command, like a garland offered as a gift of favour, and started; and Indra touched his body (as a mark of special grace) with his hand grown rough by stroking the Airávata (elephant).

23. He went to the Himálayan resort of Sthâṇu (S'iva), followed by Mádhava, his dear friend, and by Rati, with apprehension, determined to effect the work even at the cost of his body.

24. In that forest Madhu (the vernal season) manifested himself, having assumed his proper form, which was an object of pride to the Mind-born One (Kâma), acting antagonistically to the performance of austerities of the sages practising self-restraint.

25. When the hot-rayed one (sun) began to go towards the quarter guarded by Kubera (*i. e.* towards the North), out of the proper season, the Southern quarter sent forth wind from her mouth, like a sigh of anguish.

26. Then the As'oka tree put forth at once just from its stem flowers together with foliage, and did not wait for a touch from the feet, jingling with anklets, of beautiful ladies.

27. Madhu, (the vernal season), having fitted up the arrow (of Káma) in the shape of the young mango-blossom, with new leaves as its beautiful feathers, immediately inscribed on it the letters, as it were, of the name of the Mind-born (Cupid), in the shape of the bees.

28. The Karṇikára flower, though of gorgeous tints, pained the mind by its odourlessness ; generally the mind of the Creator of the world is averse to bestowing completeness of qualities on a thing.

29. The Palâs'a buds, extremely red and curved like the young moon, not being blossomed, soon shone like red marks of nails on (the persons of) the Forest-sites united with the vernal season (their lover).

30. The Vernal Beauty, having displayed on her forehead a *tilaka* (the *tilaka* flower) artistically painted with black pigment in the shape of the bees that swarmed over it, ornamented her lip in the form of the young mango-leaf with a red tint (red lac) mellow like the light of the morning sun.

31. The fawns, with their eyes blinded by the pollen-dust of the blossom of the Priyála trees, and intoxicated with passion, ran wildly against the wind in the forest-glades, full of the murmur of falling leaves.

32. What strain of sweet music was warbled out by the male Cuckoo whose voice had become impassioned by his feasting on the mango-sprouts, (that strain) became the mandate of Cupid competent to break down the pride of high-minded dames.

33. Perspiration made its appearance on the ornamental paintings (on the persons) of the Kimnara ladies, the complexion of whose faces was slightly yellow and whose lips looked bright (not being smeared with wax), owing to the passing away of the wintry season.

34. The ascetics, living in the forest of S'iva, seeing the untimely manifestation of spring, could, with difficulty, be masters of their minds whose perturbation was curbed with (great) effort.

35. When Madana reached that region, with Rati as his companion, and his flower-bow strung, all living things forming themselves into pairs manifested by their actions amorous feeling, pervaded by the sentiment of love gone to excess.

36. (Thus) the male bee, attentive to his dear mate, drank honey from the same flower-bowl; and the black antelope scratched with his horn his mate who had closed her eyes through the pleasant sensation caused by that touch.

37. The female elephant, through great love, gave to the male the water held in her mouth, fragrant with the pollen-dust of lotuses. The Chakravâka (*lit.* bearing the name of a member-wheel-of a chariot) flattered his mate by giving her a lotus-stalk half eaten (by himself).

38. The Kimpurusha, in the intervals of music, kissed his beloved's face, having its eyes rendered attractive as they rolled through intoxication caused by the floral wine, and having its paintings a little disfigured (*lit.* loosened) by the drops of perspiration brought on by exertion.

39. The trees, too, received close clasps from the arms, in the shape of tender twigs, of the creeper-wives, captivating with throbbing lips in the shape of young reddish sprouts and with breasts in the shape of dense clusters of flowers.

40. S'iva, though hearing the music of the heavenly damsels at such a time, remained absorbed in meditation; for never can obstacles disturb the contemplation of those who have complete control over themselves.

41. Then Nandî, standing at the entrance of the creeper-bower, with a gold staff resting against his left fore-arm, checked the Gaṇas, ordering them not to be mischievous, by the sign of his forefinger placed on the mouth.

42. And at his bidding the whole forest itself stood with its movements committed to a painting as it were, the trees having ceased waving

about, the swarms of bees having remained still, the birds having withheld their music, and the beasts having stopped roaming.

43. Having avoided his glance, as one does the quarter wherein shines Venus, when starting on a journey, Kâma entered S'iva's place of contemplation, screened all round with the thickly interwoven branches of Nameru trees.

44. He, the fall (destruction) of whose body was at hand, saw the Three-eyed God, absorbed in ascetic contemplation, seated on an altar of the Devadáru tree, covered over with a tiger's skin ;

45.—The fore-part of whose body was steady owing to the posture called Vîrâsana, who was sitting straight and fully drawn up, both of whose shoulders were a little bent, and on whose lap there lay as it were a full-blown lotus, owing to his two hands being placed there with the palms turned upwards ;

46.—The mass of whose matted hair was gathered upwards and tied with a serpent ; who had a double string of Rudra'kshas hanging down from his ears ; and who wore a black antelope's hide with knots, appearing still more darkish on account of the complexion of his neck ;

47.—Who was looking steadfastly at (the tip of) his nose with his eyes, the fierce pupils of which were motionless and shining but a little, which had desisted from the habit of knitting the brows, the thick lashes of which were not moving, and the vision of which was turned downwards ;

48.—Who, on account of the suspension of the vital airs (*lit.* the airs moving inside), appeared like a cloud not blustering up to burst into a shower, or like a reservoir of water unruffled with ripples, or like a lamp (burning) steady in a place free from wind ;

49.—Who was putting into shade the grace, softer than that of lotus-fibres, of the young moon, by the rays of light shooting forth from his head, having got a passage through the eye in the cranium;

50.—And who, having fixed in his heart his mind, with its operations through the nine gates (of sense) entirely suspended and completely under the influence of concentration, was realizing in himself his own Self, whom the seers call the Eternal.

51. Smara (Cupid), while looking at him, the three-eyed one, not to be assailed even in thought, in that posture, his hand drooping through fear, did not notice the bow and arrow dropped down from his hand.

52. Just then was seen the daughter of the Lord of immovables (Hima'laya) accompanied by the sylvan deities, reviving, as it were, by the beauty of her person, his prowess, almost deadened;

53.—Who wore a decoration of spring flowers, in which the *As'oka* flowers put into shade the rubies, the *Karnika'ras* bore the lustre of gold and the *Sindhuvàras* shone like a necklace of pearls;

54.—Who stooped a little with (the weight of) her breasts, and wore a garment of the hue of the morning sun, thus looking like a walking creeper covered with foliage and bending under the breast-like clusters of flowers;

55.—Who was again and again drawing up with her hand her zone composed of Bakula flowers, slipping down her hips, which was, as it were, a second string for his bow deposited there by Cupid who knew the appropriate place for it;

56.—And who, her eyes agitated through confusion, was keeping off, every moment, with a sportive lotus, a bee hovering round her Bimba-like nether lip, with its thirst (desire) excited by her fragrant breath.

57. On seeing her, faultless in all her limbs, and putting even Rati to shame, the flower-arrowed god (Cupid) again hoped for the accomplishment of his object respecting the Trident-holder (S'iva) who had conquered his senses.

58. Umá approached the entrance (to the abode) of S'iva, her future lord; and at the same time, he, too, having realized in himself the eternal light called *Parama'tman*, desisted from contemplation.

59. Then the Lord, slowly releasing all the vital airs in the body, the portion of the earth under him being, with great difficulty, upborne with the tops of his hoods by the lord of serpents, (S'esha) loosened the firm Vira'sana.

60. To him, Nandi, having saluted, announced the coming of the daughter of the Mountain-lord through a desire of waiting upon him, and ushered her into the presence of his lord, her admittance having been permitted (by him) with a mere sign of his eye-brow.

61. By her two friends was scattered a collection of spring-flowers, mixed with bits of leaves gathered with their own hands, at the feet of the Three-eyed God, with a bow.

62. Umà made a bow to the Bull-emblemed God with her head, when the tender leaf on her ear dropped down and the fresh Karṇikára flowers shining in the midst of her black tresses got loosened.

63. She was indeed told the truth by S'iva when he said—"*Do* you get a husband, who will not attend to another woman:" For, the words of the mighty do not in this world foster a sense contrary to their meaning.

64. Kàma, having seized this as the proper opportunity for (discharging) his arrow, being as if desirous of entering the fire like a moth, touched again and again the string of his bow, having fixed his eye on S'iva, while Umá stood hard by (*lit.* in the presence of Umá).

65. Then Párvatî offered to S'iva, given to asceticism, a rosary of the seeds of lotuses grown in the Mandákinî and dried up by the rays of the sun, with her hand which had a rosy complexion.

66. The three-eyed God, through his love for devotees, made ready to take that rosary; and at that very moment the flower-arrowed God placed on his bow his unfailing arrow called Sammohana (the Captivator).

67. S'iva, his firmness a little shaken, like the sea (agitated) at the rising of the moon, cast his eyes on Umá's face, the lower lip of which was like the Bimba fruit.

68. The daughter of the Mountain too, betraying her emotion by limbs that looked like the blooming Kadamba flowers (on account of the hair standing on end), stood with a half-averted face, wherein the eyes were agitated (through shyness) and which (therefore) appeared the lovelier.

69. Then S'iva, having strongly restrained the perturbation of his senses by means of his (perfect) self-control, and desiring to find out the cause of the disturbance of his heart, directed his eye towards the quarters.

70. Then he saw the mind-born one (Cupid), his clenched fist resting at the corner of his right eye,. his shoulders bent (forward) and his left foot drawn in, ready to sirike with his beautiful bow bent to (the figure of) a circle.

71. All at once a blazing fire with rising flames sprang from the third eye of him, whose ire was roused by the disturbance of his austerities, and whose face was terrible to look at owing to the knitting of the eye-brows.

72. Ere the cries of the gods—"Restrain thy ire, restrain thy ire, O Lord"—could rise in the sky, the fire, born of the eye of S'iva, left only the ashes of Madana.

73. While Rati, who for a time stood unconscious of the death of her husband, had a favour conferred upon her, as it were, by her swoon, occasioned by the sharp discomfiture, which stifled all the operations of her senses.

74. Having quickly destroyed him, the obstacle to his austerities, as the bolt of Indra does a tree, the Great ascetic, the Lord of beings

together with his followers, vanished from sight, in order to avoid the vicinity of women.

75. The daughter of the Mountain, knowing that the desire of her exalted father as well as her lovely body had been proved to be vain, and overwhelmed with shame all the more, because it happened in the presence of her two friends, somehow or other went homeward, like one dazed.

76. Just then the Mountain, having taken into his arms his daughter who deserved to be sympathized with and who had closed her eyes in fear of the anger of S'iva, went along his path, as does the elephant of the gods holding a lotus sticking to his tusk, with his body stretched to its full length on account of his great speed.

CANTO IV.

1. Then the wife of Káma, who was beside herself, being entirely in the power of the trance, was awakened by Fate, wishing to make her experience new widowhood with its unbearable pangs.

2. She made her eyes, opened at the close of the swoon, gaze attentively; (but) she did not know that the sight of her dear lord was for ever lost to her never-satiated eyes.

3. "O Lord of my life, art thou alive?"—so saying she got up; (but) she saw on the ground merely a heap of ashes, in a man's shape, due to the fire of the anger of S'iva.

4. Then she, again distracted (with grief), her breasts dusty from the touch of the ground, and her hair dishevelled, wailed, as if making that region (*i.e.* the creatures living therein) a sharer in her grief (*lit.* equally miserable).

5. "Thy body, which served as a standard for all amorous persons by reason of its resplendency (handsomeness), has been reduced to this condition; and yet I do not burst through grief! Hard-hearted, indeed, must be women!

6. Where hast thou fled, abruptly leaving me whose (very) life depends upon thee, forgetting thy love in a moment, as does a torrent of water adandoning a lotus after breaking down a dam?

7. Thou hast never done anything that would displease me, nor have I ever acted contrary to thy wishes: why is it, then, that, without cause, thou dost not present a sight of thee to Rati who is lamenting (thy loss)?

8. Dost thou remember, O Cupid, my binding thee with the strings of my waist-band whenever I was addressed with a wrong name by thee,

or my beatings of thee with lotuses used as ear-ornaments, hurting thy eyes with pollen-dust dropping from them ?

9. I know that the speech which thou usedst to utter to please me—*viz.* "thou dwellest in my heart"—is false; if it was not an empty compliment, how is it that thou art without a body, while Rati is uninjured ?

10. I will follow the path of thee who hast started on a new journey to the other world; but this world is cheated (of its pleasure) by Fate. The happiness of embodied beings does, indeed, depend on thee.

11. Who else but thee, O beloved, can enable the sweethearts terrified by the thunder of the clouds, to reach the houses of their lovers, when the roads of the cities are shrouded in nocturnal darkness ?

12. The intoxication of young damsels by wine is now a mockery, when thou hast ceased to exist—(the intoxication) that makes the red eyes roll (from side to side) and the words falter at every step.

13. O Bodiless One, the Moon, knowing that the body of thee, his dear friend, has become a subject-matter of tales, will give up his thinness, with great reluctance, even when the dark half (of the month) has passed away, as his appearance (in the sky) would (henceforth) be useless.

14. Say, by whom will the fresh blossom of the mango-tree, the beautiful stem of which is reddish-green and the sprouting of which is proclaimed by the notes of the male cuckoo, be now used as his arrow ?

15. The swarm of bees, which was many a time used as a string for thy bow by thee, seems by its hummings, in piteous tones, as if to sympathize with me, whose distress is great.

16. Rise again, recovering thy graceful form, and once more appoint the cuckoo, naturally clever in sweet (persuasive) talk, to the post of a messenger in love.

17. There is no peace for me, O Cupid, remembering as I do our secret sports, so familiar to us, and our embraces, accompanied by tremor and solicited by bowing down the head.

18. O thou expert in love-matters, here I bear on my person the vernal decoration of flowers arranged by thyself, but that beautiful body of thine is not to be seen.

19. Come, then, and finish the colouring of my left foot (*lit.* other than the right foot), before finishing the decoration of which, thou wast called away by being) remembered by the cruel gods.

20. As long as thou art not deceived (into loving them) in heaven, O dear, by the artful damsels of heaven, I will come to sit once more on thy lap, following thee by the way of locusts (*i.e.* burning myself on the funeral pyre).

21. O beloved, though I follow thee, this reproach will stand in connexion with me, *viz.* that Rati, bereaved of Madana, indeed lived (though it was) only for a moment.

22. How can the last decorations be done by me for thee, who hast gone to another world? For thou hast been simultaneously reduced to an unthought-of condition by (losing) both (thy) life and (thy) body.

23. I remember thy merry talk (*lit.* accompanied with smiles) with, and casting a side-glance (*lit.* looking from the corner of the eyes) at Madhu, as thou wast straightening the arrow, with the bow on thy lap.

24. Where is thy friend, Madhu, the delight of thy heart, who shaped thy bow with flowers? O, alas, can it be that he, too, is sent along the path taken by his friend, by the Trident-holder (S'iva) whose wrath is dreadful?"

25. Madhu, cut at heart by her cries of woe, as by venomed arrows, discovered himself in front of the woe-stricken Rati, to console her.

26. On seeing him she wept bitterly and beat her bosom so as to oppress her breasts; grief breaks out as if opening its flood-gates in the presence of one's own people (a relative or a friend).

27. Smitten with grief she thus addressed him—"Look, O Vasanta, what has remained of thy friend. These ashes, variegated like a pigeon, are blown about, particle by particle, by the wind.

28. Now reveal thyself to us, O Cupid. This Vasanta longs to behold thee; the love of men may be fickle towards women, but it cannot be so towards a friend.

29. By this thy comrade (*lit.* one who is always by thy side) the whole world, including the gods and the demons, is forced to own the empire of thy bow, the string of which is the lotus-fibre, and the arrows of which are the delicate flowers.

30. Gone is that friend of thine; he comes not back, like a lamp put out by a blast of wind; I am as it were the wick (of this lamp); behold me, enveloped in the smoke of unbearable misery.

31. Fate, sparing me while killing Káma, has only done half the butchery; when the firm, supporting tree is broken by an elephant, the creeper (hanging by it) tends (is bound) to come down.

32. Therefore, let this duty towards a friend, which comes next, be done by thee; pray, send me, who am afflicted, to my husband, by consigning me to the (funeral) fire.

33. The moon-light passes with the moon, and the lightning vanishes with the clouds; that the wife has to go by the way the husband has gone, is thus admitted even by lifeless things.

34. Besmearing my breasts with these ashes of the body of my beloved, I shall lay my body on fire as if on a bed of young leaves.

35. O gentle one, thou hast many a time helped to make up our bed of flowers ; do thou now pile up a pyre quickly for me, urged to do so (by me) with a bow with joined palms.

36. After that, by fannings in the shape of the south winds, speed up the fire set to me, so that it should burn quickly: it is indeed known to thee that Cupid cannot bear to live without me even for a moment.

37. Having done so, offer one handful of water for us two; that friend of thine, together with me, will drink it undivided in the next world.

38. O Vasanta, in the after-death ceremony for Káma offer the spray of mango-blossom, the leaves of which are tremulous; for the mango-blossom was dear to thy friend."

39. A speech, spoken in the sky, comforted Rati, thus prepared to abandon her life, as does the first shower (of rain) comfort a fish distressed by the drying-up of a pond ; viz.—

40. " O thou, wife of the flower-weaponed god, thy husband shall not be long unobtainable to thee : listen, how he came to the plight of a locust in the flame of the fire (sprung) from the eye of S'iva.

41. Prajâpati (the lord of creation) felt a lustful desire for his own daughter, his senses being excited by Kâma ; he then, having curbed the excitement, cursed Káma, who has thus experienced the fruit (of his own act).

42. 'When S'iva, made to look upon her with favour by her austerities, will lead P'arvatî to the altar, then, having got back his own bliss, he will unite Cupid again with his form.'

43. Thus did god Brahmá, when begged by Dharma, deliver a speech, setting forth a limit to Cupid's curse : the self-restrained and the clouds are the sources of both lightning and water (*i.e.* curses and favours).

44. So, O sweet woman, preserve this body which will be re-united with thy husband : a river, the water of which is drunk up by the sun, is again joined to a fresh current in the rainy season."

45. Thus did some being of unseen form discourage Rati's idea of seeking her death; and through his belief in that (being), Spring (*lit.* the friend of the flower-weaponed god) consoled her with words replete with good sense.

46. Then the wife of Cupid lived, (thinned by her misery), awaiting the end of the calamity, just as the crescent of the moon appearing by day and looking pale through the loss of rays, awaits the (coming of the) evening.

CANTO V.

1. Párvatí, baffled in her hopes by S'iva who burnt, in that manner, the mind-born deity (Cupid) in her presence, cursed her beauty in her heart : for beauty has for its guerdon good fortune as regards (the being liked by) one's beloved.

2. She wished to make her beauty fruitful by austerities, having recourse to *Samádhi* (contemplation); how else could she secure the two things—such love and a husband of that kind ?

3. Mená, hearing that her daughter, who had set her heart on S'iva, was resolved to practise penance, clasped her to her bosom, and spoke, dissuading her from the difficult vow of asceticism.

4. " In the house are such deities as thy heart would desire. Child, how widely different are the two—penance and thy body ! The delicate S'irísha flower can bear the tread of a bee, but not that of a bird."

5. Mená, though thus exhorting her daughter, whose desire was inflexible, could not dissuade her from her resolve : who can turn back a mind firm in its resolution to achieve a desired object, or water rushing towards a low ground ?

6. On one occasion, that steady-minded girl, through a friend who was her confidante, begged of her father, who knew her desire, a residence (*i. e.* permission to dwell) in the forest in order to perform religious austerities till their fruition.

7. Being granted permission by her great father, who was delighted at a persistence worthy of her, she repaired to a peak, full of (*i.e.* inhabited by) peacocks, which afterwards came to be known by her name among the people.

8. She, of a never-to be-shaken disposition, having given up her necklace, which used to rub away the sandal-paste (on her breast) by its tremulous threads, wore a bark-garment, tawny like the morning sun, the close union of which with her body was prevented by her elevated breasts.

9. As her face looked pretty by her decorated tresses, so it did by her matted hair also ; a lotus does not look beautiful only by the swarms of bees, but even by its union with moss.

10. The place of her waist-band was made red by that string of Muñja grass having three threads which was fastened there for the first time on that occasion,—which (string) she wore for her penance and which (by its harsh touch) caused her hair to stand erect every moment.

11. She made her hand, the fingers of which were (now) pricked while plucking the tender blades of Kus'a grass, the friend of the rosary of Aksha beads, (—her hand) which was turned away from (*i.e.* no longer employed in painting) her lower lip from which the red colour

had disappeared, and from her (play-) ball reddened by the unguent of her breasts.

12. She, who would experience pain even by the flowers dropped down from her hair in her rollings on her costly bed, sat and lay down (now) on the bare earth-platform, using her creeper-like arm as a pillow.

13. By her who was under a vow, had been left, as a deposit to be taken back, the two things with the two, *viz.* her sportive gesture with the slender creepers, and her unsteady glances with the female deer.

14. Never slack in her care, she personally reared up the saplings with outpourings from breast-like-jars—saplings, her motherly affection for which, being first-born, even Kárttikeya would not be able to set aside.

15. And the fawns, fondled by being given handfuls of forest-grain, trusted her so far, that out of curiosity she could measure (the length of) her own eyes with theirs before her friends.

16. Sages came there, desirous of seeing her, who used to take a sacred bath, to offer oblations to the fire, to wear a bark as her upper-garment, and to recite (sacred texts): age is no consideration in the case of those who are old in spiritual attainments.

17. The sacred grove, too, became holy, where the previous antipathy between warring beasts was abandoned, where the guests were well gratified with the (gifts of) desired fruit by the trees, and where the sacred fires were kindled in newly-built huts of leaves.

18. When she thought that the desired fruit was not to be attainable by that kind of penance which she had been already practising, then, disregardful of the delicacy of her body, she began a greater penance.

19. She, who was fatigued even by playing with the ball, entered upon the course of life of anchorites: verily her body was composed of gold lotuses, as it was delicate by nature and yet tough (full of substance).

20. In summer, she of sweet smiles and a delicate waist, sitting in the midst of four blazing fires, gazed at the sun with her sight not directed to anything else, having got the better of (*i. e.* being accustomed to bear) his lustre that dazzles the eye.

21. (Then) her face, greatly scorched by the rays of the sun in that manner, bore the beauty of a day-lotus; but gradually, only round the long corners of her eyes, dark colour made its appearance.

22. Only the water that came to her without any effort on her part, and the rays of the moon (*lit.* Lord of the constellations), full of nectar,

broke her fast, the means being not different from those by which trees subsist.

23. She, extremely heated by various fires—the one wandering in the sky and those lighted by means of fuel, and being drenched with the fresh showers at the end of the summer, gave out, along with the earth, (reeking) heat that ascended upwards.

24. The drops of first water (showers) rested for a moment on her eye-lashes; then, sriking against the nether lip, broke as they fell on the elevation of her breasts; and thence, stumbling through the (three) folds of her skin, reached, after a long delay, her navel.

25. The nights, the witnesses of the rigid penance of her who slept on a (bare) stone-slab, and who lived in open space (*lit.* not under a sheltered roof) and in the midst of unceasing showers accompanied by winds, watched her, as it were, with their glances in the shape of lightning (-flashes).

26. Determinately standing in water, she passed the nights of Pausha (cold season) when the (winter) winds scattered around a thick mass of snowy sleet, pitying the pair of the Chakraváka birds (which stood) before her, separated and crying for each other.

27. By her face, which was as fragrant as the lotus (itself) and which shone with the quivering leaf of the nether lip, she at night restored the (beauty of) lotuses to the waters (of the stream), the wealth of lotuses of which was destroyed by the showers of snow.

28. The sternest severity of austerities lies in subsisting on leaves fallen from the trees of their own accord; but that also she spurned; hence was that gentle-talker named Aparná by those conversant with history.

29. By this and other kinds of penance, she, wearying her frame, delicate as a lotus-fibre, day and night, left far behind the *tapas* practised by anchorites with hardened frames.

30. Then a certain ascetic (*lit.* one with matted hair) wearing an antelope's skin, and holding a staff of Palás'a, of ripe speech and burning, as it were, (*i. e.* refulgent) with Bra'hmanic lustre, entered the penance-forest, like the first stage of life (Brahmacharya) in bodily form.

31. Pa'rvatí, kindly disposed towards (all) guests, went forth to receive him, offering worship with great reverence; even when there is equality, the acts of the firm-minded towards great personages are such as are full of extreme reverence.

32. Having accepted the worship (hospitality) offered according to proper rites, and apparently eased his fatigue for a moment, he, look-

ing at Umâ with quite innocent eyes, began to speak to her, without giving up the proper mode (*or* decorum).

33. "Are sacrificial wood and Kus'a grass easily obtainable for holy rites? Is the water suitable for thy bathing? And dost thou practise austerities proportionate to thy strength? For, the body is the ultimate means of performing religious duties.

34. Are the young leaves of these creepers, made to sprout by the water sprinkled by thee, thriving?—the leaves which vie with thy nether lip, red though long bereft of the scarlet of Alaktaka (red lac).

35. Is thy mind pleasingly disposed towards the fawns, who take the Kus'a grass from thy hands through their love (for thee), and who, O lotus-eyed one, present a close resemblance to thy eyes by their unsteady glances?

36. O Mountain-born lady, the remark that beauty never leads to a sinful course of life is not false (*lit.* not a deviation from a general rule), since, O thou of noble form, thy conduct has become worthy of imitation even for the ascetics.

37. This Up-holder of the earth (Mountain) together with his family, has not been so sanctified by the waters of the Ganges, dropping from the firmament and resplendent with the offerings of flowers scattered by the seven (heavenly) Sages, as he has been by thy pure (*lit.* free from the taint of sin) acts.

38. O thou of pure intentions, on account of this thy conduct, Dharma (*i. e.* pursuit of religion) strikes me pre-eminently as the best of the group of the three (*viz.* Dharma, Artha and Ka'ma), since this only has been selected and followed by thee, with a mind from which all thought of *Artha* (wealth) and *Kâma* (desire) has been cast out.

39. It does not behove thee to regard me as a stranger, to whom special hospitality was accorded by thee; for, O thou of stooping body, the friendship of good people is declared to be formed after seven words have been exchanged between them (*or*, after seven steps have been walked together).

40. Hence, O thou to whom penance is a treasure, I, in whom curiosity, natural to the twice-born (a Bra'hmaṇa), is aroused, am desirous of asking something to thee, a lady of great forbearance. If it be not a secret, thou wilt kindly give a reply.

41. Thy birth is in the family of Brahma', the first progenitor (of mankind); thy body is as if it were the manifestation of the collected beauty of the three worlds; the happiness of affluence need not be sought after by thee (since it is already present); and thine youth is fresh. Say, what blessings, other than these, can be the reward of penance?

42. Such a course of action is possibly followed by high-minded ladies when overtaken by an unbearable evil; but, O thou of slender waist, no such evil can be discovered in thy case by the mind directed through the channel of thought.

43. O thou of beautiful brows, this thy form is incapable of the humiliation of grief; and whence can there be disrespectful treatment under the parental roof? Nor can there be any insult from strangers; (for) who can stretch his hand to snatch away the jet of the lustre of the serpent's gem?

44. Why is it that, having abandoned ornaments, thou hast, in youth, put on a bark-garment suitable to old age (only)? Say if the night at its beginning, with the moon and the stars prominently displayed, is fit to receive the (approach of) dawn.

45. If thou art seeking heaven, thy effort is vain, (since) the regions (on the slopes) of thy father are the land of gods. And if thou dost desire a (suitable) husband, cease from thy austerities; (for) a jewel is sought after, and has not to seek.

46. Thy hot sighs have betrayed (thy secret); and yet my mind is still more plunged in doubts; I see not that there is any one who (as a husband) is at all to be sought after by thee; how can there be one then, who is unobtainable when sought after?

47. The young man thou yearnest after, must indeed be hard-hearted, since he still holds off, seeing the matted hair, tawny like the tips of the blades of paddy, hanging loosely on thy broad cheeks from which the ear-lotus has been long cast off.

48. Of what person, having a heart, the mind is not afflicted, on seeing thee, extremely emaciated by the observance of saintly vows, with the places of ornaments scorched mercilessly by the sun and therefore looking like the crescent of the moon by day?

49. I take thy lover to be cheated by the pride of his beauty, since he does not, for a long time, make his face the mark for (*i. e.* present himself to the view of) thy eyes of lovely glances and arching eye-lashes.

50. O Gauri, how long wilt thou torture thyself? I too have religious merit accumulated in my first stage of life. Do thou get thy desired husband by (the grant of) a half of it; him, however, I desire to know well (fully)."

51. She, thus addressed by the Bráhmaṇa, having entered (divined) the inmost secret (of her heart), could not speak out the desire of her mind (through bashfulness). So she only looked at her friend standing by her side, with eyes devoid of collyrium.

52. Her friend said to the ascetic—" O sage, know thou then, if such be thy curiosity, him for whom this lady has made her body a means of practising religious austerities, as one should (make) a lotus (a means) of warding off the sun.

53. This lady, disdaining all the lords of the four quarters, the great Indra and others, of exalted dignity, seeks a husband in the holder of the Pinàka bow (*i. e.* S'iva), who is not to be conquered by charms, as is evinced by his destruction of the mind-born (Cupid) formerly.

54. The arrow of the Flower-bowed god, whose point failed to reach the enemy of the (three) cities (*i. e.* S'iva), being hurled back with the Huṃkàra sound, difficult to be borne, struck her in the heart with a cruel blow, although his body had been destroyed.

55. From that time forth, powerfully affected by love, and with her curling tresses whitened by the sandal-paste applied to her forehead, the maiden never felt at ease even when reclining on the surfaces of snow-slabs while in her father's house.

56. Many a time did she make the daughters of the Kiṃnara kings, her companions in the songs sung in the woods, burst into tears, by her words (of grief) scarcely articulate in the throat choking with tears, while the exploits of the Pináka-holder (*i, e.* S'iva) were being sung.

57. At night, when its third part only remained, she, having closed her eyes for a moment, all of a sudden woke up with incoherent cries of—" O thou of azure neck, where dost thou go ? "—having her arms thrown tight round an imaginary neck.

58. And He (S'iva) of the cresent-crest, drawn (*i. e.* painted) with her own hands by this silly girl, was upbraided in private with the words: " Thou hast been considered all-pervading by the wise ; how, then, dost thou not know this person, (as being a) slave to thy love ? "

59. At last, when she could find no other way to win the Lord of the universe (S'iva), though she searched (long and well), she, with the permission of her father, came with us to this sacred forest for practising austerities.

60. This our friend has seen fruit appearing on these trees which have been planted (*lit.* given birth to) by herself and which have been the witnesses of her austerities : and yet the craving of her heart, which has for its basis the moon-crested God, does not seem even to be near sprouting-time (*i.e.* about to bear fruit).

61. I do not know when he, difficult to be secured though sought after, will favour this our friend, worn by penance and looked at

by us, her friends, with tears, as Indra favours (with showers) the earth, distressed by his holding off (the rain)."

62. Thus informed by her, who knew the secrets of Pârvatî's heart, so as to make her noble intention clear, that handsome Brahmachárin, without showing signs of delight, asked Uma' whether it was so, or (merely) a joke.

63. Then the daughter of the mountain, putting the rosary of crystal beads on (*or*, into) her forehand, with the fingers drawn together so as to resemble a bud, spoke, with great difficulty, in measured words, having (first) adjusted her speech (in her mind) for a long time.

64. "O thou, who art chief among those who know the Vedas, thou hast heard the truth (*lit.* as it is); this (humble) person is ambitious of attaining the highest post. These austerities are a means of getting that; nothing is inaccessible to desire (fancy)."

65. Then said the ascetic—"Mahes'vara is well known; and yet thou hast a yearning after him; knowing him as possessing a love for inauspicious things, I cannot see my way to approve of thy desire.

66. O thou who hast fixed (thy mind) on a worthless object, how can this thy hand, with the nuptial string tied round it, bear the first clasp of S'iva's hand decked with circling snakes?

67. Do thou thyself consider adequately, whether these two things should ever deserve to be brought together—(your) bridal silks gleaming with the (figures of) swans, and (S'iva's) elephant-hide dripping with blood?

68. Who, even an enemy, would consent (to see) the foot-prints, leaving marks of *alaktaka* (red dye), of thy feet accustomed to tread upon flower-decorations (on the floors) of the saloons, traced upon burning-grounds spread over with the hair (of corpses)?

69. Say—Is there anything more ungainly than this, that the ashes of the funeral pyres, easy to be obtained from the bosom of the three-eyed God, will make their home on thy bosom, which has (hitherto) been a (fitting) place for sandal-wood paste?

70. Then again, this another humiliation will await thee—great men will have smiling countenances, on seeing thee, fit to be borne by a lordly elephant, striding (S'iva's) old bull, after marriage.

71. By their earnest (desire) for union with S'iva, two things have now become objects of commiseration: that bright digit of the moon, and thyself who art the moonlight of the eyes of this world.

72. His body possesses monstrous eyes, his parentage is obscure (not to be found out), and his wealth is shown by his nudity (*lit.* having the quarters for a garment). O thou having eyes like those of a

young gazelle, whatever is expected in a husband,—is that, even in part, found in the three-eyed One ?

73. Turn thy heart from this evil desire; what a distance is there between one of that kind, and thee with auspicious marks ? A stake in the cemetery is not to be treated by the good with the Vedic rites proper for a sacrificial post."

74. By her, whose anger could be guessed from her quivering nether lip, were cast askance upon the twice-born, talking adversely, her eyes, red at the corners, with her creeper-like brows contracted in a frown.

75. And him she thus addressed :—" Indeed, thou dost not know S'iva aright, since thou talkest thus to me. The dull-witted find fault with the course of life of the magnanimous, which is not in common with that of other people, and the motive of which is difficult to divine.

76. Auspicious things are resorted to by one, who is anxious to ward off calamities or to attain prosperity. What has he, who is the protector of the world and has nothing to wish for, to do with these, which corrupt the functions of the soul by generating desires ?

77. Himself poor, he is the spring of wealth ; living (*lit.* found) in the cremation-ground (*lit.* the abode of the dead), he is the lord of the three worlds ; being of terrible form, he is (still) called S'iva (*lit.* of gentle aspect). None are there who know the Trident-holder for what he really is.

78. The shape of him whose form is the universe cannot be determined : it may be resplendent with ornaments or entwined with serpents, or it may be dressed in elephant-hide or in silken garments, or it may have on its crest a vessel of skull or the moon.

79. Certainly the particles of the ashes of the funeral pyre become sanctifying by having obtained a touch of his body; and hence they are rubbed on their heads by the dwellers of heaven, (*i. e.* gods) when (they are) dropped down in the act of exhibiting the gestures of dancing.

80. Indra, having for his vehicle the rutting elephant of the (eastern) quarter, touches, with his crest, the feet of that wealthless God who goes about on a bull, and makes their toes red with the pollen-dust of the full-blown flowers of the heavenly trees.

81. Thou, of depraved soul, although wishing to speak the faults of the Lord, hast said one good thing about him. How can he, who is considered the parent of even the self-existent Brahma, have his origin known ?

82. Enough of disputing : let him be, without any reservation, what you have heard him to be. My heart, however, pervaded by the

one sentimet of love, is set on him: one who wants to act as one likes, does not regard (*i. e.* care for) criticism (*i.e.* ill-talk).

83. O friend, stop this boy who seems desirous of saying something, as his upper lip is quivering. Not only he who talks ill of the mighty, but also he who listens to him, is a sinner.

84. Or rather, I (myself) will go from this place ;" so saying the maiden, with the bark-garment slipping from her bosom, started: and the bull-emblemed God, assuming his own form, held her, with a smile.

85. On seeing him, the daughter of the Mountain-lord, all a-trembling and her body covered with perspiration, and having one foot raised to walk away, was uncertain whether to go or to stay, like a river hampered by the impediment of a mountain in the path.

86. " O thou of stooping limbs, henceforth I am thy slave, bought by thy austerities "—as the Moon-crested God said these words, she immediately forgot (all) her exhaustion caused by the austerities : for, fatigue gives fresh vigour again by the fruition (*i.e.* the achievement of the desired object).

CANTO VI.

1. Thereafter Gaurî instructed her companion, when alone (with her), to give (the following) message to S'iva (*lit.* the soul of the universe)—" The lord of mountains (Himálaya) is my giver (in marriage): let him be recognized as an authority (*i. e.* he should be applied to for my hand)."

2. She, who had communicated her message through her friend, and who remained relying on (*or,* firmly devoted to) her beloved, shone when near (him), like a young mango tree speaking through the cuckoos, and steadily awaiting the spring when near at hand.

3. Having promised, ' It will be so ' and sent away Uma' with great difficulty, he, the chastiser of Cupid, though of (*i. e.* mentally called) the seven luminous sages.

4. Illumining the sky with the haloes of their lustre, the great sages (*lit.* those whose penance was their treasure) immediately appeared before the Lord (S'iva), accompanied by Arundhatî ;

5.—(The sages) who had bathed in the streams of the celestial Ganges, the waves of which bear along the flowers of the wish-granting trees grown on its banks, and which are scented with the temporal juice of the quarter-elephants;

6.—Who wore sacred threads of pearls, were dressed in gold bark-garments and carried jewel-rosaries, (thus) looking like the heavenly trees that had betaken to the ascetic mode of life (retirement from the world);

7.—Who were looked up to with a bow by the thousand-rayed (sun) himself, having placed his horses below and bent his flag;

8.—Who had rested, at the time of the calamity of universal destruction, on the tusk of the great Boar, along with the earth, that was lifted up (from water), with her creeper-like arms attached to it (the tusk);

9—Who, on account of their finishing the work of the remaining part of creation, after Brahmâ, are mentioned (described by those conversant with history) as the primeval creators;

10.—And who, although enjoying the fruits of their exceedingly pure penance, which they had practised in previous lives and which had now come to fruition, remained (continued to be) ascetics still.

11. The chaste Arundhatî who was in their midst with her eyes directed to the feet of her husband, shone exceedingly, as though she were the success incarnate of their asceticism.

12. The Lord (S'iva) looked upon (*or*, received) her and the sages without any distinction of honour; for, with the good, whether one is male or female is no consideration, character alone being the object of honour.

13. At her sight S'iva's desire for a wife became stronger: good wives, indeed, are the prime cause of religious performances.

14. Religious duty having made S'iva take a step with regard to (*i.e.* think of marrying) Pàrvatî, the mind of Cupid, full of fear at previous guilt, breathed with relief (*or*, hope).

15. Then all those sages, who were adepts in the Vedas with their accessory branches, having duly honoured the Lord of the universe, (thus) spoke to Him, with the hair of their bodies standing on end from joy:—

16. " The Veda that was duly studied by us, the sacrifices that were offered into the fire in the prescribed form, and the penance that was practised,—the fruit of all that has ripened for us to-day,

17.—inasmuch as by Thee, Lord of all the worlds, we have been made to be the object of Thy mind which (by itself) is beyond the reach of our wish.

18. He, in whose mind Thou abidest, is, indeed, the greatest of all blessed persons: what then to say of him who dwells in the mind of Thee, the cause of Brahmâ (*or*, of the Vedas)?

19. It is true that we occupy a station higher than that of the sun and the moon; but to day (it has become) far higher than theirs, owing to the favour of Thy remembrance of us.

20. We think highly of ourselves, (having been thus) honoured by Thee: generally the regard of superiors creates confidence in one's own merits.

21. O Thou with diverse eyes, where is the necessity to express to Thee the delight caused to us by Thy having remembered us! (For) Thou art the in-dwelling soul of all embodied creatures.

22. Thou art seen visibly, and yet we know Thee not in Thy real nature; be pleased and explain Thyself: (for) Thou liest not within (*i.e.* art beyond) the range of mental faculties.

23. Which (of the three) is this form of Thine?—whether that by which Thou manifestest the universe, or that by which Thou preservest it, or that which resolves the universe back (into its original state)?

24. Or rather, O God, let this our high-soaring request stand aside: in the first place command us, who have presented ourselves at Thy mental call. What shall we do?"

25. Then the great God replied to them, heightening the scanty lustre of the moon on his head with the bright rays of his teeth.

26. "It is known to you that none of my activities are for my own self; and verily I am shown to be of such nature by my eight forms.

27. That I (*or*, I who am of such kind) have been solicited for progeny (*i.e.* to beget a son), by the gods tormented by their enemies, as the (lightning-bearing) cloud is (solicited) for a shower by the Chátaka birds oppressed by thirst.

28. For this reason I wish to take (for wife) Pàrvatî for (begetting) a son, as a sacrificer secures *arani* (particular pieces of wood) for the generating of a holy fire.

29. Hima'laya should be requested by you to bestow her (in marriage) on me: (For) the connexions (relationships) brought about by the good do not lead to bad results.

30. Know me also to be not deluded, (since I shall be) joined in relationship with him who is exalted (lofty), who keeps within proper bounds (has stability), and who bears the burden of the earth.

31. That he should be addressed in such and such a way for his daughter, need not be told to you; for the learned inculcate (those very) rules of conduct (which are) prescribed by yourselves.

32. The revered Arundhati too will do well to take part therein: generally in a matter of this nature matrons have great competency.

33. Set out then for Oshadhiprastha, the (capital) city of Himâlaya, for the accomplishment (of the business) ; we shall meet again just at this cataract of the Mahakos'î."

34. When he, the foremost of ascetics, became inclined to marriage, the ascetics, born of Brahma', gave up their shame for having wives.

35. Then having said 'Very well,' the group of sages departed. And the Lord also went to the place first settled.

36. The great sages, too, having jumped into the sky, which was dark like a sword, and equalling the mind in velocity, reached Oshadhiprastha;

37.—(The city) which was built as it were, by transplanting Alaka' itself, the repository of wealth and abundance (*or*, abundant wealth), and peopled, as it were, by causing an exodus of the redundance of heaven;

38.—Which was encircled by the streams of the Ganges, which had herbs blazing within its ramparts, the wall of which was built of large jewel-stones, and which was charming even in (*i.e.* notwithstanding) its fortifications;

39.—Wherein the elephants had overcome their fear of lions, where the horses were of the *Bila* breed, and of which the Yakshas and the Kimpurushas were the male citizens and the sylvan goddesses the females;

40.—In which, in the houses, with clouds clinging to their tops, the sounds of tabors, confounded with the echoes of the thunderclaps, are distinguished by the strikings of hands accompanying them;

41.—Where the beauty of flags planted on the staves of the houses is produced, without any attempt on the part of the citizens, by the desire-granting trees themselves, having garments fluttering on their branches ;

42.—Where in the wassail-grounds attached to the crystal mansions the reflections of stars get at night to the position of (*i. e.* serve as) offerings (of flowers);

43—Where at night, amorous females going out to meet their lovers are ignorant of (*i. e.* do not experience) nocturnal darkness (even) on cloudy days, the paths being shown by the light of the (glittering) herbs;

44.—Wherein life had youth for its last stage (*i.e.*, there was neither old age nor death) ; where no other destroyer was known than (Cupid), the flower-arrowed god; and where sleep brought on by sexual exhaustion was (the only) suspension of consciousness;

45.—In which lovers are made supplicants till favour (reconciliation) is shown, by the (jealous) anger of beloveds; in which there are contractions of the eye-brows, quiverings of lips and threatenings with graceful fingers

46.—(And) whose outer garden is the fragrant Gandhamâdana, in which the Vidyádhara travellers sleep in the shades of the Saṃtānaka (heavenly) trees.

47. Now, the divine sages, on seeing the capital of Himálaya, thought their performance of holy rites with the object of attaining heaven to be a deception.

48. Being looked at by the door-keepers with faces raised up, they, with the masses of their matted hair steady like painted (flames of) fire, descended with speed into the palace of the Mountain.

49. The row of sages, (when it) alighted from the sky, with the seniors preceding in due order, shone like a series of the reflections of the sun in water.

50. Bending the earth by the plantings of his feet, heavy with inward substance, the mountain (Himâlaya), taking the materials of worship, advanced from a distance to receive them, (who were) worthy of adoration.

51. With lips mineral-red (*also*, having red minerals for his ruddy lips), tall, with arms huge like fir trees (*also*, having the large fir trees for his arms), and with a chest naturally strong like a rock (*also*, having rocks for his chest), he was clearly known to be Himálaya.

52. Himself leading the way, he made them, to whom reception was accorded in the due form and who were of holy practices, enter his harem.

53. Having taken his seat, the lord of mountains, with joined palms, addressed this speech to the divine (*lit.* powerful) sages who were already seated in cane seats:—

54. "Your unexpectedly-obtained sight appears to me like a shower without the (previous) rise of clouds, or like a fruit without the (previous) appearance of a flower.

55. By (this) your favour I consider myself like one enlightened, having been ignorant, or as if transformed into gold, having been made of iron, or as if raised to heaven from the earth.

56. From this day I am to be approached for purification by creatures; for, that is called a holy (*i. e.* purifying) place which is resorted to by the deserving.

57. O you, the most eminent of the twice-born (Brâhmaṇas), I consider myself sanctified by these two only, by the fall of the Ganges on my head, and by the water from your washed feet.

58. I consider even my two-fold body, as separately favoured: the movable (body) by being in the position of your servant, and the immovable (body) by being marked by your feet.

59. My limbs, though spreading to (*i.e.* covering all space within) the extremities of quarters, are ill sufficient to contain the growing joy caused by the honour done (to me) by you.

60. By the sight of you, resplendent (illustrious) ones, not only the darkness in my caves is removed, but even my internal darkness (ignorance), which is beyond Rajas (the quality of passion), is dispelled.

61. I do not see that there is anything to be done by you; and if there be any, what is there that cannot be accomplished (by you)? I think your arrival here is simply for my purification.

62. Still, be pleased to give me a command in some matter (to do something for you): for, in respect of their masters, servants consider an order as a favour.

63. My own self, my wife here, and this my daughter, who is the life of my family: say which of us you want to be at your service: about external things I speak not with any regard (*i.e.* no need to say that they *will be* at your service)."

64. Hima'laya, who spoke thus, said the same thing twice, as it were, by its echo resounding from the mouths of the caverns.

65. Thereupon the sages urged Aṅgiras, best skilled (*lit.* the foremost speaker) in matters to be spoken, to speak: he replied (thus) to the Mountain—

66. "All this (that you have said) is befitting to you and even more; the loftiness of your mind and of your peaks is alike.

67. Rightly are you called Vishṇu in your immovable form: for your middle (*or*, interior) portion has become the support of all beings, movable and immovable.

68. How could the Serpent (S'esha) have borne the earth on his hoods as delicate as lotus-stalks, had you not sustained it from the bottom of the nether world?

69. Your glories and your rivers, having their currents unbroken and unstained, and being unobstructed by the waves of the seas, purify the worlds owing to their sanctity.

70. Just as Gaṅgà is lauded by (her birth from) the foot of the supreme Lord, so she is by you of lofty peaks, (who are) her second source.

71. The greatness of Hari pervaded all space, cross-wise, upwards and downwards, when attempting to take the three steps: but with you it is natural.

72. By you having got a place among those enjoying a share of the sacrificial food, the lofty golden peak of Meru is rendered futile (*i.e.* made of less consequence).

73. All hardness has been transferred by you to your immovable form. But this your animate form, given to the propitiation of the good, is humble (*lit.* bent low) with devotion.

74. Hear, then, the business which has brought us here. It is, however, your own business; but we are participators in this by our advising in beneficial matters (*i.e.* inasmuch as we have to advise you in what is to your benefit).

75. He, who bears, along with the crescent moon, the sublime title of 'Lord', which is endowed with the attributes *animan* (the power to become atomic) and others, and which does not apply to any other person;

76.—By whom is sustained this universe by means of his forms, Earth and others, adding to one another's power, as a carriage is held by horses on the road;

77.—Whom residing in the interior of the body (the heart) the ascetics seek, and whose abode, as the wise declare, is free from the fear of the recurrence of birth.

78. That S'iva himself, the witness of the doings of the world and the giver of desired objects, asks for your daughter, through us (*lit.* by words addressed through us).

79. You will then do well to unite him with your daughter, like sense with words: for, a daughter given to a good husband is not to be regretted by (*i. e.* is no matter of regret for) the father.

80. Let all these creatures, immovable and movable—as many as they are—consider her their mother; for, S'iva is the father of the universe.

81. Let the gods, after having bowed down to the dark-necked God, tinge her feet with the rays of their crest-jewels.

82. Uma' is the bride; you, her giver in marriage; here are we soliciting her; and S'iva is the bridegroom: This combination (of circumstances) is enough for the exaltation of your family.

83. By forming an alliance through your daughter, be the father (-in-law) of the father of the universe, who praises none, but is praised by all, who adores none, but is adored by all."

84. While the divine sage (Añgiras) was speaking thus, Pa'rvati, who was by her father's side, counted the petals of her sportive lotus with a down-cast look.

85. The Mountain, though his desire was entirely fulfilled, looked up to the face of Mena': Generally in matters relating to daughters, householders are guided by their wives (*lit.* have wives for their guiding eyes).

86. Mena', too, approved of all that, the much-desired object of her husband. Wives devoted to their husbands never disagree with their lords with regard to their desired objects.

87. He, having thought in his mind after reflection—'this would be the proper reply to this'—took hold of his daughter, auspiciously adorned, at the conclusion of the (sage's) speech.

88. "Come on, dear daughter: thou art made alms to S'iva (the soul of the universe). The sages are the petitioners: I have obtained the fruit of a householder's (*or*, married) life."

89. Having said so much to his daughter, the Mountain said to the sages—" Here bows to you all the bride of the three-eyed God (S'iva)."

90. Having commended the speech of the Mountain. noble on account of his acting up to their wishes, they (the sages) magnified Ambiká with benedictions that were soon to fructify.

91. Arundhatí placed on her lap that blushing girl, whose two gold ear-rings slipped down in her hurry (*lit.* earnest desire) to make a bow.

92. And by (mentioning) the virtues of the bridegroom who had no other wife before, she consoled her mother whose face was suffused with tears. and who was distracted on account of her affection for her daughter.

93. At that very moment, being asked by S'iva's (future) kinsman about the (auspicious) day for marriage, the bark-clothed sages, saying that it would be after three days thence, departed.

94. Having taken leave of Hima'laya and returned to S'iva, they told him that their mission had been succesful; and, being dismissed by him, (they) flew up into the sky.

95. The Lord of creatures (S'iva), too, eager for union with the Mountain's daughter, passed those days with difficulty. What other person, who is swayed (by the senses), will these emotions not distract, when they affect even the Almighty (S'iva)?

CANTO VII.

1. Then (after the settling of the wedding-day), in the waxing (fortnight) of the moon (*lit.* the Lord of herbs), and on the day endowed with the virtue (auspiciousness) of the Jâmitra (seventh position from the zodiacal sign fixed as auspicious for marriage), Himálaya, with his relatives gathered, performed the ceremonies preliminary to the wedding of his daughter.

2. On account of the ladies being busily engaged, out of affection, in every house, in getting up the auspicious things fit for the marriage-ceremony, the city and the inner apartment of the mountain (Hima'laya) were comparable to (*i.e.* appeared to form) one house.

3. The city, the high roads of which were strewed with heavenly flowers, the row of flags in which was made of China-silk, and which was ablaze with the brilliance of its golden outer-gates, appeared as if it was Heaven transplanted.

4. Although they had a number of children, Umâ alone, like one seen after a long time or like one revived after death, especially became the life of (*i. e.* an object of special love to) her parents, as she was about to be given away in marriage.

5. Having a benediction pronounced (upon her every time), she passed from lap to lap and enjoyed ornamentation after ornamentation: though shared by (other) relatives, the love of the mountain's family was centred in her (*lit.* was focussed on that one object).

6. During the Muhúrta (= period of 48 minutes) sacred to the sun, and when the moon was in conjunction with Uttara phalgunî (its twelfth mansion), such of her kinswomen as had their husbands and male children living, put decorations on her body.

7. She adorned the dress which she wore for being smeared with oil (previous to bathing), the beauty of which was heightened by the tender sprouts of *dúrvá* mixed with white mustard seeds, in which a silk cloth was worn reaching beyond the navel (*or,* in which the silk cloth worn round the navel was removed), and in which an arrow was held (in the hand).

8. The maiden holding (*lit.* having come in contact with) the arrow (to be held) at the ceremony previous to the marriage-rite, shone like the digit of the moon stimulated (*i.e.* waxing) by the ray of the sun, at the termination of the dark fortnight.

9. The women conducted her, to the four-pillared saloon,—her, the oil applied to whose body was removed by the powder of Lodhra, whose person was besmeared with the slightly dry Ka'leya unguent, and who had worn a cloth fit for bathing.

10. In that (saloon) which had a pavement of sapphire stones placed in it and which was variegated by being inlaid with ornamental rows of pearls, they bathed her with water poured out of gold pots, to the accompaniment of (the music of) the *túryas*.

11. She whose body looked brighter by the auspicious bath and who had put on a dress (*lit.* a pair of bleached garments) fit for approaching the bridegroom, shone like the earth, that had received a washing from rain-water and that had the (white) Kâs'a flowers full-blown.

12. From that place she, being clasped, was conducted by ladies devoted to their husbands to the middle of the auspicious altar which had a canopy and four jewelled pillars (at its four corners) and which was provided with a seat.

13. Having seated that girl of a slender frame upon it, so that she faced the east, the ladies sitting before her, having their eyes attracted by real (*i. e.* unartificial) beauty, delayed for some time, though the articles of decoration were at hand.

14. One of the ladies tied the beautiful mass of her hair, the moisture of which was removed by the smoke of incense and which had flowers inside it, with a garland of yellow Madhúka flowers intermixed with *dúrvá* grass, so as to form a charming knot.

15. They (the ladies) applied white aloe paste to her body, and decorated it with ornamental paintings drawn with *gorochaná* (yellow pigment): she (thus) stood surpassing the beauty of the three-coursed river (Ganges), the sandy banks of which are marked with the Chakravâka birds.

16. Excelling (the beauty of) the lotus with bees adhering to it, or the moon's disk with streaks of (dark) clouds, the grace of her face (set off) by her decorated tresses left no occasion for (even) the talk of comparison (*or*, equalization).

17. The barley-sprout placed on her ear, by its having attained excellence (as it hung) over her cheek roughened with the besmearing of *lodhra* powder and excessively yellow with the paint of *gorochana'*, arrested eyes (*i.e.* held riveted upon it the eyes of the onlookers).

18. The lower lip of that lady of symmetrical limbs, which was parted by a line (in the middle), the redness of which was heightened by a thin layer of wax, and which had the fruition of its loveliness at hand, gave rise to an indescribable beauty by its throbbings.

19. When blessed by her friend after dyeing her feet (with lac-dye), jocosely saying—"Touch (strike) the digit of the moon on thy husband's head with this"—she (Párvatí) struck her (friend) with a wreath of flowers, without uttering a word.

20. The ladies decorating her, seeing that her eyes were as graceful as the petals of a lovely (*lit.* well-grown) lotus, took up collyrium (for putting it into them), not because they thought it would add to their beauty, but because it was auspicious to do so.

21. While the ornaments were being put on (her person), she shone like a creeper with flowers springing up, or like the night with stars rising therein, or like a river with the Chakraváka birds resorting thereto.

22. Observing in a mirror her form looking magnificent (by that dress), she, with her long eyes steady, became eager to approach S'iva: surely the dressing of women has for its fruit (*i.e.* object) the sight of (*i.e.* its being seen by) their husbands.

23, 24. Then her mother Mená, taking with her two fingers the auspicious wet yellow orpiment and the red arsenic and having raised her face, on the two ears of which hung two bright ear-rings, made with great difficulty the *tilaka* mark, required for the marriage-rite, (on the forehead) of her daughter, giving shape thereby just to the desire which rose in her mind for the first time, and which attained growth (was intensified) after the development of Umá's bosom.

25. She (Mená) also fastened the marriage-string of wool round her (Umá's) hand, which was misplaced as her eyes were filled with tears of joy, but which was being pushed back (to its right place) by the nurse with her fingers.

26. She, clad in a fresh silk (white) garment and holding a new mirror, appeared to great advantage, like the shore of the milky ocean with a mass of foam on it, or like the autumnal night with the full moon.

27. The mother, expert in what was to be done (*lit.* what one should be made to do) (on such an occasion), having made her, the main-stay (*or*, glory) of the family, bow down to the worshipped tutelary deities, caused her to seize (*i.e.* to fall at) the feet of chaste ladies in due order.

28. "Do thou obtain the ever-continuous (*lit.* uninterrupted or undivided) love of thy husband"—thus was Umá, bowing before them, spoken to (blessed) by them; but by her, sharing half of his body, the blessings of her loving relatives were outstripped.

29. The Mountain, well-versed (in things to be done) and polite, having finished the ceremonies connected with her in a manner befitting (*or*, proportionate to) his wishes and his wealth, sat in the reception-hall, attained by his friends, (and) awaiting the arrival of S'iva (the bull-emblemed God).

30. In the meantime, on Kubera's mountain (Kaila'sa), before S'iva, the destroyer of the cities, too, were placed the decorations suited to his

marriage, the first of its kind, by the divine Mothers, diligently engaged (*or*, full of respect).

31. Out of respect for them, the Lord simply touched that wealth of auspicious decorations : the very dress of the almighty God assumed the forms (of different decorations) necessary for a bridegroom. Thus—

32. The ashes themselves became the white unguent for body, and the skull attained the beauty of the bright crest-ornament ; while the elephant's hide itself was transformed into a silk garment having on its borders marks (of swans &c.) made with *rochana'* (yellow pigment).

33. The eye itself, which shone in the middle of the frontal bone, and which had the clear tawny pupil in its interior, stood on the side of the presence of (*i. e.* served as) the *tilaka* mark of *Haritàla* (yellow orpiment).

34. Only the bodies of big snakes underwent a change, as they transformed themselves into different ornaments in their proper places; the brilliant gems in their hoods remained just as they were.

35. What was the use of putting on the crest-jewel to S'iva whose crest is always united with the moon, which sheds even during the day the brilliance of its rays, and which does not manifest the spot on account of its being merely a digit ?

36. He, the sole source of wonderful things, who had (thus) created all the well known articles of dress by his divine power, saw his image reflected in a sword brought by a *gana* (servant) who was near.

37. He, reclining on Nandî's arm, mounted the lordly bull whose broad back was covered with a tiger's skin, who looked like the mountain Kailása, and who had contracted his huge bulk out of devotion to him, and set out.

38. The Mothers, following the God and having their ear-rings agitated by the motion of their vehicles, made the sky a bed of day-lotuses, as it were, with their faces reddish-white with the pollen (in the shape) of their encircling effulgence.

39. Behind them who had the brilliance of gold, shone the goddess Kálî, wearing ornaments of white skulls, (and thus looking) like an array of blue clouds with cranes (assembled) and throwing flashes of lightning far in the front.

40. Then the auspicious sound of music which was sent forth by the *ganas*, marching in front of S'iva (the trident-holder) and which pervaded the domes of their celestial vehicles, told the gods that it was right time (for them) to wait upon (S'iva).

41. The sun held the new umbrella made by Tvashṭṛi (the heavenly architect); and the god, with his head at no great distance

from its silk fringe, appeared to have the Ganges, as it were, falling on his head.

42. Gaṅgá and Yamuná also, assuming visible forms and holding *chauries*, served the god ; at that time they appeared to have as it were a flight of swans, although their river-forms were changed.

43. The primeval Creator (Brahmá), and the god bearing the mark S'rívatsa (Vishṇu), came incarnate to him, magnifying his glory with the words ' Be victorious,' like fire with clarified butter.

44. That was but one form which divided itself in three ways. Their seniority or juniority is common (interchangeable); sometimes S'iva is prior to Vishṇu or Vishṇu to S'iva ; sometimes Brahmá to them both ; and sometimes the two to Brahmà.

45. The protectors of worlds, with Indra chief among them, appearing in modest (humble) dresses, the signs of royalty being cast off, and betokening Nandi to allow them an interview, bowed with joined palms when ushered in.

46. He honoured Brahmá with a nod of the head, Vishnu with spoken words, Indra with a smile, and the other gods with a mere look, according to seniority.

47. The seven sages first pronounced a benediction, saying, ' May you prosper,' and he said to them with a smile,—" In this nuptial sacrifice that is commenced, you have already been chosen by me as the officiating priests."

48. S'iva (*lit.* the wearer of a portion of the Moon (the Lord of stars), who cannot be overpowered by dark passions and whose glory of his destruction of the three cities was sung by celestial lute-bearers, (*or*, skilled choristers) with Vis'vávasu as their leader, (then) crossed the way.

49. The bull bore him on, moving charmingly through the sky with his golden little bells resounding, and repeatedly shaking his horns, which piercing through the clouds appeared as if covered with mud by being struck against a bank.

50. He (the bull), drawn as if by the glances of S'iva extending forward like golden strings, arrived, in a moment, at the city protected by Himálaya, the lord of mountains, which had never experienced an attack from an enemy.

51. The god with his neck dark like a cloud, alighting in its vicinity from the path marked by his own arrow (*i.e.* from the sky), being looked at by the townsmen with faces raised up through curiosity, went to the surface of an adjacent (piece of) ground.

52. The lord of mountains, delighted at his arrival, went forth to receive him, with arrays of elephants mounted by his rich kinsfolk, as though with his own ridges full of trees having full-blown flowers.

53. The two parties of the gods and the mountains, with their bustle reaching far, met at the gate of the city with its doors thrown open, like two streams of water breaking through the same bridge, with their commotion spreading to a distance.

54. The mountain felt ashamd at being saluted by S'iva, who is adorable to the three worlds. For he did not know that his own head was already bent far low by his (S'iva's) glory.

55. He (Himálaya), with his beautiful face brightening through joy, led the way (*lit.* walked in front) of his son-in-law, and conducted him to his wealthy city, in whose market-streets flowers were scattered knee-deep.

56. At that time, the beauteous ladies of the city, eager to obtain a good sight of S'iva, spontaneously acted in the following manner, in the rows of palaces, all other occupations being set aside.

57. A certain lady, going in haste to the window, did not at all think of tying up her mass of hair, which was loosened from its tie with its wreath of flowers dropped down, though she held it in her hand.

58. Some lady, snatching her fore-foot held by her dressing maid, while the red dye on it was yet wet, and having given up her graceful gait, stretched, as far as the latticed window, a line of footprints marked with red lac.

59. Another lady, having adorned her right eye with collyrium, while her left eye was without it, went, in that very state, to the vicinity of the window, holding (in her hand) the painting pencil.

60. Another of the fair sex, who was looking (*lit.* directed her eye) through the lattices of the window, did not fasten the knot (of her under-garment) loosened by her hasty movement, but stood holding up her garment with her hand, the brilliance of whose ornaments had penetrated her navel.

61. Of another lady who rose in haste, the half-strung waist-band, the gems of which dropped at every ill-placed step, had only its string left at the time, fastened to the root of her big toe.

62. The windows, having their openings filled up with the faces of those ladies, stirred up with great curiosity, with the scent of wine remaining within and the rolling eyes like black bees hovering about, looked as if they were decorated with lotuses.

63. In the meantime S'iva. (*lit.* the moon-crested God) came to the royal road with numerous flags flying and adorned with ornamental

arches raised,—S'iva who doubled, even in day-time, the splendour of the tops of palaces by shedding moonlight on them.

64. The women, ardently looking at him, the one object of sight, with their eyes, did not think of any other object of sense: thus the functions of all their other senses in their entirety had as it were entered their eyes.

65. "Rightly did Párvati, though of delicate frame, practise penance, hard to perform, for him. Blessed will be the woman (*lit.* she will have the mission of her life fulfilled) who obtains the privilege of even serving him; what to say then of her who can repose on his lap?"

66. "Had not the Creator united with each other this pair, of covetable beauty, then the effort of that Lord of creation to endow these two with beauty would have been fruitless."

67. "Surely the body of Ka'ma (the flower-arrowed god) was not burnt by him, with his anger roused; it was from shame, I think, that Kāma relinquished his body of his own accord.'

68. "Having, through good luck, entered into relationship, ardently desired by the mind, with this lord, O friend, the lord of mountains will hold higher his head, already lofty by his sustaining the earth."

69. The three-eyed god, thus hearing the talks gratifying to the ear, of the gay ladies of Oshadhiprastha, came to the abode of Himálaya, where the handfuls of fried rice were pulverized by armlets.

70. Being assisted by Vishṇu who offered him his arm, he then descended from his bull, like the sun from an autumnal cloud, and entered the apartments of the lord of mountains previously entered into by Brahma'.

71. Just after him there arrived, at the house of the mountain, the gods headed by Indra, the great sages preceded by the seven sages, and the attendants of S'iva, as great achievements follow an excellent beginning (measure).

72. There the lord, seated on a seat, duly accepted the offering of worship with jewels, honey, curds and clarified butter, and a pair of new silk garments—all of them presented by the mountain, with the recitation of the holy *mantras*.

73. He, clad in silk garments, was conducted to the bride by the well-behaved keepers of the inner apartments, as the (water of the) sea is carried near the shore by the rays of the rising moon (*lit.* the new rays of the moon).

74. Being united with her, the beauty of whose moon-like face was heightened, like the world united with the autumnal season (the beauty o

whose face, the moon, is increased), S'iva had the lotuses of his eyes expanded, and had the water of his mind rendered clear (*i. e.* delighted).

75. The eyes of the two, eagerly longing to see each other, which shrank back as they met and which were withdrawn after being steadied a little, experienced at that moment the restraint of bashfulness.

76. S'iva (*lit.* the God of eight forms) received her hand, the fingers of which were red, and which was offered by her father, the mountain (*or*, by the mountain's priest), as if it were the first sprout of the God of love, whose form was concealed in the body of Umâ through his fear of him (S iva).

77. By the joining of their hands the hair on Umà's body stood on end, while S'iva (*lit.* the bull-bannered God) had his fingers perspired it was as though the action of the mind-born one (Cupid) was equally divided between the two.

78. Since an ordinary bride and bridegroom, on being married, attain excellent splendour (beauty) from the presence of these two, how can the beauty of the two be described, when they themselves are brought in contact with each other ?

79. By going round the blazing fire, keeping it to the right, that couple, now united, shone like the day and night closely joined to each other and revolving round the sides of Meru.

80. The priest, having conducted the bride and the bridegroom round the fire, with their eyes closed owing to mutual contact, made the bride offer fried rice into the kindled fire.

81. She, following the instructions of the priest, bent her face towards the smoke, of agreeable smell, arising from the (burning) handful of fried rice; the smoke, touching her cheek with its forepart, attained for a moment the state of the ear-lotus.

82. By receiving the smoke as required by the religious custom, the face of the bride had the orbs of its cheeks a little moistened and ruddy, had the tint of the black collyrium flushed in the eyes, and had the barley-sprout worn as ear-ornament withered away.

83. The Bráhmaṇa (priest) said to the bride, " Dear child, this fire is the witness to the conclusion of your marriage-rite: practise righteousness with S'iva, your husband, giving up argumentation (*i.e.* with implicit acquiescence)."

84. Those words of the preceptor were drunk (*i.e.* listened to attentively) by Párvatí, with ears stretched up to the borders of the eyes, like the first water of the rains (*lit.* come from the great Indra) by the Earth extremely parched by the sultry season.

85. Directed by her eternal lord, charming to look at, to see the polar star, she, raising her face, with her throat choked with bashfulness, said, with difficulty,—' Seen.'

86. With their marriage-ceremony thus performed by the family-priest versed in the ceremonial, the two parents of creation (S'iva and Pàrvatî) bowed to the Creator, seated on a lotus.

87. The bride was greeted by the Creator with the words—"Blessed one, be you the mother of a hero." Though the master of speech, he became slow to think (*i.e.* was at a loss to know) as to what blessing to pronounce in the case of S'iva.

88. Thereafter, the two, the bride and the bride-groom, came to the four-cornered altar furnished with decorations, and, sitting on gold seats, experienced the application of wet whole-rice to the forehead, which is customary with the world and (one) to be coveted.

89. The goddess of wealth (Lakshmî) held over them the lotus-umbrella, which possessed the beauty of a network of pearls by means of the drops of water attached to its petals, and the long stalk of which served as its pole.

90. The goddess of speech (Sarasvatî) praised the couple with speech of a two-fold composition : the laudable bridegroom in a speech refined by grammatical purity, the bride in language easily comprehensible.

91. They saw, for a while, the first representation (of a play), in the combination of the different incidents of which the styles of description were properly brought out, in which the different sentiments were delineated by proper modes of music, and in which there were graceful bodily movements (*i.e.* gesticulations).

92. At its termination the gods, with joined palms placed across their diadems, prostrated themselves before S'iva, who had married a wife, and begged that the service of Káma, who had got back his body at the expiration of the curse pronounced on him, should now be accepted.

93. The Lord, whose anger was gone, permitted the operation of Káma's arrows even on him. Surely a request, preferred to their master at the right time by those who know their business, bears success.

94. Now, having dismissed the hosts of gods, the moon-crested god, taking the mountain's daughter by the hand, went to the nuptial apartment in which pots of gold were placed, which was furnished with decorations (of flowers, jewels &c.), and in which a bed was spread on the ground.

95. There in secret the Lord made Párvatî laugh, by the fantastic distortions of the faces of his followers,—Párvatî who looked graceful on account of bashfulness due to her being newly married, who turned away her face though drawn towards himself by him, and who replied with difficulty even to her friends who used to sleep with her.

CANTO VIII.

1. After the wedding-ceremony, as the daughter of the Lord of mountains experienced fear mixed with love, towards S'iva, he (S'iva) enjoyed thrilling pleasure which heightened his desire.

2. Although she did not reply when addressed, desired to go away when held by her garment, and slept on the bed with her face turned aside, still she gave delight to S'iva.

3. When her lover, full of curiosity, feigned to be asleep, Párvatî turned her eyes towards his face; but as he smilingly opened his eyes, she closed hers as if (they had been) struck by lightning.

4. Trembling, she obstructed the hand of S'amkara as it was placed near the region of her navel; but her garment of its own accord had its tying knot completely loosened.

5. When her lover was before her she became confused and did not remember the advice given by her friends, *viz.* "O friend, in this manner you should wait upon S'iva in private, restraining your fear."

6. When S'iva, the destroyer of the bodiless god (Cupid), was assiduously asking her questions in order to start conversation even on some irrelevant topic, Párvatî (merely) looked at him and gave a reply consisting (only) of a nod of the head.

7. In private, with her garment taken off, she closed S'iva's (two) eyes with her two palms; but, as his (third) eye on the forehead continued looking, she had her efforts foiled and became helpless.

8. Dear to S'iva was the union with his bride, although it obstructed passion, and in which response was difficult to obtain, there being no offering of the lower lip (on her part) while kissing, while her hands hung loose when very firmly embraced.

9. Párvatî could endure only that, and nothing else, on her lover's part, *viz.* kissing without biting the lower lip, marking with nails without wounding, and enjoyment in moderation.

10. At morning-time she did not, owing to bashfulness, satisfy the curiosity of her friends who began to ask her questions about the night's happenings; but her heart was eager to tell.

11. And, while observing in a mirror (the marks of) enjoyment, when she saw immediately behind her own reflection that of her lover seated at the back,—what was it that she did not do in shame?

12. The mother (Mená) was pleased when she saw her (Párvatí) whose youth was enjoyed by S'iva, the black-necked God. For brides dispel their mothers' mental grief by their being the favourites of their lords.

13. After a few days S'iva, with great difficulty, caused his beloved to incline to (*or*, to be reconciled to) (love sport). Having known the taste of love, she gradually abandoned her perverseness towards enjoyment.

14. Pressed to his bosom, she embraced her lover. She did not turn away her face when it was desired (to be turned towards him) by him. She became slack in obstructing his hand as it tremblingly searched for her girdle-zone.

15. In a few days only, their affection for each other grew (*i. e.* waxed) strong—(the affection) which was manifested by their gestures, in which displeasure was not to be seen, which was full of pleasing talk, and which could not tolerate separation even for a moment.

16. Just as the bride loved the bridegroom worthy of her, so too did he love her. For the Ganges does not leave the ocean, and the ocean, too, finds the greatest delight in tasting (the nectar of) her mouth.

17. The skill, proper for young ladies, which she learnt when she became the disciple in private of S'iva who taught her enjoyment,—that same (skill) she offered to him by way of teacher's remuneration.

18. Shaking in pain her hands, (tender) like (young) spronts, as her lower lip was released after it was bitten by S'iva, Pa'rvati cooled it in a moment with the cool crescent-moon on his head.

19. S'iva, too, when his (third) eye on the forehead was pained by her hair-powder in the act of kissing, held it to the breath of Pàrvati's mouth, whose fragrance was like that of a full-blown lotus.

20. Taking favour on Cupid by thus enjoying (following) the path pleasing to the senses, S'iva, the bull-bannered God, lived for one month only, in the house of the lord of mountains in the company of Pa'rvatî.

21. Having taken the permission of Himálaya who was distressed with sorrow at being separated from his daughter, that Self-born One (S'iva) sported in various places, moving about on his bull whose speed was immeasurable.

22. He, the blessed one, whose vehicle was as fleet as the wind, came to the mountain Meru; and, being embraced by Párvatí's breasts, and being intent on enjoyment, enjoyed (there) a night when his bed was made up of broken leaves of gold.

23. And, becoming the bee on the lotus of Párvatí's mouth, he lived on the slopes of the mountain Mandara, where the stones were marked with the (impressions of the) bracelets of Vishṇu (having a lotus springing from his navel) and which had obtained the fresh drops of nectar (as it was churned out of the ocean).

24. Being closely clasped round his neck by the tender arms of Pa'rvatí as she was frightened at the roar of Rāvaṇa, the Father of the universe (S'iva) enjoyed bright moonlight on the mountain of Kubera (Kaila'sa).

25. Once, while he sported on the grounds of the Malaya mountain, the breeze from the South, like an adulator (readily doing agreeable things), removed the fatigue of his beloved (Pa'rvatí)—(the breeze) which had shaken the branches of sandal trees (was cool), and which wafted the filaments of Lavaṃga flowers (was fragrant).

26. Pa'rvatí struck her lover with a golden lotus, and had her eyes closed, (when struck) by the water from his (S'iva's) hands; she sported in the river (Ganges) in the sky, her girdle being rendered superfluous by the row of fish (in the river, gathering round her waist).

27. In the Nandana garden, as he decorated her with the flowers of the Párijáta, usually worn in her hair by S'achí, the daughter of Puloman, the odd-eyed one (S'iva) was longingly looked at, for a long time, by celestial damsels.

28. S'iva in the company of his wife, having thus enjoyed happiness Heavenly as well as Earthly, once repaired to the mountain Gandhamádana, when the sunshine was becoming red (*i. e.* in the evening).

29. There, being seated on a slab of golden rock, he saw that the sun was observable with the eyes (alone), and (thus) addressed his lawfully wedded wife who was reposing on his left (*lit.* other than the right) arm—

30. "Having as it were transferred the beauty of the lotuses to your eyes which are reddened in their third part (corners), this lord of the day (*i.e.* the Sun) is ending the day, like the Lord of Creation (ending) the Universe at (the time of its) destruction.

31. As the low-sinking Sun is removing the contact of his rays with the spray, these streams on your father (*i.e.* the Himálaya) become deprived of their encircling rain-bows.

32. In the lake, the small distance has (now) become great, between the crying and helpless Chakravâka birds, who have dropped the half-bitten lotus-filaments, and whose necks are turned round (in order to obtain a sight of each other).

33. Having abandoned the place they occupied by day, the elephants are taking water to last them for consuming till morning--(water) which is rendered fragrant with pieces of the branches of the Sallakî trees, and in which the bees are confined within lotuses.

34. O lady of measured speech! See--by his elongated reflection, the Sun, as he hangs over the ridge of the western quarter, has formed a golden bridge as it were, upon the waters of the lake.

35. Leaving the pond wherein the mud is deep, the leaders of the herds of wild hogs are coming out, having passed the sunny day, and looking as though they had eaten the tender (*or*, curling) sprouts of lotus-stalks, by reason of their having (white) tusks.

36. O thou with plump thighs, this peacock who has taken his position on the top of a tree and whose circular tail is yellow like molten gold, is as it were drinking the lessening sunshine at the close of the day.

37. The sky, which on account of the appearance of darkness in the eastern region, has become like a lake wherein the mud has been exposed, and from which the Sun has taken off the water in the form of its light, appears like a lake in which very little (water) is left.

38. With deer entering the court-yards of the cottages, and with the small trees moistened with the sprinkling of water at their roots, these hermitages, wherein sacrificial cows are entering, and wherein (sacred) fires are kindled, present a charming appearance.

39. The lotus, although it is closed like a bud, still for a while remains with a hole left in it, as if to give, with affection, entrance to the bee desirous of residing therein.

40. With the reddish Sun whose rays are shooting widely apart and lessening (in number), the western quarter appears like a damsel adorned with the *tilaka* (mark) of a Bandhujîva flower having filaments.

41. Thousands of the Sun's followers (*i.e.* sages, Va'lakhilyas and others), drinking (*i.e.* subsisting upon) the heat of his rays, are panegyrizing him as he deposits his lustre with Fire, with hymns whose notes charm his chariot-horses.

42. This Sun here, having deposited the Day with the great ocean, is going to the setting mountain, with his steeds whose necks are bent down, whose eyes are rubbed by the *chauries* on their ears, and whose manes are twisted by the yoke.

43. When the Sun has set, the sky is as if it were fast asleep. Such is the course of great lustre : whatever it illumines when shining, that same it surely closes up (*i. e.* darkens), when no longer present there.

44. Twilight, also, has followed the revered body of the Sun as it reposes on the top of the setting mountain. How should she not follow him in his trouble, when she was formerly, in his prosperity (*i. e.* in the morning), placed in front (by him) in that manner ?

45. O thou with curly hair ! Here shine the edges of clouds, red, yellow and brown, as though the twilight-time has cleverly painted them with brushes for you to look upon.

46. See, the mountain has himself divided the evening sunshine, as it were, among the tangled manes of lions, and among the trees putting forth new foliage, and among the summits rich in minerals.

47. In the evening these ascetics, who know the proper mode, with their heels lifted up from the earth and offering handfuls of sacred water, respectfully and in privacy praise, for (their own) purification, the Supreme Soul.

48. You should, therefore, permit me, too, for a while to perform the necessary holy vows. O thou of charming speech ! Your friends, who are skilled in amusing, will divert you (during the interval)."

49. Then, treating the words of her lord with contempt, and curling her lip, the daughter of the king of mountains talked at random with Vijayá who was near.

50. S'iva, too, performed, with the proper *mantras*, the (holy) rites belonging to the close of the day, and again coming to Párvatí who refused to speak to him owing to her anger, said with a smile—

51. " O thou who are angry without any cause ! Give up your anger ; I was caused to bow down by Twilight : it is not otherwise (as you seem to think). Do you not know your lawful husband (myself) as conducting himself like a chakravàka bird (towards you) ?

52. O beautiful-bodied one ! This is that form,—which is waited upon (by all) at sunset and sunrise,—which was formerly abandoned by Brahmá after he had created the Pitṛis ; hence, O proud lady, I have respect for this (Saṃdhyá).

53. See that Twilight here, obstructed by the prevailing darkness, and lying now as though fixed on the ground, appearing like a stream of liquid minerals and decked on one of its banks with a row of *tamála* trees.

54. The western direction bears the evening sunshine, remaining as a red streak after what has gone down, as a battle-field bears a blood-covered scimitar, standing up obliquely.

55. O thou with long eyes! Now that the light appearing at the (interval) between the night and the day is hidden behind Meru, here this intense darkness spreads unchecked in all directions.

56. The eyes cannot see above, nor below, nor around, nor before, nor behind. At night this world, enveloped by the membrane in the shape of darkness, is as it were residing in the womb.

57. Pure and turbid, stationary and moving, curved and what possesses the quality of straightness,—all these have been equalized by the darkness. Fie upon the greatness of bad things (or persons), since it destroys all distinction!

58. Here indeed is rising the moon, the lord of sacrificing Bráhmaṇas, in order to dispel the darkness of the night. See, O lotus-faced lady, the face of the eastern quarter is as it were covered with the pollen of Ketaka blossoms.

59 Having the moon whose form is hidden behind the Mandara mountain, the night with the stars appears like you surrounded by your dear female friends, with me listening to your words at the back.

60. The (eastern) quarter, urged on by the night, gives out this orb of the moon, like a secret, whose coming out was prevented until the day ended, and before which was seen a slight moonlight like a smile (*also,* a slight smile like moonlight).

61. See: a pair of chakraváka birds between whom there is great distance, is imitated by the moon, whose lustre is like that of a ripe *Phalinî* fruit, by having marked both the sky and the water in the lake by his orb (and its reflection).

62. It is possible to cut (*i.e.* divide), with the cavities at the ends of nails, the newly-spreading rays of the moon (the lord of herbs), which are tender like the fresh sprouts of barley, in order to provide you with ear-ornaments.

63. Having collected darkness with his rays, as if it were a mass of hair (collected) with fingers, the moon is as though kissing the mouth of the night, wherein the eyes in the shape of (day-) lotuses have been closed like buds.

64. See, O Párvatí; the surface of the sky, wherein the darkness is half removed by the new rays of the moon, is looking like the Mánasa lake, becoming clear after it was made turbid by the bathing of elephants in it)

65. Giving up its reddened state, this moon has again become white as orb. Truly, in the case of persons who are pure by nature, any change brought about by the fault of time does not exist permanently.

66. The light of the moon is stationed on lofty things, while the nocturnal darkness has taken to low places. Surely, the Creator himself has assigned places to merits and faults, as befit each.

67. By the drops of water from the moon-stone, the appearance of which is produced by the moon's rays, this mountain is awakening, at the wrong time, these peacocks who have been asleep on the tree on its slopes.

68. O thou who art beautiful beyond argument! With his rays throbbing on the tops of the Wish-yielding trees, the moon is now as if actively curious in forming strings of necklaces.

69. On this mountain, as it abounds with high and low regions, this moonlight, along with (this) darkness, appears like the (decorative) ashes applied in various designs to the body of an elephant in rut.

70. As though unable to bear (contain) the liquid of the moon's light, drunk in the acts of blooming, this lotus, suddenly emitting the hum of bees, bursts to its stem (*i. e.* expands fully).

71. O angry one! See : the silk-garment which is hanging from the Wish-granting tree, a confusion about whose form is produced by the bright moonlight, is made distinct only when it turns in the blowing breeze.

72. It is possible to fasten up your hair with these pieces of moonlight which fall brokenly, through their leaves, under the trees, and which are delicate like flowers fallen under them, being lifted up with the fingers.

73. O sweet-faced one! Here is the moon united with the usual star, whose orb is twinkling, as a bridegroom (is united) with a newly-wedded girl who is trembling through fear.

74. O thou whose eyes are fixed on the lunar orb! The moonlight is growing as it were from the region of your cheeks, which is white like the stalk of the S'ara grass blossomed when ripe, and which is illumined with the flashing reflection of the moon therein.

75. Bringing in her own person the wine provided by the Wish-giving trees placed in a goblet of red sunstone, here comes this presiding deity of the Gandhamādana forest, towards you who are staying (here).

76. O sportive lady! Your face is as fragrant as new *bakula* flowers, and your eyes are naturally red. What other quality can wine impart when it finds a place here (*i. e.* when it is drunk by your mouth)

77. Or rather, the devotion of your friend must be honoured, (therefore) drink this, which will excite passion"---having thus spoken charmingly, S'iva made that Pārvatī drink that wine.

78. Just as a common mango-tree should be changed into one of the kind called *Sahaka'ra* owing to the inscrutable working of the Creator, Párvatî underwent a change, born of drinking that (wine), but which, though a change, was attractive.

79. Immediately that beautiful-faced one came under the influence of the two, S'iva and Passion, who deprived her of her shyness, who wanted to take her to bed, and whose lust was kindled.

80. Then S'iva drank for a long time, not with his mouth but with his eyes, the mouth of Párvatî whose eyes were rolling, wherein words stammered, which was covered with drops of perspiration, and which was smiling for no (apparent) reason.

81. Carrying her, whose golden girdle was hanging loose and who was heavy to bear on account of the weight of her hips, S'iva entered an abode built of gems and furnished with articles of comfort called into existence by his power of (*i.e.* obtained by) meditation.

82. With his beloved for his companion, he there slept on a bed, like the moon (the lord of Rohiṇi) on an autumual cloud,—a bed on which lay an upper sheet white like swans, and which looked as lovely as the sandy bank of the Ganges.

83. He was not satisfied with that enjoyment of Párvati, in which his moon was pained by the merciless seizures of her hair, in which nail-marks were made heedlessly (*i.e.* at the wrong places), in which there was (mutual) emulation, and in which her girdle was broken.

84. Only through compassion for his beloved, he, whose bosom was clasped by her, showed a desire to close his eyes (in sleep) when the rows of stars were hanging low (in the west).

85. He, accustomed to be praised by the wise, woke up at dawn along with the beds of golden lotuses, auspicious songs being sung for him by Kinnaras who took up the Kais'ika melody in a series of rising notes.

86. Breezes from the forest-regions of Gandhamádana, which were skilled in causing lotuses to bloom, and which had produced waves in the Mānasa lake, served for a while that couple (S'iva and Pa'rvatî) when they had relaxed their embrace.

87. His eyes being captivated at that moment by the series of nail-marks at the root of her thighs, S'iva prevented his beloved as she was tying up her garment which had become very loose.

88. He enjoyed amorous sports, being impassioned at seeing the [illegible] of his beloved, whose eyes were reddened owing to want of sleep, whose lower lip was injured owing to the deep tooth-marks, whose hair was dishevelled, and whose *tilaka* (mark) was wiped away.

89. When the night ended, even though it was bright day-break, he did not leave the bed, the upper sheet of which had become uneven with folds, in the middle of which the girdle with its thread broken was lying huddled together, and which was marked with the dye applied to the feet.

90. Wishing to taste, day and night, the nectar of the mouth of his beloved, which enhanced his delight, he became invisible to all who sought to see him, being (merely) informed (of their coming) by Vijayā.

91. While S'iva was sporting there, treating day and night both equally, he passed a hundred and fifty seasons as though it was one night. He did not lose his thirst for amorous pleasures, as the fire inside the ocean (is never satiated) with its rolling waters.

KUMARASAMBHAVA

NOTES

---:o:---

Canto I.

कुमारसंभवम्—कुमारस्य संभवः the birth of Kumâra or Kârttikeya; स एवाभेदोपचारात् कुमारसंभवं (also ०संभवः) काव्यं, the same denotes the composition descriptive of it by 'the transference of an epithet.' *Cf.* रघुवंश, रत्नावली &c.; see Sid.-Kau. on Pâṇ. IV. 3. 87. It is not a good way to take this as कुमारस्य संभवो यस्मिन् (काव्ये), a व्यधिकरण बहु० being ungrammatical; also because संभव has to be taken in the sense of संभववर्णन

Śl. 1. अस्ति &c.—A poet may introduce a poem by invoking a blessing (आशीः) on his readers or the audience, or by a salutation (नमस्क्रिया) to his favourite deity, or by indicating the subject (वस्तुनिर्देश) at once, as here. See Malli. The letter अ as representing Vishṇu (अकारो विष्णुरुद्दिष्टः; see our note on प्रणव Ragh. I. 11) is auspicious (Mângalika). उत्तरस्यां दिशि—That is the region to the north of Central India (मध्यदेश) which is considered as the land of gods and therefore holy *Cf infra* V. 45. देवतात्मा—having a divine being for its presiding or animating deity (*i. e.* who is a deity himself) and so having another and a divine form as distinguished from the *Sthâvara* form. The purpose served by this epithet is explained by Malli. (एतेनास्य...सिद्धि. *i. e.* capacity to discharge the functions of a living being). हिमालयः—हिमवान्हेमकूटश्च निषधस्तस्य दक्षिणे । नीलश्वेतश्च शृङ्गी च उत्तरे वर्षपर्वताः ॥ V. P. One Commentator strangely derives this as हि निश्चितं स्फुटं मा लक्ष्मीस्तस्या आलयः । अधिराजः—a Prádi Tat. comp. Chár. dissolves it as अधिकस्य राजा. तोयनिधिः—तोयानि निधीयन्तेऽस्मिन्। अवगाह्य—According to the grammarian Bhâguri the अ of अव and अपि is dropped; and according to the परिभाषा 'आचार्यग्रहणे च विभाषा वक्तव्या' *i. e.* when a rule is stated mentioning the name of an Âchârya, the rule becomes optional; so पिधान, अपिधान, &c. See H. Gr. p. 220, foot-note. *Cf* पूर्वापरसमुद्रावगाढः सानुमान् Śâk. VII. p. 181; अश्वाः स्यधुर्वैसुमतीमतिरोचमानाः । Śiś. V. 4; मन्दारमाला हरिणा पिनद्धा । Śâk. VII 2; वितस्य शार्ङ्गं कवचं पिनह्य । Bhaṭṭi. III. 47. मानदण्डः—The great length of the mountain justifies the *Utprekshâ*. मान—may be taken to mean, as done by Malli.; (1) measure; or (2) the instrument of measuring. Or मान may mean the whole measure, according to the Śruti यावन्मात्रा पृथिवी तावन्मात्रो हिमालयः । यावन्मात्रो हिमालयस्तावन्मात्रा पृथिवी ।

Śl. 2. सर्वशैलाः—For the comp. see Malli. and H. Gr. § 227 (*g*). वत्सं—shows the importance of Himálaya as being the chief of them (ranking only next to Meru). See the Śl. from B. P. quoted on the next page सर्वे स्वयुद्यवत्सेन &c. मेरौ—According to the Purâṇas, Meru, the home of the gods, forms the central point of the universe, all the planets revolving round it; it is in shape like the cup or seed-vessel of a lotus, the different Dvîpas spreading out from it like leaves. It is formed of gold, having jewels on it, and is 84,000 *Yojanas* in height, 16,000 of which are buried in the earth. The Ganges falls from heaven on its peak and thence flows to the sea. Its summit is the residence of Brahmâ and the meeting-place of the gods, Rishis, Gandharvas &c. मेरुर्मध्ये भुवनानां च भर्ता Kál. P. मेरुस्तु शुशुभे दिव्यो राजवत्समधिष्ठितः । आदित्यतरुणाभासो विधूम इव पावकः ॥ योजनानां सहस्राणि चतुरशीतिरुच्छ्रितः । प्रविष्टः षोडशाधस्तादष्टाविंशातिविंशातिः । विस्तारात्त्रिगुणस्तस्य परिणाहः समन्ततः ॥ Mat. P. The learned author of the A. H. V. shows that Meru is the terrestrial North Pole and quotes the following verses from the Mah. Bhâr. Van. Ch. 163 as describing its Polar characteristics—एनं त्वहरहर्मेरुं सूर्याचन्द्रमसौ ध्रुवम् । प्रदक्षिणमुपावृत्य कुरुतः कुरुनन्दन ॥ ज्योतींषि चाप्यशेषेण सर्वाण्यनघ सर्वतः । परियन्ति महाराज गिरिराजं प्रदक्षिणम् ॥ स्वतेजसा तस्य नगोत्तमस्य महौषधीनां च तथा प्रभावात् । विभक्तभावो न बभूव कश्चिदहर्निशानां पुरुषप्रवीर । बभूव रात्रिर्दिवसश्च तेषां संवत्सरेणेव समानरूपः ॥ See A. H. V. pp. 67, 69. भास्वन्ति—Ekaśosha Dvan.; see com.

पृथूपदिष्टाम्—Pointed out as possessing such-and-such characteristics by Pṛithu; *i. e.* as being in the form of a cow; see com. 'Advised to be favourable to the act of milking' (जनानामभीष्टदोहनार्थं त्वयानुकूलया भवितव्यमित्युपदिष्टप्रकारः ।) One Calc. Com. interprets this as—पृथुः उपदिष्टः दोहनकर्मणि नियुक्तो यया ताम्. Pṛithu was a mighty king, the son of Vena, son of Aṅga. Vena, by his wicked deeds and blasphemous language towards Vishṇu, offended the sages who killed him with their Huṃkâras (इति तेऽसत्कृतास्तेन द्विजाः पण्डितमानिना । भग्नायां भव्ययाच्ञायां तस्मै विदुर चुक्रुधुः ॥ हन्यतां हन्यतामेष पापः प्रकृतिदारुणः ॥ इत्थं व्यवसिता हन्तुमृषयो रूढमन्यवः । निजघ्नुर्हुंकृतैर्वेनं हतमच्युतनिन्दया ॥ B. P. IV. 4. 30, 31, 34.) The sages afterwards rubbed the right arm of the dead king and from it sprang the majestic Pṛithu glowing like Agni. He was immediately declared king. From him the earth received the name Pṛithvî. The subjects of Pṛithu being troubled by a famine applied to the king for the edible fruits and plants which the earth had withheld.

Pṛithu took up his bow to compel the earth to yield the supply. She, however, fled in the form of a cow, but submitted to the king afterwards and promised to yield the supply if a suitable calf were given to her so as to be able to secrete milk. Pṛithu, thereupon, made Svayambhû Manu the calf, milked the earth, and received the milk thus got in his hand, from which were produced corn, vegetables, fruits &c. For other particulars see Apte's Dic.; B. P. IV. Chs. 15-18. The Earth was also milked in their turns by the sages, mountains &c. *Cf.* इति प्रियं हितं वाक्यं भुव आदाय भूपतिः । वत्सं कृत्वा मनुं पाणावदुहत्सकलौषधीः ॥ तथा परे च सर्वत्र सारमाददते बुधाः । ततोऽन्ये च यथाकामं दुदुहुः पृथुभाविताम् ॥ ऋषयो दुदुहुर्देवीमिन्द्रियेष्वथ सत्तम । वत्सं बृहस्पतिं कृत्वा पयश्छन्दोमयं शुचि ॥.........गिरयो हिमवद्वत्सा नाना धातून् स्वसानुषु । सर्वे स्वमुख्यवत्सेन स्वे स्वे पात्रे पृथक् पयः । सर्वकामदुघां पृथ्वीं दुदुहुः पृथुभाविताम् ॥ B. P. IV. 18. 12-20. Also Mat. P. गिरिभिर्वसुधा दुग्धा रत्नानि विविधानि च । औषधानि च दिव्यानि दोग्धा मेरुर्महाचलः ॥ वत्सोऽभूद्धिमवांस्तत्र &c. Śl. quoted in S.-D. as an instance of the fault of the personal pronoun being understood.

Śl. 3. सौभाग्य—Der. सुभग+य; Vṛiddhi is substituted for the first vowels of both the members of a comp. ending in हृत्, भग &c. (see com.) before a nominal aff. having an indicative ण्, म् or क्. दुदुहुः—According to the commentators दुह must be here taken in its causative sense, as मेरु was the milker; दुदुहुरित्यत्रान्तर्भूतण्यर्थत्वं द्रष्टव्यम् । अन्यथा मेरोर्दोग्धृत्वनिर्देशानुपपत्तेः । निमज्जति—merges in, is lost sight of, *i. e.* is not noticed or taken into account. इन्दु—इन्दु is ordinarily derived as उनत्यमृतमिति or उनत्ति चन्द्रिकया भुवनमिति, fr. उन्द् to ooze and the Uṇâdi aff. उ. In the Veda, however, it is said to mean a bright or sparkling drop of the Soma juice; *cf.* सुतास इन्दवः । Rig. I. 16. 16. It then came to signify a round little body, and finally became a name of the moon, like the word *Soma* itself. एको हि &c.-*cf.* the humorous retort on this (said to be composed by Achyutarao Modak, the celebrated rhetorician of Nâsik)—एको हि दोषो गुणसंनिपाते निमज्जतीन्दोरिति यो बभाषे । न तेन दृष्टं कविना यथैको (नूनं न दृष्टं कविनाऽपि तेन*) दारिद्र्यदोषो गुणराशि (कोटि) नाशी ॥ *Cf.* रहितरत्नचयान्न शिलोच्चयानपलताभवना न दरीभुवः । विपुलिनाम्बुरुहा न सरिद्वधूरकुसुमान् दधतं न महीरुहः ॥ Kir. V. 10.

Śl. 4. अप्सरसः—The courtesans of Heaven. अद्भ्यः सरन्तीत्यप्सरसः sprung from water: so called because, according to the

---

* It is said that the poet Ghaṭakarpara, being vanquished by Kâlidâsa in his Nalodaya as regards the composition of stanzas containing यमक, had this fling at the latter on this s'loka of the Kumârsambhava. कविनाऽपि तेन may also be read as कवि-नापितेन (a barber).

Râmáyaṇa, they came out of the churned ocean—अप्सु निर्मथनादेव रसात्तस्माद्वरस्त्रियः । उत्पेतुर्मनुजश्रेष्ठ तस्मादप्सरसोऽभवन् ॥ Or because they are supposed to bathe frequently. Although the word is generally used in the plural, it is also found used in the sing. (as in the Bhâshya on Pâṇ. VIII. 4. 47) and dual (अप्सरसाविति श्रुतिनिर्देशात्); *cf.* Vik. अनप्सरेव प्रतिभासि. According to the Mah Bhâr. they are the daughters of Kâśyapa and Pradhá—इमं त्वप्सरसां वंशं विदितं पुण्यलक्षणम् । प्रधासूत महाभागा देवदेवर्षितः पुरा ॥ For the principal *Apsarasas* see note on III. 17. विभ्रमार्थं मण्डनानि विभ्र० । विभ्रम is used here in the sense of विलास 'amorous sport.' 'Decorations which added grace to their amorous gestures.' *Cf* विलासिनीविभ्रमदन्तपत्रम् Ragh. VI. 17. The second sense given by Malli. following Dak. N., *viz.*, the misplacing of ornaments on the person through hurry and confusion, does not seem to be natural. It has been adversely criticized by the Com. Ar. संपादयित्री—The provider of, which supplies. बलाहक—a compound of the पृषोदरादि class. The comp. पृषोदर (पृषतः उदरं) is formed by the dropping of त्; so a comp. of irregular formation is explained by classing it under the head of पृषोदर (Páṇ. VI. 3. 109); here वारि is changed to ब and व to ल. ०च्छेदाः—संध्यावायुना विच्छिन्ना मेघाः. *cf.* दिनान्तसुप्रानिलभिन्नमेघम् । Ragh. XVI. II. अकालसंध्याम्—Twilight out of the proper time. The large mass of red minerals imparted a red hue to the clouds overhanging it, so that to a looker-on from a distance the whole scene, the mineral-covered peaks together with the clouds, presented an aspect of the evening sky. धातुमत्ता—The affix मत् is added प्राशस्त्ये, the excellence here consisting in the plentifulness of the minerals. *Cf.* for a similar description नवविनिद्रजपाकुसुमत्विषां द्युतिमतां निकरेण महाश्मनाम् । विहितसांध्यमयूखमिव क्वचिन्निचितकाञ्चनभित्तिषु सानुषु ॥ Kir. V. 8. Sl. quoted in the Kâv.-Pr. VII. as an instance of the fault 'Obsoleteness.' The word मत्ता forming part of the word धातुमत्ता and signifying 'possession' has that meaning overpowered by the sense of 'intoxicated' which it usually has as the feminine of मत्त—अत्र मत्ताशब्दः क्षीबार्थेन निहतार्थः ।

Sl. 5. आमेखलं—Here आ indicates limit inceptive (अभिविधौ) *i. e.* including the मेखला. मेखला—The middle part of a mountain. Avya. comp.; *cf.* पृथुनितम्बविलम्बिभिरम्बुदैः । Kir. V. 6. छायाम्—छायामिषे *V. l.*=छायां इषे 'in the month of Âśvina'.; but this does not seem to be the original reading. Kâli. is not likely to use such an obscure word. Besides there is no propriety of saying 'in Âśvina'; why not in Bhádrapada also. अधःसा०—Nar. reads ०गताः which seems to be better. आतपवन्ति—Perpetually exposed to the sun, being above the region of clouds. सिद्धाः—देवयोनिविशेषाः (विश्वावसुप्रभृतयः Aruṇ.) A class of semi-divine beings characterized by great holiness and purity and possessing the eight superhuman faculties or *Siddhis*, *viz.* अणिमा महिमा चैव लघिमा गरिमा तथा । प्राप्तिः प्राकाम्यमीशित्वं वशित्वं चाष्ट सिद्धयः ॥ (Sometimes कामावसायिता is mentioned instead of गरिमा ; see Apte's Dic) They are said to inhabit the region between the earth and the sun. According to some their region is below the world of the moon, while the V. P. makes them occupy the region north of the sun and south of the seven Ṛishis. The poet, however, seems to refer here probably to those who had partially or fully acquired the eight Siddhis mentioned above by the practice of *Yoga* (सिद्धिरेषां विद्यते) and who lived on the mountain.

Śl. 6. धौत—*P. p. p.* of धाव् 1 P. A'. to wash, to run &c.; also धावित. The option is allowed by the अनित्यत्व (not being absolutely binding) of the rule यस्य विभाषा Pán. VII. 2. 15 (*i. e.* any root which takes इ optionally somewhere does not take इ before त). नृती गात्रविक्षेपे इत्यत्र इदित्करणं यस्य विभाषेत्यस्यानित्यत्वज्ञापनार्थम् । तेन धावितभिराजधियेत्यादि सिध्यति । Bhaṭṭoji in his Manoramâ. द्विपाः—द्वाभ्यां (with his trunk and mouth) पिबतीति द्विपः । Huge elephants are supposed to develop pearls in their heads. See the verse quoted by Malli करीन्द्र &c. According to Nár. who reads द्विपेन्द्र for करीन्द्र this quotation is from अगस्त्य (who has written on रत्नपरीक्षा). These pearls are often described by poets as sticking to the nails of lions splitting open the temples of elephants. विदन्ति—The root विद् occurs in several conjugations; *cf.* सत्तायां विद्यते ज्ञाने वेत्ति विन्ते विचारणे । विन्दते विन्दति प्राप्तौ श्यन्लुक्श्नम्शेष्विदं क्रमात् ॥ केसरिणां—For Himálaya's being the home of lions, *cf.* Ragh. IV. 72. किराताः—Name of a wild tribe or class of mountaineers like the Bhillas, Pulindas &c. and classed as Mlechchhas—भेदाः किरातशबरपुलिन्दा म्लेच्छजातयः । Amar. The characteristics of a म्लेच्छ are गोमांसभक्षको यस्तु लोकबाह्यं च भाषते । सर्वाचारविहीनोऽसौ म्लेच्छ इत्यभिधीयते ॥ This name is thus derived—किरं पर्यन्तभूमिमतन्ति गच्छन्तीति who live on the borders of hills or mountains. *Cf.* पर्यन्ताश्रयिभिर्निजस्य सदृशं नाम्नः किरातैः कृतम् । Ratn. II. 3. For further particulars see notes on śl. 15.

Śl. 7. कुञ्जरबिन्दु०—See Malli. Elephants when about fifty years old (पञ्चाशद्वर्षदेशीयाः) are said to have red spots appearing on their skin. The age of an elephant may be known from these. The characters on the barks resemble the red dots. The comp.

may also be taken as बिन्दुभिः शोणाः बिन्दुशोणाः; कुअरा इव बिन्दुशोणाः. विद्याधरसुन्दरी—विद्याया मन्त्रादेः गुटिकाअनादिविषयिण्याश्च धराः विद्याधराः kinds of demi-gods, thus described by Wilson—"A class of spirits who reside upon the loftiest peaks of the Himâlaya mountains, who possess superhuman longevity and faculties and the knowledge of what is passing beyond their presence. They have in many cases been mortals and are constantly connected with human beings in friendship and enmity, love and hate." Wilson's works Vol. IV. p. 115. The *Vidyádharas*, the *Kiṃnnaras*, the *Kiṃpurushas* and the *Gandharvas*, so often mentioned as residing on the peaks of the Himálayas and the mountain Hemakúṭa, a hill to the North of the Himâlayas, were probably some hardy races who on account of their superior strength, beauty of person, and the knowledge of magic, were at first looked upon with admiration and afterwards magnified into semi-divine beings by the A'ryas. अनङ्गलेख—Epistles expressive of love, often in verse (मदनावस्थासूचकाः श्लोकगाथाः).

Śl. 8. कीचक—Bamboos with holes which, as the wind passes through them, produce musical sounds. For a similar idea *cf.* स कीचकैर्मारुतपूर्णरन्ध्रैः कूजद्भिरापादितवंशकृत्यम् । Ragh. II. 12: शब्दायन्ते मधुरमनिलैः कीचकाः पूर्यमाणाः संसक्ताभिस्त्रिपुरविजयो गीयते किंनरीभिः ॥ Megh. I. 58. The bamboos are here compared to flutes or pipes which the mountain fills with his breath in the shape of the wind blown from the mouth-like caves. किंनराः—कुत्सिता नराः केषांचिन्नरमुखाश्वकायत्वादन्येषामश्वमुखनरशरीरत्वात्; A Nitya-samâsa. So called because some have a human figure with the head of a horse, while others have a human head with the form of a horse. See Śiś. IV. 38. They are classed with the Gandharvas and are described as heavenly minstrels. Like the Yakshas, they are the attendants of Kubera and are described as the sons of Pulastya—राक्षसाश्च पुलस्त्यस्य वानराः किंनरास्तथा । यक्षाश्च मनुजव्याघ्र पुत्रास्तस्य च धीमतः ॥ B. P. See Wilson's V. P. Vol. I. pp. 82, 87. तान—A kind of protracted tone giving rise to different tones and on which depend the *Râgas*; see Malli. The full śl. is द्विकत्रिकचतुष्काः स्युर्ज्ञेया वंशगताः स्वराः । अधोधस्तारतां प्राप्तास्तानस्त्वंशस्वरो मतः ॥ अंशस्वरलक्षणे भरतः—रागो यस्मिन्निवसति यस्माच्चापि प्रवर्तते । नेता च तारमन्द्राणां योऽत्यर्थं चोपलभ्यते ॥ ग्रहोपन्यासविन्यासंसंन्यासन्यासगोचरः । अनुवृत्तश्च यश्चेह सोंऽशः स्याद्दशलक्षणः ॥ इति भरतः । *cf.* यथा तानं विना रागः Bv. I. 119. The number of these is said to be 49. विस्तार्यन्ते प्रयोगा ये मूर्च्छनाशेषसंभवाः । तानास्तेऽप्यूनपञ्चाशत्सप्तस्वरसमुद्भवाः ॥ स्थानप्र०—*V. l.* wishes to take up the place of the singers, *i. e.* wishes to relieve them by taking up the chorus &c. 'स्थानप्रदायी पार्श्वस्थगानविच्छेदकारकः ।' इति विश्वः ।

Śl. 9. कपोल०—See Ragh. II. 37. सरल—देवदारुविशेष । °द्रुमाणां—सरलाश्च ते द्रुमाश्च । A Karm comp. According to some, such a comp. is not desirable. We should say तक्षकः सर्पः, रामो जामदग्न्यः, &c. The भाष्यकार says तर्हि इमौ द्वौ शब्दौ एकस्मिन्नर्थे युगपद्वरुध्येते । वृक्षः शिंशपेति । नैतयोरावश्यकः समावेशः । &c. Some say such a comp should be taken as of the शाकपार्थिवादि class; सरलनामानो द्रुमाः सरलद्रुमाः इति कथंचित् शाकपार्थिवादित्वम् । Kaiyaṭa says such a comp. may be allowed to make the sense clear; विशेषणविशेष्ययोः सबन्धिकतया अन्यतरोपादानमात्रेणेतराक्षेपसंभवे उभयोपादानं स्पष्टार्थम् । The poets use such compounds and the later grammarians justify them. See further on स देवदारुद्रुमवेदिकायां &c. III. 44. *Cf* अथ जयाय नु मेरुमहीभृतः &c. Kir. V. 1. सुरभीकरोति—न सुरभीणि असुरभीणि तानि सुरभीणि संपद्यमानानि करोति. A च्वि—formation.

Śl. 10. वनितासखानां—Mark the comp. which must be dissolved as Gen. Tat. according to Pâṇ. V. 4. 91. Had it not been for this restriction it would have been readily taken as a Bah. See our note on महिषीसखः Ragh. I. 48. अतैल०—तैलेन पूर्यन्त इति तैलपूराः न तैल० अतैलपूराः । *Cf.* आसन्नोषधयो नेतुर्नक्तमस्नेहदीपिकाः । Ragh. IV. 75. सुरत०—Malli. takes this as a Loc. Tat.; the authority for it is सप्तमी (a noun may be compounded with another noun in the Loc.) detached from the Sûtra सप्तमी शौण्डैः Pâṇ. II. 1. 40. It may also be taken as a comp. of the शाकपार्थिवादि class. सुरतार्थं सुरतोपयोगिनो वा प्रदीपाः. Quoted in Sar.-K. and S.-D. as an instance of Vibhâvanâ. According to Vámana this is a विशेषोक्ति; Káv. Sû. IV. 5. 23; he also remarks रूपकं चेदं प्रायेण. *Cf.* श्रीमल्लताभवनमोषधयः प्रदीपाः शय्या नवानि हरिचन्दनपल्लवानि । अस्मिन्रतिश्रमनुदश्च सरोजवाताः स्मर्तुं दिशन्ति न दिवः सुरसुन्दरीभ्यः ॥ Kir. V. 28.

Śl. 11. शिलीभूत—न शिला अशिला; अशिला शिला संपन्नं शिलीभूतं a च्वि formation. इव—इवशब्दोऽयमुत्प्रेक्षाद्योतकः अचेतनेषु भयासंभवात् । हेतूत्प्रेक्षा चेयम् । N. दुर्वहं—दुःखेन उह्यते । वोढुं वा शक्यं दुर्वहं; कृच्छ्रार्थे खल्; now see com. आर्ताः—*i.e.* by their weight.; *P. p. p.* of ऋ with आ. भिन्दन्ति—change, or abandon, give up; *i.e.* do not accelerate. अश्वमुख्यः—also ०मुखाः.

Śl. 12. दिवाकर—*Upapada* Tat. दिवा भीतं—There is a side reference to the owl (दिवाभीत) which also does not venture out during day-time. अपि—though there was cause for making haste. ममत्वं—मम इत्यस्य भावः । Fr. मम (treated as an Avyaya

ममेति विभक्तिरूपो निपातः) and त्वम्. (Can it be originally a compound of मम त्वं thou art mine ?). उच्चैःशिरसां—उच्चैः शिरो येषां ते उच्चैःशिरसः। Who ever seeks their protection—whether a good or a bad man—the noble-minded regard him as their own and extend their protection to him. *Cf.* Bg. V. 18.

This śl is quoted in the K.-Pr. as an instance of अनुचितार्थता दोष or the fault in an Arthântaranyâsa called 'groundlessness' which amounts to improper signification. निर्विषयस्य (अर्थान्तरन्यासस्य) अप्युत्प्रेक्षादूषणमनुचितार्थत्वमेव । Kâv.-Pradîpa. अत्र अचेतनस्य तमसो दिवाकरात् त्रास एव न संभवतीति कुत एव तत्प्रयोजितमद्रिणा परित्राणम् ।

Śl. 13. बालव्यजनैः—These are parts of the *insignia* of royalty. See Ragh. III. 16. चमर्यः—The Chamarî is a kind of cow or the Yak of Tartary (it is a deer according to Amara,) from the bushy tails of which *Châmaras* are made. The Chamarîs, by waving Châmaras over Himâlaya, showed that he was really a King. *Cf.* व्याधूयन्ते निचुलतरुभिर्मञ्जरीचामराणि । Vik. IV. 4.

Śl. 14. अंशुक—अंशून् सूत्राणि कायति or अंशवः विषयोऽस्य (अंशु + क) a thin garment of fine texture. For अंशुकाक्षेप *cf.* Megh. II. 7. यदृच्छया—या ऋच्छा अभिप्रायः (wish) यदृच्छा तया a Tat. of the मयूरव्यंसकादि class; accidentally; hence, without any effort on the part of the women. तिरस्करिण्यः—तिरस्करोतीति (णिनिः), तिरस्क्रियतेऽनया (ल्युट्) इति वा. There is no Vriddhi, by the परिभाषा—संज्ञापूर्वको विधिरनित्यः. The fig. here is परिणाम according to Malli. ; according to K.-P., which does not recognize परि० as a separate figure, it will be रूपक.

Śl. 15. भागीरथी—भगीरथस्येयं; तस्येदमित्यण्; so called because the river was brought down from heaven by Bhagîratha. ०शीकराणां वोढा—This leads to the inference that the breeze was cool. शीकरः—drops of water scattered by the wind; शीकरोऽम्बुकणाः स्मृताः । Amara. According to some सीकर also. अन्विष्टमृगैः किरातैः—The Kirâtas are hillmen living by hunting and clad in a dress made of peacock's feathers. In the Purânas they are mentioned along with the Mlechchhas and are described to be of a dark complexion, dwarfish in stature, with short arms and legs, projecting chin, broad flat nose, red eyes and tawny hair. In some passages they are described as fierce bow-men, clad in hides and living upon fruits and roots. भिन्नशिखण्डिबर्हः—Malli. understands that the wind agitates the peacock's feathers attached by the Kirátas to their waists; but according to other commentators, the expression refers generally to peacocks in forests. This latter explanation is certainly preferabla. The peacocks are particularly mentioned because they have a long plumage which can be easily acted upon by the wind. It also indicates the abundance of peacocks on the mountain and explains why the breeze was gentle. The wind, having met with obstruction from the peacocks' feathers in its passage, lost some of its force and became gentle. We have thus three different epithets to indicate respectively that the breeze was cool, fragrant and gentle. कविसमये वायुस्त्रिविधो वर्ण्यते । शीतो मन्दः सुरभिश्च । भागीरथीस्पर्शाच्छीतः । देवदारुस्पर्शात्सुरभिः । भिन्नशिखण्डिपिच्छत्वान्मन्दः । *cf.* Ragh. I. 38, II. 13; Śák. III. 5 (शक्यमरविन्दसुरभिः कणवाही मालिनीतरङ्गाणाम् ।... पवनः ॥). Malli. says that the hunters wore girdles of peacocks' feathers round their waists to accelerate their motion, and the wind broke through them. How far the feathers could have quickened their motion is a question. Perhaps the Kirátas wore the feathers for the sake of ornamentation. The fig. of speech is स्वभावोक्ति.

Śl. 16. सप्तर्षि०—This is a संज्ञा (name of a particular class of Ṛishis) and so the comp. is allowed. The names of the seven Ṛishis generally given are-मरीचिरात्रिः पुलहः पुलस्त्यः क्रतुरङ्गिराः । वसिष्ठश्च महाभागाः सप्तैते ब्रह्मणः सुताः ॥ The Kâliká P. enumerates them thus—कश्यपोऽत्रिर्वसिष्ठश्च विश्वामित्रोऽथ गोतमः । जमदग्निर्भरद्वाज एते सप्तर्षयो मताः ॥ They are described as चित्रशिखण्डिनः । *Cf* Pratâpamârtaṇḍa—मरीचिरङ्गिरा अत्रिः पुलस्त्यः पुलहः क्रतुः । वसिष्ठश्चेति सप्तैते ज्ञेयाश्चित्रशिखण्डिनः ॥ In the Satapatha Bráh. and elsewhere they are mentioned as कश्यपोऽत्रिर्भरद्वाजो विश्वामित्रोऽथ गोतमः । जमदग्निर्वसिष्ठश्च सप्तैते ऋषयः स्मृताः ॥ In another list Daksha is substituted for Vasishṭha. Astronomically represented the seven Ṛishis form the constellation Ursa Major or the Great Bear. The Ṛishis pluck the flowers for offering worship after they bathe in the Ganges. *Cf.* our note on V. 37. हस्ताव०—केचिद्वचितावित्यत्र पदभङ्गं कुर्वन्ति *i. e.* हस्तावचितौ अशेषाणि । तत्र चर्मणि द्वीपिनं हन्तीतिवत् निमित्त सप्तमी । Châr.; but this is far-fetched. By केचित् he probably refers to Ar. who says अथ वा सप्तर्षिहस्तावचितौ इति निमित्तसप्तमी । on which Nár. says—यत्र सूर्यः सप्तर्षीणामुपयोगार्थं समस्तानि पद्मानि प्रबोधयतीत्यर्थः । "उत्तमान्यरुणः प्रातर्मध्यमानि च भास्करः ॥ प्रबोधयति पद्मानि अधमान्यातपो महान् ॥" From Jin.'s com. as quoted by D. विवस्वान्--विविधं वस्ते (wearing a varied garment of light or rays) or विवांसि rays अस्य सन्ति. अधः परिवर्तमानः-Because the course of the sun is below that of the

Saptarshis.* *Cf. infra* अधःप्रस्थापिताश्वेन समावर्जितकेतुना &c. and सत्यमर्कोच्च सोमाच्च परमध्यास्महे पदम् । VI. 7, 19. The seven Rishis pluck the lotuses in the lakes on the highest peaks (अग्रसरोरुह— otherwise this will lose its propriety) of the Himâlayas. Therefore the path of the sun must be below the peaks. See B. G. Tilak's A. H. V. p. 147.

Śl. 17. यज्ञाङ्ग—The essential things at a sacrifice, such as the Soma plant, a Khadira post, Palâśa sticks and others. प्रजापति—Brahmâ. The name, however, is commonly applied to the ten patriarchs, the sons of Brahmâ, sprung from the different parts of his body while engaged in meditation, *viz.* मरीचिरत्र्यङ्गिरसौ पुलस्त्यः पुलहः क्रतुः । भृगुर्वसिष्ठो दक्षश्च दशमस्तत्र नारदः ॥ B. P. III. 2. 22. See Manu. I 32. कल्पितयज्ञभागं—This shows that the mountain was raised to the rank of the gods entitled to a share of the oblations offered at a sacrifice. ०भागः—*V. l.* qualifies प्रजा०, who alloted the respective shares of deities. अन्वतिष्ठत्—स्था with अनु is used transitively; *cf.* VII. 1 *infra* and Ragh. VII. 32. Some needlessly take it in the sense of the causal (अन्तर्भावितण्यर्थः).

Śl. 18. मेरुसखः—Because one of the three mind-born daughters of the Pitris was given in marriage to Meru. मानसीं—The

* The late V. S. Chiplunkar finds fault with Malli.'s explanation and says that the peaks of the Him. need not be supposed to be above the sun's course. According to him the poet describes the sun who is yet below the horizon as touching the lotuses with his slanting rays and so causing them to bloom. (See Kavi. P. pp. 49, 50). But it will be seen, that Malli. gives us the poet's meaning. We in modern times may well be shocked at what might appear to be an extraordinarily high flight of the poet's imagination. But in such cases, before we pronounce our judgment, we must look to the ideas that prevailed when a particular poet lived. In the first place, how can we make the sun below the horizon emit rays that could reach the top of the mountain and not the mountain itself? Secondly, such a description would apply more or less to any other mountain. Thirdly, such descriptions are not rare. In the Van. P. of the Mah. Bhâr. we are told that the mountain Vindhya also, in jealousy of Meru, once rose so high as to obstruct the path of the Sun and other heavenly bodies and the gods had to request Agastya to check the upward progress of the mountain. See our notes on Ragh. VI. 61. Here the poet follows the Purâṇas which confounded the mountain Himâlaya with Meru and transferred their characteristics to either. Thus the Ganges is described as falling on the tops of both; the Gandharvas &c. are said to reside on both ; and so on. See our note on Meru, *supra* I. 2.

idea is something like that of the 'production of Minerva from the brain of Jupiter.' B. K. पितॄणां—The Pitṛis, as divine beings, possessed the power of creating with an effort of the mind alone; originally probably the deified ancestors of men to whom Śráddhas were offered and balls of rice presented. Seven classes of these are mentioned:—अग्निष्वात्ताः सोमपाश्च हविष्मन्तस्तथोष्मपाः । सुकालिनो बर्हिषद् आज्यपाः पितरः स्मृताः ॥ In the Veda पितृ is an epithet of बृहस्पति, वरुण, प्रजापति, and especially of the heaven or sky. See note on पितॄणां, *infra* II. 14. पितॄणां कन्यां—The Pitṛis meant are अग्निष्वात्त and बर्हिषद्; by them स्वधा had two daughters, both well acquainted with theological truth, given to meditation and accomplished in perfect wisdom. Mená became the wife of Himálaya and Dhâriṇî was married to Meru. V. P. स्थितये—Here स्थिति may mean 'stability, perpetuality of the family by begetting progeny; *cf.* प्रजायै गृहमेधिनां Ragh. I. 7, 69; or the observance of duties proper for a family. स्थितये स्थिरत्वाय न कामार्थमित्यर्थः । अनेनातिसत्त्वोत्तरत्वादस्य शान्तनायकत्वमुक्तम् । Nár. मेनां—मेना, derived from मन्; the other form मेनका (see com.) is छान्दस (used in the Veda); if used in ordinary language it must be taken as a word of the पृषोदरादि class. छन्दसीति मेनकेत्यादि भाषायां न प्राप्नोति । यदि सिध्यते पृषोदरादित्वाद्भविष्यति । Kaiyaṭa. मुनीनामपि माननीयां—This shows that Mená was superior to the Munis by her Yaugic and ascetic practices. It was thus from her mother that Párvatî got the power both physical and mental to practise the kind of hard penance she did to propitiate Śiva. See *infra* V. 28, 29. आत्मानुरूपां—अनुगतं रूपमस्या अनुरूपा; आत्मनोऽनुरूपा आ० ताम्. उपयेमे—यम् with उप is Âtm. in the sense of marrying or accepting in general. See Malli Mark the alliterations in this S'loka. अत्र कामव्यपोहाय कुलस्य स्थितय इत्युक्तमिति परिसंख्यालंकारः । किंचित्पृष्टमपृष्टं वा कथितं यत्प्रकल्पते । तादृगन्यव्यपोहाय परिसंख्या तु सा स्मृता ॥ इति ॥ Nár.

Śl. 19. कालक्रमेण—may better be taken with गर्भोऽभवत्. The Instr. is explained by the Várttika प्रकृत्यादिभ्य उपसंख्यानम् on कर्तृकरणयोस्तृतीया । Pâṇ. II. 3. 18. स्वरूप०—स्वरूप or सौन्दर्य includes the idea of bodily make also. The second sense given by Malli. does not seem to be natural. मनोरमं—The Commentator अवचूरि as quoted by D. says—मनोरमाभिधानं यौवनम् । कामं मनोरमं चैव जवरं जावरं तथा । चतुर्धा यौवनं प्रोक्तं कामशास्त्रविशारदैः ॥ यौवनं—*fr.* युवन्+अ (अण्) while यौवत means 'a collection', अ (अञ्) being added समूहार्थे. This s'l. is not found in the Triv. S. S. Ed. Probably it is an interpolation.

Sl. 20. नागवधू—The Nâgas, the offspring of Kâśhyapa and Kadru, are described as semi-divine beings having a human face and the tale of a serpent, and living in Pátála. They could also assume a perfect human form at will. Their chief town is called Bhogávatí. The Nága damsels were known for their beauty. ०पभोग्यं—*i. e.* who was to have a Nága damsel for his wife. भोग्य *fr.* भुज्+य (ण्यत्); the other form is भोज्य by the rule भोज्यं भक्ष्ये. मैनाकं—The son of Menakâ (मेनकायां भवः । अण्) said in the Mahábhárata to be situated north of Kailása. According to some it stood in Central India, and according to others between the Southern extremity of the Indian Peninsula and Ceylon. अम्भोनिधि०—When Maináka saw Indra lopping off the wings of mountains he fled to the sea for protection which the latter readily granted, and so the two became friends. Indra's thunderbolt had no power over the waters of the sea. The reason of mentioning the brother is given by Malli.; *cf.* also Manu. III. 11.

पक्षच्छिदि—In the Kṛitayuga the mountains had wings—according to the Harivaṃśa the demon Hiraṇyâksha endowed them with wings—कदाचित्तु सपक्षास्ते पर्वता धरणीधराः । प्रस्थिता धरणीं त्यक्त्वा नूनं तस्यैव (*i. e* हिरण्याक्षस्य) मायया ॥; according to the Agnipuráṇa, Vishṇu gave them the wings—(see below ततोऽद्रयो &c.). Having got wings the mountains became refractory, moved from place to place and tormented the world and the people in general. On seeing this, Indra clipped their wings with his thunderbolt and fixed them in their proper places. *Cf.* ततोऽद्रयो जातपक्षा विष्णोश्चैव तु मायया । प्रस्थिता मेदिनीं त्यक्त्वा यथापूर्वं निवेशिता ॥ ....धरण्यां तु गिरीन् स्थाप्य स्वेषु स्थानेषु गोपतिः । चिच्छेद पविना पश्चात् सर्वेषां भुवि चारिणाम् ॥ एकः सपक्षो मैनाकः सुरैस्तत्समये कृतः ॥ Agni P.; also Rámá.—पूर्वं कृतयुगे तात पर्वताः पक्षिणोऽभवन् । तेऽपि जग्मुर्दिशः सर्वा गरुडा इव वेगिनः । ततस्तेषु प्रयातेषु देवसंघा महर्षिभिः । भूतानि च भयं जग्मुस्तेषां पतनशङ्कया । ततः क्रुद्धः सहस्राक्षः पर्वतानां शतक्रतुः । पक्षांश्चिच्छेद वज्रेण ततः शतसहस्रशः ॥ See Sundar-Káṇ. I. 115-119. एकः सपक्षो मैनाकः सुरैस्तत्समये कृतः । H. V. । वृत्रशत्रौ—Vṛitra, a mighty demon, the leader of the Káleyas. Endowed with mighty power he discomfited the gods with Indra and drove them out of heaven. The gods, however, instructed by Brahmá, got a mighty weapon with six sides, called Vajra, prepared out of the bones of Dadhichi, with which Indra killed Vṛitra. The Vedic conception of Vṛitra (*lit.* the coverer, obstructer) is that of an imaginary malignant influence, the demon of darkness and drought, supposed to take possession of the clouds, make them obscure the sky and keep back the waters. He is variously designated as Vṛitra, Ahi, Śambara, Namuchi, Bala, &c. Indra is represented as battling successfully with this influence and letting loose the pent-up waters to the delight of the world. Vṛitra, in the Veda, also means a cloud. The stories about Indra cutting the wings of mountains (trains of clouds), or piercing with his bolt the aerial cities of the demons, or killing Vṛitra and the Káleyas, are probably due to the misconception of the phenomenon and the movements of the clouds, dissolving into rain, with thunder and lightning &c. See, however, Prof. Tilak's A. H. V. pp. 295, 296. अवेदनाज्ञं कुलि०—कुलिनः पर्वतान् श्यति इति कुलिशं, also *mas.*; *fr.* शो + कः (अ), by आतोऽनुपसर्गे कः (Roots ending in आ not preceded by a prep. take the aff. क). अवेदनाज्ञं is connected with कुलि०; the comp. (सापेक्ष०; see com.) is allowed by the authority of the भाष्यकार (on Páṇ. II. 1. 1) who says भवति च प्रधानस्य सापेक्षस्यापि समासः। *Cf.* what another poet has got to say on this—वरं पक्षच्छेदः समदमघवन्मुक्तकुलिशप्रहारैरुद्गच्छद्बहलगहनोद्गारगुरुभिः। तुषाराद्रेः सूनोरहह पितरि क्लेशविवशे न चासौ संपातः पयसि पयसां पत्युरुचितः॥ Bh. N. 36.

Śl. 21. अवमानेन &c.—Daksha once performed a sacrifice; but he did not invite his daughter, Sati, nor her husband Śiva, to be present at it. Sati, however, went to the sacrifice against the advice of her husband, but as she was not taken notice of there by her father she felt greatly insulted and threw herself into fire (see however below) and perished. For fuller particulars see B. P. IV. 4; and दक्ष in Apte's Dic. *Cf.* Ratn. I. 3. दक्षस्य—Daksha, the chief of the ten Prajâpatis, was born from the thumb of Brahmâ (दक्षस्त्वजायताङ्गुष्ठाद्दक्षिणाद्भगवानृषिः। ब्रह्मणः पृथिवीपाल शान्तात्मा सुमहातपाः॥). He had many daughters by different wives. According to one account he had sixteen by his wife Prasûti, daughter of Manu. Out of these he gave one in marriage to Śiva (प्रसूतिं मानवीं दक्ष उपयेमे ह्यजात्मजः। तस्यां ससर्ज दुहितॄः षोडशामललोचनाः॥ त्रयोदशादाद्धर्माय तथैकामग्नये विभुः। पितृभ्य एकां युक्तेभ्यो भवायैकां भवच्छिदे॥) B. P. VI. 1. 47, 48. योगविसृष्टदेहा—who relinquished the body by generating fire into it by concentrating her mind on the fiery element. योग here means sitting in a steady posture and fixing the mind on one particular object having withdrawn it from others. (सर्वविषयेभ्योऽन्तःकरणवृत्तेर्निरोधः) The following extract from B. P. will explain the process:—इत्यध्वरे दक्षमनूद्य शत्रुहन् क्षितावुदीचीं निषसाद शान्तवाक्। स्पृष्ट्वा जलं पीतदुकूलसंवृता निमील्य दृग्योगपथं समाविशत्॥ कृत्वा समानावनिलौ जितासना सोदानमुत्थाप्य च नाभिचक्रतः।

शनैर्हृदि स्थाप्य धियोरसि स्थितं कण्ठाद्भ्रुवोर्मध्यमनिन्दितानयत् ॥ एवं स्वदेहं महतां महीयसा मुहुः समारोपितमङ्कमादरात् । जिहासती दक्षरुषा मनस्विनी दधार गात्रेष्वनिलाग्निधारणाम् ॥ ततः स्वभर्तुश्चरणाम्बुजासवं जगद्गुरोश्चिन्तयती न चापरम् । ददर्श देहो हतकल्मषा सती सद्यः प्रजज्वाल समाधिनाग्निना ॥ IV. 4. 24-27. *Cf.* समानजयाज्ज्वलनम् । Pât. Y. S. III. 40; also एवं दाक्षायणी हित्वा सती पूर्वकलेवरम् । जज्ञे हिमवतः क्षेत्रे मेनायामिति शुश्रुम ॥ B. P. IV. 7. 58.

Śl. 22. समाधिमती—Samâdhi means here a religious observance or vow; मत् shows excellence; hence 'she who led a perfectly pious life.' This is put in to explain why she was accepted as her mother by the Mother of the universe (Satî). Malli. says संतत्यर्थं; but this does not seem to be necessary as she already had a son. She did not live a life of perfect austerity with a particular object in view but did it as a duty and so won the admiration and praise of even the sages; (मुनीनामपि माननीयां) śl. 18. This epithet corresponds to अपरिक्षता in the simile. What the poet means is that just as policy rightly employed and never marked by a wrong step naturally leads to prosperity, so she whose virtuous life was never disfigured by a blemish or breach of duty was naturally blessed with the birth of such a daughter. The student should mark the different senses in which the word Samâdhi has been used in this poem; *cf.* I. 59; III. 40, 50; V. 2, 6, 24, 45, &c. उदपादि—'उत्पत्तिश्चात्र नित्याया देव्या देवकार्यार्थम् । तदुक्तं देवीमाहात्म्ये—देवानां (सुराणां, इ पा०) कार्यसिद्ध्यर्थमाविर्भवति सा यदा । उत्पन्नेति तदा लोके सा नित्याप्यभिधीयते ॥ इति ।' Nâr. भव्या—The blessed one; one who exists and exists pre-eminently; whose life is a blessing. The aff. यत् is added कर्तरि by Pâṇ. III. 4. 68. सम्यक्प्र०—The proper employment of; the propriety lies in taking into consideration one's own power as well as that of one's enemy, &c.; see Ragh. XVII. 59 (परात्मनोः परिच्छिद्य शक्त्यादीनां बलाबलम् । &c.). अपरिक्षता—not frustrated or checkmated. नीति—statesmanship, state-policy. उत्साह—The chief of the three Śaktis or powers which a king must possess. शक्तयस्तिस्रः । प्रभावोत्साहमन्त्रजाः; *viz.*, (1) the power or pre-eminent position of a king by virtue of a good treasury and good government (कोषदण्डजं तेजः); (2) the personal energy or valour (विक्रमबलमुत्साहशक्तिः); (3) the power arising from good counsel, diplomacy (सन्ध्यादीनां सामादीनां च यथावत्स्थापनं न तु केवलं ज्ञानम्). *Cf.* उत्साहो मन्त्रमूलं स्यादिति नीतिविदां मतम् । ०गुणेन—उत्साहस्य गुणः the excellence or efficacy of; if it be taken as a कर्मधारय (उत्साह एव गुणः) गुण has no propriety.

Śl. 23. पुष्पवृष्टि—The gods showered down flowers, delighted at the birth of one whose son was to kill their enemy. प्रसन्न०, पांसु०, शङ्खस्व०—Those three epithets show that P.'s birth gratified the four organs of sense respectively, *viz.* the eyes, the skin, and the nose and ears. स्थावर—Fr. स्था and aff. वर, one that stands by habit (स्थानशील:); 'स्थेशभासपिसकसो वरच्' : so ईश्वर, भास्वर, पेस्वर &c. By स्थावर here is meant such of the mountains as have presiding deities and trees which are considered as living bodies (*i. e.* having sensation) though fixed (which alone are capable of feeling the pleasure). स्थावराणां तु पत्रपुष्पफलादीनां सातिशयोत्पत्तिदर्शनेन सुखं जातमित्यवसेयम् । उक्तं च श्रीकृष्णविलासे—तद्दर्शनालच्युतमच्युतस्य गीतामृतं साधु निषेव्य वृक्षाः । चिरं जराजर्जरितत्वचोऽपि बाला इवासन्नवपल्लवाढ्याः ॥ इति । Nâr. जङ्गम—The opposite of स्थावर; जङ्गम्यन्ते वक्रं गच्छन्ति इति जङ्गमाः । गत्यर्थानां नित्यं कौटिल्ये इति यङ् (Freq.) । स्वाम्यादिमते भृशार्थे यङ्-which is better. *Cf.* दिशः प्रसेदुः पवनः सुखं ववौ शङ्खान्निदध्मुर्गगनेचरास्तथा । पपात मौलौ कुसुमाञ्जलिस्तदा बभूव तज्जन्मदिनं सुखप्रदम् ॥ S'. P. The birth of great men is similarly described; *cf.* दिशः प्रसेदुर्मरुतो ववुः सुखाः &c., and निर्दोषमभवत्सर्वमाविष्कृतगुणं जगत् । Ragh. III. 14., X. 72. वाता ववुः स्पर्शसुखा मनोज्ञा दिव्यानि सूनान्यवपातयन्तः । सूर्यः स एवाभ्यधिकं चकासे जज्वाल सौम्यार्चिरनीरितोऽग्निः ॥ Bud. ch. I. 41.

Śl. 24. सुतरां—अत्यन्तं; compar. of सु. स्फुरत्प्रभा०—Heavenly beings are described as having a halo of light about them; *cf.* स्फुरत्प्रभामण्डलमध्यवर्ति कान्तं वपुर्व्योमचरं प्रपेदे । Rag. V. 61., XIV. 14. विदूर—Name of a mountain (said to be in Ceylon.) from which the jewel sapphire or the *lapis lazuli* is brought. उद्भिन्नया—The idea is—When it thunders, the ground where the sapphires lie, splits up and reveals the streaks or germs of the gems. 'यदाह भोजः—अस्ति शैलो विदूराख्यः पर्यन्ते तत्र काचन । मही रत्नाकरीभूता वैदूर्यं तत्र जायते ॥ मेघशब्देन जायन्ते तत्र रत्ननवाङ्कुराः । क्रमात्परिणतास्ते स्युर्मणयो राजपूजिताः ।' as quoted by Nâr. What Vidûra is cannot be definitely known. बालवाय is another name for वैदूर्य and the ancients believed that it was the hill बालवाय or the region about it that produced these gems and they were refined or polished at Vidûra. Kátyâyana thus justifies the use of the two terms—बालवायो विदूरं च प्रकृत्यन्तरमेव वा । न वै तत्रेति चेद् ब्रूयाज्जित्वरीवदुपाचरेत् (*i.e.* as merchants call the city of Vârâṇasî by the name जित्वरी) ॥ See Malli. on Śiś. III 45. For the idea *cf.* मेना तया पूर्णनिशेशवक्त्रया स्फुरत्प्रभामण्डलया रराज ह। यथा विदूराचलभूमिरञ्जसा घनोत्थया रत्नशलाकया सुने ॥ S'. P.

Śl. 25. चान्द्रमसी लेखा—The comparison implies lustrous beauty and the capacity to develop more. लावण्य—लावण्य is defined as the appearance in the bodily complexion of a quivering lustre like that of pearls. See Malli.; लवणस्य भावः लावण्यम्; this shows that beauty (lustrous complexion) has certainly to do with a proper consumption of salt (लवण). विशेषान्—अवयवान्; the शब्दार्णव also confirms this meaning—विशेषोऽवयवे द्रव्ये द्रष्टव्योत्तमवस्तुनि। ज्योत्स्नान्तराणि—*i. e.* blending of additional light (shed by the new digit every day) with the light of the previous digits: अन्तर means व्यवधान 'its being concealed or swallowed up by'; what is meant is—'Pârvatî's bodily complexion appeared more and more lustrous every day. कलान्तराणि—additional Kâlas. Malli. takes the comp. सुप्सुपा; but गणरत्नकार includes such compounds under the head of the मयूरव्यंसकादि Tatpurushas. *Cf.* यथा चान्द्री लेखा ज्योत्स्नायुक्ताः कलाः प्रत्यहं वर्धयति तथा। चान्द्रीलेखा कलान्तराणीवेत्युपमानोपमेयसिद्धौ। यद् द्वितीयमिवशब्दोपादानं तत्र पौनरुक्त्यं न चिन्त्यम्। यद्वा कर्तृकर्मणोरौपम्ये- क्रियाभेदादिवद्वयोपादानम्। तत्र वृद्धिक्रियया सह देव्याश्चन्द्रलेखोपमा। पोषण- क्रियया च विशेषणं कलान्तरोपमानम्। Châr.

This śl. is quoted in S.-K. as an instance of वाक्योपमा. Kâlidâsa often uses this उपमान (the waxing or waning of the moon) to express उत्कर्ष or अपकर्ष; *cf.* Ragh. V. 16.

Śl. 26. बन्धुप्रियां—बन्धूनां प्रिया बन्धुप्रिया ताम्। आभिजनेन—see com.; or अभिजनः तन्निमित्तमाभिजनं तेन; it has its root meaning here—derived from the parent. उमा—is generally derived as ओमिहेशस्य मा लक्ष्मीः; or उं शिवं माति पतित्वेन मन्यते इति. Kâli. probably refers here to Ś. P.—उ मा गच्छ वनं घोरं सर्वविघ्नास्पदं सदा। *Cf.* तपसो वारयामास उमेत्येवाब्रवीच्च सा। तदेव माता नामास्याश्चक्रे पितृसुता शुभा॥ Vâmana P.; तां पार्वतीत्याभिजनाच्च नामतो जुहाव तद्बन्धुजनः स्वभावतः। मात्रा निषिद्धा तपसे यदा तु सा ययावुमाख्यां भवभक्तिभाविनी॥ Ś. P.

Śl. 27. पुत्रवतः—see com.; the rivers are also poetically spoken of as the daughters of mountains; *cf.* अपशङ्कमङ्कपरिवर्तनोचिता- श्चलिताः पुरः पतिमुपैतुमात्मजाः। अनुरोदितीव करुणेन पत्रिणां विरुतेन वत्सलतयैष निम्नगाः॥ Śiś. IV. 47. अपत्यं—न पतन्ति पितरोऽनेनेत्यपत्यं (अ+पत्+य); or अपततं भवति पितुः सकाशादेस्य पृथक्तं भवति। अनेन जातेन सता पिता नरके न पतति इति वा। Yáska. The birth of a child is considered as preventing parents from falling into hell. चूत—Here चूत signifies flower; चूतस्य विकारः पुष्पं चूतं the aff. अण् being dropped by the Várttika—'the affix denoting flowers and roots is dropped in most cases'; (see com.); *e. g.* मल्लिकायाः पुष्पं मल्लिका. द्विरेफ—a term derived from the word भ्रमर which contains two रs. Probably so called from having two रेफ-like hairs one on each side of its mouth. ०माला—This represents the eye of Madhu. सविशेष०—*cf.* न हि प्रफुल्लं सहकारमेत्य वृक्षान्तरं काङ्क्षति षट्पदाली। Ragh. VI. 69.

This śl. is cited in the K. P. VII. as an instance of 'the violation of the uniformity (प्रक्रमभङ्ग) of a synonym', to avoid which the reading महीभृतोऽपत्यवतोऽपि is suggested. अत्रापत्येषु बहुषु सत्स्वपि तस्मिन्नपत्ये स्नेहातिशयविवक्षणादपत्यशब्दे प्रयोक्तव्ये पुत्रशब्दप्रयोगात्पर्यायप्रक्रमभङ्गः। Pra. अनन्तपुष्पस्य—Nâgojibhatta in his Uddyota remarks on this—पूर्वार्धे उत्तरं दृष्टान्तः। अनन्तपुष्पविशिष्टमधुसंबन्धिन्यपि द्विरेफमाला चूतपुष्पे सविशेषसङ्गेत्यर्थः। अत्र द्विरेफमाला सादृश्याद्वसन्तदृष्टित्वेनाध्यवसिता बोध्या। For a similar idea *cf.* निवातपद्मस्तिमितेन चक्षुषा नृपस्य कान्तं पिबतः सुताननम्। महोदधेः पूर इवेन्दुदर्शनाद्गुरुः प्रहर्षः प्रबभूव नात्मनि॥ Ragh. III. 17.

Śl. 28. प्रभामहत्या—प्रभया महती great by *i.e.* shedding or emitting powerful light. त्रिमार्गगा—*Lit.* flowing in three courses; the river Ganges, respectively called Mandâkinî, Bhágîrathî and Bhogâvatî, as it flows in heaven, on earth and in the nether world. त्रिदिव—mark the comp.; here त्रि is equivalent to तृतीय; the third world. See also Malli. संस्कारवत्या—Possessed of grammatical purity; refined; polished. मनीषी—मनीषा (talent) अस्यास्ति. Here Malli. explains this word as the Sid.-Kau. does (fr. मनस्+ईषा+इन्), according to the Várt. शकन्ध्वादिषु पररूपं वाच्यम्। Here अस्+ई (in मनस्+ईषा) are combined into ई and thus there is पररूपसंधि. Elsewhere (Ragh. I. 11) he follows the Bhâ. (which is perhaps better, as the word here is मनीषिन् and the meaning is more directly got), and says मनसः ईषिणः धीराः विद्वांस इति यावत् with the remark पृषोदरादित्वात्साधुः. Note Malli.'s remarks on the use of the epithets प्रभामहत्या and संस्कारवत्या.

Śl. 29. मन्दाकिनी—मन्दमकितुं शीलमस्याः flowing gently; here refers to the Ganges on earth (भूगङ्गा); the current flowing down the valley of Badarikedâr in the Himâlayas. The heavenly Ganges fell on the peak of the mount Meru (Himâlaya) and thence flowed to the nether world (then called पातालगङ्गा). Originally the name of a tributary of the Ganges, but afterwards identified with the Ganges. See Ragh. XIII. 48. सैकत—a sandy place; सिकता सन्त्यस्मिन्; अ (अण्) being added in the sense of 'possession' (मत्वर्थे); see com. वेदिकाभिः—This shows the religious tendency of her mind from girlhood. Young girls are described as fond of sports of this kind; *cf.* तत्र खलु मन्दाकिन्याः पुलिनेषु सिकतापर्वतकेलिभिः क्रीडन्ती &c. Vik. IV. p. 91. मन्दाकिन्याः... ......अन्वेष्टव्यैः कनकसिकतामुष्टिनिक्षेपगूढैः संक्रीडन्ते मणिभिरमरप्रार्थिता यत्र कन्याः॥ Megh. II. 6. कन्दुकः—This is also a favourite pastime of young maidens: *cf.* कराभिघातोत्थितकन्दुकेयं &c. Ragh. XVI. 83. बाल्ये—Chár. reads बाल्यं and takes क्रीडारसं (क्रीडाया रसो रागो यत्र तादृशं) as an *adj.* to it; enjoying childhood wherein one ...

passion for play. Ar. reads क्रीडारसात्......बाल्यम्. This śl. is quoted in the Sar.-K. as an instance of क्रीडित or sportiveness.

Śl. 30. महौषधीं &c.—*cf.* नक्तं ज्योतिरिवौषधिः Ragh. X. 66. ओषधिषु तेजः स्थापयित्वा रविरस्तं यातीत्यागमः। स्थिरोपदेशाः—With whom instruction (knowledge acquired) was permanent, *i. e.* who retained a permanent impression of what she had learnt (in her former existence) and hence (उपदेशकाले) at the time of her education, the different lores of her past life manifested themselves to Pâr., without being taught; see Malli. This cannot be taken here in the sense of 'on whom instruction took a firm hold' as प्रपेदिरे &c. would lose its force. प्राक्तन—प्राक् भवं प्राक्तनं, प्राक्तनं च तज्जन्म च तस्य विद्याः। *Cf.* Ragh. III. 30. The sons of Râma had the knowledge of the use of the Jṛimbhaka missiles manifested to them without instruction. See Uttar. II. p. 52. *Cf.* गङ्गां यथा हंसगणाः शरत्सु वै रात्रौ स्वभासस्तु यथा महौषधीः। गुरूपदेशादुपदेशपण्डितां तां पूर्वसंस्कारगणा ययुर्मुदा ॥ Ś. P.

Śl. 31. असंभृतं—(अकृत्रिम) *lit.* not brought about by outer (artificial) means. अङ्गयष्टेः—अङ्गं यष्टिरिव a slim or slender body; or मयूरव्यंसकादित्वात् a comp. of the Nitya class; हस्तयष्टिलतादयः प्रशंसावचना इत्युक्तत्वात्। Nâr. अनासवाख्यं—आसव इति आख्या यस्य तदासवाख्यं; तन्न भवतीति चेतोविकारजनकं Châr.; *cf.* तस्या उन्मादयितृ रूपं प्रेक्ष्य। Śâk. I. p. 31; or मद may mean here मदविकार to which youth gives rise; *cf.* मधु नयनयोर्विभ्रमादेशदक्षं। Megh. II. 12; see also *infra* IV. 12. पुष्पव्यतिरिक्त०—पुष्पेभ्यः (*i. e.* the flowers forming his arrows) व्यतिरिक्तमधिकं (in excess over, other than) अस्त्रम्। The five flowers forming the arrows of Kâma are अरविन्दमशोकं च चूतं च नवमल्लिका। नीलोत्पलं च पञ्चैते पञ्चबाणस्य सायकाः ॥ Some substitute शिरीष for नवमल्लिका—अरवि०...शिरीषं नीलमुत्पलम्। चूतं चेति प्रकीर्त्यन्ते पञ्च० ॥ बाल्यात्परं—So in Ragh. बाल्यात्परामिव दशां V. 63. Critics are at variance as regards the figures of speech in this śl. *Cf.* सर्वत्र विभावनेति भोजराजः। द्वितीयपाद एव विभावनेति मङ्खुकः। वामनः पुनः एकगुणहानिकल्पनायां साम्यदार्ढ्यं विशेषोक्तिः इति लक्षणमाश्रित्य विशेषोक्तिरलंकार इत्युक्तवान्। यौवनस्य मण्डनत्वादिरूपणाद् रूपकालंकार एव स्फुटः। Nâr. This śl. is quoted in S.-D. as an instance of यौवनशोभा, and in Sar.-K. as of चित्रा नाम कारणान्तरविभावना.

Śl. 32. उन्मीलितं—gradually made manifest or unfolded (like a flower opening up). भिन्न—split up into its different parts, opened. अरविन्द-अराकाराणि पत्राणि विन्दति इति; *lit.* having petals resembling the spokes of a wheel; अर + विद् + अ (शः) by Vârttika on Pâṇ III. 1. 138. चतुरस्रशोभि—beautiful in (the four, hence) all parts. चतुरस्र—See com.; the final अ is added by the Sûtra सुप्रातसुश्वसुदिवशारिकुक्षचतुरस्रैणीपदाजपदप्रोष्ठपदाः । Páṇ. V. 4. 120. विभक्तं—the different parts being brought into prominent relief; symmetrically developed. Quoted in Sar.-K. as an instance of यौवनसंपत्.

Śl. 33. उद्गिरन्तौ—The use of this word (which primarily means 'vomiting') is vulgar; but it is not so here as it is used in a metaphorical sense: see Malli. This shows the extreme delicacy of her feet. *Cf.* विद्रुमरसनदीमिव चरणाभ्यां प्रवर्तयन्तीं Kád. अव्यवस्थाम्—अविद्यमाना व्यवस्था यस्यास्ताम्। Not fixed or stationary, moving about. This is necessary to bear out the comparison to स्थला॰ which is stationary. Whenever she walked such a scene was displayed. *Cf.* तत्पादपाथोजभुवा श्रिया मुने स्थलारविन्दच्छविरूपनिन्दनम्। S. P.

Śl. 34. राजहंसैः-राजहंस being a जातिवाचक term हंसानां राजानः राजहंसाः; a comp. of the राजदन्तादि class. Some regard it as a नित्यसमास like कृष्णसर्प having no विग्रह. संनताङ्गी—See Malli.; *cf.* स्तोकनम्रा स्तनाभ्याम् Megh. II. 22. संनतांसा—*v. l.*—This reading is perhaps better as bearing better comparison with swans; *cf.* संनतांसाः स्त्रियः पूज्या उन्नतांसास्तु पूरुषाः । इति सामुद्रिकाः । हंसा हि संनताङ्गतया प्रसिद्धाः स्मर्तव्याः शिथिलांसहंसरुचयो गोदावरीवीचयः इत्यादिषु । Nár· लीला॰- in which the steppings were graceful on account of sportiveness or dalliance. अञ्चित॰—*Lit.* that which is worshipped or respected; hence beautiful; charming. *Cf.* उभावलंचकतुरञ्चिताभ्यां तपोवनावृत्तिपथं गताभ्याम् । Ragh. II. 18; लीलाञ्चितभ्रूलता D.-K. The gait of beautiful women is often compared to that of royal swans. *Cf.* भवनदीर्घिकामत्तमरालिकागमनरीत्या लीलालसगतिविलासम् &c. D.-K. व्यनीयत—Was taught or given instruction in. For the reverse of this idea *cf.* Vik. IV. 16 (मदखेलपदं कथं नु तस्याः सकलं चोर गतं त्वया गृहीतम्।). प्रत्युपदेश॰ &c.—The royal swans taught her how to step beautifully because they themselves longed to learn from her in return how to utter notes sweet like the jingle of her foot-ornaments. ॰शिञ्जितानि—must be taken in the secondary sense of 'cooings beautiful like the jinglings' &c. Malli. commenting on Megh. II. 19 says शिञ्जिधातुरयं तालव्यादिर्न तु दन्त्यादिः (*i. e.* should not be written as सिञ्ज्); but according to Nágeśabhaṭṭa it is दन्त्यादि also. *Cf.* Ś. P. सुनूपुरभ्राजितपादपद्मयोरादित्सया हंसगणा गतं ययुः ॥.

Śl. 35. वृत्तानुपूर्वे—For comp. see com. The thighs of beautiful ladies are often compared to plantain-stems or the trunks of elephants, but the poet does not use that comparison here for reasons given in the next S'loka. *Cf.* such expressions as रम्भोरूः, करभोरूः &c. to be met with in Sanskrit works, and used by the poet himself elsewhere (क नु खलु रम्भोरूर्गता स्यात् Vik. IV. p. 94; Ragh. VI. 35; अङ्के निधाय करभोरु यथासुखं ते &c. Śák. III. 9.) न चातिदीर्घे—The Com. Ar. remarks that the नञ् here must be taken as पर्युदास and not प्रसज्यप्रतिषेध. But Nár. remarks—अतिदीर्घे च न नाप्यतिह्रस्वे चेति भावः । दीर्घजङ्घा प्रपद्यायुर्दीर्घकालं सुखं त्यजेत् । ह्रस्वजङ्घा श्रियं त्यजेत् । इत्यादिसामुद्रिकोक्तस्त्रीदोषनिषेधपरमिदं विशेषणम् । निर्माणविधौ-निर्माणमेव विधिः तत्र in the matter of the act of creation (here विधि is almost redundant). Ar. takes the loc. as निमित्ते; ०निर्माणविधौ 'निमित्तात्कर्मसंयोगे' (Vârt. on Pâṇ. II. 3. 36) इति सप्तमी चर्मणि द्वीपिनं हन्तीतिवत् । The same com. further remarks दक्षिणावर्तेन तु धातुप्रदीपकारमतमनुसरता लावण्य उत्पाद्य इवास यत्नः इति पाठोऽङ्गीकृतः गत्यर्थत्वं च । तत्र विसंधिदोषोऽर्थासङ्गतिश्च । गत्यर्थयोगे कर्मणोऽपेक्षितत्वात् । But this criticism is needless. It is better to take the loc. as वैषयिक as Malli. does. विभ्रातुः—is used in a different sense in śl. 57. लावण्ये उत्पाद्ये—The meaning of Malli.'s remark on this is this—A कार्य cannot be produced without its उपादानकारण (material cause, as earth in the case of a घट); now लावण्य the उपादानकारण of her limbs was exhausted in the creation of her thigh, and so Brahmá had to make an effort &c. इवास यत्नः—may also mean:—In fashioning her thighs so beautifully the Creator made a preliminary attempt, as it were, to see how he was to create exquisite beauty in her other parts. आस—The root अस् 'to be' is defective in the Perfect, and yet Káli. is found using the form आस in the sense of बभूव; *cf.* प्रादुरास बहुलक्षपाछविः; निष्प्रभश्च रिपुरास भूभृताम्; Ragh. XI. 15, 81; तेनास लोकः पितृमान् विनेत्रा। *Ibid.* XIV. 23; &c. So Malli. (see com.) tries to defend it by quoting शाकटा० who says that it is a verbal ind. in the sense of बभूव. Vâmana defends the form by taking अस् as a different root altogether, *viz.* of the 1st. conj. (meaning to go, to shine, to take &c.) and not of the 2nd; अस गतिदीप्त्यादानेषु इति भ्वादिः; आसेरयसतेः । Kâv. Sû. V. 2. 27. See the Vritti on it स्वरितेतः (Malli.'s अनुदात्तेत् seems to be an oversight) लिटि रूपम्. *Cf.* निर्माय पङ्केरुहसंभवं मुखं जानू तदीये ह्यनुवृत्तपूर्वके । शेषाङ्गनिर्माणविधौ जडोऽभवद्विमोहितस्तन्मुखदर्शनेच्छया ॥ Ś. P.

Śl. 36. त्वचि कर्क०—Aru. takes it as an *aluk* comp.; त्वचिकर्कशत्वादिति अमूर्धमस्तकात्स्वाङ्गात् (Pâṇ. VI. 3. 12) इत्यलुक्।' एकान्त०—Always cold, never changing their nature. कदलीविशेषाः—may also mean सरसकदल्यः; *cf.* यास्यत्यूरुः सरसकदलीस्तम्भगौरश्चलत्वम् ।

Megh. II. 36 where Malli. says सरसी रसाईः न परिपक्वः शुष्कश्च। तत्रैव पाण्डिमसंभवात्। Nár. says—कदलीविशेषाः विशिष्टाः कदल्यः न तु सामान्यकदल्यः। नन्दनोद्यानादिप्ररूढाः कनककदलीकाण्डा इति भावः। यथोक्तं सौन्दर्यलहर्याम्—करीन्द्राणां शुण्डाः कनककदलीकाण्डपटलीमुभाभ्यामूरुभ्यामुभयमपि निर्जित्य भवती। इति। परिणाहि—परिणाहः hugness, bulk, अस्यास्तीति. उपमान—उपमाने उपमायां बाह्याः; where उप० means comparison; or उपमानेषु बाह्याः excluded from, *i. e.* which could not be used as standards of comparison. That with which the thing in hand is compared is उपमान (येन सादृश्यज्ञानं भवति) as चन्द्र, कमल &c. as opposed to उपमेय or the thing compared, as मुख, पद &c. the Fig. of speech is व्यतिरेक.

37. एतावता—एतत्परिमाणमस्य तत्तेन। अनु०—may also be explained as अनुमेया शोभा अनुमेयशोभा साऽस्यास्तीति, by adding इन्; but Malli.'s way is better. For the *Matub* aff. is not allowed after a Karm., by the rule न कर्मधारयान्मत्वर्थीयः बहुव्रीहिश्चेत्तदर्थप्रतिपत्तिकरः (although it may be used in exceptional cases, the rule being supposed not to be all-binding as the भाष्यकार himself has said असुक्वत् in his Bháshya on Páṇ. VII. 3. 44). Some explain it as अनुमेयं यथा तथा शोभि; *cf. supra* चतुरस्रशोभि. It may also be explained as अनुमेयेन शोभते इति तच्छीलम्. पश्चात्—*i. e.* after her marriage with Śiva; one can easily infer how beautiful her S'roṇi was from the fact that it could attract even S'iva, &c. अतिक्रम्य—goes with both राजि and आर्चैः. सिते०—सितादितरस्तस्य; Abl. Tat.

Śl. 38. नतनाभि०—This is considered a mark of beauty; *cf.* गङ्गावर्तसनाभिर्नाभिः D.-K.; नाभिह्रदैः परिगृहीतरयाणि निम्नैः। Śis. V. 29; प्रजापतेः स्पृशतः सौकुमार्यादङ्गुलिमुद्रामिव निमग्नां नाभिमण्डलीमावर्तिनीमुद्वहन्तीं; त्रिभुवनविजयप्रशस्तिवर्णावलीमिव लिखितां मन्मथेन रोमराजिमञ्जरीं बिभ्राणाम्। Kád. p. 284; रोमावली विलासिन्याः प्रविष्टा नाभिमण्डलम्। कियद्गाम्भीर्यमत्रेति तात्पर्यमिव बिभ्रती॥ Vik.-Ch. VIII. 28.

प्र० श्लो०—गम्भीरश्चासौ नाभीह्रदश्च the deep pool-like navel. मुखेन्दु०—as if dropped down from the beak of the Chakraváka in the form of her breast, afraid of the moon in the form of her face. The Chakraváka is separated from his mate during the night and hence he is afraid of the moon (thinking of the night). See Śák. IV. 15. Fig.—उत्प्रेक्षा.

Śl. 39. वेदिविलग्न—वेदिरिव विलग्नमस्या कृशमध्या by उपमानानि सामान्यवचनैः। Páṇ. II. 1. 55; or वेद्याः इव विलग्नः मध्यः यस्याः; the two boundary lines of a Vedi come close in contact with each other in the centre. Hence the comparison. विलगति ह्रसतीति विलग्नं

कंशम्. Char. takes Vedi here in the sense of 'a seal ring' (see Apte's Dic.), meaning that her waist could go into a ring as it was as slender as a finger; but this will be carrying the comparison too far. वलित्रयं—Also one of the items in the description of a beautiful lady by Sanskrit poets; *cf.* मध्येऽस्याश्चिवलीतरङ्गविषमे। Ratn. II. 11; सौधारोहणपरिपाट्या वलित्रयं D.-K.; विततवलिविभाव्यपाण्डुलेखा &c. S'is. VII. 33. बाला—बाला षोडशवार्षिकी। *Cf.* मध्ये च तस्यास्त्रिवली रराज सा कामोत्सवार्थं नवयौवनोद्भवा। Ś. P.

Śl. 40. उत्पीडयत्—Pressing hard (against each other). As the word अन्योन्यं is used here, उत्पीडयत् is Pars.; otherwise it should have been A'tm. by the rule कर्तरि कर्मव्यतिहारे *i. e.* when there is mutual exchange of action and the agent is to be denoted (*i. e.* is used actively) the A'tm. is used. अन्तरं—room covered by; *cf.* स्तनद्वयं वै ववृधे तथा मुने यथा न सूत्रं किल मध्यगं भवेत्। Ś. P. न सूक्ष्मतन्तोरपि तावकस्य तत्रावकाशो भवतः किमु स्यात्। Ratn. II. 15. Aru. notices the reading ०सूत्रेण पदं न लब्धम् and remarks किंत्वपेरपेक्षित्वान्न्यूनपदं (but it has the fault of न्यूनपदत्व as अपि is wanting).

Śl. 41. शिरीषपुष्पा०—*Cf.* शिरीषपुष्पाधिकसौकुमार्यः Ragh. XVIII. 45. The *S'irîsha* is mentioned as one of the arrows of Kâma. See *supra,* notes on śl. 31. Now the poet's idea is this—Kâma who always uses delicate weapons tried his arrow S'irîsha but failed; and finding nothing softer than that, had to yield; but now that he used Pârvatî's arms as his weapons, they must have been softer than the *S'irîsha* flower even. According to those who do not include S'irîsha among the arrows of Cupid the idea is this—Kâma is called Kusumâstra; and as such he ought to have used *S'irîsha,* the softest of flowers, as his weapon against S'iva. But since he did not do that but used Pârvatî's arms as his weapon, they must have been considered by him, thinks the poet, as softer than the *S'irîsha* flower. The figure of speech here is व्यतिरेक.

निर्भर्त्सित &c.—(Śl. in the foot-note) निर्भर्त्सिता तिरस्कृता thrown into the background (by its redness) अशोकदलस्य प्रसूतिः production, *i. e,* the tender leaves येन। चारवो नखा यस्य तच्चारुनखम्। नवोदितः—newly-risen य इन्दुस्तस्य प्रतिमा (form) यस्मिन्। विफलीचकार— *i. e.* surpassed. The idea is this—Her palms were red and so they resembled the red, evening sky; but they displayed ten lunar curves in the form of the nails and thus surpassed the beauty of the evening sky which had but one lunar curve displayed in it. प्रदोषैकचन्द्रोदयाद् व्योम्नो दशनखचन्द्रोदयस्य पाणिद्वयस्य शोभाधिक्यम् । Vijayagaṇi.

Śl. 42. बन्धुर—bulged out at the base and tapering (like a conch); *cf.* जयशङ्खो बन्धुरा लावण्यधरा कन्धरा D.-K. स्तन०—The propriety of the epithet is this—Her neck was flattened at its base on account of her elevated breasts so that the pearl-necklace remained close fitting round it and did not slip down on the bosom. The idea is—Generally it is a pearl-necklace that adds beauty to the neck; but in Párvatí's case the necklace too was set off by her neck; so they helped to enhance each other's beauty. तनुबन्धु०—*v. l.* तनुर्नात्यन्तपीवरश्चासौबन्धुरः सुन्दरश्च तस्य.

Śl. 43. भुङ्क्ते—Enjoys, experiences. भुज् is A'tm. except in the sense of 'protecting' (अनवने). लोला—*Cf.* येन श्रियः संश्रयदोषरूढं स्वभावलोलेत्ययशः प्रमृष्टम्। Ragh. VI. 41. लक्ष्मी—The deity presiding over beauty. Párvatí's face combined in itself the special beauties of both, the lotus and the Moon, such as unfading freshness, fragrance, liveliness, &c. and thus excelled both; this is very poetically and strikingly described in this śloka.

This śl. is quoted in the K.-P. as an instance of those cases wherein the non-statement of the हेतु when it can be easily known is not a fault. अत्र रात्रौ पद्मस्य संकोचः दिवा चन्द्रमसश्च निष्प्रभत्वं लोकप्रसिद्धमिति न भुङ्क्ते इति हेतुं नापेक्षते. Here the causes, *viz.* the withering of lotuses by night and the paling of the moon by day, of Lakshmí's not obtaining the qualities of the lotus or the moon, are well-known and can be obtained by implication and so there is no fault. चञ्चलायामपि तादृशप्रीतिदानेनोमामुखस्योत्कर्षः । Uddyota.

Śl. 44. प्रवाल—A tender leaf (which is red). स्फुट—bright or clean (not soiled with dust). विशदस्य स्मितस्य—स्मित is defined as ईषद्विकसितैर्दन्तैः कटाक्षैः सौष्ठवान्वितम् । अलक्षितद्विजद्वारमुत्तमानां स्मितं भवेत् ॥ A smile is described, according to poetic convention, as white; मालिन्यं व्योम्नि पापे यशसि धवलता वर्ण्यते हासकीर्त्योः । S.-D. कृ with अनु is generally used by poets with the Gen.; as यश्च मनसि वसता धर्मेण......अनुकरोति भगवतो नारायणस्य । Kád.; sometimes with the Acc. as in शैलाधिपस्यानुचकार लक्ष्मीम् । Bhaṭṭi. II. 8. पर्यस्तरुचः—By the rule नहिवृतिवृषिव्यधिरुचिसहितनिषु क्वौ । Páṇ. VI. 3. 116 (*i. e.* when derivatives from the roots नह्, वृत् &c. formed with the aff. क्विप् are used as the second members of compounds, the final vowel of the first member is lengthened; *e. g.* उपानत्, नीरुक् &c.) this should be पर्यस्तारुक् ; but Bhaṭṭoji says (see Sid.-Kau. on the above Sûtra)—this rule applies when the पूर्वपद is a गति or कारक

word and not when it is a विशेषण ; and so we have पर्यस्तरुक्. This Śl. is quoted in S.-K. as an instance of स्मित, a kind of हास.

Śl. 45. अमृत०—अमृतं स्रवतीति अमृतस्रुत् तच्छीलेन । प्रजल्पितायां—Here क्त (त of the p. p. p.) is used कर्तरि; see com.; some explain it as प्रजल्पितमस्या अस्तीति by adding अ मत्वर्थे. अभिजात०—अभिजात properly means nobly-born; speaking like a lady of family; hence sweet-speaking, or genetly speaking. See Śl. 26. अन्यपुष्टा—The Indian *kokil* or cuckoo. The female is supposed to deposit her eggs in the nest of some other birds—generally the crows—which hatch them: hence such names as परभृता, परपोषिता &c. for the cuckoo. *Cf.*. प्रागन्तरिक्षगमनात्स्वमपत्यजातमन्यैर्द्विजैः परभृताः खलु पोषयन्ति । Śák. V. 22. प्रतिकूलशब्दा—प्रतिगतः कूलं or प्रतीपः कूलात् *lit.* going against the bank or current; discordant, adverse, unfavourable, hence harsh. *Cf.* आमत्तकोकिलरुतव्यथिता तु हृद्यामद्य श्रुतिः पिबतु किंनरकण्ठि वाचम् ॥ Mál.-Mádh. VIII. 4; "यथोक्तं सौन्दर्यलहर्यां—विपञ्च्या गायन्ती विविधमपदानं पशुपतेस्त्वयारब्धे वक्तुं चलितशिरसा साधुवचने । तदीयैर्माधुर्यैरपहसिततन्त्रीकलरवां निजां वीणां वाणी निचुलयति चोलेन निभृतम् ॥ इति ।" Nár. श्रोतृ-one who has an ear for music. वितन्त्री—see Malli; or विरुद्धा तन्त्री; a Prádi. Tat., with strings not properly tuned. Mark that the words अवी, लक्ष्मी, तन्त्री (see com.) do not drop the स् of the Nom. sing. उत्पाद्यानां स्वरादीनां विहितं ताडनक्रमम् । विना या ताड्यते मन्दैः सा वितन्त्रीरिहोच्यते ॥ अत्रामृतस्रुतेवेत्युत्प्रेक्षा माधुर्यसौकुमार्यादिगुणैः परभृताविरुताद्देवीसंजल्पितस्य व्यतिरेकं द्योतयति । प्रतिकूलशब्दश्च तमभिद्योतयतीति व्यतिरेकालंकारो ध्वन्यते । Nár.

प्र० श्लो०—ताटङ्क—A kind of ear-ornament, roundish in shape, made of jewels, sometimes of gold. पुष्पवन्तौ—The sun and the moon (used in the dual only). एकयोक्त्या पुष्पवन्तौ दिवाकरनिशाकरौ । Amar. The poet says that the two Táṭaṅkas were not *Táṭaṅkas* but the sun and the moon in disguise coming to wait upon her, knowing that she was to be the wife of Śiva. *Cf.* for a similar idea मुक्ताफलस्रग्भिरवाप शोभां पतिंवरा विभ्रमवेदिका सा । चन्द्री बहुस्त्रीक इति प्रवक्तुं भियेव ताराभिरुपास्यमाना । Vik. Ch. IX. 50 (where the pearls of the necklace are said to be stars).

Śl. 46. प्रवात—प्रकृष्टो वातो यत्र, *i. e.* held in play by the wind. ०नीलोत्पलात् निर्गतो विशेषो यस्य । अधीरं च तद्विप्रेक्षितं च । आयताक्ष्याः—Long eyes are considered as a mark of beauty. *Cf.* तदेतदुन्मीलय चक्षुरायतं Vik. I. 5; सरोषकषायितायताक्षी । Śis. VII. 11. तया गृहीतं नु &c.—The मृगाङ्गनाs meant here are चकितमृ० to whose eyes the eyes of females are often compared; *cf.* त्रस्तैकहायनकुरङ्गविलोलदृष्टेः । Uttar. III. 28; चकितहरिणीप्रेक्षणे दृष्टिपातं Megh. II. 44; अत्यन्तमात्म-

सद्दरीक्षणवल्लभाभिराहो निवत्स्यति समं हरिणाङ्गनाभिः । Śák. I 24; also Śák. II. 3.

Śl. 47. शलाका०—शलाकायुक्तमञ्जनं; a comp. of the शाकपार्थिवादि class; see com. Nâr. reads लेखयोः सा यां वीक्ष्य. लीलाचतुरां-Attractive, charming by, or clever in, amorous or sportive gestures. लीला केलिविलासश्च शृङ्गारभावजा क्रिया । In this consisted the superiority of her eye-brows. The curved eye-brows of beautiful ladies form the staff of Madana's bow. *Cf.* चापयष्टिश्रिया भ्रूलते D.-K. कामकार्मुकतया कथयन्ति भ्रूलतां मम पुनर्मतमन्यत् । Subh. For the idea in the last two lines *cf.* (यत्र) मायश्चापं न वहति भयान्मन्मथः षट्पदज्यम् । सभ्रूभङ्गप्रहितनयनैः कामिलक्ष्येष्वमोघैस्तस्यारम्भश्चतुरवनिताविभ्रमैरेव सिद्धः ॥ Megh. II. 14. The Fig. is व्यतिरेक.

Śl. 48. तिरश्चां—तिरः अञ्चतीति तिर्यङ्; fr. तिरस् changed to तिरि when the root अञ्च् does not drop its अ. See Pâṇ. VI. 3. 94. कैशo—नै well-known, famous; *cf.* K.-P. प्रकान्तप्रसिद्धानुभूतार्थविषयस्तच्छब्दो यदुपादानं नापेक्षते । बालप्रियत्वं—By the Várt. 'वा प्रियस्य' the word प्रिय may stand first or second in a Bah. comp.; *cf.* प्रियमण्डना Śák. IV. 9; प्रियारामा Uttar. II. Mallinátha's reference to the आहिताग्न्यादि class seems to be due to oversight. His defence of the पुंवद्भावः (०प्रियत्वं for प्रियात्वं) by the Várttika त्वतलोः &c. is inaccurate, (being against the Bhâshya) if not wrong. For, the meaning of गुणवचन in the Vârttika is restricted :—शुक्लादय एव गुणाः इति प्रौढमनोरमा । अत्र संज्ञाजातिकृदन्ततद्धितान्त-समस्त-सर्वनाम-संख्याशब्द-व्यतिरिक्तः शब्दो गुणवचनशब्देनोच्यते । आकडारसूत्रभाष्यतस्तथैव लाभात् । Nâges'abhaṭṭa in his शब्देन्दुशेखर. Grammarians defend it by the Vârttika 'सामान्ये नपुंसकमिति वाच्यम्' । on Páṇ. II. 4. 17. ननु इह जातिसंज्ञाव्यतिरिक्तं धर्ममात्रं गुण इति यत्प्राचीनैरुक्तं तत्स्वीकर्तव्यम् । अन्यथा निरीक्ष्य मेने शरदः कृतार्थता (Kir. IV. 9); सा मुमोच रतिदुःखशीलताम् (Kum. VIII. 13) इत्यादिषु पुंवद्भावप्रवृत्त्या दीर्घश्रवणं स्यादित्यत आह सामान्ये नपुंसकमिति । एवं च—नेष्टं पुरो द्वारवतीत्वमासीत् (Śis. III. 69) इत्यादिप्रयोगो निर्बाधः । Tattvabodhinî. The idea—Pârvatî's hair was more luxuriant and graceful than the tails of the Chamarîs, and yet they did not give up their regard for their own hair; hence the conclusion follows that lower animals are incapable of having any sense of shame.

Śl. 49. उपमाद्रव्य०—The Upamánas (उपमा उपमानं स्यात् Amara.) *i. e.* the standards of comparison, such as the moon (without the spot), the lotus &c.; *cf.* the more poetical and felicitous though less forcible description of Śak.'s beauty—चित्रे निवेश्य परिकल्पितसत्त्वयोगा रूपोच्चयेन मनसा विधिना कृता नु । Śák. II. 9; also सा रामणीयकनिधेरधिदेवता वा सौन्दर्यसारसमुदायनिकेतनं वा । तस्याः सखे नियतमिन्दुसुधामृणाल-

ज्योत्स्नादि कारणमभून्मदनश्च वेधाः ॥ Mál.-Mádh. I., which is equally vigorous with the description here. यथाप्रदेशं—प्रदेशं स्थानमनतिक्रम्य यथा तथा । विश्वसृजा—Even the Creator of the universe had to make an effort to create a form so exquisitely beautiful. प्रकृष्टः यत्नः प्रयत्नः ।

Ṡl. 50. नारदः—Son of Brahmá and the most celebrated of the divine sages (देवर्षि). Though reckoned as one of the ten Prajâpatis he does not seem to have taken any part in the creation of the world. The name is variously derived.—नारं (नरस्य धर्म्यं) तद्ददाति; यद्वा नारं नरसमूहं याति कलहेन; अथ वा नुरिदं नारमज्ञानं तद् द्यति or नारं पानीयमित्युक्तं तत्पितृभ्यः सदा भवान् । ददाति तेन ते नाम नारदेति भविष्यति ॥ इत्यागमः Bhán. D. He is a great devotee of Vishṇu (परमभागवत); see नारद Śák. p. 173 and our note *ad loc.* He is represented as of a bright complexion, wearing gold ornaments, clad in white raiment bright as the moon, wandering, Vîṇá (which instrument he is said to have invented) in hand and singing the praise of God, from world to world, a bearer of news from the gods to men and from men to the gods &c. See Śis'. I. 4–10. His Vîṇâ is called Mahatî; see Śis. I. 10. ज्वलिताग्निप्रतीकाशो बालार्कसदृशेक्षणः । सव्यापवृत्तं विपुलं जटामण्डलमुद्वहन् ॥ चन्द्रांशुशुक्ले वसने वसानो रुक्मभूषणः । वीणां गृहीत्वा महतीं कक्षासक्तां सखीमिव ॥ कृष्णाजिनोत्तरासङ्गो हेमयज्ञोपवीतवान् । दण्डी कमण्डलुधरः साक्षाच्छक्र इवापरः ॥ वेत्ता जगति गुह्यानां विग्रहाणां गुहोपमः । महर्षिर्विग्रहरुचिर्विद्वान् गान्धर्ववेदवित् ॥ देवगन्धर्वलोकानामाविवक्ता मुनिः परः । गाता चतुर्णां वेदानामुद्गाता प्रथमर्त्विजाम् ॥ स नारदोऽथ विप्रर्षिर्ब्रह्मलोकचरोऽव्ययः ॥ Harivamśa. कदाचित्—Once, there being an occasion for it (कस्मिंश्चित्प्रस्तावे). प्रेम्णा—प्रेमन् abs. n. fr. प्रिय+affix इमनिच्. शरीरार्धहरां—The comp. here is a disputed point. Malli. takes first अर्धहरा as an Upapada Tat. and then connects it with शरीर. For as the word अर्ध here means 'exactly a half' we cannot get the comp. शरीरार्ध; it will be अर्धशरीर by अर्धं नपुंसकम् । Pâṇ. II. 2. 2.). But the authority of this Sútra is rejected by Patañjali (see भाष्य on II. 4. 26; अथपुनरयमेकदेशिसमासः आरभ्यमाणः षष्ठीसमासं बाधते । इष्यते च षष्ठीसमासोऽपि । &c.); and Bhaṭṭoji Dîk. says in his शब्दकौस्तुभ—अर्धपिप्पलीति कर्मधारयेण सिद्धम् । न च समप्रविभागे षष्ठीसमासं बाधितुमिदं सूत्रमिति वाच्यम् । षष्ठीसमासस्यैवेष्टत्वादिति । तथा च कालिदासः मायुक्त-प्रेम्णा शरीरार्धहरां हरस्य इति । So we can have शरीरस्यार्धं हरतीति also. किल—We are told; it is known from history (ऐतिह्य). *Cf.* एषा भार्या जगद्भर्तुर्वृषाङ्कस्य महीधर । शरीरार्धहरा देवी भविष्यति न संशयः ॥

Ṡl. 51. प्रगल्भेऽपि &c.—shows that some girls at least were married at an advanced age in those days. कृशानु—कृशयतीति कृशानुः । that reduces the mass of things; hence, fire. Fire only is हव्यवाह्, being the mouth of the gods. हव्य—see Malli.; also हूयन्ते देवा अनेन ; an offering made to the gods as opposed to कव्य which is offered to the manes; हव्यकव्ये देवपैत्रे अन्ने इत्यमरः । This Śl. is quoted in the Sar.-K. as an instance of महाभाग्य.

Śl. 52. देवदेव—gives the reason why Himálaya could not offer, unasked, his daughter to Śiva, the most High, fearing a refusal. अयाचितारं सुतां &c. The Commentators Ar. and Avachûri quote—अयाचितानि देयानि (दीयन्ते) (सर्वदानानि) सर्वद्रव्याणि भारत । अन्नं विद्या तथा कन्या अनर्थिभ्यो न दीयते ॥ (अर्थिभ्यः सम्प्रदीयते) ॥ सुतां ग्राहयितुं—Some grammarians take ग्रह् Cau. as a द्विकर्मक root, on the authority of Patañjali's Káriká नीवह्योर्हरतेश्चापि गत्यर्थानां तथैव च । द्विकर्मकेषु ग्रहणं कर्तव्यमिति निश्चयः ॥ By च in the कारिका, Sudhâkara, Mádhava and others include such roots as मुच् cau. (Megh. II. 33), त्यज् cau. (Megh. II. 36), ग्रह् cau. and some others. The grammarian हरदत्त is against the inclusion of ग्रह् ; *cf.* Mádhava जयतेः कर्षतेर्मन्थेर्मुषेर्दण्डयतेः पचेः । तारेर्ग्राहेस्तथा मोचेस्त्याजेर्दीपेश्च संग्रहः ॥ कारिकायां च शब्देन सुधाकरमुखैः कृतः । ग्राहेरिह ग्रहो नैव हरदत्तस्य संमतः ॥ Malli. commenting on Ragh. XV. 88 says ग्रहित्यज्योर्ण्यन्तयोर्द्विकर्मकत्वम् । *Cf.* अजिग्रहत्तं जनको धनुस्तत् । Bhaṭṭ. II. 42. Those who do not accept this view explain away the difficulty either by saying स्वतन्त्राः कवयः, or by taking ग्राहयितुं in the sense of बोधयितुम्. साधुः—This word is emphatic; when a man is अर्थी the poet has a different defence to give; *e. g.* याच्ञा मोघा वरमधिगुणे नाधमे लब्धकामा । Megh. I 6. माध्यस्थ्यं—मध्यस्थस्य भावः । *Cf.* एवं सर्वगुणोपेतामुमामालोक्य भूधरः । क्रमेण योजयामास तां हरार्चनकर्मणि । हिमवानुवाच–शृणु गौरि वचोऽस्माकं शंकरो वर्तते मयि । इहामुत्र फलार्थं च तं पूजय समाहिता ॥ Ś.-P.

Śl. 53. यथैव पूर्वे—*Cf. Supra* s'l. 21. सुदती—To get this form there must be indication of age which is not the case here.; so we should have सुदन्ती or सुदन्ता. This form is, therefore, somehow justified by supposing that the poet here adds an epithet which, expressing her beauty, also indicates that stage of her age when the teeth are fully grown. *Cf.* कथं तर्हि सा दक्षरोषात्सुदती ससर्ज इति । न ह्यत्र वयो गम्यते । अतः सुदन्तीति भाव्यम् । अत आहुः-शोभना दन्ता अस्याः समस्ता जाता न तु न्यूना इति कथंचिदिहापि वयो गम्यते एव । Praudhamanoramâ. Vámana, in his Kâv. Sût. says सुदत्यादयः प्रतिविधेयाः । V. 2. 68 see his Vṛitti on this. But Bhaṭṭoji's opinion is preferable and so it is given above. The Com. Dakshiṇávarta proposes to read सा दक्षरोषात्तु सती. परिग्रहः—परिगृह्यते what is entirely taken possession of, a wife. सङ्ग—attachment to worldly objects. *Cf.* यदा देहं सती देवी दक्षरोषात्ससर्ज ह । ततो विमुक्तसङ्गोऽभूच्छंकरस्त्वपरिग्रहः ॥ Ś.-P. The Com, Ar. remarks

अत्र पूर्वप्रवृत्तत्वेन सूचितस्य शृङ्गारस्य विरोधी तपश्चर्यानुभावकः शान्तो रसस्तृतीयसर्गान्तं यावदनुवर्तते । तयोश्च विरोधस्तदुभयाविरुद्धेन देवीदेहत्यागसूचितेन मध्ये पतता करुणेन प्रशमितः । तदुक्तं ध्वनिकृता—रसान्तरान्तरितयोरेकवाक्यस्थयोरपि । निवर्तते हि रसयोः समावेशविरोधिता ॥ इति ।

Śl. 54. कृत्तिवासस्—कृत्तिः चर्म वासो यस्य. When Śiva killed the elephant-demon (Gajásura) the son of Mahishásura, the latter begged of him as a boon that he should wear on his person his (the demon's) hide and should thenceforward be known by the name of Krittivâsas. महिषासुरपुत्रोऽसौ समायाति गजासुरः । प्रमथ्नन् प्रमथान्सर्वान् निजवीर्यमदोद्धतः ॥......गजासुर उवाच-त्रिशूलपाणे देवेश जाने त्वां स्मरहारिणम् । तव हस्ते मम वधः श्रेयानेव पुरान्तक ॥ यदि प्रसन्नो दिग्वासास्तदा नित्यं वसान मे । इमां कृत्तिं विरूपाक्ष त्वच्छिूलाग्निपाविताम् । नामास्तु कृत्तिवासास्ते प्रारभ्याद्यतनं दिनम् ॥ Kâśikhaṇḍa. तपसे—The Dat. may be तादर्थ्ये as Malli. has it, or it may mean तपश्चरितुं by क्रियार्थोपपदस्य च कर्मणि स्थानिनः । यतात्मा—is significant; it shows why Śiva selected a peak which was मृग० and कण्कि०-attractions which draw away the mind from asceticism. अन्त्येन विशेषणद्वयेन रमणीयत्वप्रतिपादकेन विरोधिसंनिधावप्यतिधीरत्वाद् देवस्य धैर्यलोपशङ्का नास्तीति द्योत्यते । Ava. *Cf.* Śâk VII. 12. गङ्गाप्रवा०—implies its purity; *cf.* गङ्गाम्बुसंपर्कविशुद्धिभाजः । Bhaṭṭi.: III. 39. मृगनाभिगन्धि—मृगनाभेर्गन्धः मृगनाभिगन्धः स विद्यते अस्य; not a Bah. Comp., as the smell is not inseparably connected with the peak. See Gr. § 256 (*c*). *Cf.* स कृत्तिवासास्तपसे यतात्मा वर्तते मम । प्रस्थं चालकनन्दायां सदाशीकरशीतलम् ॥ Ś.-P.

Śl. 55. गणाः—Inferior deities or a troop of demigods called Pramathas, who attend on Śiva and are under the superintendence of Gaṇes'a, one of the demigods. विचित्ररूपाभरणा जटाचन्द्रार्धमण्डिताः । आकाशमार्गे गच्छन्तमनुगच्छन्ति नित्यशः ॥ ध्यानस्थं परिचर्यन्ति सलिलादिभिरीश्वरम् । नानाशस्त्रधराः शंभोर्गणास्तु प्रमथाः स्मृताः ॥ अपरे गायनास्तालमृदङ्गपणवादिभिः । नृत्यन्ति वाद्यं कुर्वन्तो गायन्ति मधुरस्वरम् । षट्त्रिंशत्कोटयश्चैते हरस्य संकला गणाः ॥ Káliká P. नमेरु०—नमेरोः प्रसवः (flower) अवतंसः (an ear-ornament or head ornament) येषां ते. ०विच्छुरिताः—bedecked or besmeared with. स्पर्शवतीः—of excellent *i. e.* soft touch. शैलेय—a kind of fragrant resin. नद्ध—over-grown. With the description here *cf.* विशश्रमुर्नमेरूणां छायास्वध्यास्य सैनिकाः । दृषदो वासितोत्सङ्गा निषण्णमृगनाभिभिः ॥ Ragh. IV. 74; शैलेयगन्धीनि शिलातलानि *Ibid.* VI. 51; आसीनानां सुरभितशिलं नाभिगन्धैर्मृगाणां तस्या एव प्रभवमचलं प्राप्य गौरं तुषारैः ॥ Megh. I. 54.

Śl. 56. तुषारसंघात—तुषाराणां संघाताः masses of snow closely adhering together (संघात close union); now see com. दर्पकलः—Some take कल to mean मनोज्ञ charming, eminent by. This explains why he did not bear the roar of the lions. समुल्लिखन्—*Cf.* क्वचित

त्र्यम्बकवृषभाविषाणकोटिखण्डिततटशिलाखण्डं Kád.; शैलादाशु त्रिनयनवृषोत्खातकूटान्निवृत्तः । Megh. II. 53. गवय—A species of the gayal, erroneously classed by Hindu writers as a species of deer. M.-W. (But the term मृग is not restricted to the deer but means a beast in general). असोढ०—*Cf.* प्रकृतिः खलु सा महीयसः सहते नान्यसमुन्नतिं यया । Kir. II. 21.

Śl. 57. आधाय--Having duly consecrated (for continued worship); *cf.* Uttar. I. 8. समित्—अर्कपलाशखदिरन्यग्रोधपिप्पलोदुम्बरशमीदूर्वाकुशाः समिधः क्रमात् । Ava. स्वमेव मूर्त्यन्तरं—Fire is one of the forms of Śiva. अष्टमूर्तिः—For the eight forms see Malli.; भूत means the five elements, which include तेजस् or fire. Also, वसुधागन्धवाहश्च यजमानजलाग्नयः । सूर्यश्चन्द्रो नभश्चेता अष्टौ शंकरमूर्तयः ॥ See our notes on Śák. I. 1. केनापि कामेन—with some object in view which none could divine; for there is no object which he could wish for; *cf.* हृदयस्थमनासन्नमकामं त्वां तपस्विनम् । Ragh. X. 19. The object may be to oblige the world or to guide it or the like. Nár. quotes from the B.-P. ईजे च भगवान्रामो यत्रास्पृष्टोऽपि कर्मणा । लोकानां ग्राहयञ्शीलं यथाऽन्योऽप्याप्नुत्तये ॥ Mark the alliterations in this and the next two ślokas.

Sl. 58. अर्घ्य—See Malli.; similarly दण्डमर्हतीति दण्ड्यः, वध्यः, युग्यः &c. अर्घ्येण—An *arghya* is a respectful offering offered to a deity or a distinguished guest and generally consists of eight ingredients :—आपः क्षीरं कुशाग्रं च दधि सर्पिः सतण्डुलम् । यवः सिद्धार्थकश्चैव अष्टाङ्गोऽर्घः प्रकीर्तितः ॥ See also our note on the word at Ragh. V. 2. अद्रिनाथः—Here the न should be changed to ण by the rule पूर्वपदात्संज्ञायामगः । Páṇ. VIII. 4. 3 (*i. e.* न् is changed to ण् when the letter occasioning the change occurs in the first member and the whole is a name, except when ग intervenes); but it is not changed to ण् here, as the term अद्रिनाथ is not limited to one mountain and is not therefore a संज्ञा; similar instances are रघुनाथ, रघुनन्दन, वृषवाहन, &c. (एकाधिकवस्तुनिष्ठत्वाकिंमहत्वादत्र असंज्ञात्वम्). अर्चयित्वा—For Śiva, coming, to dwell of his own accord on one of his peaks, was his guest, and it is usual with house-holders to depute their daughters to wait upon guests; *cf.* दुहितरं शकुन्तलामतिथिसत्काराय नियुज्य &c. Śák. I. p. 15; गृहमेधिनो हि अतिथिसत्काराय कन्यकां नियुञ्जन्ति यथा दुर्वाससः कुन्तीं कुन्तिभोजः । Ar. प्रयतां—self-restrained and therefore pure and capable of enduring trouble; this shows that she was a fit person to wait on Śiva. Mark the alliterations in the first two lines. *Cf.* ईश्वराणां सदा सेवा जायते सर्वमङ्गलम् । तस्मात्तदर्चनासक्ता भव त्वं भवभाविनि ॥ पितृर्वाक्यमिदं श्रुत्वा जहास मनसा ...

तथेत्युक्त्वा स्वपितरं परिचर्यापराभवत् ॥ जया च विजया तस्याः सख्यौ द्वे परिचारिके । ताभ्यां साकं चन्द्रमुखी चन्द्रशेखरमार्चयत् ॥

Śl. 59. प्रत्यर्थि०—प्रतिकूलमर्थयते तच्छीला; प्रत्यर्थिनी भूता प्रत्य०; see Malli. The masculinization (पुंवद्भाव) of प्रत्यर्थिनी is due to स्त्रियाः पुंवत् &c. Pâṇ. VI. 3. 34. Some take it as a Tat., under श्रेण्यादयः कृतादिभिः । (तत्र कृतादिषु भूतशब्दः पठितः । श्रेण्यादिः आकृतिगणः इति च शाकटायनः । see Malli. on एकौघभूते Kir. III. 35). समाधेः—has not its technical meaning in the Yoga philosophy here, but simply means contemplation, penance, ascetic practices. शुश्रूषमाणां—Because she desired to serve him. श्रु is A'tm. in the Desiderative. विघ्नियन्ते—Malli. takes this as Pass. Pres., तेन हेतुना being understood. It may also be taken कर्मकर्तरि. This is amply borne out by subsequent events; see *infra* III. 40, 69, 71 &c. *Cf.* एवमुक्त्वा तु तां देवीं सेवायै जगृहे हरः । इदमेव महद्धैर्यं यद्विघ्नो न हि विघ्नयेत् ॥ Kâlikâ-P.; समाधेरनुमेने तां गिरिशः परिपन्थिनीम् । प्राप्योऽहं तपसा सत्यमिति लोकांश्च दर्शयन् ॥ S.-P.

Śl. 60. बलि०—बल्यर्थं बल्यर्थानि वा पुष्पाणि बलि०. नियम०—The fixed rites Śiva had to perform as required by the particular form of penance he had been practising; तेषां विधिः अनुष्ठानम् । Religious observances are of two kinds; नियत or नित्य (as सन्ध्योपासनं in the case of a Bráhmaṇa), the performance of which cannot be neglected; and अनित्य or काम्य, those recurring at particular times or performed with a view to gain some end (as स्वर्गकामो यजेत). गिरिशं—Malli. commenting on the word at Ragh. XVI. 51 says—गिरिरस्यस्य निवासत्वेन गिरिशः । लोमादित्वात् शप्रत्ययः । (the *mat.* aff. श being added) and remarks—गिरौ शेते इति विग्रहे तु गिरौ शेतेर्ड इति छन्दसि विधानात् लोके प्रयोगानुपपत्तिः स्यात् । तस्मात्पूर्वोक्तमेव विग्रहवाक्यं न्याय्यम् । सुकेशी—also सुकेशा. The Com. Ar. remarks that the words परिखेद and सुकेशी indicate the peculiar grace imparted to her body by exhaustion (अत्र परिखेदसुकेशीशब्दाभ्यां श्रमावस्थासुलभः शोभातिशयः प्रत्याय्यते) and explain why she was peculiarly attractive in that condition. *Cf* गिरिशमुपचचार प्रत्यहं सा सुकेशी स्वजनकवचनाज्ञापालनायेशभक्ता । सकलभुवननाथः शंकरश्चन्द्रमौलिर्भवतु मम हि भर्ता भावयन्तीति लाभम् ॥ S.-P.

CANTO II.

Śl. 1. तारक—A demon, son of Vajraṇakha and Varâṅgî. Brahmâ conferred upon him a boon that he would not be killed by any one except a child seven days old. Kârttikeya slew the demon on the 7th day of his birth. दिवौकसः—Fr. दिव + ओकस ;

if derived from दिव् the form will be दिवोकस् (or दिवौकस् if classed under पृषोदरादि as Malli. says). तुरासाह्—*Lit.* who overpowers or defeats the mighty or impetuous तुरं वेगवन्तं साहयति अभिभवति; or तुरं or तुरा (quickly) साहयति अरीन्; fr. तुर+सह् cau.+क्विप् । अन्येषामपि दृश्यते । Pân. VI. 4. 137 इति पूर्वपदस्य दीर्घः । स्वायंभुवं—Here the ऊ of स्वयंभू does not take Guṇa substitute as it should by the rule 'ओर्गुणः' (The उ or ऊ of a *Bha* base takes Guṇa before a Taddhita affix; Pâṇ. VI. 4. 116) by the maxim संज्ञापूर्वको विधिरनित्यः—'a rule is not universally applicable when what it teaches is expressed by a technical term such as by गुण here'. See Malli. *Cf.* एतस्मिन्नन्तरे काले तारकेण दिवौकसः । आजौ पराजिता आसन् शक्रदर्पविघातिना ॥ तदा सर्वे तुरासाहं कृत्वाग्रे हतविक्रमाः । स्वायंभुवं ययुर्धाम सत्यलोकमिति श्रुतम् ॥ Ś.-P.; also Ragh. X. 5.

Śl. 2. आविरभूद्ब्रह्मा—This was a good omen; for अभ्याक्षेपी भविष्यन्त्याः कार्यसिद्धेर्हि लक्षणम् । Ragh. X. 6. आविस् has optionally गतिसंज्ञा (*i. e.* is treated as a *prep.* or उपसर्ग) and then must precede the root connected with it. When it is a mere निपात it may stand apart from a root; *cf.* वारुणीमदविशङ्कमथाविश्चक्षुषोऽभवद्-साविव रागः । Śiś. X. 19. सुप्तपद्मानां—The lotuses correspond to the faces of the gods. For a similar idea comp. सुप्तमीन इव ह्रदः । Ragh. I. 73. दीधितिमानिव—The comparison implies power in Brahmâ to cause the lotuses of their faces to bloom again. *Cf.* Vik. I. 5 महोत्पलं प्रत्युषसीव पद्मिनी. *Cf.* दृष्ट्वा तत्र जगन्नाथं विकसत्सु मुखश्रियः । बभूवुः पङ्कजानीव प्रातर्दृष्ट्वा दिवाकरम् ॥ Ś.-P.; Ragh. X. 6, 7.

Śl. 3. सर्वस्य धातारं—*cf.* चतुर्वर्गफलं ज्ञानं कालावस्थाश्चतुर्युगाः । चतुर्वर्णमयो लोकस्त्वत्तः सर्वं चतुर्मुखात् ॥ Ragh. X. 22, where Malli. quotes the Śruti—इदं सर्वमसृजत यदिदं किंचित् । वागीशं—Brahmâ is represented as the lord of speech, being the source of the Vedas; *cf.* Uttar. I. 2. In वागीशं, वाचां is Gen. (and not an object of ईश्) by कर्तृकर्मणोः कृति; Pâṇ. II. 3. 52; and thus we have the comp. by कृद्योगा च षष्ठी समस्यते । If वाचां be taken as the कर्म of ईश् then the comp. would be precluded by the Vârttika प्रतिपदविधाना षष्ठी न समस्यते । Further discussion of this point will be uninteresting here. अर्थ्याभिः—*Lit* not departing from their senses. All that was said was no idle compliment but entirely true in the case of Brahmâ; *cf.* स्तुत्यं स्तुतिभिरर्थ्याभिरुपतस्थे सरस्वती; भूतार्थव्याहृतिः सा हि न स्तुतिः परमेष्ठिनः । Ragh. IV. 6, X. 33; उपतस्थिरे—स्था with उप is A'tm. in the sense of 'waiting upon a deity;' see com. *Cf.* ततस्ते लोकधातारं वागीशं सर्वतोमुखम् । प्रणिपत्य यथान्यायमिदमाहुस्तदा मुने ॥ Ś.-P., also Ragh. X. 15.

Śl. 4. त्रिमूर्तये—The same Saguṇa Brahman appears in a three-fold form as it identifies itself with Rajas, or Sattva, or

'Tamas (गुणत्रयवि०). See com. and our note on Ragh. X. 16. Ar. reads नमस्त्वमूर्तये 'a bow to thee that hast no form or forms before creation'. केवलात्मने—*i. e.* existing as Brahman only, without being associated with any conditions. *Cf.* आत्मा वा &c. Ait. A'r. II. 4. 1. 1 quoted in the com.; सदेव सोम्येदमग्र आसीदेकमेवाद्वितीयम्। Chhând. Up. VI. 2. 1; भगवानेक आसेदमग्र आत्मात्मनां विभुः। B. P. III. 5. 23. गुणत्रय०—The three guṇas are the constituents of nature (Máyá or the Prakṛiti of the Sâṃkhyas) in which they exist potentially. All that is good—such as knowledge, joy &c is the result of Sattva (the quality of goodness); activity, energy &c. spring from Rajas (the quality of foulness); and all that is bad or terrible—such as destruction, misery, wickedness &c., is the result of Tamas (the quality of ignorance). पश्चाद्भेद०—Malli. takes भेद in the sense of भेदोपाधि or limiting conditions, leading to the multiformity of forms and names (नामरूपविकारभेदोपाधिविशिष्टं ब्रह्म &c. Śâr. Bhâ.). Brahman, at the time of creation, first associates itself with the three qualities and then manifests a diverse creation. *Cf.* तदैक्षत बहु स्यां प्रजायेयेति; इदं सर्वमसृजत यदिदं किं च; सच्च त्यच्चाभवत् &c.; also पुरश्चक्रे द्विपदः पुरश्चक्रे चतुष्पदः। पुरः स पक्षी भूत्वा पुरः पुरुष आविशत्। रूपं रूपं प्रतिरूपो बभूव। Brih. II. 5. 18. 19. Kaṭhop. V. 9. Also रसान्तराण्येकरसं यथा दिव्यं पयोऽश्नुते देशे देशे गुणेष्वेवमवस्थास्त्वमविक्रियः॥ and Châ.'s remark तत्त्वतो निरुपाधिकस्वरूपेऽपि त्वयि स्रष्टृत्वादिव्यवहारो गुणोपाधिनिबन्धन इति भावः। *Cf.* ब्रह्मणे सृजते विश्वं स्थितौ पालयते नमः। रुद्ररूपाय कल्पान्ते नमस्तुभ्यं त्रिमूर्तये॥ S.-P.; Ragh. X. 17.

Śl. 5. यदमोघं &c.—अमोघं—not futile; full of potentialities. *Cf.* महाप्रलयकालान्त एतदासीत्तमोमयम्। प्रसुप्तमिव चातर्क्यमविज्ञातमलक्षणम्॥ अविज्ञेयमविज्ञातं जगत्स्थास्नु चरिष्णु च। ततः स्वयंभूरव्यक्तः प्रभवः पुण्यकर्मणाम्॥ व्यञ्जयन्नेतदखिलं प्रादुरासीत्तमोनुदः। योऽतीन्द्रियः परोऽव्यक्तादणुर्ज्यायान्सनातनः नारायण इति ख्यातः स एकः स्वयमुद्बभौ॥ यः शरीरादभिध्याय सिसृक्षुर्विविधं जगत्। अप एव ससर्जादौ तासु बीजमवासृजत्॥ तदेवाण्डं समभवद्धेमरूपमयं महत्। संवत्सरसहस्रेण सूर्यायुतसमप्रभम्॥ प्रविश्यान्तर्महातेजा स्वयमेवात्मसंभवः। तदन्तर्भगवानेष सूर्यः समभवत्पुरा। आदित्यश्चादिभूतत्वाद् ब्रह्मा ब्रह्म पठन्नभूत्॥ दिवं भूमिं समकरोत्तदण्डशकलद्वयम्। जरायुर्मेरुमुख्याश्च शैलास्तस्याभवंस्तदा॥ नद्योऽण्डनाम्नः संभूताः पितरो मनवस्तथा। &c., Mat. P. चराचरं—may also be from the Frequentative base of चर् + अ (अच्). प्रभवः गीयसे—As in यतो वा इमानि भूतानि जायन्ते। Tait. Up. III. 1. जन्माद्यस्य यतः Ved. S. I. 1. 2, &c the commentators Ar. and Nar. prefer the reading प्रभावस्तस्य गीयते and construe तस्य चीजस्य अतः चराचरं विश्वं प्रभावः (प्रकृष्टो भावः विभूतिः the great manifestation) इति गीयते। मन्वादिभिरिति शेषः। and the former remarks—प्रभवस्तस्य गीयसे इति पाठे सर्वस्मिन्नपि अनन्तरस्य

पौनरुक्त्यं स्यात् । Malli notices the reading प्रसवः गीयते which is the best; *cf.* त्वया यत्क्षिप्तममलं बीजं जलधिसंचये । स्तूयते प्रसवस्तस्य चराचरमिदं जगत् ॥ Ś.-P.

Śl. 6. तिसृभिः &c.—ब्रह्मत्वे सृजते लोकान् विष्णुत्वे पालयत्यपि । रुद्रत्वे संहरत्येव तिस्रोऽवस्थाः स्वयंभुवः ॥ उदीरयन्—pre-eminently manifesting, proclaiming. महिमानं—Such as अस्य जगतो नामरूपाभ्यां व्याकृतस्यानेककर्तृभोक्तृसंयुक्तस्य प्रतिनियतदेशकालनिमित्तक्रियाफलाश्रयस्य मनसाप्यचिन्त्यरचनारूपस्य जन्मस्थितिभङ्गं यतः सर्वज्ञात् सर्वशक्तेः कारणाद्भवति तद् ब्रह्म । Śár. Bhá. बालिर्बन्धे जलधिर्मन्थे जह्नेऽमृतं दैत्यकुलं विजिग्ये । कल्पान्तदुःस्था वसुधा ततोहे येनैष भारोऽतिगुरुर्न तस्य ॥ Bhaṭṭi. II. 39. पक्ष्मालीपिङ्गलिम्नः कण इव तडितां यस्य कृत्स्नः समूहः । यस्मिन्ब्रह्माण्डमीषद्विघटितमुकुले कालयज्वा जुहाव ॥ &c. Mál.-Mádh. I. *Cf.* दर्शयन्महिमानं त्वं तिसृभिर्मूर्तिभिः प्रभुः । उत्पत्तिस्थितिनाशानामेकोऽभूः कारणं स्मृतम् ॥ Ś.-P.; Ragh. X. 16.

Śl. 7. स्मृतौ—are authoritatively stated to be. स्मृत in such cases has a technical meaning; it means 'told in the Smṛitis.' The Smṛitis (*lit.* what is remembered) are the codes of memorial law written by inspired sages like Manu, Yâjñavalkya and others, and are so called in contradistinction to श्रुति (what is heard, *i. e.* directly revealed). They rank next to the Śrutis in authority. *Cf.* Manu. I. 32 quoted in the com. *Cf.* स्त्रीस्वरूपो भवानेव पुमानसि जगत्पते । तस्मात्सर्वेषु सत्त्वेषु विख्यातौ पितरौ भवान् ॥ Ś.-P,

Śl. 8. स्वकाल°—The four Yugas (Kṛita, Tretâ, Dvâpara and Kali, which take up 4,320,000 human years) rolling on one thousand times form a day of Brahmâ and the same is the length of his night. *Cf.* कृतं त्रेता द्वापरं च कलिश्चेति चतुर्युगम् । प्रोच्यते तत्सहस्रं तु ब्रह्मणो दिनमुच्यते ॥ V.-P. Read before यदा स देवो &c.—चत्वार्याहुः सहस्राणि वर्षाणां तत्कृतं युगम् । तस्य तावच्छती (*i. e.* 400) संख्या संध्यांशश्च तथाविधः ॥ (*i. e.* 4,800 years of gods which multiplied by 360 amount to 1,728,000 years of men) इतरेषु ससंध्येषु ससंध्यांशेषु च त्रिषु । एकापायेन वर्तन्ते सहस्राणि शतानि च । (*i. e.* 4800 Kṛita, three-fourths of this, *i.e.* 3600 Tretâ; half of that, *i.e.* 2400 Dvâpara, and one-fourth, *i e.* 1200 Kali.) एतद् द्वादशसाहस्रं देवानां युगमुच्यते । दैविकानां युगानां तु सहस्रं परिसंख्यया । ब्राह्ममेकमहर्ज्ञेयं तावतीं रात्रिमेव च ॥ See B.-P. III. 11. 17-22. व्यस्तरात्रिंदिवस्य—There is some technical difficulty of gram. about this comp; रात्रिंदिव is allowed as a Dvandva only in the sense of the Loc. while it is here used in the sense of the Nom.; Malli. defends this by saying—Since the भाष्यकार has used दोषा and दिवा in the Acc. in दोषामन्यमहः । दिवामन्या रात्रिः, here the words दिवा and रात्रि in the comp. may somehow be considered as taking प्रातिपदिकार्थ and have the Nom. यौ तु स्वमा°—अनेन स्वापुषोऽपि स्वयमेव व्यवस्थापक इत्युक्तं भवतीति । जगदीश्वरस्य नेतरजनवत्कालाधीनत्वं नापि

कर्माधीनत्वमिति लोकतो व्यतिरेको भन्यते । Nâr. *Cf.* तवावबोधो भगवन् भूतानामुदयाय च । मलयाय भवेद्राविर्नमस्ते कालरूपिणे ॥ S'.-P.

Śl. 9. जगद्योनिः—An allusion to the Vedântic theory of creation (Śl.s 9th and 10th). योनिश्च हि गीयते । Ved.-S. I. 4. 27. जगत् all created things (*lit.* that which undergoes change constantly; according to the Vedântic theory there is nothing like absolutely dead matter); पञ्चमहाभूतेन्द्रियविषयात्मकं तु जगत्. जगतः योनि- जगद्योनिः, अयोनि—कथं न योनिरिति विरोधः; the *Virodha* is removed by taking अयोनि as a Bah.; see Malli.; and so on. जगदादिः— Here आदिः means 'existing previously to;' *cf.* एष सर्वेश्वर एष सर्वज्ञ एषोऽन्तर्याम्येष योनिः सर्वस्य प्रभवाप्ययौ हि भूतानाम् । Mâṇḍ. Up. सर्वज्ञस्त्वमविज्ञातः सर्वयोनिस्त्वमात्मभूः । सर्वप्रभुरनीशस्त्वमेकस्त्वं सर्वरूपभाक् ॥ *Cf.* जगदीशस्त्वमेवासि त्वत्तो नास्त्येव ईश्वरः । जगदादिरनादिस्त्वं नमस्ते स्वात्मवेदिने ॥ Ś.-P.; Ragh. X. 20.

Śl. 10. आत्मानं &c.—आत्मना स्वयमात्मानं वेत्सि सृजसि आत्मन्येव प्रलीयसे एतेन तव ज्ञाता कर्ता संहर्ता नान्योऽस्तीति दर्शितम् । नित्यस्य भगवतो धर्मरक्षणार्थः- मधर्मनिबर्हणार्थं च शरीरस्वीकारपरिहारवशादौपचारिकौ सृष्टिसंहारौ । Châr. God being the material and efficient cause of the Universe there can be nothing beyond him. He is the knower and the known. He is the real Vastu; manifested universe is an illusion. This is the Advaita doctrine. *Cf.* नान्योऽतोऽस्ति द्रष्टा नान्योऽतोऽस्ति विज्ञाता । Bṛih. III. 7. 23. कृतिना—प्रशस्तं (implying his omnipotency) कृतं कर्म अस्य; the all-powerful. *Cf.* एवं सर्वं स सृष्ट्वेदं मां चाचिन्त्यपराक्रमः । आत्म- न्यन्तर्दधे भूयः कालं कालेन पीडयन् ॥............यदा स्वपिति शान्तात्मा तदा सर्वं निमीलति ॥ Manu. I. 51, 52; and आत्मानमात्मना चेदं सृजस्यवसि हंसि च। आत्मज्ञानविदो नित्यं त्वां विदुर्नेतरे जनाः ॥ Ś.-P.

Śl. 11. संघात०—*i. e.* परमाणूनां; close adhesion of atoms. Here there is a reference to the atomic theory of Kaṇâda. The Naiyâyikas maintain that action first takes place between two atoms which combine and form what is called a Dvyaṇuka, three Dvyaṇukas form a Tryaṇuka and so all substances, up to the earth, are formed. प्राकाम्यं— absolute power (to enforce one's will) over. विभूतिषु— *i. e.* Siddhis; for which see I. 5. नमः समुद्ररूपाय संघातकठिनाय च । स्थूलाय गुरवे तुभ्यं सूक्ष्माय लघवे नमः ॥ व्यक्ताव्यक्ताय देवाय सर्वलोकेश्वराय च । सर्वान्तःसाक्षिणे तुभ्यं निर्जराजरदायिने ॥ Ś.-P. The com. Ar. omits this śl.

Śl. 12. उद्घातः—उद्धननं fr. हन् + अ (घञ् added भावे). उद्गीथः— *V. l.* is a designation of the sacred syllable *Om* (composed of अ, उ, म्); *cf.* ओमित्येतदक्षरमुद्गीथमुपासीत; Chhân. Up. I. 1. प्रणवः—The monosyllable *Om*, representing Brahman and repeated at the beginning of the recital of any Vedic passage (fr. प्र and नु to praise). According to some accounts it was the source of all the Vedas, while according to the Aitareya Brâhmaṇa it arises from the Vedas. It must be repeated at the beginning and end of a Vedic passage; otherwise what one learns will slip away from or not long remain with one; *cf.* ब्रह्मणः प्रणवं कुर्यादादावन्ते च सर्वदा । स्रवत्यनोंकृतं पूर्वं परस्ताच्च विशीर्यति ॥ Manu. II. 74. It is called एकाक्षरं ब्रह्म; see Manu. II. 83, and our note on प्रणव Ragh. I. 11. It is said to represent the three Vedas, the three worlds, the three holy fires &c.; ओमित्येतत्त्रयो वेदास्त्रयो लोकास्त्रयोऽग्नयः । विष्णुक्रमास्त्रयस्त्वेते ऋक्सामानि यजूंषि च ॥ Its repetition dissipates sin, its meditation ensures final emancipation. इत्येतदक्षरं ब्रह्म परमोङ्कारसंज्ञितम् । यस्तु वेदयते सम्यक्तथा ध्यायति वा पुनः । संसारचक्रमुत्सृज्य मुक्तसंचितबन्धनः ॥ अचलं निर्गुणं स्थानं शिवं प्राप्नोत्यसंशयम् ॥ ओङ्कारं परमं ब्रह्म सर्वमन्त्रेषु नायकम् । प्रजापतेर्मुखोत्पन्नं तपःसिद्धस्य वै पुरा ॥ यथा पर्णं पलाशस्य शङ्कुनैकेन धार्यते । तथा जगदिदं सर्वमोङ्कारेणैव धार्यते ॥ जपेन दहते पापं प्राणायामैस्तथा मलम् । ध्यानेन जन्यनिर्याणं धारणाभिस्तु मुच्यते ॥ See also ओम् in Apte's Dic.

न्यायैस्त्रिभिः—is explained in different ways:—as संहितापदक्रमरूपैः, ऋग्यजुःसामभिः (See Apte's Dic. under न्याय); तार-(high-as a note) मन्द्र-(low) मध्य-(intermediate in pitch) रूपैः; but Malli. seems to be more to the point. He takes न्याय to mean स्वर tones or accent-pitches. These are उदात्त raised or acute, अनुदात्त not raised, or grave and स्वरित or a combination of the two, or circumflex (*i. e.* a naturally grave syllable following an acute in the same or another word). See Gr. § 3. In the Veda, स्वरित is marked by a small upright line above the syllable, अनुदात्त or नत्तर by a small horizontal line and the उदात्त is left unmarked. Malli. quotes from the Śikshâ of Pâṇini—यथेन्द्रशत्रुः &c.; the full verse runs thus—मन्त्रो हीनः स्वरतो वर्णतो वा मिथ्या प्रयुक्तो न तमर्थमाह । स वाग्वज्रो यजमानं हिनस्ति यथे० ॥ इन्द्रशत्रु when आद्योदात्त or accented on the first syll. is a Bah. (इन्द्रः शत्रुः *i. e.* killer यस्य) and when अन्त्योदात्त or accented on the 2nd syll. is a Tat. The allusion —Once Indra killed Viśvarûpa, a son of the sage Tvashṭṛi (त्वष्टृ), whereupon Tvashṭṛi performed a maledictory sacrifice wishing to beget a son (called वृत्र) who would be the killer of Indra. But when repeating the Mantra इन्द्रशत्रुर्वर्धस्व he misaccentuated the word इन्द्रशत्रु । *i. e.* instead of pronouncing it with an acute उ (in शत्रु) pronounced it, through carelessness, with an acute इकार which made the comp. a Bahuvrîhi and thus Indra became the killer of his son, instead of the son being the killer of Indra.

कर्म यज्ञ:—This is the doctrine of the Mîmâṃsakas who hold that the Vedas enjoin action or the performance of the ritualistic rites as the means of getting heaven. *Cf.* चोदनालक्षणोऽर्थो धर्मः । आम्नायस्य क्रियार्थत्वादानर्थक्यमतदर्थानाम्। and विधिना त्वेकवाक्यत्वात्स्तुत्यर्थेन विधीनां स्युः &c. Jai. I. 1. 2; II. 1. 7. दृष्टो हि तस्यार्थः कर्मावबोधनम् Śábarabháshya on Jai. I. 1. 2. फलं—*i. e.* through the performance of the ritual. Malli. remarks on this—कर्मस्वर्गौ ब्रह्मापवर्गयोरप्युपलक्षणे. He is evidently a follower of the school of the later theologians who propounded the philosophy of Brahman (or Upanishad-Vidyá) and whose doctrines were systematically set forth by the venerable S'aṃkaráchárya and others. These, *i. e.* the Vedántins, maintain that *Karman* cannot lead to *Moksha* but that it simply prepares the way for the knowledge of Brahman which alone leads to *Moksha.*

गिराम्—The Vedas which comprise the Saṃhitás, *i. e.* the body of the chief *Mantras*, the Bráhmaṇas consisting of Vidhi and Arthaváda and the Âraṇyakas and Upanishads. प्रभव:—*cf.* अस्य महतो भूतस्य नि श्वसितमेतद्यदृग्वेद: &c. Bṛih. II. 4. 10. Also the Smṛiti—अनादिनिधना नित्या वागुत्सृष्टा स्वयंभुवा । आदौ वेदमयी दिव्या यतः सर्वाः प्रवृत्तयः । According to the Upanishads the Vedas are eternal. Brahmá does not create them, but merely sends forth the syllables afresh at the time of every creation, while the Puráṇas regard them as created by Brahmá and hence Mallinátha remarks—प्रणेता स्मर्ता वा &c. *Cf.* त्वत्तो वेदाः समुद्भूता ऋग्यजुःसामसंज्ञकाः । कर्मयज्ञाः स्वर्गफलाः साङ्गोपनिषदः शुभाः ॥ S.-P.

Śl. 13. आमनन्ति—आम्ना (म्ना-अभ्यासे) to hand down traditionally, to lay down as in a sacred text:; hence, to mention authoritatively. प्रकृति—A technical term of Sâṃkhya philosophy. The two principal categories of the Sâṃkhya philosophy are—Prakṛiti (nature) also called *Pradhána* (the chief), from its being the origin of the seven principal evolutes and sixteen other products, and *Purusha* or Supreme soul. मूलप्रकृतिरविकृतिर्महदाद्याः प्रकृतिविकृतयः सप्त । षोडशकस्तु विकारो न प्रकृतिर्न विकृतिः पुरुषः* ॥ The seven Principles are बुद्धि or intellect; अहंकार or egotism, and पञ्च तन्मात्राणि or the five subtile rudiments. The sixteen productions are:—the five organs of sense (बुद्धीन्द्रियाणि), the five organs of action (कर्मेन्द्रियाणि), the mind, and the five elements (महाभूतानि). See Sâṃ. K. 3 and the Bháshya on it. प्रकृतेर्महांस्ततोऽहंकारस्तस्माद्गणश्च षोडशकः । तस्मादपि षोडशकात्पञ्चभ्यः पञ्चभूतानि ॥ २२ ॥

* Thus there are 25 *Tattvas* or Principles, a correct knowledge of which, with a proper discrimination of Purusha from the rest, leads to final emancipation. Kapila is the founder of this philosophy.

अभिमानोऽहंकारस्तस्माद् द्विविधः प्रवर्तते सर्गः। एकादशकश्च गणस्तन्मात्रः पञ्चकश्चैव ॥ &c. (ईश्वरकृष्ण, सांख्यकारिका). Prakriti is represented as सत्वरजस्तमसां साम्यावस्था (in which the three qualities are in equipoise). According to the Sáṃkhyas the universe is the development of Prakṛiti. Purusha takes no part in its creation, but is passive, a mere looker-on, while Prakṛiti evolves the world. Prakriti acts for the benefit of the Purusha: the one is blind, the other is lame; their union is necessary for the purpose of creation. This system agrees with Vedânta in being synthetical, and so differs from the analytical Nyâya or Vaiśeshika; but its great points of divergence from the Vedánta are—It admits two principles which the Vedânta denies; it does not recognize God, as the Vedânta does, as the Creator and controller of the universe; and it maintains the plurality of souls. पुरुषार्थ—तदुक्तं सांख्यसप्तत्यां—रङ्गस्य दर्शयित्वा निवर्तते नर्तकी यथा नृत्तम्। पुरुषस्य तथात्मानं प्रकाश्य विनिवर्तते प्रकृतिः ॥

तद्दर्शनं—This is a refutation of the Sâmkhya doctrine, which regards प्रकृति as quite distinct from Purusha, while according to the Vedânta प्रकृति is identical, at least inseparable from, Purusha (तत्त्वान्यत्वाभ्यामनिर्वचनीया हि सा माया &c. Samk. on Br. Sût. I. 41). This shows that Káli. was a follower of the Advaita Philosophy as propounded by Bádaráyaṇa in his Brahma-Sútras. The Vedántins have no objection to those principles of the Sámkhyas which do not go counter to their own. यत्तु दर्शनं न विरुध्यते तेनेष्टमेव सांख्ययोगस्मृत्योः सावकाशत्वं Brah. Bhá. on Vedá. Sú. II. 1. 3. उदासीनं—cf. औदासीन्येन वर्तितुम्। Ragh. X. 25; असङ्गो ह्ययं पुरुषः Brih. IV. 3. 15. The Śruti quoted by Malli. runs thus-अजामेकां लोहितशुक्लकृष्णां बह्वीः प्रजाः सृजमानां सरूपाः। अजो ह्येको जुषमाणोऽनुशेते जहात्येनां भुक्तभोगामजोऽन्यः ॥ Sve. IV. 5. See B. P. III. 26. 5, 10 &c. *Cf.* धर्मार्थकाममोक्षाणामादिभूतां सनातनीम्। त्वामामनन्ति प्रकृतिं पुरुषार्थविदः प्रभो ॥ S. P.

Śl. quoted in the S.-D. as an instance of unintelligibility (as of the terms प्रकृति and पुरुष here) being a merit when the speaker and the person addressed are wise, *i. e.* quite conversant with the terms used.

Śl. 14. Aruṇ. reads this Śl. before the preceding. पितॄणां—एत इति वै प्रजापतिर्देवानसृजतासृग्रमिति मनुष्यानिन्दव इति पितॄन्-इति श्रुतिः। quoted by Sáṃk. in his Bhá. on Brah. Sû. I. 3. 28; see *supra* I. 18 मनोर्हैरण्यगर्भस्य ये मरीच्यादयः सुताः। तेषामृषीणां सर्वेषां पुत्राः पितृगणाः स्मृताः ॥ विराट्सुताः सोमसदः साध्यानां पितरः स्मृताः। अग्निष्वात्ताश्च देवानां मारीच्या लोकविश्रुताः ॥ दैत्यदानवयक्षाणां गन्धर्वोरगरक्षसाम्। सुपर्णानां नराणां च

स्मृता बर्हिषदोऽग्निजाः ॥ कव्यवालोऽनलः सोमो यमश्चैवार्यमा तथा । अग्निष्वात्ता बर्हिषदः सोमपाः पितृदेवताः ॥

परतोऽपि—The passage इन्द्रियेभ्यः &c. is from Kaṭhop. वेधसां—For the names of the Prajápatis see *supra* I. 17. विदधाति इति वेधाः । विधाञो वेध च इति वेधादेशः असिमत्ययश्च । Uṇádi. IV. 225. *Cf.* इन्द्रादीनां च देवानां देवो भगवते नमः । मरीच्यादिविधातॄणां विधातासि जगद्गुरो । परतोऽपि परोऽसि त्वं सर्वेन्द्रियविगोचरः ॥ Ś. P.

Śl. 15. त्वमेव हव्यं &c.—*Cf.* ब्रह्मार्पणं ब्रह्महविर्ब्रह्माग्नौ ब्रह्मणा हुतम् ॥ भोज्यं &c.—भोज्यं fr. भुज् when the sense is 'food'; otherwise भोग्यं. *Cf.* अहमन्नमहमन्नादः । Tait. Up. III. 10. 6. Ar. reads भोग्यं शाश्वतं on which Nár. remarks अग्निहोत्रादिफलं तु नित्यमेव न कर्मविनाशे नश्यतीति भावः । अनेन पूर्वकाण्डप्रतिपाद्यानामर्थानां ब्रह्मात्मकत्वं प्रतिपादितम् । शाश्वतः—Fr. शश्वत्+अण्; see Malli. शश्वत् being an *adv.* of time should properly take ठञ् (इक) by the rule कालात् ठञ् । Páṇ. IV. 3. 11, and the form should be शाश्वतिक; but Malli. defends the use of अण् by citing Vámana's remark that it is authorized by usage. It may, however, be defended on the authority of the Bhâshyakára who says एवं तर्हि शाश्वते प्रतिषेधो वक्तव्यः । शाश्वतम् । on which Kaiyaṭa remarks—शाश्वतमिति भाष्यकारवचनप्रामाण्यादण् प्रत्ययः इति । So Vámana's remark 'शाश्वतमिति प्रयुक्तेः' is unnecessary. वेद्यं च वेदिता—*cf.* स वेत्ति वेद्यं न च तस्यास्ति वेत्ता । Śve. III. 19. नान्योतोऽस्ति द्रष्टा नान्योतोऽस्ति विज्ञाता । Bṛih. III. 7. 23. ज्ञेयं यत्तत्प्रवक्ष्यामि यज्ज्ञात्वामृतमश्नुते । अनादिमत्परं ब्रह्म न सत्तन्नासदुच्यते ॥ ज्ञानं ज्ञेयं ज्ञानगम्यं हृदि सर्वस्य धिष्ठितम् । Gítá, XIII. 12,17. ध्याता—One who contemplates with the mind concentrated on one object. ध्येय—the object of contemplation, *i.e.* the Supreme Soul. This refers to the identity of the Individual Soul with the Supreme One. ध्यान means the continuous flow of one cognition as the means of seeing the Supreme Soul; Malli. *Cf.* हव्यहोतृस्वरूपेण भोज्यभोक्तृस्वरूपतः । सर्वेषां यजनादेव भवान् स्वर्गफलप्रदः । वेद्यवेतृस्वरूपेण ध्येयध्यातृस्वरूपतः ॥ Ś. P.

Śl. 16. यथार्थाः—अर्थमनतिक्रम्य वर्तन्ते इति; or यथा proper, worthy अर्थः यासाम्. *Cf.* भूतार्थव्याहृतिः सा हि न स्तुतिः परमेष्ठिनः । Ragh. X. 33. हृदयंगमाः—see com.; गम् takes the aff. खच् (अ) by the Vârttika गमेः सुपि on प्रियवशे वदः खच् । Páṇ. III. 2. 38, and a nasal is added to the words अरुष्, द्विषत् and bases ending in अ, when the latter member ends in an aff. having an indicatory ख. प्रसादा°—प्रसादस्याभिमुखः । Chá. takes it as प्रसादेन प्रसन्नत्वेनाभिमुखः, which will also do. वेधाः—विदधाति इति fr. धा with वि changed to वेध and the Uṇâdi aff. अस्, one who ordains things, one who has power to control the course of things. Hence this is peculiarly appropriate after the preceding.

Śl. 17. पुराणस्य कवेः—पुरा भवः पुराणः । fr. पुरा + ट्युल् (तन); the त् does not come in as the word is so given (निपातनात्); so पुरातन is also allowed; or पुरापि नवः (पुरा + नव) Pāṇ. IV. 3. 105; a compound of the पृषोदरादि class; in both cases the word is irregular. कवेः—Malli. here rightly paraphrases कवेः by कवयितुः; वेदरूपस्य काव्यस्य स्रष्टृत्वाद्भगवतः पुराणकवित्वम् । तथा च स्मृतिः-अनादिनिधना &c. See notes, śl 13; *cf.* कविं पुराणमनुशासितारं &c. Bg. VIII. 9. चतुर्मुख°—the comp. presents a grammatical difficulty. We cannot take it as चत्वारि मुखानि as that will give चतुर्मुखी; for we cannot have recourse to the Vârttika पात्रादेर्नेति वाच्यम् and have चतुर्मुखं like पञ्चपात्रं, as the पात्रादि group is limited. To avoid this difficulty Malli. takes it as an उत्तर°; see com.; but this is also inaccurate. For a त्रिपद तत्पुरुष is not allowed unless the latter member is परिमाणि, *i. e.* signifies a measure (as in द्विमास-जातः &c.). So compounds like the present or त्रिलोकनाथेन सता मखद्विषः (Ragh. III. 45) should be taken, according to the भाष्यकार, as of the शाकपार्थिवादि class, there being उत्तरपदलोप here. चतुर्दिग्दर्शि मुखं चतुर्मुखं तेन समीरिता. It is unneussary to enter further into the discussion here; the curious student may see Bhaṭṭoji's शब्दकौस्तुभ. चतुष्टयी शब्दानां प्रवृत्तिः—चत्वारोऽवयवा यस्याः सा चतुष्टयी. These four stages as given by Malli. are—(1) वैखरी or articulate speech (as that of a newly born child); (2) मध्यमा or the same rendered audible (the words being distinct); (3) पश्यन्ती or of clear import (the words being syntactically arranged); and (4) सूक्ष्मा or making a permanent impression. According to some the order is परा, पश्यन्ती, मध्यमा and वैखरी (सर्वशास्त्ररूपा सर्वव्यवहारप्रदर्शिका). Words are also of four kinds, those referring to (1) द्रव्यs or substances, as पृथ्वी &c.; (2) to गुणs or qualities, as white &c.; (3) to कर्मन् or action, as पाकः गमनं &c.; and (4) to जाति or species, as a Brâhmaṇa, a cow &c. चरितार्था—see com.; *cf.* Ragh. X. 36.

Śl. 18. स्वागतं—may be an *adv.* (निपात) or a noun. स्वागतं वचनविशेषः । सपद्युपस्थिते मित्रे कुशलं नागतं त्वया । इति यत्प्रश्नवचनं तत्स्वागतमुदाहृतम् ॥ Chār. अधीकार—When the aff. घञ् (अ) is added, the final vowel of a *prep.* may be optionally lengthened; *e. g.* प्रति-तीकार' &c. प्रभाव—Divine power. Malli. remarks काकुश्च &c.—Kâku is the change of voice due to different feelings, such as joy, fear, anger &c. काकुः स्त्रियां विकारो यः शोकभीत्यादिभिर्ध्वनेः । Amara. He means—Brahmâ addressed these words to the gods in such a way as to indicate his concern or apprehension on their account. *Cf.* स्वागतं वो महाभागाः सर्वदैत्यविमर्दनाः । स्वर्गं च स्वभुजाक्रान्तैर्भवन्तः पालयन्ति हि ॥ S.—P.

Śl. 19. क्लिष्ट—Oppressed; hence dimmed, rendered faint. *Cf.* रूपमक्लिष्टकान्ति Śák. V. 19. *Cf.* also इदानीं तु कथं सर्वे नष्टभासोऽभवन्सुराः। तुषारच्छन्नतेजांसि ज्योतींषीव विहायसि ॥ Ś. P.

Śl. 20. सुरायुधम्—The rain-bow; by लक्षणा, a varied lustre. सुरस्य इन्द्रस्य आयुधं सुरा०, न उद्गीर्णमनु०, अनुद्गीर्णं सुरायुधं येन तत्। Chár. remarks—कुलिशरश्मिसमूहादिन्द्रचापोदय इत्याहुः। अनुद्गूर्ण—*v. l.* गूर्ण *p. p. p.* of गुर् 1. 6. A'. to make an effort; this may be interpreted as अनुद्गूर्णानि सुरायुधानि यस्मात् which does not allow the weapons of the other gods to be lifted up (there being no necessity for them). For वृत्र, see *supra* I. 20. *Cf* पुरुहूतस्य यद्वज्रमधःकृतसुरायुधम्। तदिदानीं महाभागा दृश्यते हतयौवनम् ॥ Ś. P.

Śl. 21. दुर्वारः—दुःखेन वार्यते इति। कर्तृकरणे कृता बहुलमिति समासः। प्रचेतस्—Varuṇa, the lord of the western quarter and the regent of water. He has a noose for his weapon. हतवीर्यस्य—*cf.* Ragh. II. 32. *Cf.* वरुणस्य तु यः पाशो बद्धासुरबलः सदा। सोऽयं वै दृश्यते सर्पो मन्त्राहतबलो यथा ॥ Ś. P.

Śl. 22. कुबेर—कुत्सितं बेरं शरीरमस्य कुत्सितत्वात्। कुत्सायां कितिशब्दोऽयं शरीरं बेरमुच्यते। कुबेरः कुशरीरत्वान्नाम्ना तेनैव सोऽङ्कितः॥ Vá P ; or कुम्बति धनं. He is the son of Viśravas and Iḍâviḍâ and thus the half brother of Rávaṇa. He is the lord of the Yakshas and Kiṃnaras and a friend of Rudra. His abode is Kailása and his capital Alakâ. He is represented as deformed in body, having three legs, eight teeth and a yellow mark in place of one eye. He is the lord of riches and the regent of the northern quarter. His weapon is a mace. कुबेरस्य भुजः शून्यो गदया दृश्यते सुराः। Ś. P. The figures in this śl. are a fusion of उत्प्रेक्षा, उपमा and रूपक.

Śl. 23. यमः—Like Indra, Varuṇa and others, Yama is one of the Lokapálas or Dikpâlas and the regent of the southern quarter. He is the ruler (पितृपति) over the पितृलोक or the world of the departed souls, and is the dispenser of justice or punishment to the dead according to their good or bad deeds. As such, he is called धर्मराज and has a rod for a weapon (दण्डधरः). दण्डेन—Daṇḍa is the special weapon of Yama; *cf.* दण्डी यमो माहिषगो &c. Bṛih. Saṃ. Chap. 58. 57. अमोघेऽपि—At least Yama's rod ought to have free scope everywhere, but that too has experienced a rebuff and hence the surprise. निर्वाण०—निर्वाण is the *p. p. p.* of वा with निर् when वात is not the subject; as निर्वाणोऽग्निर्मुनिश्च। वाते तु निर्वातो वातः। Sid.-Kau. लघोर्भावः लाघवं the low state of, the miserable condition of. *Cf.* यमोऽपि विलिखन् भूमौ दण्डेनास्तमितत्विषा। Ś. P.

Śl. 24. आदित्याः—अदितेः अपत्यानि the sons of Aditi and Kaśyapa. They are twelve, being probably the representations of the sun in the twelve months. Their names as given in the V. P. are–तत्र विष्णुश्च शक्रश्च जज्ञाते पुनरेव हि। अर्यमा चैव धाता च त्वष्टा पूषा तथैव च॥ विवस्वान् सविता चैव मित्रो वरुण एव च। अंशुर्भगश्चादितिजा आदित्या द्वादश स्मृताः॥ There is a different आदित्य presiding over each month; *cf.* आदित्यहृदय—"अरुणो माघमासे तु सूर्यो वै फाल्गुने तथा। चैत्रे मासि च वेदज्ञो (वेदाङ्गो) वैशाखे तपनः स्मृतः॥ ज्येष्ठे मासि तपेदिन्द्र आषाढे तपते रविः। गभस्तिः श्रावणे मासे यमो भाद्रपदे तथा॥ इषे हिरण्य(सुवर्ण)रेताश्च कार्तिके च दिवाकरः। मार्गशीर्षे तपेन्मित्रः पौषे विष्णुः सनातनः॥ इत्येते द्वादशादित्याः काश्यपेयाः प्रकीर्तिताः॥" See our note on पाहुर्द्वादशधा स्थितस्य मुनयो यत्तेजसः कारणं। Śák. VII. 27. प्रकामा॰—प्रकामम् आलोकनीयः प्रकामालोकनीयस्तस्य भावस्तत्ताम्। *Cf.* Ś. P.—त एते द्वादशादित्या दृश्यन्ते गततेजसः। भित्तिभागे गृहाणां च चित्रकैर्लिखिता इव॥

Śl. 25. पर्याकुलत्व—Obstructed motion. मरुतां—The wind-gods are the children of Diti and said to be seven, or seven times seven, in number. According to a legend, Diti, when her sons, the Daityas, were destroyed by Indra, implored her husband to give her an Indra-destroying son. But when she was pregnant Indra cut the embryo in 49 pieces which began to utter cries of pain. Indra, however, took compassion upon them and changed them into Maruts. प्रतीप—*Lit.* against the current of water; fr. प्रति+अप्+अच् (प्रतिगता आपोऽत्र); द्व्यन्तरुपसर्गेभ्योऽप ईत् इति ईकारः। ऋक्पूरब्धूःपथामानक्षे इति अकारः समासान्तः; । hence, in a contrary direction. *Cf.* प्रतिकूल further on (IV. 7); also I. 45. *Cf.* वेगभंगाः कथममी सर्वे च मरुतोऽभवन्। Ś. P.

Śl. 26. आवर्जित॰—जटानां मौलयः जटामौलयः। आवर्जिताश्च ते जटामौलयश्च आव॰ लयः। शशिनः कोटिः शशिकोटिः। ॰मौलिषु विलम्बिन्यः &c. see com. रुदतां—fr. रुद् to cry. The child, when born, began to cry; *cf.* the Śruti सोऽरोदीयदरोदीत्तद्रुद्रस्य रुद्रत्वम्। Also रोदनात्तव रुद्रेति नामधेयं भविष्यति। Kûrm. P. यदरोदीः सुरश्रेष्ठ सोद्वेग इव बालकः। ततस्त्वामभिधास्यन्ति नाम्ना रुद्र इति प्रजाः॥ B. P. III. 12, 10. According to Paurâṇic accounts, when Brahmâ asked his sons, Sanaka, Sananda and others, who were inactive, without passion &c. (मुनीन्निष्क्रियानूर्ध्वरेतसः) to take part in the creation and found them to be unwilling to do so, he got mightily angry with them. Before he could check his anger, from the middle part of his forehead, darkened with angry frowns, sprang Rudra resplendent as the noon-day sun. His was a fierce and bulky form composed of male and female. At Brahmâ's command he became twofold, separating the two forms. The male part was again divided into eleven portions, and so there came to be eleven Rudras, some fierce in form, some of hideous aspect, some mild and others agreeable in appearance. They are regarded as the manifestations of Śiva, who is their chief. *Cf.* रुद्राणां शंकरश्चास्मि Bg. X. 23. According to the Bṛih. Up. the Rudras are ten vital breaths (prâṇas) with *Manas* as the eleventh. They use the sound 'Hum' for their weapons of destruction. हुं is a mystical sound occurring in spells and charms. *Cf.* रुद्राणां मौलयश्चैव कथं चन्द्रार्धवर्जिताः । S. P.

Śl. 27. लब्धप्र०—लब्धा प्रतिष्ठा यैः । प्रतिष्ठा–(1) stability, firm position; (2) operation, general application. अपवाद—अपोद्यतेऽनेन (by which is spoken away, *i. e.*, set aside, thrown into the background) इति अपवादः विशेषविधिः 'an exception or a special rule' as opposed to उत्सर्ग or 'a general rule (सामान्यशास्त्रं)'–as मा हिंस्यात्सर्वाणि भूतानि (one should not kill any kind of creature) इति उत्सर्गः; अग्नीषोमीयं (sacred to Agni and Soma) पशुमालभेत (one should kill) इत्यपवादः; or इको यणचि (Páṇ. VI. 1. 11) इत्युत्सर्गः; अकः सवर्णे दीर्घः (Pâṇ. VI. 1. 10) इत्यपवादः । भूयो दर्शनमुत्सर्गो बाधस्तस्यैकदेशगः । अपवादः स विज्ञेयो मृग्यो व्याकरणादिषु ॥ *Cf.* अपवाद इवोत्सर्गं व्यावर्तयितुमीश्वरः । Ragh. XV. 7. Malli. paraphrâses व्यावृत्ति by विषयसंकोचः narrowing of the field of, limitation of the province or of the application of. न खलु स्थ बलोत्तरैः—*V. l.* is to be read with a *kâku* (a change in the voice to indicate the intended sense), 'Are you not', I should like to know (I think you are); खलु is here जिज्ञासायां (in the sense of inquiry). बलेन उत्तरैः बलोत्तरैः । conspicuous by valour.'

Śl. 28. ब्रूत–Tell distinctly (व्यक्तं वदत); the use of this word shows his impatience to hear. वत्साः—shows affection and readiness to help them on the part of the speaker. इतः—from me. समागताः—their coming in a body indicated that they had come with some important object in view.

Śl. 29. कमला०—The simile beautifully expresses Indra's turning his thousand eyes to Bṛihaspati. The eyes of gods are described as steady and not winking; hence Malli.'s remark अनिमेषाणां &c.; or perhaps Indra simply turned his eyes towards his Guru by a motion of his body and so urged him to speak. नेत्रसह०—स्वतो निर्निमेषाणां नेत्राणामिच्छावशाच्चालनं युज्यते । Chár. वासवः—वसवो देवाः वसूनि रत्नान्यस्य वा सन्तीति । ज्योत्स्नादित्वादण् ।

Śl. 30. विनेतृ—*V. l.* read by Ar. which he explains as विनयोपदेशकं; but this is not a good reading, as it involves a sort of tautology with चक्षुः. द्विनेत्रः—which Ar. explains as द्वे नेत्रे यस्य धर्मदृष्टिरर्थदृष्टिश्च । अनेन भगवतो बृहस्पतेः शुक्राद्व्यतिरेको ध्वनितः । स हि बलियज्ञे विरोधमाचरन् भगवता विष्णुना धर्मदृष्ट्या विकलीकृतः । हरेश्चक्षुः—चक्षुः in such cases has the secondary sense of 'an instrument of seeing things;' his counsellor and guide. सहस्र०—for he was वाचस्पति· वाचस्पतिः—वाचः पतिः वाचस्पतिः (or वाक्पतिः when there is no अलुक्)· To account for the change of Visarga to स् and the अलुक् Malli. refers the word to the कस्कादि group (गण). But this rule provides only for the सत्व and not for अलुक्. So grammarians like Bhaṭṭoji and Haradatta explain the Aluk by तत्पुरुषे कृति बहुलम् (Pāṇ. VI. 3. 14) *i e.* by the बाहुलक प्रमाण. Svâmî explains the सत्व by referring to the rule पतिपुत्रपृष्ठ...(Pāṇ. VIII. 3. 53); but as this rule belongs to Veda, Malli. is opposed to this (see com.), and therefore refers to the कस्कादि group. It is not necessary for ordinary students to enter deeper into this controversy. द्विनेत्रः हरेश्चक्षुः शतचक्षुःशताधिकम् *v. l.*—In this case द्विनेत्रः qualifies सः; चक्षुषां शतं चक्षुःशतं; दशगुणितं चक्षुःशतं दशचक्षुःशतं (otherwise we shall have चक्षुःशती by the Vârttika अकारान्तोत्तरपदो द्विगुः स्त्रियामिष्टः); तस्माद्‌-धिकम्. प्राञ्जलिः—प्रसृतः प्रबद्धो वा अञ्जलिर्येन ।

Śl. 31. आत्थ—present in the sense of the immediate past, see com. Vâmana condemns this form as remarked by Malli.; see Kâv. Sût. V. 2. 44. Similarly ज्ञास्यसि is used in the sense of the present tense. This is by the rule लृट् (2nd Fut.) शेषे च (उक्तादन्यः शेषः). भगवत्—One possessed of भग or षड्गुणे-श्वर्य; ऐश्वर्यस्य समग्रस्य वीर्यस्य (धर्मस्य) यशसः श्रियः । ज्ञानवैराग्ययोश्चैव षण्णां भग इतीरणा ॥ आमृष्ट-snatched away from; forcibly taken. ज्ञास्यसि—जानासि or जानीयाः. प्रत्येकं &c.—*Cf.* the Śrutis तत्सृष्ट्वा तदेवानुप्राविशत्; स च त्यच्चाभवत् । &c. ईश्वरः सर्वभूतानां हृद्देशेऽर्जुन तिष्ठति; समं सर्वेषु भूतेषु तिष्ठन्तं परमेश्वरम् । &c. Bg. यदेतदुक्तं भवता नानृतं सत्यमेव तत् । सर्वभूतान्तरात्मासि कथं न ज्ञास्यसि प्रभो ॥ S.-P.

Śl. 32. उदीर्ण—Puffed up, grown haughty. लङ्घितमर्यादः (acting in a way trangressing all bounds of propriety). Châr. उपप्लव—a universal calamity, general oppression; at IV. 46 it means 'personal distress.' धूमकेतुः—धूमः केतुरस्य the appearance of a comet is considered to be ominous; आग्नेयेषु च दृष्टेषु लोकानां संक्षयो भवेत् । नित्योद्विग्नाः प्रजाः सर्वा भवन्ति हि न संशयः ॥ यदा रौद्राः प्रदृश्यन्ते दुर्भिक्षं निर्दिशेत्तदा । धूमकेतौ च प्रजाः सर्वा मृत्युक्षुद्रोगपीडिताः ॥ उक्तं च गार्ग्यसंहितायां—उत्तिष्ठति यदा भीमो धूमकेतुर्नभस्थले । तदा विनश्यति क्षिप्रं जगदे-तच्चराचरम् ॥ इति. *Cf.* महासुरस्तारकाख्यस्त्वत्तः प्राप्तपराक्रमः । सर्वलोकविनाशाय केतुराजिरिवोत्थितः ॥ S.-P.

Sl. 33. सारस्त्—तत्परिमाणमस्य । दीर्घिका—दीर्घा इव । संज्ञायां कन् । a pleasure-tank, oblong in shape and containing lotus-plants in it. यावन्मा॰—यत्परिमाणमस्य यावान्; यावानेव यावन्मात्रं तेन; by just as much &c. *Cf.* तदन्तःपुरवर्तिन्यो दीर्घिकाः सन्ति याः प्रभो । तासां पद्मोदयायैव विवस्वान् भाति केवलम् ॥ Ś. P.

Śl. 34. निषेवते—The स् of सेव् is changed to ष् after the prepositions परि, नि and वि; see Páṇ. VIII. 3. 70. हरचूडा॰—A *Chvi* formation. नाद्रते—because Śiva was the favourite deity of the Asuras. *Cf.* चन्द्रस्तु तं सदाकालं कलाभिः परिषेवते । चन्द्रशेखरमूर्धस्थां कलामेकां विहाय च ॥ Ś. P.

Śl. 35. कुसुमस्तेय॰—From fear of the consequence of the theft (the carrying away of the flowers which would deprive the trees of their beauty). A strong wind has such an effect. *Cf.* वृन्ताच्छ्लथं हरति पुष्पमनोकहानाम् । Ragh. V. 69. यद्यहमधिकं वहेयं तर्हि कदाचिदुद्यानपुष्पापहारादपराधी भवेयमिति भावः । Chár. Nár. takes साहस in the sense of दण्ड and says—दण्डो दमः साहसोऽस्त्री इति वैजयन्ती; he takes साहसात् as ल्यब्लोपे पञ्चमी, साहसमाशङ्क्येत्यर्थः । *Cf.* शनैः शनैर्वाति वायुस्तद्युद्याने च भीरुवत् । पतने कुसुमानां च पुष्पस्तेयी भविष्यति ॥ Ś. P.

Śl. 36. पर्याय—Fr. इ to go + अ (घञ्); आनुपूर्वी स्त्रियां वावृत्परिपाटी अनुक्रमः । पर्यायः, Amara. उपलङ्घ्य—*i. e.*, his garden presented the flowers, fruits and other beauties of all seasons at all times. ऋतवः—वसन्तश्च तथा ग्रीष्मः प्रावृट् च शरदेव च । हेमन्तः शिशिरश्चैव षडेते ऋतवः स्मृताः ॥ *Cf.* ऋतवस्ते स्वकालं च विहायासुरभीरवः । युगपच्च तदुद्यानं फलपुष्पैरुपासते ॥ Ś. P.

Śl. 37. कथमपि-(With great difficulty; anxiously)—shows the impatience of the Sea to wait upon the demon with the jewels. *Cf.* समुद्रः सर्वरत्नानि तस्मै योग्यानि वै ददौ । Ś. P.

Śl. 38. ज्वलन्मणि॰—Some take the comp. as ज्वलन्तः मणय एव शिखा येषां or शिखाश्च येषां ते. वासुकि—वसुना शिरस्थरत्नेन कायति (कै शब्दे ग्वादिः); or वसु रत्नं के मूर्ध्नि यस्य । वसुकस्य अपत्यमिति वा । नागाः काद्रवेयास्तदीश्वरः । शेषोऽनन्तो वासुकिस्तु सर्पराजः । Amara. Śesha is represented as the king of Nágas, and Vásuki of Sarpas. *Cf.* सर्पाणामस्मि वासुकिः । अनंतश्चास्मि नागानां; Bg. X, 28, 29. They are sometimes spoken of as one. *Cf.* ज्वलन्मणिशिखो रात्रौ वासुकिस्तं निषेवते । Ś. P.

भुजंगाः—भुजः वक्रः सन् गच्छतीति भुजंगः भुजेन कौटिल्येन गच्छतीति वा; fr. भुज+गम् + खच् (अ) before which a nasal is inserted + डित् (अ) before which the final consonant of a root is dropped; when खच् only is added we have भुजंगम by the Várttika खच्च डिद्वा on Páṇ. III. 2. 38.

Śl. 39. अनुकूलयति—A Denom. from अनुकूल favourable; अनुगतः कूलं अनुकूलः *lit.*, going along the bank or the current; hence favourable. कल्प०—the decorations (flowers, ornaments) produced by the Kalpa trees; *cf.* एकः सूते सकलमबलामण्डनं कल्पवृक्षः । Megh. II. 12. Idea—Even the lord of gods seeks to conciliate him; what of other gods then?

Śl. 40. एवमारा०—For दुर्जनो नार्जवं याति सेव्यमानोऽपि नित्यशः । उपकार—doing service to, conciliatory behaviour. नोपकारेण &c.–*Cf.* चतुर्थोपायसाध्ये तु रिपौ सान्त्वमपक्रिया । स्वेद्यमामज्वरं प्राज्ञः कोऽम्भसा परिषिञ्चति ॥ Śiś. II. 54. एवमाराधितश्चापि स क्लिश्नाति जगत्त्रयम् । शाम्येत्प्रत्यपकारेण नोपकारेण दुर्जनः ॥ Ś. P.

Śl. quoted in the S.-D. X. as an instance of अर्थान्तरन्यास by वैधर्म्य or contrast (अत्र सामान्यं a general statement विशेषस्य समर्थकम् strengthens a particular one).

Śl. 41. अत्र कार्यभूतेन छिन्नपातज्ञापनेन कारणभूतं पातनं प्रतीयते इति कार्यद्वारेण पातनस्यैवाभिधानात्पर्यायोक्तमलंकारः । Nār. *Cf.* आवर्ज्य शाखाः सदयं च यासां पुष्पाण्युपात्तानि विलासिनीभिः । वन्यैः पुलिन्दैरिव वानरैस्ताः क्लिश्यन्त उद्यानलता मदीयाः ॥ Ragh. XVI. 19. चिच्छेद नन्दनतरून्देवस्त्रीपरिपालितान् । Ś. P.

Śl. 42. संसुप्तः—When asleep he was fanned gently, lest a strong current might disturb his sleep. संतप्तः *v. l.*—has no propriety, as there is no reason why he should not have been fanned though not heated when there was no breeze: again if he was heated श्वाससा० would not have sufficed. Ar. reads संतप्तश्वास० and explains संतप्तश्वासैः साधारणः सदृशः अनिलो येषां but without propriety; for the point of the poet is the extreme gentleness of the wind; if it is meant to indicate the warmth of the wind, then that purpose is served by the epithet बाष्पशीकर०, for the tears were warm; *cf.* शोकोष्णैः पार्थिवाश्रुभिः Ragh. XII. 4; so if this is at all the original reading it will be better to take साधारणं in the sense of 'mixed with;' संतप्तश्वासैः साधारणो मिश्रोऽनिलो यथा तैः. श्वाससाधा०—श्वासेन साधारणाः श्वास० तैः । सुरबन्दी—वन्द्यते इति बन्दीः; fr. वन्द्+इ (इन् Uṇādi) +ई; one who has to bow; hence a woman forcibly carried away (हठाद्दृतस्त्री); the word occurs also at Ragh. X. 47.

Śl. 43. हरितां—Of the horses of the sun, seven in number and all of green colour. In the Ṛigveda the sun is called हरिदश्वः; see our note on हरितः Śák. I. p. 12. आक्रीड०—See Malli.; *cf.* for a similar use words like क्रीडासर, क्रीडापर्वत, क्रीडागृहवापी &c.; or it may mean आक्रीडेषु उद्यानेषु पर्वताः आक्रीडापर्वताः ॥ *Cf.* कनकाचलशृङ्गाणि समुत्पाट्य महासुरः । क्रीडास्थलेषु तान्येव स्थापयामास वेश्मनि ॥ Ś. P.

Śl. 44. मन्दाकिनी—The celestial Ganges. शेषम्—is left to it; fr. शिष्+अ (घञ्) added कर्मणि (शिष्ट); see com. on I. 16. When घञ् is added भावे, the word is mas.; otherwise it may be of any gender. दिग्वारण०—This explains why the water was not taken away. एतेन मन्दाकिन्या दिग्गजानां मदोष्मनिवृत्तिमात्रमुपयोगो न तु देवविद्याधरादीनां कोऽप्युपयोगः श्रीकनककमलानामपहृतत्वात् । Châr. The quarter-elephants are described as sporting in the water of the heavenly Ganges. *Cf.* नदत्याकाशगङ्गायाः स्रोतस्युद्दामदिग्गजे । Ragh. I. 78. Their names are ऐरावतः पुण्डरीको वामनः कुमुदोऽञ्जनः । पुष्पदन्तः सार्वभौमः सुप्रतीकश्च दिग्गजाः ॥ खातानां—The golden lotuses are so called because they were uprooted and then planted. यदुत्खाय प्रतिरोप्यते तत्खातं; see Malli. on Ragh. IV. 37. *cf.* मन्दाकिन्याः पयः सर्वं स्ववाप्यां स्थापितं प्रभो । Ś. P.

Śl. 45. भुवना०...ना नुभूयते—तद्भयात्संकुचिता देवा गृहादपि बहिर्भवितुं न शक्नुवन्ति । Châr. खिलीभूते—खिल्+च्वि+भू+क्तः । खिल--untrodden ground; hence, waste or fallow land. The sudden appearance of Râvaṇa's *Vimâna* was similarly dreaded; *cf.* Ragh. X. 46. तदापात—तदाघात० *V. l.* where आघात means a stroke or an attack.

Śl. 46. अध्वर—A sacrifice. The word is variously derived. (1) नास्ति ध्वरा हिंसा sinful killing यस्मिन्, see Manu. V. 44. (2) According to Sâyaṇâchârya, न ध्वरतीति अध्वरः not disturbed by the Râkshasas; (न ह्यग्निना सर्वतः पालितं यज्ञं राक्षसा हिंसितुं प्रभवन्ति) Sây. on Ṛig. I. 1. 4. Later writers derive it as अध्वानं राति ददाति that which opens up the way to heaven; or न ध्वरति कुटिलो भवति that which never becomes crooked, *i. e.*, never fails to give its reward. जातवेदस्—an epithet of Agni. This is also variously derived:—(1) जातं सद्योजातं विन्दति gets to every one newly born (जातमात्रस्य जठरानलसंपर्कोत्तथात्वम्); (2) जातं वेत्ति वेदयते वा knows every one born, or makes every creature know him; or (3) जातं वेदो धनं यस्मात् who is the source of wealth. *Cf.* Yâska—जातवेदाः कस्माज्जातानि वेद जातानि वैनं विदुः । जाते जाते विद्यते इति वा जातवित्तो वा जातधनः । ०मुखात्—Because the gods get the oblations offered to them only through Agni; *cf.* the Śruti अग्निमुखा वै देवाः । अग्निर्वै देवानां मुखम् । मायी—माया अस्य विद्यते; also मायाविन् and मायिक; this explains how he took the oblations meant for the gods before their very eyes. *Cf.* अचिरायज्वभिर्भागं कल्पितं विधिवत्पुनः । मायाविभिरनालीढमादास्यध्वे निशाचरैः ॥ Ragh. X. 45. यज्ञभागं स चाश्नाति विनिवार्य दिवौकसः । Ś. P. Śl quoted in Sar.-K. as an instance of वाह्विवाच्यभावलक्षणम्.

Śl. 47. उच्चैः—tall; उन्नतत्वमश्वानां प्रधानगुणः; or noble, famous. उच्चैःश्रवाः—उच्चैः श्रवसी ears श्रवो यशो वा यस्य; long-eared or far-famed; or loudly neighing; name of the horse of Indra obtained at the churning of the ocean, and considered as the prototype and king of horses. देहबद्धं—बद्धो देहः येन; the परनिपात (coming second in the comp.) of बद्ध is to be explained by taking the comp. as one of the आहिताग्न्यादि class, where we have अग्न्याहित also. देहबन्धं—*V. l.* (देहं बध्नातीति । कर्मण्यण्) means the same thing. यशः—दानपुण्यकृता कीर्तिः पराक्रमकृतं यशः । एकदिग्व्यापिनी कीर्तिः सर्वदिग्विस्तृतं यशः । यशस् or fame is considered as white by Sanskrit poets, and as the horse is also white he may be taken to be an embodiment of Indra's fame. *Cf.* शुभ्रं यशो मूर्तमिवातितृष्णः । Ragh. II. 69. शरदिन्दुकुन्दघनसार...मूर्त्या कीर्त्याभितः सुरभितः । D.-K.

Śl. 48. उपायाः—*i. e* , भेदो दण्डः सामदानमित्युपायचतुष्टयम् । Amara. (1) सामन् or a policy of conciliation, negotiation; (2) दान or giving gifts, bribery; (3) भेद or sowing dissensions; and (4) दण्ड or punishment, declaration of hostilities. क्रिया—application or operation. सांनिपातिक—A disease, such as malignant fever, caused by the simultaneous disturbance of a serious nature of the three humours—phlegm, bile and wind—which baffles the power of medicine. Nár. quotes—वातपित्तकफानां च संनिपातो यदा भवेत् । तदा जातो ज्वरस्तीव्रो ह्यसाध्यः सर्वभेषजैः ॥ Fig *Upamá*. *Cf.* अस्माकं सकलोपाया आत्मन्नस्ता महामुने । मेघच्छन्ना रविकरा यथा तेजस्विनो भुवि ॥ S. P.

Śl. 49. हरिचक्र—Said to be given to Vishṇu by Śiva after being made out of the energies of the gods and therefore radiant with lustre and irresistible to the enemies. अथ विष्णुप्रमुखा देवाः स्वतेजांसि ददुस्तदा । तेनाकरोन्महादेवः सहसा शस्त्रमुत्तमम् ॥ चक्रं सुदर्शनं नाम ज्वालामालातिभीषणम् । ततः प्रातः प्रभुः प्रादाद्विष्णवे प्रवरं वरम् । प्रत्यक्षं तेजसं श्रीमान् दिव्यं चक्रं सुदर्शनम् ॥

Śl. 50. पुष्करा०—A class of mighty clouds said to cause dearth or famine or appearing at the time of the destruction of the world *Cf* छन्नं मेघैनं गगनतलं पुष्करावर्तकाद्यैः । Veṇ. III. 5; see Megh I. 6. "Clouds, agreeably to the Brahmáṇḍapuráṇa, are divided into three classes, according to their origin from fire, the breath of Brahmá, or the wings of the mountains, which were cut off by Indra. These latter (Pushkaras) are also called पुष्करावर्तक, being especially the receptacles of water. Thus in the Puráṇasarvasva—पुष्करा नाम ते मेघा बृहन्तस्तोयमत्सराः (insatiable of water) (पूरिताः *v. l.*) । पुष्करावर्तकास्तेन कारणेनेह शब्दिताः ॥ नानारूपधरास्ते तु महाघोरस्वनास्तथा । कल्पान्त वृष्टिकर्तारः संवर्ताग्नेर्नियामकाः ॥ * * *. They are the largest and most formidable, and those, which at the end of the Yugas and Kalpas pour down the waters of the deluge." Wilson on Megh. I. 6.

तटाघातं—Also called वप्रक्रीडा, (Megh. I. 2) is the sport of butting enjoyed by an elephant or a bull against a mound or a mountain-skirt. तडाघातं—*V. l.* striking with the sound *tad*; *cf.* येनोन्नमाः स्फुटन्तस्तडिति तिलतुलां यान्त्यगेन्द्रा युगान्ते । Súryaśataka. ऐरावत—इरा आपः तद्वान् इरावान् समुद्रः तत्र भवः । Indra's elephant, produced at the churning of the milky ocean, and the prototype of the elephant race. तत ऐरावतो नाम वारणेन्द्रो विनिर्गतः । दन्तैश्चतुर्भिः श्वेताद्रेर्हरन् भगवतो महीम् ॥ B. P. VIII. 8. 4. He is the guardian-elephant of the east. Also called ऐरावण; इरया जलेन वणते शब्दायते इरावणः समुद्रस्तत्र भवः । श्वेतैर्दन्तैश्चतुर्भिस्तु महाकायस्ततः परम् । ऐरावणो महानागोऽभवद्वज्रभृता धृतः ॥

Śl. 51. स्रष्टु—स्रष्टं (त्वया) *V. l.* 'created by you' seems to be better as it accords well with the reply of Brahmâ न त्वस्य सिद्धौ &c. śl. 54. कर्मबन्धच्छिदं—The comp. कर्मबन्ध may also be taken as कर्मजनितः बन्धः. धर्म—*i. e.*, निवृत्तिलक्षणधर्म or ज्ञानमार्ग (called) पराविद्या (अथ परा यया तदक्षरमधिगम्यते । Muṇḍ. I. 1. 5). Karma is नित्य, नैमित्तिक and काम्य. The performance of this three-fold Karman, together with the non-performance of the *Nishiddha* or prohibited Karman, leads to reward (the enjoyment of happiness in heaven &c.) and its omission to punishment (नरक or condemnation to hell &c.). It thus serves in either case as fetters to tie down the soul to a continued embodied existence. A total annihilation of this Karman, to be attained by *jñâna*, can alone lead to Moksha. ज्ञानादेव तु कैवल्यं is the doctrine of the Vedântins. [*Cf.* परीक्ष्य लोकान् कर्मचितान् ब्राह्मणो निर्वेदमायान्नास्त्यकृतः (मोक्षः) कृतेन (कर्मणा) । Muṇḍ. ब्रह्मविदाप्नोति परम् । क्षीयन्ते चास्य कर्माणि तस्मिन्दृष्टे परावरे । Muṇḍ.; also तरति शोकमात्मवित् । ब्रह्मविद् ब्रह्मैव भवति &c. कर्मजं बुद्धियुक्ता हि फलं त्यक्त्वा मनीषिणः । जन्मबन्धविनिर्मुक्ताः पदं गच्छन्त्यनामयम् ॥ Bg. II. 51; also ज्ञानाग्निः सर्वकर्माणि भस्मसात्कुरुते तथा । *Ibid.* IV. 37. The passage 'नाभुक्तं क्षीयते कर्म कल्पकोटिशतैरपि' applies to one who is not ज्ञानी.] The Jñâna meant is of this sort:—अहमेवाहं समः शान्तः सच्चिदानन्दलक्षणः । नाहं देहो ह्यसद्रूपो ज्ञानमित्युच्यते बुधैः ॥

मुमुक्षवः—मोक्तुम् इच्छुः मुमुक्षुः (noun in उ from the Desid. base of मुच्) one who wishes to be free from Saṃsâra or continued birth and re-birth; a sage seeking final emancipation.

Śl. 52. बन्दीमिव—like one made a captive. *i. e.*, forcibly. *Cf.* रिपुश्रियं साञ्जनबाष्पसेके बन्दीकृतानामिव पद्धती द्वे । Ragh. VI. 55. or, बन्दी (जातौ एकवचनं) बन्दीः सुरश्रियं च; *cf.* for a similar use of इव—बन्दैः पुलिन्दैरिव वानरैस्ताः क्लिश्यन्त उद्यानलता मदीयाः । Ragh. XVI. 19.

Cf. हन्तारं परसैन्यानां गोप्तारं त्रिदिवौकसाम् । दातारं शक्रलक्ष्म्याश्च महावीर्यपराक्रमम् ॥ Ś. P.

Śl. 53. अवसिते—*p. p. p.* of सो with अव. आत्मभूः—आत्मना स्वयमेव भवतीति; आत्मनो विष्णोर्वा भवतीति । गर्जिता॰—Bṛihaspati's speech is compared to thunder on account of its breathing an air of fear and plaintive tone.

Śl. 54. कालः कश्चित् &c.—*i. e.,* a favourable time; *cf.* तदा वयं विजेष्यामो यदा कालः प्रदक्षिणः । B. P. X. Ch. 54. 16, as quoted by Nár. The reason of this is thus given in Ś. P.—तपःफलविपाकस्तु तस्यामीदधुना महान् । Even God, who is bound by his laws, cannot punish any one unless his treasure of religious merit is exhausted. आत्मना—आत्मनः *v. l.* आत्मन इति कर्मणि षष्ठी । आत्मांशेनैवात्मानं न स्रक्ष्यामीत्यर्थः । *Cf.* भविष्यति भवत्कामः सहत्वं सुरपुंगवाः । Ś. P.

Śl. 55. विषवृक्षोऽपि—Nár. quotes—यस्य स्पर्शनमात्रेण वायुसंस्पर्शनेन वा । म्रियन्ते जन्तवः सर्वे विषवृक्षः स कीर्तितः ॥ As the relation of the object and verb is expressed here by a particle, विषवृक्ष is put in the Nom. case, असाप्रतं being equivalent to अनर्हः (न युज्यते); see Malli.; अनभिहिते, कर्मणि द्वितीया (Páṇ. II. 3. 1-2). When the relation is not expressed, the object is put in the Acc.; but when it is expressed, the Nom. is used; and the relation is expressed by a verb, or a Kṛit or Taddhita aff., or a comp. अभिधानं तु प्रायेण तिङ्कृत्तद्धितसमासैः । तिङ्-हरिः सेव्यते । कृत्-लक्ष्म्या सेवितः तद्धित-शतेन क्रीतः शत्यः । समास—प्राप्त आनन्दो यं स प्राप्तानन्दः क्वचिन्निपातेनाभिधानं यथा विषवृक्षोऽपि &c.; सांप्रतमित्यस्य तु युज्यते इत्यर्थः Sid.-Kau. The meaning of परिगणनं &c. (in the quotation from Vámana, see com.) is—the enumeration of the cases by which अभिधान takes place, as mentioned by the Vârtika तिङ्कृत्त॰, is प्रायिक, *i. e.,* in most cases, and is not exhaustive, hence निपातेनापि &c.; *cf.* मया तस्मै वरो दत्तो न हन्तव्यो ह्यसौ मम । विषवृक्षोऽपि &c. S'. P.

Śl. quoted in the Kávya-Pradîpa to show that in this, the word इदं (in इतः इतः) is restricted to the speaker by अपदेश (the speaker's pointing to himself; अत्रापदेशेनेदंशब्दस्याभिधा वक्तरि नियम्यते).

Śl. 56. इदं—*viz.,* exemption from death at the hands of anyone except the son of Śiva or a child seven days old. The penance practised by the demon is thus described—एवं कष्टतरं तप्तं शृण्वतामपि दुःसहम् । तस्यैव शिरसस्तत्र तेजश्च निसृतं महत ॥ तेनैव देवलोकास्ते दग्धप्राया बभूविरे । इन्द्रश्च भयमापेदे स्वपदं कर्षयिष्यति ॥ अत्यन्तदुःखमापन्नाः सर्वे देवास्तथा विभो । अकाण्डे चैव ब्रह्माण्डं संहरिष्यति वै प्रभुः ॥ यदि ब्रह्मा वरं ह्यस्य न दास्यति सुदुष्करम् । तथापि सर्वलोकानां नाशश्चैव भविष्यति ॥ as quoted by

Mr. Deshpande. The demon was to die as desired by him at the hands of the son of Śiva only:—त्वया च निर्मिते लोके मत्तुल्यो बलवान्न हि। शिववीर्यसमुत्पन्नः पुत्रः सेनापतिर्यदा। धृत्वा शस्त्रं क्षिपेन्मह्यं तदा मे मरणं भवेत् ॥ S. P. शमितं—अशमितं *v. l.* qualifies तपः; तस्य तपः वरेण अशमितं सत् लोकान्दग्धुमलं हि अभविष्यदिति शेषः।

Śl. 57. सांयुगीनं—fr. संयुग a battle and aff. खञ् (इन) in the sense of 'an expert in'; see com; संमुखीनं—*V. l.* confronting or opposing; fr. संमुख+ईन (खः) by यथामुखसंमुखस्य दर्शनः खः; सर्वस्य मुखस्य दर्शनः संमुखीनः. उद्गद—*V. l.* with the mace raised. नीललोहितः—See Malli.; नीलं येन ममाङ्गं तु रसाक्तं लोहितं त्विषा। नीललोहित इत्येव ततोऽहं परिकीर्तितः ॥ युध्यन्तमाहवे तं च महाबलपराक्रमम्। समर्थः को भवेज्जेतुं विना शंभुसुतं सुराः ॥ S. P.

Śl. 58. देवः—Fr. दिव् to shine; not only this, but he is परं ज्योतिः (the source of all intelligence, knowledge and bliss) and hence तमःपारे. *Cf.* तद्देवा ज्योतिषां ज्योतिरायुर्होपासतेऽमृतम्। Brih. Up. IV. 4. 16. परिच्छिन्न—what is cut all round; hence, definitely or accurately known. प्रभावर्द्धिः—ऋद्धि excellence, excess; परिच्छिन्ना प्रभावर्द्धिर्यस्य सः. *Cf.* तवैश्वर्यं यत्नाद्यदुपरि विरिंचो हरिरधः परिच्छेत्तुं यातावनलमनलस्कन्धवपुषः &c., *Mahimnastotra.*

Śl. 59. ते—You who wish to have a leader (ये इत्थं सेनानीसर्जनार्थिनः). शंभोः—शं सुखं भवति शंभुः; he who proves to be a source of happiness. The word is very appropriate here. Their labour will not be ill-spent. लोहवत्—A grammatical inaccuracy; here वत् is simply used in the sense of इव (लोहमिव); here उमारूप corresponds to अयस्कान्त and शंभोर्मनः to लोह. It is difficult to get the affix वत् in the sense intended here, as Malli. remarks; for according to the Sûtra quoted by Malli., there ought to be तुल्यक्रियत्व of the subject and its उपमान as in ब्राह्मणवदधीते; and so the meaning will be 'as iron would attract,' which is absurd. *Cf.* उमा श्रयति गौरीशं तत्परिग्रहणेच्छया। ततस्तत्र प्रयत्नं च कुरुध्वं विबुधेश्वराः ॥ S. P.

Śl. 60. वा—अवधारणे Châr.; *cf. infra* III. 16, मूर्तिर्जल०—*cf.* अप एव ससर्जादौ तासु बीजमवासृजत्। Manu. I. 8. मम—प्रसंगात्सा-क्षाद्यथीतनायात्मनोऽभिधानम्। Châr.

Śl. 61. आत्मा—see com.; and आत्मा वै पुत्र उत्पन्न इति वेदानुशासनं; B. P. X. Ch. 78, 36. शिति०—शितिः कालः कण्ठः यस्य। It was the effect of the Hâlâhala poison which Śiva swallowed at the time of the churning of the milky ocean. एवमामन्त्र्य भगवान्भवानीं विश्वभावनः। तद्विषं जग्धुमारेभे प्रभावज्ञान्वमोदत ॥ ततः करतलीकृत्य व्यापि हालाहलं विषम्। अभक्षयन्महादेवः कृपया भूतभावनः ॥ तस्यापि दर्शयामास स्ववीर्यं जलकल्मषः।

यश्चकार गले नीलं तच्च साधोर्विभूषणम् ॥ B. P. VIII. 7. 41-43. He is also called श्रीकण्ठ for this reason; धृतं कण्ठे विषं घोरं ततः श्रीकण्ठतामगात् । According to another account, Śiva's neck turned black on account of a stroke given by Indra with his thunderbolt—वृत्तः प्रहारः कुलिशेन पूर्वं तवेशान सुरराज्ञातिवीर्यः । कण्ठे नैलं तेन ते यत्प्रवृत्तं तस्मात्ख्यातस्त्वं नीलकण्ठेति कल्प्यः ॥ While according to a third account the black colour of the neck was due to its being seized by Nârâyaṇa in a duel: ततः प्रसभमाप्लुत्य रुद्रं विष्णुः सनातनः । जग्राह कण्ठे भगवान्नीलकण्ठस्ततोऽभवत् ॥ *Cf.* अद्यप्रभृति श्रीवत्सः शूलाङ्को मे भवत्वयम् । मम पाण्यङ्कितश्चापि श्रीकण्ठस्त्वं भविष्यसि ॥ मोक्ष्यते—will liberate, set free, for the locks that were once braided were never let loose as the celestial ladies were in bondage. Probably their braids were roughly seized by the demon; *cf.* स्वर्गस्त्रैणकचग्रहं रचयितुं निःशङ्कमुद्युञ्जते । Pár. P. II. 2; Ragh. X. 47.

Śl. 62. तिरोदधे—*cf.* कृष्णमेघस्तिरोदधे । Ragh. X. 48. आहित—Firmly laid, determined or fixed in mind. इत्युदाहृत्य तान्देवान् गृहान्प्राविशत्प्रभुः । देवास्ते कृतकृत्यास्तु नमस्कृत्य ययुर्दिवम् ॥ Ś. P.

Śl. 63. तत्र—May mean (1) in Indra's heaven, *i. e.*, in the council of gods; or (2) to execute the business, as Malli. takes it. कंदर्पः—कं सुखं तत्र तेन वा दृप्यति । पचाद्यच् । पाकशासनः—पाकान् बालान् शास्तीति; it originally meant—the instructor or discipliner of the ignorant or illiterate, Indra being the god of infinite wisdom. In the Purâṇas Indra is described as the killer of the demon Pâka, brother of Bali. (See B. P. VIII. 11) पाकं जघान तीक्ष्णाग्रैर्मार्गणैः कङ्कवाससैः । तत्र नाम विभुर्लेभे शासनत्वाच्छरैर्दृढैः । पाकशासनतां शक्रः सर्वामरपतिर्विभुः ॥ Vám. P. कार्य०—कार्यसिद्धिविषये या त्वरा &c. *Cf.* तस्मिन्कार्ये विनिश्चित्य कंदर्पं सिद्धिदायकम् । मघवास्मरमुवाचेदं पुष्पबाणधनुर्धरम् ॥ Ś. P.

Śl. 64. सललित—Châr. reads सुललित and translates सुललिता विलसन्ती &c. शृङ्ग—Point or end. अनेन चापविशेषणेनास्मत्कार्यमसौ साधयिष्यत्येवेति शतमखस्य बुद्धिर्व्यन्यते । Nâr. पद—the marks left on the neck by. चूताङ्कु०—See III. 27. अनेन सहायसंपत्तिः सहायस्य स्वाधीनता च दर्शिता । Nâr. शतमख—The god of hundred sacrifices (*i. e.* who owes his position to the performance of a hundred Aśvamedha sacrifices). मख is a syn. of क्रतु which originally meant 'counsel, wisdom'; and Indra was the god of hundred wisdoms; *i. e.*, infinitely wise. क्रतु, however, came to mean 'a sacrifice' in post-Vedic times and the position of Indra was made dependent on the performance of a hundred Aś. sacrifices. See our note on शतक्रतु Ragh. III. 38. उपतस्थे—The Âtm. by उपाद्

देवपूजासंगतिकरणमित्रकरणपथिष्विति वाच्यम् । Vârttika on I. 3, 25; *i. e*, in the senses of worshipping a deity, uniting or joining &c.; See com. *Cf.* मुखरमधुपमालाचारुमौर्वीसनाथं त्रिभुवनजययोग्यं चापमंसे दधानः । मुखमुदितविलासं वीक्षमाणः प्रियायाः सहमधुरिह मन्दं मन्दमायाति कामः ॥ Pâr. P. II. 8.

CANTO III.

Śl 1. मघवन्—An epithet of Indra. Originally this was a word of regular formation, fr. मघ a gift, present or wealth and वत् or वन्; one possessing riches or distributing gifts; the whole then signifying—'the munificent Indra *i.e.* the sun, the bestower of plentiful rain and thereby of wealth.' In post-Vedic times the term came to be applied to Indra and explained as मह्यते पूज्यते इति, irregularly derived by the Uṇâ. Sû. श्वन्नुक्षन्&c., from मह् to adore and the aff. अन् (कनिन्) with the augment व्.

त्रिदशाः—The gods. जन्मसत्ताविनाशाख्यास्तिस्रो दशा येषां or तृतीया यौवनाख्या दशा येषाम्; or the gods taken collectively; see Malli.; thirty standing for 33. According to the Śat. B. the gods are 33—"कतमे ते त्रयस्त्रिंशदिति अष्टौ वसव एकादश रुद्रा द्वादशादित्यास्त एकत्रिंशदिन्द्रश्चैव प्रजापतिश्च त्रयस्त्रिंशदिति ।" त्रिदशान्विहायेत्युक्त्या त्रिदशगतं गौरवमेकोपभुक्तं कामगतमिति दर्शितम् । Ar. प्रयोजना &c.—प्रयोजनमपेक्षते इति प्रयोजनापेक्षि (गौरवं) तस्य भावस्तत्ता तया; or प्रयोजनमपेक्षितुं शीलमेषामिति प्रयोजनापेक्षिणस्तेषां भावस्तत्ता तया ।

Śl. 2. आसन्न०—Used adverbially. Malli. remarks शेषषष्ठ्या &c. The meaning of Śesha is कारकप्रातिपदिकार्थव्यतिरिक्तः स्वस्वामिभावादिसंबन्धः । Sid.-Kau.; संनिकृष्टमासनं आसनसंनिकृष्टम् । आहिताग्न्यादिषु पाठात्साधुत्वम् । Ar. तद्यथा भवति तथा विसृष्ट०. मिथः—अनेन मन्त्रगुप्तिर्दर्शिता । Nâr. प्राक्रमत—क्रम् with प्र and उप is Âtm. in the sense of 'beginning'; see com. समर्थौ तुल्यार्थौ प्रारम्भेऽनयोस्तुल्यार्थता । Sid.-Kau.; but प्रक्रामति goes, उपक्रामति comes. समर्थ means तुल्यार्थ; when the root क्रम् with प्र or उप has the same meaning, *viz.* आरम्भ, it takes तङ् (is Âtm).

Śl. 3. ज्ञातविशेष—He who knows the special merit of a person. ज्ञातविशेष इत्यनेनात्मन इतरेभ्य उत्कर्षो द्योतितः। (Châr.). By using this epithet Kâma compliments Indra on his readiness to appreciate merit and to show respect to those who deserve it. He says आज्ञापय as he knows that Indra could not have thought of him unless he had in view some business requiring his special service. *Cf.* पुरुषान्तरविदो महेन्द्रस्य Vik. I. Here ०विशेष should not have been compounded, as पुंसः is left out; or the whole should have been compounded as ज्ञातपुंविशेष; but as the connexion can be plainly seen the comp. may be allowed; and hence Malli.'s remark सापेक्षत्वे &c. लोकेषु—by this Káma shows that he has power over the three worlds. अनुग्रहं—Kâma feels particularly flattered, as he, of all the gods, was specially remembered by his chief. His speech is quite in keeping with court language. संवर्धितं—Malli notices the reading संवर्धितुं and remarks that if it is admitted an effort should be made to explain it by attaching a causal sense to the root without the termination; for if णिच् be added the form will be संवर्धयितुम्. आज्ञया—by getting a command from you; this is a polite way of saying 'what command of yours shall I execute.'

Śl. 4 पदकाङ्क्षिणा—Having been often employed in similar duties, this is Káma's first thought. He thinks that his master has some rival practising penance to wrest his post from him and asks the question accordingly. Indra is often represented as being alarmed whenever a mortal practises unusual austerities, lest he might aim at his post. *Cf.* अस्त्येतदन्यसमाधिभीरुत्वं देवानां Śâk.: चरतः किल दुश्चरं तपस्तृणबिन्दोः परिशङ्कितः पुरा। प्रजिघाय समाधिभेदिनीं हरिरस्मै हरिणीं सुराङ्गनाम् ॥ Ragh. VIII. 79; also XIII. 39, 42. यावत्—Malli. takes this in the sense of यतः, but without stating authority; it may be taken in the sense of 'साकल्ये'—'will fully be' (भवति); or better with भवति giving it a future sense, by the rule यावत्पुरानिपातयोर्लट्। कार्मुकं—कर्मणे प्रभवति इति (कर्मन्+उक).

Śl. 5. असंमतः &c.—Now he says—Even if a man does not seek your post, but merely aims at *Moksha* and has not your approval, him I will fetter down to the world. मुक्तिमार्गं प्रपन्नः—seeking ब्रह्मविद्या, having renounced the world. See *supra* II. 51. *Cf.* तद्विज्ञानार्थं स गुरुमेवाभिगच्छेत् समित्पाणिः श्रोत्रियं ब्रह्मनिष्ठम्। Muṇḍ. I. 2. 12; ब्रह्मविदाप्नोति परं Tait. II. 1. 1; न जायते म्रियते वा विपश्चित्। Kaṭh. II. 18. &c. आरेचित—रेचन is the graceful raising of one eyebrow; Ar. quotes रेचितं पुनरेकस्या ललितोत्क्षेपणं भ्रुवः। Samgîta-Sástra; or रेचिताभिः नर्तिताभिः sportively moved; आरेचितं नर्तितं स्यादिति भोजः। कटाक्षैः—विलासैः *v. l.* blandishments; amorous gestures *Cf.* D.-K. रेचितभ्रूलतैरपाङ्गवीक्षितैः &c. चतुर—beautiful, engaging, charming. *Cf.* I. 47; V. 49. असंमतः कस्तवेन्द्र मुक्तिमार्गमपेक्षते। तं सुन्दरीकटाक्षैस्तु बध्नाम्याज्ञापयस्व मे ॥ Ś.P.

Śl. 6. This question refers to a future enemy (अनागतापत्प्रतीकारविषयः). उशनस्—Sukrâchârya, son of Bhrigu and preceptor of the demons In the Vedic as well as post-Vedic literature the epithet Kâvya 'the wise' is applied to him. He is also known as a writer on civil and religious law and is one of the authorities cited on civil polity. उशनसापि—न कश्चिन्नापनयते

पुमानन्यत्र भार्गवात् । इति दर्शनात् । Ar. नीति—Nîti is used here in a wider sense–that which gives rules for the conduct of human affairs or regulates the daily life of individuals enabling them to secure अर्थ and काम without infringement of religious law. राग—Love for carnal pleasures (clouding reason). अर्थधर्मौ—also धर्मार्थौ by the Várttika (on Páṇ. II. 2. 31) धर्मादिष्वनियमः। Sole attention to Kâma would destroy the other two. These are the three of the four objects of human pursuit, the forth being मोक्ष. पीडयामि—obstruct, overpower, *i. e.* whom shall I make a helpless sensualist? कस्य शत्रोरपि हरे धर्मार्थौ पीडयाम्यहम् । S. P.

Śl. 7. Next Kâma thinks that his master might have set his heart on a woman beyond his reach but whose love he seeks through his means; and hence this question. दुःखशीलां—दुःखं दुर्धर्षं शीलं स्वभावो यस्याः whose disposition is difficult to be challenged, who cannot be made to move from her vow; or habitually suffering the misery or hardships of; *cf.* दुःखशीले तपस्विजने Śák. VI. Or दुःख may mean दुःखकरं (शीलं यस्याः) giving pain to others on account of. स्वयंग्राह॰—This should be स्वयंग्रह; *cf.* स्वयंग्रहाश्लेषसुखेन निष्क्रयम् । Śiś. I. 50. Malli.'s view seems to be—In the sense of an alligator we have ग्राह alone; but in the sense of 'seizing &c.' we may have ग्रह or ग्राह. But this does not seem to be supported by the leading grammarians. By the rule विभाषा ग्रहः, ण (अ) is added to ग्रह् in the sense of 'an alligator' only, as the optionality is fixed, as remarked by Vâmana–व्यवस्थितविभाषा चेयम् । जलचरे नित्यं ग्राहः । ज्योतिषि नेष्यते तत्र ग्रह एव । This view is held by Haradatta and Bhaṭṭoji also. Some say-निरङ्कुशाः कवयः । others derive ग्राह by affixing घञ् or अच् to ग्रह् cau. in the primitive sense (स्वार्थण्यन्ताद्) स्वयं ग्रहो यस्याः सा स्वयंग्राहा; ग्रहे ग्राहः Amara.; or ग्रह् in the causal sense; ग्राह्यते असौ, घञ् being added कर्मणि; स्वयं ग्राहा स्वयंग्राहा सुप्सुपेति समासः; now see com. विषक्त—*V. l.* closely cast, or entwined. Malli. refers here to Indra's seduction of Ahalyâ.

Śl. 8. Now he forms a different conjecture and asks accordingly. कामिन्—भूयान् कामोऽस्यस्य; इन् shows excess; see Gr. मतुप् aff; foot-note, भूमनिन्दाप्रशंसासु &c. सुरता॰—सुरते अपराधस्तस्मात् । सहसा॰—*V. l.* thoughtlessly. कोपना—कुप्यति तच्छीला । दृढानुतापं—Repentance for having slighted the prostration. प्रवालशय्या—one of the usual appliances for allaying the torment caused by love-affection.

Śl. 9. Lastly Kâma thinks that Indra might have got some demon to cope with and expresses his readiness to reduce him to a helpless condition through the agency of the fair nymphs of heaven, his followers. वीर—He purposely uses this, lest Indra might feel offended at his telling him to cast off his Vajra. मोघीकृत०—न मोघममोघं अमोघं मोघ संपद्यमानं कृतं मोघीकृतं बाह्वोर्वीर्यं यस्य सः. *Cf.* वज्रं तव सुराधीश यत्कार्यं न करिष्यति । तत्करिष्यामि पुष्पास्त्रः सर्वासुरविमोहनम् ॥ Ś.-P.

Śl. 10. तव प्रसादात्—He pays his master a compliment, as is usual with subordinates; *cf.* सिध्यन्ति कर्मसु महत्स्वपि यन्नियोज्याः संभावनागुणमवेहि तमीश्वराणाम् । Śāk. VII. 4. पिनाकपाणेः—And hence the more formidable; see com.; mark the contrast between this and कुसुमायुधोऽपि. पाति इति पिनाकः the bow of S'iva; according to some the trident or three-pronged spear of Śiva. धन्विनः—fr. धन्व+इन्; (अत इनि ठनौ इति इनिः); or धन्वन्+इन् (व्रीह्यादिभ्यश्चादिनिः). Śl. referred to in the S.-D. to show that the epithet पिना० is fitly used here and not redundant; (अत्र तु विशेषप्रतिपत्त्यर्थमुपात्तत्वाद्युक्तमेव ।); and quoted in Kuv. as an instance of परिकर. *Cf.* Ś-P. धैर्यच्युतिं करिष्येऽहं भवस्यापि तवाज्ञया । अन्येषां चैव देवानामसुराणां च का कथा ॥ and दनुजो वा मनुजो वा मुनिरपि वा मुग्धचन्द्रचूडो वा । सुरलोकसुन्दरीणां स भवतु बद्धः कटाक्षशृङ्खलया ॥ Pâr. P. II. 12.

Śl. 11. ऊरुदेशात्—the use of the word देश indicates the expanse of the thigh. संभावित—'honoured;' it was an honour to the foot-stool that Indra placed his foot on it. Some read संमानित. आखण्डलः—आखण्डयति परबलानि, the slayer of the enemy's armies; or अखण्डमैश्वर्यं ज्ञानं वा लाति इति अखण्डलः; अखण्डल एव आखण्डलः । 'अन्येषामपि दृश्यते' इति दीर्घः ।

Śl. 12. सर्वं—all that is contained in s'ls. 4-10. सखे—Mark how Indra flatters him by calling him a friend. *Cf.* III. 1. उपपन्नं—is proved to exist in; or proper in. कुलिशं—कुलो in the hand शेते or कुलिनः पर्वतान् श्यति reduces the bulk of इति. कुण्ठं—कुण्ठो मन्दः क्रियासु यः Amara.; what is unable to perform its function; fr. कुण्ठ् 1. P. to be blunted. सर्वत्रगामि—and hence superior to Kuliśa; qualifies ०अस्त्रं. By this Indra indicates that he accepts Kāma's declaration of his power (as in प्रसीद विश्राम्यतु वीर वज्रं) as a statement of facts and not a mere vaunting on his part.

Śl. 13. अवैमि ते सारं—*Cf.* अवैमि तेऽनङ्ग वीर्यं हरधैर्यहरं परम् । Ś.-P. आत्मसमं-आत्मना समं my equal. भूधरतां—Sesha's supporting the earth is often referred to by Sanskrit poets; *cf. infra* ततः भुजङ्गाधिपतेः फणाग्रैः &c. III. 50; धत्ते धरित्र्याः फणिना ततोऽधः । Śiś. VI. 25; किं शेषस्य भरव्यथा न वपुषि क्ष्मां न क्षिपत्येष यत् । Mud. II.; Ragh. XV. 83 &c. कृष्णेन—by Vishṇu (in his divine form which is of immense proportion). *Cf.* Ragh. X. 7. शेषः—king of the Nâgas, see Vâsuki; *supra* II. 38. He has a thousand hoods. He is regarded as the emblem or personification of eternity and hence is called Ananta (the infinite). Vishṇu is represented as sleeping on him during the intervals of creation; *cf.* योगनिद्रां यदा विष्णुर्जगत्येकार्णवीकृते । आस्तीर्य शेषमभजत्कल्पान्ते भगवान्प्रभुः ॥ Mârk.-P. See Ragh. X. 7; also during the four months beginning with the 11th of A'shâḍha to the 11th of Kártika S'uddha.

Śl. 14. आशंसता—Here शंस् with आ must be taken in the sense of 'declaring.' See Malli. who criticizes Nâtha's comment as wrong. शंस् with आ in the sense of इच्छा or soliciting or hoping is A'tm., while the meaning याच्ञा or 'seeking' is without authority. अनयोरभावाद्योगाच्च means—these two meannings do not exist and do not suit in कुर्यां हरस्यापि &c. Ar. takes it as आ ईषत् शंसता । ईषद्वचनमत्र तदेव देवकार्यमिति निश्चयाभावात् । गति—The effective fall on; power to hit. निबोध—We have this again in V. 52. यज्ञांशभुजां—The word is significant: the gods specially suffered because their sacrificial portions were obstructed from reaching them by Târaka; see *supra* II. 46. उच्चैस्तरामि°—*v. l.* see foot-note; the highest object of the gods rests herein, *i e.*, in Śiva's being induced to marry.

Śl. 15. उशन्ति—The root वश् is a छान्दस root (*i.e.* used in the Veda); but it is sometimes used in ordinary language also; Kâli. has again used it in S'ák. VII. 20 (भवनेषु रसाधिकेषु पूर्वं क्षितिरक्षार्थमुशन्ति ये निवासम् ।); *cf.* वष्टिभागुरिरल्लोपं &c. Sid.-Kau. निःस्वो वष्टि शतं &c. Śântiśataka. ब्रह्माङ्गभूः—It is difficult to know what this exactly means. Different commentators have given different interpretations. The meaning that would readily suggest itself to the mind is—'born of Brahmâ' (and some commentators have taken it in that sense ब्रह्मणः अङ्गभूः, ब्रह्मणोऽङ्गात् भूरुत्पत्तिर्यस्य *i. e.* रुद्र); see our note on रुद्रः II. 26; and *cf.* स रुद्रो यो रुद्रः स ईशानो य ईशानः स भगवान्महेश्वरः । Atharvaśira-upanishad Or, the source of the Vedas and their Upâṅgas; (ब्रह्मवेदः अङ्गानि च तेषां भूः). Châr. says—ब्रह्मा अङ्गभूः पुत्रो यस्य; which the poet may have intended, see *infra* V. 81. *Cf.* for the two meanings:—'भ्रुकुटीकुटिलात्तस्य ललाटात्परमेष्ठिनः (ब्रह्मणः) । समुद्भूतो महादेवः कुमारो नीललोहितः' ॥ and Śiva's words to Brahman—'त्वमात्मज्योतिः पुरुषो मम देहसमुद्भवः' । Kûrma Puráṇa. Malli. understands by this—Who is the repository of the Mantras सद्योजात and others, by having made the Nyâsa, *i. e.*, touching the six parts of the body हृदय and others and assigning deities to them by repeating the proper Mantras; *cf.* अथ वा ब्रह्मणोऽङ्गानि पञ्च शैवसिद्धान्ते प्रोक्ता मन्त्रविशेषास्तेषामुत्पत्तिस्थानम्। आयात-ईशान-वामदेव-तत्पुरुष-सद्योजात-लक्षणानि पञ्चाङ्गानि। Sukhâvabodhatîkâ, as quoted by Mr. Deshpande. सद्योजात &c. (*i.e.* their deities) are simply शिवमूर्तिभेदs. One Calcutta commentator suggests an optional interpretation of the last two lines as—यद्वा स सेनानीः त्वदेकेषुनिपातेन साध्यः उत्पादनीयः। कीदृशः। ब्रह्मणा नियोजितः आत्मा यत्नो यस्मै सः। यतः स्वं ब्रह्माङ्गभूः। ब्रह्मणोङ्गादुत्पत्तिर्यस्य तथा।

ब्रह्मणि—ब्रह्मन्, the one supreme Ens, is, according to the Vedántins, the material and efficient cause of the universe. It is नित्य 'over-lasting', शुद्ध 'pure', बुद्ध intelligent', and मुक्त 'unfettered by any conditions' (अस्ति तावन्नित्यशुद्धबुद्धमुक्तस्वभावं सर्वज्ञं सर्वशक्तिसमन्वितं ब्रह्म। Śâr.-Bhâ.). The two great texts (Mahávâkyas) setting forth the nature of Brahman are सत्यं ज्ञानमनन्तं ब्रह्म (Tait.) and सत्यं विज्ञानमानन्दं ब्रह्म (Brih.). The word is derived from बृह् to be great,-what has become great, all-pervading. Or ब्रह्मणि may mean 'in the heart'. योजितात्मा-indicates his तपोवीर्यमहत्त्वं (śl. 13); hence त्वदेकेषु etc. *Cf.* तस्कुरुष्वामराणां च स्थितये त्रिदिवस्य च। हिमवच्छिखरं गत्वा यत्रास्ते भगवान्हरः। उमा गिरिसुता चैव तं च तस्यां नियोजय॥ Ś. P.

Śl. 16. प्रयतां—Self-restrained, pure; the adj. shows that Pârvatî is the proper person to win over Śiva who is यतात्मा, and Kâma's effort in that direction will not be vain. *Cf.* क्रिया हि वस्तूपहिता प्रसीदति. सैवक्षमेति—see II. 60.

Śl. 17. And these are favourable circumstances for our attempt; for, गुरोः &c. स्थाणु—Śiva. नित्यमव्यय एव तिष्ठतीति; from स्था+नु. He who exists for ever without change, the eternal one; or one who stands like a tree; *cf.* वृक्ष इव स्तब्धो दिवि तिष्ठत्येकः। Śve.; also ततः प्रभृति विश्वात्मा न प्रसूते शुभाः प्रजाः। स्थाणुवन्निश्चलो यस्मात्तस्मात्स्थाणुरिति श्रुतः॥ अधित्यका—पर्वतस्यारूढं स्थलमाधि०; उपाधिभ्यां &c. (see com.), Pâṇ. V. 2. 34. त्यक is added to उप and अधि in these technical senses. These are instances of nouns formed from prepositions. अन्वास्ते—waits on; *cf.* अन्वासितमरुन्धत्या Ragh. I. 56 where Malli. explains अन्वासित by पश्चादुपवेशनेनोपसेवितम्. अप्सरसां-See notes on I. 4 *supra.* The Apsarases are generally mentioned as 12 in number; the principal of them are-घृताची मेनका रम्भा उर्वशी च तिलोत्तमा। सुकेशी मञ्जुघोषाद्याः कथ्यन्तेऽप्सरसो बुधैः॥ प्रणिधिः—प्रकर्षेण निधीयते ज्ञेयमत्र; *lit.* one to whom information to be culled is entrusted, and hence who can be trusted.

Śl. 18. अर्थोऽयं-Malli. seems to take अर्थ as referring to स्थाणुवशीकरण; it rather refers to देवकार्यं *i. e.*, the gods' getting a leader, by the birth of a son to Śiva (see śl. 16), while अर्थान्तर would mean Śiva's espousing Pârvatî; सिद्धये indicating success in Kâma's inducing Śiva to love Pârvatî (रोचयितुं यतस्व). Châr. also says— सेनानीजन्मलक्षणोऽर्थः । Some read अर्थोत्तर for अर्थान्तर and take it as हे अर्थोत्तर धर्मार्थाभ्यामुत्तर काम । प्रत्यय—Ultimate cause; for this sense, *cf.* Ragh. X. 3. (अतिष्ठत्प्रत्ययापेक्षसंततिः स चिरं नृपः ।) Śl. quoted in K. P. with the reading प्रत्ययमङ्गलब्धये for प्र० मुत्तमं त्वां as an instance of the fault 'harshness of sound (cacophony)'. In this śloka which contains a solicitation, sweet words only should appropriately be used, but they are not. The conjunct consonants द्धये (in सिद्धये) and ब्धये (in लब्धये) sound harsh to the ear. अङ्गलब्धये *v. l.*—आत्मोत्पत्तये for its production.

Śl. 19. नाम—Malli. takes this संभावनायां; you only can be well expected to direct your weapon successfully. We may also take it प्राकाश्ये. 'It is well known;' it is acknowledged on all hands. For Indra is speaking here assertively (*cf. supra* स च त्वदेकेषु० śl. 15, also 12) to please Káma. नाम प्राकाश्यसंभाव्यक्रोधोपगमकुत्सने । Amara. अप्रसिद्धं—insignificant. Its अनन्यसाधारणत्व (requiring the employment of one's special talent) is the cause of glory.

Śl. 20. सुराः—The gods, themselves the granters of boons, now solicit you. विष्टप—विशन्त्यस्मिन्सुकृतिनः इति विष्टपं; from विश् and the Uṇâdi. aff. अप before which तु is inserted; the श् is changed to ष्. Pâṇ. VIII. 2. 36. न चातिहिंस्रं—हिनस्ति इति हिंस्रं. *Cf.* यतः प्रयोक्तुर्न चातिहिंसा विजयश्च हस्ते । Ragh. V. 57. अहो—expresses wonder; बत—joy or satisfaction (संतोष.)

Śl. 21. मन्मथ—मत् चेतना; मथतीति मथः (fr. मथ् 1. P. to shake off); मतो मथः । The epithet is aptly used here. *cf.* D.-K. मन्मथो मां मथ्नन् निजनाम सान्वयं करोति । सहायः—*Cf.* the root-meaning सह अयते (goes) इति; अय्+अ (अच्). समीरणः &c.—Poets describe the following as natural friends:—मेघपर्वतयोरब्जसूर्ययोरब्धिचन्द्रयोः । शिखिजीमूतयोर्मैत्री वाताग्न्योश्च स्वभावतः ॥ According to Nâr. there is a fusion of the figures पर्यायोक्त and प्रतिवस्तूपमा in this śl.; अत्रोक्तिभङ्ग्या वसन्तस्य नियोग एवोक्त इति पर्यायोक्तमलंकारः । तेन च प्रतिवस्तूपमायाः संसृष्टिः ।

Śl. 22. शेषा—A garland or wreath, such as is taken from an idol, or from his body by a holy personage, and given as a mark of favour or a token of good wishes. इव—Malli. has this discussion on this–What is the force of इव here? If शेषा was actually given, इव stands for यथा and the fig. is उपमा; if it was not given, it indicates उत्प्रेक्षा (as if it were); and as there is no proof for or against the actual gift of शेषा (साधकबाधकप्रमाणाभावात्) the fig. is संदेहसंकर of उपमा and उत्प्रेक्षा; see com. मूर्ध्ना—*Cf.* तस्याज्ञां...दधुः शिरोभिर्भूपालाः &c. Ragh. XVII. 79; and गुणानुरागेण शिरोभिरुह्यते नराधिपैर्माल्यमिवास्य शासनम् ॥ Kir. I. 21. कर्कशेन—indicates Indra's habit of constantly stroking his elephant. *Cf.* सुरद्विपास्फालनकर्कशाङ्गुलौ । Ragh. III. 55; see also Ragh. VI. 73. This does not seem to be intended to convey any hidden meaning, although Chár. remarks—कर्कशशब्दं प्रयुञ्जानेन कविना भावि मरणं मन्मथस्य सूचितम् । पस्पर्श—This (moving the hand along the body) is the highest token of affection and regard.

Śl. 23. साशङ्कं—Fearing some mishap to her husband as she knew with whom he had to deal, for अतिस्नेहः पापशङ्की. अनुप्रयातः-For as a पतिव्रता she could not leave him in the hour of trial. अङ्गव्यय—For he too knew that the attempt might cost him his body even. प्रार्थित—Sought in right earnest. हैमवतम्—हिमवत् + अण् (अ); तत्र भव इत्यण् । *Cf.* इत्युक्तस्तेन कंदर्पः स जगाम हिमालयम् । नियोजयितुकामस्तु उमायां चन्द्रशेखरम् । पुष्पबाणधनुर्बाहुरेकया सह वै स्त्रिया ॥ Ś.-P.

Śl. 24. मुनीनां—is put in to imply that the advent of the spring would have adverse influence on the ascetic practices of ordinary sages only, but would not affect Śiva in any way. Otherwise he would have simply said तपःस॰ and not मुनीनां &c. तपःसमाधेः—practice of penance with a concentrated mind or undisturbed attention. अभिमानभूतं—as indicated in सहायमेकं मधुमेव लब्ध्वा । Ar. quotes—संकल्पप्रभवं कामं रतिं प्रीत्यभिमानिनीम् । अभिमानात्मकं तस्य मधुं मदनविग्रहम् । आराधयेयुः क्षितिपाः सस्त्रीका रूपकाङ्क्षिणः ॥ *Cf.* तस्मिन्वने संयमिनां मुनीनामूर्ध्वरेतसाम् । समाधेः प्रतिकूलस्तु कामो विजयते मुने ॥ तस्मिन् शरदि कालेऽपि सर्वसंभारसंवृतः । बभूव कामसंसर्गाद्वसन्तो देहवानिव ॥ Ś. P. वाचालयन्नथ कुलानि वनप्रियाणामङ्कूरयन्मलयमारुतकन्दलानि । सख्युः प्रसूनविशिखस्य भुजावलेपं संवर्धयन्मधुरजृम्भत काननेषु ॥ Pár. P. III. 2.

Śl. 25. This verse has a side-meaning, *viz.* "A certain kind-hearted damsel heaved out a sigh of pain from her mouth, when her lover, an adventurous gallant, started to go to another woman, kept by some deformed person, having broken the engagement with her." The Sun is here represented as a साहसिक नायक (bold or unscrupulous lover), the Southern Quarter as a खण्डिता नायिका (ज्ञातेऽन्यासङ्गविकृते खण्डितेर्ष्याकषायिता । D.-R. II. 25) or a lady offended at her lover's infidelity, and the North as a प्रतिनायिका or a rival-mistress (being the wife of Kubera).

कुबेरगुप्तां दिशं—The North; for Kubera, see II. 21. समय—(1) दक्षिणायन; when the sun in its apparent annual revolution begins to proceed to the north of the equator (about the 23rd of December, after the winter solstice takes place), spring sets in. Here although it was दक्षिणायन (winter), yet the sun changed its course at once and began to travel towards the north. (2) The fixed time of meeting or union. *Cf.* Ragh. जिगमिषुर्धनदाध्युषितां दिशं XI. 25. उष्णरश्मि—(1) the sun; (2) an adventurous lover. दक्षिणा-(1) the southern quarter; (2) a lady acting according to the wishes of her husband or lover. गन्धवहं—Mark the comp.; if we add अण् (कर्मणि) the form will be गन्धवाहः; words like पच (as in श्वपच), धर (चापधर &c.), वह &c. are derived by means of अच् under Pâṇ. III. 1. 134; and वाह, धार (दण्डधार), by अण् (Pâṇ. III. 2. 1). As soon as summer sets in, southerly breezes from the Malaya mountain begin to blow. व्यलीक—offence, wrong; or pain, grief. The southerly breeze is fancied as the sigh of the Southern quarter lamenting the separation of the sun. *Cf.* क्षिप्त्वा गुहासु तिमिरं विहितव्यलीकाः। Vik.-Ch. XI. 89; सुतनु हृदयात्प्रत्यादेशव्यलीकमपैतु ते। Śâk. VII. 24; एवं प्रत्यक्षदृष्टव्यलीकः किं ब्रवीमि। Rat. III., and III. 15. For the idea, *cf.* Ragh. IX. 25, and आधूय चन्दनतरूनुत्तमनयास्तरङ्गमालिङ्गय। आदाय कमलसौरभमङ्कुरितो मलयशैलपवमानः॥ Pâr.-P. III. 4.

Śl. 26. From here are described the effects of the influence of Madhu. The description here and in some other places is according to poetic convention (कविसंकेत). The poets think that the Aśoka requires to be struck by females with their feet adorned with anklets, so that it is able to put forth flowers. *Cf.* नूपुरान्वितपादेन तरुण्या ताडितो भृशम्। अशोकः केसरी वक्रसीधुसिक्तश्च फुल्लति॥ Prayogaratnâvalî. See Malli.; also स्त्रीणां स्पर्शात्प्रियंगुर्विकसति बकुलः सीधुगण्डूषसेकात्पादाघातादशोकस्तिलककुरबकौ वीक्षणालिङ्गनाभ्याम्। मन्दारो नर्मवाक्यात्पटुमृदुहसनाच्चम्पको वक्त्रवाताच्चूतो गीतान्नमेरुर्विकसति च पुरोनर्तनात्कर्णिकारः॥ *Cf.* आकर्ण्याशोकपादाहतिषु च रणतां निर्भरं नूपुराणां। Rat. I. 18; कुसुमं कृतदोहदस्त्वया यदशोकोऽयमुदीरयिष्यति। Ragh. VIII. 62. नापैक्षत—did not wait for, did not stand in need of. For, Vasanta himself exerted such an influence. वसन्तकालस्य बलवत्तरत्वात्तदपेक्षा नासीत्। Châr. *Cf.* रक्ताशोकश्चलकिसलयः केसरश्चात्र कान्तः प्रत्यासन्नौ कुरबकवृतेर्माधवीमण्डपस्य। एकः सख्यास्तव सह मया वामपादाभिलाषी काङ्क्षत्यन्यो वदनमदिरां दोहदच्छद्मनास्याः। Megh. II. 18. चूताः कोरकिता विनापि सुदृशां हस्ताम्बुजामर्शनात्तत्पादाम्बुजताडनैरपि विना फुल्लाः पुष्पिताः। तत्संगीतकमन्तरेण हसिता रम्याः प्रियालद्रुमा मुक्त्वा तद्वदनासवं मुकुलिता गन्धोत्तराः केसराः॥ Pâr. P. III. 6. Śl. quoted in D.-R. as marking the beginning of the spring season which acts as an incentive to शृङ्गार (love).

Śl. 27. सद्यः—'the moment the arrow was finished' goes with निवेशयामास. Some take it with नीतं,-the arrow being at once (and not gradually as ordinarily) fully equipped. सहयुः—*v. l.* goes with मनोभवस्य. चूत०--the mango blossom is one of the arrows of Cupid. See Notes on IV. 14. *Cf.* Śâk. VI. 8 (धनुषि चूतशरश्च निवेशितः). द्विरेफाः--A word said to be based on the word भ्रमर which contains two *refas.* *Cf.* Vâmana—लक्षणाशब्दाश्चातिप्रयुक्ताः प्रयोक्तव्याः। यथा द्विरेफरथचरणशब्दौ भ्रमरचक्रवाकार्थौ लक्षणापरौ। अनतिप्रयुक्ताश्च न प्रयोक्तव्या यथा द्विकः काक इति। See also Malli. further, on Śl. 36. नामाक्षर०—It was usual with great warriors to have their names inscribed on their arrows. See Vik. V. 7; बाणाक्षरैरेव परस्परस्य नामोर्जितं चापभृतः शशंसुः। Ragh. VII. 38.

Śl. 28. कर्णिकार--has flowers of a bright red colour or of a golden hue but without smell; see III. 53. सामग्र्यविधौ—सामग्र्यस्य विधिस्तस्मिन्; सामग्र्य *fr.* समग्र + य (ष्यञ्); also सामग्री by adding ई. *Cf.* शशिनि खलु कलङ्कः कण्टकाः पद्मनाले युवतिकुचनिपातः पक्वता केशजाले। जलधिजलमपेयं पण्डिते निर्धनत्वं वयसि धनविवेको निर्विवेको विधाता॥ चन्द्रे कलङ्कः सुजने दरिद्रता सुखप्रसादः अधनेषु सर्वदा। विकाशलक्ष्मीः कमलेषु चञ्चला यशो विधातुः कथयन्ति खण्डितम्॥ यः सुन्दरस्तद्वनिता कुरूपा या सुन्दरी सा पतिरूपहीना। यत्रोभयं तत्र दरिद्रता च विधेर्विचित्राणि विचेष्टितानि॥ Subh.

Śl. 29. In this Śloka Vasanta is represented as a lover inflicting nail-wounds on the persons of the forest-sites. अविकासभावात्—owing to the state of not being full blown. *Cf.* उपहितं शिशिरापगमश्रिया मुकुलजालमशोभत किंशुके। प्रणयिनीव नखक्षतमण्डनं प्रमदया मदयापितलज्जया॥ Ragh. IX. 31. Śl. quoted in Kuv. as an instance of स्वरूपोत्प्रेक्षा.

Śl. 30. भक्ति—a beautiful arrangement of little dots making up the *tilaka* or ornamental mark on the fore-head. *cf.* अलिभिरञ्जनबिन्दुमनोहरैः कुसुमपङ्क्तिनिपातिभिरङ्कितः (तिलकः) Ragh. IX. 41. तिलकं—The *tilaka* flower with bees perched on it is here figured as the ornamental mark on the forehead of Spring-Beauty while the young sun is the red paint for her with which to adorn her lip, the tender mango-leaf. ०चित्रं—read by Ar. and Nâr. is not a good reading; for it then becomes an epithet of मुखं, which is absurd, as the whole face is not dotted with collyrium. राग—(1) red colour; (2) the same serving as लाक्षाराग Fig एकदेशविवर्तिरूपकम्.

Śl 31. प्रियाल—*Chironjia Sapida* M.-W. विघ्नित—विघ्न एषां संजातः ते विघ्निताः; now see com. मदोद्धताः—exhilarated with passion. मर्मर—is the sound of dry leaves falling; मर्मरः शुष्कपर्णानाम् इति यादवः। अयं च शुक्लादिशब्दवद्गुणिन्यपि वर्तते प्रयुज्यते च-'मर्मरैरगुरुधूपगन्धिभिः' इति। Malli. on Ragh. IV. 73

Sl. 32. कषाय०—may also be taken in the sense of सुरभित (*i. e.*, the throat; as is done by Jag. on केसरकषायकण्ठ &c. Mâl-Mâdh. VII. p. 153) and hence capable of uttering sweet sounds; सुस्वरकण्ठ इत्यर्थः। Nâr. पुंस्कोकिलः—कोकिलासैन्यसंयुक्तो हिमाद्रिं प्रययौ स्मरः॥ Brah. P. मनस्विनी—High-minded ladies; ladies having a proper sense of their honour. मान०—स्त्रीणामीर्ष्याकृतः कोपो मानोऽन्यासंगिनि प्रिये; or मानश्चित्तसमुन्नतिः Amara. वचनं स्मरस्य—*viz.*, 'त्यजत मानमलं बत विग्रहैर्न पुनरेति गतं चतुरं वयः'। परभृताभिरितीव निवेदिते स्मरमते रमते स्म वधूजनः॥ Ragh. IX 47. *Cf.* प्रियसखीसदृशं प्रतिबोधिताः किमपि काम्यगिरा परपुष्टया। प्रियतमाय वपुर्गुरुमत्सरच्छिदुरयाऽदुरयाचितमङ्गनाः॥ Śiś. VI. 8; दत्तं प्रियाभिर्बहुमानपूर्वमासाद्य चूतासवमन्यपुष्टाः। आमोदिभिः पद्मपरागभेदैः मावोधयन्पत्रशरावलेपम्॥ Pa'r. P. III. 3.

Śl. 33. विशद०—Being no longer smeared with wax-salve. Women are described as applying a kind of wax-salve to their lips to protect them from the effects of the winter cold. *Cf.* व्रणगुरुप्रमदाधरदुःसहं &c. Ragh. IX. 32. पत्रविशेषक—Ornamental paintings drawn by young women generally on their cheeks and bosoms with cosmetics. (Probably the custom arose originally out of the necessity to keep the upper half of the body uncovered in the hottest days of the sultry season, the paintings being devised as a substitute for the upper garment.) *Cf.* कस्तूरीमकरीः पयोधरयुगे गल्लद्वये च श्रियाः। Pras. घर्माम्भोविसरावितर्नैरिदानीं मुग्धाक्ष्याः परिजनचारुसुन्दरीणाम्। तत्पातविहितविचित्रपत्रलेखावैदग्ध्यं जहति कपोलकुङ्कुमानि॥ Mâl.-Mâdh. I. 37.

Śl. 34. आकालिकी—समानकालावाद्यन्तौ यस्याः; (the word आकाल is substituted for समानकाल by Pâṇ. V. 1. 114 quoted in the com.); (पूर्वेद्युने मध्याह्नादावुत्पद्य दिनान्तरे तत्रैव नश्वर इति वा Sid.-Kau.); here it means-unseasonable, untimely; and may be derived from अकाल; see com. विक्रिया—a change or alteration in a particular condition or state; hence (1) perturbation, agitation as here; *cf.* IV. 41; (2) see *infra* Śl. 47 (अविक्रिया); (3) any sudden change; V. 10; (4) any undesirable or unwelcome change, evil; VI. 29.

Śl. 35. काष्ठा—प्रकर्ष excess, from काश् to shine. स्नेह-love linking together two hearts. रस—रस्यते इति what is enjoyed and which thus produces a lasting sensation of pleasure, pain &c. Here it is the sentiment of love which completely pervaded all nature. द्वन्द्वानि—couples of both the vegetable and the animal kingdom. भाव—Malli. understands by this रत्याख्यशृङ्गारभाव. Rati is the Sthâyî bhâva (lasting or permanent feeling) of Śriṅgâra 'the Erotic sentiment.' विभावैरनुभावैश्च सात्त्विकैर्व्यभिचारिभिः। आनीयमानः

स्वाद्यत्वं स्थायी भावो रसः स्मृतः ॥ Stháyíbháva is that which is rendered capable of being enjoyed or felt by means of Vibhávas &c. For the meanings of these see Sâh.-Dar. or D.-R. Here we are concerned with अनुभाव which is defined as अनुभावो विकारस्तु भावसंसूचनात्मकः—Any outward effect indicating the internal state of mind or feeling, such as कटाक्षक्षेपण &c. in the case of रति. अनुभावो भावबोधकः Amara. भावस्य सूचको गुणक्रियादिः; अनुभावयतीत्यनुभावः । S.-D. defines रति as—रतिर्मनोनुकूलेऽर्थे मनसः प्रवणायितं III. 176. Its आलम्बनकारण is नायकनायिका, and उद्दीपन (excitant) अभिमतदेशकालादि. क्रियया—by their actions *i. e.* gestures &c. as described in the following slokas. *Cf.* आदाय चापमधिरोपितषट्पदज्यं तस्मिन्हिमाचलमुपेयुषि पञ्चबाणे । वेलातिलम्बि किमपि प्रणयातिरेकाद् द्वन्द्वानि लौल्यमभजन्त विमोहितानि । Pâr. P. III. 5.

Śl. 36. Now the poet proceeds to particularize the general statement made in the preceding śloka. द्विरेफः—*Lit.* a word having two *refas* in it, *i. e.* भ्रमर ; and then by उपचार it signifies 'a bee.' See Malli. अनुवर्तमानः—'following his mate' (Malli.); but it seems better to take it in the sense of 'acting agreeably to, or ministering to the wishes of; pleasing, serving.' The two drank the honey together out of the same flower-bell. पिबन्तः पर्याप्तं सह सहचरीभिर्मधुरसं समन्तादापानोत्सवमनुभवन्तीह मधुपाः । Nág. III. 8. *Cf.* प्रभुचित्तमेव हि जनोऽनुवर्तते । Śis. XV 41. The Com. of S.-D. too says सेवमानः. Sl. quoted in D.-R. as an instance of कालविभाव or season serving as an excitant (inflamer of passion). विभाव is defined as ज्ञानमानतया तत्र विभावो भावपोषकृत् । Vibhâva is that, which being perceived or enjoyed, nourishes the main sentiment (नायकादिरभिमतदेशकालादिर्वा D.-R.); also in S.-D. as an instance of रसाभास or semblance of Rasa, as it is manifested by lower animals (which is regarded as real when located in mankind ; अत्र हि संभोगशृङ्गारस्य तिर्यग्विषयत्वाद्रसाभासः).

Śl. 37. रसात्—through love, the reading सरःपङ्कज॰ has no propriety. *Cf.* for a similar act, Vik. IV. 23. Mark the alliterations. अर्धोपभुक्तेन—a comp. सुप्सुपा. संभावयामास-honoured, pleased. रथाङ्गनामा—Chakravâka is also called Chakra. Śl. quoted in Sar.-K. as an instance of रसाभास in beasts and birds. चिरविरचितचाटुश्चन्द्ररेखायमाणः प्रथमरसबिसाग्रग्रासलीलार्पणेन। इह रमयति हंसीं राजहंसो रिरंसुः पुलकयति च चञ्चूकोटिकण्डूयनेन ॥

Śl. 38. समुच्छ्वासित—Loosened (by being wet) and made to puff up. पुष्पासव—wine prepared from flowers (the Madhûka flowers) called माध्वी; गौडी माध्वी च पैष्टी च विज्ञेया त्रिविधा सुरा. ॰आघूर्णित—*cf.* मधु नयनयोर्विभ्रमादेशदक्षम् । Megh. II. 12; and *infra*

IV. 2. चुचुम्ब—The reading found in the printed editions is चुचुम्बे; but the reading चुचुम्ब is preferred as the root चुम्ब् is Paras. Had Malli. read चुचुम्बे he would have made some remark on the Âtm. use of the root. One Calc. commentator says—चुचुम्बे इति चुबि वक्रसंयोगे इत्यस्य परस्मैपदित्वेऽपि कर्मव्यतीहारे आत्मनेपदम् । But कर्मव्यतिहार (mutual kissing) is not meant here, as clearly shown by the words प्रियामुखं किंपुरुषः (and not किंपुरुषौ). Śl. quoted in Sar.-K. as an instance of किंनरेषु रसाभास.

Śl. 39. पर्याप्त—Large (fully developed); स्तबक a cluster of flowers.—०स्तननम्रः also, ई being optionally added. प्रवालोष्ठ—We have already had this comparison in śl. 30.

Śl. 40. श्रुताप्सर०—We already know that the nymphs were in attendance on Śiva (see *supra* 17); their songs were particularly attractive at this times (अस्मिन्क्षणे) of the spring reason. प्रसंख्यान—*Lit.* Proper enumeration; right knowledge; hence thought; and lastly, deep meditation, abstract contemplation, the mind being withdrawn from external objects and fixed on the inward soul. See Yog. S. Those who hold that ख्या is used in the conjugational tenses only, derive प्रसंख्यान fr. चक्ष् with प्र and सम् (ख्या being substituted for it). The न्यासकार remarks संपूर्वस्य ख्यातेः प्रयोगो नास्ति. समाधि—concentration or resting the mind on one object. भेद—disturbance of. Śl. quoted in D.-R. as an instance of सत्त्व (विकारहेतौ सत्यप्यविकारकं सत्त्वं that quality of the mind which does not allow its equilibrium to be disturbed even in the presence of causes of disturbance), and in S.-D. as one of धैर्य or firmness (व्यवसायादचलनं धैर्यं विघ्ने महत्यपि).

Śl. 41. लतागृह—लता एव लतामयं वा गृहं लतागृहं &c. नन्दी—one of the principal Gaṇas and the door-keeper of Śiva. He is a part-manifestation of Śiva and the son of Sâlaṅkâyana (also called Śaláka; see Śiv. P. Sa. Sam. Ch. 44). *Cf.* (महेश्वरः) सुन्दरं तु परं रूपं धृत्वा हस्तिमुखावहम् । शालङ्कायनपुत्रत्वं योगमायामुपाश्रितः ॥ In another Kalpa he was the son of शिलादमुनि. Sometimes three Nandis are mentioned—आद्यः कनकनन्दी च गिरिकाख्यो द्वितीयकः । सोमनन्दी तृतीयस्तु विज्ञेया नन्दिनस्त्रयः ॥ ०वेत्रः—वेत्र a cane-staff, the badge of a warder or door-keeper.

Śl. 42. निष्कम्पवृक्षं- On this Malli. remarks—इदमुद्भिज्जोपलक्षणं *i. e.* an indirect indication of all उद्भिज्ज (the vegetable kingdom). The four classes of generation are—नृगवाद्या जरायुजाः (viviparous); स्वेदजाः (born from moisture) कृमिदंशाद्याः पक्षिसर्पाद्या अण्डजाः (oviparous—born of eggs); उद्भिदस्तरुगुल्माद्याः ।

Amara. निभृत—still, silent. चित्रार्पितारम्भं—आरम्यत इति आरम्भः action; रभ् + अ (घञ् कर्मणि); *cf.* Ragh. II. 31. It appears that at Nandî's command all creatures and things just stood in the condition they were in, so that their actions were transferred to a painting, as it were. Before Nandî gave the command, the trees were shaken by the Malaya breeze, the bees were astir, moving from flower to flower, the birds being impassioned were singing and the excited deer were moving about (*supra* Śl. 31).

Śl. 43. दृष्टिप्रपातं—प्रपतत्यतेऽस्मिन्निति प्रपातः; पत् + घञ् (अ) अधिकरणे; दृष्टेः प्रपातः दृष्टिप्रपातः the place where the eye would fall; hence the range of the eye. ०प्रतीपं—*V. l.* the opposite part or front of. पुरःशुक्रं—may also mean the planet Venus shining in the front (पुरः संमुखे स्थितं शुक्रम्). Nár. quotes मुहूर्तशास्त्र—आग्नेयाद्यास्तारकाः साभिजित्काः प्रागाद्याशाः संस्थिताः सप्त सप्त। यस्यां तिष्ठेद्भार्गवो दिश्यमुष्यां यात्रा पुंसां प्राणमानार्थहन्त्री ॥ प्रान्तेषु—All the sides of the place where Śiva was sitting. Nameru trees had formed an arbour there, their branches forming a canopy. This shows that it was a good place for Káma to hide himself from Śiva.

Śl. 44. देवदारुद्रुम०—देवदारुः द्रुमः तस्य वेदिका (a dais or raised ground near the root) शिलादिभिर्बद्धे मूलप्रदेशे इत्यर्थः। Nár. देवदारुद्रुमाणामधोभागविरचितस्थण्डिले Châr. त्रियम्बकं—for त्र्यम्बकं to meet the exigencies of the metre, by poetical licence (or through inadvertence); the form त्रियम्बक is considered छान्दस; *cf.* Patañjali on the Vârttika इयङादिप्रकरणे तन्वादीनां छन्दसि बहुलम्—तन्वं पुषेम, तनुवं पुषेम; विष्वं पश्य, विषुवं पश्य; स्वर्गं लोकं, सुवर्गं लोकं; त्र्यम्बकं यजामहे, त्रियम्बकं यजामहे ॥ Such a deviation from grammar is excusable in the case of great sages and authors. Such instances are not very rare in Kâli.; see our note on तं पातयां प्रथममास Ragh. IX. 61. The use of some such epithet as त्र्यम्बकं is necessary after ०शरीरपातः to account for it. One Calc. commentator reads तं त्र्यम्बकं, but तं has no propriety here. Malli. must have been quite sure of his reading as the genuine one and hence his remark केचित्साहसिकाः &c. The following six Ślokas are to be taken with this, the seven ślokas thus forming what is called a *Kulaka*; द्वाभ्यां युग्ममिति प्रोक्तं त्रिभिः श्लोकैर्विशेषकम्। कलापकं चतुर्भिः स्यात्तदूर्ध्वं कुलकं स्मृतम् ॥

Śl. 45. पर्यङ्कबन्ध—पर्यङ्कस्य बन्धः; now see com.; पर्यङ्क also called Vîrâsana or the heroic posture, is one of the postures assumed by ascetics when practising contemplation. See Malli. Śiva sat in that posture, with the upper half of his body drawn straight up and motionless, the shoulders a little depressed owing to the lotus-like palms with their concave surfaces turned upwards being placed on the lap. The palms were placed one over the other. Some take पर्यङ्क in the sense of उत्तरासङ्ग, an upper garment or a piece of cloth worn round the loins (परिकर). *Cf.* वैकक्षमुत्तरासङ्गः प्रोक्ता बृहतिका तथा । पर्यस्तिका परिकरः पर्यङ्कश्चेति कथ्यते ॥ इति हलायुधः । Some say पर्यङ्कस्य योगपट्टस्य बन्धः योगपट्टेन पृष्ठजानुजङ्घाबन्धनम् । The Com. Ava. reads ऋज्वायतांसं० and explains ऋजू सरलौ आयतौ दीर्घौ, आ ईषत्संनमितौ उभौ अंसौ यस्य । समकायं सुखासीनं समाधिस्थं महेश्वरम् । Bra. P. *Cf.* पर्यङ्कग्रन्थिबद्धद्विगुणितभुजगाश्लेषसंवीतजानोरन्तःप्राणावरोधव्युपरतसकलज्ञानरुद्धेन्द्रियस्य । आत्मन्यात्मानमेव व्यपगतकरणं पश्यतस्तत्त्वदृष्ट्या शंभोर्वः पातु शून्येक्षणघटितलयब्रह्मलग्नः समाधिः ॥ Mr. ch. I. 1.

Śl. 46. भुजङ्गम—भुजं वक्रं गच्छतीति, भुज+गम्+खच् (अ); see *supra* II. 38. भुजङ्गमेन वासुकिना Châr. द्विगुणा०—द्वौ गुणौ परिवृत्ती यस्य तद् द्विगुणं; कर्णे (on the right ear) अवसक्तं द्विगुणमक्षसूत्रं यस्य. अक्षसूत्रं—Madhyamapadalopî comp. अक्ष is a seed of which rosaries are made (also called रुद्राक्ष). प्रभासङ्ग०—प्रभाभ्यङ्ग *v. l.* कण्ठप्रभायाः अभ्यङ्गेन व्याप्त्या by being covered with; here अभ्यङ्ग has no propriety and it has to be taken in its secondary sense. ग्रन्थिमती—Having knots (which held it round the neck).

Śl. 47. किंचित्प्रकाश—Because the eyes were only slightly opened. विरत०—On account of the absence of all emotions. प्रसङ्ग—effort, intentness or operation. लक्ष्यी०—See Malli.; also समं कायशिरोग्रीवं धारयन्नचलं स्थिरः । संप्रेक्ष्य नासिकाग्रं स्वं दिशश्चानवलोकयन् ॥ Bg. VI. 13. *Cf.* ददर्श तत्र चेशानं नासाग्रकृतलोचनम् । Brah. P.

Śl. 48. अवृष्टि०—वृष्ट्यां संरम्भः (an impetuous effort) वृष्टिसं०, न विद्यते वृष्टिसंरम्भो यस्य not going to pour down rain; this shows that the प्राणवायु was restrained in its sphere and not allowed to go down; see Malli. अपामिव &c.—*Cf.* सुप्तमीन इव ह्रदः Ragh. I. 73. This shows that *apána* was restrained in its place. see Malli. Some *yogins* do this; see the quotation from Bg. अन्तश्चराणां मरुतां—These are five in number, *viz.*—हृदि प्राणो गुदेऽपानः समानो नाभिसंस्थितः । उदानः कण्ठदेशस्थो व्यानः सर्वशरीरगः ॥ निरोधात्—The restraining of. *Cf.* अपाने जुह्वति प्राणं प्राणेऽपानं तथा परे । प्राणापानगती रुद्ध्वा प्राणायामपरायणाः । अपरे नियताहाराः प्राणान्प्राणेषु जुह्वति । Bg. IV. 29, 30. निवात &c.—*cf.* यथा दीपो निवातस्थो नेङ्गते सोपमा स्मृता । योगिनो यतचित्तस्य युञ्जतो योगमात्मनः ॥ Bg. VI. 19.

Śl. 49. कपालनेत्र—escaping through the hole of the eye of the skull of Brahman worn by Śiva on his head; see *infra*, VII. 32.

शिरस्तः—*i. e.* from the ब्रह्मरन्ध्र or an aperture on the crown of the head which is said to be extremely brilliant and which is connected with the Sushumṇá. Yogins, with breath restrained, kindle the fiery energy in them, make it pass through the Kuṇḍalinî, then through the central vein, Sushumṇâ, and then carrying it successively through the navel region, the heart and the middle of the eye-brows, finally cause it to issue out of the Brahmarandhra. See Pát. Yog. S. III. 32 and com. on it.

Śl. 50. नवद्वार०—The nine gates (openings in the body) through which the mind has communication with the external world. These are—द्वे श्रोत्रे द्वे चक्षुषी द्वे नासिके च मुखमेकमिति शीर्षस्थानि सप्त द्वे पायूपस्थे अधःस्थे इति नव छिद्ररूपाणि द्वाराणि देहे सन्ति । 'नयनश्रवणे द्वे द्वे नासिके वदनं तथा। पायूपस्थौ च देहेऽस्मिन्नवद्वाराणि देहिनाम्' ॥ The mind must be made अन्तर्मुख (*i. e.* turned inward from external objects). हृदि—The abode and resting place of the mind; see com. अक्षर—*Lit.* not decaying, immutable, the Supreme Soul or कूटस्थ ब्रह्म. *Cf.* अक्षरं ब्रह्म परमम् Bg. VIII. 3; द्वाविमौ पुरुषौ लोके क्षरश्चाक्षर एव च। क्षरः सर्वाणि भूतानि कूटस्थोऽक्षर उच्यते ॥ *Ibid.* XV. 16. क्षेत्रविदः—Those who know the body, *i. e.* its real nature and functions; hence, men learned in the Brahma-lore, also called शारीरकशास्त्र. *Cf.* इदं शरीरं कौन्तेय क्षेत्रमित्यभिधीयते । एतद्यो वेत्ति तं प्राहुः क्षेत्रज्ञ इति तद्विदः ॥ तत्क्षेत्रं यच्च यादृक् च यद्विकारि यतश्च यत् । स च यो यत्प्रभावश्च तत्समासेन मे शृणु ॥ महाभूतान्यहंकारो बुद्धिरव्यक्तमेव च । इन्द्रियाणि दशैकं च पञ्च चेन्द्रियगोचराः ॥ इच्छा द्वेषः सुखं दुःखं संघातश्चेतना धृतिः । एतत्क्षेत्रं समासेन सविकारमुदाहृतम् ॥ Bg. XIII. 1, 3, 5, 6.

Śl. 51. तथाभूतं—*i. e.* sitting in an awe-inspiring posture as described above. अधृष्यं—Not to be assailed even in thought; *cf.* सा दुष्प्रधर्षा मनसापि हिंस्रैः Ragh. II. 27. स्रस्त—With its nervous power lost, drooping, utterly unnerved.

Śl. 52. निर्वाण०—Conspicuous or great by its extinction, *i. e.* greatly, almost destroyed; Malli. We may also take the comp. as निर्वाणं भूयिष्ठं यस्य on the analogy of अभिरूपभूयिष्ठा Śák. or उदितभूयिष्ठः Mál.-Mádh. I., the comp. being reckoned as one of the आहिताग्नि class, where we have अग्न्याहित also. Mark the *p. p. p.* of वा with निर् which is निर्वाण when 'wind' is not the subject, निर्वाणोऽग्निर्मुनिश्च । वाते तु निर्वातो वातः । Sid.-Kau. संधुक्षयन्ती—stirring up, reviving; the word is appropriate as Kâma's वीर्य is compared to fire, as suggested by the use of the word निर्वाण. वपुर्गुण—the excellence (charms or grace) of her person. वनदेवताभ्यां—These were her friends, already referred to in I. 58, where Malli. gives their names as Jayá and Vijayá; Ar. and Nâr. give them as विजया and मालिनी (एते च विजया मालिनी चेति प्रसिद्धे); they are called वनदे॰ because all the females of the city of Himálaya were such ; see VI. 39 *infra*.

Śl. 53. Here it will be seen that Párvatî had put on a simple dress and worn sylvan ornaments in place of costly jewel-ornaments she wore in her father's house. Thus she wore a wreath of Aśoka flowers in place of rubies &c. This is poetically described here. अशोक—*i. e.* the red Aśoka. The Aśoka flowers were so fresh and deep-red as to throw into shade the rubies. "The vegetable world scarcely exhibits a richer sight than an Aśoka tree in full blossom." Sir W. Jones. पद्मराग—पद्मस्य इव रागो यस्य। आकृष्ट॰—possessed; from this it appears that the Karnikára flowers were yellowish red; *cf.* सुपुष्पितांस्तु पश्यैतान्कर्णिकारान्समन्ततः । हाटकप्रतिसंछन्नान्नरान्पीताम्बरानिव ॥ Râmâ. Kiś. K. I. 1. Women are described as wearing these flowers in their hair; *cf.* कर्णेषु योग्यं नवकर्णिकारं चलेषु नीलेष्वलकेष्वशोकम् &c. Rit. VI. 5. आकृष्ट *v. l.*—condemned or censured, *i. e.* put into the background. This at first sight seems to be a better reading as better agreeing with निर्भर्त्सित in the previous line. But the poet does not seem to mean this. He describes the Aśoka flowers as prominently attracting attention first, and so they are described as निर्भर्त्सित &c. Secondly, he describes the Karnikára flowers as resembling gold ornaments, while he describes the wreath of Sinduvâra flowers as exactly filling the place of a pearl necklace. In the D.-R. also we have the reading आकृष्ट. मुक्ता॰—The wreath of Sindh.-flowers served as a thick necklace of pearls. Śl. quoted in D.-R. as an instance of वेषविभाव.

Śl. 54. तरुणार्क॰—She wore a red garment as befitting the Vasanta dress ; *cf.* अरुणरागनिषेधिभिरंशुकैः Ragh. IX. 43. आवर्जिता &c—*Cf.* स्तोकनम्रा स्तनाभ्याम् Megh. II. 22; Rat. I. 1, 16. पर्याप्त—Fat and round. सुजात *v. l.*, read by Ar., does not explain the अवनम्रत्व. पल्लविनी—richly covered all over with red foliage.

Śl. 55. न्यासीकृतां—Deposited there so that he may have it ready for use when required. स्थान॰—That is the नितम्ब which was the proper place for it (as assisting in exciting passion); *cf.* व्याजार्धसंदर्शितमेखलानि Ragh. XIII. 42. Śl. quoted in K.-P. with the reading द्वितीयमौर्वीमिव as an instance of the fault अविमृष्टविधेयांश 'the not-mentioning of the emphatic prominently.' Here द्वितीय is emphatic, and should not have been compounded. अत्र द्वितीयत्वमात्रमुत्प्रेक्ष्यम् । मौर्वीं द्वितीयामिति तु युक्तः पाठः । स्थानविदा स्वाभ्रभूता पार्वत्येव स्वीयमौर्वीस्थापनस्थानमिति जानता।

मन्नाशेऽपि अनयैव शिवं वशीकरिष्यामीति जानता वा । आश्रयगुणप्रकर्षेणाधेयगुणप्रकर्ष इति योग्यमिदं स्थानामीति जानता वा । अत्र मौर्वीपदादेव कार्मुकसंबन्धे लब्धे कार्मुकपदमयुक्तम् । Uddyota. Nár. does not think this criticism to be just. He says—न चात्र द्वितीयात्वमात्रमुपेक्ष्यमपि तु स्मरेण न्यासीकृतत्वं मौर्वीत्वं च । तत्र मौर्वीत्वोत्प्रेक्षयैव तदितरोत्प्रेक्षासिद्धिरिति मौर्वीत्वमेवात्र विधेयांश इति नाविमृष्टविधेयांशत्वदोषः ।

Śl. 56. सुगन्धि०—शोभनः गन्धः अस्यास्तीति सुगन्धिः । सुगन्धिः निःश्वासः; now see com.; the comp. may also be taken as ०निःश्वासे विवृद्धा तृष्णा यस्य. संभ्रम—confusion due to fear. बिम्बाधरा०—Notice the comp.; it may also be taken as बिम्बाकारः अधरः; see com.; otherwise we shall get अधरबिम्ब. *Cf.* the similar description of a bee that hovered round Śak.'s lip. लीलारविन्दं—लीलाया (लीलार्थे) अरविन्दं ; तादर्थ्ये षष्ठीसमासः (and not च. त.) प्रकृतिविकृतेरभावात्. Persons of either sex are represented as having a sportive lotus in the hand. *Cf.* लीलाकमलपत्राणि गणयामास पार्वती । *infra* VI. 84. काश्चित्क-राभ्यामुपगूढनालमालोलपत्राभिहतद्विरेफम् । रजोभिरन्तःपरिवेषबन्धि लीलारविन्दं भ्रमयांचकार ॥ Ragh. VI. 13. हस्ते लीलाकमलमलके बालकुन्दानुविद्धं &c. Megh. II. 2. अत्रान्तरे हरमुपासितुमभ्ययासीद्वासन्तिकप्रसवकाल्पितमण्डनश्रीः । शृङ्गारवीरतपसामधिदेवतेव साकं सखीभिरवनीधरराजकन्या ॥ Pár. P.

Sl. 57. अनवद्या—अवद्य what deserves condemnation or reproach. वद् preceded by the negative particle takes यत् only in the sense of गर्हा, by अवद्यपण्यवर्या गर्ह्यपणितव्यानिरोधेषु । Pâṇ. III. 1. 101. अवद्यं पापम् । गर्ह्यं किम् । अनुद्यं (not to be uttered out of respect) गुरुनाम । Sid.-Kau. रतेरपि—*Cf.* for a similar idea but more forcibly expressed, प्रत्यादेशो रूपगर्वितायाः श्रियः Vik. I. ह्रीपदं—the object, *i. e.* cause, of shame; ह्रीतिं—*V. l.* shame (fr. ह्री + ति); ह्रीमतिं—*v. l.* sense of shame (लज्जाबुद्धिं). शूलिनि—पुष्पचापः—The two epithets explain why Kâma had lost hope of success :—The one armed with the well-known trident, the other, with a flowery bow.

Śl. 58. च च—show simultaneousness of both the actions. योग—ध्यान which is defined as 'तत्र प्रत्ययैकतानता ध्यानम्' Pát. Yog. S. III. 2; *i. e.*, the state of having one object only present to the mind continuously to the exclusion of every other thought; concentration of the mind on one object only. अन्तः—*i. e.* हृदयकुहरे in the cavity of the heart; *cf.* अथ यदिदमस्मिन्ब्रह्मपुरे दहरं पुण्डरीकं वेश्म &c. Chhân. Up. VIII. 1. 1.

Sl. 59. कथंचित्—As the pent-up vital airs were released, the downward pressure was so great that S'esha for the time found the task of supporting the earth very difficult. *Cf.* for a similar idea Śiś. I. 13. प्राणविमुक्तिः—*i. e.* by exhaling the breath through one nostril, so as to allow the five *práṇas* to perform their usual functions. निबिडं—very close, so as to leave no cavity (अच्छिद्रं).

Śl. 60. शुश्रूषया—with the object of serving;—noun in आ from the desid. base of श्रु. एनां—Properly एतां should have been used; but the optional form is sometimes used even when there is no अन्वादेश (see Gr § 137) as in अथैनमद्रेस्तनया शुशोच Ragh. II. 37; तदेनमुल्लङ्घितशासनं विधेः Śiś. I. 73. भ्रूक्षेप०—भ्रुवः क्षेपः भ्रूक्षेपः भ्रूक्षेप एव भ्रूक्षेपमात्रं; now see com.

Śl 61. शिशिरात्यय—Properly, the passing of the winter-season; hence, the succeeding season. पुष्पोच्चयः—As the flowers were plucked with the hand, this should be पुष्पोच्चायः; hence Malli.'s remark हस्तादाने &c. Vámana calls this the play of childish ignorance—अवतरावचायशब्दयोर्दीर्घह्रस्वत्वव्यत्यासो बालानाम् । Kâv.-Sâu. The insertion of what looks like a Vârttika in the Káśiká, *viz.* उच्चयस्य प्रतिषेधो वक्तव्यः is an interpolation. In the sense of 'collection' we have चयः. त्र्यम्बक—त्रीणि अम्बकानि यस्य । or त्रयाणां लोकानां (ब्रह्मविष्णुशिवानां Ved.) पिता इति वा; or त्रीन् लोकान् अम्बते शब्दायते इति ।

Śl. 62. नीलालक०—The dark hair set off the Karṇikâra of golden hue. विस्रंसयन्ती—causing it to drop down; this shows that Pâr. bent her head very low in reverence to Siva.

Śl. 63. तथ्य—तथा सत्ये साधु. भव्यं—*v. l.* what was sure to come to pass; न केवलमाचारसिद्धं किं तु भावि. न हीश्वर—*Cf.* न हीश्वराणां व्याहृतयो व्यभिचरन्ति । Pâr. P. II. ऋषीणां पुनराद्यानां वाचमर्थोऽनुधावति Uttar. I. 10. लोके—पाके *v. l.* परिणामे in their result.

Śl. 64. बाणावसर—The fit time for discharging the arrow. उमासमक्षं—for the comp. see com ; *i. e.* white Umá stood near, as her presence would aid the action of his arrow. *cf.* कामो धनुषि संयोज्य पुष्पबाणं तदा मुने । पार्वतीसंमुखे स्थाणौ मोक्तुकामो व्यवस्थितः ॥ Ś. P.

Śl. 65. उपनिन्ये—The A'tm. is used as the fruit of the action is intended to be enjoyed by the agent (कर्त्रभिप्राये क्रियाफले तङ्); for the Par. use *cf.* स न्यस्तशस्त्रो हरये स्वदेहमुपानयत्पिण्डमिवामिषस्य । Ragh II. 59. गिरिशाय—The dat. by the rule कर्मणा यमभिप्रैति स संप्रदानम् ।. गौरी—योगाग्निदग्धदेहा सा पुनर्जाता हिमालये । शङ्खेन्दुकुन्दधवला ततो गौरी तु सा स्मृता ॥ पुष्करबीज०—*i. e.* पद्माक्षमाला.

Śl. 66. प्रणयिप्रियत्वात्—This must be taken in a general sense although Párvatî is the offerer here; प्रणयिनः प्रिया यस्य स प्रणयिप्रियस्तस्य भावः प्र०त्वम् ; also प्रियप्रणयित्वं as प्रिय takes परनिपात optionally. Or प्रणयिनि प्रियत्वं तस्मात्. It cannot be dissolved as प्रणयिनी प्रिया यस्य, as in that case we shall get प्रणयिनीप्रिय०, the पुंवद्भाव being precluded by Pâṇ. VI. 3. 35. उपचक्रमे—क्रम् with उप is A'tm. संमोहनं—One of the five arrows of Káma ; संमोहनस्तापनश्च शोषणः स्तम्भनस्तथा । उन्मादनश्च कामस्य पञ्च बाणाः प्रकीर्तिताः ॥ Nár. gives them differently, as द्रावणः क्षोभणश्चैव वशीकरण इत्यपि । आकर्षणश्च कामस्य बाणः संमोहनोऽपरः ॥ च च—show that the two actions were in immediate succession. धनुष्यमोघं &c.—*Cf.* Ragh. III. 53. The fig. of speech is समुच्चय.

Śl. 67. परिलुप्त—परिवृत्त *v. l.* turned back, changed. धैर्य—(1) Firmness of mind; (2) स्थैर्य motionlessness of water. चन्द्रोदयारम्भे—when the flood-tide sets in. अम्बुराशिः—The comparision implies that though Hara allowed his mind to be ruffled a little he was not to transgress the bounds of steadiness (as the sea does not its). *Cf.* एतस्मिन्नन्तरे देवो विकासितविलोचनः । सस्मार नगराजस्य तनयां रक्तमानसः ॥ Brahma P. as quoted by D. बिम्बफला°—The comp. is like बिम्बाधर, *supra* Śl. 56;—shows that it deserved such an attention from Śiva. Śl. quoted (1) in D.-R. as an instance of भाव or the first manifestation of the feeling of love in the mind; (2) in S.-D. as an instance of उद्बुद्धमात्रस्थायिभाव (the permanent feeling, *i. e.* रति, just manifested); and (3) in K.-P. IV. as of संदिग्धप्राधान्यव्यङ्ग्यकाव्य; अत्र परिचुम्बितुमैच्छदिति किं प्रतीयमानं किं वा विलोचनव्यापारणं वाच्यं प्रधानमिति संदेहः । विलोचनानीति बहुवचनेन उत्कण्ठातिशयो व्यज्यते । Com.

Śl. 68. विवृण्वती—Manifesting, betraying. भावं—The feeling of love first striking root in her mind (हृदयाभिप्रायं); कामाभिलाषं Châr. स्फुरद्बाल°—कचित् *v. l.* for स्फुरत् is to be taken with तस्थौ. बालकदम्ब—*i. e* the buds; the reading कुचद्बाल° of Ar. and Nár. does not give a good sense; Nâr. says कुचन्तः संकुन्चतः संकुचत्पुष्पा इत्यर्थः; *i. e.* closing flowers and therefore looking bud-like; but then these would not stand straight like fresh buds The comparison is based on the fact of Pârvatî's hair suddenly standing on end just like the Kadamba's suddenly putting forth buds on being sprinkled with the drops of water of the first thunder-cloud. The comparison is common enough. *Cf.* प्रथमप्रियावचनसंश्रवस्फुरत्पुलकेन संप्रति मया विडम्ब्यते । घनबद्धनूतनपयःसमुक्षणक्षणबद्धकुड्मलकदम्बडम्बरः ॥ Mâl.-Mádh. III. 7. सस्वेदरोमाञ्चितकम्पिताङ्गी जाता प्रियस्पर्शसुखेन वत्सा । मरुन्नवाम्भःप्रविधूतसिक्ता कदम्बयष्टिः स्फुटकोरकेव ॥ Uttar. III. 42. साचीकृता—made to stand turning sideways; fr. साचि *ind.* obliquely, in a side-long manner; the reading साचिक्रियाचारु° of Ar. and Nâr. is better; the face looked more graceful on account of its turning sideways. *Cf.* निनाय साचीकृतचारुवक्त्रः । Ragh. VI. 14. Also Mâlav. IV. 15. (साचीकरोत्याननम्) and न च प्रियेष्वायतलोचनानां

समग्रपातीनि विलोचनानि *Ibid.* 8. पर्यस्त०—पर्यस्त cast aside or turned back; it may also mean 'bent down;' पर्यस्तः पतिते हते । Medinî. Śl. quoted as an instance of अशब्दा शृङ्गारप्रतीति by अनुरागजन्यावस्थाविशेषानुभाववद्विभावोपवर्णन in D.-R. and of हाव (भाव एवाल्पसंलक्ष्यविकारः) in S.-D. *Cf.* also तदनु युगपदीशः पार्वतीवक्त्रपद्मे स्मितविकसितगण्डे प्राहिणोल्लोचनानि । पुलकिततनुरन्तर्भावमावेदयन्ती दरमुदितमुखेन्दुः सा च सव्रीडमस्थात् ॥ Pár. P. III. ७.

Śl. 69. इन्द्रिय—इन्द्रस्य आत्मनः लिङ्गम् fr. इन्द्र + इय; that which is a sign, *i. e.*, leads to the inference of the existence of the soul (इन्द्र आत्मा स चक्षुरादिना करणेनानुमीयते । नाकर्तृकं करणमस्ति Vâmana). See our note on the word, Ragh. I. 55. Or इन्द्रेणात्मना दुर्जयं Sid.-Kau. ०क्षोभं—The senses are often compared to horses which if not properly governed, would prove restive. इन्द्रियाणि हयानाहु Kathop.; मा भूवन्नपथहरास्तवेन्द्रियाश्वाः । Kir. V. 50 वशित्वं—वश अस्यास्तीति वशी तस्य भावः । The state of having self-control; by virtue of his power to control his senses. अत्र शान्तरसव्यभिचारिण्या मतेरुदय इन्द्रियक्षोभनियमने हेतुः । क्षोभकारणदर्शनौत्सुक्यं तादृश्या मतेर्व्यभिचारि दृष्टिविसर्गस्तस्या अनुभावः इति विवेकः । Nâr. *Cf.* हरस्तु धैर्यमालम्ब्य किमेतदिति चिन्तयन् । ददर्श पृष्ठतः कामं पुष्पबाणधनुर्धरम् ॥ ततो भगवानन्तःकरणविक्रियां तपोबलेन संयम्य तत्कारणाय विश्वग्विलोचनानि व्यापारितवान् । Pâr. P.

Śl. 70. दक्षिणा०—अपाङ्गति तिर्यक् चलति नेत्रं यत्रासौ अपाङ्गः; the corner of the eye; this shows that the bow was drawn to its utmost. चारु—attractive because made of flowers (and not fierce). आत्मयोनि—आत्मा चित्तं (the mind) योनिर्यस्य; आत्मा चित्ते धृतौ यत्ने धिषणायां कलेवरे । इति हेमचन्द्रः । Mark this meaning of आत्मन्; *cf.* मनोभूः; आत्मयोनि more usually means, 'the self-born', ब्रह्मा; *cf.* ब्रह्मात्मभूः &c. Ak. Malli. says that Kâma was here in the आलीढ posture which is one of the five attitudes assumed by archers when striking. आलीढ is one in which the right foot is advanced and the left one drawn in and contracted; प्रत्यालीढ is the reverse of this; समान is with the two feet evenly placed, वैशाख with the feet a span apart, and मण्डल is with both the knees bent. *Cf.* आरादपश्यदधिसंहितमोहनास्त्रं कर्णावतंसपदकल्पितकार्मुकज्यम् । आकुञ्चितैकपदमञ्चितपूर्वकायं लक्ष्यीकृतात्मवपुषं मदनं महेशः ॥ Pár. P.

Śl. 71. परामर्श—Properly an attack on; hence disturbance. भ्रूभङ्ग—Contraction of the eye-brows; frowning. दुष्प्रेक्ष्य—fr. प्र + ईक्ष् + ण्यत्; दुःखेन प्रेक्ष्यः, कुगतिप्रादयः इति समासः । अत्र स्फुरन् उदर्चिः निष्पपातेति पदत्रयेण कृशानुस्वभावसिद्धः क्रमो विवक्षितः । Nâr. *Cf.* विवृद्धमन्योस्तस्याथ तृतीयनयनान्मुने । स्फुरन्नुदर्चिरग्निस्तु पपात मदनोपरि ॥ S. P.

Śl. 72. यावत्—So soon as; just as; *i. e.* both the actions took place simultaneously. स वह्निः—the word कृशानु, 'the reducer' would have been more appropriate here. *Cf.* क्रोधं संहर हे देव इति यावद्वदन्ति खे । इन्द्रादिसकला देवास्तावद्भस्मीचकार तम् ॥ तदा स भगवान् शंभुः पृष्ठभागे ददर्श ह । धनुर्धरं हि पुरुषं तं ददाहाक्षिवह्निना ॥ Ś. P. Śl. quoted in the K. P. VII. to show that anger, without its external signs such as the knitting of the eye-brows &c., and producing an instantaneous effect, may properly be represented concerning the divines only (इत्युक्तवदनभ्रुकुट्यादिविकारवर्जितः क्रोधः सद्यःफलदो दिव्येष्वेव).

Śl. 73. अभिषङ्ग—From सञ्ज् with अभि; *lit.* that which closely sticks to the heart, *i. e.* is keenly felt; hence, here, a terrible calamity, a sudden blow. मोहेन—one of the eight Sáttvika *bhâvas* and an accessory of Karuṇa. संस्तम्भयता—She was stunned by the blow and became unconscious. कृतोप०—Because the trance she was in did not allow her to feel the poignant pain to be caused by the calamity. *Cf.* तस्याः सुमित्रात्मजयत्नलब्धो मोहादभूत्कष्टतरः प्रबोधः । Ragh. XIV. 56. Śl. quoted in the D.-R. and S.-D. as an instance of मोह (मोहो विचित्तता भीतिदुःखावेशानुचिन्तनैः ।)

Śl. 74 वनस्पति—वनस्य पतिः; the स् comes in when वन is followed by पति; Pâṇ. VI. 1. 157. Here it means 'a tree.' *Cf.* वनस्पतिर्ना द्रुमात्रे विना पुष्पं फलिद्रुमे । वज्र इव—Like a stroke of thunderbolt; the *Upamána* shows the insignificance of Káma before Śiva. स्त्रीसंनि०—Because he thought that the present obstacle was due to Pârvatî's presence there. सभूतः—भूतैः (his followers, the *gaṇas*) सहितः. *Cf.* उपस्थितं विघ्नमिमं ज्ञात्वा च चन्द्रशेखरः । ततश्चान्तर्दधे सोऽपि भगवान्प्रमथैः सह ॥

Śl. 75. उच्छिरस्—(1) उन्नतं शिरः शृङ्गं यस्य—having high peaks; (2) उद्गतं शिरः अस्य—he who can hold up his head on account of his noble deeds; hence, noble, great; hence also, one who would feel the disappointment more bitterly. व्यर्थ—Because she knew that she could not make conquest of Śiva's heart either by her personal charms or by the high position of her father. सख्योः—see com. समक्षं—अक्ष्णोः समीपे; see Várt. on Páṇ. V. 4. 107. शून्या—dejected, down-cast, vacant-minded. Śl. quoted in Sar.-Kaṇ. as an instance of Mánitá.

Śl. 76. सपदि—goes with आदाय. अनुकम्प्यां—Because she did not deserve to be discomfited like that. प्रतिपथ०—a Prádi Tat.; see com प्रतिपथ+आ *fem.*; the final अ is added to पथिन् by the rule ऋक्पूरब्धूःपथामानक्षे । दीर्घीकृताङ्ग—As a divine being he had that power *V. l.* ०कृताभ्रः—lengthening the clouds—has no propriety. *Cf.* आगत्य दोर्भ्यामादाय मूर्च्छामुकुलितेक्षणा । नीता निताम्तवात्सल्याद्गौरी हिमवता गृहम् ॥ Pâr. P.

CANTO IV.

Śl. 1. मोहपरायणा—Who was solely in the power of or under the protection of, (totally had lost), consciousness. प्रतिपादयिष्यता—wishing to explain to her or make her understand; hence, to make her experience; or, wishing to give, *i. e.* teach her; प्रतिपादनं तु दाने प्रतिपत्तौ प्रबोधने । इति मेदिनी ।

Śl. 2. अवधानपरे—attentively fixed; *i. e.* in order to see where her husband was (for she had only seen the terrible fire dart forth from Śiva's eyes when she fell into the swoon). प्रलय—the swoon she was in. अतृप्तयोः—not satisfied with looking, *i. e.* she kept on looking for Káma (दर्शनोत्सुकयोः सतोः इत्यर्थः). अत्यन्त—utterly, *i. e.* for ever. *Cf.* अत्यन्तलुप्तप्रियदर्शनेन Ragh. XIV. 49; सा चात्यन्तमदर्शनं नयनयोर्यातेति कोऽयं विधिः । Vik. IV. 2.

Śl. 3. अयि—see Malli.; कोमलामन्त्रणे वा. पुरुषाकृतिः—*V. l.* here the cons. is तया पुरुषाकृतिः ददृशे । कीदृशी सा—केवलं हरकोपानलभस्म एव. It was simply the ashes of the fire. Śl. quoted in the D.-R. as an instance of (इष्टनाशात्करुण) the Karuṇa *rasa* consequent on the destruction of a beloved person (इष्टनाशादनिष्टाप्तौ शोकात्मा करुणः).

Śl. 4. समदुःखामिव &c.—स्थली by Lakshaṇá means the 'plants and creatures in that place,' poetically represented as sharing Rati's grief; *cf.* अकरोत्पृथिवीरुहानपि स्रुतशाखारसबाष्पदुर्दिनान् । Ragh. VIII. 70; गुरुतरशोकोपहता कुररीव प्रियवियोगमापन्ना । आक्रन्ददार्तनादं बाष्पस्नपितोन्नतस्तनी बाला ॥ Pár. P. III. 11. For the idea, *cf.* also Śák. त्वयोपस्थितवियोगस्य तपोवनस्यापि समवस्था दृश्यते । उद्गलितदर्भकवला मृग्यः परित्यक्तनर्तना मयूराः । अपसृतपाण्डुपत्रा मुञ्चन्त्यश्रूणीव लताः ॥ IV. 12; see also Ragh. XIV. 69.

Śl. 5. उपमान—Standard of comparison; *cf.* I. 36. उपमानस्यापि सखे प्रत्युपमानं वपुस्तस्याः । Vik. II. 3. विलासिनां—विलासः अस्यास्तीति विलासी; for Viláea see com.; or विलासो भूषणालापगतिकर्मसु चारुता the gracefulness of ornamentation, sweetness of address, a charming gait and action. This is the meaning here. It is elsewhere defined as प्रियसमीपगमने यः स्थानासनगमनविलोकितेषु विकारोऽकस्माच्च क्रोधस्मितचमत्कारमुखविकूवनं स विलासः; *i. e.* the sudden change of place, posture, gait, or look, as also the manifestation of feigned anger, smile &c., on the approach of, or on approaching, a lover. कान्तिमत्तया—अतिशयिना प्रशस्ता वा कान्तिरस्यास्तीति कान्तिमत् तस्य भावः कान्तिमत्ता तया । न विदीर्ये &c.—which she ought to have done as a Pativratâ. *Cf.* the śl. आर्तार्ते मुदिते &c quoted by Malli. further on (sl. 33); and the similar thoughts of Sítá मनो मे न विना

रामायत्पुरफोट सहस्रधा । &c. Bhaṭṭi. XIV. 56; also 57, 58; and *infra* notes on Śl. 21. The form विदार्य must be explained by taking दॄ as a root of the 4th Conj. although not actually given in the list, the one in the 1st & 9th Conj. being Paras.; the words of the भाष्यकार दृणातिर्दार्यतेर्वा justify such a supposition.

Śl. 6. स्वदधीन—त्वयि अधि स्वदधीनं; the aff. ख (ईन) is always added when अधि forms the latter part of a Loc. Tat. क्षण-भिन्न०—क्षणेन भिन्नं destroyed, lost, सौहृदं यस्य सः । *Cf.* कथमेकपदे निरागसं जनमाभाष्यमिमं न मन्यसे । Ragh. VIII. 48. सेतु०—सौहृद is here compared to *Setu* or a dam, the common ground of comparison being, as remarked by Malli., स्थितिहेतुत्व—the one keeping together Rati and Madana, the other, water and the lotus-plant. सौहृद—This is formed from सुहृदय which being mentioned in the युवादि group takes अण्; and by virtue of this its आदिवृद्धि and the substitution of हृत् for हृदय take place by the rule 'हृदय is changed to हृद् before the word लेख, the affixes यत् and अण् and before लास' (see com.); if हृदय be changed to हृद् in the sense of 'a friend' by Pâṇ. V. 4. 150, then अण् being added the form will be सौहार्द. See com. Malli. refers to Kâv. Sût. V. 2. 84. The absence of the उत्तरपदवृद्धि (*i. e.* हार्) should rather be explained by the general maxim संज्ञापूर्वको विधिरनित्यः ।

Śl. 7. कृतवानसि विप्रियं—*Cf.* मनसापि न विप्रियं मया कृतपूर्वं तव किं जहासि माम् । Ragh. VIII. 52. प्रतिकूलं—प्रतीपं कूलात्; against the bank or slope, against the current; contrary to one's wishes. *Cf.* 'When was the hour, I ever contradicted your desire,' Shaks. *Henry VIII.* II. 4. विलपन्त्यै—this implies—'this is no time for joke; show yourself to me at once.'

Śl. 8. Rati means to say that knowingly she had given Kâma no offence. But in their love-sports she had sometimes taken liberty with him and that might have displeased him. गोत्रस्खलितेषु—Lovers are often represented as misnaming their sweethearts or wives (calling them by the name uppermost in their minds), through absentmindedness while lost in thoughts about other ladies. *Cf.* गोत्रेषु स्खलितस्तदा भवति च व्रीडाविलक्षश्चिरम् । Śák. VI. 5; अज्ज जंणिमित्तं भट्टा उक्कण्ठिदी ताए इश्ि...ए णामधेएण भट्टिणा देवी आलविदा । Vik. II.; लोलुपं बत मनो ममेति तं गोत्रविस्खलितमूचुरङ्गनाः । Ragh. XIX. 24. बन्धनं—*Cf.* मेखलाभिरसकृच्च बन्धनं वञ्चयन्प्रणयिनीरवाप सः । Ragh. XIX. 17.

Śl. 9. वससि—the subj. is त्वं (addressed to Rati). कैतवं—कितवस्य भावः a false assertion made to mislead me; for this sense of कितव, *cf.* दृष्टः स्वप्ने कितव रमयन्कामपि त्वं मयेति । Megh. II. 51; for

कैतव, *cf.* ध्रुवमस्मि शठः शुचिस्मिते विदितः कैतववत्सलस्तव । Ragh. VIII. 49. Rati's idea is this—If she really lived in Káma's heart, as he would say she did, she should have been reduced to ashes along with his body. But she was safe; hence what he said was simply an empty compliment. Śl. quoted in Sar.-Kaṇ. as an instance of करुण.

Śl. 10. नवप्र०—Since you have recently gone I can find out you track. विधिना जन एष—Ar. and Nâr. take एष to refer to Rati. This person, *i. e.* myself, was deceived by Fate by causing me to be under the influence of a swoon (otherwise I should have followed you just then). But this is not a good way. For in the first part she says that she would follow him to the next world and so she would not be the sufferer. It is the people who would suffer. This is supported by the 4th line.

Śl. 11. रजनीतिमिरा०—*cf.* रुद्धालोके नरपतिपथे सूचिभेद्यैस्तमोभिः । Megh. I. 39. घनशब्द०—*cf* जलधर निर्लज्जस्त्वं...यन्मां स्तनितेन भीषयित्वा &c. Mṛich. V. 28; घनागमनसमये निरस्तमाना इति च व्यज्यते । Nâr. प्रियाः—the Abhisârikâs are meant here; *i. e.* damsels who being overpowered by love go to the residence of their lovers under the cover of nightly darkness (कामार्ताभिसरेत्कान्तं सारयेद्वाभिसारिका । D.-R.).

Śl. 12. पदे पदे—At every step; and, at each word. वारुणी—A kind of wine or spirit (prepared from hogweed ground with the juice of date or palm and then distilled. M.-W.). *Cf.* रागमादर्शयन्नेष वारुणीयोगवर्धितम् । तिरोभवति घर्मांशुरनङ्गश्च विजृम्भते ॥ Daṇḍin. प्रमदानां—Wine seems to have been freely used by young ladies in ancient times. It was thought that it improved their beauty by imparting a red flush to their cheeks and enabled them to better enjoy the company of their lovers or husbands. See Śiś. X. 19; Malli. refers to X. 33. See *infra* VII. 62. मद is defined as संमोहानन्दसंभेदो मदिरादिकृतो मदः ।

Śl. 13. कथीकृतं—Made the subject of stories, *i. e.* no longer in actual existence. प्रियबन्धोः—प्रिया बन्धवो यस्य; or प्रियश्चासौ बन्धुः तस्य. बहुलेऽपि &c.—*i. e.* the moon will wax but with a heavy heart now; for the love-exciting influence of moonlight will now have no effect.

Śl. 14. कल०—The voice of the cuckoo becomes clear and sweet when it tastes the mango-sprouts. Hence the melodious voice of the cuckoo indicates the presence of mango-blossoms. See *supra* I. 31, III. 32. कस्य बाणतां—For the five arrows of Kâma see *supra* I. 31 (notes); *cf.* Śâk. VI. 5; and *supra* III. 27.

Śl. 15. **अलिपङ्क्तिः—The row of bees is poetically represented as forming the string of Kâma's bow;** मौर्वीमधुकरपंक्तिलीलया &c. D.-Ch. p. 49; प्रायश्चापं न वहति भयान्मन्मथः षट्पदज्यं Megh. II. 14; ज्या यस्यालिकुलं &c. Ṛit. VI. 28. **अनुरोदिति—It is natural for a female to sympathize more readily with another female.**

Śl. 16. **रतिदूतिपदेषु—To the post or duty of a love-messenger.** रति is love-sport enjoyed by youthful persons. रत्यर्थे दूती रतिदूती. The Kokilâ is often spoken of as Káma's messenger, inasmuch as its voice is an inflamer of passion. *Cf.* त्वां कामिनो मदनदूतिमुदाहरन्ति मानावभङ्गनिपुणं त्वममोघमस्त्रम्। तामानय प्रियतमां मम वा समीपं मां वा नयाशु कलभाषिणि यत्र कान्ता ॥ Vik. IV. 11; परभृताविरुतैश्च विलासिनः स्मरबलैरबलैकरसाः कृताः। Ragh. IX. 43;...कोकिलानां च नादैः। इषुभिरिव सुतीक्ष्णैर्मानसं मानिनीनां। तुदति कुसुमचापो मन्मथोद्दीपनाय। Ṛit. VI. 27. See also *supra* III. 32 and notes thereon. दूति—see Malli.; the word is, however, often used with a short ending by the poet. *Cf.* Vik. quoted above. See Ragh. XIX. 18 (तेन दूतिविदितं निषेदुषा), XVIII. 53; दूत्यां दूतिरपि स्मृता इति शब्दभेदप्रकाशे। Hemâdri on Ragh. XIX. 18. The shortening of ई may also be explained by the rule ङ्यापोः संज्ञाछन्दसोर्बहुलम्। See Malli. on वैदेहिबन्धोर्हृदयं विदद्रे। Ragh. XIV. 33. The reading रतिदूत॰ कोकिलान् is not good as females are generally employed as messengers; see Mud. III. 9. **पुनः—For else the voice of the cuckoo will not enkindle the passion of love.**

Śl. 17. **उपगूढानि—उपगुह् + त added to form a noun (नपुंसके भावे क्तः), an embrace.** *Cf.* सद्यः कण्ठच्युतभुजलताग्रन्थिगाढोपगूढम्। Megh. II. 37; Śiś. X. 88. **संस्मृत्य—This is grammatically incorrect as the gerund in य substituted for त्वा must have the same subject as the main verb; so some supply संस्मृत्य स्थितायाः मम.** *Cf.* **for a similar construction** निरीक्ष्य संरम्भनिरस्तधैर्यं राधेयमाराधितजामदग्न्यम्। असंस्तुतेषु प्रसभं भयेषु जायेत मृत्योरपि पक्षपातः॥ Kir. III. 21; see also Ragh. IV. 2 and our note *ad loc.*

Śl. 18. **आर्तवं—of the season; fr. ऋतु + अण् (अ). ध्रियते—stands as it was, continues to exist;** *cf.* ध्रियते स्वेदलवोद्गमोऽपि ते। Ragh. VIII. 51. **कुसुम॰—कुसुमान्येव प्रसाधनं (a decoration) or कुसुममयं प्रसा॰ a comp. of the शाकपार्थिवादि class. For the former** *cf.* **Ragh. IX. 28 (कुसुममेव न केवलमार्तवं नवमशोकतरोः स्मरदीपनं &c.); for the latter see** ***supra*** **III. 53.**

Śl. 19. दारुणैः—Because they deputed him to execute a business which was sure to cost him his life. स्मृतः—called away by being remembered. परिकर्मन्—The act of decorating. दक्षिणेतरं—दक्षिणात् (दक्षिणस्माद्वा) इतरस्तम् । निर्मितरागमेहि मे—For a similar idea *cf.* Ragh. VIII. 64.

Śl. 20. पतङ्गवर्त्मना—पतन्सुप्लवन् गच्छति इति पतंगः a locust; पतङ्गः अग्निरेव वर्त्म तेन Châr. In the manner of a locust or grasshopper that drops of its own accord into a flame; *i. e.* I will burn myself. विलोभ्यसे दिवि—Rati in her distraction forgets that Káma was himself a celestial being as she also was; or she may be referring to some higher world.

Śl. 21. वचनीयमिदं—Bad talk, ill report. For people would say that she was not a real Pativratâ as she did not die the very moment she saw her husband dead. See *supra,* notes on Śl. 5. *Cf.* ममर्थ चातिघोरां मां धिग्जीवितलघूकृताम् । मृतेऽपि त्वयि जीवन्त्या किं मयाणकभार्यया ॥ Bhaṭṭi. XIV. 57, 58. व्यवस्थितं—विशेषेण अवस्थितं has remained firmly *i. e.* permanently.

Śl. 22. अन्त्यमण्डनं—The last *i. e.* funeral decoration, such as putting a garland on the dead body, applying sandal to the head in case of males, tying a pearl to each of the ears, and so on, before it is cremated; *cf.* Ragh. VIII. 71. कथं क्रियतां—The reason of this is given in the last two lines. समं—at one and the same time; simultaneously.

Śl. 23. ०धन्वनः—see com.; धनुस् is changed to धन्वन् when at the end of a Bah. ०विलोकितं—may be at Madhu or herself; नयनस्य उपान्तः the corner or angle of the eye तेन विलोकितं a side-glance.

Śl. 24. हृदयंगमः—हृदय + गम् + खच् ; before the affixes खच् and खश् (अ) the words अरुष्, द्विषत् &c. and such as end in अ take the augment म्; see Malli.. Similarly मितंगम an elephant, विहंगम &c. कुसुमायो०—prepared or formed thy bow with &c. (Malli.); or fitted with flowers (as arrows), or bedecked with flowers.

Śl. 25. विग्धधारैः—०फलैः; *v. l.* where फल means 'the point of an arrow.' आहतः—अर्दितः. *v. l.* is better. अभ्युपपत्तुं—*Lit.* to favour her, *i. e.* to offer consolation to her, to sympathize with her. Ar. read अभ्यवपत्तुं and says अभ्यवपत्तिरनुग्रहः ।

Śl. 26. स्तन०—The Namul is used when the whole part of the body is oppressed or suffers pain. See com. विवृतद्वारं—to which a passage is opened; when an oultet is given to a liquid pent up it rushes forth with all its force; so grief flowed forth all the more poignantly in the presence of a relative. *Cf.* संतानवाहीन्यपि मानुषाणां दुःखानि सद्बन्धुवियोगजानि । दृष्टे जने प्रेयसि दुःसहानि स्रोतःसहस्रैरिव संप्लवन्ते । Uttar. IV. 8.

Sl. 27. दुःखिता—दुःखमस्याः संजातमिति । सुहृदः—Ar. and Nâr. read सुहृदं and have to give an awkward construction. Says Nâr.—वसन्त सुहृदं पश्य । सुहृद्दर्शनं त्वरितमेव कर्तव्यं नायं कालक्षेपस्यावसर इत्याह—स्थितमवस्थानम् । भावे निष्ठा । किम् । *i.e.* why do you stand thus waiting? कालक्षेपं मा कुरु इत्यर्थः । स्थित इति पाठे किमर्थं तूष्णीं स्थितो भवसीत्यर्थः । तदिदं &c.—एतद्दर्शनसौकर्यार्थम् । यावन्न निःशेषं प्रकीर्यते तावद्भस्मापि पश्येति भावः । अत्र दैन्यम् । Ar. All this roundabout way of explaining the reading is saved by adopting Malli.'s reading.

Sl. 28. माधवः—मधुरेव माधवः; स्वार्थे अण् (अ). न खलु प्रेम &c.—The idea is this–The love of men for their wives may not be always steady, but that for their real friends *is*; this consideration ought to induce you to show yourself to him at least.

Sl. 29. अमुना—Herein she tells Káma how much indebted he is to his friend Mâdhava for the valuable service rendered to him by the latter. ससुरा°—सुष्ठु राति ददाति अभीष्टमिति सुरः । The Râmâ. thus accounts for the name—सुरा (the nectar churned out of the ocean) प्रतिग्रहाद्देवाः सुरा इत्यभिविश्रुताः । असुर derived as अस्यन्ति क्षिपन्ति देवान्; or सुरविरुद्धाः the negative particle न expressing विरोध. असुर, however, is the older of the two words and meant in the Veda the mighty (असु प्राणस्तेन तद्वन्तो भवन्ति) and was used for the Supreme Spirit and also as an epithet of the gods, Indra, Agni &c. See असुर in Apte's Dic. बिसतन्तु—Sometimes the lotus-fibres are said to form Madana's bow-string. जगदाज्ञां &c.—The passion of love is very strong in Spring and so Madhu may be said to be helping Káma in the work of subduing the world. The Act. const. is अयं जगत् जगता वा धनुषः आज्ञां कारितवान्; the Pass. cons. therefore is—अनेन जगद् धनुषः आज्ञां कारितं or अमुना जगता धनुष आज्ञा कारिता. See com.

Sl. 30. गत एव &c.—*i. e.* असंनिवृत्तये गतः, gone never to come back, once for all, *i. e.* dead. धूमिता—धूमः अस्याः संजातः असौ धूमिता ता; implies continuous and tormenting grief. The wick of a lamp that is blown out also emits smoke for some time. This implies that she also would suffer the torment for a short time (as she was going to immolate herself shortly after).

Sl. 31. वैशसं—abst. noun fr. विशस a killer, a cruel man, from शस् with वि to kill; and अ (अञ्); see com. Rati means to say, as Madana's wife she formed a half of him and as she was spared, the work of destruction was but half-done by cruel fate. Fate is cruel because it left the other part to perish by itself. अर्धस्य वैशसमर्धवैशसम्; *cf.* अथ वा मम भाग्यविप्लवादशनिः कल्पित एष वेधसा । यदनेन तरुर्न पातितः क्षपिता तद्विटपाश्रिता लता ॥ Ragh. VIII. 47. अनपायिनि—अनपेतुं शीलमस्य never leaving, always standing by. The reading अनघापि or अहतापि is better.

Śl. 32. तत्—Because Fate left the cruel deed half-done-which is more painful. बन्धुजन०—The business of a friend; Rati, as Káma's wife, was the *Bandhu* of Madhu. विधुरां—विगता धूः कार्यभारो यस्याः one not able to do one's duty; helpless. ननु—अनु *v. l.* afterwards.

Śl. 33. An instance of rich poetic imagery and wealth of illustration. सह मेघेन—As soon as the cloud dissolves into rain *i. e.* ceases to exist as a cloud, the lightning-flash also disappears. *Cf.* शशिनं पुनरेति शर्वरी दयिता द्वंद्वचरं पतत्रिणम् । Ragh. VIII. 56. विचेतनैः—Those having no sense; Malli. takes this in the sense of those having little sense (see com.), probably following the theory that everything has अनुद्भूतचैतन्य, like earth.

Śl. 34. विभावसु—विभा वसु wealth यस्य. रचयिष्यामि—*i. e.* I shall welcome a fiery bed just as much as a leafy one. *Cf.* for the reverse of the idea—नवपल्लवसंस्तरेऽपि ते मृदु दूयेत यदङ्गमर्पितम् । तदिदं विषहिष्यते कथं वद वामोरु चिताधिरोहणम् ॥ Ragh. VIII. 57.

Śl. 35. आवयोः सहायतां—The state or position of being a helper. She means—you have formerly willingly helped us in making our flowery bed; now you should do it the more readily being requested with folded hands. Ar. reads विनिष्याचितां making it qualify चितां. मे चिताम्—Aja, although similarly circumstanced, could not do the same for the reason given in Ragh. VIII. 72.

Śl. 36. मदर्पितं—see com.; or मह्यमर्पितं; or better still मयार्पितं according to the precept स्वयमेवार्पयेदग्निम्. दक्षिणवात०—It is but fit that Rati should here refer to the Malaya-breeze, the agent of Káma himself and a willing helpmate of Madhu. For the breeze from the south, especially the mountain Malaya, blows in the Spring season. The fire thus fanned would burn briskly and enable Rati to go to her husband the more quickly. *Cf.* मुकुलायितबहुचूतको वाति दक्षिणपवनकः । Rat. I. 14. खलु—Certainly. Ar. takes it अनुनये-I beseech you.

Śl. 37. एक एव—One only and not two; for though physically different, as husband and wife they formed but one whole. *Cf. supra* अर्धवैशसं śl. 31.

Śl. 38. परलोकविधौ--परलोकस्य परलोकाय वा विधिः तस्मै । परलोकः means मृतः according to some (परो लोकः यस्य). निवपः—वप् with नि to make an offering to the deceased; पितृदानं निवापः स्यात् Amara.

Śl. 39. शफरी—The Saphara is described as a small glittering fish, which darting rapidly through the water is not unaptly compared to the twinkling glances of a sparkling eye. (Wilson, notes on the Megh.) See Kir. VI. 16 (शफरीपरिस्फुरितचारुदृशः). अन्वकम्पयत्—took pity on; *i.e.* cheered her up. *Cf.* ततो वह्निं समादाय सा रतिः कामवल्लभा । अनुगन्तुं स्वभर्तारमुद्योगमकरोन्मुने ॥ ततो रतिं कामपत्नीं स्थितां देहविमुक्तये । आकाशसंभवा वाणी प्राहेदं मधुराक्षरम् ॥ S. P.

Śl. 41. उदीरित—stirred up, excited; ०न्द्रियः—his sensuality being roused, owing to the working of Kâma. स्वसुतायां—Malli. says सरस्वत्यां. Sarasvatî is the name of the evening twilight or संध्या; *cf.* गायत्री नाम पूर्वाह्णे सावित्री मध्यमे दिने । सरस्वती च सायाह्ने सैव संध्या त्रिधा स्मृता ॥ Some commentators give the name of Brahman's daughter as तिलोत्तमा. अकरोत्प्रजा०—Allusion to the Kâli. Pu. Brahmâ fell in love with his daughter Saṁdhyâ (also called Sarasvatî); but being laughed at by the sages and by Śiva for this weakness of mind, he cursed Káma, as the author of the mischief, in the manner stated here. *Cf.* ब्रह्मापि तनयां संध्यां दृष्ट्वा पूर्वमथात्मनः । कामायाशु मनश्चक्रे त्यक्त्वा बुद्धिं सुतेति वै ॥ तस्याश्च चलितं चित्तं कामबाणविलोडितम् । ऋषीणां प्रेक्षतां तेषां मानसानां महात्मनाम् । भर्गस्य वचनं श्रुत्वा सोपहासं विधिं प्रति ॥ आत्मनश्चलाचित्तत्वममर्यादमृषीन्प्रति । कामस्य तादृशं भावं मुनिमोहकरं तदा । दृष्ट्वा संध्या स्वयं तत्र त्रपामापातिदुःखिता । ततस्तु ब्रह्मणा शप्ते मदने तदनन्तरम् । × × अमर्षवशमापन्ना संध्या ध्यानपराऽभवत् ॥ (quoted by Mr. Deshpande). Her form is thus described in the B. P. Sk. III. Ch. 20—तां क्वणच्चरणाम्भोजां मदविह्वललोचनाम् । काञ्चीकलापविलसद्दुकूलाच्छन्नरोधसम् । अन्योन्याश्लेषयोत्तुङ्गनिरन्तरपयोधराम् । सुनासां सुद्विजां स्निग्धहासलीलावलोकनाम् । गूहन्तीं व्रीडयात्मानं नीलालकवरूथिनीम् ॥ 29-31.—According to another version Saṁdhyâ on seeing her father affected by passion assumed the form of a female deer, on which Brahmâ became a deer and followed her. Siva seeing him in that state shot an arrow from his Pinâka, whereupon Brahmâ, with his head lopped off, remained suspended in the sky in the form of the constellation मृगशीर्ष and the arrow of Śiva became the constellation आर्द्रा chasing it.

The fable is thus explained by Kumârila Bhatta—प्रजापतिस्तावत्प्रजापालनाधिकारादादित्य एव उच्यते । स चारुणवेलायामुषस्युदयन्नभ्येति । सा तदागमनादेवोपजायत इति तद्दुहितृत्वेन व्यपदिश्यते । तस्यां चारुणकिरणाख्यबीजनिक्षेपात्स्त्रीपुरुषसंयोगवदुपचारः ।

Śl. 42. प्रवणीकृतः—inclined to favour; from प्रवण. सरस्वती—*Cf.* यदा कुर्याद्गिरिसुतां हरः पाणिगृहीतिकाम् । तदा भवान् शरीरेण समेष्यति समग्रताम् ॥ Kâlikâ P.

Śl. 43. आह—is strictly a form of the pres. tense, here used in the sense of the past tense by the rule वर्तमानसामीप्ये वर्तमानवद्वा । Vâmana says—आहेति भूते &c. Káv. Sût. V. 2. 44, but remarks that स्म should be supplied in such cases. धर्म—one of the Prajâpatis and the father of Káma, by his wife Śraddhâ, a daughter of Daksha. He was created by Brahmâ for maintaining the creation in order. He is represented as having the form of a bull, losing one of his legs at the end of each age. (*Cf.* स सिसृक्षुः प्रजास्त्वादौ पालनं तास्वचिन्तयत् । तस्य चिन्तयतः स्वाङ्गाद्दक्षिणाच्छ्यात् सकुण्डलः । प्रादुर्बभूव पुरुषः श्वेतमाल्यानुलेपनः । तं दृष्ट्वोवाच भगवांश्चतुष्पादं वृषाकृतिम् । पालयेमाः प्रजाः पुत्र त्वं ज्येष्ठो जगतो भव । इत्युक्तः स समुत्तस्थौ चतुष्पादः कृते युगे । त्रेतायां स त्रिभिः पादैर्द्वाभ्यां वै द्वापरेऽभवत् । कलावेकेन पादेन प्रजाः पालयते विभुः ॥ वराहपुराण (as quoted by Mr. Deshpande). अशनिः &c.—The destructive curse is compared to the stroke of thunderbolt (lightning); and its termination, owing to clemency, to Amrita (water; also favour acting like *amrita.*). *Cf.* for a similar idea—वज्रादपि कठोराणि मृदूनि कुसुमादपि । लोकोत्तराणां चेतांसि को हि विज्ञातुमर्हति ॥ Uttar. II. 7. The Poet, however, says elsewhere—(In the case of great sages) उष्णत्वमग्न्यातपसंप्रयोगाच्छैत्यं हि यत्सा प्रकृतिर्जलस्य । Ragh. V. 54.

Śl. 44. शोभने—'O blessed one !'—implies that she will not remain a widow for ever. भवितव्य—is here Active, तव्य being कर्तरि by कृत्यल्युटो बहुलं *i. e.* the affixes called कृत्य and the aff. ल्युट् (अन) may be used in other places than those ordained by the rules. According to Char. भवितव्य may also be from भू प्राप्तौ (to get): भवितव्यः प्राप्तव्यः प्रियसंगमो येन. युज्यते—may be active as taken by Malli. (युज् being of the 4th cl.) or pass. fr. युज् 7 cl.

Śl. 45. व्यवसाय—Fixed purpose, determination. सुचरितार्थपदैः—The meaning of which was well attained; hence, of agreeable import; or very significant. This he did because Rati was not in a condition of mind to take a proper view of the utterance.

Śl. 46. दिवातनस्य—दिवा भवः दिवातनः । The affix तन is added to the particles स्वयं, चिरं, प्राह्णे, प्रगे and adverbs of time in the sense of—'of that time.' Páṇ. IV. 3. 23. Fig. *Upamâ.*

CANTO V.

Sl. 1. तथा समक्षं &c.—This is made clear in V. 53. निनिन्द रूपं—*cf. infra* III. 75. This she did because Śiva disappeared from the place even after he had fully seen her beauty; *cf.* III. 67. प्रियेषु &c.—सुभगाया भावः सौभाग्यं good fortune. Beauty has for its fruit 'good fortune as regards the husband or a love', *i. e.*, if a woman's beauty attracts her husband and makes him love her then only that can be called beauty; otherwise it is useless, howsoever great it may be in the eyes of others. *Cf. infra*—स्त्रीणां प्रियालोकफलो हि वेषः। VII. 22. येन रूपेण प्रियवल्लभा न भवति तद्रूपं व्यर्थमित्यर्थः। Chá.

Śl. 2. अवन्ध्यरूप०—The negation here is prominent (प्रसज्यप्रतिषेध), and so it should not have been compounded; see our note on Ragh. I. 21, or Megh. II. 52. But according to the Bháshyakára such नञ् may be compounded (प्रसज्यप्रतिषेधेऽपि नञ्समास इष्यते); or the comp. may be taken as न वन्ध्यमवन्ध्यं, अवन्ध्यं च तद्रूपं च तस्य भावः। समाधिम्—seems to mean here नियम or a rigid rule of conduct; see *infra* sl. 18. Malli. takes it in the sense of contemplation. Śl. quoted in Sar.-K. as an instance of तपश्चरणादिजन्मा नैमित्तिकानुरागः।

Śl. 3. गिरीश०—Some read as गिरिशं प्रति सक्तमानसां in which case प्रति is a कर्मप्रवचनीय governing गिरिशं. When the whole is taken as a comp. प्रति is an Upasarga after which म् is changed to ण्. गिरीश—the lord of the mountain Kailása. See note on गिरिशं *supra* I. 60.

Śl. 4. मनीषिताः—Such as the mind would long for; as would satisfy the cravings of the mind. Mark the Saṁdhi (मनस्+ईषित); see com. The reading मनीषितायाचं &c. 'worship *i. e.* propitiate the deities for the obtainment of your desired object' seems to be better as it gives the intended sense directly. देवताः प्रतिमारूपेण वर्तमानाः सौभाग्यप्रदा इन्द्राण्याद्याः। Nár. क—क—*Lit.* where is the one—where is the other; hence by Káku (intonation) this means-How great is the distance between the two; the two how unequal! The repetition of क shows the great disparity between the two. *Cf.* क सूर्यप्रभवो वंशः क चाल्पविषया मतिः Ragh. I. 2; क भूपतीनां चरितं क जन्तवः। Kir. I. 6; also *infra* sl 73. पतत्रिन्—पतत्रि इति from पत्+अत्रिन्. *Cf.* परुषस्तपोभिरिदमत्र पुनरङ्गं शिरीषसुकुमारम्। व्यवसितमेतत्कठिनं पर्वाति तद्दुष्करमिति प्रतिभाति॥ Pár. P. III 16 इति स्वजनयावाक्यं श्रुत्वा तु गिरिजा मुने। उवाचदुःखिता भूत्वा बाष्पगद्गदया गिरा॥ नम्रमारं भक्तियुक्तेन पूजयस्व गृहे शिवम्। उ मा गच्छ वनं घोरं सर्वविघ्नास्पदं सदा॥ S. P.

Sl. 5. ध्रुवेच्छां—This is preferable to the other readings as it explains why her mother failed to dissuade her from going to practise penance. ईप्सित—*p. p. p.* of the Desid. of आप् निम्नाभिमुखं—Dissolve निम्नस्याभिमुखम् । प्रतीपयेत्—A Denom. verb from प्रतीप.

Sl. 6. मनोरथज्ञं—Who knew her cherished desire and who was therefore expected to grant the permission readily. मनस्विनी—of sound judgment, thoughtful, *i. e.*, who knew when and how to make a request. Or she who was firm-minded or resolved to gain her object at any cost. Nár. quotes महाकार्ये कृतोद्योगो विघ्नैराहतमानसः । प्रारब्धं न त्यजति यः स मनस्वीति कथ्यते ॥

Sl. 7. अनुरूपा०—रूपस्य योग्यः सदृशो वा अनुरूपः. अभिनिवेश—a determined purpose, firm resolution; or it may mean strong attachment, love, as in Śak. III—सखि दिष्ट्यानुरूपस्तेऽभिनिवेशः । The first meaning, however, will better suit the context. गरीयसा—exalted; and hence कृताभ्यनुज्ञा. According to some मातुरपि पूज्यत्वाद् गरीयसा (but this does not seem to be intended). शिखण्डिमत्-abounding in peacocks; this indicates the absence of venomous serpents and also of ferocious animals like tigers &c. and thereby shows that the place was beautiful and fit for practising penance. It may have been also used for alliteration, like गरीयसा above. *Cf.* Ava. मयूरा निस्सङ्गा भवन्ति । सङ्गदर्शनेन समाधिभङ्गो भवति । According to some this was the original name of the peak (*cf.* गृध्रकूट &c.). *Cf.* गौरी विजयया सख्या जयया च सुनेत्रया । साकं सखीभ्यां सुमुखी सा गौरीशिखरं ययौ । चकार वसतिं यस्माद्गौरीशिखरमुच्यते ॥ Ś P.

Sl. 8. सा हारं—The Com. Ava. reads these two words as connected and says सा आहारं विसृज्य &c. ; he also separates विलो० as अविलोलयष्टिः (*i. e.* देहयष्टिः) and takes प्रविलुप्त० as an adj. of वल्कलं. But this explanation is faulty. In the first place she did not give up her आहार then (unless we take it in the restricted sense of her usual food); she did it afterwards. Secondly there is also greater propriety in saying that she gave up her हार, as it requires a great restraint of mind on the part of women to give up wearing ornaments which they love very much. Again, अवि० does not yield a good sense and has no propriety. प्रविलुप्त indicates a past action and therefore does not fit in well with वल्कल. Again the चन्दन was not there when they put on the bark-garment. अहार्यनिश्चया—and hence, at the time of putting her resolution into practice, she quietly removed her ornaments and put on the bark-garment. यष्टि—the strings of pearls forming the necklace. बालारुण—Some separate this as बाला अरुण संहतं—close-fitting, close contact with the body. अत्र परिवृत्तिरलंकारः । परिवृत्तिर्विनिमयो योऽर्थानां स्यात्समासमैः । Nár. Quoted in S-K. as an instance of वर्णोत्कटकाव्य. Śls. 8, 12 give the usual accoutrements of a तपस्विन्. See notes on śl. 30 further on.

Śl 9. प्रसिद्धैः—Decorated. सशैवला०—*Cf.* सरसिजमनुविद्धं शैवलेनापि रम्यं मलिनमपि हिमांशोर्लक्ष्म लक्ष्मीं तनोति । इयमधिकमनोज्ञा वल्कलेनापि तन्वी किमिव हि मधुराणां मण्डनं नाकृतीनाम् ॥ Śa'k. I. 18. Also न रम्यमाहार्यमपेक्षते गुणम्; रम्याणां विकृतिरपि श्रियं तनोति । Kir. IV. 23; VII. 5.

Śl. 10. त्रिगुणां—त्रयो गुणा यस्यास्तां made of a triple string; मुञ्जाय विकारो मौञ्जी made of *muñjá* grass, अ (अण्) being added in that sense. त्रिगुणाः प्रदक्षिणा मेखलाः । Prachetas; मौञ्जी त्रिवृत्समा श्लक्ष्णा कार्या । Manu. II. 42. तत्पूर्वनिबद्धा—Fastened there for the first time then; and hence its harsh touch caused horripilation every moment. रशनागुणास्पद is periphrastic for जघन.

Śl. 11. विसृष्ट०—As she had to practise penance, Párvatí could no more attend to such decorations of the person as the painting of the lips &c., nor to such pastimes as playing with the ball &c. She willingly (as the use of the word प्रणय shows) exchanged these everyday duties for those of plucking the *kus'a* grass, counting the beads, &c. कन्दुकात्—कञ्चुकात् *v. l.* has no propriety, as the hand is not required to be particularly busy with the कञ्चुक. कन्दुकात् is appropriate, because we know that Pârvatî was fond of that play; see I. 19 and 19 further on. Śl. quoted in the S.-D. as an instance of पर्याय (अत्र एकं वस्तु कररूपं अनेककर्मणि कृतम्).

Śl. 12. महार्हशय्या—नवपल्लवसंस्तरेऽपि ते मृदु दूयेत यदङ्गमर्पितम् । Ragh. VIII. 57. बाहुलता०—प्रशस्तो बाहुः ०लता tender arm; तामुपहन्तीति ०घातिनी; here इन् (णिनि) indicates the observance of a vow; by व्रते (णिनिः) Pâṇ. III. 2. 80. अशेत—*Cf.* स्वप्याद्भूमौ शुची रात्रौ दिवसं प्रपदैर्नयेत् । स्थानासनविहारैर्वा योगाभ्यासेन वा तथा ॥ Yâj. III. 51; प्रपदैः अटनैः Com. निषेदुषी—(and) sat. स्थण्डिले—on a purified piece of ground; स्थण्डिलं संस्कृता भूमिः । Hala'yudha. *Cf.* शेते या किल हंसतूलशयने निद्राति सा स्थण्डिले वस्ते या मृदुलं दुकूलमबला गृह्णाति सा वल्कलम् । या वा चन्दनपङ्कलेपशिशिरे धारागृहे वर्तते पञ्चानामुदितोष्मणां हुतभुजां सा मध्यमासेवते ॥ Pár. P.-IV. 2.

Śl. 13. द्वयेऽपि—The reading द्वयीषु is grammatically faulty, remarks Malli.; for द्वयी *fem.* of द्वय means 'having two parts' (द्वौ अवयवौ यस्याः); see Páṇ. V. 2. 42, 43 (संख्याया अवयवे तयप्, द्वित्रिभ्यां तयस्यायज्वा); so the dual and plural terminations cannot be affixed to it, unless different sets of things possessing two parts are meant. लतासु &c.—For the idea *cf.* कलमन्यभृतासु भाषितं कलहंसीषु

मदालसं गतम् । पृषतीषु विलोलमीक्षितं पवनाधूतलतासु विभ्रमाः ॥ &c. Ragh. VIII. 59; for a poetic description of लताविलास *cf.* Ragh. IX. 35. विलासचे०—Actions due to coquetry, blandishments; from the quotation given above it will appear that the poet uses विलास and विभ्रम promiscuously; for विलास see *supra* IV. 5. विभ्रम means wantonness of action due to मद, राग, &c. (मद्रागहर्षजनितो विपर्यासो विभ्रमः).

Sl. 14. अतन्द्रिता—तन्द्रा (drowsiness, lassitude) अस्याः संजाताऽसौ तन्द्रिता, न त० अतन्द्रिता; without being slack, assiduously. स्वयमेव वृक्षकान् &c.—One of the favourite avocations of maidens leading a hermit's life. *Cf.* Ragh. I. 51; II. 36 (यो हेमकुम्भस्तननिःसृतानां स्कन्दस्य मातुः पयसां रसज्ञः) Śák. I. &c. घटस्तन०—As Pârvatî was not yet married, the idea that she reared the trees like children by the flow from her water-jar-breasts is not very happy. गुहः—गूहति देवसेनां इति; or according to the Mah.-Bhàr.—स्कन्दत्वात्स्कन्दतां प्राप्तो गुहावासाद्गुहोऽभवत् । So called because he was reared in a cave. पुत्रवात्सल्यं—*cf.* Ragh. II. 37; संवर्धितानां सुतनिर्विशेषम् । *Ibid.* V. 6.

Sl. 15. अरण्यबीजाञ्जलि &c.—*Cf.* Ragh. I. 50; Śa'k. IV. 14. श्यामाकमुष्टिपरिवर्धितको (मृगः &c.); करकमलवितीर्णैरम्बुनीवारशष्पैस्तरुशकुनिकुरङ्गान्मैथिली यानपुष्यत् । Uttar. III. 25. अमिमीत लोचने—*cf.* परस्पराक्षिसादृश्यमदूरोज्झितवर्त्मसु । मृगद्वंद्वेषु पश्यन्तौ स्यन्दनाबद्धदृष्टिषु ॥ Ragh. I. 40. The construction as given by Malli. is (स्वकीये) लोचने सा सखीनां पुरः अमिमीत.Chár. takes पुरः independently and construes (स्वस्य) पुरः सा सखीनां लोचने अमिमीत. But the construction given by Malli. is better; since the poet's object is evidently to describe the resemblance of Párvatî's eyes to those of the fawns, as at Sl. 35 *infra*, and he is not concerned with the description of the eyes of her female friends. Moreover, in the latter case we would expect सखीनां लोचनानि (plural), and not लोचने (dual).

Sl. 16. कृताभिषेकां &c.—This was the daily course of her life. Without bathing no sacred rite can be performed; *cf.* अस्नात्वा नाचरेत्कर्म जपहोमादि किंचन । स्नानमूलाः क्रियाः सर्वाः श्रुतिस्मृत्युदिता नृणाम् ॥ स्वगुत्तरासङ्ग०—The comp. must be taken as Malli. has done it. *Cf.* Chár. स्वग् उत्तरासङ्गमस्या अस्तीति । अत्र बहुव्रीहिमत्वर्थीययोः समानार्थत्वात्कथं मतुप् । उच्यते । एकीयमतमेतदिति कर्मधारयादपि मत्वर्थीयः । यद्वा त्वचा उत्तरासङ्गवतीति तृतीयासमासः । अधीतिनां—one more reference to the social customs of those times, which shows that women were educated. To see her who led such a life &c. *Cf.* जजाप परमं मन्त्रं शैवं पञ्चार्णसंज्ञकम् । S. P. ऋषयोऽभ्युपागमन्—*cf.* तपःप्रधानाः क्षतवृष्यथोऽपि तं द्रष्टुमीयुर्न मठानभीयुः । Bud.-Ch. VII. 4. न धर्मवृद्धेषु-

—For गुणाः पूजास्थानं गुणिषु न च लिङ्गं न च वयः। Also because कामिवेशते रमयितुं न गुणाः। Kir. VI. 24; तेजसां हि न वयः समीक्ष्यते Ragh. XI. 1; प्रकृतिरियं सत्त्ववतां न खलु वयस्तेजसो हेतुः। Bh. N. 58; and शिशुत्वं स्त्रैणं वा भवतु ननु वन्द्यासि जगताम्। Uttar. VI. 11.

Śl. 17. विरोधि०—Such an effect of the presence of a holy person in a penance-grove is not unusual. *Cf.* Ragh. II. 14 अस्य भगवतः प्रसादादेवोपशान्तवैरमपगतमत्सरं तपोवनम्। अहो प्रभावो महात्मनाम्। अत्र हि शाश्वतिकमपहाय विरोधं &c. Kád. p. 79. द्रुमैरभीष्ट &c.—Such descriptions are common enough; *cf.* तस्यातिथीनामधुना सपर्या स्थिता सुपुत्रेष्विव पादपेषु। Ragh. XIII. 46; see also Bhaṭṭi. III. 42.

Śl. 18. तपःसमाधि—The degree of austerity as at first undertaken. सर्वसमा—*V. l.* सर्वत्र शीतोष्णप्रियाप्रियादिषु द्वन्द्वेषु समबुद्धिः। Nár. Treating everything equally, not minding cold or heat. सर्वसमाधिसा०—*v. l.* is explained as सर्वसमाधीन् साधयति इत्येवंशीलम्. प्रचक्रमे—See *supra,* note on प्राक्रमत III. 2.

Śl. 19. ध्रुवं—Indicates उत्प्रेक्षा. *Cf.* मन्ये शङ्के ध्रुवं प्रायो नूनमित्येवमादिभिः। उत्प्रेक्षा व्यज्यते शब्दैरिव शब्दोऽपि तादृशः। Káv. D. II. 234. काञ्चन०—The word काञ्चन is happily chosen; it not only bears resemblance to her bodily complexion, but indicates softness and at the same time power to resist any destructive influence.

Śl. 20. शुचौ—Mark the two senses of शुचि in this śl. चतुर्णां &c.—This is what is called the Pañchâgnisâdhana Tapas. शुचिस्मिता, सुमध्यमा—The two epithets are significant:—The first shows that her strong will-power had so hardened her body that it scarcely felt the effects of heat, since she could smile as brightly before; the second shows that she should have felt the fatigue. but did not. विजित्य—At first the solar rays dazzled her eyes: but by and by she got used to the powerful light of the sun and could fix her gaze on the luminary; *cf.* हविर्भुजामेधवतां चतुर्णां मध्ये ललाटंतपसप्तसप्तिः। Ragh. XIII. 41. सवितृ—सुवति इति he who impels creatures to action, or the producer of things, the vivifier. *i. e.* the sun. In the Veda he is sometimes spoken of as a different deity from the sun. *Cf.* पञ्चमः पञ्चतपसस्तपनो जातवेदसाम्। Śiś. II. 51.

Śl. 22. अयाचितो०—*i.e.* rain-water and dew-water. रसात्मकस्य-जलमयस्य watery; *cf.* सलिलमये शशिनि रवेर्दीधितयो मूर्च्छितास्तमो नैशम्। क्षपयन्ति। Vará. Bṛihatsaṁhitá. The moon is supposed to be watery on account of its cooling rays; or रस may mean 'nectar'; *cf.* the name सुधाकर; Malli.'s अमृतमयस्य may have either meaning. पारणाविधिः—Páraṇá has a technical meaning; it means food taken after a fast. Malli. says अभ्यवहारकर्म, *i. e.* eating, taking her daily food; but it may have its usual meaning also. Párvatî observed a fast during the day and subsisted only on the dew-drops and lunar rays obtained at night. *Cf.* अप्राम्यमन्नं सलिलप्ररूढं पर्णानि तोयं फलमूलमेव । यथागमं वृत्तिरियं मुनीनां &c. Bud.-Ch. VII. 14.

Śl. 23. विविधेन—Fivefold; see śl. 20 *supra.* द्विविधेन—*v. l.* twofold, *i. e.* that in the sky (the sun) and that on earth (fire kindled with fuel). This reading seems to be better as the four earthly fires were of the same sort (इन्धनसंभृत). वह्निना—वह्नि is used here in the sense of 'burning energy.'

Śl. 24. स्थिताः क्षणं—Indicates the thickness of her eyelashes. उत्सेध—bulk, protrusion. Śl. quoted in S.-D. as an instance of पर्याय परिकर.

Śl. 25. शिलाशया—During the rainy season she sat or slept in open space (अनिकेतवा॰ not in the house) on a stone-slab, exposed to the rain and winds, &c. उन्मिषितैः—The flashes of lightning are fancied as the twinklings of the eyes of the nights.

Śl. 26. हिमोत्किरा॰—Scattering frosts; हिमोत्तरा॰ *v.l.*-abounding in, bearing a large quantity of. उदवास—उदक is changed to उद before पेष &c.; उदपेषं, उदवाहन, उदधिः; see Malli. परस्परा॰—By the rule 'कर्मव्यतिहारे सर्वनाम्नो द्वे वाच्ये,' the pronouns अन्य, पर, इतर and उत्तर are doubled when reciprocity of action is expressed, and स् replaces the case of the first part of अन्य and पर and does not disappear even in a comp.; this doubled form may further be compounded on the authority of the Bháshyakára (as he has used it in अन्योन्यसंश्रयत्वे तद्). चक्रवाक—a kind of ruddy goose; according to VII. 15, there appears to be a yellow species of these birds; the female and the male are supposed to be separated at night which they spend in crying for each other's company; see Śák. IV. 16; and Vik. IV 20. हेमन्ते जाह्नवीतोये करकाभ्यधिशीतले । आकण्ठमग्ना ध्यायन्ती संस्थिता चन्द्रशेखरे ॥ S. P.

Śl. 27. प्रवेपमाना॰--अधरः एव पत्रं the leaf of the lotus. Her excessively trembling lip looked like the petal of the lotus of her face. तुषार &c —तुषारवृष्ट्या (by the shower of frost) क्षता (destroyed) पद्मसंपत् (the abundance of lotuses) यासां. *Cf.* हिमसेकविपत्तिरत्र मे नलिनी पूर्वनिदर्शनं मता । Ragh. VIII. 45. सरोज—Her lotus-like face being reflected in the rippling water made up for the loss of lotuses which thus still appeared to be there. ॰संतानं—continuation of the line of.

Śl. 28. प्रियंवदा—Although thus mortifying herself she did not lose her habit of sweet-speaking; mark the nasal coming in;

see com. and note on *supra* II. 38. The reading वदन्त्यपर्णामिति तां is grammatically faulty as remarked by Malli.; Cha'r. also remarks— अत्रेतिशब्दे कर्मणोऽभिहितत्वादपर्णामिति चिन्त्यम्। The reading अपर्णा किल तां is not faulty. *Cf.* चतुर्थं त्यक्तपर्णा च अपर्णाख्यामवाप सा Ś. P.

Śl. 29. मृणालिका &c.—So in Vik. अनेन कल्याणि मृणालकोमलं व्रतेन गात्रं ग्लपयस्यहर्निशम्। III. 13. *Cf.* एषा शिरीषसुकुमारशरीरयष्टिश्चान्द्री कलेव नयनोत्सवमावहन्ती। संचेतुमिच्छति शिलाकठिनैः शरीरैः संपादितान्यपि तपांसि तपोधनानाम्॥ Pâr. P. IV. 1; and तपः......तथा स राजर्षिरसाधयद्यथा महर्षयोऽस्मादपकर्षमाययुः Vikr. Ch. II. 44.

Śl. between 29–30. This seems to be necessary; *cf.* सोऽहं तृष्णातुरैर्वृष्टिं विद्युत्वानिव चातकैः। अरिविप्रकृतैर्देवैः प्रसूतिं प्रतियाचितः॥ VI. 27.

Śl. 30. अथ—After this, *i. e.* when Pârvatî had reached, in her practice of penance, a point far higher than that attained by ascetics. अजिना०—Śiva came disguised as an ascetic to try Pârvatî's devotion. अजिन—The skin of a black antelope on which a Brahmachârin sits. *Cf.* Âpastamba—हारिणमैणेयं वा कार्ष्णं वा ब्राह्मणस्य; see Manus. II. 41. आषाढ:—The Palâśa staff carried by an ascetic. See Manus. II. 45 (ब्राह्मणो बैल्वपालाशौ). प्रगल्भवाक्—whose powers of speech were highly developed; eloquent in speech. ज्वलन्निव &c.—he was refulgent with the lustre which the study of the Vedas gives. जटिलः—Wearing matted hair, which a Brahmachârî may do; *cf.* मुण्डो वा जटिलो वा स्यादथ वा स्याच्छिखाधरः। Manu. शरीरबद्धः—Also बद्धशरीरः; see com. प्रथमाश्रमः &c.—He looked, as it were, the very embodiment of the 1st Âsrama, *i. e.* the perfect type of a Brahmachârin. The religious life of a Dvija (especially a Brâhmaṇa) is divided into four stages:—(1) Brahmacharya or the life of a student (ब्रह्मचारिन्) passed at the Guru's house in acquiring sacred knowledge, (2) गार्हस्थ्य or that of married life which he leads as a householder; (3) that of वानप्रस्थ or the life of an anchorite when he retires to a forest with or without his wife; and (4) संन्यास wherein renouncing all worldly concerns he fixes his mind on Brahman to attain *Moksha.* ब्रह्मचारी गृही वानप्रस्थो भिक्षुश्चतुष्टये। आश्रमोऽस्त्री Amara; Manus. VI. 87. A Brahmachârin, while at his Guru's house, must wear the proper girdle, deer's skin &c., learn the prescribed portion of the Vedas, bathe every day, offer prayers to the gods, sages and the Pitṛis, fetch holy sticks and so on. He must not frequent the company of women, must not think of personal decorations &c.; in short he must live a perfectly holy life. *Cf.* तपोविपाककाले तां जिज्ञासुर्भगवान् शिवः। ब्रह्मचर्यव्रतधरो विवेश तपसोऽचलम्। अजिनाषाढधारी च प्रगल्भवचनो मुने।

ज्वलन्निव जटाधारी ब्रह्मज्ञो ब्रह्मतेजसा ॥ Ś. P. The Pâr. P. thus describes the divine ascetic :—अंसे कृष्णाजिनश्रीस्त्रिगुणविरचिता मेखला श्रोणिभागे पाणावाषाढदण्डो भसितविरचितं पुण्ड्रकं भालदेशे । दर्भैः क्लृप्तं पवित्रं श्रवसि परिणमन्मानतुङ्गा पिशङ्गी मौलौ पंक्तिर्जटानां जपवलयमिदं स्फाटिकं च प्रकोष्ठे ॥ IV. 6.

Śl. 31. आतिथेयी—one good *i. e.* hospitable to guests; see com.; fr. अतिथि + एय (ढञ्) + ई fem. affix; similarly पाथेयं, स्वापतेयं (wealth) &c. निविष्ट०—And hence not ruffled by feelings of jealousy &c. साम्येऽपि &c.—साम्येऽभिनि० the reading of Ar. means 'of those who have set their hearts firmly on equality,' or are free from likes and dislikes (रागद्वेष). But this reading is bad as then वपुर्विशेषेषु loses its propriety (as such persons cannot observe distinctions). *Cf.* दृष्ट्वा तमातिथिं गौरी पूजयामास सादरात् । भक्ष्यभोज्यैरशेषैश्च सशय्यासनवारिभिः ॥ Ś. P. वपुर्विशेषेषु—*Cf.* आकृतिविशेषेष्वादरः पदं करोति । Mâlav. I.

Śl. 32. सत्क्रिया—Here सत् is treated like a preposition by आदरानादरयोः सदसती । Pâṇ. I. 4. 63. नाम—He showed that he took rest although not really fatigued. The disguise required this. *Cf.* विश्रम्य विष्टरे नाम । Kir. XI. 9. ऋजुना—By casting a simple, meaningless glance at her. He did not at all betray his feeling of love by his looks. क्रमः—परिपाटी *i. e.* the regular order or course; hence proper method, propriety.

Śl. 33. क्रियार्थं—क्रियायै इदं; a Nityasamása. समित्कुशं—Sam. Dvan. by the rule जातिरप्राणिनां Pâṇ. II. 4. 6, *i. e.* of words expressive of द्रव्यs (not qualities &c.) and not denoting animals when the species is prominently referred to (जातिप्राधान्य एवायमेकवद्भावः Sid.-Kau.; else बदरामलकानि). *Cf.* अपि क्रियार्थं सुलभं पुष्पवारिसमित्कुशम् । अपि देवी तपोमूर्ध्नि स्वशक्त्यापि प्रवर्तसे ॥ Ś. P.; see also Ragh. V. 5. अपि स्वशक्त्या—*i. e.* hast thou the strength to bear the great strain of thy penance and practise it ? For अविरभसकृतानां कर्मणामाविपत्तेर्भवति हृदयदाही शल्यतुल्यो विपाकः । Bh. Nît. 99. शरीरमा०—शीर्यते इति शरीरं fr. शॄ and the uṇâdi aff. ईर; that which is shattered, easily falls off; hence what must be greatly taken care of.

Śl. 34. वीरुधां—विरुध् fr. रुह with वि with the aff. क्विप्, the ह् being changed to ध् and वि lengthened irregularly (निपातनात्). दन्तवाससा—दन्तानां वास इवाच्छादकत्वात् that which covers the teeth (lip), तेन. According to Pâṇ. II. 3. 72, the Inst. cannot be used with the word तुला. Malli. defends this by saying that here the word तुला is सादृश्य (noun) वाची and so the Inst. may be used while the सूत्र negativing the Inst. requires it to be सदृश (*adj.*) वाची

(but there is no such distinction in the Sûtra). Bhoja also takes the same view, when he says सदृशपदार्थवाची सादृश्यमात्रवाची चेति द्वौ तुलाशब्दौ । सादृश्यमात्रवाचकतुलाशब्दयोगे तु तृतीयाऽप्यिष्यत एव । Some defend this by supplying सह after वासना.

Śl. 35. करस्थदर्भ०—The deer were allowed such liberty by the ascetics. अपराधिषु—*V. l.* guilty by their seeking the Kuśa grass lying in your hand; this is not a good reading. *Cf.* Ragh. V. 7; *cf. supra* sl. 15. उत्पलक्षेपचलैः—*V. l.* unsteady like lotuses tossed about; see com.

Śl. 36. पापवृत्तये न रूपं—For beauty of person presupposes a degree of religious merit on the part of the person endowed with it; hence such a person cannot be expected to lead a sinful life (*cf.* आकारो रुचिरः &c. Bhar.). *Cf.* यत्राकृतिस्तत्र गुणा वसन्ति; and न ह्याकृतिः सुसदृशं विजहाति शीलम् Mrich. IX. 16. उदारदर्शने—Malli. takes दर्शन in the sense of 'the eye'; it may also mean form, appearance ; 'O beautiful one'. शीलं &c.—*cf.* न तुलाविषये तवाकृतिर्न वचोवर्त्मनि ते सुशीलता । त्वदुदाहरणाकृतौ गुणा इति सामुद्रिकसारमुद्रणा ॥ Nai. II. 51.

Śl. 37. विकीर्ण० &c.—The seven Ṛishis are described as bathing in the heavenly Ganges and sitting in its waters practising Práṇáyâma &c. *Cf.* ततः सप्तर्षयो यस्यां प्राणायामपरायणाः । तिष्ठन्ति वीचिमालाभिः सिच्यमानजटाजले ॥ V. P. बलि—*i. e.* the flowers therein which are poetically regarded, on account of their white colour, as the smiles of the Mandâkinî. ०प्रभासिभिः *V. l.*—प्रभासितुं शीलमेषामिति तैः bright with. अनाविलैः—indicates the greater sanctity of Párvatí's action than that of the waters of the Ganges. Fig.—व्यतिरेक implied.

Śl. 38. अनेन धर्मः &c.—*Cf.* अप्यर्थकामौ तस्यास्तां धर्म एव मनीषिणः । Ragh. I. 25. The reading भाविनि one having excellent, *i. e.* pure thoughts—is preferable to भामिनि which means either a beautiful (or fortunate) or passionate woman, and is out of place here. मनो०-मनसः निर्विषयौ (not the objects of) अर्थकामौ यस्याः; whose mind is entirely free from all thoughts about अर्थ and काम.

Śl. 39. संप्र०—सा प्रति० v. l. सा त्वं. संनत०—stooping; hence, beautiful. नतं चारु संनतमिति भोजः। Nár. सासपदीनं-Formed when seven words are uttered. Fr. सप्तपदं Dvigu + खञ् (ईन); formed irregularly by Páṇ. V. 2. 22. *Cf.* संबन्धमाभाषणपूर्वमाहुः &c. Ragh. II. 58. According to some पद means 'a footstep'; formed by walking over seven steps together. The Sûtra admits of both these senses. सतां

सप्तपदा मैत्री सत्सता त्रिपदा स्मृता। सत्सतामपि ये सन्तस्तेषां मैत्री पदे पदे ॥ Avachûri as quoted by Mr. Deshpande.

Śl. 40. बहुक्षमां—Much forgiving; gives the reason why he makes bold to ask the question. द्विजाति०—Although the term द्विजाति refers to the first three classes, it here means the Bra'hmaṇa class alone. मातुर्यदग्रे जायन्ते द्वितीयं मौञ्जिबन्धनात्। ब्राह्मणक्षत्रियविशस्तस्मादेते द्विजाः स्मृताः ॥; see also Manus. II. 169. चापल—want of patience, loquacity. प्रष्टुमनाः—The nasal of the *inf.* is dropped before काम and मनस्. तुं काममनसोरपि is part of a परिभाषा quoted by ancient grammarians and sanctioned by Pâṇ. Its full text is लुम्पेदवश्यमः कृत्ये तुंकाममनसोरपि। समो वा हिततयोर्मांसस्य पचि युड्घञोः ॥ प्रतिवक्ष्य०—प्रतिबोधयिष्यसि *V. l.* 'You will please let me know or tell; the 2nd future is used in the sense of the Imp. as a courteous way of asking one to do a thing. परिगोपायिष्यसि—*V. l.*—'If you will not conceal the secret;' but this is not a good reading, as it presupposes the possibility of Pârvatî's hiding her secret from him.

Śl. 41. प्रथमस्य वेधसः—For the mountain Hima'laya was created by Brahmâ, the primeval creator; see com. त्रिलोक०—Dissolve व्यवधवो लोकस्त्रिलोकस्तस्य; otherwise we should expect त्रिलोकीसौ०. *Cf. supra* I. 49. ऐश्वर्यं—For her father's city was the home of wealth of every kind. See *infra* VI. 73. *Cf.* Pár· P. जन्मान्ववाये प्रथमस्य धातुः पिता गरीयान् गिरिसार्वभौमः। वपुर्मनोहारि वचश्च रम्यं पदं च लोकादतिलोकमस्याः ॥ IV. 11.

Śl. 42. अनिष्टात्—अनिष्ट anything untoward or undesirable, an insult. Dakshiṇâvartanâtha says भर्तृकृतात् but that does not seem possible, as Pârv. was unmarried. कृशोदरि—तलोदरि *V. l.* has the same meaning.

Śl. 43. अलभ्य०—It is a supposition that graceful persons cannot be subject to misery; *cf.* अहो दुर्निवारता व्यसनोपनिपातानां यदीदृशीमप्याकृतिमनभिभवनीयामात्मसात्कुर्वन्ति । Kád. सुभ्रु—Properly the Voc. sing. of सुभ्रू should be सुभ्रूः as it is not a नदीसंज्ञक word. The poets, however, use the form with a short उ. Malli. defends it thus—According to the Bháshyakára, the shortening of the final vowel may be allowed in rare cases; for in his com. on the Vârttika on Páṇ. IV. 1. 66 he has instanced अलाबू, कर्कन्धू thereby indicating that sometimes ऊकारान्त words may take ऊङ् and be नदीसंज्ञक so that they can shorten their vowel in the Voc. sing.; see Malli. Va'mana also upholds this view, saying ऊकारान्तादप्यूङ् प्रवृत्तः। K.-S.-V. V. 2. 48. पर०—परेणाभिमर्शः; being touched carnally, an outrage; *cf.* Śák. V. 20. ०सूचये—सूचि the sharp point of; *i. e.* to catch it by its end. °सूतये—*V. l.* where सुति means चालनं—for the removal of.

Śl. 44. वार्द्धक°—Malli. derives वार्द्धक by adding वुञ् (अक) to वृद्ध by including the word in the group मनोज्ञादि (Pâṇ. V. 1. 133); but the word वृद्ध is not found in that list. वुञ् is added to वृद्ध in the sense of समूह or multitude by the Vârttika वृद्धाच्च on Pâṇ. IV. 2. 39; but that is not the sense here; hence it is explained by including it in the मनोज्ञादि group. यदि वृद्धत्वेऽपि वार्द्धकमिति प्रयोगोऽस्ति तर्हि मनोज्ञादित्वं कल्पनीयमित्याहुः ॥ Tattvabodhinî. प्रदोषे &c.—When the night is in its youth, as it were. अरुण—The son of Kaśyapa and Vinatá and the elder brother of Garuḍa. He was born without thighs and is hence called 'Anûru.' He is the charioteer of the Sun, and the harbinger of the dawn. Here अरुण means 'the dawn.' बदि कल्पते—As the night in its vigour does not think of the dawn, so you should not also think of putting on bark garments &c. in youth. *Cf.* एषा ते यौवनावस्था तपः कर्तुं न युज्यते । तपसे मुनयश्चाहुरुत्तरं वपुषो वयः ॥ वृद्धकालोचिते शेषे जटावल्कलवाससी। कथं बिभर्षि सुश्रोणि मया त्वयि न लक्ष्यते । S. P.

Śl. 45. श्रमः—also means penance; अभ्यासे शास्त्रविद्यादौ वेदे तपसि च श्रमः । इति भोजः as quoted by Nâr. अलं समाधिना—समाधि penance; *cf.* अस्त्येतदन्यसमाधिभीरुत्वं देवानाम् । Śák. I. न रत्नम°—*cf.* घोरेण तपसा देवी भर्तारं यदि वाञ्छसि । रजनीया तदा मत्रो त्वं भवत्या न वै पतिः ॥ S. P.

Śl. 46. निवेदितं निःश्वसितेन—I am told that by the sigh (your warm breathing); for Párvatî heaved a sigh when the ascetic referred to her desire for a suitable husband. न दृश्यते &c.—He means—you have not to seek the bridegroom; the bridegroom must come seeking you.

Śl. 47. स्थिर—may mean firm, not easily affected or moved; hence 'stern, relentless'; or quiescent, incapable of feeling passion. There may also be a covert reference to 'Sthâṇu.' ईप्सितः—*p.p.p.* of the Desid. of आप् to obtain. कर्णोत्पल°—कर्णालंकारभूतमुत्पलं कर्णोत्पलं तेन शून्यः कर्णोत्पलशून्यस्तस्य भावः कर्णोत्पलशून्यता ताम्. श्लथ°—श्लथाश्च ता लम्बिन्यश्च ताः; °बन्धिनीः *v. l.*—श्लथः बन्धो यासां विद्यते ताः श्लथबन्धिन्यः ताः with their tie loosened.

Śl. 48. अतिमात्र°—अतिक्रान्ता मात्रा यस्मिन्कर्मणि तदतिमात्रं; now see com. दिवाकरा°—Those parts of the body on which ornaments are usually put are sun-burnt. शशाङ्क°—with thy lustrous complexion paled. कस्य मनः—I too feel pain on your account—implied.

Śl. 49. सौभाग्य—The good fortune lies in being loved by Pârvatî. वञ्चितं—Because he has been foolish by denying himself the pleasure of seeing your face. लक्ष्य—The mark or object of sight. Ar. reads लक्ष्यं रविं makes the sun the mark for your eye, *i.e.* still forces you to practise the *Pañchâgni* penance. आत्मीयं—आत्मन इदं ; fr. आत्मन्+छः (ईय). अराल०—अरालानि पक्ष्माणि यस्य with curved, *i. e.* beautiful eyelashes.

Śl. 50. पूर्वाश्रम—प्रथमाश्रम *i. e.* Brahmacharya. तदर्धभागेन &c.—अत्र निगूढोऽर्थः—तपःशब्देनात्र तपःसाधनभूतं शरीरं लक्ष्यते । साध्यसाधनभावश्च संबन्धः । पूर्वाश्रमसंचितं पूर्वं जगत्सर्गादौ अश्रमेण । मायामात्रेणेत्यर्थः । संपादितं यत्तपः शरीरं तस्यार्धभागेन कांक्षितं लभस्व । मम शरीरार्धभागमेव ते दास्यामि । इ० Nár.; this is of course far-fetched. साधु—Properly, fully. *Cf.* किमाकाङ्क्षसि सुश्रोणि कथयस्व ममाग्रतः । कुतूहलेन शुश्रूषुरहं तव नगेन्द्रजे ॥ S. P.

Śl. 51. प्रविश्य—Having entered into or penetrated her mind; having divined her inmost thoughts. मनोगतं सा &c.—This shows the modesty of Párv., as became a high-born maiden. एतेन कुलस्त्रीणां परपुरुषैः सह साक्षात्संभाषणं न कर्तव्यमिति गम्यते Com. of Ś. P. The Ś. P. thus accounts for this–एषा गिरिसुता विप्र सती कमललोचना । वाचं परस्य साक्षान्नो ददाति मवसेविनी ॥. अथो वयस्यां—This was Jayâ. वयसा तुल्या वयस्या; fr. वयस्+यत् by नौवयोधर्म &c. Pâṇ. IV. 4. 91. विवर्तित०—Adv. comp.; विवर्तितं (turned towards); अविद्यमानमञ्जनं यस्य तदनञ्जनं; now see com.

Śl. 52. वर्णिन्—वर्णः प्रशस्तिः अस्यास्तीति वर्णिन्; a Brahmachârin; a religious student. The aff. इन् is added to वर्ण in this sense alone; otherwise वर्णवान्; see Kâśiká on the Sútra quoted by Malli. (Pâṇ. V. 2. 134). In his com. on Kir. I. 1, Malli. explains प्रशस्ति as स्मरणं कीर्तनं केलिः प्रेक्षणं गुह्यभाषणम् । संकल्पोऽध्यवसायश्च क्रियानिर्वृत्तिरेव च ॥ एतन्मैथुनमष्टाङ्गं प्रवदन्ति मनीषिणः ।एतदष्टविधमैथुनाभावः प्रशस्तिः । वाञ्छितं—*v. l.* her desired object. साधो—साध्नोति परकार्यमिति; one who accomplishes another's business, hence Pârvatî's friend fitly addresses him as साधु (since he had said तदर्धभागेन &c.).

Śl. 53. चतुर्दिगीशान्—चतसृणां दिशां समाहारः चतुर्दिक् तस्य ईशान् । Malli. takes the comp. as उत्तरपदलोपी (शाकपार्थिवादि); then it will have to be dissolved as चतुर्विदिक्सहिताः दिशः चतुर्दिशः, विदिक् being dropped, तासामीशान्; but this is inaccurate, as that will include Śiva himself, the lord of the North-east. अधिश्रियः—अधिका (अधिगता वा) श्रीः येषां (यैर्वा); pre-eminently rich or refulgent.

Śl. 54. असह्य—terrible to hear. हुङ्कार—This is the weapon of Śiva as Rudra. पुरारि—Śiva; also called त्रिपुरारि, from his having destroyed the three cities of gold, silver and iron, built in the sky, the ethereal region and on earth, by the demon Maya.

and presided over by himself, Vidyunmâlî and Târakâsura. To achieve this feat Śiva had to stand for one thousand years awaiting the coming together of the cities; *cf.* Mah. Bhâr. त्रिपुरस्य वधार्थाय स्थाणुः प्रहरतां वरः । स्थानं माहेश्वरं कृत्वा दिव्यमप्रतिमं प्रभुः । अतिष्ठत्स्थाणुभूतः स सहस्रं परिवत्सरान् । यदा त्रीणि समेतानि अन्तरिक्षे पुराणि च । त्रिपर्वेण त्रिशल्येन तदा तानि बिभेद सः ॥ See also B. P. VII. 10. Ś. P. 53-68. व्याहतपार्श्व—Adj. comp.; so as to make a deep wound (into Pârvatî's heart); being hurled back with great force.

Śl. 55. उन्मदना—उद्गत उत्कटो वा मदनो यस्याः सा her passion being greatly excited. ललाटिका०—Fr. ललाट+कन् (क) by कर्णललाटात्कन् अलंकारे Pâṇ. IV. 3. 65; an ornamental mark on the forehead; see com. To allay the fever caused by her love-torment sandal-paste was applied to her forehead; but that too brought her no relief. *Cf.* शश्वद्व्यापृतचन्दनाद्रिपवनस्पर्शं न संमन्यते शय्यां पल्लवकल्पितां न सहते चन्द्रातपं निन्दति । नो वा पद्मपलाशनिर्मिततनुप्रावार-माक्षम्यते सा नीहारशिलातले शृणु परं तापातुरा वर्तते ॥ Pâr. P. IV. 4.

Śl. 56. उपात्तवर्णे—वर्ण properly letters; hence the arrangement of words in a song;-begun to be sung in due order. किंनरराज०—Because Pârvatî was a princess so she would have princesses only for her companions. The Kiṃnaras are known for the extreme sweetness of their voice; *cf.* Ragh. XV. 64. ०अन्त—A forest-spot; *cf.* यत्र रम्यो वनान्तः । Uttar. II. 25.

Śl. 57. त्रिभाग०—See Malli. She got a little sleep, but only to be broken the next moment when a fourth or third part of the night remained. अलक्ष्यवाक्—अविद्यमानं लक्ष्यं यस्याः सा अलक्ष्या; now see com. She uttered words but without there being any person present to whom the words could be addressed. Śl. quoted in the S.-D. as an instance of प्रलाप (one of the ten conditions induced by love-affection when intense; अलक्ष्यवाक्प्रलापः स्याच्चेतसो भ्रमणाद्भृशम्).

Śl. 58. यदा—सदा *V. l.* is perhaps better; always present everywhere. भावस्थं—love-smitten; Malli.; Ar. also says भावोऽभिलाषः; it may also mean 'abiding in my heart.' This is the special reason why she had the first claim on his attention. स्वहस्तो०—Drawing the beloved's picture is one of the four ways by which lovers in separation beguile longing. *Cf.* वियोगावस्थासु प्रियजनसदृक्षानुभवनं ततश्चित्रं कर्म स्वपनसमये दर्शनमपि । तदङ्गस्पृष्टानामुपगतवतां स्पर्शनमपि प्रतीकारः कामव्यथितमनसां कोऽपि कथितः ॥ मुग्धया—The innocent one, who in her love-mania did not know that it would be of little avail to address a picture. रहसि—in private. Malli. remarks

सखीमात्रसमक्षम्; but this is not necessary. The friends might have overheard her ejaculations at times.

Śl. 60. तपःसाक्षिषु—Because the trees were planted there by her as soon as she went there to practise penance. प्ररोहाभिमुखः—has not even shown signs of sprouting up; she has not got even a distant glimpse of the fulfilment of her object.

Śl. 61. प्रार्थित०—प्रार्थितश्चासौ दुर्लभश्च; see *supra* śl. 46. अस्रोत्तरं-अस्रैः उत्तरं यथा स्यात्तथा; see com. अस्रान्तरं *V. l.* अस्राणामन्तरे उद्गमनिपतनयोरन्तराले. वृषा—वर्षति इति the showerer; Indra, originally regarded as the god of rain (and then as the god of wealth, the showerer of gifts; see Ṛig. I. 2. 7, 8). सीता—Properly a furrow or line of a plough-share; hence, ploughed land; tilled ground. तदवग्रहक्षताम्—Malli. proposes to take तद् separately as the object of न वेद्मि. But this does not seem to be natural. The poet intends the whole as a comp. word (तस्यावग्रहः तद०): तद् referring to वृषन् is put in for the sake of force. The friend wishes to bring to the ascetic's notice the obstinacy of both—Indra and Śiva—in withholding their favours respectively from the ground and Pârvatî who are quite innocent in the matter. Both are sufferers, but it is not an evil of their own seeking.

Śl. 62. अगूढ०—अगूढः सद्भावो यस्मिन्कर्मणि तद्यथा तथा. सद्भाव—Honest intentions; innocent thoughts. नैष्ठिक—निष्ठा मरणं तत्पर्यन्तं (उपनयनोत्तरं) ब्रह्मचर्येण तिष्ठति इति; fr. निष्ठा इक (ठञ्) भवार्थे; a life-long religious student who lives at his Guru's house and observes the vow of celibacy. See Yâj. S. I. 49. ०सुन्दरः—the handsome ascetic; see śl. 30 *supra*; or सुन्दर may mean by Lakshaṇâ श्रेष्ठ. Malli. takes this in the sense of Vilâsin, probably because Śaṃkara had come there as a lover as suggested by अत्यजितहर्षलक्षणः; the ascetic was rejoiced at heart to see how deep Pârvatî's love for him was, but he betrayed no sign of joy. अपीरं—*V. l.* is better.

Śl. 63. अग्रहस्ते—The comp. must be dissolved as Malli. has done it. Here अग्र is the अवयव (part) and हस्त the Avayavin. In a Karm. comp. such as नीलोत्पल, the उत्पल and its नीलत्व are identical. But in this case अग्र and हस्त are not identical; they may, however, be so regarded metaphorically, through their relation of Avayava and Avayavin, as remarked by Vâmana; K.-S.-V. V. 7. 20; see com. For a fuller discussion of the point see our notes on Śâk. p. 92. स्फटिका०—स्फटिकानां स्फटिकनिर्मिता वा अक्षमालिका; here अक्ष० merely means a rosary.

Śl. 64. वेदविदां—वेदं वेदार्थं विदन्तीति वेदविदः । तथा may be supplied after यथा, यथा श्रुतं तत्तथा । लङ्घन—going up to, attainment of. किल—indeed; or, as Malli. takes it, falsely; this penance is a means of attaining it; but it does not seem to be so. Ar. and Nâr. also take it अपरमार्थे. मनोरथानां—*i. e.* desire can aspire to attain anything. मनसो रथो मनोरथः.

अद्रेस्तनया—This has its significance. Although the daughter of the mountain and therefore स्थिरचित्ता, she was so much overpowered by emotion that she could not for a long time adjust her words and make an effort to speak. मिताक्षरं—मितानि अक्षराणि यथा स्युस्तथा. चिर०—चिरेण व्यवस्थापिता वाग्यया ।

Śl. 65. आह—Strictly, the use of आह in the sense of the past tense is to be impugned. विदितः—Malli. says मया; it may as well be त्वया or सर्वैः. With मया the meaning will be—I know Śaṃkara as one who once insulted you by ignoring your beauty and burning Madana. महेश्वरः—ironical. पुनरेव—Ar. reads पुर एव and thus comments on it—पुर एव मद्दर्शनात्प्रागेवारभ्य । यदि मम त्वद्दर्शनं प्रागेवाभविष्यत्तर्हि तदर्थिनी त्वं नाभविष्यः इति भावः । अनुवृत्ति &c.—I cannot follow you in this; I cannot advise you to follow such a course. *Cf.* आलेपो भसितं विभूषितमहिर्वासः पितॄणां वने वेतालाः परिचारकाः प्रतिदिनं वृत्तिश्च भिक्षामयी । इत्थं यस्य शुभेतराणि चरितान्याख्यान्ति सर्वे जनास्तस्मिन्मोग्ध्यवशान्मतिस्तव रुचिं बध्नाति किं ब्रूमहे ॥ अन्यच्च । जगत्त्रयीलोचनबालचन्द्रिका कुलस्य रत्नं भवती क भूभृतः । क कृत्तिवासाः पितृकानने वसन्नमङ्गलाचाररतिस्त्रिलोचनः ॥ Pár. P. IV. 12, 13.

Śl. 66. अवस्तु—an unworthy object, *viz.* love for Śiva. Here अ has the sense of अप्राशस्त्य; not the proper or worthy person. The negative particle has six senses:—तत्सादृश्यमभावश्च तदन्यत्वं तदल्पता । अप्राशस्त्यं विरोधश्च नञर्थाः षट् प्रकीर्तिताः ॥ निर्बन्ध—persistence in. कौतुक—the nuptial thread tied round the wrist; see Ragh. VIII. 1. वलयी०—*Cf.* श्मशानचारी सततं व्यालाभरणभूषितः । निन्दितः सर्वलोकेषु स कथं वाञ्छ्यते त्वया ॥ तस्योद्वाहनकाले च हा हा कर्तुं भविष्यति । फणिकंकणसंयोगं यदा ते कंकणं भवेत् ॥ S. P.; अस्मिन्नगृह्यत पिनाकभृता सलीलमाबद्धवेपथुरधीरविलोचनायाः । विन्यस्तमङ्गलमहौषधिरीश्वरायाः स्रस्तोरगप्रतिसरेण करेण पाणिः ॥ Kir. V. 33.

Śl. 67. तावत्—sufficiently, fully (Malli.); quickly (Ar.); in the first place, first of all (Châr). स्वयं-स्वतः-*V. l.* naturally, goes with योग. कलहंसलक्षणम्—कलहंसाः लक्षणं यस्य. The figures of swans painted or impressed upon it with Gorochanâ or turmeric. गोरोचनादिलिखितहंसमिथुनसनाथपर्यन्तभागमित्यर्थः । Nâr. गजाजिनं—It is said that Śiva, when he killed Gajásura, danced with his body covered with the skin stripped off from the body of the demon and wet with blood, and wore it afterwards as a trophy. For further information see our note on the word at Megh. I. 38. Ar. reads क च इंस० ए भ्राजिरं &c., but the incongruity expressed by the two कs is already expressed by the question in the 2nd line.

Śl. 68. चतुष्क—चत्वारोऽवयवा यस्य, fr. चतुर्+क (कन्) added to form a name (संज्ञार्थं); see Pâṇ. V. 1. 58. A hall supported by four pillars, a saloon; here it seems to be used for चतुःशालं or a house formed with four halls facing each other. अवकीर्ण—placed or set on. The flower-covered floors of the halls are contrasted with the cemetery grounds, the favourite resorts of Śiva, frightful with the hairs of dead bodies scattered all round. परेत-परं लोकं इतः gone परा दूरं इतः इति वा परेतः a dead person.

Śl. 69. अनुरूपं—अतिशयेन युक्तं युक्तरूपं, तत्र भवतीस्य०; now see Malli. त्रिनेत्रवक्षःसुलभं—See Malli.; it is better, however, to take the whole as one comp. word (०वक्षसि सुलभं). The construction, too, would thus become simple; तथापि अस्मिन्...स्तनद्वये त्रिनेत्रवक्षः-सुलभं चिताभस्मरजः पदं करिष्यति &c. There is no objection to the change of न to ण in त्रिणेत्र (by पूर्वपदात्संज्ञायाम्); see Malli. on Śiś. XIII. 27; but, as the word is generally written as त्रिनेत्र, Malli. defends it by including it in the क्षुभ्नादि group; see com. on VII. 69 *infra*. हरिचन्दनं—हरेर्विष्णोरिन्द्रस्य वा चन्दनम् । Or, घृष्टं च तुलसीकाष्ठं कर्पूरागुरुयोगतः । अथ वा केशरैर्योज्यं हरिचन्दनमुच्यते ॥ Padma-Purâṇa.

Śl. 70. पुरः—before you *i. e.* will inevitably follow when you are married. विडम्बना—matter for laughing or derision; fr. डम्ब् with वि+अन (णिच्)+*fem.* आ. ०हार्यया—who are accustomed to be borne on a lordly elephant. ०भार्यया *V. l.*-excellent female-elephant. वृद्धोक्ष:—वृद्धश्चासौ उक्षा च; उक्षन् is changed to उक्ष at the end of a Karm. by Pâṇ. V. 4. 77. महाजन:—includes the idea of men, many and good or respectable; see Malli. on न लङ्घयामास महाजनानां शिरांसि नेवोद्धतिमाजगाम । Śiś. III. 28. Nâr. says—ओषधिप्रस्थवास्तव्यो लोकः तेषामन्यथैव पूर्वं परिचयात्. स्मेर—smiling; from स्मि+र, by नमिकम्पिस्म्यजसकमहिंसदीपो रः Pâṇ. III. 2. 167. र is added कर्तरि; नम्रः, कम्प्रः; स्मेरः, अजस्रं (जसिर्नञ्पूर्वः क्रियासातत्ये वर्तते Sid.-Kau.) &c.

Śl. 71. पिनाकिनः—कपालिनः *V. l.* better suits the context as indicating Śiva's misery; पिनाकिनः bespeaks power on his part. This appears to be the original reading from śl. 78, where reference is made to Śiva's कपालित्व. कला च सा—*i. e.* which Śiva holds on his crest. Śl. quoted in K.-P. V. with the remark—द्वयं गतमित्यादौ पिनाक्यादिपदवैलक्षण्येन किमिति कपाल्यादिपदानां काव्यानुगुणत्वम् । K.-

Pradîpa says—इत्यादौ न पिनाक्यादिपदमनुकूलं किं तु जुगुप्साव्यञ्जकतया कपालिपदमेव ।–and also in VII. as remarked by Malli., to show that when the sense can be easily known the relative pronoun may be left understood. Here सा refers to the digit of the moon which is well known. It is again quoted further on as an instance of the fault अक्रमत्व or the absence of the syntactical order of words. Here the proper position of च is immediately after त्वं; for it is the word त्वं and not लोक that is meant to be conjoined with कला as an object to be deplored. Also quoted in S.-D. in this connexion with the remark अत्र त्वमित्यनन्तरमेव चकारो युक्तः । नेत्रकौमुदी—A beautiful woman is often compared to moon-light (on account of her complexion); hence the giver of delight or the cause of joy. *Cf.* त्वं कौमुदी नयनयोः Uttar. III. 29; मम तु यदियं याता लोके विलोचनचन्द्रिका; या कौमुदी नयनयोर्भवतः सुजन्मा; Mâl.-Mâdh. I. 36, 34; Ragh. VI. 85.

Ś1. 72. विरूपाक्षं—विरूपमक्षि यस्य the third eye being fiery and tawny-coloured (भीषणत्वात्पिंगलत्वाच्च । Ch.). The eyes are so deformed; why talk of the other limbs then? (सर्वाङ्गप्रधानं चक्षुरेव यस्य विरूपं तस्येतराङ्गं किं वक्तव्यमित्यर्थः Uddyota). Again, the additional eye is an ominous sign. Śl. quoted in K.-P. VII. as an instance of अविमृष्टविधेयांश or the prominent non-mention of the predicate. Here (in अलक्ष्यजन्मता) unknowability is intended to be predicated of birth; but the predicate अलक्ष्य is subordinated as it is compounded. To avoid this the readings अलक्षिता जनिः, अलक्षितं जनुः are suggested. वरेषु &c.—*Cf.* कुलेन कान्त्या वयसा नवेन गुणैश्च तैस्तैर्विनयप्रधानैः । त्वमात्मनस्तुल्यममुं वृणीष्व &c. Ragh. VI. 79.

Śl. 73. असदी०—असच्च तदीप्सितं च तस्मात्. द्व न्द्व—See Śl. 4. वैदिकी—as ordained in the Veda; वेदे भवाः fr. वेद+ठञ् (इक) added by the rule 'अध्यात्मादिभ्यश्च' the अध्यात्मादि being an आकृतिगण. *Cf.* तत्परित्यज्य गिरिशमुपेन्द्रं वा शचीपतिम् । वरय त्वं विशालाक्षि वरयोग्यौ तु तौ तव ॥ S. P. श्मशानशूल—which is used for unholy purposes only, criminals being impaled on it, while the यूप is used exclusively for holy purposes. This must have insulted Pârvatî the most.

Śl. 74. प्रतिकूल—प्रतीपं कूलात्प्रतिकूलं *lit.* against the current; hence, in opposition to one's wishes; प्रतिकूलं वदतीति तद्विरः. विकुञ्चित०—In a manner in which her creeperlike eye-brows were greatly bent or contracted. तिर्यगाहिते—*i. e.* she cast at him a look of contempt.

Śl. 75. परमार्थतः—परमार्थः the highest sense or object; hence, the truth or reality; you do not know Hara as to his real nature;

you only know him superficially. This is a refutation of the ascetic's assertion विदितो महेश्वरः śl. 65. अलोकसामान्यं—न विद्यते लोके सामान्यं यस्य Avachûri. For, उपसर्गाः क्षयं यान्ति छिद्यन्ते विघ्नपल्लवाः । मनः प्रसन्नतां याति पूज्यमाने महेश्वरे ॥ मन्दाः—the dull-minded who cannot know the real nature of great men's actions; *cf.* दह्यमानाः सुतीव्रेण नीचाः परयशोग्निना । अशक्तास्तत्पदं गन्तुं ततो निन्दां प्रकुर्वते ॥

Śl. 76. विपत्प्रतीकार०—विपदः प्रतीकारः विप०, स परं यस्य । मङ्गल—Sing. for the plural (as it refers to the whole class of *Mangalas*); see Malli. भूतिस०—भूतौ prosperity समुत्सुकः eager to obtain तेन. जगच्छरण्यस्य—and therefore not विपत्प्रतीकारपर. निराशिषः—of him who is free from desires, being always परिपूर्ण (not only that, but पूर्णात्पूर्णमदुच्यते) and therefore not भूतिसमुत्सुक. This is a reply to अमङ्गलाभ्यासरतिं &c. śl. 65. Pâr. means to say—It matters very little whether he is मङ्गलरति or अमङ्गलरति—he who has nothing to wish for but is the fulfiller of the wishes of all; who has not a calamity to ward off but is the warder off of the calamities of the world. आशोपहता०—which vitiate or overpower the functions of the mind by generating desires or holding forth hopes—qualifies मङ्गलैः. आभिः आशो०-*v. l.* dissolve आशया उपहतः आत्मा येषां ते आशोपहतात्मानः तेषां वृत्तिभिः; by these doings (course of action) of those whose minds are overpowered by desire.

Śl. 77. अकिंचनः—See com. Tat. comp. of the मयूरव्यंसकादि class, and not a Bah. त्रिलोकनाथः—Malli. taks this a an उत्तरपदत०, but this is grammatically inaccurate; see our note on चतुर्मुख० II. 17. It is better to dissolve this as त्र्यवयवो लोकः त्रिलोकस्तस्य नाथः. Having nothing, he is the source of wealth of every kind; lord of (pervading) the three worlds, he can be found (delights to live) in the cremation ground; so in fact no one can form an adequate conception of Śiva. *Cf.* प्राकाम्यं ते विभूतिषु II. 11. This is a reply to विकीर्णकेशासु परेतभूमिषु śl. 68.

Śl. 78. पिनद्धभोगि—पिनद्धः भोगी a serpent यत्र; the अ of अपि may optionally be dropped; so अपिनद्ध also. भोगिन्—Fr. भोग a serpent's body or hood+इन्. कपाली—Śiva, according to the Kâśîkhaṇḍa, once got very angry with Brahmâ on hearing the latter's proud declaration that he (Śiva) had sprung from his forehead &c. and created in anger the fierce Kâlabhairava, who severed one of the heads of Brahmâ with his nails. Śiva, thereafter, wore, as Kâlabhairava, the skull of Brahmâ's head. *Cf.* स (पितामहः) मायया महेशस्य मोहितो लोकसंभवः । हिरण्यगर्भस्तं प्राह जाने त्वां चन्द्रशेखर ॥ भालस्थलान्मम पुरा रुद्रः प्रादुरभूद्भवान् । अथेश्वरः पद्मयोनेः श्रुत्वा गर्ववतीं गिरम् ॥ स कोपतः समुत्पाद्य पुरुषं भैरवाकृतिम् । प्राह पङ्कजजन्मासौ शास्यस्ते

कालभैरव ॥ (स) वामाङ्गुलिनखाग्रेण चकर्त च शिरो विधेः । (शिवः) प्राह स्वमूर्तिमपरां भैरवं तं कपर्दिनम् ॥ कपालं वैधसं चापि नीललोहित धारय। चर त्वं सततं भिक्षां कपालिव्रतमास्थितः ॥ काशीखण्ड (as quoted by Mr. Deshpande). न विश्वमूर्तेः &c.—*Cf.* विष्णोरिवास्यानवधारणीयमीदृक्तया रूपमियत्तया वा। Ragh. XIII. 5. This is a reply to Ślokas 66, 67, and 71.

Śl. 79. नृत्या°—The dance of Śiva is called ताण्डव (तण्डुना प्रोक्तं) which is a kind of vehement dance. अभिनय–हृद्गतभावाभिव्यञ्जकशरीरचेष्टाः movements of the body indicative of internal feelings; gesticulations. विलुप्यते *v. l.*—is taken off, as it sticks to their foreheads in the act of bowing.

Śl. 80. प्रभिन्न°—With the temples split open, *i e.*, shedding rut. वृष and दिग्वारण are contrasted. 'Who can describe the greatness of Śiva before whom even Indra bends his head?' A retort flung with equal force at the Brahmachârin, saying इयं च तेऽन्या पुरतो विडम्बना &c. śl. 70. उपनम्य—*v. l.* is unnecessary as the idea of bowing is implied by मौलिना. विनिद्र &c.—विनिद्राणि (full-blown) च तानि मन्दाराणि विनिद्रमन्दाराणि; see com. *Cf.* महोक्षः खट्वाङ्गं परशुरजिनं भस्म फणिनः कपालं चेतीयत्तव वरद तन्त्रोपकरणम् । सुरास्तां तां सिद्धिं दधति तु भवद्भ्रूप्रणिहितां न हि स्वात्मारामं विषयमृगतृष्णा भ्रमयति ॥ Pushpadanta's महिम्नस्तोत्र śl. 8.

Śl. 81. विवक्षता—*Pre. p.* of the Desid. of वच्. We may also construe दोषं विवक्षता अत एव च्युतात्मना (मान्यानां निन्दाकरणात्). विवृण्वता—*v. l.* pointing out, telling.

Śl. 82. अलं विवादेन—Here अलं has the sense of वारण; the meaning is—साध्याभावाद्विवादो न कर्तव्यः। गम्यमानसाधनक्रियापेक्षया विवादस्य करणत्वात्तृतीया। गम्यमानापि क्रिया कारकविभक्तौ प्रयोजिकेति नियमात्। See Malli. on Ragh. II. 34. भावैक°—Solely attached by the feeling of love; entirely swayed by the sentiment of love. स्थिर–*v. l.* firmly set on. वचनीयं—see IV. 21.

Śl. 83. बटुः—fr. बट् 10 cl. to tell and the Uṇâdi aff. उ; वाचाटः a garrulous fellow. स्फुरितोत्तरा°—स्फुरितमुत्तर अधिकं यस्मिन् would be the natural way of taking the comp. (see Malli. on Ragh. VII. 49); but as this would require the पूर्वनिपात of उत्तर, we analyse it as स्फुरितेन उत्तरः mixed with, conspicuous with. उत्तरशब्द आधिक्यं ब्रुवाणः सन् मिश्रत्वमाह । तथा च–निनाय सात्यर्थहिमोत्तरानिलाः । हिममिश्रा इत्यर्थः। Hemâdri on Ragh. VI. 50. Some take उत्तर to mean the upper lip; स्फुरितौ उत्तराधरौ यस्मिन्. *Cf.* निवार्यतामयं भिक्षुर्विवक्षुः स्फुरिताधरः । न तावन्निन्दकः पापी यथा शृण्वन् शशिप्रभे ॥ Vámana-P.; यः करोति महादेवनिन्दामात्मविनाशिनीम् । स पापिष्ठतरस्तस्माद्यः शृणोति स पापभाक् ॥ S. P.

Śl. 84. स्तन०—स्तनाभ्यां भिन्नं वल्कलं यस्याः सा. वृषराज०—केत्यते ज्ञायते अनेन इति केतनं a distinguishing mark, a flag; वृषराजः केतनं यस्य *Cf.* इत्युक्त्वोत्थाय गच्छन्त्यां पिधाय श्रवणावुभौ । स्वरूपं समुपाश्रित्य जग्रहे वसनं हरः ॥ Brahma-P.

Śl. 85. वेपथु—Tremor; from वेप्+अथु. This is one of the Sâttvika Bhávas:—स्तम्भः स्वेदोऽथ रोमाञ्चः स्वरभङ्गोऽथ वेपथुः । वैवर्ण्यमश्रुप्रलया-वित्यष्टौ सात्त्विका गुणाः ॥ सरसा०—full of perspiration (स्वेद). निक्षेप एव—*V. l.* निक्षेप इति निमित्तसप्तमी । निक्षेपणार्थं यत्पदमुद्धृतं तत्तथैवो-द्वहन्तीत्यर्थः । Nár. निक्षेप एव...मर्पयन्ती *V. l.*—उद्धृतं पदं निक्षेपे निक्षिप्यते यस्मादिति निक्षेपः पूर्वस्थानम् । तत्र अर्पयन्ती स्थापयन्ती । व्यतिकर—forcible contact; hence, an obstruction. Śl. quoted in D.-R. as an instance of साध्वस (agitation at the sight of a lover), and in S. K. B. of रसरूपेणैव रससिद्धिः. *Cf.* पार्वती सविस्मयप्रहर्षं पुलकिततनुः प्रस्विन्नगण्डा प्रतिपत्तिमूढा तिष्ठति । Pâr. P.

Śl. 86. अनवमाङ्गि—*V. l.* न अवमं low or base अनवमं the best अङ्गं यस्यास्तत्संबुद्धिः । चन्द्रमौलौ—साभिप्रायं पदम् । अन्यस्यापि क्रीतदासस्य मौला अङ्गी भवति । Sukhâvabodha com. (Deshpande). फलेन—*i. e.* the attainment of fruit; imparts fresh vigour which removes fatigue and refreshes one; some separate फलेन हि as फले (सति) हि नवतां &c., *i. e.* when the fruit is obtained it does not certainly remain fresh, *i. e.* is forgotten. This is not so forcible as the first. नवतां पिधत्ते *V. l.*—प्रत्यग्रतामाच्छादयति conceals its freshness, *i. e.* is not felt as anything. *Cf.* तव हस्तदानचतुरस्तपसा हि क्रीतोऽयमस्मि दासजनः । Pár. P.

CANTO VI.

Śl. 1. संदिदेश—Sent as a messenger, *i. e.* sent a message through her. प्रमाणीक्रियताम्—should be approached or referred to as an authority (not being so approached before), *i. e.* should be formally applied to for my hand and his consent obtained (the father being the proper authority for the disposal of his daughter in marriage).

Śl. 2. व्याहृत०—व्याहृतः संदेशो यस्याः । निभृता प्रिये—निभृता appears to mean 'keeping quiet'; silently waiting for her espousal by Śiva, thereby indicating her modesty; as one Com. says, सलज्जत्वाद्विनीता. चूतयष्टिः—should rather mean a young mango-tree (*cf.* अङ्गयष्टि). अभ्यासे—near at hand. The meaning is—Párvatí, having sent word to Śiva as to the course he was to adopt, stood silently waiting for her marriage, just as a young mango-tree stands expecting the advent of summer (when it is about to set in), sending the call for it through the *kokila*. The notes of the cuckoo always herald the spring. आभाष्ये—*V. l.* constr. मधौ आभाष्ये—'when Vasanta is to be addressed.' परभृतो०—see Malli.; it is better to take परभृता as Instr. sing, as suggested by Mallinátha.

Śl. 3. कथमपि—With difficulty (as he was now irresistibly drawn towards her, being won over by her unflinching devotion and love); see Malli. ऋषीन् सप्त—For their names see notes on I. 16. ज्योतिर्मयान्—*i. e.* having astral bodies as apart from their physical ones. The Ṛishis in their astral forms constitute the constellation of stars called 'Ursa Major,' or the 'Great Bear.' कलया चरन्ति रात्रिषु दिवि ये सप्तर्षयो मरीच्याद्याः । Parâśara-Saṃhitâ. *Cf.* त्रिम्यो निमन्त्रिताश्चैनमभिजग्मुर्महर्षयः । न भौमान्येव धिष्ण्यानि हित्वा ज्योतिर्मयान्यपि । Ragh. XV. 59. सस्मार—In the original no mention is made of the Ṛishis being deputed to Himâlaya.

Śl. 4. सारुन्धतीकाः—Arundhatî, wife of Vasishṭha, was one of the nine daughters of Kardama Prajâpati by Devahûti. She is regarded as the highest pattern of conjugal excellence and wifely devotion, and as such is invoked by the bridegroom at nuptial ceremonies. The Ṛishis are invariably associated with Arundhatî and are always so invoked. See foot-note. Astronomically represented she is the smallest star in the constellation Ursa Major. प्रभोः—explains why they readily appeared before Śiva.

Śl. 5. आप्लुताः &c.-The sages bathed as they had to approach the supreme Deity. They are described as bathing in the heavenly Ganges; *cf.* Ragh. X. 63 (कृताभिषेकैर्दिव्यायां त्रिस्रोतसि &c.). उत्किरन्तीति उत्किराः 'which throw up'; now see com. दिङ्नाग—Quarter-elephants are represented as sporting in the water of the celestial Ganges; *cf.* Ragh. I. 78.

Śl. 6. रत्नाक्षसूत्राः—The Kalpa trees bore strings of pearls and jewels, and so the Ṛishis are compared to them. *Cf.* एषां गिरेः सकलरत्नफलस्तरुः स प्राग्दुग्धभूमिसुरभेः खलु पञ्चशाखः । मुक्ताफलं फलनसान्वयनाम तन्वन्नाभाति बिन्दुभिरिव च्छुरितः पयोधिः ॥ Nai.-Ch. XI. 10. प्रव्रज्यां—Malli. understands by this the Samnyâsâśrama or the fourth order in the religious life of a Brâhmaṇa, and then takes it to refer to the Vânaprasthâśrama by Lakshaṇâ; see his remarks. This, however, is not necessary, as the abandonment of wife, the sacred thread, &c., is not necessary in every kind of Saṃnyâsa. By Pravrajyâ we might understand the विद्वत्संन्यास, such as was practised by

Yájñavalkya and others (सम्यगनुष्ठितैः श्रवणमननं निदिध्यासतैः परतत्त्वं विदितवद्भिः संपद्यमानो विद्वत्संन्यासः ।). See also Bg. VI. 1, 2; XVIII. 2. Looking to the general drift of the śl. it appears better, however, to take प्रव्रज्या in the sense of 'going, motion.' The Ṛishis had jewels, gold &c. on, and so looked like the Desire-granting trees in motion. If we accept Malli.'s sense, the comparison to Kalpa-trees become meaningless. *Cf.* हेमपरोह इव जङ्गमकल्पवृक्षः Vik. V. 19.

Śl. 8. आसक्तबा°—आसक्ता या बाहुलता ; Malli. takes बाहुलता to belong to the earth and he is right. We can hardly call the sages' arms 'लता,' which is an expression that goes naturally with the arms of ladies, not of big men. तया उद्धृतया भुवा-The earth which was submerged in the oceanic waters was drawn up by Vishṇu, assuming the form of a Boar. *Cf.* Gîtagovinda-वसति दशनशिखरे धरणी तव लग्ना । शशिनि कलङ्ककलेव निमग्ना । केशव धृतशूकररूप जय जगदीश हरे ॥ See also B. P. III. 13.

Śl. 9. प्रणयन—Mark the root-sense—'carrying' forward (the work of), completing. पुरातनाः—पुरा भवाः । See दिवातन *supra* IV. 46. धातारः &c.—The seven sages were the mind-born sons (प्रजापतिs) of Brahmâ created for the purpose of carrying on the work of creation. "The descendants of the daughters of Daksha were married to these Brahmarshis. Mârkaṇḍeya was the son of Mṛikaṇḍu the grandson of Bhṛigu. The 49 fires, the 60,000 Válakhilyas, &c., were the progeny of these sages. V. P. I. 10." Deshpande.

Śl. 10. तपस्विनः—*i. e.* they kept their minds under control although enjoying the fruits of their penance. For the fruit of penance, *cf.* Śák. VII. 12.

Śl. 11. पत्युः पार्श्व°-The whole should have been compounded; but it is not compounded as the connexion can be easily known. पार्श्वार्पित°—For such is the mode of conduct prescribed for a lady of honour.

Śl. 12. ईश्वरः—fr. ईश् + वरच् by स्थेशभासपिसकसो वरच् । Pâṇ. III. 2. 175; स्थावर, भास्वर, पेस्वर &c. स्त्री पुमान्—*Cf.* शिशुत्वं स्त्रैणं वा भवतु ननु वन्द्यासि जगतां गुणाः पूजास्थानं गुणिषु न च लिङ्गं न च वयः । Uttar. IV. 11. सतां महितं—is esteemed by the wise ; सतां should not be taken with वृत्तम्.

Śl. 13. दारार्थे—दारेभ्य इति; दारक्रिया *v. l.* marriage. धर्म्य—*lit.* not departing from, keeping to, duty ; see com. Similarly पथ्य, अर्घ्य &c. पत्नी—is the *fem.* when the meaning is 'she who shares in the fruit of the sacrificial acts performed by the husband.' मूल०—For the precept is सस्त्रीको धर्ममाचरेत्। *Cf.* Mah.-Bhá. भार्या मूलं त्रिवर्गस्य भार्या मूलं तरिष्यतः ।

Śl. 14. धर्मेण—*i. e.* by the God of religious duties or righteousness (depending upon married life), and not by Râga or sensual desire. शर्व—Śiva in the form of क्षिति; *cf.* शर्वाय क्षितिमूर्तये नमः । Bhav. P.; fr. शॄ-शृणातीति the destroyer; this accounts for the fear of Káma. पदं का०— पदं कृ 'to set foot on'; hence, to bring under influence; *cf.* III. 33, V. 21 &c. *Cf.* हञ्जे पश्य कारितैव बकुलावलिकया एतस्मिन्पदं मालविका । Mâlav. III. p. 54. Chár. प्राग्धर्मेण प्रार्थितो ब्रह्मा यदा हरो गौरीं परिणेष्यति तदा स्मरः स्वं वपुः प्राप्स्यतीति शापान्तं चक्रे । अतो धर्मेण गौरीं प्रत्युद्यमः कारितो न तु रागेण ।

Śl. 15. जगद्गुरु—गुरु may mean (1) the father, *i. e.* creator of the world; *cf.* जगतः पितरौ वन्दे &c. Ragh. I. 1; or (2) adorable to. अनूचान—one who has studied the Vedas with their *aṅgas* (accessary works) and is able to expound them; see com. It is formed from वच् with अनु with the affix आन (कानच्) added कर्तरि. वेदस्यानुवचनं कृतवान् Sid.-Kau. The six *aṅgas* are—शिक्षा कल्पो व्याकरणं निरुक्तं छन्दसां चयः । ज्योतिषामयनं चैव वेदाङ्गानि षडेव तु ॥ प्रीतिक०—कण्टका आसां संजाताः कण्टकिताः; now see com. ०कितं वचः-*V. l.* प्रीत्या कण्टकितं गद्गदं obstructed, faltering यथा तथा वचः ऊचुः.

Śl. 16. आम्नातं—studied and acted upon; अनेन ब्रह्मचर्याश्रमधर्मोनुष्ठानमुक्तम् । Nâr. तस्य—*i. e.* कृत्स्नस्य तस्य कर्मणः; or पृथगन्वयादेकवचनम्. विपक्वं—'has pre-eminently borne fruit'.

Śl. 17. मनोरथ—*lit.* the car of the mind; hence, the mind moving from one object to another like a car; hence, desire. ०स्याविः०—beyond the province of desire; not to be thought of even by the mind. ०स्याप्यपथं—*V. l.* has the same meaning, and is better, inasmuch as it avoids the repetition of विषय. मनोविषय०-may mean—the object of our minds, *i. e.* thyself; or (we have been made) the object of thy mind, thou having remembered us.

Śl. 18. यस्य चेतसि &c.—*Cf.* केवलं स्मरणेनैव पुनासि पुरुषं Ragh. X. 29. कृतिनां—प्रशस्तं कृतमस्यास्तीति; here इन् shows excellence; who has a good stock of merit, blessed. तावत्—surely (अवधारणे). ब्रह्म—the Vedas; *cf.* the Śruti निःश्वसितमस्य वेदाः, and the Bâd. Sûtra शास्त्रयोनित्वात् I. 1. 3. It may also mean ब्रह्मा; ब्रह्मणः योनिः the source, generator of.

Śl. 19. अर्क—fr. अर्क् 10. P. to praise अर्कयते; or fr. अर्च्, च् being changed to क् by Unâdi III. 40.

Śl. 20. स्वसंभावितं—contains the fault अविमृष्टविधेयांशत्व. प्रत्ययं-When eminent men show respect, one gets confidence in one's merits. *Cf.* for the idea differently expressed—आ परितोषाद्विदुषां ....बलवदपि शिक्षितानामात्मन्यप्रत्ययं चेतः। Śák. I. 2.

Śl. 21. विरूपाक्ष—This is variously derived as विविधानि रविचन्द्राग्निरूपाणि अक्षीण्यस्य; or विरूपेष्वपि अक्षि कृपादृष्टिर्यस्य; or विविधरूपाणि विविधरूपेषु वा अक्षाणि इन्द्रियाणि यस्य। Any of these will do here. त्वदनुध्यान०—Ar. reads तव निध्यान० (revelation or sight of you), and remarks त्वदनुध्यानेति पाठे स्मरणानुग्रहात्तव (śl. 13) इति पुनरुक्तं स्यात्। निध्यानात्स्वरूपसाक्षात्कारात्। Nár. अन्तरात्मा—see Manus. XII. 12, 13.

Śl. 22. साक्षात्—*i. e.* in a form perceptible to the senses. अञ्जसा—(Instr. sing. of अञ्जस् used as an *adv.*) correctly; as regards thy true nature; तत्त्वे त्वञ्जाञसा द्वयोः। Amara. *Cf.* याथार्थ्यं वेद कस्तव। Ragh. X. 24. न धियां पथि वर्तसे—*Cf.* यतो वाचो निवर्तन्ते अप्राप्य मनसा सह। Tait. Up.

Śl. 23. व्यक्तं—The distinct or manifested world (developed from अव्यक्त or the indistinct originating principle). *Cf.* अव्यक्तो व्यक्तकारणम्। Ragh. X. 18. भागः—not a portion or a part, but a phase of; 'thou art the same in these three capacities.' *Cf.* the Smṛiti—ब्रह्मत्वे सृजते लोकान्विष्णुत्वे पालयत्यपि। रुद्रत्वे संहरत्येव तिस्रोऽवस्थाः स्वयंभुवः॥

Śl. 24. सुमहती—गुह्यार्थबोधनाद् दुर्लभा Chár.; one to which we cannot aspire just now. करवाम किम्—अत्र मुनीनां देवविषया प्रीतिर्दर्शिता। सैव भाव इति व्यपदिश्यते। रतिर्देवादिविषया व्यभिचारी तथाञ्जितः। भावः प्रोक्तः। K.-P. IV. 35.

Śl. 25. इन्दुः—उनत्त्यमृतमिति; irregularly derived fr. उन्द् to ooze, and the Uṇádi aff. उ; or उनत्ति क्लेदयति चन्द्रिकया भुवनम्। Originally इन्दु meant a sparkling drop of the Soma juice or the Soma juice itself; *cf.* सुतास इन्दवः Ṛig. I. 16. 6. It then meant 'a small round body', and finally came to mean 'the moon', when Soma became a name of the moon. उपचिन्वन्—adding to the mass of, augmenting.

Śl. 26. स्वार्थो न मे &c.—*Cf.* लोकानुग्रह एवैको हेतुस्ते जन्मकर्मणोः। Rah. X. 31. ननु—surely. मूर्तिभिः &c.—The eight forms are: the five elements, the sun, the moon and the sacrificer; see Śák. I. 1. They are thus given in the Bháv. P.—शर्वाय क्षितिमूर्तये नमः। भवाय जलमूर्तये नमः। रुद्रायाग्निमूर्तये नमः। उग्राय वायुमूर्तये नमः। भीमायाकाशमूर्तये नमः। पशुपतये यजमानमूर्तये नमः। महादेवाय सोममूर्तये नमः। ईशानाय सूर्यमूर्तये नमः। All these are for the welfare of the world, and so they show that God exists for the good of the world.

Śl. 27. चातकैः—The Chátaka bird has wholly to depend upon the clouds for water; *cf.* Bhar. त्वमेव चातकाधारोऽसीति केषां न

गोचरः । Śiva means by the simile that the gods are quite helpless and have solely to depend upon him for a deliverer, and hence his seemingly strange procedure.

Śl. 28. आत्मजन्०—आत्मनः स्वस्य जन्मने; *cf.* the Śruti आत्मा वै पुत्रनामासि । and पतिर्जायां प्रविशति गर्भो भूत्वेह मातरम् । quoted by Malli. in his com. on Ragh. II. 1;—or आत्मनो जन्म यस्य । अवर्ज्यो व्यधिकरणो बहुव्रीहिर्जन्माद्युत्तरपदः । Vâmana. उत्पादाय-*V. l.* for the production of. यजमान इव—The simile is very appropriate, and indicates the holiness of the purpose. The sacrificer performs his sacrifices for the benefit of the world; *cf.* Manus. अग्नौ प्रास्ताहुतिः सम्यगादित्यमुपतिष्ठते । आदित्याज्जायते वृष्टिर्वृष्टेरन्नं ततः प्रजाः ॥ Śiva's act, too, was for the benefit of the world.

Śl. 30. The epithets in the first half have a double application as referring to the physical and divine body of the mountain. उन्नत—(1) high; (2) lofty in character. स्थितिमान्—(1) firmly rooted; (2) keeping within the bounds of propriety. धुरं—(1) burden; (2) the responsibility of guiding the affairs of.

Śl. 31. भवत्प्रणीतं—Because the sages were the writers of smritis. आचारं—Rules for the guidance of the daily course of conduct. आमनन्ति—Malli. translates this by उपदिशन्ति proclaim or point out to others. It may also mean 'study and follow'.

Śl. 32. आर्या—आर्यते मान्यते इति; fr. ऋ + य (ण्यत्); आर्यो ब्राह्मणः प्रोक्तव्यः इति हरदत्तः । Bhaṭṭoji. व्यापारं—taking part in; कार्यार्थं—*V. l.* is simpler. पुरन्ध्रीणां—पुरं गृहं धारयतीति; or according to some पुरं धरतीति; fr. धृ + अ (च्) by Uṇâdi IV. 139; the chief woman of the house; one whose children and husband are living. For the idea *cf. infra,* Śl. 85.

Śl. 33. ओषधिप्रस्थं—ओषधीनां प्रस्थं शृङ्गं (properly a peak of the mountain). The town is probably a creation of the poet's fancy. It is not mentioned in the Śiva P., but is mentioned in the Pár. P. where Nàrada enters it by शैलेयगन्धिकटवर्त्म. The poet describes it further on in Pauráṇic style. महाकोशीप्रपाते—Mr. Deshpande's note on this is—" Śiva's departure from गौरीतपोवन which we find in Ś. P. is not authorized by Br. P. which Kálidâsa closely follows in this Canto. It must be understood, therefore, that Ś. P. strengthens the following account in relating that Śiva was not to the south of Káśī or Benares at this time. In the exhaustive list of Jambudvîpa rivers mentioned in B. P. I cannot find anything of this name. It is, however, passingly mentioned in the Kâlikâ

Puráṇa—महाकोशीप्रपाते च यद्वारि पतितं तु तैः । कौशिकी नाम सा जाता &c. Hence it appears that the junction of the महाकोशी and other streamlets form the Kausikī mentioned in B. P. with the tributaries of the Ganges—गोमतीं धूतपापां च गण्डकीं च महानदीम् । कौशिकीं निश्चितां &c. We have still a tributary of the Ganges by name कोशिका or कुशा. Properly, then, we may suppose the two Kausikis to be one and the same. Mahákosī, therefore, may be a small river in the south of Nepál or somewhere near it."

Sl. 34. संयमिनां—Ascetics (fr. संयम mental restraint); or practisers of Yoga or mental abstraction (ध्यान-धारणा-समाधि-त्रयमेकत्र संयमः ।). आद्यं—(1) first; because God practised contemplation before the creation of the universe; स तपोऽतप्यत । स तपस्तप्त्वेदं सर्वमसृजत यदिदं किं च । *Tait.*; or (2) foremost, chief. जहुः व्रीडां—In the S. P. it is Siva who gives up shame. अरुन्धत्यां तथा युक्ताः । ...तान्दृष्ट्वा सूर्यसंकाशाञ्जहौ लज्जां हरः स्वयम् ॥ (See intro.) Kálidása improves upon the original.

Sl. 35. परमम्—A particle of assent (मते *i. e.* अनुमतौ); very well; so we will do. उद्दिष्ट—mentioned, fixed upon.

Sl. 36. परमर्षयः—परमाः च ते ऋषयश्च । अनेनाकाशगमनसामर्थ्यं द्योत्यते । अतिश्यामं—दूरोपलक्ष्यमाणस्यैवाकाशस्यातिश्यामत्वादुत्पनसमय एव तादृशदेशप्राप्तिरनेनोक्ता । Når.

Sl. 37. अलका—A Pauráṇic town, the capital of Kubera, the god of wealth and regent of the North. It is also called वसुधारा, वसुस्थली and प्रभा. The three peaks of Meru, situated in the middle of Ilávarsha, form the abodes of Vishṇu, Siva and Brahmâ, called Vaikuṇṭha, Kailâsa and Brahmapura; and below them are the cities of the eight *Lokapálas*—तेषामधः शतमखज्वलनान्तकानां रक्षोम्बुपानिलशशीशपुराणि चाष्टौ ॥ Siva P. According to Dr. Bhau Daji, its situation must be looked for in Kashmir. Mr. Deshpande quotes the following from B. P.-तपसा निर्मिता राजन्स्वयं वैश्रवणेन सा । शशिप्रभाप्राकारा कैलासशिखरोपमा ॥ दिव्या हेममयी तुङ्गैः प्रासादैरुपशोभिता । महारत्नवती चित्रा दिव्यगन्धा मनोरमा ॥ अतिवाह्य—having cut off from all sides and then transplanted (Malli.); or, surpassing, excelling. स्वर्गाभि०—स्वर्गस्य अभिष्यन्दः *lit.* overflow; hence, excess or surplus of population and other things. 'Formed as if by drawing off the superfluous portion of.' By अनुविपर्यभिनिभ्यः स्यन्दतेरप्राणिषु । (Pàṇ. VIII. 3. 72) the स् of स्यन्द् is optionally changed to ष् when it does not refer to animals alone; यदि तु अतिवृद्धिपदेन केवलं प्राणिन एव गृह्यन्ते

तदा न षत्वम् । The same line occurs in Ragh. XV. 29 on which Hemâdri remarks—यत्र ग्रामादेरारम्भे यावत्संख्यो जनो व्यवस्थापि स्वस्थानादाधिक्येन यो जनः सोऽभिष्यन्दशब्देन लक्ष्यते । तस्यान्यत्रानयनं वमनशब्देन लक्ष्यते । स्वर्गादधिकस्थितिरित्यर्थः । Châr. explains it there as स्वर्गस्याभिष्यन्दवमनं शाखानगरं कृत्वेव विनिवेशिता । and here he says स्वर्गस्याभिष्यन्दः सारस्तस्य वमनमुद्गिरणम् । वमनं—means here removal (and not vomiting). The use of such words when used in a metaphorical sense does not constitute a blemish (ग्राम्यतादोषः) as remarked by Daṇḍin-निष्ठ्यूतोद्गीर्णवान्तादि गौणवृत्तिव्यपाश्रयम् । अतिसुन्दरमन्यत्र ग्राम्यकक्षां विगाहते ॥ K.-D. I. 95. भूतपूर्वमभूतपूर्वं वा जनपदं परदेशापवाहनेन स्वदेशाभिष्यन्दवमनेन वा निवेशयेत् । Kau. Arth. II. 1. 19. व्यवस्थितादभ्यधिकोऽप्यभिष्यन्दो जनादिकः । Bhoja as quoted by Nâr.

Śl. 38. गङ्गा—The streams of the Ganges encircling the city served as a ditch. वप्र—mounds of earth next to the ditch supporting the surrounding wall or rampart. ०सालं—साल a rampart. There were three things—first, the ditch or moat; then, the mounds fiery with the blazing herbs; and lastly, the wall of precious stones. The city was thus a type of ancient cities.

Śl. 39. जितसिंह०—The elephants in the city only are meant here; see Malli.; otherwise the statement will be in conflict with I. 6.—वीतवीतभयाः *v. l.* means वीतं वीतात् driving by means of a goad भयं येषाम्. बिलयोनयः—*i. e.* they were not of mortal breed, not being produced in the ordinary way. For the seven ordinary ways in which horses are produced see com.

Śl. 40. शिखरासक्त०—This shows that the city was situated on a plateau below or near the middle of the mountain (as the poet's object is to describe the great height of its mansions). संदिग्धाः—Confounded with. This shows that the sound of the drums (*murajas*) also was loud and deep. करणैः—Beatings of hands, cymbals &c. accompanying the sound of the tabor and marking the musical halts or pauses (which distinguished the sound of the *murajas* from the rumblings of the drum which were not marked by such accompaniments). See com. *Cf.* विपुलकनकशृङ्गोपान्तविश्रान्तमेघं सुरतरुवरवाटीशोभमानोपकण्ठम् । मणिभवनमहोभिः सृज्यमानेन्द्रचापं मदयति मम चेतो मन्दिरं विस्मयानाम् ॥ Pâr. P. I. 13.

Śl. 41. विलोल०—*Cf.* Śâk. शाखालम्बितवल्कलस्य च तरोः VI. 7. The clothes might have been the productions of the trees; *cf.* वासश्चित्रं मधु नयनयोर्विभ्रमादेशदक्षं......एकः सूते सकलमबलामण्डनं कल्पवृक्षः । Megh. II. 13; or dissolve विलोलानि विटपा एव अंशुकानि येषाम् । The boughs with their thick foliage looked like banners. गृहयन्त्र—

Mechanical contrivances attached to houses for holding up the flags. अपौरयत्न॰—*i. e.* without any effort on the part of the citizens.

Śl. 42. आपानभूमिषु—Parts of the mansions set apart for drinking purposes. सोपानपङ्क्तिषु *v. l.*—in the lines or rows of the flights of steps. उपहार—flowery decorations (flowers strewn over the ground; or garlands, bouquets &c. suspended from windows &c.); *cf.* भवति विरलभक्तिर्म्लानपुष्पोपहारः । Ragh. V. 74; यस्यां यक्षाः सितमणिमयान्येत्य हर्म्यस्थलानि ज्योतिश्छायाकुसुमरचितान्युत्तमस्त्रीसहायाः । आसेवन्ते मधु &c. Megh. II. 5.

Śl. 43. संचरः-a path. दुर्दिनेषु—Supply अपि after this; 'even on cloudy days' (much less on ordinary days); for clouds hide only moon-light and not herb-light. अभिसारिका-अभिसारयते कान्तं या मन्मथवशंवदा । स्वयं वाभिसरत्येषा धीरैरुक्ताभिसारिका ॥ S.-D. तमिस्रं—extensive darkness; तमिस्रं तिमिरं तमः । Amara. Or the word may be तमिस्रा, 'a dark night'; the *abhisārikās* do not know what dark nights are.

Śl. 44. यौवनान्तं—Because the inhabitants were all divine beings (त्रिदशाः). अन्तकः—Properly, the god of death, the destroyer; hence, the destroyer of happiness, afflicter. आतङ्कः—'anxiety', the reading adopted by Ar. Ch. &c., is better. *Cf.* the quotation from Megh. below. निद्रा—and not death (the long, long sleep). संज्ञाविः॰—The opposite *i. e.* loss of consciousness. *Cf.* आनन्दोत्थं नयनसलिलं यत्र नान्यैर्निमित्तैर्नान्यस्तापः कुसुमशरजादिष्टसंयोगसाध्यात् । नाप्यन्यस्मात्प्रणयकलहाद्विप्रयोगोपपत्तिर्वित्तेशानां न च खलु वयो यौवनादन्यदस्ति ॥ Megh. II. 4.

Śl. 45. भ्रूभेदिभिः—भ्रूभेदः (contraction or bending of the eyebrows) एषां विद्यते तैः; or भ्रुवौ भेत्तुं शीलमेषामिति तैः. अङ्गुलि॰—अङ्गुलिभिः तर्जनानि अङ्गुलित॰; now see com. अर्थिनः—*i. e.* they have no other object to seek. They had only to submit to ladies charming in their anger and not to the frowns of the enemies &c. अप्रसादार्थिनः *v. l.*—the reading of Ar. Châr. &c. seems to be better, as otherwise the epithets will have no significance. The ladies looked more charming in their anger, and so their husbands were not anxious to seek a reconciliation, as they were sure that their beloveds would themselves come to terms of their own accord. If the husbands sought reconciliation the proper reading would have been प्रसादार्थिनः.

Śl. 46. संतानक—One of the five trees of heaven. ॰च्छाया—See Malli.; or we may separate as च्छाये आ समन्तात् सुमाः &c.

The original reading as remarked by Malli. is सुगन्धिर्गन्धमादनः। It was probably changed owing to Amarasiṃha's line गन्धमादनमन्ये च हेमकूटादयो नगाः। गन्धमादन—name of a mountain situated to the east of Meru and known for its forests having odoriferous herbs which give it the name. According to the V. P. it is to the south of Meru, being one of its props; विष्कम्भा रचिता मेरोर्योजनायुतमुच्छ्रिताः। पूर्वेण मन्दरो नाम दक्षिणे गन्धमादनः। (तत्र च केतुवृक्षो जम्बुस्तत्र वनं गन्धमादनाख्यं) विपुलः पश्चिमे पार्श्वे सुपार्श्वश्चोत्तरे स्थितः॥ II. 16.

Śl. 47. अथ ते—तत्कान्तं *V. l.* is better as it gives the हेतु for considering residence in heaven as a deception. स्वर्गाभिसंधि०—स्वर्गस्याभिसंधिः intention to obtain स्वर्गाभि०; now see com. Châr. reads ०संधि सु० and explains स्वर्गस्याभिसंधिर्यत्र तत्. Ar. reads स्वर्गाभिसंधिसुकृतां the desire to obtain heaven, of those who perform holy deeds. This reading is better. वञ्चनां मेनिरे—For the Ṛishis themselves were दिव्याः (seekers of heaven and similarly deceived).

Śl. 48. लिखितानल०—Because their matted hair of a bright tawny colour looked like painted flames of fire. The hair remained motionless on account of their great velocity; *cf.* चित्रन्यस्तमिवाचलं (वेगानिलात्) हयशिरस्यामवञ्चामरं Vik. I. 4.

Śl. 49. यथावृद्ध०—वृद्धमनतिक्रम्य यथावृद्धं; यथावृद्धं पुरःसराः यस्यां; their order is thus given in Paráśarasamhitá—मरीचिः पूर्वभागस्थो वसिष्ठः परतस्ततः। ततोऽङ्गिरास्ततश्चात्रिः पुलस्त्यः पुलहः क्रतुः॥ See also Var. Bṛih. भास्करालो—*i. e.* भास्करप्रतिबिम्बाली. तोयान्तः—because the brilliance of the sages was not burning.

Śls. 50, 51. दूरात्—shows his great respect for the sages. For गृहानुपैतुं प्रणयादभीप्सवो भवन्ति नापुण्यकृतां मनीषिणः। Śiś. I. 14. (अतः कृच्छ्रलभ्याः सन्तः पूज्या एव Malli.). सारगुरु०—Because his bodily form represented the weight of his physical form. *Cf.* for the idea धीरोद्धता नमयतीव गतिर्धरित्रीम्। Uttar. VI. 19. धातुताम्राधरः—This and the other epithets apply to both the Sthâvara and the Jaṅgama forms of the mountain; *e.g.* (1) having lips red like red minerals, (2) having red minerals for lips; (1) having huge arms like the cedar trees, (2) having huge cedar trees for arms; &c. Comp. with this the description of Dilîpa, Ragh. I. 13, 14. सुव्यक्तः—it was clear from his form that he was the representative of the mountain.

Śl. 52. आक्रमयामास—Made them enter; see Malli.; otherwise we should have expected the Acc. of तद् (तान्). Some explain away the Instr. as सहार्थे; तैः सह आक्रमयामास प्रविवेश—taking क्रम् as a root of the चुरादि class on the principle 'सर्वे धातवो वा चुरादौ पठ्यन्ते' mentioned by the author of the Manoramá. शुद्धान्तं—शुद्धः अन्तः the interior as well as surroundings यस्य. Curiously enough, the Arabic word *Harem* also radically means 'sacred or pure', thus showing a common idea underlying the two. शुद्धकर्मभिः—explains why he took them to the harem. Their sight would be purifying.

Śl. 53. कृतासन०—अनासनप० *v. l.* who did not take a seat, but sat on the ground; this reading perhaps better brings out his modesty.

Śl. 54. अपमेघोदयं &c.—अपगतः मेघोदयः यस्मिन्. अतर्कि०—अतर्कित यथा तथोपपन्नं happening unexpectedly, and therefore quite a matter of your favour. *Cf.* तुल्या भवद्दर्शनसंपदेषा वृष्टेर्दिवो वीतबलाहकायाः। Kir. III. 5. For the thought comp. also उदेति पूर्वं कुसुमं ततः फलं घनोदयः प्राक्तदनन्तरं पयः। Śák. VII. 30; किमयममभ्रः सुधावर्षः। Mál.-Mádh. X. 10.

Śl. 55. मूर्द्ध &c.—and हैमीभूतं refer to his moral and physical elevation, while the third indicates the result of the two.

Śl. 57. द्विजोत्तमाः—द्विजेषु उत्तमाः; or even द्विजानामुत्तमाः। हलादिः शेष इत्यादौ भाष्यकृता षष्ठीसमासस्य विधानात्। See Kaiyaṭa on Mahâbhâshya on Pâṇ. V. 3. 57. गङ्गाप्रपातेन—Gaṅgâ being विष्णुपादोद्भवा. *Cf.* also कमण्डलुत्था कमलासनस्य विनिःसृता विष्णुपदान्नदी सा। भागीरथी भर्गजटावतीर्णा जगत्त्रयं जह्नुसुता पुनीते॥ Udâr. I. 21; see *infra* X. 31. धौतपादाम्भसा—the water used for washing the feet of the sage is as holy as the Ganges flowing from Vishṇu's feet. Thus the sages are indirectly praised as Vishṇu's equals. वः—is connected with धौत०; so we have a सापेक्षत्वेऽपि गमक समास.

Śl. 58. प्रैष्य—प्र+एष्यः; one who is sent on an errand, a servant; the Vṛiddhi is by प्रादूहोढोढ्येषैष्येषु Várt. on Pâṇ. VI. 1. 89. See Gr. § 20 (*a*). प्रैष्यभावेन-*v. l.* by having been made the object of your sight. द्विरूपमपि—Ar. reads द्वैरूप्यं तेन मे कृतम्—द्विरूपं एव द्वैरूप्यं by adding य स्वार्थे (चतुष्पदादित्वात्स्वार्थे ष्यञ्). Constr.—तेन प्रैष्यभावेन. चरणन्यासेन च मे रूपं विभक्तानुग्रहं विभक्तः अनुरागो यस्य तत्तथा कृतं मन्ये.

Śl. 59. मूर्छति—grading, pervading the body. अपि स्यात &c.—He speaks of himself as identical with his physical form. *Cf.* युगान्तकालप्रतिसंहृतात्मनो जगन्ति यस्यां सविकासमासत। तनौ ममुस्तत्र न कैटभद्विषस्तपोधनाभ्यागमसंभवा मुदः॥ Śiś. I. 23. प्रभवन्ति—भू with प्र in the sense of अलं governs the Dative; *cf.* विधिरपि न येभ्यः प्रभवति Bh. II.

Śl. 60. रजसोऽपि परं तमः—तमः (1) darkness; (2) the quality of तमस् (the 3rd of the three qualities) next after रजस् (the 2nd). See *supra*, notes on II. 4. The word परं indicates that not only तमस् but रजस् also is अपास्त, pure सत्त्व being left. रजस् is the cause of passions and emotions; *cf.* सत्त्वं ज्ञानं तमोऽज्ञानं रागद्वेषौ रजः स्मृतम् । Manu.; रजो रागात्मकं विद्धि &c. Bg. XIV. 7; see also 12, 13. *Cf.* न ह्यम्मयानि तीर्थानि न देवा मृच्छिलामयाः । ते पुनन्त्युरुकालेन दर्शनादेव साधवः ॥ B. P.

Śl. 61. कर्तव्यं वो &c.—(1) I do not see you have to do anything or gain any object by coming here; or (2) you want me to do anything for you. For अस्मास्वधीनं किमु निःस्पृहाणां Kir. III. 9. प्रस्थानं—Nâr. takes this in the sense of समागम and says—'प्रशब्दस्तु प्रकर्षं च द्योतयेच्च समागमम्' इति उपसर्गवृत्तिः ।.

Śl. 62. तथापि तावत् &c.—So in Ragh., तवार्हतो नाभिगमेन तृप्तं मनो नियोगक्रिययोत्सुकं मे । V. 11. प्रभविष्णु—Fr. भू with प्र+इष्णु (च्). Properly the aff. इष्णु is added to भू in the Veda only, by भुवश्च Pâṇ. III. 2. 138. But poets use such forms by poetic license. *Cf.* यत्प्रभविष्णवे रोचते । Śák. P. 49. Bhattoji (Sid.-Kau.) remarks—कथं तर्हि—जगत्प्रभोरप्रभविष्णु वैष्णवमिति (माघे)-निरङ्कुशाः कवयः । Elsewhere he says—चकारोऽनुक्तसमुच्चयार्थः । तेन भ्राजिष्णुरिति काशिका । एवं च क्षयिष्णु इति केषांचित्प्रयोगः संगच्छते । किं तु चकारस्यानुक्तसमुच्चयार्थत्वं भाष्ये नोक्तम् । अतो बहवो न पुरस्कुर्वन्ति । Śabdakaustubha.

Śl. 63. कन्येयं &c.—called कुलप्रतिष्ठा further on (VII. 27). कुलजीवितं—*cf.* जीवितमिव सिद्धराजान्वयस्य Nág. II. अनास्था—He means-I do not mention other things as not worth offering to you. The नञ् (अ) here ought not to be compounded and it should be न आस्था अस्ति. But Malli. remarks प्रसज्यप्र० &c. Writers on rhetorics mention two kinds of negation, *viz.* प्रसज्यप्रतिषेध and पर्युदास. अप्राधान्यं विधेर्यत्र प्रतिषेधे प्रधानता । प्रसज्यप्रतिषेधोऽसौ क्रियया सह यत्र नञ् ॥ The नञ् is called प्रस० when the negation, instead of the affirmation, is prominent and the नञ् is expressed with the verb. And when a word enters into a compound, it is subordinated and cannot be emphatic (समासे गुणीभूतत्वादप्राधान्यम्). But this general principle cannot be applied to every case. Páṇ. himself often compounds an emphatic नञ्; and Vámana commenting on Páṇ. III. 3. 19 says प्रसज्यप्रतिषेधेऽपि समासोऽस्ति. The नञ् here, therefore, must be taken as प्रसज्य० (emphatic) and not as पर्युदास. For other particulars see our note on अत्रस्तः &c. Ragh. I. 21.

Śl. quoted in D.-R. as an instance of औदार्य (in the form of सदुपग्रह), one of the manly qualities of the hero proceeding from Sattva.

Śl. 64. ऊचिवान्—According to grammarians this is an instance of poetic license. For the Perf. p. in वस् (which is used only in the Veda) is not to be used in ordinary language except in the case of सद्, वस्, and श्रु. But poets often use the participles of other roots also. *Cf.* कसुकानचावपि छान्दसौ इति त्रिमुनिमतम् । कवयस्तु बहुलं प्रयुञ्जते । तं तस्थिवांसं नगरोपकण्ठे (Ragh. II. 29). श्रेयांसि सर्वाण्यधिजग्मुषस्ते (V. 34) इत्यादि । Sid.-Kau. on Pāṇ. III. 2. 107. भाषायामपि क्वसुर्भवतीति भाष्यविरोधादुपेक्ष्यम् । उत्तरसूत्रानर्थक्यं च यदि भाषायामपि क्वसुर्भवति । Haradatta. The *sthâvara* form of the mountain too said the same thing. The poet is fond of describing such an effect of an echo; *cf.* Ragh. II. 51; Vik. IV. 27.

Śl. 65. अङ्गिरस्—One of the ten mind-born sons (according to B. P. III. 12, 24, he was born from Brahmá's mouth) of Brahmá; they were Prajápatis. He is the author of the hymns of R.-V. IX., of a code of law and of a treatise on astronomy. His wife was Śraddhá, by whom he had three sons. Besides Śraddhá he is said to have married Smṛiti, two daughters of Maitreya, several daughters of Daksha &c. He is also regarded as a teacher of Brahma-Vidyá which he is said to have learnt from Satyaváha, a descendant of Bharadvâja. In astronomy he is Brihaspati, the regent of Jupiter, and a star in Ursa Major. For other particulars see Apte's Dic. अग्रण्य—अग्रं नयति अग्रे नीयते वा, fr. अग्र+नी+क्विप्; the ई is changed to य् by एरनेकाचोऽसंयोगपूर्वस्य । Pāṇ. VI. 4. 82. The change of न् to ण् must be explained by ज्ञापकप्रमाण from the analogy of ग्रामणी. *Cf.* अग्रण्यमैन्द्रकृताग्रुषीणां Ragh. V. 4. उदाहरणवस्तु—उदाहरण a loud clear speech; वस्तु the subject-matter, hence well-organized speech; or things to be said, the topic of conversation. *Cf.* पत्रे निवेशितमुदाहरणं प्रियायाः । Vik. II. 13.

Śl. 67. विष्णुमाहुः—विष्णु fr. विष् 3rd conj. to pervade; वेवेष्टि सर्वमिति । यस्माद्विष्णुमयं सर्वं यच्चराचरमुच्यते । तस्मात्स गीयते विष्णुर्विशधातोः प्रवेशनात् । V. P. *Cf.* Bg. X. 25. This is according to the doctrine laid down further on in यद्यद्विभूतिमत्सत्त्वं &c. Bg. X. 41. आधारतां गतः—The mountain being in the centre of the world.

Śl. 68. अधारयत्—See Malli. Here the use of the Conditional is ungrammatical, since it is used when there is क्रियातिपत्ति *i. e.* अनिष्पत्ति or non-fulfilment or non-achievement of the act.

Śesha's inability to hold the earth is never described or known. रसातल°—रसातलमेव मूलं तस्मात्; see com.

Śl. 69. अमल—(1) Free from taint, spotless; (2) free from turbidity, clear. °निवारिता:—(1) spreading beyond the seas; (2) not driven back by the waves; rushing with great force into the sea; mighty.

Śl. 70. श्लाघ्यते—In such passages as विष्णुपादप्रसूतासि वैष्णवी विष्णुपूजिता &c. परमेष्ठिन्—परमे व्योमनि चिदाकाशे वा तिष्ठतीति; fr. परम+स्था+इन्. Malli. quotes here the latter part of the Sûtra अम्बाम्बगो &c. Pâṇ. VIII. 3. 97 to account for the change of स् to ष्; but it is not the proper one. It must be explained by the Vârt. स्थास्थिन्स्थूणाम्; see Bhân. on Amara. Malli. rightly explains it in his com. on Ragh. X. 33. Ar. reads यथैव श्लाघ्यते गङ्गा पातेन परमेष्ठिनि । प्रथमेन, द्वितीयेन.........सि त्वयि and explains श्लाघते as आत्मानं बहु मन्यते. In this case परमेष्ठिनि means शिवे.

Śl. 71. तिर्यक्—Horizontally spreading all round. हरे:—*i.e.* Vishṇu in his Vâmanâvatâra. त्रिविक्रमोद्यतस्य-त्रिषु विक्रमास्तत्रोद्यतस्य। Vishṇu, having assumed the form of a dwarfish Brâhmaṇa boy, appeared before the demon Bali (son of Virochana who was proud of his empire over the three worlds), and asked for as much land as could be covered by his three steps. Bali pressed him to ask for more; but, the dwarf refusing, he granted his request. Thereupon Vâmana expanded himself, filled up heaven and earth with his two steps, and with the third pressed down Bali to Pâtâla, the sovereignty of which was, however, left to him. The Vedic version of the story where Vishṇu means the Sun is not to the point here. त्रिविक्रमो° and स्वाभाविक are contrasted. Vishṇu's greatness filled up all space at a particular time; the mountain does so always. अत्र व्यतिरेकोऽलंकार:। Nâr.

Śl. 72. यज्ञभागभुजां—See *supra* I. 17. उच्चै: and हिरण्मयं—Meru has these two advantages over him., *viz*, its peaks are loftier and its constituent material is gold and yet the mountain is not allowed to partake of sacrificial food at sacrifices. For the Śruti हिमवतो हस्ती, see *supra* com. on I. 17. शृङ्ग—also has the side-meaning of 'superiority'; see com.

Śl. 73. भवतां—भवत: *v. l.*; in this case supply भवता or ईश्वरेण (अर्पितं). सता°—अर्हदाराधनं *v. l.* (Ar.); अर्हतां पूज्यानामाराध्यते अनेनेति आराधनं the means of pleasing.

Śl. 74. श्रेयसां &c.—The plural shows that the course they were going to advise Himâlaya to follow would prove of benefit not only to him but to the world and also to them.

Śl. 75. अणिमादि०—For the 8 Siddhis, see *supra* I. 5. अणिमा is the power to be as small as an atom; महिमा to be as great as anything; लघिमा to be light; गरिमा to be heavy; प्राप्तिः to obtain anything desired; प्राकाम्यं unobstructed power; ईशित्वं supremacy or the power of being the master of all; and वशित्वं the power to control the senses &c. Some mention कामावसायिता 'the power of ending passion or desire' instead of गरिमा. अस्पृष्ट०—अन्यः पुरुषः पुरुषान्तरं; now see Malli. Here a grammatical difficulty arises. पुरुषान्तर is a comp. of the मयूरव्यंसकादि class (see Pán. II. 1. 72), and words of the मयूर० class, तिष्ठद्गुप्रभृति class &c. are prohibited from being further joined in a comp.; and so the question arises—कथं तर्हि अस्पृष्टं पुरुषान्तरं येनेति पुनरस्य समासः। Says the Bháshya—किमर्थश्चकारः। एवकारार्थः। मयूरव्यंसकादय एव। क मा भूत्। परमो मयूरव्यंसक इति। The question is discussed by many eminent grammarians, but it is unneccessary to quote all those discussions here. The gist of the whole is that only Karmadháraya is prohibited from being further compounded. Some take this as a case of poetic license; others take पुरुषान्तर as a Gen. Tat.; पुरुषस्यान्तरं विशेषः। ततो बहुव्रीहिः। *Cf.* ईशानः सर्वभूतानामीश्वरः Tait. Up.; यस्मिन्नीश्वर इत्यनन्यविषयः शब्दो यथार्थाक्षरः Vik. I. 1. *Cf.* शब्दोऽयमीश्वर इति श्रुतिगोचरः सन्नानीलकण्ठमवतंसितचन्द्रलेखम्। त्वामेव बोधयति नाथ निजार्थपोषादन्यं पुनः प्रकरणार्थनिपीडनेन॥ सार्धचन्द्रं—Here अर्ध means a part, a digit; अर्धः चन्द्रो यस्य सोऽर्धचन्द्रः; अर्धचन्द्रेण सहितः सार्धचन्द्रः शब्दः.

Śl. 76. कलितान्योन्य०—Which impart power to each other by their mutual action and reaction and maintain the phenomenal world in its working order. *v. l.* कल्पित also means कृत. The five elements, being the constituents of the universe, are interdependent. The sun being the centre of activity also helps to keep up the universe; *cf.* the Śrutis सूर्य आत्मा जगतस्तस्थुषश्च, मित्रो दाधार पृथिवीमुत द्यां &c. For a similar office performed by the moon comp. ṚV. X. 85. 2 सोमेनादित्या बलिनः सोमेन पृथिवी मही &c. where Sâyaṇa remarks अमृतसेकेनौषध्यभिवृद्ध्या पृथिव्या बलवत्त्वम्। The sacrificer also augments the power of the sun and thereby sustains the creation; *cf.* Manu. अग्नौ प्रास्ताहुतिः.........ततः प्रजाः॥ quoted above (śl. 28). Thus the eight forms together contribute to maintain the stability of the universe. येन—यस्य *v. l.* goes with आत्मभिः. धुर्यैः—must be taken as करणे तृ०. Śiva is the driver of the chariot of the universe, the 8 forms the horses &c. Here Śiva is considered as existing outside his 8 forms. Otherwise the simile would lose its force. *Cf.* the Śruti—यो रुद्रोऽग्नौ योऽप्सु

य ओषधीषु । यो रुद्रो विश्वा भुवना विवेश । Also Parâśara—तदेतत्सकलं विश्वं स हि विश्वाधिकः शिवः । Perhaps the simile is suggested by the well-known passage in the Kaṭh. Up. आत्मानं रथिनं विद्धि &c.

Śl. 77. योगिनः—Those who practise योग, which is defined as चित्तवृत्तिनिरोध—controlling the functions of the mind and setting it on one particular object; तां योगमिति मन्यन्ते स्थिरामिन्द्रियधारणाम्। Kaṭh. Up. See also *supra* III. 58. यं विचिन्वन्ति—*Cf.* Vik. अन्तर्यश्च मुमुक्षुभिर्नियमितप्राणादिभिर्मृग्यते । I. 1 and the Śruti तमेव विदित्वातिमृत्युमेति नान्यः पन्था विद्यतेऽयनाय । Also, स्वाराद्याख्यस्य देवस्य हृदयाम्भोजमध्यमे । उमासहायो भगवान्नीलकण्ठस्त्रिलोचनः । यो नृत्यति ह्यसौ नित्यं परमानन्दचिद्घनः । तं दृष्ट्वा मनुजः सर्वो विमुक्तो भवतीति हि ॥ Ś. P. क्षेत्राभ्यन्तर०—*i. e.* in the दहराकाश; for क्षेत्र see *supra* III. 50. अन्तर्वृत्ति०—see Bg. XV. 5; also 6 (यद्गत्वा न निवर्तन्ते तद्धाम परमं मम).

Śl. 78. वृणुते—This was necessary for Himálaya to be able to offer his daughter to Śiva; see I. 51. संक्रमितैः—The Causal of क्रम् is संक्रमयति. The root क्रम् is one of the roots marked as मित् *i. e.* the penultimate vowel of which remains short. But the form संक्रामयति also occurs. So if the reading be संक्रामितैः it is to be thus explained according to the Vṛittikára (a commentator on Páṇ.)—मितां ह्रस्व इति सूत्रे वा चित्तविकारे इत्यतो वा इत्यनुवर्त्य व्यवस्थितविभाषाश्रयणात् ह्रस्वाभावः । *i. e.* from the previous Sûtra वा (the optionality of the rule) should be imported in the rule मितां ह्रस्वः in some fixed (व्यवस्थित) cases such as संक्रामयति, विश्रामयति &c. *Cf.* Malli. on धुर्यान् विश्रामयेति सः Ragh. I. 54; *cf.* also रजो विश्रामयन् राज्ञां Ragh. IV. 85.

Śl. 79. अर्थमिव &c.—Refers to the inseparable connexion between the two, see Malli. *Cf.* शब्दजातमशेषं तु धत्ते शर्वस्य वल्लभा। अर्थरूपं यदखिलं धत्ते मुग्धेन्दुशेखरः ॥ V. P. as quoted by Malli. in his com. on वागर्थाविव संपृक्तौ Ragh. I. 1. अशोच्या &c.—*cf.* वत्से सुशिष्यपरिदत्ता विद्येवाशोचनीयासि संवृत्ता । Śák. IV. कुलं च शीलं च मनोज्ञता (सनाथता) च विद्या च वित्तं च वपुर्यश (वय) श्च । एतान् गुणान् सप्त निरीक्ष्य कन्या वराय देया पितुरप्यशोच्या ॥ (देया कन्या बुधैः शेषमचिन्तनीयम् ॥)

Śl. 80. यावन्त्येतानि—Ar. reads यावद् द्वयानि (of two kinds).

Śl. 81. शितिकण्ठाय—शितिः (black) कण्ठः यस्य, Śiva. चरणौ &c.—See *supra* V. 79, 80.

Śl. 82. विधिः—The combination of (these happy) circumstances (Malli.); Ar. takes विधि in the sense of 'marriage-rite'.

Śl. 83. अस्तोतुः—one who has none to praise ; *cf.* केवलं दधति कर्तृवाचिनः प्रत्ययानिह न जातु कर्मणि । धातवः सृजति संहशास्तयः स्तौतिरत्र विपरीतकारकः ॥ Śiś. XIV. 66; and विपरीतं कारकं यस्य स विपरीतकारकः ।

स्तूयते स्तुस्य इत्यादि कर्मप्रत्ययान्त एव । न तु कदाचित्स्तौति स्तोता इत्यादि कर्तृप्रत्ययान्तः । सकललोकस्तुत्यस्य तस्य स्तुत्यन्तराभावात् । Malli. on *Ibid.* गुरु:—an elderly relation; *cf.* the Smṛiti-पित्रादयस्त्रयो भ्राता पितुर्माता-महस्तथा । ज्येष्ठभ्राता मातुलश्च श्वशुरो गुरवस्त्विमे ॥

Śl. 84. देवर्षिः—देव इव or देवानामपि ऋषिः; one or the seven classes of sages, *viz.* Ṛishi, Maharshi, Paramarshi, Devarshi, Brahmarshi, Káṇḍarshi and Śrutarshi. Śl. quoted in D-R. S.-D. &c. as an instance of अवहित्था dissimulation or the concealment of the outward effects of the feeling of shame, fear &c.

Śl. 85. संपूर्णकामः—This काम is refered to in I. 55, V 1 &c. गृहिणी°—नेत्र the eye, *i. e.* guide ; *cf. supra* स द्विनेत्रं हरेश्चक्षुः II. 30. कन्यार्थेषु—कन्याया अर्थाः कन्यार्थाः; *cf. supra* śl. 32.

Śl. 86. मेने—accepted (as proper to be done); hence, consented to; or अभीप्सितं कार्यमिति मेने. अव्यभि°—न व्यभिचरितुं शीलं यासां; not habitually departing from, always going with. This Śl. is omitted by Ar. and by the Bengal Commentator Râmagovinda.

Śl. 87. इदं—refers to the import of the next Śloka. न्याय्यं—just: fit for the occasion. बुद्धिः—The reasoning faculty.

Śl. 88. भिक्षा—A gift made to an ascetic (See Com.), Śiva being pre-eminently such ; *cf. supra* śl. 34 (संयमिनामाद्ये). गृहमेधिन्—is derived by Malli. (see Ragh. I. 7) as गृहैर्दारैः मेधते संगच्छते इति; some derive it as गृहमेधो विवाहः अस्त्यस्य; according to others it should be derived as गृहमेधः यज्ञः कर्तृत्वेन विद्यते अस्य; the sacrifice to be daily performed by a householder is fivefold:—अध्यापनं ब्रह्मयज्ञः पितृयज्ञस्तु तर्पणम् । होमो दैवो बलिर्भौतो नृयज्ञोऽतिथिपूजनम् ॥ Manu. III, 70, 71. °फलं—*Cf.* the Smṛiti गृहस्थः श्रद्धया दद्याद्भक्ष्यं भिक्षार्थिने सदा । भिक्षामददतः पुंसो गार्हस्थ्यं निष्फलं भवेत् ॥.

Śl. 91. जाम्बूनदं—जम्बूनद्यां भवं. According to Pauráṇic accounts it is the gold found in Jambûnadî, a river supposed to be formed of the fruit-juice of a gigantic Jambû tree in the middle of Jambûdvipa and flowing round the mountain Meru and then bending its course down to the Northern Kurus. दक्षिणेन तु नीलस्य निषधस्योत्तरेण तु । सुदर्शनो नाम महाजम्बूवृक्षः सनातनः । ...तस्या जम्ब्वाः फलरसो नदी भूत्वा जनाधिप । मेरुं प्रदक्षिणं कृत्वा संप्रयात्युत्तरान् कुरून् ॥ *Cf.* B. P. एवं जम्बूफलानामत्युच्चनिपातविशीर्णानामनस्थिप्रायाणामिभकायनिभानां रसेन जम्बूर्नाम नदी मेरुमन्दरशिखरादयुतयोजनादवनितले निपतन्ती दक्षिणेनात्मानं यावदिलावृत्तमुपस्यन्दयति । तावदुभयोरपि रोधसोर्या मृत्तिका तद्रसेनानुविध्यमाना वाय्वर्कसंयोगविपाकेन सदामरलोकाभरणं जाम्बूनदं नाम सुवर्णं भवति ॥ V. 16, 12, 20. वतंस—also अवतंस (55).

Śl. 92. अनन्यपूर्वस्य—अन्या पूर्वा married before (not living) यस्य; see com. अन्या पूर्वं न विद्यते यस्य Ar.; according to some नास्ति

अन्यः पूर्वः यस्य; आदिपुरुषस्येत्यर्थः । विशोकामकरोत्—This bears out the statement in VI. 32.

Śl. 94. आमन्त्र्य—bidding adieu to. अस्मै निवेद्य तद्वि०—As तद् is used after अस्मै there is the fault of भग्नप्रक्रमता. Śl. quoted in S.-D. and K.-P. VII. as an instance of the प्रक्रमभङ्ग (violation of the uniformity) of a pronoun; for here शूली is first referred to by इदम् (अस्मै) and then by तद् instead of by इदम् or its synnonym; so तद्विसृष्टाः should have been अनेन विसृष्टाः. Also quoted in the Káv.-Sû. under II. 3 as an instance of ओजस् depending on समास or cumulation of statements.

Śl. 95. पशुपतिः—The name is explained in various ways; पशूनां जीवानां पतिः; or पशूनां (जीवानां) पाशनं (नाशः) यस्मात्तस्मात्पशुपतिः स्मृतः । S. P. ब्रह्माद्याः स्थावरान्ताश्च देवदेवस्य शूलिनः । पशवः परिकीर्त्यन्ते संसारवशवर्तिनः । तेषां पतित्वाद्देवेशः शिवः पशुपतिः स्मृतः ॥ Ś. P. Vâyusaṃ. II. 9. According to one account the gods called themselves Paśus before Śiva, their lord, when they requested him to destroy the three Puras of the demons. व्यग्रोत्कः—The description of Śiva as a lover, in this śl. and in the following Cantos, is not only inconsistent with his own declarations in śls. 26, 27, but unworthy of a deity. The poet describes Śiva an as ordinary lover probably to meet the exigencies of a Mahákávya. He, however, does it very guardedly, as appears from his use of the word स्पृशन्ति and not विकुर्वन्ति. विभुं—*i. e.* able to control his senses; see *supra* III. 69. Śl. quoted in D.-R. as an instance of औत्सुक्य, one of the Vyabhichâribhávas (feelings not confined to a particular Rasa, but serving as accessories to any permanent sentiment).

CANTO VII.

Śl. 1. ओषधीनामधिपस्य—The moon is called the 'Lord of herbs,' as they thrive under the influence of the lunar rays. *Cf.* सोमेनादित्या बलिनः सोमेन पृथिवी मही । Ṛg. X. 85. 2, commenting on which Sáyaṇa says—अमृतसेकेनौषध्यभिवृद्ध्या पृथिव्या बलवत्त्वम्. *Cf.* also ततस्तस्मै ददौ राज्यं ब्रह्मा ब्रह्मविदां वरः । बीजौषधीनां विप्राणामपां च जनमेजय । H. V. and बीजौषधीनां तोयानां राजाभूद्द्विजन्मनाम् ॥ Káśíkh. According to some it was सोम the plant, that was originally regarded as the king of plants; and when by a curious misapplication Soma became a name of the moon, the latter came to be called the *king of plants*. वृद्धौ—*i. e.* the bright half of a month which is preferable; *cf.* उदगयन आपूर्यमाणपक्षे कल्याणे नक्षत्रे चौलकर्मो-

पनयनगोदानविवाहाः । A's.-G.-S. I. 4. 1. तिथौ—Some read तनौ which means लग्ने as the जामित्रगुण belongs to a लग्न; see Malli. जामित्र—The seventh zodiacal sign or house in a diagram representing the aspect of heavens at the time of a person's birth from his natal sign (the one just rising above the horizon at the moment) and which is the house of the wife or the husband. तस्य गुणाः—purity, it being free from any adverse influence exerted by a planet such as the moon &c.; see Malli. *Cf.* पापग्रहाश्चन्द्रो यदि सप्तमस्थः स्यात्तदा जामित्रवेधो नाम दोषान्तरं जायते। Also रविमन्दकुजाक्रान्तं मृगाङ्कात्सप्तमं त्यजेत्। विवाहयात्राचूडासु गृहकर्मप्रवेशने ॥ Some consider the word जामित्र to be a contracted form of जायामित्र, the seventh sign indicating the future good luck of one's wife. But it may be directly derived from जामि [which means a वधू or daughter-in-law; see Manus. III. 57; Mah. Bhár. XIII. 15; —or a woman in general; see Bṛih. Saṃ. 74. 10] and त्र (त्रायते इति). Western scholars connect the word with the Greek *diametron*. समेतबन्धुः—Meru, Mandára, Vindhya, Gandhama'dana and others; see Pa'r. P. V. 7. विवाहदीक्षा—Ar. and Nâr. take दीक्षा in its technical sense, and say, विवाह एव दीक्षा विवाहदीक्षा; दीक्षाशब्दस्यात्रोपनयनमर्थः। विवाह एव हि स्त्रीणामुपनयनम्। यथाह मनुः—वैवाहिको विधिः स्त्रीणामौपनायनिकः स्मृतः इति। अन्वतिष्ठत्—*Cf.* Ragh VII. 32.

Śl. 2. कौतुक॰—Properly means a मङ्गल (an auspicious ceremony); hence, here, the things (उपकरणानि) necessary for a मङ्गल. संविधान—getting ready. Cha'r. says—मङ्गलार्थं सुधागैरिकलेपादि यत्क्रियते तत्कौतुकमुच्यते। चैक॰—shows the love which the citizens bore to their king.

Śl. 3. संतानक—Properly, one of the five trees of heaven; but here used as a general term. महापथं—महत् is compounded with पथिन् by the rule सन्महत्परमोत्तमोत्कृष्टाः पूज्यमानैः। Pa'ṇ. II. 1. 61. There is, however, a rule prohibiting the use of महत् with such words as पथिन्; *viz.* शङ्खे तैले तथा मांसे वैद्ये ज्यौतिषिके द्विजे। यात्रायां पथि निद्रायां महच्छब्दो न दीयते ॥ But we find the word so compounded by great authors. *Cf.* महाब्राह्मण Śâk.; महाब्रह्मसमूहजुष्टः; पर्यङ्कलान् महाब्रह्मैराट नैकटिकाश्रमान्। Bhaṭṭi. So the rule seems to be of later growth. See Vámana on Pâṇ. VI. 2. 69. चीनांशुक—Fine silk-cloth imported from China (which was famous for its silks from the earliest times) and much used for flags, not only for its beauty but also for its toughness. *Cf.* चीनांशुकमिव केतोः प्रतिवातं नीयमानस्य। Śâk. I. 31; उच्चित्रचीनांशुकपस्तारस्थगिता &c. Mâl.-Mâdh. VI. 5. ॰तोरणाङ्कं *v. l.* (read by Ar.)—marked with &c.; but in this case there is nothing left to which the भास can refer. स्थानान्तरं

This comp. is of the *neu.* gender (*cf.* पुरुषान्तरं), and so used with a *masc.* noun.

Śl. 4. पुत्रपङ्क्तौ—It is difficult to see what the poet means by this, even though the comp. be taken as Malli. does. For according to the Ś. P. Himâlaya had two sons and two daughters only, *viz.* Mainâka and Krauñcha and Gaurî and Gaṅgâ. मेना हिमवतः पत्नी मेनाकं क्रौञ्चमेव च। गौरीं गङ्गां च सुषुवे भवाङ्गाश्लेषपावनीम् ॥ Ś. P. Vây. Saṃ. XV. 52, 53. Some say—मेनाकपर्यन्तपर्वतनद्यादिरूपायाम्, *i. e.* the adjoining hills and rivers are considered as the sons and daughters of a mountain; see *supra* notes on I. 27, where Malli. purposely takes the word पुत्र as a comp. मृतोत्थिता—The direct mention of death is inauspicious and should have been avoided. उच्छ्वसितं—*Cf.* सा कुलपतेरुच्छ्वसितमिव Śâk. III. Ar. reads °च्छ्वसिता and says उमा विशेषेण उच्छ्वसिता उल्लसिता। अधिकलालितेत्यर्थः ; but this is twisting the word.

Śl. 5. उदीरिताशीः—*scil.* as she left the lap of each relative. मण्डनान्म°—Every relative gave her an ornament or some kind of decoration.

Śl. 6. मैत्रे मु°—मित्रो देवताऽस्येति मैत्रः fr. मित्र + अण् (अ) by सास्य देवता। Pâṇ. IV. 2. 24. According to Malli. this is the third muhûrta (a period of 48 minutes) from sunrise, *i. e.* after 1 hour and 36 minutes after sunrise. According to another view this *muhûrta* is the period of the sun's apparently passing througu the lunar mansion Anurâdhâ (part of the zodiacal sign Scorpion) during the course of the day. The sun is the presiding deity of this constellation. उत्तरफ°—The twelfth lunar mansion (part of the signs Leo and Virgin and one of the Nakshatras mentioned as auspicious for the performance of ceremonies). *Cf.* रोहिण्यैन्दव रेवत्यश्विसनभं मूलानुराधा मघा हस्ताश्चोत्तरभत्रयं च शुभदं वैवाहिके कर्मणि। Subodhinî. पतिपु°—For, women who have lost their husbands or who are sonless are thought to be unfit for taking part in such ceremonies.

Śl. 7. सिद्धार्थ—सिद्धोऽर्थोऽस्मात्; white mustard which keeps off evil influences; *cf.* सरीषपः......सिते तस्मिन् रक्षोघ्नो भूतनाशनः। Rabhasa. दूर्वाप्र°—the दूर्वा grass is also held sacred by the Hindus, and is worn by ladies along with flowers as auspicious (see Vik. III. 12) and is offered to deities &c. निर्नाभिकौ°—निर्नाभि may be explained as निष्पतितं नाभिं covering the navel, or as Malli. does. Some take निर्नाभि to mean 'musk' (निर्गतो नाभेः produced from the navel of the musk-deer); 'musk and silk-cloth,' or a silk-cloth scented with musk. Chár. takes the comp. as निर्गतं नाभिकौशेयं यत्र—in which the silk-cloth worn round the navel was removed (as she was to be anointed); but, as if dissatisfied with this way of taking it, (for the spoiling of a silken cloth was no consideration in the case of Himálaya), he also interprets it as Malli. does. Ar. reads उन्नीवि० and explains—उन्नीवि उद्गतनीविबन्धनं कौशेयं यत्र। अनेन पाणिग्रहणात्प्राक्तनः परिधानप्रकार उक्तः। यथा विद्धशालभञ्जिकायां-कन्येति सूचयति वेषविशेष एव यन्नीलचोलकवती लिखितात्र चित्रे । पाणिग्रहात्प्रभृति तु प्रमदाजनस्य नीवीनिवेशसुभगः परिधानमार्गः ॥ इति। कौशेयं—कोशे संभूतं by कोशाड्ढञ् Páṇ. IV. 3. 42 (रूढिरेषा तेन क्रिमौ न भवति Káśiká). This shows that in Páṇini's days the art of making cloth from cocoons of silk–worms was known and cultivated.

उपात्तबाणम्—This refers to the custom, according to which when there was a marriage between a husband of exalted rank or higher class and a woman of lower rank, a Kshatriya girl had to catch hold of an arrow held by her hand, as she had not the privilege of directly joining her hand with that of her husband. *Cf.* शरः क्षत्रियया ग्राह्यः प्रतोदो वैश्यकन्यया। वसनस्य दशा ग्राह्या शूद्रयोत्कृष्टवेदने ॥ Manu. III. 44 (See also Yájñavalkya I. 62). This passage is differently explained by different Commentators —क्षत्रियया पाणिग्रहणस्थाने ब्राह्मणविवाहे ब्राह्मणहस्तपरिगृहीतकाण्डैकदेशो ग्राह्यः। Kullûka. Medhâtithi nearly says the same and adds पाणिग्रहणस्थाने शरस्य विधानात्। Nârâyaṇa, however, says क्षत्रियया धृतं शरं पाणिग्रहण-मन्त्रैर्वरो गृह्णीयात्। Râghayánanda says—शरः पाणिना क्षत्रियया गृहीतो यस्तं पाणिस्थानीयं विप्रो गृह्णीयात्...अन्यथा मन्त्रलिङ्गविरोधः। Following probably this statement, the poet makes Párvatî take an arrow in her hand as she was to marry Śiva, vastly her superior in rank. अभ्यङ्ग—अभ्यङ्गार्थं नेपथ्यं dress suited to the auspicious bath (see *infra* śl. 10); or अङ्गेष्विति अभ्यङ्गः अभ्यङ्गं नेपथ्यं (decoration of each part of the body, सुप्सुपेति समासः. अलंचकार—The grace of her person lent charm to her dress (see *infra*, śl. 13) instead of the dress setting off her person. *Cf.* आभरणस्याभरणं प्रसाधनविधेः प्रसाधनविशेषः &c. Vik. II.; असमग्रभूषणायास्तनुतरकौशेयवासधारिण्याः। आलिप्तमङ्गमखिलं तैलेन सुगन्धिना तस्याः ॥ Pár. P.

Śl. 8. दीक्षाविधि०—Perhaps the custom was prevalent in Kâlidâsa's time. करेण—सुषुम्णाख्येन Châr.; by the ray called Sushumṇâ—(also called सुषुम्न)—one of the seven principal rays of the sun, supplying heat to the moon. *Cf.* सूर्यरश्मिः सुषुम्नो यस्तर्पितस्तेन चन्द्रमाः। कृष्णपक्षेऽमरैः शश्वत्पीयते वै सुधामयः ॥ V. P. II. 2. 22. अथाप्यस्यैको रश्मिश्चन्द्रमसं प्रति दीप्यते...। सुषुम्णः सूर्यरश्मिश्चन्द्रमा गन्धर्व इत्यपि निगमो भवति। Nirukta, II. 2. .2 संभुक्ष्य०—Châr.

reads संधुक्षमाणा which is better (उपमानसाधर्म्यात्); Malli. also probably read thus. संधुक्षणं दीपने स्याद्वर्धने दहनेऽपि च इति भोजः। The quotation given by Malli. (read, after क्षपयन्ति, दर्पणोदरनिहिता इव मान्दिरस्यान्तः ॥) is from Varâhamihira's Bṛih. Saṃ.; *cf.* also पुपोष वृद्धिं हरिदश्ववीधितेरनुप्रवेशादिव बालचन्द्रमाः। Ragh. III. 22.

Śl. 9. ०कल्क—The *lodhra*-bark pounded with water. आश्यान—*p. p.* of श्यै with आ. कालेय—कालेयक is given in Amara. as a synonym of दारुहरिद्रा, but that does not seem to be intended here; it is given again as a kind of fragrant yellow pigment—अथ जायकम्। कालीयकं च—which Malli. follows here. According to Haláyudha, it means 'saffron'—काश्मीरजं च विद्वद्भिः कालेयं जागुडं स्मृतम्—and this will also do here. Malli. himself, commenting on Siś. XII. 14 (कालीयकक्षोदविलेपनश्रियं दिशद्दिशामुल्लसदंशुमद्द्युति) understands it in this sense and quotes Sâśvata in support of it. ०रागां—This was done to remove the dryness caused by the *lodhra-kalka.* अभिषेक०—*i. e.* a cotton-cloth. चतुष्क—चत्वारोऽवयवा अस्य। A small quadrangular house supported by four pillars.

Śl. 10. विन्यस्त० &c.—Malli. seems to take this in the sense of 'a floor laid with' &c.—see trans.; it may also be taken in the sense of—'in which a large slab formed of settings of Vaidúryas was placed'. Chár. reads ०शिले च तस्मिन्. भक्ति—Ornamental arrangement. Châr. reads अविद्ध (unperforated) मुक्ता०. Ar. and Nâr. read आविद्धमुक्ताकृतभक्तिलेखे which the latter explains as आविद्धाभिः सूत्रप्रोताभिः मुक्ताभिः कृता भक्तिलेखा विन्यासविशेषरचना यत्र तस्मिन्। अष्टापद—अष्टौ धातवः पदानि अस्य. The अ of अष्ट is lengthened by अष्टनः संज्ञायाम्। Pâṇ. VI. 3. 125, when the comp. formed is a name; otherwise अष्टपुत्रः. स्नप०—also स्नापयां०. *Cf.* मणिपीठवर्तिनीं तां मङ्गलशङ्खेषु मन्द्रघोषेषु। अम्भोभिरमरनद्याः सखीजनो विहितमज्जनामकरोत्॥ Pâr. P.

Śl. 11. उद्गमनीय—A bleached or white cloth. According to Amara. (see com.) it refers to a pair of washed (whitened) garments. No stress is to be laid on युग. According to Kshîrasvâmin it means 'that which is seen' (यल्लक्ष्यं तदेव); the upper garment is also seen as well as the one put underneath; hence the term applies to both. प्रत्युद्गमनीय is the reading of Chár.; it means—'fit for going forth to meet or for welcoming the bridegroom.' गृहीतप्रत्युद्ग० *v. l.* is simpler, but is not symmetrical with प्रफुल्लकाशा below. निर्वृत्तपर्जन्य०—निर्वृत्त accomplished; निवृत्त *v. l.* ceased, finished. पर्जन्य fr. पृष् to shower + अन्य Uṇádi III. 103; पर्षति वृष्टिं ददातीति; ष् being irregu larly (निपातनात्) changed to जू. प्रफुल्लकाशा—corresponds to ०नीयवस्त्रा; for the Kâśa flowers compared to a garment *cf.* Ṛit. III. 1, 28. *Cf.* मङ्गलमज्जनविषदा कर्पूरक्षोदपाण्डुरं क्षौमम्। साऽधत्त जलदधौता द्यौरिव शरदिन्दुचन्द्रिकोद्रेदम् ॥ Pâr. P.

Śl. 12. चतुष्टय—चत्वारोऽवयवा अस्य। परिगृह्य—See Malli.; or, 'having taken her with them'. कौतुक०—कौतुकार्था वेदिः; कौतुक 'the ceremony of tying the marriage-thread round the wrist;' see *supra* V. 66 and Ragh. VIII. 1.

Śl. 13. भूतार्थ०—Ar. and Nâr. dissolve: भूतार्थश्चासौ शोभा च भूतार्थशोभा. ०नेत्राः—Because they knew that her natural beauty would only be soiled by the decorations, and so it could not be seen afterwards; see *supra,* śl. 7. This Śl. is quoted in the D.-R. as an instance of शोभा (one of the seven natural ornaments of young women).

Śl. 14. त्याजित—*p. p.* of the caus. of त्यज् here used as a root governing two accusatives. Some grammarians, Sudhâkara and others, include roots like त्यज्, मुच् &c. in the list of the द्विकर्मक roots on the authority of च in Patañjali's Kârikâ—नीवह्योर्हरतेश्चापि गत्यर्थानां तथैव च। द्विकर्मकेषु ग्रहणं द्रष्टव्यमिति निश्चयः ॥ *Cf.* त्याजितैः फलमुत्खातैः &c. Ragh. IV. 33; भरतस्तत्र गन्धर्वान्युधि निर्जित्य केवलम्। आतोद्यं ग्राहयामास समत्याजयदायुधम् ॥ *ibid.* XV. 88. Others do not adopt this view. Kaiyaṭa on अकथितं च Pâṇ. I. 4. 51 says गवा पयस्त्याजयति; *cf.* Bhaṭṭi. संत्याजयांचकाराथ सीतां विंशतिबाहुना। केशान्तं—Here अन्त indicates excellence; प्रशस्ताः केशाः केशान्तः तं; *cf.* अन्तः स्वरूपे पर्यन्ते मृत्यौ मध्यावसानयोः इति भोजः। उदार—excellent; hence, charming. *Cf.* आगुल्फलम्बमस्याः कुन्तलमन्तर्निगूढमन्दारम्। संयम्य चतुरबन्धं सखीजनः स्तिमितनेत्रमास चित्रम् ॥ Pâr. P.

Śl. 15. विन्यस्त०—Ar. reads प्रसन्नशु०, where प्रसन्न means 'bright, prominent'. शुक्लागुरु—a kind of अगुरु or fragrant aloe-wood, also called राजार्ह. पत्र—ornamental paintings. विभक्त—diversified or variegated with. ०विभङ्ग *v. l.* (Châr.)—गोरोचनायाः पत्रविभङ्गाः पत्रलताः, (linear ornamental figures) यत्र. सैकत—sandy bank; fr. सिकता + अण् by सिकताशर्कराभ्यां च। Pâṇ. V. 2. 104 (सिकताः सन्त्यस्मिन्देशे इति सैकतो देशः).

Śl. 16. लग्न—Châr. reads लीन; for the idea *cf.* न पङ्कजं तद्यदलीनषट्पदम् Bhaṭṭi. 11. 19. प्रसिद्ध—decorated; see V. 9. अलकैः—Malli. takes the Instr. उपलक्षणे; it may also be taken करणे—'on account of'. Châr. remarks—कमलशशिनौ किल मुखस्योपमानभूतौ। अभिमते तु प्रसाधनमेव हेतुः। चिच्छेद &c.-*Cf.* जातास्तदूर्वोरुपमानबाह्याः I. 36.

Śl. 17. कषाय—An unguent or thick juice of. As it is astringent it made the cheek a little rough. See *supra*, śl 9. Malli. takes रूक्ष in the sense of 'bright by being painted with;' and Nâr. says रूक्षे अत्यन्तधवलत्वात् दुर्निरीक्ष्ये । मनोहरे इत्यर्थः । ०रूषे *v. l.* -०कषायेण रूषो रूषणं being painted or coloured यस्य. भेद *v. l.*—intermixture with. गोरोचनापत्र *v. l.*—drawings with *gorochaná*. परभाग—*lit.* the chief or excellent portion; a position of advantage; hence, supreme excellence. परभागो गुणोत्कर्षः Haláyudha and Abhi. Chin.; *cf.* Ragh. V. 78.

Śl. 18. सुविभक्त—well-proportioned, symmetrical. *Cf. supra* I. 3. मधूच्छिष्ट—*cf.* सिक्थकमलक्तकं चोष्ठयोर्दत्वा &c. Vátsyáyana. विमृष्ट—polished off. Char. reads विसृष्ट. कामप्य०—*cf.* सूर्यापाये न खलु कमलं पुष्यति स्वामभिख्याम् । Megh. II. 20; वपुरभिनवमस्याः पुष्यति स्वां न शोभां Śák. I.

Śl. 19. स्पृष्ट—That is—When Śiva would bend his head before you when angry. To make the heroines strike their lovers with their foot in love-sport seems to be a favourite idea with Kálidâsa; *cf.* Mâlav. III. 12, 19; Megh. II. 18. Śl. quoted in D.-R. as an instance of वचोहास्यनर्म.

Śl. 20. सुजातो०—Well-developed; else it would not bear comparison with her eyes. *Cf.* सुजातयोः पङ्कजकोशयोः श्रियम् Ragh. III. 8. कान्तिविशेष—The enhancement or setting off of the beauty of.

Śl. 21. त्रियामा—त्रयः यामा यस्याः. Yâma is a period of three hours. The night proper has three such periods; only the first half of the first and the second half of the last being left out, as they are almost like day, there being some light and the people being as active as during the day; or त्रीन्यापयतीति that which dismisses the three, *viz.* धर्म, अर्थ and मोक्ष—the time being especially suited to काम.

Śl. 22. स्तिमिता०—with eyes steady on account of the thoughts of her husband; for such an effect on the eyes, *cf.* Ragh. I. 73. प्रियालोक०—प्रियस्य प्रियकर्तृकः आलोकः, 'its being seen by the husband'. Śl. quoted in D.-R. IV. as an instance of औत्सुक्य.

Śl. 23. हरिताल—Yellow orpiment. माङ्गल्य—मङ्गले साधु मङ्गल्यं (which Ar. reads) by adding य (यत्) by तत्र साधुः Páṇ. 10. 4. 98; मङ्गल्यमेव माङ्गल्यं by adding य (ष्यञ्) स्वार्थे by taking it as a word of the ब्राह्मणादि class. मनःशिला—red arsenic, *i. e.* its paste. दन्तपत्र—an ear-ornament made of ivory (much used in ancient times). बद्धमध्य—Ar. and Nâr. read उज्झिनाय and the latter remarks—

तिलकविधानार्थं मुखमुन्नमय्य मुखदर्शनकुतूहलात्किंचित्कालं तूष्णीमेव स्थितवतीत्यर्थः । अत एव उन्नयनमात्रे वाक्यसमाप्तिः ।

Śl. 24. स्तनोद्भेद—See I. 40. मनोरथ—*viz.* to bestow her in marriage on Śiva. प्रथमं-see I. 50. तमेव—The same, as indicative of that marriage. कथंचित्—With difficulty, being unnerved by excessive joy. *Cf.* तस्या ललाटसीमनि चन्दनपङ्केन मेनया लिखितम् । आसीत्सितातपत्रं तिलकमनङ्गस्य दर्शितच्छायम् ॥ Pár. P.

Śl. 25. स्थानान्तरे क॰—She fastened it in the wrong place. कौतुक॰—Malli. takes कौतुक in the sense of मङ्गल 'auspicious;' it may be taken in its usual sense also, the comp. being taken as one of the Śákapârthivâdi class (कौतुकाभिधानं हस्तसूत्रं), or कौतुकं च तद्धस्तसूत्रं च, a comp. सुप्सुपा.

Śl. 26. क्षीरोद॰—The milky ocean is selected on account of its whiteness. पर्यास॰—The moon corresponds to the mirror she held in her hand as required by custom. क्षौम—This was of a white colour as the comparison to फेनपु॰ shows. नवं नवं *v. l.*—goes with बभौ; 'she shone more and more'.

Śl. 27. कुलप्रतिष्ठा—वंशयशस्करी Chár.; called कुलजीवितं in VI. 63. तां प्रणमय्य—Here नम् is taken as an intrans. root and hence governs one object in the causative form, and so कुलदेवताभ्यः is in the dative by क्रियार्थोपपद &c., the meaning being कुलदेवताः अनुकूलयितुम्. नम् is used intransitively by 'धातोरर्थान्तरे वृत्तेर्धात्वर्थेनोपसंग्रहात् । प्रसिद्धेरविवक्षातः कर्मणोऽकर्मिका क्रिया ॥. क्रमेण—अनुज्येष्ठं according to seniority.'

Śl. 29. कृती—कृतमस्यास्तीति skilled in the things to be done. ॰प्रतीक्षः—An Upapada Tat., ण (अ) being added by ईक्षिक्षमिभ्यां च Várt. on Páṇ. III. 2. 1. Malli.'s statement कर्मण्यण् seems to be due to oversight. ॰नं प्रतीक्ष्य—*v. l.* is bad; we should expect प्रतीक्षमाणः.

Śl. 30. तत्पूर्व॰—तदेव पूर्वमप्र्यं श्रेष्ठं वा, and not प्रथमं, as Śiva was first married to Daksha's daughter सती; or तत्पूर्वस्य पाणिग्रहणस्य similar to that of his first marriage. मातृभिः—The divine mothers attending on Śiva. They are seven—ब्राह्मी माहेश्वरी चैव कौमारी वैष्णवी तथा । माहेन्द्री चैव वाराही चामुण्डा सप्त मातरः ॥; or—ब्राह्मी माहेश्वरी चैन्द्री वाराही वैष्णवी तथा । कौबेरीत्यपि कौमारी सप्तैवं मातरः स्मृताः ॥; or eight according to some—ब्राह्मी...... । कौमारी चैव चामुण्डा चर्चिकेत्यष्ट मातरः ॥ According to others they are sixteen, but they are not meant here, as गौरी forms one of that list. आदृताभिः—आदृतौ सादरार्चितौ Amara.; full of respect, or worshipful. पुरशासनः—पुरस्य शासनः; it is better to take this as a Gen. Tat.; if we follow Malli., the बहुलत्व (in most cases and not in a few) provided by कृत्यल्युटो बहुलम् will have to be resorted to to keep off अण्.

Śl. 32. सिता°—unguent of white *aguru*; see *supra*, śl. 15. कपालं—*scil.* ब्रह्मकपाल; see *supra*, IV. 49, V. 78. शेखरश्रीः—*i. e.* श्रीमान् शेखरः—the beautiful head-ornament. रोचनाङ्कः—Marked (decked) with figures of swans &c. drawn with *gorochaná*; *cf.* गोरोचनाचित्रितदशमनुपहतं दुकूलयुगलं वसाना Kád. p. 115.

Śl. 33. शङ्ख—The frontal bone. सांनिध्यपक्षे—सांनिध्ये साध्ये in the matter of the *tilaka* mark being got ready, *i. e.* made.

Śl. 34. यथाप्रदेशं—in their respective places; हारस्थाने हारत्वं अङ्गदस्थाने अङ्गदत्वं काञ्चीस्थाने काञ्चीत्वं च । Nâr.

Śl. 35. निष्ठ्यूत— *p. p.* of ष्ठिव् with नि; 'emitted,' sent forth. °भाजा *v. l.*—having the rays &c. बाल्यात्—on account of its smallness, *i. e.* being only a digit. °लक्षणेन—*v. l.* has the same sense. ग्रहणं—Ar. and Nâr. take this in the sense of वचन (as in नामग्रहण B. P. VI. 2. 14); हरस्य चन्द्र एव चूडामणिरासीदिति वचनं निरर्थकमित्यर्थः । Nâr. चूडामणेः—'उभयप्राप्तौ कर्मणि' इति षष्ठी. हरस्य—the gen. is कर्तरि.

Śl. 36. अद्भुतैकप्रभवः—अद्भुतो निरूप्यमाणविस्मयनीयः संसारस्तदात्मभूत तत्त्वजातं च । तस्यैकप्रभवः प्रधानं जन्मकारणम् । प्रसिद्ध—as known to the world (and required by custom). खड्गे—Ar. reads टङ्के; टङ्के परशौ (an axe). 'टङ्कः परशुश्च परश्वधः' इति भोजः । Nár.

Śl. 37. नन्दि°—See III. 41. संक्षिप्त—Contracted (in order to enable Śiva to mount him), as elephants also do by bending down; this may rather be taken with कैलास—as though he rode Kailása, with its form contracted &c.—as done by Chár. Nár. also says गोपतिमुत्प्रेक्षते—तद्भक्ति° कैलासमिवेति । नित्यं भगवदावासस्थानभूतः कैलास एव भगवतः प्रस्थानसमये भगवद्भक्त्या वाहनभावोचितं वेषमादाय सहैव गन्तुमुद्युक्त एवायमिति जनैरुत्प्रेक्ष्यमाणमित्यर्थः । The Calc. comm. Rámagovinda says—तद्भक्त्या संक्षिप्तं ह्रस्वीकृतं पश्चात् बृहद् वर्धितं प्रमाणं शरीरं येन तम् । अत एव कैलासमिवेत्यपि साधु संगच्छते । कैलासमिव—Kailása is the site of Kubera's capital and the favourite abode of Śiva. It is white, and the bull is compared to it on account of his whiteness and large size; see Ragh. II. 35.

Śl. 38. स्ववाहन°—स्ववाहनानां हंसवृषमयादादीनां Nâr. रेणु°-मण्डलराजि (the row of) *v. l.* is better, as रेणु read by Malli. has no propriety. पद्माकरं—A bed of lotuses of golden hue (as the deities were of golden complexion; see next ś'l.). अन्तरीक्षं—द्यावापृथिव्योरन्तः ईक्ष्यते इति; fr. ईक्ष् + अ (घञ् कर्मणि); or अन्तः ऋक्षाणि stars अस्य; in this case the word is अन्तरिक्ष.

Śl. 39. काली—The fierce blood-thirsty consort of Śiva in his character of the destroyer of the world. She is represented as of a black colour, with a hideous and terrible countenance, dripping with blood, encircled with snakes, and hung round with skulls and human heads &c. She killed the demon Raktabîja. On account of her black colour and huge form she is compared to a line of dark clouds, the skulls resembling cranes. बलाकिनी—बलाकाः अस्याः विद्यन्ते. The rainy season is the period of the gestation of the cranes, and they are represented as congregating in the sky at the first appearance of clouds. *Cf.* Malli. on गर्भाधानक्षणपरिचयान्नूनमाबद्धमालाः सेविष्यन्ते नयनसुभगं खे भवन्तं बलाकाः। Megh. शतह्रदा—शतं ह्रदा अर्चींषि rays, flashes अस्याः.

Śl. 41. सहस्ररश्मिः—The Pár. P. makes Śesha the umbrella-bearer; *cf.* चन्द्रार्कावपि चामरे विधुनुतां छत्री भवाहीश्वरः । V. 24. तद्दुकूल—the white silken cloth of the umbrel'a which looked like the white current of the Ganges when falling from heaven. Malli. explains the Abl. by the optionality given by दूरान्तिकार्थैः &c. Pâṇ. II. 3. 34. His remark नाथेनोक्तं &c. means—'Nâtha's statement आराच्छब्दस्य &c. is without authority from original grammar. Again, if this optionllity (of अन्यारा०) be accepted, that of दूरा० becomes rejected, and the use of the Gen. in दूरं ग्रामस्य cannot be defended. So Nâtha's statement must be dismissed as untenable.'

Śl. 42. मूर्त—*p. p.* of मूर्छ्. सहंसपाते—The *chauries* which were being waved resembled swans alighting on the banks.

Śl. 43. प्रथमः—The first of the प्रजापतिs, मरीचि and others; *v. l.* प्रथमं would be better. श्रीवत्स०—*lit.* the favourite of Śrí; a peculiar auspicious mark—according to some, a curl of hair—on the breast of Vishṇu. According to the Mah.-Bhâr. Śân. P. it is the mark left by the stroke of Śiva's शूल, and according to the Bhâg. P., of Bhṛigu's foot. See our note on the word, Ragh. X. 10.

Śl. 44. एकैव &c.—See *supra*, II. 4, 6; *cf.* Ragh. X. 16. Here the poet states his own belief in the unity of the three gods. It is the same god, one and alone, regarded in the three aspects of creating, protecting and withdrawing the manifested universe. This clearly shows that Kälidâsa was not a bigoted Śaiva. His Śaivism was like that of the poet Bhartṛihari, perhaps not even so pronounced (see Vair. Śa. 85). The natural propensity of his mind led him to be a worshipper of Śiva, that is all. See our note on Vik. I. 1.

Śl. 45. लोकपालाः—These are इन्द्रो वह्निः पितृपतिः (=यमः) नैर्ऋतो वरुणो मरुत् (=वायुः) । कुबेर ईशः पतयः पूर्वादीनां दिशां क्रमात् ॥ Amara. पुरुहूतः—पुरु (fr. पॄ+कु Uṇâdi I. 24) many; पुरुभिर्हूतः पुरु प्रचुरमाह्वानं यज्ञेष्वस्य पुरूणि हूतानि नामान्यस्य इति वा । श्री०—श्रियाः लक्षणानि श्रीलक्षणानि; now see com.

Śl. 46. कम्पेन—with a slight bow (इति गौरवं Nâr.) शतपत्र०—शतपत्रं (a lotus) योनिर्यस्य. वाचेति मित्रभावः । स्मितेनेति प्रसादः । Nâr. The description here shows how an Indian imperial king received his guests and subordinates.

Śl. 47. जयाशीः—जयस्याशीः; or जयेत्या०, तिङन्ते न मयूरव्यंसकादयश्चेति तत्पुरुषः । अध्वर्यवः—अध्वर्यु is a particular priest officiating at a sacrifice; अध्वर्यूद्गातृहोतारो यजुःसामर्ग्विदः क्रमात् ; it is used here in the sense of a priest, the marriage being compared to a यज्ञ; Der.-अध्वर+या+उ (कुः) Uṇâdi I. 38; अध्वरस्याकारलोपश्चेत्युज्ज्वलदत्तः. पूर्ववृत्ताः—as indicated in VI. 33.

Śl. 48. विश्वावसु—विश्वं वसु यस्य. The अ of विश्व is lengthened by विश्वस्य वसुराटोः Pân. VI. 3. 128. Name of a chief of the Gandharvas and a musician (like तुम्बुरु) in the court of Indra; the name of his lute was Brihatî. प्राग्रहर—chief; प्रकृष्टमग्रं प्राग्रं the foremost point; प्राग्रे हरति; हरतेरनुद्यमनेऽच् (अ); Pân. III. 2. 9. प्रवीणैः—निपुणैः; or प्रकृष्टा वीणा येषाम् । यद्वा वीणया प्रगायन्तीति । सत्याप० (Pân. III. 1. 25) इति णिजन्तात्पचाद्यच्; 'versed in playing on the lute;' skilful musicians. त्रिपुरावदानः—see Malli.; the valorous or glorious deed in connexion with Tripura —*i. e.* his destroying with an arrow the three cities of gold, silver and iron built in the sky, in the mid-space, and on earth by Maya for the demons. त्रिपुर may also mean the demon (त्रीणि पुराण्यस्य) and अवदान his destruction (संगीयमानं त्रिपुरस्य अवदानं यस्य). अध्वान्त०—see *supra*, II. 58. Nâr. says—तमसि निपातितोऽध्वान्तशब्दस्तद्गतज्ञाननिरोधकत्वगुणयोगादविद्यायां गौणो वर्तते । तस्य विकारास्तु परमार्थज्ञाननिरोधादयः । तद्रहिता अध्वान्तविकारास्तैर्लङ्घ्यः प्राप्यः । ये परमार्थज्ञानवन्तस्तैः सर्वैरपि सेव्य इत्यर्थः । But this is far-fetched.

Śl. 49. खे—may be taken with खेलगामी or उवाह. खेलगामी—gracefully (gently and with dignity). वाहः—though usually meaning 'a horse', here the word mean 'a bull', by the maxim रूढा अपि शब्दा यौगिकमवगाहन्ते (may have their etymological sense). चामीकर—चमीकरे स्वर्णाकरभेदे भवम् ; तत्र भवः इति अण् ; यद्वा चामीं शोभां करोतीति; चामीकरस्य किंकिण्यः; यद्वा चामीकरस्य विकाराः चामीकराः । विकारार्थे अण् । क्वचिदपवादविषयेऽपि उत्सर्गोऽभिनिविशते इति भाष्यात् ; now see Malli. तदाभि०—See I. 56. धुन्वन्—to get rid of the obstruction, as is usual with bulls when their horns are covered with mud. प्रोतघने—प्रोतो घनो याभ्यां; प्रोत *p. p. p.* of वे I. U. with प्र to sew, to pierce.

Śl. 50. सः—Châr. takes this to refer to Śiva. पराभियोग—attack by the enemy. मुहूर्तात्—ल्यब्लोपे कर्मण्यधिकरणे चेति वक्तव्यात्पञ्चमी । दृष्टिपातैः—the glances darted from the third eye (हरतृतीयनयनपातैः Châr.) which had a golden brightness. कृष्यमाणं—Śiva had fixed his glances on the city; on account of the great speed of the bull, the city appeared to be drawn to him by the ropes of his glances as it were; *cf.* केनाप्युत्क्षिपतेव पश्य भुवनं मत्पार्श्वमानीयते । Śák. VII. 8.

Śl. 51. घननील०—घन may mean a cloud; dark like &c., or deep-dark. स्वबाण०—the path marked by the flight of his arrow, *i. e.* the aerial region; see Malli. Some take it to refer to the arrow shot by Śiva at Brahmâ when running, with his passion inflamed, after his daughter (स्वकन्यागमनोद्यतं ब्रह्माणमाहन्तुं निक्षिप्त आर्द्रानक्षत्ररूपेण स्थितः शिवस्य बाण एव चिह्नं यस्य). See *supra* IV. 41. *Cf.* प्रजानाथं नाथ प्रसभमभिकं स्वां दुहितरं गतं रोहिद्भूतां रिरमयिषुमृष्यस्य वपुषा । धनुष्पाणेर्यातं दिवमपि सपत्राकृतममुं त्रसन्तं तेऽद्यापि त्यजति न मृगव्याधरभसः ॥ Pushpadanta's Mahimna. 22. The constellation मृगशिरस् (Orion) is Brahmâ; आर्द्रा is the arrow. Ar. and Nâr. read स्ववाहचि० and the former remarks—मेघवाहनकल्पे भगवान्विष्णुर्मेघो भूत्वा देवासुरयुद्धे (युद्धसंनद्धं) हरमवहदिति पुराणे । Hence the name मेघवाहन of Śiva.

Śl. 52. प्रतीतः—pleased; ख्याते हृष्टे प्रतीतः Amara.; प्रतीतः सादरे ज्ञाते हृष्टप्रख्यातयोस्त्रिषु । Medinî. *Cf.* for this meaning Ragh. III.12; V. 26. प्रफुल्ल—*p. p.* of फुल्ल् 1. P. to bloom, or फल् 1. P to burst open; (फुल्ल or फुल्त in this sense; फलित in other senses).

Śl. 53. उद्घटित—*p. p.* of घट् with उद् 7 conj.; *cf.* कृष्णा संधिं भीमो विघटयति यूयं घटयत । Veṇî. I. 10; आनीय झटिति घटयति विधिः । Rat. I.; घट् 10 Conj. has घाटित. अपिधान—also पिधान. भिन्नैक०—The simile vividly expresses the idea of the two pressing crowds mingling together.

Śl. 54. त्रैलोक्य—त्रयो लोकाः त्रैलोक्यं by adding य (ष्यञ्) स्वार्थे (चतुर्वर्णादित्वात्) by Vârt. on Pâṇ. V. 1. 134. आवर्जितं &c.—When Himálaya saw Śiva he unconsciously bent his head in veneration; but he did not remember it.

Śl. 55. प्रीतियोगा०—When at the end of a comp, योग almost means 'in consequence of, by reason of'; *cf.* रक्षायोगादयमपि तपः &c. Śâk. II. 14; सांनिध्ययोगात्किल तत्र शच्याः &c. Ragh. VII. 3.

अमेसरतां—Shows his great reverence for Śiva. आगुल्फ०—Ar. reads आगुल्फगाढार्पित०—आगुल्फं गाढं यथा तथा अर्पितानि मार्गे पुष्पाणि यस्मिन् ; this is better, as it does not limit the showering of flowers to the market-streets only.

Śl. 56. Now the poet proceeds to describe the confusion of the ladies of the town hurrying to obtain a good view of Śiva and the procession. Such descriptions are common enough in Sanskrit; *cf.* Śiś. XIII. 30-48, Bud.-Ch. III. 13-24, Vikram. VI. 11-19. This śl. occurs with necessary modifications in Ragh.; see VII. 5.

सुन्दरीणाम्—सुष्ठु उनत्ति इति; fr. सु + उन्द् + अर, like शकन्धु ; see Vârt. on Pâṇ. VI. 1. 94; *fem.* सुन्दरी. ०लालसानां—may also be taken as ईशानसंदर्शने लालसा eagerness, ardent desire यासां तासां. लालसा may be from लल् 10 A'. to desire and the Uṇâdi aff. अस (णू), or from the Freq. base of लस् to shine with the fem. aff. आ. *Cf.* अवलोकनाय सुरविद्विषां द्विषः पटहप्रणादविहितोपहूतयः। अवधारितान्यकरणीयसत्वराः प्रतिरथ्यमीयुरथ पौरयोषितः ॥ Śiś. XIII. 30.

Śl. 57. Ślokas 57-62 are almost the same as in Ragh. VII. (6-11). आलोकमार्गे—आलोक्यतेऽनेन इत्या० a window; or आलोक may mean 'light'; तस्य मार्गम्. उद्वेष्टन &c.—उद्गतं वेष्टनमस्य स उद्वेष्टनः। प्रादिभ्यो धातुजस्य वाच्यो वाचोत्तरपदलोपः इति बहुव्रीहिः। वान्तं माल्यं येन। आदौ उ० पश्चाद्वान्तमाल्यः। मालैव माल्यम्। चतुर्वर्णादिष्यञ्। Vârt. on Pâṇ. V. 1. 124; or मल्यते इति ण्यत् (य) by Pâṇ. III. 1. 124. वान्त—The use of the word is not objectionable here as it is used in a metaphorical sense, *viz.* that of 'thrown down'; see note on वमन VI. 37. वेष्टन here may mean a string by which it was tied up. तावत्—here adds emphasis—'not at all'. Malli. says ध्यर्यन्तं, but not in good taste. For if the lady did not think of tying up her hair when making for the window, it was less likely that she should think of it when actually at the window where her attention would be more engrossed. रुद्धोऽपि—This shows how great her absent-mindedness was. Châr. says—केशपाशो बन्द्धुं तावन्न संभावित एव नापि रुद्धः, but without propriety, as it does not bring out the lady's absent-mindedness so prominently. केशानां कलापः केशपाशः, a Nityasamâsa. See also I. 38, notes

Śl. 58. अग्रपादम्—See Malli. If dissolved as पादस्याग्रं the comp. will be पादाग्रम्. Malli. quotes Vâmana who states that the compounds हस्ताग्र and अग्रह० are obtained by taking गुण (अग्रत्वं) and गुणी (हस्त) as distinct and as identical respectively. In the present case the गुण, अग्रत्व, resides in the foot which is the गुणी. The poet here speaks of them both as identical, disregarding the distinction between the whole पाद् and its forepart, to which alone the अग्रत्व properly belongs. See our note on this at Ragh. VII. 7. गवामक्षीव गवाक्षः । The word signifies a window by Rúḍhi (usage). See notes on 62, further on. *Cf.* with this Śiś. XIII. 33.

Śl. 59. दक्षिण—This implies extreme hurry; see Malli.; *cf.* वामभागस्तु नारीणां श्रेष्ठः पुंसां तु दक्षिणः । दाने देवादिपूजायां शृङ्गारकरणेऽपि च ॥ Nimittanidána. सङ्क्षित—Because she did not give to the right eye what it had a right to expect.

Śl. 60. जाला०—जालान्तरे ेन्तरेण वा प्रेषिता दृष्टिर्यया । प्रस्थान०—Ar. reads ०भिन्नानवबद्धनीविः—प्रस्थानेन भिन्ना अनवबद्धा च नीविर्यस्याः—This reading is better as it gives the subject directly. But Kâlidâsa is not likely to use such a word as अनवबद्ध where अव has no propriety. The lady was in such a hurry that when she heard that the procession was advancing she besmeared her right eye and then at once ran to the window. नाभिप्र०—The word प्रविष्ट indicates depth of the navel, which is supposed to be a mark of beauty. See *supra,* I.38; *cf.* Ragh. VI. 52 (आवर्तमनोज्ञनाभिः). *Cf.* हरिवीक्षणाक्षणिकचक्षुषान्यया करपल्लवेन गलदम्बरं दधे । Śiś. XIII. 44.

Śl. 61. अर्धा०—A comp. सुप्सुपा. दुर्निमिते—fr. मि 5 P. A'. to measure, to establish (—the root is rarely used in classical literature); ill-measured, ill-placed. The woman was stringing her girdle with pearls, fastening one end of the string to her big toe. But when she heard of the approach of the procession she ran to the window, forgetting in her hurry to secure that part of the waist-band which had been strung, and so all the pearls dropped down, the string only being left hanging by her great toe.

Śl. 62. आसवगन्धगर्भैः—The word गर्भ takes परनिपात by the Vârt. गड्वादिभ्यः परा सप्तमी. Drinking wine seems to have been a fashionable vice with the men and women of the higher classes in ancient India, if it be not a mere poetical fiction. *Cf.* Śiś. X. 33 quoted by Malli. while commenting on IV. 12 *supra*; *cf.* also ककुभिकन्यावक्त्रान्तर्वासलब्धाधिवासया । मुखामोदं मदिरया कृतानुव्याधमुद्वमन् ॥ Śiś. II. 20. सान्द्र०—This shows that the women remained stationary and so their faces looked like lotuses. भ्रमरैः—भ्रमन् रौतीति । भ्रमतीति वा भ्रमरः । fr. भ्रम्+अर (अर्तिकमिभ्रमिचामि—इति करन् Uṇádi III. 132). It is customary with poets to describe lotuses with bees hovering about them. गवाक्षाः—गो means 'a ray of light'; अक्षि something like an eye, a hole. अक्षि becomes अक्ष at the end of a compound when it does not mean 'an eye', by अक्ष्णोऽदर्शनात्। Pâṇ. V. 4. 76. Hence गवाक्ष means 'a hole for admitting light;' and so a window, by Rûḍhi or usage. Though the word ought to be *neu.* (it is so given in Kâśikâ) it is *masc.* by custom (पुंस्त्वं लोकात्) (Manoramá and Tattv.-Bodh.). ०पत्रावरणाः—*V. l.* covered with &c.; सहस्रपत्रमयमावरणं येषां Ar.

Śl. 63. इन्दुमौलिः—इन्दुर्मौलौ यस्य Vyadh. Bah.; मौलि takes परनिपात by गड्वादिभ्यः &c.; see last śl. उत्तोरणं—उत्क्षिप्तं तोरणं यत्र. राजपथं—राज्ञः पन्थाः; or पथां राजा the chief road; here पथिन् takes परनिपात by राजदन्तादिषु परम् Pâṇ. II. 2. 31.

Śl. 64. दृष्टिभिः पा—is a Sanskrit idiom for 'to look intently at'; see Ragh. II. 19, 73. नार्यः—*i. e.* by their senses. विषया०—अन्ये विषयाः वि० राणि। विषिण्वन्ति निबध्नन्ति इन्द्रियाणि इति विषयाः 'those which attract the senses;' hence the objects of senses. 'तद्गतमनस्कत्वाच्च शृण्वन्ति न स्पर्शमनुभवन्ति न जिघ्रन्ति' Chár. The women were looking at Śiva so intently that the power of perception of the other senses seemed to be quite paralysed, ears caught no sound, the skin felt no touch &c. *Cf.* Ragh. VII. 12. Notice the reading ताः शङ्करं in this connexion. Ar. reads the last line as विनोपघातेन जडीबभूव and comments विनोपघातेन शक्तिनिरोधमन्तरेण जडीबभूव कुण्ठिताऽभवत्।

Śl. 65. अपर्णया—For the name see *supra* V. 28. It seems that the name had been well-established among the ladies of Oshadhiprastha by this time. पेलवा—पेलवं विरलं तनु Amara.; hence, delicate tender. अङ्कया०—Ar. takes अङ्क in the sense of उरस् and Nâr. quotes Yádava- 'अङ्कश्चिह्नेऽन्तिकोरसोः'-in support.

Śl. 66. परस्परेण— may also be taken with स्पृह०; इन्दुमत्याः शोभाऽजेन स्पृहणीयासीदजस्य शोभा चेन्दुमत्या इत्यर्थः ॥ शोभयतीति शोभा Hemádri. द्वन्द्वं—द्वौ द्वौ इति। द्विशब्दस्य द्विर्वचनं पूर्वपदस्याम्भावः अत्वं चोत्तरपदस्य। By द्वंद्वं रहस्यमर्यादावचन &c. Pâṇ. VIII. 1. 15. *Cf.* Ragh. VII. 14, and निशा शशाङ्कं गिरिशं तथोमया श्रिया हरिं योजयतः प्रतीतः। विधेरपि स्वारसिकः प्रयासः परस्परं योग्यसमागमाय ॥.

Śl. 67. व्रीडात्—व्रीड fr. व्रीड् 4. P. to be ashamed + अ (घञ्); with आ व्रीडा by Pâṇ. III. 3. 103 (गुरोश्च हलः). According to Vâmana, the आ may be sometimes optionally dropped; *e. g.* बाधा, बाधः; ऊहा, ऊहः; व्रीडा, व्रीडः; see Ar. *Cf.* व्रीडमावहति मे स संप्रति Ragh. XI. 73; व्रीडादिवाभ्यासगतैर्विलिल्ये Śiś. III. 40.

Śl. 68. मनोरथ०—*Cf. supra* I. 51, V. 7.

Śl. 69. त्रिनेत्र—Malli. here avoids the णत्व by rejecting its संज्ञात्व on the authority of Pâṇ. VIII. 4. 39. केयूर० लाजमुष्टि—It

was customary for ladies, young and old, to shower handfuls of *lâjas* **&c. (rice-grains parched without being husked which swell considerably and lose the husk in the process of parching) on a distinguished person, as an auspicious sign (माङ्गलिकत्वात्).** See Ragh. II. 10. *Cf.* पदे पदे विवाहानल इव कुसुममिश्रैर्लाजाञ्जलिभिरवकीर्यमाणश्चन्द्रापीडः &c. Kâd. p. 140. The word लाज is *mas.* and used in the plural; दाराक्षतलाजासूनां बहुत्वं च इति लिङ्गानुशासनसूत्रम्। चूर्णीकृत—पुरन्ध्रिजनसंबन्धातिशयोक्तिः। Malli. The *lâjas* were powdered rather as they came in contact with the *keyûras* worn by the large assemblage of men (केयूरेति जनसंबाध उक्तः। Ar.). The *keyúras* are worn by men; *cf.* Ragh. VI. 68; Bhar. Nît. 19. *Cf.* Ragh. VII. 16. Ar. reads ०लाजमुष्टिः (चूर्णीकृता लाजमुष्टयः यस्य *i. e.* thrown on him).

Śl. 70. अच्युत—नास्ति च्युतं स्वपदात्स्खलनमस्य। उक्षन्—a bull; fr. उक्ष् सेचने भ्वादिः + अन् (कनि) by श्वन्नुक्षन् &c. Uṇâdi I. 152. कक्ष्या—a room or hall; also कक्षा.

Śl. 72. विष्टर—seat; the स् is changed to ष् after वि when the meaning is a tree or a seat; वृक्षासनयोर्विष्टरः। Pân. VIII. 3. 93; but वाक्यस्य विस्तरः. यथावत्—यथार्हम्। तदर्हमिति वतिः। *Cf.* ततो यथावद्विहिताध्वराय। Ragh. V. 19; अध्यापिपद्गाधिसुतो यथावत्। Bhaṭṭi. II. 21. गव्यं—गोरिदम्; by गोपयसोर्यत्। Pâṇ. IV. 3. 160; clarified butter and curds. All these form the ingredients of what is technically called मधुपर्क. It is to be offered to a distinguished guest, or to the bridegroom on his arrival at the door of the bride's father. *Cf* अलंकृतः सितच्छत्रोऽपदातिर्ज्ञातिबान्धवैः। वृतो वधूगृहं गत्वा मधुपर्कादिपूजितः॥ A'śvalâyana.

Śl. 73. This is the same as Ragh. VII. 10, where the reading is रक्षैः for ऋक्षैः. विनीतैः—Well-trained, behaving respectfully. स्फुटफेन०—Large masses of foam give a white appearance to the sea. नवैः—This is put in because the rays of the new moon give a mild light and compare well with the humble attendants of the seraglio. The fig. is उपमा, and not दृष्टान्त as some have it.

Śl. 74. Here Pârvatî is compared to autumn, her face to the autumnal moon which appears brighter in that season (*cf.* चन्द्रे च विशदप्रभे Ragh. IV. 18), and Śiva's eyes to lotuses. The attributes may be taken with शरद् and लोक; प्रवृद्धा आननभूतस्य चन्द्रस्य कान्तिर्यस्याम्। प्रफुल्लानि चक्षूंषीव कुमुदानि यस्मिन्। प्रसन्नं चेत इव सलिलं यस्मिन्. *Cf.* in this respect प्रससादोदयादम्भः कुम्भयोनेर्महौजसः। Ragh. IV. 21. संसृज्यमानः—कर्तरि देवादिकात् शानच्। *Cf.* संसृज्यते सरसिजैररुणांशुभिन्नैः। Ragh. V. 69.

Śl. 75. समापत्ति—Accidental or fortuitous meeting; *i. e.* when they happened to meet; *cf.* समापत्तिद्दष्टेन Vik. I. ह्रीयन्त्रणा–The restraint of bashfulness; *i. e.* they could not look freely at each other. *Cf.* Ragh. VII. 23.

Śl. 77. रोमाञ्च and स्वेद are two of the eight Sâttvikabhávas which are manifested at the first meeting. As to the question whether the statement made here goes counter to Vátsyâyana's teathing, see Malli. समं–'equally'; or, 'at one and the same time.' इव—indicates Utprekshâ. *Cf.* Ragh. VII. 22.

Śl. 78. वधूवरं—There is no special rule in Pâṇini's grammar for the समाहारत्व of this. So we must have recourse to the Paribhâshá सर्वो द्वन्द्वो विभाषया एकवद्भवति which is admitted by the Bhâshyakára. We shall have वधूवरौ also. अंस्यौ—fr. अंस+य (यत्) by तत्र साधुः. उभयस्य—According to Kaiyaṭa this is not used in the dual; according to Haradatta it is; (उभयशब्दस्य द्विवचनं नास्तीति कैयटः। अस्तीति हरदत्तः। Sid.-Kau. on Pâṇ. VII. 1. 52); *cf.* तस्य मित्राण्यमित्रास्ते ये च ये चोभये नृपाः। Śiś. II. 101; रुचमदधुरुभय्यः कल्पिता भूषिताश्व। *ibid.* XI. 27; तद्गुश्चोभये भटाः। Bhaṭṭi. XIV. 30.

Śl. 79. This is the same as Ragh. VII. 24. प्रदक्षिण°—प्रदक्षिणं यथा तथा प्रक्रमणं तस्मात्। कृशानोः–कृशयतीति that which reduces the mass of a thing; hence, fire; fr. कृश्+आनु (क्) by Uṇâdi IV. 2. मेरोः—For मेरु see notes on I. 2. मेरोरिवान्ते परिवर्तमानं—*v. l.* adopted by Ar. is preferable as it better corresponds with प्रदक्षिणप्रक्रमण. अहस्त्रियामम्—For त्रियामा see *supra* śl. 21. The sing. may be accounted for by the rule विप्रतिषिद्धं चानधिकरणवाचि। Pâṇ. IV. 4. 13; *i. e.* words not denoting द्रव्यs or concrete things and incapable of existing together, optionally become *sing* and *neu.* (form a समाहारद्वंद्व). But, if day and night be regarded as द्रव्यs, this will not apply, and then recourse must be had to the Paribhâshâ सर्वोऽपि द्वन्द्वः &c. quoted before.

Śl. 80. पुरोधाः—पुरो धीयते इति the family priest; fr. पुरः and धा+अस् Uṇâdi IV. 230. वधूं—also वध्वा; see Malli. समिद्धा°—समिद्धमर्चिर्यस्य तस्मिन्. लाजमोक्षं—The offering of *lájas* on the fire is enjoined by the most ancient writers on marriage-rites; *cf.* इमान् लाजानावपामि समृद्धिकरणान् मम तुभ्यं (अग्नये) च संवरणं तदाग्निरनुमन्यतामयम्। इत्यभिधायेयं नार्युपब्रूतेऽग्नौ लाजानावपन्ती—दीर्घायुरस्तु मे पतिरेधन्तां ज्ञातयो मम स्वाहा। Hiraṇyakeśi-Sûtra XIX. 6. 2. *Cf.* Ragh. VII. 25.

Śl. 81. लाजधू°—is equivalent to लाजाञ्जलिधूमम्; लाजानां धूमयुक्तः अञ्जलिः तम्. Nár. says—लाजाञ्जलिं विसृज्य धूमाग्रं समाजिघ्रेत्

इति प्रयोगवृत्तिकारवचनमत्र प्रमाणम् । ०संसर्पि०—कपोलयोः संसर्प्तुं (संस्रप्तुं) वा शीलमस्याः । ०त्पलतां—उत्पल is taken here as it is blue and compares well with धूम. *Cf.* Ragh. VII. 26.

Śl. 82. गण्ड०—प्रशस्तौ कपोलौ गण्डलेखे. उच्छ्वासि—flushed, being wetted. यवा०—*i. e.* sprouts of *yavas* artificially grown in shade and watered with any dye, generally yellow, and worn as ornaments on the ears. आचार०—the customary inhaling of smoke; see Malli.; अन्ये वृद्धाचाराद्धूमग्रहणमित्याहुः. *Cf.* Ragh. VII. 27.

Śl. 83. द्विजः—Ar. reads गिरिः, but the advice is better put in the mouth of the priest. कर्मसा०—साक्षी fr. साक्षात्+इनिः by साक्षाद्द्रष्टरि संज्ञायाम् । Pâṇ. V. 2. 91. चर्या—practising of; from चर्+य (with the fem. affix, या) by गदमदचरयमश्चानुपसर्गे । Pâṇ. III. 1. 100. मुक्तविचारया—*i. e.* implicitly; without inquiring into the reason of it.

Śl. 84. आलोचनान्तं—supply स्थिते श्रवणे her ears which stood on the borders of the eyes, *i. e.* of the long-eyed one. श्रवणे वितत्य—is a strange expression. It refers to the mental effort to direct the ears to what was said, and simply means-'with sole attention'. उल्बण—fr. वण् 1 P. to sound, with उद्+अ (च्): उद्वणति ; a word of the पृषोदरादि class. It means 'what is clearly seen,' or is prominent; hence, something which has great size.

Śl. 85. ध्रुवदर्शनाय—It is a part of the marriage-ceremony that the bride should see Dhruva (the polar star) actually if possible, or look in that direction, expessing a hope, in the words ध्रुवमसि ध्रुवाहं पतिकुले भूयासम्, to confirm which the bridegroom is to say—ध्रुवा द्यौर्ध्रुवा पृथिवी ध्रुवं विश्वमिदं जगत् । ध्रुवासः पर्वता इमे ध्रुवा स्त्री पतिकुले इयम् । सन्न—*p. p.* of सद् to waste away, to be destroyed. कण्ठ—voice. Mark the alliterations in this śl.

Śl. 86. उपचार—Rite, ceremony. For another meaning see śl. 88. प्रणेमतुः—Siva bowed to Brahmâ as he now stood in the relation of an elderly kinsman to him, as Himâlaya, was created by him. *Cf.* यज्ञार्थं हि मया सृष्टो &c. quoted by Malli. in his com. on V. 41. प्रथमं लोकमान्यत्वाद् ब्रह्मा देवेन शिरःकम्पेन संभावितः इदानीं तु वधूकुलकूटस्थत्वात्प्रणामेनेति विशेषः । Ar. प्रजानां पितरौ—see Malli. on Ragh. I. 1. पद्मा०—Brahmâ is always represented as sitting on a lotus; *cf.* his epithet कमलासन. पितामह—लोकपितॄणां मरीच्यादीनामर्यमादीनां पिता; the affix मह is added to मातृ and पितृ in the sense of 'father of' by the Vârt. मातृपितृभ्यां पितरि डामहच् ।.

Śl. 87. वाचस्पतिः &c.—Though the lord of speech, *i. e.* though whatever he said was sure to come to pass, he paused;

he did not know what blessing to confer on Śiva; because Śiva was अष्टमूर्ति the whole universe was his, there was nothing that he could have wished for. आशास्य°—Pot. p. used as a noun; 'a blessing or benediction,' *cf.* आशास्यमन्यत्पुनरुक्तभूतं Ragh. V. 34.

Śl. 88. °पचारां—Such as the placing of pots filled with water, the fastening of garlands of flowers and strings of leaves etc. लौकिकं—लोकविहितं, enjoined by custom; fr. लोक + इक (ठञ्) added in this sense, by लोकसर्वलोकाट्ठञ् Pāṇ. V. I. 44. अक्षता:—whole (unbroken) grains of rice. एषणीयं—much coveted by relations (especially women). Châr. reads एषितव्यम्. *Cf.* Ragh. VII. 28.

Śl. 89. पत्रान्त°—Nâr. reads °लम्बै: (hanging down from) जलबिन्दुवर्षै:, the falling drops of water. आकृष्ट—drawn to it; possessed. आक्रुष्ट *v. l.*—cried down, *i. e.* surpassed.

Śl. 90. वाङ्मय—वाचो विकारो वाङ्मयं a composition. संस्कार—grammatical purity or faultlessness. सुखग्राह्य°—The arrangement (construction and import) of which could be easily understood; see Malli. This refers to the custom of ancient times which made women and persons of the lower ranks speak in Prakrit which is almost as old as Sanskrit itself.

Śl. 91. Here the poet has used some technical terms used in dramas. Saṃdhi is defined as अन्तरैकार्थसंबन्ध: संधिरेकान्वये सति । *i. e.* the proper union of the main plot with episodes and other minor incidents. These are five in number; see com. For these see our Introduction to Śák. or Vikr. व्यश्रित—properly brought out. वृत्ति—The style of procedure prescribed for the hero, or of description (तद्व्यापारात्मिका वृत्तिश्चतुर्धा; नाटके वृत्तय: प्रोक्ताश्चतस्रो नाट्यवेदिभि: ।). For the Vṛittis and the sentiments to which they are suited, see com. रस—The nine well-known Sentiments. राग—a mode of music (in certain fixed melodies). The chief Râgas are—भैरव: कौशिकश्चैव हिन्दोलो दीपकस्तथा । श्रीरागो मेघरागश्च रागा: षडिति कीर्तिता: ॥ Each Râga has six Râgiṇîs as its consorts and their unions give rise to several musical modes. प्रयोग—representation of situations with Rasa and proper acting. अप्सरसां—अप्सरस् is derived as अद्भ्य: सरन्तीति fr. अप् + सृ + असु by Uṇâ. IV. 237; अप्सु निर्मथनादेव रसात्तस्माद्वरस्त्रियः । उत्पेतुर्मनुजश्रेष्ठ तस्मादप्सरसोऽभवन् ॥ Râmâyaṇa. The *Apsarasas* are a class of celestial women, regarded as the courtesans of gods and as such the servants of Indra. अङ्गहार-dancing, the pantomimic representations. The presence of women was necessary for the proper exhibition of the Kaiśikî style. Nâr. quotes the following from Bharata—

भरतः प्रार्थयामास प्रोवाचेनमथात्मभूः । लास्यप्रयोगो भवता नैव शक्यः कथंचन ॥ लास्ये हि कैशिकी वृत्तिराधिका सा न पुरुषैः । प्रयोक्तुं या ततो लास्ये नारीणामेव नैपुणम् ॥ कैशिकी श्लक्ष्णनेपथ्या शृङ्गाररससंभवा । अशक्या पुरुषैः साधु प्रयोक्तुं स्त्रीजनादृते ॥ इत्युक्त्वा तत्प्रयोगार्थं सृष्टैवाप्सरसां गणम् । शिक्षयामास ललितं लास्यं तस्मात्तदादिकम् ॥.

Śl. 92. ऊढभार्य—ऊढ *p. p.* of वह् to marry; it takes पूर्वनिपात optionally by वाहिताग्न्यादिषु । Pâṇ. II. 2. 37; so भार्योढं also; *cf.* भार्योढं तमवज्ञाय तस्थे सौमित्रयेऽसकौ । Bhaṭṭi. IV. 15. बद्धाञ्ज०—*v. l.* दृष्टाञ्जलयः with their joined hands placed in close contact &c. शापा०—See *supra*, IV. 41-43.

Śl. 93. तस्यानुमेने—The meaning is:—Śiva allowed himself to be influenced by passion. कार्य०—*v. l.* कालविद्धिः, which is noticed by Malli., is better.

Śl. 94. भक्ति०—Ornamental drawings with powder etc.; offerings of flowers etc. Ar. reads ०रक्षाभक्तिशोभा which Nâr. explains as कनकमयः कलशः पूर्णकुम्भः । रक्षार्था शक्तिः रक्षाशक्तिः । शक्तिरायुधविशेषः । दीक्षागृहे शक्तिनिक्षेपो दुर्देवतापरिहारार्थः । स च देशाचारसिद्धः । This was done merely because custom required it. कौतुका०—The house for conjugal sports. Malli. quotes Âśv.-Gr.-S. I. 8, 10.

Śl. 95. ०भूषणं—She appeared the more graceful by her bashfulness. See com. on Vâts.-Kâm.-Sût. III. 2. 10. तत्कृता०—drawn towards himself and raised up. Notice the reading ०कृताक्षेपं. *Cf.* Śâk. III. 23. प्रमथ०—Name of a class of beings (goblins) attending on Śiva. See com. विकारैः—distortions of faces as they danced. गूढं—Pârvatî laughed gently. The हास्य was intended for the abatement of her bashfulness.

CANTO VIII.

In this Canto the Poet describes the amorous sports of Śiva and Pârvatî (ultimately leading to the birth of Kumâra). Śiva spent a month after his marriage in the palace of Himâlaya (see śl. 30). In the first eleven ślokas the goddess is represented as a मुग्धा नायिका (one who has just attained youth and is yet inexperienced in love-sports). See Malli.'s introduction.

Śl. 1. Consture शैलराजदुहितुः हरं प्रति भावसाध्वसपरिग्रहात्, हरस्य कामदोहदसुखं अभूत् । See translation. Because Pârvatî felt fear mixed with love, Śiva felt delight. पाणिपीडन—पाणेः पीडनं seizing firmly of; marriage; more commonly पाणिग्रहण *supra* VII. 4, 30 &c.; *cf.* न प्रमाणीकृतः पाणिर्बाल्ये बालेन पीडितः Utt. VII. 5. ०विधेः—

is either abl. or gen., as enplained by Malli. on विश्वयोनेरनन्तरम् *supra* VI. 9. हरं प्रति—(परिग्रह) 'with reference to Hara;' प्रति is here a कर्मप्रवचनीय. भावसाध्वस should rather be explained as a Śâkapârthivádi comp., as is done by Nâr. (भावमिश्रं साध्वसं), or भावप्रयुक्तं साध्वसं as Malli. seems to do, than as a Dvandva (भावश्च साध्वसं च), as साध्वस is more prominently represented in the following ślokas. भाव°—is the feeling of love arising in the mind caused by the presence of the lover &c.; बाह्यार्थालम्बनो यस्तु विकारो मानसो भवेत् । स भावः कथ्यते सद्भिः तस्योत्कर्षो रसः स्मृतः ॥ Haláyudha. It also means 'love cherished in the heart;' see Malli. on V. 58 (भावस्थमिमं जनं). कामदोहद is adjectival in sense, being equivalent to कामसंवर्धक, 'which heightened his desire.' दोहद primarily means the 'ardent longing' supposed poetically to exist in plants, desiring to be kicked by fair ladies &c., in order to put forth flowers or fruits; then secondarily it is applied to anything which produces such desire. See Śabdârṇava quoted by Malli. The com. on Naish. I. 82 also says अतिशयितफलादिसमृद्धिः येन भवति तद्दोहदम्. कामसौहदसुखं *v. l.*—कामेन सौहदं मैत्री यत्र तत्सुखं, *i. e.* happiness springing from love.

Śl. 2. रतये—supply बभूव after this. It brought pleasure to Śiva. *Cf.* प्रणयविशदां दृष्टिं वक्त्रे ददाति न शङ्किता &c. Ratn. III. 9; and दृष्टा दृष्टिमधो ददाति कुरुते नालापमाभाषिता शय्यायां परिवृत्य तिष्ठति बलादालिङ्गिता वेपते । &c. Nág. III. 4. Śl. quoted in the D.-R. as an instance of a Náyiká who is रतवामा (opposed to enjoyment) and again as one of साध्वस. Some rhetoricians object to the description of the love of Śiva and Pârvatî as though they were common mortals; the com. Aruṇ. gives the following reply to these, which is doubtless an ingenious defence ; he says—अत्र दक्षिणावर्ते आह—'अस्य प्रकरणस्य शिवयोः संभोगविषयत्वात् रसभावान्विविच्य वक्तुं बिभेमि तस्मादन्वयमात्रादि क्रियते' इति । एतदल्पज्ञताविलसितं, यतः प्रसिद्धलौकिकोत्तमनायकव्यवहारमनुकुर्वतोरनयोः महानटयोः लीलामात्रात्मिकासु प्रवृत्तिषु परमार्थबुद्धिर्यस्यास्ति तस्यैव अयं दोषः; यस्य तु सा नास्ति तस्य तद्विवेचनमपि शिवयोः स्तुतिः पर्यवस्यति ।

Śl. 3. कैतव—pretence (see *supra* IV. 9); Śiva was not really asleep, he only pretended to be so. प्रतिमुखं—*adv.* 'towords his face'. The constr. is पार्वती प्रतिमुखं निपातितं (आत्मनः) चक्षुः न्यमीलयत्. प्रिये उन्मिषति—'as her beloved opened his eyes;' उन्मिष् is an intrans. verb meaning 'to open the eyes'; *cf.* उन्मिषन्निमिषन्नपि । Bg. V. 9.

Śl. 4. नाभिदेश°—In this and the following three ślokas Kálidâsa follows Vâts.-K.-Sû. II. 2. 30-38 in making Śiva gain the confidence of his wife. Loosening of the knot of the garment is an indication of extreme love (रतिपारवश्य) which Párvatî was unable to prevent showing itself. Nár. quotes Amaru—कान्ते तल्पमुपागते विगलिता नीवी स्वयं बन्धनात् &c. verse 101; such descriptions are very frequent in Sanskrit literature; *cf.* लोलदृष्टिवदनं दयिताया श्चुम्बति प्रियतमे रभसेन । व्रीडया सह विनीवि नितम्बादंशुकं शिथिलतामुपपेदे ॥ Kir. IX. 47. दूरं—is an adverb to be construed with उच्छ्वसित 'extremely loosened'; for this meaning of उच्छ्वसत् comp. नीवीबन्धोच्छ्वसितशिथिलं Megh. II. 7.

Śl. 5. एवं—refers to the actual words in which the advice was conveyed. आलि—See *supra* V. 83. उपदिष्टं—Supply वचनं understood, as is done by Malli.; it may also be taken as a noun (=उपदेशं) by 'नपुंसके भावे क्तः.' आकुला—confused or overcome by fear (in his presence).

Śl. 6. अवस्तुन्यपि—*lit.* 'even about a thing that did not exist so that she should say 'no' at least', or about a trifling topic ; goes with प्रश्नतत्पर०. He somehow wanted to make her talk; and for that purpose he was starting discussions on any topic at random (यत्किंचित्पृच्छन्तम् Malli.). Nár. understands अवस्तुनि in its literal sense, which seems unnecessary; he remarks—अवस्तुनि अत्यन्तशून्ये वस्तुनि । अद्य प्रभाते गगनमण्डले गन्धर्वाणां नगरमाविर्भूतम् । तत्र च गन्धर्वराजः सभार्यः प्रतिवसति स्म । तत्किं त्वया दृष्टं अथ वाऽदृष्टं—इत्यादीनि शून्यानि वस्तूनि परस्परवाक्श्रिवणमात्राकाङ्क्षया पृच्छन्तमित्यर्थः ।

Śl. 7. मोघयत्नविधुरा—dissolve मोघयत्ना चासौ विधुरा (distressed) च । She became helpless, her efforts having failed, as with her two hands she could not close the three eyes of Śiva.

Śl. 8. The वधूरत was क्लिष्टमन्मथ because it was दुर्लभप्रतिकृत ; and how it was दुर्लभ० is explained in the first half. अधरदान—by Párvatî. स्रस्तहस्तं (*adj.* of वधूरतं)—in which the hands hung loose by her sides, as she made no efforts on her part to embrace him; स्रस्तौ (nerveless) हस्तौ यस्मिन् तत्. The phrase has occurred above at III. 51 (नालक्षयत्साध्वससन्नहस्तः). अदयोपगूहन—on the part of Śiva. क्लिष्ट—*lit.* troubled, pained, distressed, inasmuch as it failed to obtain complete satisfaction for lack of response; क्लिष्टशब्देनात्र असंपूर्णत्वं लक्ष्यते Nár. प्रतिकृत—*lit.* 'acts in return,' *viz.* kisses and embraces in response. Nár. says चुम्बने सीत्कृतं ताडने ताडनं इत्यादिप्रतिव्यापाररहितम्.

Śl. 9. अक्षताधरं—without biting her lower lip, which would give her pain. यत् च नखं दत्तं—stands for यत् च नखस्य दानम्; (the impressing of) the नखदान was अव्रणपद, *i. e.* it left no marks by way of scratches or wounds in the skin, which would give her pain. सदयं—प्रहरणादिरहितं (Nâr.); प्रहरण or striking with the fists would have given her pain. With this verse *cf.* सदयं बुभुजे महाभुजः सहसोद्वेगमियं व्रजेदिति । अचिरोपनतां स मेदिनीं नवपाणिग्रहणां वधूमिव ॥ Ragh. VIII. 7.

Śl. 10. अनुयुज्—to ask; प्रश्नोऽनुयोगः पृच्छा च Ak. विभात-morning. तत्वरे—Her heart was eager to recount those things, but her bashfulness held her back. ह्रिया—*v. l.* रहः 'in private;' *i. e.* to each one separately.

Śl. 11. परिभोग—enjoyment, *i. e.* its outward marks, such as nail-scratches &c. With this verse compare the almost similar one in Ragh. (XIX. 28)–दर्पणेषु परिभोगदर्शिनीर्नर्मपूर्वमनुपृष्ठसंस्थितः । छायया स्मितमनोज्ञया वधूर्ह्रीनिमीलितमुखीश्चकार सः ॥ पृष्ठतः—Śiva was sitting just behind her, and so she saw him, too, reflected in that mirror. निषेदुषः—gen. sing. of निषेदिवस् Perf. Part. from नि+सद्+क्वसु by Páṇ. III. 2. 108. *Cf.* निषेदुषीमासनबन्धधीरः Ragh. II. 6. The constr. is आत्मनः बिम्बमनु प्रणयिनः बिम्बं प्रेक्ष्य ; अनु is a कर्मप्रवचनीय and governs the acc. case. See A. G. § 37. कानि कानि–referring to the bodily movements and gestures she would naturally make in her bashfulness; नयननिमीलनवदनविनमनादीनि Nár. कानि कान्यपि *v. l.*—'did this thing and that thing'. Śl. quoted in the Sar.-K.

Śl. 12. परिभुक्तयौवनां विलोक्य—referring to the परिभोग of the previous stanza. समाश्वसत्—*i.e.* she was pleased at heart to find that her daughter was beloved by her husband; *cf.* प्रियेषु सौभाग्यफला हि चारुता *supra* V. I. मानसी *fem.* (adj. of शुच्)—mental, which she felt within her. The Fig. of Speech is अर्थान्तरन्यास.

Śl. 13. वासराणि कतिचित्—accusative of time; taking some days for it. स्थाणुना प्रिया पदमकार्यत—(passive of the causal)—'was made to step towards'; some such word as रतिकर्मणि or संभोगरसज्ञाने (Nár.) should be supplied before पदम्. Such an omission, which can be easily understood, constitutes a merit when the inclusion of the words would have read rather crude. पदं कृ, in the fig. sense of 'to make one inclined towards', is a favourite expression of our poet; *cf. supra* VI. 14 (धर्मेणापि पदं शर्वे कारिते पार्वतीं प्रति). दुःखशीलता—perverseness, *lit.* the condition of one whose nature becomes troublesome to others ; *cf.* उपेत्य सा दोहददुःखशीलतां Ragh. III. 6; कामेकपत्नीव्रतदुःखशीलां *supra* III. 7. She became दुःखशील because of acts like those described in śl. 2 above ; that was when she was a मुग्धा (undeveloped, young) wife. Nár. quotes मुग्धा नववयःकामा रतौ वामा मृदुः क्रुधि D.-R. II. 16.

Śl. 14. This śl. amplifies the statement in the last śl. °निपीडिता°—तं *v. l.* (read by Ar. and Nār.) उरो निपीडितं नितरां पीडितं यथा भवति तथा (*adv.*); the is not a good reading, as Párv. cannot be expected to do this at this stage of her love. प्रार्थितं-when sought lovingly (desired for kissing). मेखलाप्रणयलोल—busy in seeking her girdle (for loosening the knot). प्रणय means 'acquaintance or familiarity' (as Malli. takes it); hence lovingly seizing it; *cf.* कृतोऽक्षसूत्रप्रणयी तया करः *supra* V. II. Ar. and Nár. read मेखलापनयलोल which gives the same sense more directly. शिथिलं—used adverbially; 'in a slack way', *i. e.* half-heartedly, since she was not now so particular about obstructing his hand.

Śl. 15. The constr. is कैश्चिदेव दिवसैः तयोः प्रेम रूढमभूत्—their love grew, *i. e.* it became firmly rooted. भावसूचितं—it was indicated by their various gestures indicative of love; भाव means चेष्टा such as कटाक्षनिक्षेप &c. (Malli.) विप्रिय—the opposite of प्रिय; *i. e.* an act which displeases. *Cf.* Ragh. VIII. 52. चाटुमत् (*adj.* of प्रेम)—'possessing or including in it agreeable or pleasing words;' from चाटु & the poss. affix मत्. For चाटु *cf.* चाटुकारः *infra* śl. 25. °कातरम्—afraid of, *i.e.* not tolerating. इतरेतराश्रयं—(*adj.* of प्रेम) the love of each had for its substratum that of the other; इतरेतरं आश्रयः यस्य तत्। देवीप्रेम्णो देव एवाश्रयो देवप्रेम्णस्तु देवी।

Śl. 16. Construe वधूः (पार्वती) तं वरं (शिवं) यथा अन्वरज्यत तथैव सोऽपि (वरः) तां (वधूं) अन्वरज्यत. See translation. आत्मसदृशं—suggesting that both were worthy of each other. अन्वरज्यत—अनु+रञ्ज् 4 P. Â. used transitively; *cf.* समस्थमनुरज्यन्ति विषमस्थं त्यजन्ति च। Rámá. Both Ar. and Nár. read the verb as अरज्यत only, taking अनु as a कर्मप्रवचनीय with वरं and तां in the sense of लक्षण ('the manner in which'); but this is unnecessary. अनपगा—Not going away from, always seeking; अपगच्छतीति अपगा (fem.), न अपगा अनपगा. For the simile compare सागरमुज्झित्वा कुत्र वा महानद्यवतरति Śák. III. p. 72; जलनिधिमनुरूपं जह्नुकन्यावतीर्णा Ragh. VI. 85. सोऽपि—*scil.* सागरः. सन्मुख—जाह्नवीमुख; the word मुख, which literally means 'the mouth of a river', by implication also suggests the mouth (and lips) of the woman (here, Párvatī). Similarly the word रस, which means 'water' in the case of the Ganges, signifies 'the honey of the lips' (अधरमधु) in the case of the *Náyiká*. निर्वृतः—pleased, happy; *cf.* कां निर्वृतिं चेतसि तस्य कुर्यात् &c. Śák. VII. 19.

Śl. 17. Constr.—शंकरस्य रहसि शिष्यतां प्रपन्नया तया यत् युवतिनैपुणं शिक्षितं तदेव &c. मिथुन—sexual sports. शिष्यतां प्रपन्नया—It was Śiva who first taught her whatever skill she later on showed in amorous sports; hence she is described as the 'disciple' of Śiva. युवतिनैपुणं—युवतीनां (उचितं) नैपुणं the skill which ladies ought to possess. तत् (नैपुणं) गुरुदक्षिणीकृतम्—Whenever a disciple is taught by his preceptor, the latter is entitled to his tuition fee, called गुरुदक्षिणा. [See Ragh. V. 20 for the word]. Ordinarily this दक्षिणा consists of monetary gifts; but in this case, the poet says, that Párvatî *gave him that same skill back* by way of his fee, meaning that she displayed that skill in complete response to his amorous approaches. See Malli.

Śl. 18. दष्टमुक्तं—Diss. आदौ दष्टं पश्चान्मुक्तं Karmadh. Comp. (which she could not bear a few days ago; see *supra* śl. 9). निरवापयत्—caused to cool; from निर्वापय् the causal of निर्+वा to cool. मौलिचन्द्र°—This implies growth of confidence (जातविस्रम्भतां ध्वनयति Aruṇ.).

Śl. 19. अलकचूर्ण—fragrant powder applied to the hair; this got into Śivá's third eye when he was kissing her. रूषितं *v. l.* for दूषितं means—covered or overlaid with. उच्छ्वसत्—'opening' (said of lotuses); *cf.* नोच्छ्वासिति तपनकिरणैश्चन्द्रस्यैवांशुभिः कुमुदं Vikr. III. 16. The breath of Párvatî's mouth possessed a fragrance similar to that of a full-blown lotus; गन्ध is changed to गन्धि in this compound by Páṇ. V. 4. 137. ददौ—meaning that he utilized the breath of Párvatî's mouth for blowing off the powder from his eye. गन्धवाहिन्—an epithet of wind (वायु) as the wafter of smells.

Śl. 20. इन्द्रियसुख—(adj. of वर्त्मन्) '(the path of enjoyment) which gave pleasure to the senses'. अनुगृहीतमन्मथः—compare *supra* VII. 92 देवास्तदन्ते &c. मासमात्रम्—The comm. Aruṇ. and Nár. quote the following in support of this period—'एवं भुञ्जानो नवोढां मासेन वशीकुर्यात्' इति गोनर्दीयवचनात्. Gonardîya is an authority on Kāmaśāstra. Malli. seems to have followed this when he says मासमात्रमिति वधूवशीकरणकालक्लृप्तिः प्रदर्शिता.

Śl. 21. आत्मभूः—here used as an epithet of Śiva, as at Śák. VII. 35 (पुनर्भवं परिगतशक्तिरात्मभूः). It is also used of Vishṇu (Ragh. IX. 16) and of Brahmá (Kum. V. 81). Such promiscuous use doubtles arose from the early identification of the three deities as manifestations of the One Supreme Spirit. आत्मजाविरह—implying that Śiva left along with Párvatî. संपतन्—*v. l.* संचरन् would mean the same, but it is grammatically faulty, since by समस्तृतीयायुक्तात् Páṇ. I. 3. 54 we require the A'tm. here (संचरमाणः instead of संचरन्). Some comm. defend संचरन् by supplying the word मार्गे before it; this is not so satisfactory and is obviously a subterfuge. The reading of Malli. is better as well as older. अप्रमेय—*lit.* 'immeasurable'; the standard of गति would be the mind, but the Bull of Śiva was swifter even than the mind. ककुद्मत्—*cf. supra* I. 56.

Śl. 22. मरुदाशु०—मरुदिव आशुः fleet वाहनः vehicle, the bull यस्य. पार्वतीस्तनपुरस्कृतः—'honoured by Párvatî's breasts' (with an embrace); पुरस्कृतः पूजितः । आलिङ्गित इत्यर्थः । पुरस्कृतः पूजितेऽरात्यभियुक्तेऽग्रतः कृते इत्यमरः । Náráyaṇa. This was of course when the two sat on the bull while on their way. विभङ्ग—a piece; *cf.* भङ्ग in the same sense used at पुष्पोच्चयः पल्लवभङ्गभिन्नः *supra* III. 61. Everything on the mountain Meru was of gold, the trees as well as the leaves on them. Dissolve the comp. as हेमपल्लवविभङ्गाः एव संस्तरः (bed) यस्यां तां क्षपाम्—the night in which his bed consisted of (*i.e.* was made with) golden leaves plucked from Meru's trees. Ar. and Nár. read ०संस्तरानन्वभूत्सुरतमर्दनक्षमान् which gives an easier compound.

Śl. 23. पद्मनाभ—पद्मं नाभौ यस्य; from whose navel sprang a lotus *i.e.* vishṇu. नाभि comes latter in the comp. by the Várt. गड्वादिः परा सप्तमी. वलय—a bracelet. The bracelets of Vishṇu were rubbed against the rocky projections of the Mandâra mountain being held in his arms by him when it was used as the churning-handle by the gods who churned the ocean for nectar. Its slopes are therefore described as bearing the marks left by Vishṇu's bracelets. construe नवाः अमृतविप्रुषः (acc. plu.) प्राप्तवत्सु कटकेषु—the slopes of the Mandára must have received the first spray of the liquid nectar when it was being churned out. विप्रुष्—*fem.* 'a drop'. पार्वतीवदनपद्मषट्पदः—As intent on tasting the honey of Párvatî's lips as a bee is on drinking that of a lotus-flower.

Śl. 24. रावणध्वनितभीतया-Malli. takes this to refer to the story of Râvaṇa's uprooting the mountain Kailása (for which see our note on दशमुखभुजोच्छ्वासितप्रस्थसंधेः कैलासस्य Megh. I. 62 or रामस्तुलितकैलासमरातिं बह्वमन्यत Ragh. X. 89. But it seems an anachronism to make Rāvaṇa lift up the mountain within two months from the marriage of Párvatî. If this is the original meaning the explanation seems to be this—Rávaṇa might have gone to Kailása to pay his homage to the deity he worshipped and his voice was naturally frightful (रवणाद्रावणः); its being suddenly heard might have frightened Párvatî. The other reading वारणध्वनित० is also not very happy; in this case we have to suppose that the place abounded with roaming wild elephants, whose trumpetings filled Párvatî with terror. But Párvatî who lived on the mountain Himálaya and often heard the roars of elephants was not likely to be frightened by them. एकपिङ्गल—is an epithet of Kubera who is the lord of the Kailása mountain (*cf.* कुबेरशैले *supra* VII. 30); *lit.* 'he who has a yellow mark in the place of one eye'; पिङ्गलैकनेत्रत्वादेकपिङ्गल: Kshîra. According to others—एक: मुख्य: पिङ्गल: निधिविशेषो यस्य. Nár. quotes—कोपप्रशमने भीतौ वियोगे पुनरागमे । संभोगे च समाश्लेषो विशेषेण सुखावह: ॥

Śl. 25. जातु—Once. स्थली—a piece of uncultivated ground, natural soil, as distinguished from स्थला. लता—Kálidása frequently uses this word in the sense of 'branch' (शाखा); *cf.* इमां तटाशोकलतां च तन्वीं Ragh. XIII. 32. सलवंग°—Wafting away the filaments of the *lavamga* flowers. These two epithets indicate fragrance and coolness of the beeze. आचचाम—'drank (dried) up,' *i. e.* removed; *cf.* आचचाम सतुषारशीकरो भिन्नपल्लवपुटो वनानिल: Ragh. IX 68. चाटुकार: इव—resembling a lover who utters sweet, pleasing, agreeable words to win the favour of his beloved; *cf.* सिप्रावात: प्रियतम इव प्रार्थनाचाटुकार: Megh. I. 32. दक्षिणानिल:—the Southern breeze, described in particular as blowing from the Malaya mountain which lies in the South.

Śl. 26. हेमतामरस—golden lotuses, which are described as growing in the Heavenly Ganges; *cf. supra* II. 44. खे तरंगिणी–*i. e.* आकाशगङ्गाम्. मीनपङ्क्तिपुनरुक्तमेखला—As Párvatî sported in water which was waist-deep, her girdle was rendered superfluous by being duplicated by the fish which formed another girdle, so to say, when they surrounded her on all sides near the waist; the fish, being small, bright and tremulous, had the appearance of a girdle set with brilliant, flashing jewels and pearls.

Śl. 27. पुलोमतनया—is Śachi, also called पौलोमी, the wife of Indra and the daughter of Puloman. उचित—*lit.* 'accustomed to', *i. e.* usually worn by; as the Párijáta is a celestial tree, its flowers are fitly worn in her hair by Śachî. They were now used by Śiva for decorating Párvatî's hair. प्रसाधय्—to decorate, to adorn; note the words प्रसाधिका (VII. 20), प्रसाधन (IV. 18), प्रसिद्ध (VII. 16), which are all related to the same root. नन्दन—Indra's garden; *cf. supra*, II. 41. अयुग्मलोचन:—*Cf.* अयुग्मनेत्र *supra* III. 51 and our note thereon. सस्पृहं ईक्षित:—*v. l.* ऐड्यत: this, being more direct, is a better reading than ours.

Śl. 28. अभौमं—'not earthly', *i. e.* heavenly; मेरुमन्दरादिगतं (Aruṇa.). पार्थिवं—'Earthly' (पृथिव्यां भवं); मलयगतं (Aruṇa.). वनिता°—See मेरुसख: *supra* I. 18 for comp. लोहितायू—'to become red', is a denominative from the adjective लोहित meaning 'red'. लोहितायति आतपे—*i. e.* at evening time, when sunlight assumes a reddish glow. *Cf.* गम्यतामुपगते नयनानां लोहितायति सहस्रमरीचौ। Kir. IX. 4. गन्धमादन°—See *supra* VI. 41. Ar. reads °वनात् which means °वनमुद्दिश्य। ल्यब्लोपे पञ्चमी।

Śl. 29. नेत्रगम्यम्—which could be looked at with the eye. व्यपाश्रय—or आश्रय, means 'a resting-place' (दक्षिणेतरभुजः व्यपाश्रयः यस्याः ताम्); *cf.* न चास्य सर्वभूतेषु कश्चिदर्थव्यपाश्रयः Bhag. III. 18. सहधर्मचारिणी—a common term for one's legally wedded wife, as she alone is entitled to perform religious ceremonies in company with the husband; *cf.* *supra* VII. 83 and Âśvaláyana quoted thereon by Malli. See also *infra* śl. 51.

Śl. 30. With this śloka begins the descriptive part of this Canto which is unparallaled in Sanskrit literature for the gorgeousness of its imagery and the vividness of its expression. नेत्रयोरिव संक्रमय्य—because her eyes are as beautiful as lotuses; since lotuses close when the Sun sets, they are no longer beautiful, and the poet conceives that their beauty has been deposited as it were with the eyes of Párvatî. अरुणत्रिभागयोः—'a large portion of which is red'; त्रिभाग strictly means 'a third part' (*vide* Malli. on V. 57 *supra* for the Comp.) and since the corners of the eyes roughly cover one-third of their surface, त्रिभाग here refers to those corners, whence the paraphrase of Malli. as अरुणोपान्तयोः. संश्रये—at the time of प्रलय, the lord of creatures (प्रजेश्वरः—in his capacity as destroyer) destroys all the world; *cf.* प्रजानां प्रलये तमःस्पृशे अजाय नमः Kád. Introd. Śl. 1. अहर्पतिः—also अहःपतिः; see Várt. on Páṇ. VIII. 2. 69; 'the lord of the day,' *i. e.* the Sun. प्रजेश्वरः may also be taken with अहर्पति. *Cf.* नमः सवित्रे जगदेकचक्षुषे जगत्प्रसूतिस्थितिनाशहेतवे। त्रयीमयाय त्रिगुणात्मधारिणे विरिञ्चिनारायणशंकरात्मने॥

Śl. 31. °व्यतिकरं दूरयति (सति)—When the Sun is removing the contact; for this sense of व्यतिकर *cf.* मार्गाचलव्यतिकर *supra* V. 85. When the Sun was high up in the sky, his rays fell upon the water-spray and gave rise to innumerable rain-bows; now that he is sinking below the horizon and the spray is no longer in contact with the rays, the mountain-torrents have not rain-bows displayed above them. अवनते—is an *adj.* of बिभ्रति; it is strange to find Malli. taking it as voc. sing., meaning 'O you (Párvatî) with supple limbs,' when it legitimately goes with बिभ्रति. परिवेष—an encircling halo; the rain-bows being semi-circular are described as परिवेष, which originally refers to the halo round the Sun or the Moon. तव पितुः—*scil.* of the Himálaya mountain.

Śl. 32. °स्वज्ञोः—gen. dual; the two birds are a couple of *chakravákas* eating the same bit of lotus-filament; मुखद्वयेन पक्वं इति भावः (Malli.). They are poetically represented as the types where the most perfect conjugal love abides; *cf. supra* V. 26. क्रन्दतोः—It is now night, when they are separated from each other; *cf.* चक्रवाकवधुके आमन्त्रयस्व सहचरम्। उपस्थिता रजनी। Śák. III. p. 82. निघ्नयोः—निघ्न literally means 'dependent', and some such word as दैवे is to be supplied before it; दैवे निघ्न—dependent on fate, *i. e.* rendered helpless by cruel fate; or it may mean 'condemned by fate,' miserable. Nár. proposes to read स्निग्धयोः for निघ्नयोः, but it appears to be an unjustifiable emendation. अनल्पतां गतम्—During day-time they were close to each other and there was little space between them; but now they are separated by a great distance. See *infra* śl. 61.

Śl. 33. आह्निकं—अह्नि भवं 'which they occupied by day;' from अहन्+इक (ठञ्). सल्लकी—Name of a plant whose leaves and twigs are a favouite food of elephants; *cf.* अयं (गजः) अभिलषतु तावदासवसुरभिरसं सल्लकीभङ्गम् Vikr. IV. 23. °वासितम्—adj. of वारि; it can also be taken as an adj. of स्थानं, as is done by Nár. and Sîtârâma. The Sallakî has a strong small; *cf.* शिशिरकटुकषायः स्त्यायते सल्लकीनामिभदलितविकीर्णग्रन्थिनिस्यन्दगन्धः। Mál.-Mádh. IX. 6. आविभात-चरणाय—'for consuming it till the next morning;' the meaning is that the water which they drink in the evening will last them till the next morning. Ar. and Nár. (also Malli.) interpret it as 'sufficient for the digestion of what they have eaten since the morning' (विभातमारभ्य यद्भुक्तं तस्मै पर्याप्तं), which is also possible. For चर् in the sense of 'to eat,' *cf.* भुक्तास्तृणानि पशवः कटकं चरन्तः Śiś. V. 61. Nár. quotes from Pálakápya—आतपभीता नागा वनभुवि तरुषण्डमण्डिते कुहचित्। अतिवाहयन्ति दिवसान्सलिलं गृह्णन्ति संध्यासु। गृह्णते—Âtm. 3rd pers. plural, present tense. वारिरुह°—In the evening the day-lotuses are closed, and the bees sitting on them are confined within their folded petals.

Śl. 34. This verse contains one of the finest fancies in this Canto. The sun is hanging low over the western horizon, and his orb, which is just above the water-level, would be reflected in an extremely elongated shape, the reflection covering the whole surface of the water between the beholder and the Sun; in shape it is long and narrow, and the poet describes it as though it were a golden bridge between the two shores. मितकथे—*voc. sing.* 'O you who speak measuredly'. तापनीयं-Made of gold (तपनीय).

Śl. 35. उत्तरन्ति—It is the habit of hogs to spend the hot part of the day in marshy spots; *cf.* स पल्वलोत्तीर्णवराहयूथानि (वनानि पश्यन्) Ragh. II. 77. गाढपङ्कं—full of deep mud. विनिकीर्य—leaving it after having disturbed its water. दंष्ट्रिण:—possessed of long, white tusks; the tusks sticking out from their snouts look like white lotus-stalks; hence the adj. दृढभङ्गुर &c. भङ्गुर—' fragile ', as Nár. takes it; or ' crooked ' (with Malli.), *i. e.* curved.

Śl. 36. वृक्षशिखरे—As is the habit of peacocks; *cf.* आवासवृक्षोन्मुखबर्हिणानि Ragh. II. 17. " The wild peacock, although it lays its nest upon the ground, is said by Captain Williamson to roost constantly on the loftiest trees"—H. H. Wilson (on Megh. II. 18). मण्डल—the circular tail of a peacock. हीयमानं—which is becoming less and less. अहरत्यय—' the passing of the day ', *i.e.* the evening. पिबतीव—The evening sunshine is golden in colour; it was becoming less and less every moment, and the poet fancies that it was so because the peacock must have been drinking the same, since his tail is showing the same golden colour (शिखण्डमण्डलस्य दिनान्तातपतुल्यवर्णत्वं दिनान्तातपस्य परिक्षीयमाणत्वं च उत्प्रेक्षाबीजम् Nâr.) पीवरोरु—this is a deviation from Páṇ. IV. 1. 70 which would require पीवरोरु as the voc. sing. The Tattva-B. explains the form as an irregularity to be justified by the maxim संज्ञापूर्वको विधिरनित्य:. बर्हिण:—fr. बर्ह a peacock's feather + इन a poss. affix.

Śl. 37. In this verse the sky is compared to a lake which is almost wholly devoid of water (किंचित् शेषवत्—in which only a little water remains); in a lake, when the water is being dried off, dark mud would be seen; here the darkness which is showing in the east corresponds to the mud, and the sunshine—which has disappeared—corresponds to the water. The reading किंचिदिव शोषवत्—' some portion of which is dried up '—gives the same sense more directly, and hence would be preferable. The figure in this śl. is a fusion of Upamá and Utprekshâ.

Śl. 38. In the evening the deer sit in the courtyards, the trees are watered, the cows come home, and the fires are kindled. All these four phenomena are described in this śloka. उटजाङ्गनं—*Cf.* मृगैर्वर्तितरोमन्थमुटजाङ्गनभूमिषु । Ragh. I. 52. अग्निधेनु°—अग्ने: अग्निहोमार्थं धेनव: अग्निधेनव: । A Comp. like अश्वघास (तादर्थ्ये षष्ठीसमास:); 'a cow kept for the purposes of *Agnihotra*', called होमधेनु elsewhere (*e. g.* at Ragh. II. 8). सन्दीपित—kindled.

Śl. 39. In the evening the lotuses are closed. Before their petals close round completely, they are visible for some moments in a half-closed, half-opened condition. The poet fancies that they purposely remain like that, because they are anxious to receive inside their folds the bees wandering outside. Bees are generally described as residing within the lotus-flowers during the night; see *supra*, śl. 33. कुशेशयं—कुशे on water शेते इति । fr. शी+अ (अच्); the *aluk* is by शयवास &c. Pán. VI. 3. 18.

Śl. 40. In the western quarter the small reddish orb of the Sun is lying above the horizon, and its yellow-red rays are shooting widely apart, so that one can almost count them separately. The quarter is compared to a maiden, the Sun corresponding to the small red *bandhujīva* flower which ladies often stick on their forehead as the decorative *tilaka* mark; and the rays correspond to its yellow-red filaments. दूर०—see com. for the dissolution of the comp. ०मग्नपरिवेश *v. l.*—the rays from whose halo shoot far off. वारुणी दिक्—the west, which is presided over by Varuṇa the lord of the waters. बन्धुजीव—For the practice of using this flower as a decorative mark compare मनोरमं प्रापितमन्तरं भ्रुवोरलंकृतं केसररेणुनाऽणुना । अलक्तताम्राधरपल्लवश्रिया समानयन्तीमिव बन्धुजीवकम् ॥ Kir. IV. 7.

Śl. 41. सामभिः—*Cf.* समसामोपगीतं त्वां Ragh. X. 21. सहचराः सहस्रशः—the reference is to the sages called Vâlakhilyas, 60,000 (80,000 according to Sk.-P. quoted below) in number, who accompany the Sun through the sky as the guards of his chariot. The Vishṇu-Puráṇa describes them as pigmy sages, no bigger than a joint of the thumb, chaste, pious, resplendent as the rays of the Sun. *Cf.* वालखिल्या इति ख्याताः पतङ्गसहचारिणः । अष्टाशीतिसहस्राणि मुनीनामूर्ध्वरेतसाम् ॥ Skanda-P.; and वालखिल्याः सहस्राणि षष्टिर्ब्रह्मर्षयोऽमलाः । पुरतोऽभिमुखं यान्ति स्तुवन्ति स्तुतिभिर्विभुम् ॥ Bhág. P. XII. 11. See also Ragh. XV. 10. अग्निपरिकीर्ण०—this alludes to the well-known belief that the Sun deposits his lustre with Fire during the night; *cf.* दिनान्ते निहितं तेजः सवित्रेव हुताशनः Ragh. IV. 1 and the Śruti quoted by Malli. किरणोष्मपायिन.—the Vâlakhilyas take no food, but subsist by taking in the heat of the Sun. सामभिः संस्तुवन्ति—because it is laid down that hymns from the Sâmaveda should be used for evening prayers; *cf.* ऋग्भिः प्रभाते संस्तुवन्ति, यजुर्भिर्मध्याह्ने, सामभिः संध्यायां इति च श्रुतिप्रसिद्धम् । Nârâyana.

Śl. 42. In this verse there is the fig. of speech called स्वभावोक्ति, as there is a vivid and life-like description of the behaviour of the horses of the Sun as they descend downwards with bent necks &c. कर्णचामर०—chowries are placed above the ears of horses by way of ornament (कर्णयोः अलंकारार्थं बद्धे ये चामरे &c. Nâr.); they come in hard contact with the eyes of the horses owing to their having lowered their heads. भुग्न—made to curl round. *Cf* जलनिधिजलमध्यादेष उत्तार्यतेऽर्कः ॥ पयसि सलिलराशेर्नक्तमन्तर्निमग्नः स्फुटमनिशमतापि ज्वालया वाडवाग्नेः । Śiś. XI. 44, 45.

Śl. 43. खं प्रसुप्तमिव—The presence of the Sun had lit up the sky; but now that he has set, the same appears dark and is as it were asleep. It is the nature, the poet says, of all lustrous objects to illumine their surroundings by their presence and darken the same by their absence; the glory of the surroundings is merely a borrowed one, and it does not belong to them but to the source of light. This is expressed in the second half. Construe—सत् (तेजः) उत्थितं (सत्) यावत् (स्थानं) प्रकाशयति, तावतः (स्थानात्) च्युतं (सत्) (तावतः) मलिनाय (for obscuring) खलु (भवति) । See trans. भावतश्च्युतं *v. l.*—fallen from its presence; *i. e* when it disappears.

Śl. 44. Saṃdhyá (Twilight) is visible twice, once in the morning and again in the evening; in the morning it precedes the Sun, as if the Sun, to show his honour for her, had allowed her to walk before him. Having been thus honoured, the poet says, it is but natural that she should follow him (*i. e.* be visible after he has set) in the evening. There is the suggestion of a dutiful and beloved wife following in death the body of her lord, by ascending the funeral pyre. अनुगतं—अनुपदं *v. l.* ' just after. ' वपुः—पदं *v l.*, ' his foot ', *i. e.* rays. धर्म्यं—धर्म्यं *v. l.* धर्मादनपेतं यथा भवति तथा; adv. modifying अनुपदं; "इदं नायिकात्वारोपसूचकम् । निधनेऽपि पतिमार्गानुसारित्वं नायिकाधर्मः ।" Nâr.

Śl. 45. कपिश—reddish-brown. The various kinds of hues visible on the patches of clouds in the sky are poetically conceived as having been painted thereon by Saṃdhyâ for Pârvatî to gaze at. वर्तिका—a brush used in painting; *cf.* वर्तते स्म स कथंचिदालिखन्नङ्गुलीक्षरणसन्नवर्तिकः । Ragh. XIX. 19. वर्तिताः—Malli. takes this in the sense of उत्पादिताः ' produced '; but it is etymologically connected with the word वर्तिका, and should better be understood as meaning ' painted ', as is done by Ar. who says वर्तिताः विन्यस्तरागविशेषाः. The reading वर्णिताः shows that this is the sense intended by the poet.

Śl. 46. The yellowish-red evening sunshine has disappeared, but the manes of lions, the young sprouts of trees, and the mineral clay on the mountain, all still possess that yellow-red colour; hence the poet describes that the Sunlight has been divided and deposited with those various things, as it were. केसरसटा—the two words केसर and सटा mean the same and would be tautologous; hence Ar. and Malli. propose to render सटा by समूह. भूभृता—Malli.'s interpretation of this as अस्ताद्रिणा seems to be a slip, since we expect गन्धमादनगिरिणा; the word आत्मना in the next half refers to this same mountain. The variant सिंहकेसरसटासु भूभृतां (=शैलानां)........०शिखरेषु भानुना (भास्वता v. l.) संविभक्तं is simpler and more natural, since it is the Sun, and not the mountain, who is expected to divide the sunshine. धातुशिखरेषु—धातुप्रचुराणि शिखराणि (Madhyam. compound), तेषु.

Śl. 47. पार्ष्णिमुक्तवसुधाः—standing with uplifted heels (*i. e.* on tip-toe) is a characteristic posture when offering water by way of worship; see the Smṛiti quoted by Malli. गूढं—*adv.* 'secretly', *i. e.* repeating it mentally to themselves so that nobody should hear. गृणन्ति—from गॄ 9 P. to 'praise;' the repetition of the *gâyatrî mantra* is meant here, as is pointed out by Malli. His quotation is from Yâjñavalkya I. 24.

Śl. 48. प्रस्तुताय—*scil.* तपस्विभिः; the holy *Saṃdhyâvandana* which is commenced by the ascetics as just decribed. It may also mean—उपस्थिताय for which the time has come. विनोद०—विनोदिनि पुनः *v. l.* is not happy. सखीजनः—see *supra* VII. 95. वल्गु—beautiful; *cf.* वल्गुवागपि च वामलोचना Ragh. XIX. 13. विनोदयिष्यति—A denominative from विनोद.

Śl. 49. निर्विभुज्य—having curled; showing that she felt piqued at what she conceived to be a neglect on Śiva's part to leave her even for a short while; the root is भुज् 'to bend'; the com. Râmag. takes it to be भुज् 'to bite,' which is perhaps preferable. दशनच्छद—*lit.* 'what covers the teeth', *i. e.* the lip. अवधीरणापरा—the disregard consists in not vouchsafing him the permission so humbly asked for by him. विजया—this is the name of her female companion; see *infra,* śl. 90. अहेतुकं—without any particular motive, at random, talking for talking's sake. This अवधीरणा shown by Pârvatî is what the rhetoricians call बिब्बोक भाव, which is thus defined—गर्वाभिमानादिष्टेऽपि बिब्बोकोऽनादरक्रिया D.-R. II.; it is the "neglectful behaviour, even toward one that is loved, because of haughtiness due to pride." Śl. quoted in the Sar.-K. and referred to in S.-D. (III. 198) as an instance of प्रणयमान on the part of the Nâyikâ.

Śl. 50. अनुतष्ठिवान्—Perf. participle of स्था with अनु; mark the change of स् to ष् which takes place in the case of स्था although the reduplicative त intervenes. See Pāṇ. VIII. 3. 64. विधिम्—*i. e.* his evening prayers. अवचनां—अवनतां *V. l.* 'with her head hung down.' असूया—her anger as described in the preceding śl.

Śl. 51. नान्यथा—' It is not otherwise '; he means that it was not on account of another woman that he left her temporarily, but on account of Saṃdhyā. Religion made him leave her, and not Lust. Some read नान्यया. सहधर्मचारिन्—the masculine form of the commoner word °चारिणी, for which see *supra* śl. 29; °चारिन् means the legally-wedded husband. चक्रवाकसमवृत्ति—' as faithful to you as the male *chakravâka* is to his mate '; also as unable to bear separation. *Cf.* रथाङ्गनाम्नोरिव भाववन्धनं बभूव यत्प्रेम &c. Ragh III. 24; and *supra* śl. 32. Śl. quoted in the Sar.-K.

Śl. 52. निर्वितेषु पितृषु—The allusion here is to the story of the origin of Saṃdhyá. After Brahmâ, as the creator, had created the Pitris, Agnishvátta and others (see *supra*, notes on I. 18), he gave up his body. It then became Saṃdhyâ, and began to wait upon the eastern and the western mountains; she is often personified as the daughter of Brahmâ. For other particulars see notes on *supra* IV. 41. सुतनु—Voc. sing. There is some grammatical difficulty here. If we take it as a Bah. (शोभना तनुर्यस्याः) having तनु (उ short) as its final member, the form should be सुतनो. If the word be understood to be तनू, the final क is unavoidable, and we shall have सुतनूके. Hence grammarians take the word तनु as referring to the woman-class. *Cf.* Bhattoji in his शब्दकौस्तुभ–ननु इह तनुशब्दस्य ह्रस्वान्तत्वे संबुद्धौ चेति गुणेन भाव्यम् । दीर्घान्तत्वे नदीलक्षणः कप्प्राप्नोति । सत्यम् । तनुशब्दः स्त्रीजातौ कविभिः प्रयुज्यते । तस्मादूङुत इत्यूङि कृते कर्मधारयोऽयमिति हरदत्तः । Vâmana explains it differently. See Kâv.-S. V. 2. 47—मनुष्यजातेर्विवक्षाविवक्षे । For a similar use *cf.* एते ते सुतनु पुरीजनोपभोग्या दृश्यन्ते नयनमनोरमा वनान्ताः । Bhatti. XVI. 27; सुतनु हृदयात्प्रत्यादेशव्यलीकमपैतु ते &c. Śāk. VII. 24. सेव्यते—*scil.* जनैः; अस्तं and उदयं are adverbs of time, signifying 'at sunset and sunrise'; see Malli. Ar. and Nár. read सेवते, where अस्तं and उदयं are the objects, meaning respectively the western and the eastern mountains. अत्र—towards her (Saṃdhyâ).

Śl. 53 तामिमां—*scil.* संध्याम्. पीडितां—hemmed in; obstructed by. The Saṃdhyâ is yellow-red in itself; but the growing darkness in the east is giving it a darkish appearance in that part, where it appears to be touching the ground. Hence the poet compares it to a river of liquid minerals, which would be yellow-red in colour, having dark-leaved *tamâla* trees growing on its bank. The darkness of the leaves of the *tamâla* is frequently referred to by Sanskrit poets; *cf.* मेघैर्मेदुरमम्बरं वनभुवः श्यामास्तमालद्रुमैः Gît. I. 1. भूमिलम्बम्—(adverb) भूमौ लम्बं यथा भवति तथा. Ar. and Nâr. read °लम्बमिव and °लम्बं as a Namul (समन्यन्ते उपपदे 'समासत्तौ' इति णमुल्। भूमौ लम्बित्वेत्यर्थः।). ०मालिनी-'having a row (माला) of'; from माला + इन् poss. aff. with the fem. ई.

Sl. 54. A narrow patch of red light was visible on the western horizon, which the poet compares to a blood-covered sword lying on a battle-field, the point of the sword is sticking in the ground and its blade and hilt are lying obliquely, which is supposed to be the position in the sky of that red streak of sunshine. अस्तमितशेषं—it is a stray patch of light, nearly all of it having already disappeared. रक्तलेखं—adj. of आतपं, 'appearing as a red streak.' संपराय—battle, from सं + परा + इ (to come together for fighting). मण्डलाग्र *m.-lit.* 'a bent or curved sword,' a scimitar; मण्डलाकृति अग्रं अस्य इति मण्डलाग्रः Kshîra.

Sl. 55. सुमेरुणा—Sumeru or Meru is the mountain which is described in mythology as the centre of the terrestrial world and round which the Sun revolves; hence the solar light is described as being concealed beyond it. *Cf.* सुमेरुणा व्यवहिते इति पौराणिकमतानुसारेणोक्तम्। सूर्यः सुमेरुं प्रदक्षिणीकरोतीति तन्मतम्। Nâr. अन्धतमस—*lit.* 'blinding darkness', *i. e.* intense or pitchy darkness; अ is added to the final of तमस् when it is preceded by अव, सं or अन्ध, by Pâṇ. V. 4. 79. निरर्गलं—either adj. to अन्धतमसं or adv. to विजृम्भते: अर्गला is *lit.* the bolt of a door, and *fig.* it means any check or impediment.

Sl. 56. अभितः—on all sides. तिमिरोल्ब०—उल्ब is the enveloping membrane surrounding the embryo in the womb; *cf.* यथोल्बेनावृतो गर्भः Bg. III. 38. Darkness is compared to such a membrane, the whole world being then poetically described as being in the condition of an infant shut up in the womb.

Sl. 57. Nothing can be seen in the pitchy darkness, the white cannot be distinguished from the black, nor the stationary from the moving, nor the curved from the straight. This result is brought about by the growth of darkness; the poet compares it to the prosperity of wicked people, which makes them unable to perceive any distinction between the good and the bad, between the righteous and the vicious &c. यदि असता

कश्चिन्महत्त्वमुत्पद्येत तर्हि न जनानां जातिकर्माविकृतं विशेषमीक्षन्ते इति भावः। Nár. हृतान्तरम्—removing, wiping out all distinction.

Śl. 58. यज्वनां पतिः—यज्वन् is a Brâhmaṇa who has duly performed sacrifices; the Moon is often described as यज्वनां पतिः (*cf.* गौराङ्गीवदनोपमाद्युक्तमादत्ते पतिर्यज्वनाम् *Anarghyarághava* quoted by Nár.). The reason appears to be दर्शपूर्णमासादियागप्रवृत्तिहेतुत्व of the Moon, as Malli. explains it; see also the Śruti quoted by him at Ragh. V. 23. Or it may mean विधिनेष्टवतां ब्राह्मणानां पतिः; द्विजराज is a common epithet of the Moon. शार्वर—fr. शृ + वर (ष्वरच्)+ ई=शर्वरी and then शार्वर by adding अण् तस्येदमिति; 'belonging to the night (शर्वरी).' Vámana in his Kâv.-S. (V. 2. 50) calls this form ungrammatical, and so does Bhaṭṭoji in commenting upon कालाट्ठञ् Páṇ. IV. 3. 11, according to which the form should have been शार्वरिक, ठञ् being the proper affix. कैतकैरिव रजोभिः—the pollen of the *Ketakî* flawers being extremely white, moonlight is most fitly compared to it. Bhavabhúti similarly says in the Mál.-Mádh. VIII. 1—दलयति परिशुष्यत्प्रौढतालीविपाण्डुः तिमिरनिकरमुच्चैरिन्दवः प्राक्प्रकाशः। वियति पवनवेगादुन्मुखः केतकीनां प्रचालित इव सान्द्रो माकरन्दः परागः॥

Śl. 59. Here the night corresponds to Párvatî, the stars to her female friends, the Moon to Śiva, and his lying hidden behind Mandara to Śiva's lying concealed at Pârvatî's back. श्रोष्यता-The Fut. p. in the sense of the Pres. p.

Śl. 60. The eastern direction is sending out the lunar orb, being urged on (as it were) by the night to do so; the orb is preceded by the white moonlight, and it was itself invisible during day-time. All this phenomenon serves poetically to suggest the comparison to some lady telling her love-secrets, being urged on to do so by her friend; before the secret is told she smiles, while the secret itself is withheld till the approach of night. ॰निर्गमनं—its coming out, *i. e.* being told. पूर्वदृष्ट॰—may also be separated as पूर्वदृष्टतनु (पूर्वस्यां दृष्टा तनुर्यस्य तत्; qualifying ॰मण्डलं) and चन्द्रिकास्मितं. रात्रि॰—॰देशितं *v. l.* told by the night (looked upon as her co-wife).

Śl. 61. A highly elaborate simile. The ripe fruits of the *phalinî* plant are golden-yellow in colour; the same is the colour of the Chakraváka birds (see *supra* VII. 15 and 21), and also of the lunar orb just after it has risen. There is the one orb in the sky, while another—the reflection of it—is visible in the water of the lake; these two orbs are likened to a pair of Chakravákas who, it is well-known, are described as being separated at night.

फलिनी—better known as the Priyaṅgu creeper, and poetically represented as being matched with the mango-tree; see Ragh. VIII. 61. °विवरं—here विवर has an unusual sense *viz.* that of 'space between, distance' (separated by a great distance). *Cf.* अन्तमन्तरमनल्पतां गतम् *supra,* śl. 32. °विधुरं—*V. l.* विप्रकृष्टं separated अत एव विधुरं afflicted. But there is no propriety of this here.

Śl. 62. A hyperbolical description of the rays of the moon which look so delicate that one might cut them up into bits as though they were tender sprouts of barley-corn and wear them on the ears by way of ornament. The constr. is कराः छेत्तुं शक्यम् where शक्यं is used impersonally. This is a very common construction in the works of Kâlidâsa. *Cf.* शक्यमरविन्दसुरभिः...अविरलमालिङ्गितुं पवनः Śâk. III. 5 and our note thereon; also शक्यमञ्जलिभिः पातुं वाताः केतकगन्धिनः Râm. IV. 28. 8. °कृते— might either be taken as the dative sing. of °कृत् when कृत् *f.* is a verbal noun meaning क्रिया; or कृते might be the adverb meaning 'for the sake of,' used at the end of the Comp. यवसूचि—the tender blades of. The practice of *yava* sprouts being worn as ear-ornaments by ladies has been referred to above, VII. 17 and 82; *cf.* also श्रवणलब्धपदैश्च यवाङ्कुरैः Ragh. IX. 43. अग्रनख°-For the Comp. see Malli. on अग्रहस्त *supra* V. 63. °संपुटैः—*i. e.* taking the patches of the rays by means of.

Śl. 63. The Moon is here likened by implication to a lover who is kissing his beloved mistress (Night). There is a mixture here of various Figures of Speech; there is उपमा when the rays and darkness are respectively compared to the fingers and dark hair; there is रूपक when the lotuses are called the eyes; and there is उत्प्रेक्षा when the act of touching is described as being equivalent to kissing. *Cf.* अत्रोपमारूपकोत्प्रेक्षाणां संकरः Aruṇa. रजनीमुख—*lit.* means 'the beginning of the night.', *i. e.* the evening; and the word *mukha* suggests the sense of 'the mouth of the beloved'. Instead of explaining the comp. as सरोजे एव लोचने (Rûpaka), Malli. goes out of the way to explain it as सरोजे लोचने इव (Upamá) as he wants it to harmonize with the Upamâs in the first line; the Rúpaka he takes as ध्वनित. Śl. quoted in the Sar.-Kaṇṭh.

Śl. 64. सामि - *indec.*; 'half,' *i.e.* partially. Cf. English 'semi,' and सामिभुक्तविषयाः समागमाः Ragh. XIX. 16; पूर्वं गाधिसुतेन सामिघटिता मुक्ता नु मन्दाकिनी। Naish. संप्रसीदत इव—because the waters of the Mânasa lake are naturally pure and white, though temporarily made turbid by elephants wading in them. मानसं सरः—A sacred lake on the mountain Kailâsa, so called because it was created by Brahmâ with an effort of the mind; cf. कैलासशिखरे राम मनसा निर्मितं सरः । ब्रह्मणा प्रागिदं यस्मात्तद्भून्मानसं सरः ॥ Râm.

Śl. 65. The Moon was reddish (रक्त) when it rose, but after a short time began to shine with brilliant white (परिशुद्ध) lustre as usual. The poet draws a moral from this, saying that a naturally noble-minded person, though he might be temporarily influenced by passion (रक्त) for some time, is bound to revert to his original noble (परिशुद्ध) nature; the change will not be permanent. It does not seem likely that the poet is referring to kings here; the words प्रकृति and मण्डल, which also mean 'ministers' and 'subsidiary princes under a sovereign,' have led Malli., as well as Aruṇa and Nâr. [—but not Sîtârâma—] to draw the rather far-fetched moral that in the case of a sovereign ruler whose dependent princes are disaffected, his ministers help to bring them round and make them as loyal as before. The śloka, however, reads very well without any such undue straining of sense.

Śl. 66. Moonlight, which is white, is visible on lofty places, such as hill-tops, and darkness, which is black, is to be seen sunk low, lying at the bottom of pits. The moral is that good men prosper and evil persons come to grief generally in this world (तेजस्विनः उन्नमन्ति मलिनास्तु न्यञ्चन्तीति भावः Malli.). ०पर—disposed to move towards. आत्मसदृशि—V. l. to one befitting itself. वेधसा प्रकल्पिता—'seems to have been ordained by fate.' गुणदोषयोः गतिः—viz. that virtues should be at the top and succeed, and that vicious practices should be at the bottom and fail. एव—this possesses no special force, and therefore the reading वेधसेह (इह—in this world) would seem to be preferable.

Śl. 67. चन्द्रपाद०—it is believed that the moonstones begin to liquefy when brought into contact with the rays of the moon; cf. स्फुटजललवस्यन्दिनश्चन्द्रकान्ताः Megh. II. 9; सायं शशाङ्ककिरणाहतचन्द्रकान्तनिस्यन्दिनीरनिकरेण कृताभिषेकाः Siś. IV. 58. Moonstones abound on the Gandhamâdana mountain, and their liquid flow awakens from sleep the peacocks on the trees. Peacocks do not sleep in nests, but on the trees without any additional shelter; see note above on śl. 36. निद्रित—from निद्रा+इत (इतच्) by तदस्य संजातं तारकादिभ्य इतच् Pâṇ. V. 2 36.

Śl. 68. On the mountain there are Kalpa-trees, on these trees are hanging pearl necklaces; the rays of the Moon falling on them are compared to the hands of a person who is trying as it were to count those necklaces. अविकल्पसुन्दरि—विकल्प means 'doubt'; 'O you who are beautiful beyond any possibility of doubt;' this is rather an unusual expression in Kálidása. Ar. and Nár. read इह पश्य सुन्दरि which seems more natural and better. हारयष्टि—a *hâra* consists of several strings which are separately called *yashṭis*; see *supra* V. 8.

Śl. 69. The moonlight is interlaced with patches of darkness (as described in śl. 66) and the whole appearance is like that of the dark body of an elephant decked with white ashy lines by way of decoration. उन्नता—there is moonlight in the *unnata* portions and darkness in the *avanata* ones. भक्ति—ornamental lines; or patches of painting; भक्त्यो रचनाः । लेखा इति यावत् । Malli. on Megh. I. 19. भूति—ashes. Compare भक्तिच्छेदैरिव विरचितां भूतिमङ्गे गजस्य Megh. I. 19.

Śl. 70. उच्छ्वसितपीतं—उच्छ्वसित *n.* 'act of blowing' (भावे क्तः); *cf.* the use of उच्छ्वसत् above at śl. 19; उच्छ्वसितेन पीतं उच्छ्वसितपीतं 'which was drunk by it as it bloomed'. Nár. takes पीत in the sense of yellow. (पीतं पीतवर्णम् । रक्तकुमुदापेक्षयैवमुक्तम्). ऐन्दव—*adj.* from इन्दु; 'belonging to the Moon.' मुक्तषट्पदविरावं—the bees were confined within its fold, which now opening makes their humming audible. अञ्जसा—*adv.* 'quickly'; स्राग्झटित्यञ्जसाह्नाय द्राङ्मङ्क्षु सपदि द्रुते Ak. भिद्यते=विकसति, 'opens' 'blooms'. आ निबन्धनात्—'up to its very stem,' *i. e.* opens quite completely, expands quite fully. The words सोढुमक्षममिव suggest its resemblance to a person whose belly would be bursting if he were to drink anything beyond its capacity. See Malli.

Śl. 71. The silk-garments which are hanging on the Kalpa trees are indistinguishable from moonlight, since they are dazzlingly white; one is aware of their presence only when the breeze causes them to flutter and to turn. चलित केवलं is also read as चलितके चलम्.

Śl. 72. Underneath the trees, on the ground, the moonlight has fallen brokenly through the foliage, in small and white bits; these bits are compared to flowers which appear as though they could be picked up and used to decorate Pârvatî's hair. See śl. 62 above for a similar idea. पेशल—tender, delicate, charming. पत्रजर्जर०—पत्रैः जर्जरैः शशिप्रभालवैः, bits of moonlight falling brokenly on account of the intervening leaves. उत्कचय—to coil up, to fasten, to decorate by interlacing them with flowers. अलक—*m. n.* curled hair; *cf.* śl. 62.

Śl. 73. The conjunction of the Moon with a star is compared to the union of a bridegroom with his bride. योगतारा—any star which daily comes near the Moon in its path through the sky. This is in accordance with the explanation of Malli. who says प्रत्यहं यया युज्यते सा योगतारा. Ar. and Nár. give a different explanation in that they omit प्रत्यहं; इन्दुर्यस्यां तारकायां तिष्ठति सा योगतारा (Nâr.)—meaning any star which is at that moment near the Moon. *V. l.* योग्यतारया—रोहिणीरूपया (Râmag.) नवदीक्षा—the *dîkshá* meant is विवाहदीक्षा; *cf.* the expression occurring at VII. 8 (नवेन दीक्षाविधिसायकेन).

Śl. 74. The lunar rays, as they are reflected in Pârvatî's face, appear as if they are growing on her cheeks. पाकभिन्न—blossoming because of its being ripe. शरकाण्ड—काण्ड may mean 'a cluster', or 'a stem' as Nár. understands it. For the simile compare शरकाण्डपाण्डुगण्डस्थला Málav. III. 8; उपहसित इवासौ चन्द्रमाः कामिनीनां परिणतशरकाण्डापाण्डुभिर्गण्डभागैः Śis. XI. 30 प्रतिकृति—image, reflection. गण्डलेखा—the region of the cheeks, or broad cheeks; *cf.* देश्यस्त्रीगण्डलेखानां Ragh. X. 12.

Śl. 75. अर्कमणि—the *sûryakânta* crystal; note that it is described as being red in colour. कल्पवृक्षमधु—*cf.* मधु नयनयोर्विभ्रमादेशदक्षं...एकः सूते...कल्पवृक्षः Megh. II. 13. स्थितिमती—'having residence, residing'; at VI. 30 it is used in a different sense; प्रभावयुक्तां Ar.; स्थैर्ययुक्तां Rámag.

Śl. 76. The intoxication of wine works two changes; it renders the mouth fragrant, and colours the eyes red (making them look beautiful) Since, however, Pârvatî already possessed these two things, there was nothing more that wine could accomplish in her case. केसर—the *bakula* flower. कं गुणान्तरं करिष्यति—'what other, *i. e.* more excellent, merit, special charm can it produce?'—a question of appeal, meaning that there is none to be produced. For the meaning of गुणा॰ comp. पात्रविशेषन्यस्तं गुणान्तरं व्रजति शिल्पमाधातुः । Málav. I. 6. मधुः—wine; this word is usually *neuter*, and Malli. defends its *masc.* use by pointing out that it belongs to the अर्धर्चादि group, which contains words which are used both in the neut. and the masc. The reading of Ar. and Nâr. is, however, मदः, and it is distinctly better; for it is unlikely that the poet who uses ॰मधु (*neut.*) in the preceding verse and again refers to it as इदं (*neut.*) in the next stanza would be using the same word in the masc. here.

Śl. 77.—Although there is thus no *guṇa* which the wine can produce, still it should be drunk out of respect to the goddess who comes as a friend (सखीजनः) to offer hospitality; her affection (भक्ति) should not be slighted. शंकरः अम्बिकां पानं अपाययत—Śiva made her drink that wine. Notice the use of the causal of पा 'to drink' with the accusative case (अम्बिकां); see A. G. § 44. The Âtm. is by Páṇ. I. 3. 89. मान्यभक्तिः—diss. मान्या भक्तिर्यस्य; strictly speaking the comp. should have been मान्याभक्तिः *i. e.* the first member should have retained its fem. gender; but such masculinization is allowed by practice. See Malli. and our notes on दृढभक्तिर्मयाऽऽन्या Megh. I. 40 or on दृढभक्तिरिति ज्येष्ठे &c. Ragh. XII. 14.

Śl. 78. विक्रियामपि सतीं—the change is generally for the worse (न हि विक्रिया कुत्रापि मनोहरा भवति Nár.); but the change wrought in Pârvatî was attractive, *i. e.* it made her look more beautiful. आम्र and सहकार both signify 'mango-tree'; but the latter refers to a particular species whose blossoms are exceedingly fragrant (सहकारोऽतिसौरभः Ak.). An ordinary mango-tree cannot be transformed into one of the सहकार species except by treating it with some magical charms, which is expressed by अप्रतर्क्यविधियोग (मणिमन्त्रौषधकालादियोगः Nâr.). Pârvatî underwent just a similar magical change.

Śl. 79. विपरिवर्तित—'turned away', *i. e.* made to disappear; विपरिवर्तिता अपनीता ह्रीः याभ्यां तयोः Nár. नेच्छतोः सावनं—वाञ्छतो रमणं *v.l.* desiring amorous sports. इद्धरागयोः—'who kindled (increased) her passion'; or it might mean 'whose (own) lust was kindled;' in this latter sense राग must be interpreted as 'redness' when understood with मद्. See Malli. शूलिनः मदस्य च—meaning that Śiva took hold of her for his enjoyment, and the infatuation of wine possessed all her senses. Śl. quoted in the Sar.-Kaṇṭh.

Śl. 80. Her (Pârvatî's) face looked so attractive that before kissing it Śiva remained gazing long at its entrancing loveliness. स्वेदबिन्दुमत्—possessing, *i. e.* covered with, drops of perspiration (*adj.* of उमामुखं). अकारणस्मित—as is natural under the influence of wine.

Śl. 81. The constr. is हरः तां उद्वहन् (bearing her) मणिशिलागृहं प्राविशत्. ध्यानसंभृत—See com. for diss. By virtue of his supernatural powers he endowed that house with all the articles of comfort and luxury. मणिशिलागृहं—meaning a cave in the jewelled rocks of the Gandhamádana. Nár. remarks—अत्र मणिशब्देन नित्योज्ज्वलत्वं ध्वनितं, तेन च प्रदीपनिराकाङ्क्षत्वम् । 'रत्नाङ्कुरा यत्र रतिप्रदीपाः' इत्यादिवत्.

Śl. 82. उत्तरच्छद m.—a bed-sheet (*lit.* 'the upper covering'). जाह्नवीपुलिन—which would be extremely white; पुलिनं हि सर्वासामपि नदीनां श्वेतं भवति । किं पुनः अतिश्वेतसलिलायाः जाह्नव्याः इति द्योतयितुं जाह्नवीपदोपादानम् । Nâr. अध्यशेत शयनं—the root शी with अधि governs the Acc.; see A. G. § 31. रोहिणीपतिः—an epithet of the Moon, as the lord of the starry constellation Rohiṇî, who is described as his best beloved and most favourite consort from among the 27 constellations. On हंसधवल० the com. Ar. and Nâr. quote from Vâtsyâyana—शुक्लमुभयोपधानं मध्ये विनतं शुक्लोत्तरच्छदं बद्धवितानं शयनीयं स्यात् । इति.

Śl. 83. क्लिष्टचन्द्रं—the moon was pained (*cf.* the use of क्लिष्ट *supra* śl. 8) when Śiva's matted hair, in which the moon lies, was seized by Pârvatî. उत्पथ० —nail-scratches are to be made only on certain parts of the body; the rule was forgotten in the heat of passion. समत्सरं—see the explanation given by Malli. Ar. explains differently: समत्सरं कलहरूपत्वात्सुरतस्य । तदुक्तं 'कलहरूपं सुरतमाचक्षते' इति । मत्सरेण च कृतप्रतिकृतादि द्योत्यते। यद्वधूरते दुर्लभत्वेन प्रागुक्तम् (in śl. 8)। तदुक्तं—'कृते प्रतिकृतं कुर्यात् चुम्बिते प्रतिचुम्बितम् । करणेन च तेनैव ताडिते प्रतिताडितम् ॥' इति । छिदुर—from छिद् to break + उर (कुरच्) by Pâṇ. III. 2. 162. अतृप्तये अभूत्—*i. e.* it increased his desire instead of satisfying it.

Śl. 84. केवलं प्रिय०—and not because he felt any exhaustion himself. ज्योतिषामव०—*i. e.* towards the hours of early morning when the stars (ज्योतिस् *n. plu.*) are about to set. नैमीलन०—*i. e.* he slept; the word कुतूहल shows that sleep was not necessary for him, but he played with it as it were, rest being required by Pârvatî.

Śl. 85. शातकुम्भ—gold; golden lotuses abounded in the Mânasa lake which was hard by (see śl. 86). ०करैः समं व्यबुध्यत-Śiva 'awoke', literally; while the root is to be understood figuratively to mean 'to bloom', 'to open', in the case of the lotuses. The fig. of speech here is सहोक्ति. मूर्छना०—The *Kais'ika* is a melody (राग) which is suited to the time of dawn (कैशिकः प्रभातकालोचितो रागविशेषः Nâr.); मूर्छना means 'a regulated rise and fall of the seven musical notes'; 'क्रमात् स्वराणां सप्तानां आरोहश्चावरोहणम् । सा मूर्छेत्युच्यते—' quoted by Malli. on Śiś. I. 10. Another definition is—स्वरः संमूर्छितो यत्र रागतां प्रतिपद्यते । मूर्छनामेव तां प्राहुः कवयो ग्रामसंभवाम् ॥ The Kiṁnaras were singing the Kaiśika rága with proper attention to the Múrchhanâ, or the rules about the rise and fall of notes (in that particular râga).

Śl. 86. **रश्चितमानसोर्मयः**—the epithet suggests that the breezes were laden with cool spray. **पद्मभेद॰**—implying that they were laden with the fragrance of lotus-flowers which they had caused to expand. **सिषेविरे**—*i. e.* for having their fatigue removed.

Śl. 87. **तत्क्षणं**—*i. e.* when the breezes (just referred to) blew off her garments.

Śl. 88. **प्रजागर**—the state of lying awake through most of the night. **कषाय**—red. **दन्तपद**—the marks of his teeth, visible on Pârvatî's lips. **प्रेक्ष्य अरंस्त**—meaning that the mere sight of her face, suggestive of previous enjoyment, heightened his desire. **भिन्नतिलकं**—on which the *tilaka* mark had been wiped off from the forehead.

Śl. 89. **भङ्गि** *f.*—a curve, a bend; this refers to the folds in the bed-sheet, which gave it an uneven appearance. **मध्यपिण्डित॰**—in the centre of the bed was lying in a heap the girdle of Pârvatî with its thread broken; see com. for the diss. of the comp. **निर्मलेऽपि निशात्यये**—*i. e.* although it was broad daylight. **नोज्झितं**—*i. e.* his sports continued even by day; this is clear from the word **दिवानिशं** in the next śl. **चरणराग**—the *alaktaka* dye of Pârvatî's feet.

Śl. 90. **अदृश्यतामाजगाम**—*i. e.* he refused to receive visitors who came to see him, when informed of their arrival by Vijayá. Vijayá was the female friend of Pârvatî; see śl. 49 above. **॰निवेदितां**—*v. l.* qualifies **अदृश्यता** of which (his refusal to see them) they were informed by Vijayá.

Śl. 91. **समदिवसनिशीथं**-adverb; he treated day and night equally, *i. e.* sported by day as well as by night. The word **निशीथ** generally means 'mid-night' (**अर्धरात्र**), but here it is used for a night in general. **ऋतूनां सार्धं शतं**—one hundred and fifty seasons (of mortals); this means twenty-five human years, since six seasons constitute one year. **एका निशेव**—'as though it were one continuous night,' so oblivious he was to the passage of time. **न च** &c.—*i. e.* his desire, instead of being satisfied and lessened, grew stronger day by day; *cf.* न जातु कामः कामानामुपभोगेन शाम्यति । हविषा कृष्णवर्त्मेव भूय एवाभिवर्धते ॥ Mbh. **ज्वलन इव** &c.—just as the submarine fire, intead of being quenched by the water, grows as it feeds upon them. The allusion is to the fire called Aurva or Vaḍavánala which is said to exist in mid-ocean, consuming the oceanic waters. For further information see our note on **और्व इवाम्बुराशौ** Śák. III. p. 64.

APPENDIX

The Metres used in the Poem.

1. Sanskrit verse is regulated by quantity, and not by accent, as in English. A पद्य or stanza consists of four पाद्s or quarters. A पाद् is regulated by the number of syllables (अक्षरs) or of syllabic instants (मात्राs). When a वृत्त has all the पाद्s in one metre, it is called a सम वृत्त, to which type most of the common metres conform; those are called अर्धसम वृत्तs wherein the first *pâda* corresponds with the third, and the second with the fourth, called respectively the odd and the even *pádas*; while विषम वृत्तs are those of which all the *pádas* are dissimilar.

2. The vowels अ, इ, उ, ऋ and ऌ are short and the rest long. The quantity of a syllable is determined by its vowel. A syllable with a short vowel is called लघु ('light') and one with a long vowel is called गुरु ('heavy').

3. But a लघु syllable becomes गुरु if it is followed by an *anusava'ra*, a *visarga*, or when it occurs at the end of a *pa'da*.[1]

4. Three successive syllables form a गण ('foot'); a short syllable is marked as and a long one as —; the different गणs, which are eight in number, may be exhibited as follows[2]:—
य ⏑ — —; र — ⏑ —; त — — ⏑; भ — ⏑ ⏑; ज ⏑ — ⏑; स ⏑ ⏑ —; म — — —; and न ⏑ ⏑ ⏑. A short syllable is sometimes indicated in the Definition by the letter ल, and a long one by ग.

METRES.

अनुष्टुभ्—(also called श्लोक)—Def. श्लोके षष्ठं गुरु ज्ञेयं सर्वत्र लघु पञ्चमम् । द्विचतुःपादयोर्ह्रस्वं सप्तमं दीर्घमन्ययोः ॥ There are many varieties of this metre, but the one defined is the commonest occurring. Each *páda* of it consists of 8 syllables, of which the sixth is long and the fifth short, and the seventh in the 2nd and 4th *pádas* is short and in the 1st

---

1 सानुस्वारश्च दीर्घश्च विसर्गी च गुरुर्भवेत् ।
वर्णः संयोगपूर्वश्च तथा पादान्तगोऽपि वा ॥

2 आदिमध्यावसानेषु यरता यान्ति लाघवम् ।
भजसा गौरवं यान्ति मनौ तु गुरुलाघवम् ॥

and 3rd *pádas* long. The rest of the syllables may be either short or long. *Examples*:—II. 1—63; VI. 1—94.

[इन्द्रवज्रा—See *Upajáti* below].

उपजाति—Def. [स्यादिन्द्रवज्रा यदि तौ जगौ गः उपेन्द्रवज्रा जतजास्ततो गौ ॥] अनन्तरोदीरितलक्ष्मभाजौ पादौ यदीयावुपजातयस्ताः ॥ [इत्थं किलान्यास्वपि मिश्रितासु वदन्ति जातिष्विदमेव नाम ॥]. An *Upajati* is a mixture of one or more *pádas* of इन्द्रवज्रा with one or more of उपेन्द्रवज्रा, so as to form one stanza. [इन्द्रवज्रा has 11 syllables in each quarter, the feet being त, त, ज, ग, ग; उपेन्द्रवज्रा also has 11 syllables, the feet being ज, त, ज, ग, ग] A mixture of other metres also in this manner is called an *Upajâti*. The student should always scan and find out in each case whether a *páda* is in *Indrav.* or the *Upendrav.*

Examples:—I. 1-59; III. 1—74; II. 1—93.

[उपेन्द्रवज्रा—See *Upajâti* above].

पुष्पिताग्रा—Def. अयुजि नयुगरेफतो यकारो युजि च नजौ जरगाश्च पुष्पिताग्रा। Odd *pâdas*—12 syllables; scheme of *gaṇas*—न, न, र, य. Even *pâdas*—13 syllables; scheme—न, ज, ज, र, ग. This is an अर्धसम वृत्त. *Examples*:—IV. 46; VI. 95.

मालिनी—Def. ननमयययुतेयं मालिनी भोगिलोकैः। 15 syllables; scheme न, न, म, य, य. The pause occurs after the eighth syllable. *Examples*:—I. 60; II. 64; III. 76; VII. 94, 95; VIII. 91.

रथोद्धता—Def. रान्नराविह रथोद्धता लगौ। 11 syllables; scheme—र, न, र, ल, ग, *Ex.*:—VIII. 1—90.

वंशस्थ—Def. जतौ तु वंशस्थमुदीरितं जरौ। 12 syllables; scheme—ज, त, ज, र. *Ex.*:—V. 1—84.

वसन्ततिलका—Def. उक्ता वसन्ततिलका तभजा जगौ गः। 14 syllables; scheme—त, भ, ज, ज, ग, ग. *Ex.*:—III. 75; IV. 45; V. 85, 86.

वियोगिनी—Def. विषमे ससजा गुरुः समे सभरालोऽथ गुरुर्वियोगिनी। Odd *pádas*—10 syllables; scheme—स, स, ज, ग. Even *pádas*—11 syllables; scheme—स, भ, र, ल, ग. This is an अर्धसम वृत्त. *Ex.*:—IV. 1—44.

अथ

कुमारसंभवस्थश्लोकानुक्रमणिका ।